TRUE
CHRISTIANITY

The New Century Edition
of the Works of Emanuel Swedenborg

Jonathan S. Rose
Series Editor

Stuart Shotwell
Managing Editor

TRUE CHRISTIANITY

Containing

a Comprehensive Theology

*of the New Church That Was Predicted by the Lord
in Daniel 7:13–14 and Revelation 21:1, 2*

EMANUEL SWEDENBORG

Volume 2

Translated from the Latin by Jonathan S. Rose

With Notes by Reuben P. Bell, Glen M. Cooper, Lisa Hyatt Cooper,
George F. Dole, R. Guy Erwin, Kristin King, Jonathan S. Rose,
Fitzhugh L. Shaw, Stuart Shotwell, Richard Smoley, and Lee S. Woofenden

SWEDENBORG FOUNDATION

West Chester, Pennsylvania

Originally published in Latin as *Vera Christiana Religio,* Amsterdam, 1771

Printed in the United States of America

ISBN (library)	Volume 1: 978-0-87785-484-5
	Volume 2: 978-0-87785-501-9
ISBN (paperback)	Volume 1: 978-0-87785-485-2
	Volume 2: 978-0-87785-502-6
ISBN (slipcase set)	Volumes 1 and 2: 978-0-87785-506-4

(The ISBNs in the Library of Congress data shown below are the previous, 10-digit ISBNs.)

Library of Congress Cataloging-in-Publication Data

Swedenborg, Emanuel, 1688–1772.
　　[Vera Christiana religio. English]
　　True Christianity, containing a comprehensive theology of the new church that was predicted by the Lord in Daniel 7:13–14 and Revelation 21:1, 2 / by Emanuel Swedenborg ; translated from the Latin by Jonathan S. Rose ; with an introduction by R. Guy Erwin ; and notes by Stuart Shotwell . . . [et al.].
　　　　p. cm. — (The new century edition of the works of Emanuel Swedenborg)
　　　　Includes bibliographical references and indexes.
　　　　ISBN 0-87785-506-4 (two-volume set, slipcase : alk. paper) — ISBN 0-87785-484-X (hardcover, v. 1 : alk. paper) — ISBN 0-87785-501-3 (hardcover, v. 2 : alk. paper) — ISBN 0-87785-485-8 (pbk., v. 1 : alk. paper) — ISBN 0-87785-502-1 (pbk., v. 2 : alk. paper)
　　　　1. New Jerusalem Church—Doctrines.　2. Theology, Doctrinal.　I. Rose, Jonathan S.　II. Erwin, R. Guy.　III. Shotwell, Stuart, 1953– .　IV. Title.

BX8712.T8 2006
230'.94—dc22

2004018105

This book is printed on acid-free paper that meets the American National Standards Institute Z39.48-1992 standard.

Senior copy editor, Alicia L. Dole
Cover design by Caroline Kline and Karen Connor
Text designed by Joanna V. Hill
Ornaments from the first Latin edition, 1771
Typesetting by Alicia L. Dole
Indexes by Chara Cooper Daum, Alicia L. Dole, Skye Kerr, Chad E. Odhner, Chara M. Odhner, Bruce Tracy

For information about the New Century Edition of the Works of Emanuel Swedenborg, contact the Swedenborg Foundation, 320 North Church Street, West Chester, PA 19380 U.S.A. Telephone: (610) 430-3222 • Web: www.swedenborg.com • E-mail: info@swedenborg.com

Contents

Translator's Preface to Volume 2

THE main introductory materials for this volume are to be found at the beginning of volume 1, pages 1–101. There are, however, a few additional points to be made here at the beginning of volume 2.

I. Remarks on the Back Matter of *True Christianity*

Emanuel Swedenborg's 1771 work *True Christianity,* like several of his other works (most notably the 1769 work *Survey*), has what could be termed multiple endings. The conclusion of the main text of *True Christianity* in §790 is followed by (1) a brief but significant postscript (§791); (2) fifty-four sections of additional material on the spiritual world (§§792–845); (3) six sections of an account of a memorable occurrence[1] (§§846–851); (4) an author's table of contents; (5) an author's index of the accounts of memorable occurrences; and (6) an unnumbered additional account of a memorable occurrence, here designated §[852].[2] In the first edition, these six items of back matter add 63 pages to the 478 pages of main text. They are all included in this volume, though the latter three have suffered various fates of omission and transposition in various other editions.[3]

---

1. In his last five published theological works (*Revelation Unveiled* [1766], *Marriage Love* [1768], *Survey* [1769], *Soul-Body Interaction* [1769], and the present work), Swedenborg uses the term "memorable occurrence" (Latin *memorabile,* plural *memorabilia,* traditionally translated "memorable relation") as a technical term for an extended narrative account of one of his spiritual experiences.

2. On the verso (that is, the back) of the last numbered page of the first edition, after the six items just mentioned, there occurs a brief list of typographical errors in the work, covering the first 296 of its 541 pages. For more on this list, see the translator's preface in volume 1, page 29.

3. The most extreme example of the varied placement this material has received can be seen in the case of item 6, the unnumbered additional account of a memorable occurrence. Both the second and the most recent Latin edition (Swedenborg [1771] 1857–1858; Swedenborg [1771] 2009) place this final account at the very end of the volume, in accordance with the first edition. Samuel H. Worcester's Latin edition (Swedenborg [1771] 1906) moves all three of the final items of back matter to the front of the first volume of two, but keeps them in the same sequence; this brief account, then, comes just before the main text begins with §1. In Clowes's translation (Swedenborg [1771] 1781) and Bayley's translation (Swedenborg [1771] 1933), this account is omitted altogether. In the

a. The Additional Material on the Spiritual World

The second of these items, the additional material on the spiritual world (§§792–845), is largely based on a body of text that Swedenborg had published before. Its provenance is worth reviewing briefly, and it also poses some particular problems for today's reader.

In 1758, Swedenborg published *Heaven and Hell* and *Last Judgment*. In 1763 he published supplements to both of these works under a single title: *Continuatio de Ultimo Judicio: Et de Mundo Spirituali* (Supplements on the Last Judgment and the Spiritual World). The work contained first a supplement to *Last Judgment* (*Supplements* 1–31), and then a supplement to *Heaven and Hell* (*Supplements* 32–90). It is this second supplement that forms the basis of the additional material that appears toward the end of *True Christianity*. Although the dependence of the later body of text on the earlier is still clearly visible, Swedenborg edited quite freely as he brought the material forward. Of ten headings in the earlier work, two were removed from the later version, two changed places, and two were added (see figure 2 on page 20 in volume 1, and the accompanying text on pages 19–21). Of the two headings and bodies of text that are entirely new, one concerns Martin Luther (1483–1546), Philipp Melanchthon (1497–1560), and John Calvin (1509–1564) in the spiritual world and the other concerns Germans there.[4] In the case of the eight headings that were brought forward, just over half of the accompanying text is taken more or less word for word from *Supplements,* but is interspersed sometimes section by section, sometimes sentence by sentence, with material that did not appear in *Supplements.* The parts that have been the most changed or expanded are those concerning Roman Catholics, Muslims, and Africans.

Readers should be forewarned that the additional material in §§792–845 characterizes peoples, nations, and religions in the spiritual world in

---

translations of T. G. Worcester (Swedenborg [1771] 1833), Ager (Swedenborg [1771] 1906–1907), and Dick (Swedenborg [1771] 1950), it appears at the end of the main text but *before* the index of the accounts of memorable occurrences. In Foster's translation (Swedenborg [1771] 1869) as well, it appears after the main text and before the index of the accounts of memorable occurrences, but in that work a general index supplied by the translator intervenes between the main text and the unnumbered additional account. In Chadwick's translation (Swedenborg [1771] 1988), the brief account is actually inserted into the main text between §§816 and 817 and is numbered §816A. (Chadwick explains this placement in a footnote to §816A and on page vii of his preface.)

4. In the earlier treatment in *Supplements,* there are brief mentions of Melanchthon in *Supplements* 47 (oddly placed at the end of the section on the British), and of Calvin and Luther in *Supplements* 54, 55 (oddly placed at the end of the section on the Dutch). These are markedly different from the much longer treatments in *True Christianity.*

sweeping terms[5] and contains much that will be problematic and even offensive to a wide array of modern readers. On the milder end, the Dutch are portrayed as immovably stubborn; Dutch housewives, as domineering; the British, as insular and excessively patriotic. Germans are depicted as memorizing the words of others rather than thinking for themselves. More offensively, Catholics are portrayed as foolishly worshiping saints; the saints they pray to either do not hear them or become babbling idiots. Underhanded Catholic monks try to convert Protestants to Catholicism. Muslims are characterized as generally bitter and jealous, with dwellings that smell unpleasant; Jews, as generally external and self-centered, with dwellings and streets that are full of filth and garbage. Devotees of Moses, Muhammad, Geneviève, Xavier, Luther, Melanchthon, and Calvin would all take exception to the way these and other prophets, saints, and religious leaders are portrayed here.

Alongside these disquieting characterizations are many equally sweeping comments of a neutral or positive nature. Yet the comments, whether negative or positive, are distributed quite unevenly. In §795 Swedenborg indicates that these descriptions are brief and selective, and implies that he could have written much more:

> I have conversations every day with the races and peoples of this world. I have interactions not only with people in Europe but also people in Asia and Africa. I talk to people of a variety of religions. Therefore by way of an epilogue to this work I will add a brief description of the state of *some* of them. (§795, emphasis added)

In fact, large portions of world populations are omitted entirely. The absence of any mention of spirits from Swedenborg's native Sweden or any other part of Scandinavia is particularly striking.

And indeed, some *positive* characterizations, especially those concerning Swedenborg and his theology, may also be problematic for readers. The cornerstone of Swedenborg's theology—the view that Jesus is the God of heaven and earth and that obeying the Ten Commandments is essential to salvation—is portrayed as an increasingly dominant force in the spiritual world: Moses, Luther, Melanchthon, an unnamed Catholic

---

5. The sweeping nature of this part of the text is no accident. When Swedenborg writes that because of their political and religious diversity, "Germans and their minds, inclinations, and lives are more difficult to generalize about from eyewitness experience in the spiritual world than other peoples and nationalities" (§813), he shows that it was a goal of his throughout this additional material to make such generalizations.

pope, Catholic monks in teaching positions, and Jewish governors, as well as many rank-and-file Jews, Muslims, Catholics, and Protestants in the spiritual world are described as converts to this theology. Swedenborg himself is depicted as a popular teacher and someone surrounded by protective angelic spirits. Whereas his original Lutheran readership may not have minded harsh comments about Catholics, Muslims, and Jews (since such things were commonplace then) or even his calling Calvin an "evil spirit" to his face (§798:9), surely they would have taken offense at his assertions that he was sought out by Luther as a teacher and confidant, and taught him daily concerning the nature of true Christianity, until Luther was thoroughly persuaded and laughed at his own former teachings.

Yet for all the oddities and difficulties of this section, its overall purpose is clear: to show that the life circumstances of all in the spiritual world depend on the nature of their acknowledgment and worship of God (§795).

b. The Author's Index of the Accounts of Memorable Occurrences

The inclusion of items 4 and 5 enumerated above, an author's table of contents and an author's index of memorable occurrences, is not in accordance with Swedenborg's usual custom. He provided such material in only one other title among his eighteen published theological works, namely, *Marriage Love,* published in 1768. In that work as well, the extra matter is placed at the end of the volume. Its table of contents fills ten pages, and the index of accounts of memorable occurrences fills just over a page, summarizing each memorable occurrence in very few words in a kind of headline style. Most of the entries fit on a single line, and none is longer than two lines. In the first edition of *True Christianity,* the table of contents is of a similar length—it fills thirteen pages; but the index of accounts of memorable occurrences is of quite a different nature. It fills over twenty-five pages. Its entries are generally written in whole sentences and vary considerably in length; the shortest is four lines long and many fill more than half a page each.[6]

Though one might expect an index to reflect as accurately as possible the contents of the volume being indexed, this one departs in numerous

---

6. In the first edition of *True Christianity,* the index of memorable occurrences consists of seventy-seven units sequentially numbered in roman numerals. In the current edition the original divisions have been preserved, though the roman numerals have been deleted, as they had no referent in the main text. Their function has been taken over by the section numbers of the indexed

intriguing ways from the text to which it refers. The main anomalies are of two types: discrepancies and expansions.[7]

Four definitions in §135:5 provide examples of discrepancies. They appear as follows in the main text:

> *Mediation* refers to his [that is, God's] human manifestation as the medium through which we can get closer to God the Father, and God the Father can get closer to us and teach and lead us so as to save us. This is why the Son of God, meaning the human manifestation of God the Father, is called the Savior, and in the world was called Jesus, which means salvation.
>
> *Intercession* refers to ongoing mediation. Absolute love, with its mercy, forgiveness, and grace, constantly intercedes; that is, it mediates for the people who do its commandments, the people it loves.
>
> *Ritual purging* refers to the removal of the sins that we would quickly fall into if we turned to Jehovah without mediation.
>
> *Appeasement* refers to the actions of mercy and grace that prevent us from causing our own damnation through sin and also protect us from desecrating what is holy. This has the same meaning as the mercy seat over the ark in the tabernacle.

In the index, however, both the wording and the order of the last two items are markedly different:

> *Mediation* refers to God's human manifestation as the intermediary. *Intercession* refers to his mediating as ongoing. *Appeasement* refers to God's human manifestation as providing every human being with welcome access to God. *Ritual purging* refers to this access as available even to those who have committed sins.

Discrepancies occur even in some simple facts of description. For example, in §508:1, a temple is described as square; in the corresponding index entry, it is described as round.

---

material, which have been relocated from the end to the beginning of each index entry. In the first edition most of the units appear as single blocks of text; the current edition introduces modern paragraphing throughout to make the entries easier to read. In three instances in the original (the index entries for §§25–26, 731–752, and 846–851) a new paragraph (or paragraphs) within the unit is indicated with a long dash. These paragraphs also are now indicated by modern paragraphing. Since the main translation text of this edition supplies endnote references and bracketed biblical references for allusions, those notes and references are not repeated in the author's index.

7. These discrepancies and expansions have not been documented in the annotations, since such treatment would have led to an unacceptable proliferation of notes.

Expansions can be illustrated by a close comparison of one passage, §110:1, and its index entry. It is true that some material has been cut from the passage, as one would expect. In the following quotation from the main text, shading indicates material that does not appear in the later index entry:

> I asked him why he had fallen out of heaven like that. He answered that Michael's angels had thrown him down as an angel of the dragon. "It was because I voiced some of the beliefs I had convinced myself of in the world," he said. "Among them was this one: God the Father and God the Son are not one; they are two. As it turns out, though, all who are in the heavens today believe that God the Father and God the Son are one like a soul and a body. Any statement to the contrary is like a stinging irritation up their noses or like an awl piercing their ears. They become disturbed and pained by it, so they order anyone voicing opposition to leave, and if you resist, they throw you out."

However, it appears that even while some details were being cut out, new wording was being added. The following quotation of the index entry indicates the additions with boldface text:

> I **went over to him and** asked why he had fallen out of heaven like that. He answered that Michael's angels had thrown him down, because he had said that God the Father and his Son are two, not one. He said that the entire angelic heaven believes that *God the Father and his Son are one as a soul and a body are one*—**a point the angels support with many passages from the Word. They also use rational argumentation as support: they say the Son's soul came from nowhere else but the Father; therefore that soul was an image of the Father, and the body that came from it contained that image. He added that when he was in heaven he of course spoke of one God, just as he used to do on earth; but because his verbal statements to this effect did not match what he was thinking, the angels said he did not believe in any God, because the two views cancel each other out. He said this was why he was thrown out of heaven.**

The end result is that the index entry for this part of the memorable occurrence is actually longer than the corresponding main text by about a third. Although the essential outline is the same, the later version is more a revision than a condensation. When one reads the main and index texts in combination, a different, more complete understanding of the account emerges.

In another significant example, Swedenborg takes the opportunity to expand on the nature of his spiritual calling. The beginning of the main text of §846 reads as follows (again, shaded text indicates material that is not reflected in the index entry):

> On one occasion I was carried up in my spirit to the angelic heaven, to a particular community there. Some of the wise people of that community met with me and asked, "*What are the latest developments on earth [in regard to wisdom]?*"
>
> "This is new," I said: "The Lord has recently revealed secrets that are more excellent than any that have ever been revealed since the church first came into existence."
>
> "What are they?" they asked.
>
> "They are as follows," I said.
>
> (1) "In the Word, within each and every detail of it, there is a *spiritual meaning. . . .*"

In the index, the material quoted above is presented as follows (again, the boldface indicates material added):

> **This account deals with *this revelation*.** The Lord **chose to manifest himself to me and open the inner levels of my mind, allowing me to see what is in heaven and what is in hell. By so doing, he** revealed secrets that are of greater excellence **and importance** than any other secrets that have been disclosed before. They are as follows: (1) In each and every detail of the Word there is a *spiritual meaning. . . .*

The main text is presented as a story of an experience Swedenborg had. The index entry makes no mention of the experience—where Swedenborg was, who asked him what question, and so on. Instead Swedenborg appears to address the reader, providing a brief but unusually direct summary of the process by which his spiritual awakening occurred, none of which corresponds to any material in the main text.

These examples of discrepancies and expansions are not chosen at random; they are some of the more striking examples. Nonetheless, they reflect trends that are visible throughout the author's index of the accounts of memorable occurrences. Swedenborg is constantly rewording and rephrasing and even rearranging the material as he summarizes it.

It is possible that the discrepancies and expansions may reflect an earlier, fuller draft of the main text.[8] That is, Swedenborg may have edited down the longer version twice: first to create the main text we have, and

---

8. For a discussion of the various drafts of this work, see the translator's preface in volume 1, pages 10–27.

then to make the index. During each edit, according to this theory, he chose different details to retain. Rather than moot the existence of such a longer draft, however, we should probably give preference to a simpler scenario in which Swedenborg compiled the index from the main text we have, but saw ways in which he wanted to elucidate the account even as he edited it. After all, years of repeatedly reframing his theological ideas for new publications had made him an old hand at editing and recasting text. One could even say that it would have been more remarkable if the index had adhered strictly to the main text.

Swedenborg's index of the accounts of memorable occurrences, then, is not simply a superfluous mirror of the text in question, but a brief retelling from a slightly different point of view.

In addition to discrepancies and expansions, this index also contains a third type of material that one would consider most unusual in an ordinary index. Some ten times its text specifically directs readers to consult the main text itself (see the entries for §§137, 185, 334, 459, 462, 508, 567, 625, 665–666, 692), when in the ordinary course of things it would be taken for granted that the main text is where the details are. In fact, twice the author of the index indicates that there is simply too much material to be readily transcribed:

> They [the speakers in the story] all gave ample support for their own definition; because there was a great deal of this supporting material, it cannot be copied here—see the account itself. (Author's index of §459)

> The arguments I used were too extensive to copy here; see the account itself. (Author's index of §462)

The details for which readers are sent to the main text concern matters that one could expect they would have remembered had they *already read* the accounts in question. Therefore this index, although it appears at the end of the volume, apparently was not written in the assumption that those reading it would have any familiarity with the earlier portions of the volume. Rather, it was created in the expectation that it would be the first part of the book that readers would encounter.

This interpretation is supported by two cover letters that Swedenborg sent out with his earlier work *Revelation Unveiled* (published in Amsterdam in 1766). In the letters he draws the addressees' attention to the accounts of memorable occurrences, and suggests that they be read first. To his friend Gabriel Beyer (1720–1779) Swedenborg writes:

> At the end of every chapter are Memorabilia separated from the text by asterisks. The Herr Doctor [Beyer] will be so good as to read these first.

From them one gets a fundamental knowledge of the miserable state into which *Faith Alone* has brought the churches of the Reformed. (Acton 1948–1955, 610)

And to the Swedish ambassador to France at the time, Swedenborg writes,

In the same work are inserted various Memorable Accounts of my interaction with the Spiritual World; they are separated from the text of the work by asterisks, and are to be found at the end of the explanation of each chapter; since they contain some remarkable material, they will probably draw the reader's attention as material that ought to be read first. (Rephrasing of the versions in Acton 1948–1955, 612, and Tafel 1877, 242)

Swedenborg also arranged for a handbill in England promoting *Revelation Unveiled* that specially advertised its accounts of memorable occurrences, giving the section reference for each one (Hyde 1906, entry 2195). Again, this seems an invitation to read this material first.

In conclusion, Swedenborg provided this volume with what could be termed multiple endings or at least items of back matter, and one of those was markedly different from anything he had published before. Furthermore, Swedenborg did not intend to finish here. There is evidence that he had plans and possibly even drafts of not only an appendix to this volume but also several other works (see volume 1, pages 1–2 and footnote 1; see also page 689 note 71, page 716 note 240 there). The present title, however, turned out to be the last volume he saw through the press. To the end, then, he kept fine-tuning his approach and presenting his message in new ways.

II. Acknowledgments

For acknowledgments of people who assisted with volume 1 (almost all of whom helped with this volume as well) and of foundations that gave financial support, please see my preface to volume 1, pages 43–44. Let me here acknowledge those whose work especially or exclusively concerned this second volume.

It is some indication of the breadth of Swedenborg's interests that experts from a wide range of fields must be consulted to clarify some of the obscurities of his many metaphors. I would like to thank Michael A. Ivie and Chris Carlton for entomological information, Fritz W. Huchzermeyer for his expertise in the anatomy and lore of crocodiles, and Richard L. Doty at the Smell and Taste Center at the University of Pennsylvania School of Medicine for his expertise in the history of olfactory studies.

I am grateful to the annotators whose work on *True Christianity* began with this second volume: Reuben P. Bell, Lisa Hyatt Cooper, Kristin King, Fitzhugh L. Shaw, Richard Smoley, and Lee S. Woofenden. The knowledge, intelligence, and expertise brought by them and the annotators who also worked on volume 1 have not only contributed to the notes but often shed a welcome light on puzzling passages in the Latin text.

I am thankful to Skye Kerr, who prepared the indexes, supplied missing cross-references, and checked more or less everything numerical; to Chad E. Odhner for index checking and bibliographical research; to Sarah Mae Allard for reading the annotations in context with an objective eye; and to Emily Latta Klippenstein for tracking down many of the sources of Swedenborg's quotations from the *Book of Concord* and carefully comparing his Latin versions with the originals.

I am especially indebted to those who took on additional responsibilities for me and protected my time so that I could complete this volume—most notably Chara Cooper Daum, James P. Horigan, Skye Kerr, Chara M. Odhner, Stuart Shotwell, and Marlyn F. Smith.

Finally, I wish to express my deep affection, gratitude, and admiration for the late Alice B. Skinner (1925–2010), who as president of the Swedenborg Foundation shepherded the New Century Edition and its editorial committee into existence, and supported it in countless ways thereafter. I found the timing of her passing heartbreakingly poignant. I finished translating the first draft of this volume on the afternoon of September 15, 2010, and placed a call to her in Maine the next morning with the intention of letting her know that this milestone had been reached, only to learn from her husband, Wickham Skinner, that she had passed away suddenly the previous afternoon. Although the New Century Edition is the result of many combined dreams and efforts, her role was central; she always gave others the credit, but the truth is that without her it would not have come into being.

JONATHAN S. ROSE
Bryn Athyn, Pennsylvania
March 2012

Works Cited
in the Translator's Preface to Volume 2

Acton, Alfred. 1948–1955. *The Letters and Memorials of Emanuel Swedenborg.* 2 vols. Bryn Athyn, Pa.: Swedenborg Scientific Association.

Hyde, James. 1906. *A Bibliography of the Works of Emanuel Swedenborg, Original and Translated.* London: Swedenborg Society.

Swedenborg, Emanuel. [1771] 1781. *True Christian Religion Containing the Universal Theology of the New Church: Which Was Foretold by the Lord, in Daniel, Chap. vii. 5, 13, 14, and in the Apocalypse, Chap. xxi. 1, 2.* 2 vols. [Translated by John Clowes.] London.

———. [1771] 1833. *The True Christian Religion Containing the Universal Theology of the New Church Foretold by the Lord in Daniel VII. 13, 14; and in Revelation XXI 1, 2.* Translated by T. G. W[orcester]. Boston: John Allen.

———. [1771] 1857–1858. *Vera Christiana Religio, Continens Universam Theologiam Novae Ecclesiae a Domino apud Danielem Cap. VII: 13–14, et in Apocalypsi Cap. XXI: 1, 2. Praedictae.* 2 vols. Edited by J. F. Immanuel Tafel. Tübingen: Verlagsexpedition, and London: Swedenborg Society.

———. [1771] 1869. *The True Christian Religion Containing the Entire Theology of the New Church, Foretold by the Lord in Dan. vii. 13, 14; and Rev. xxi. 1, 2.* 2 vols. Translated by R. Norman Foster. Philadelphia: J. B. Lippincott.

———. [1771] 1906. *Vera Christiana Religio Continens Universam Theologiam Novae Ecclesiae a Domino apud Danielem VII: 13, 14, et in Apocalypsi XXI: 1, 2, Praedictae.* 2 vols. Edited by Samuel H. Worcester. New York: American Swedenborg Printing and Publishing Society.

———. [1771] 1906–1907. *The True Christian Religion Containing the Universal Theology of the New Church Foretold by the Lord in Daniel VII. 13, 14; and in Revelation XXI. 1, 2.* 2 vols. Translated by John C. Ager. New York: American Swedenborg Printing and Publishing Society.

———. [1771] 1933. *The True Christian Religion Containing the Universal Theology of the New Church.* [Translated by F. Bayley], with an introduction by Helen Keller. London and Toronto: J. M. Dent and Sons, and New York: E. P. Dutton.

———. [1771] 1950. *The True Christian Religion Containing the Universal Theology of the New Church Foretold by the Lord in Daniel vii 13, 14, and in the Revelation xxi 1, 2.* Translated by William C. Dick. London: Swedenborg Society.

———. [1771] 1988. *The True Christian Religion Containing the Complete Theology of the New Church as Foretold by the Lord in Daniel 7:13,14 and in Revelation 21:2,3.* 2 vols. Translated by John Chadwick. London: Swedenborg Society.

———. [1771] 2009. *Vera Christiana Religio Continens Universam Theologiam Novae Ecclesiae a Domino apud Danielem Cap. VII:13–14, et in Apocalypsi Cap. XXI:1,2, Praedictae.* 2 vols. Edited by Freya H. Fitzpatrick. Bryn Athyn, Pa.: Academy of the New Church.

Tafel, R. L. 1877. *Documents Concerning the Life and Character of Emanuel Swedenborg.* Vol. 2. London: Swedenborg Society.

Short Titles and Other Conventions
Used in This Work

ALTHOUGH *True Christianity* was originally published as a single volume, in this edition it has been broken into two volumes.

Following a practice common in his time, Swedenborg divided his published theological works into sections numbered in sequence from beginning to end. His original section numbers have been preserved in this edition; they appear in red boxes in the outside margins. Because many sections throughout Swedenborg's works are too long for precise cross-referencing, Swedenborgian scholar John Faulkner Potts (1838–1923) further divided them into subsections; these have since become standard. They are indicated by bracketed arabic numbers that appear in the text itself: [2], [3], and so on. Since the beginning of the first subsection coincides with the beginning of the section, it is not labeled in the text.

As is common in Swedenborgian studies, text citations of Swedenborg's works refer not to page numbers but to section numbers, which are uniform in most editions. Thus "*Secrets of Heaven* 29" refers to section 29 (§29) of Swedenborg's *Secrets of Heaven*. Subsection numbers are given after a colon; a reference such as "29:2" indicates subsection 2 of section 29.

Biblical citations in this edition follow the accepted standard: a semicolon is used between book references and between chapter references, and a comma between verse references. Therefore "Matthew 5:11, 12; 6:1; 10:41, 42; Luke 6:23, 35" refers to Matthew chapter 5, verses 11 and 12; Matthew chapter 6, verse 1; Matthew chapter 10, verses 41 and 42; and Luke chapter 6, verses 23 and 35.

Some features of the original Latin text of *True Christianity* have been modernized in this edition. For example, Swedenborg's first edition relies on context or italics rather than on quotation marks to indicate passages taken from the Bible or from his other works. The manner in which these conventions are used in the original suggests that Swedenborg did not belabor the distinction between direct quotation and paraphrase; neither did he mark his omissions from or changes to material, whether biblical or his own. In this edition, passages quoted more or less directly by Swedenborg from his sources are indicated by block quotations or quotation marks, but passages that he only paraphrased are not specially marked. His practice of not indicating omissions or changes in quotations has been followed here. Words in italics in the biblical quotations of this edition almost always reflect a similar emphasis in the first edition; in a few instances, however, italics have been added where consistency demanded them. In passages of dialog as well, quotation marks have been introduced that were not present as such in the original.

This translation is based on the first Latin edition, published by Swedenborg himself. It incorporates the silent emendation of minor errors, not only in the text proper but in Bible verse references and in section references to Swedenborg's other published theological works. The text has also been changed without notice where the verse numbering of the Latin Bible cited by Swedenborg differs from that of modern English Bibles. Throughout the translation, references or cross-references that were implied but not stated have been inserted in square brackets; for example, [John 3:27]. By contrast, biblical references that occur in parentheses reflect the first edition. These may be found even in passages of dialog, where they are presumably intended to indicate a reference by the author, not the speaker. Unless an endnote indicates otherwise, all brackets represent an insertion of material that was not present in the first edition.

Comments on the text are printed as endnotes, which are referenced by superscript numbers appearing in the main text. A reverse reference is given in the endnote itself. To find the location of the text treated in endnote 62, for example, the reader would turn back to the indicated section, §472, and the indicated subsection, [3]. The initials of the writer or writers are given in square brackets at the end of each note. Translations of material quoted in the endnotes are those of the indicated writer, except where otherwise specified or in cases in which the cited source is a translated text. In this second volume, when a topic arises in the text that is covered by a detailed endnote on the same topic in volume 1, a brief endnote appears here with a cross-reference to that endnote in volume 1. Indexes to the entire work appear at the end of this volume.

References to Swedenborg's works in this volume accord with the short titles listed below, except where he gives his own version of a title in the text of the translation, or where other translations are cited by the annotators. In this list, the short title is followed by the traditional translation of the title; by the original Latin title, with its full translation; and finally by the place and date of original publication if Swedenborg published it himself, or the approximate date of writing if he did not. The list is chronological within each of the two groups shown—the published theological works, and the nontheological and posthumously published works. The titles given below as theological works published by Swedenborg are generally not further referenced in lists of works cited in the preface and endnotes.

Theological Works Published by Swedenborg

Secrets of Heaven
Traditional title: *Arcana Coelestia*
Original title: *Arcana Coelestia, Quae in Scriptura Sacra, seu Verbo Domini Sunt, Detecta: . . . Una cum Mirabilibus Quae Visa Sunt in Mundo Spirituum, et in Coelo Angelorum* [A Disclosure of Secrets of Heaven Contained in Sacred Scripture, or the Word of the Lord, . . . Together with Amazing Things Seen in the World of Spirits and in the Heaven of Angels]. London: 1749–1756.

Heaven and Hell
Traditional title: *Heaven and Hell*
Original title: *De Coelo et Ejus Mirabilibus, et de Inferno, ex Auditis et Visis* [Heaven and Its Wonders and Hell: Drawn from Things Heard and Seen]. London: 1758.

New Jerusalem
Traditional title: *New Jerusalem and Its Heavenly Doctrine*
Original title: *De Nova Hierosolyma et Ejus Doctrina Coelesti: Ex Auditis e Coelo: Quibus Praemittitur Aliquid de Novo Coelo et Nova Terra* [The New Jerusalem and Its Heavenly Teaching: Drawn from Things Heard from Heaven: Preceded by a Discussion of the New Heaven and the New Earth]. London: 1758.

Last Judgment
Traditional title: *The Last Judgment*
Original title: *De Ultimo Judicio, et de Babylonia Destructa: Ita Quod Omnia, Quae in Apocalypsi Praedicta Sunt, Hodie Impleta Sunt: Ex Auditis et Visis* [The Last Judgment and Babylon Destroyed, Showing That at This Day All the Predictions of the Book of Revelation Have Been Fulfilled: Drawn from Things Heard and Seen]. London: 1758.

White Horse
Traditional title: *The White Horse*
Original title: *De Equo Albo, de Quo in Apocalypsi, Cap. XIX: Et Dein de Verbo et Ejus Sensu Spirituali seu Interno, ex Arcanis Coelestibus* [The White Horse in Revelation Chapter 19, and the Word and Its Spiritual or Inner Sense (from *Secrets of Heaven*)]. London: 1758.

Other Planets
Traditional title: *Earths in the Universe*
Original title: *De Telluribus in Mundo Nostro Solari, Quae Vocantur Plane-tae, et de Telluribus in Coelo Astrifero, deque Illarum Incolis, Tum de Spiritibus et Angelis Ibi: Ex Auditis et Visis* [Planets or Worlds in Our Solar System, and Worlds in the Starry Heavens, and Their Inhabitants, As Well as the Spirits and Angels There: Drawn from Things Heard and Seen]. London: 1758.

The Lord
Traditional title: *Doctrine of the Lord*
Original title: *Doctrina Novae Hierosolymae de Domino* [Teachings for the New Jerusalem on the Lord]. Amsterdam: 1763.

Sacred Scripture
Traditional title: *Doctrine of the Sacred Scripture*
Original title: *Doctrina Novae Hierosolymae de Scriptura Sacra* [Teachings for the New Jerusalem on Sacred Scripture]. Amsterdam: 1763.

Life
Traditional title: *Doctrine of Life*
Original title: *Doctrina Vitae pro Nova Hierosolyma ex Praeceptis Deca-logi* [Teachings about Life for the New Jerusalem: Drawn from the Ten Commandments]. Amsterdam: 1763.

Faith
Traditional title: *Doctrine of Faith*
Original title: *Doctrina Novae Hierosolymae de Fide* [Teachings for the New Jerusalem on Faith]. Amsterdam: 1763.

Supplements
Traditional title: *Continuation Concerning the Last Judgment*
Original title: *Continuatio de Ultimo Judicio: Et de Mundo Spirituali* [Supplements on the Last Judgment and the Spiritual World]. Amsterdam: 1763.

Divine Love and Wisdom
Traditional title: *Divine Love and Wisdom*
Original title: *Sapientia Angelica de Divino Amore et de Divina Sapientia* [Angelic Wisdom about Divine Love and Wisdom]. Amsterdam: 1763.

Divine Providence
Traditional title: *Divine Providence*
Original title: *Sapientia Angelica de Divina Providentia* [Angelic Wisdom about Divine Providence]. Amsterdam: 1764.

Revelation Unveiled
Traditional title: *Apocalypse Revealed*
Original title: *Apocalypsis Revelata, in Qua Deteguntur Arcana Quae Ibi Praedicta Sunt, et Hactenus Recondita Latuerunt* [The Book of Revelation Unveiled, Uncovering the Secrets That Were Foretold There and Have Lain Hidden until Now]. Amsterdam: 1766.

Marriage Love
Traditional title: *Conjugial Love*
Original title: *Delitiae Sapientiae de Amore Conjugiali: Post Quas Sequuntur Voluptates Insaniae de Amore Scortatorio* [Wisdom's Delight in Marriage Love: Followed by Insanity's Pleasure in Promiscuous Love]. Amsterdam: 1768.

Survey
Traditional title: *Brief Exposition*
Original title: *Summaria Expositio Doctrinae Novae Ecclesiae, Quae per Novam Hierosolymam in Apocalypsi Intelligitur* [Survey of Teachings of the New Church Meant by the New Jerusalem in the Book of Revelation]. Amsterdam: 1769.

Soul-Body Interaction
Traditional title: *Intercourse between the Soul and Body*
Original title: *De Commercio Animae et Corporis, Quod Creditur Fieri vel per Influxum Physicum, vel per Influxum Spiritualem, vel per Harmoniam Praestabilitam* [Soul-Body Interaction, Believed to Occur either by a Physical Inflow, or by a Spiritual Inflow, or by a Preestablished Harmony]. London: 1769.

True Christianity
Traditional title: *True Christian Religion*
Original title: *Vera Christiana Religio, Continens Universam Theologiam Novae Ecclesiae a Domino apud Danielem Cap. VII:13–14, et in Apocalypsi Cap. XXI:1, 2 Praedictae* [True Christianity: Containing a Comprehensive Theology of the New Church That Was Predicted by the Lord in Daniel 7:13–14 and Revelation 21:1, 2]. Amsterdam: 1771.

Nontheological and Posthumously Published Works by Swedenborg Cited in This Volume

Draft on Discovering Mines
Traditional title: *Discovering Mines*
Original title: *Nya anledningar till grufwors igenfinnande . . .* [New Hints for the Discovery of Mines . . .]. Written before or during November 1719.

Height of Water, Second Edition
Traditional title: *Height of Water*
Original title: *Om wattnens högd, och förra werldens starcka ebb och flod* [On the Height of Water, and the Great Ebb and Flow of the Primeval World]. Uppsala: 1719.

Miscellaneous Observations, Volume 2
Traditional title: *Miscellaneous Observations,* Part 4
Original title: *Pars Quarta Miscellanearum Observationum circa Res Naturales, et Praecipue circa Mineralia, Ferrum, et Stallactitas in Cavernis Baumannianis* [Miscellaneous Observations of Phenomena in Nature, Part Four, Especially Regarding Minerals, Iron, and the Stalactites in Baumann's Cave]. Schiffbeck: 1722.

Draft of "The Infinite" on the Soul-Body Mechanism
Traditional title: *Mechanism of the Soul and Body*
Original title: *De Mechanismo Animae et Corporis* [Mechanism of the Soul and Body]. Written between late 1733 and early 1734.

Basic Principles of Nature
Traditional title: *Principia*
Original title: *Principia Rerum Naturalium sive Novorum Tentaminum Phaenomena Mundi Elementaris Philosophice Explicandi* [Basic Principles

of Nature or of New Attempts to Explain Philosophically the Phenomena of the Elemental World]. Dresden and Leipzig: 1734.

Philosophical and Metallurgical Works III: Copper and Brass
Original title: *Regnum Subterraneum sive Minerale: De Cupro et Orichalco* . . . [The Subterranean or Mineral Kingdom: On Copper and Brass . . .] Dresden and Leipzig: 1734.

The Infinite
Traditional title: *The Infinite*
Original title: *Prodromus Philosophiae Ratiocinantis de Infinito, et Causa Finali Creationis: Deque Mechanismo Operationis Animae et Corporis* [Precursor to a Philosophy Reasoning about the Infinite and about the Final Cause of Creation; Also about the Operative Mechanism between the Soul and the Body]. Dresden and Leipzig: 1734.

First Draft of Three Transactions on the Brain
Traditional title: *The Cerebrum*
Original title: [Untitled]. Written before or during August 1738

Dynamics of the Soul's Domain
Traditional title: *Economy of the Animal Kingdom*
Original title: *Oeconomia Regni Animalis in Transactiones Divisa* [Dynamics of the Soul's Domain, Divided into Treatises]. 2 vols. Amsterdam: 1740–1741.

Quotations on Various Philosophical and Theological Topics
Traditional title: *A Philosopher's Note Book*
Original title: [Untitled]. Written around 1741.

Draft on the Soul and the Body
Traditional title: *Soul and Body*
Original title: *Transactio Prima de Anima et Ejus et Corporis Harmonia in Genere* [First Treatise on the Soul and the Harmony between It and the Body in General]. Written before or during 1742.

Draft on the Origin of the Soul
Traditional title: *Origin of the Soul*
Original title: *De Origine et Propagatione Animae* [On the Origin and the Propagation of the Soul]. Written before or during 1742.

Draft on Action
Traditional title: *Action*
Original title: *De Actione* [On Action]. Written before or during 1742.

Draft of a Rational Psychology
Traditional title: *Rational Psychology*
Original title: [Untitled]. Written before or during 1742.

Draft on the Fiber
Traditional title: *The Fiber*
Original title: [Untitled]. Written around 1742.

Draft on the Reproductive Organs
Traditional title: *Generation*
Original title: [Untitled]. Written around 1743.

The Soul's Domain
Traditional title: *The Animal Kingdom*
Original title: *Regnum Animale, Anatomice, Physice, et Philosophice Perlustratum* [The Soul's Domain Thoroughly Examined by Means of Anatomy, Physics, and Philosophy]. 3 vols. The Hague, London: 1744–1745.

Worship and Love of God
Traditional title: *Worship and Love of God*
Original title: *Pars Prima de Cultu et Amore Dei; Ubi Agitur de Telluris Ortu, Paradiso, et Vivario, Tum de Primogeniti seu Adami Nativitate, Infantia, et Amore. Pars Secunda de Cultu et Amore Dei; Ubi Agitur de Conjugio Primogeniti seu Adami, et Inibi de Anima, Mente Intellectuali, Statu Integritatis, et Imagine Dei. Pars Tertia, de Vita Conjugii Paris Primogeniti.* [Part 1: Concerning the Worship and Love of God; In Which Is Discussed the Earth's Origin, Paradise, and the Garden, and Then the Birth of the Firstborn, or Adam, His Infancy, and Love. Part 2: Concerning the Worship and Love of God; In Which Is Discussed the Marriage of the Firstborn, or Adam, and Therein the Soul, the Understanding Mind, the State of Wholeness, and the Image of God. Part 3: Concerning the Life of the Firstborn Married Couple]. London: 1745.

The Old Testament Explained
Traditional title: *The Word Explained*
Original title: *Explicatio in Verbum Historicum Veteris Testamenti* [The Historical Word of the Old Testament Explained]. Written from November 1745 to February 1747.

Spiritual Experiences
Traditional title: *The Spiritual Diary*
Original title: *Experientiae Spirituales* [Spiritual Experiences]. Written from 1747 to 1765.

Greek Orthodox Religion
Traditional title: *Greek Religion*
Original title: *Religio Graeca* [Greek Religion]. Written during 1748.

Revelation Explained
Traditional title: *Apocalypse Explained*
Original title: *Apocalypsis Explicata secundum Sensum Spiritualem, Ubi Revelantur Arcana, Quae Ibi Praedicta, et Hactenus Recondita Fuerunt* [The Book of Revelation Explained as to Its Spiritual Meaning, Which Reveals Secret Wonders That Were Predicted There and Have Been Hidden until Now]. Written from 1758 to 1759.

Draft of "Sacred Scripture"
Traditional title: *De Verbo*
Original title: *De Scriptura Sacra seu Verbo Domini ab Experientia* [On Sacred Scripture, or the Word of the Lord, from Experience]. Written around 1762.

Draft of "Supplements"
Traditional title: *Last Judgment (Posthumous)*
Original title: *De Ultimo Judicio* [On the Last Judgment]. Written around 1762 to early 1763.

Draft on Divine Love
Traditional title: *On Divine Love*
Original title: *De Divino Amore* [On Divine Love]. Written around late 1762 to early 1763.

Draft on Divine Wisdom
Traditional title: *On Divine Wisdom*
Original title: *De Divina Sapientia* [On Divine Wisdom]. Written in early 1763.

Sketch on Goodwill
Traditional title: *Charity*
Original title: *De Charitate* [On Charity]. Written between April and September 1766.

Draft of Five Memorable Occurrences
Traditional title: *Five Memorable Relations*
Reported original title: *Memorabilia* [Memorable Occurrences]. Written around 1766.

Sketch for "True Christianity"
Traditional title: *Canons of the New Church*
Reported original title: *Canones Novae Ecclesiae, seu Integra Theologia Novae Ecclesiae* . . . [Canons of the New Church, or the Entire Theology of the New Church . . .]. Written around 1769.

Draft for "Coda to True Christianity"
Traditional title: *Coronis*
Original title: *Coronis seu Appendix ad Veram Christianam Religionem* . . . [Coda or Appendix to "True Christianity" . . .]. Written around 1771.

Biblical Titles

Swedenborg refers to the Hebrew Scriptures as the Old Testament and to the Greek Scriptures as the New Testament; his terminology has been adopted in this edition. As was the custom in his day, he refers to the Pentateuch (Genesis, Exodus, Leviticus, Numbers, and Deuteronomy) as the books of Moses or simply as "Moses"; for example, in §787:2 he writes "in Moses we read that no one can see God and live" and then cites a passage from Exodus. Similarly, in sentences or phrases introducing quotations he sometimes refers to the Psalms as "David"; to both the Gospel and the Epistles of John as simply "John"; and to the various Epistles of Paul as simply "Paul." The exact source of passages identified in this generic fashion is given in parentheses at the end of the quotations.

TRUE CHRISTIANITY

By Emanuel Swedenborg
Servant of the Lord Jesus Christ

Chapter 8

Free Choice

BEFORE even preparing to present what the new church[1] teaches regarding free choice, I must first lay out what the church of today says about it in its doctrinal texts. Otherwise, devout and rational readers may think there is no point in my trying to write something new about it, since they would say to themselves, "Who doesn't know we have free choice in spiritual matters? Why else would ministers preach that we need to believe in God, turn ourselves around, live according to the precepts of the Word,[2] fight against the lusts of our flesh, and prepare ourselves as new creatures,[3] not to mention many other things of the same kind?" They cannot avoid the conclusion that if there were no free choice in matters of salvation, such words would be nothing but hot air; and that it is insane to deny free choice, because such denial goes against common sense.

Nevertheless, the church of today is in fact headed in the opposite direction. It casts the idea of free choice out of its sanctuaries, as is clear from the following teachings taken from the book called the *Formula of Concord*—a book Lutherans swear to observe.[4] From the religious treatises of the Reformed churches,[5] it is clear that there are similar teachings and a similar belief about free choice throughout the entire Christian world, and thus in Germany, Sweden, Denmark, England, and the Netherlands. The statements just following are copied from the *Formula of Concord* in the Leipzig edition of 1756:

1. The teachers of the Augsburg Confession[6] assert that we human beings have been so deeply corrupted through the fall of our first parents[7] that in spiritual matters concerning our conversion and salvation we are by nature blind. When the Word of God is preached we do not and cannot understand it. Instead, we regard it as foolishness. Of our own accord we never move closer to God; on the contrary, we are an enemy of God, and remain so until from pure grace without any cooperation

on our part we are converted, given faith, regenerated, and renewed by the power of the Holy Spirit through the Word as it is preached and heard. (Page 656)[8]

[2] 2. We believe that in spiritual and divine matters, the mind, heart, and will of unreborn human beings are entirely unable to understand, believe, comprehend, think, will, start, finish, enact, work, or cooperate through their own natural powers. Instead, we are utterly corrupt and dead to what is good, so that in our nature after the Fall but before our regeneration not the least spark of spiritual power remains that would enable us to prepare ourselves for the grace of God, or accept it once it was offered, or adapt ourselves to it, or make room for it on our own; or contribute to, perform, bring about, or cooperate in our own conversion, in whole or by half or to the least extent, either by acting on our own or even by seeming to act on our own. Instead, we are a slave of sin and the property of Satan, who supplies our driving force. Therefore because of our corrupt powers and depraved nature, our earthly free choice is active and effective only in areas that are displeasing and hostile to God. (Page 656)[9]

[3] 3. In civic and earthly matters we human beings are industrious and ingenious, but in spiritual and divine matters, which concern the salvation of our souls, we are like a log, a stone, and Lot's wife when she became a pillar of salt,[10] which have no functioning eyes, mouth, or senses. (Page 661)[11]

[4] 4. We human beings do retain locomotive power to control our outer parts, to hear the Gospel, and to meditate on it to some extent, but nevertheless in our private thoughts we despise it as foolishness and cannot believe it. In this respect we are worse than a log, unless the Holy Spirit begins to work within us and kindles and develops faith, obedience, and other God-pleasing virtues. (Page 662)[12]

[5] 5. According to a certain kind of reasoning it could be said that we are not a stone or a log, because a stone and a log do not fight back, nor do they comprehend or even feel what is being done to them. But until human beings have been converted to God, of their own will they fight against God. It is true that before conversion we human beings are rational creatures that have understanding—but not in divine matters. And we do have a will—but we do not will anything that is good for our salvation. We have nothing to contribute to our own conversion, and in this sense we are worse than a log or a stone. (Pages 672, 673)[13]

[6] 6. Conversion is entirely the work, gift, and product of the Holy Spirit, which brings it about and develops it by its own strength

and power through the Word in our mind, heart, and will, as if we were a passive subject. We do nothing for the process; we only experience it. Yet this does not take place the way a statue is formed from a block of stone or a seal is pressed into wax, because the wax lacks both awareness and will. (Page 681)[14]

[7] 7. Some church fathers and more recent theologians say, "God draws, but he draws the willing,"[15] meaning that our will plays some role in our conversion. But this does not square with sacred words,[16] which confirm that human free choice plays no role in conversion. (Page 582)[17]

[8] 8. In the outer things of the world, which are subject to reason, we still have a little bit of intellect, power, and our faculties left, although these wretched remnants are profoundly disabled, and what little is left is itself infected and contaminated with poison resulting from hereditary disease,[18] so that before God they are inconsequential. (Pages 640, 641)[19]

[9] 9. In our conversion, in which we turn from children of wrath [Ephesians 2:3] into children of grace, we do not cooperate with the Holy Spirit. In fact, the conversion of human beings is a task that belongs solely to the Holy Spirit. (Pages 219, 579 and following, 663 and following; appendix page 143)[20]

Nevertheless, people who have been reborn *are* able to cooperate, through the power of the Holy Spirit, although they remain profoundly weak. They function well as far and as long as they are led, ruled, and governed by the Holy Spirit. But even then they do not cooperate with the Holy Spirit the way two horses pull a wagon together. (Page 674)[21]

[10] 10. Original sin is not some wrong that we perpetrate in act; instead it is something deeply embedded in our nature, substance, and essence. It is the fountainhead of all actual sins, with the result that the things we think and say are depraved and the things we do are evil. (Page 577)[22]

That hereditary sickness, which has corrupted our whole nature, is dreadful sin. It is indeed the beginning and origin of all sins; all transgressions flow from it as their root and source. (Page 640[a])[23]

Even in our inmost parts and the deepest recesses of our heart, our nature is totally infected and corrupted before God by that sin, as if it were a spiritual leprosy. Because of this corruption our character is accused and damned by the law of God, so that by nature we are children of wrath and the property of death and damnation, unless with the aid of Christ's merit we are liberated and kept safe from this evil. (Page 639[b])[24]

As a result there is a total absence or deprivation of the original righteousness that was ours from creation in paradise, [namely,] the image of God, and this absence has led to the impotence, incompetence, and stupidity that render us completely inept in regard to all divine and spiritual matters. In place of the lost image of God in us, there lies within our mind, intellect, heart, and will the inmost, worst, deepest, unfathomable, unspeakable corruption of our entire nature and of all our powers, especially the higher and principal faculties of our soul. (Page 640[b])[25]

465 These then are the precepts, dogmas, and tenets of the church of today regarding human free choice in spiritual and earthly matters and regarding original sin. The reason I have presented these here is so that the precepts, dogmas, and tenets of the new church on these topics may appear more clearly. Truth appears in the light when two forms are set side by side like this, just as sometimes in paintings a misshapen face is placed next to an attractive one; since we can see the faces at the same time, the beauty of the one and the ugliness of the other stand out clearly before the eye.[26] The tenets of the new church are as follows.

The Fact That Two Trees—the Tree of Life, and the Tree of the Knowledge of Good and Evil [Genesis 2:9]— Were Placed in the Garden of Eden Means That Free Choice in Spiritual Matters Has Been Granted to Humankind

466 Many have come to believe that Adam and Eve in the Book of Moses[27] do not mean the first created people. They support their position with evidence that people existed before Adam,[28] which is based on calculations and the chronologies of various peoples. They also point to what Cain, the firstborn of Adam, said to Jehovah:[29]

"I will be a wanderer and an itinerant on the earth—whoever encounters me will kill me." Therefore Jehovah placed a mark on Cain so that whoever encountered him would not kill him. (Genesis 4:14, 15)

And after he left the presence of Jehovah, he lived in the land of Nod and built a city. (Genesis 4:16, 17)

Therefore the land was inhabited before Adam.

But Adam and his wife mean the earliest church[30] on this planet. This is demonstrated in a number of ways in *Secrets of Heaven,* which I published in London.[31] That work also indicates that the Garden of Eden means the wisdom of the people of that church; the tree of life means the Lord[32] is in us and we are in the Lord; the tree of the knowledge of good and evil means we are not in the Lord but in a sense of our own autonomy instead, like people who believe that they do everything, even what is good, on their own; and eating from this tree means incorporating evil into ourselves.[33]

In the Word the Garden of Eden does not mean some garden but a state of understanding; and a tree does not mean some tree but a human being. You can see that the Garden of Eden means understanding and wisdom from the following passages: "*With your understanding and wisdom* you had made wealth for yourself"; and in the following verses there: "Full of *wisdom,* you were in *Eden, the garden of God.* Every precious stone was your covering" (Ezekiel 28:4, 12, 13). These things are said of the prince and of the king of Tyre. The king is said to possess wisdom because *Tyre* in the Word means the church's concepts of truth and goodness, which lead to wisdom. The precious stones that cover him also mean these concepts of truth and goodness. The prince and the king of Tyre were not in the Garden of Eden.

[2] Elsewhere in Ezekiel: "Assyria was a cedar in Lebanon. The cedars in *the garden of God* could not hide it. No tree in *the garden of God* was equal to it in beauty. All *the trees of Eden in the garden of God* were jealous of it" (Ezekiel 31:3, 8, 9). And again: "To which among *the trees of Eden* did you become comparable in glory and size?" (Ezekiel 31:18). This is said of Assyria, because in the Word Assyria means rationality and understanding. [3] In Isaiah: "Jehovah will comfort Zion and turn her wilderness into *Eden,* and her desert into *the garden of Jehovah*" (Isaiah 51:3). Zion here means the church; Eden and the garden of Jehovah mean wisdom and understanding. In the Book of Revelation: "To those who overcome I will give [food] to eat from *the tree of life,* which is in *the middle of the paradise of God*" (Revelation 2:7). "In the middle of the street [and] of the river, on this side and that, will be the tree of life" (Revelation 22:2). [4] From these verses it is very clear that the garden in Eden in which Adam was placed means understanding and wisdom, because similar things are said about Tyre, Assyria, and Zion.

Elsewhere in the Word as well, a *garden* means understanding; for example, in Isaiah 58:11; 61:11; Jeremiah 31:12; Amos 9:14; Numbers 24:6. A garden has this spiritual meaning because of symbolic representations in the spiritual world.[34] In that world, garden paradises appear wherever there are angels who have understanding and wisdom; the understanding and wisdom they have from the Lord causes such things to appear around them. This occurs because of correspondence, for all things that exist in the spiritual world are correspondences.

468   The following passages in the Word show that a *tree* means a human being:

> All the trees of the field must recognize that I, Jehovah, will humble the tall tree; I will exalt the humble tree; I will wither the thriving tree and cause the dried-out tree to germinate. (Ezekiel 17:24)

> Blessed are the people who take good pleasure in the law. They will be like a tree planted by streams of water, which will produce fruit in its time. (Psalms 1:1, 2, 3; Jeremiah 17:7, 8)

> Praise Jehovah, you fruit trees. (Psalms 148:9)

> The trees of Jehovah are drenched. (Psalms 104:16)

> The axe lies against the root of the tree. Every tree that does not produce good fruit will be cut down. (Matthew 3:10; 7:16–20)

> Either make the tree good and its fruit good or make the tree rotten [and its fruit rotten], for a tree is recognized by its fruit. (Matthew 12:33; Luke 6:43, 44)

> I will start a fire that will consume every thriving tree and every dried-out tree. (Ezekiel 20:47)

Since a *tree* means a person, therefore it was decreed that "in the land of Canaan a tree's fruit that is good to eat should be circumcised" (Leviticus 19:23, 24). Since olive oil means a person of the heavenly church,[35] we read of "the two witnesses who were prophesying, that they were two olive trees standing next to the Lord of the whole earth" (Revelation 11:4). Likewise Zechariah 4:3, 11, 12, 14; and in David,[36] "I am an olive tree, thriving in the house of God" (Psalms 52:8); and in Jeremiah, "Jehovah has called your name 'a thriving olive tree, beautiful in its fruit'" (Jeremiah 11:16, 17), besides many more passages, which because of their abundance are not presented here.

469   Everyone today who is inwardly wise is capable of perceiving or divining that what is written [in Scripture] about Adam and his wife involves spiritual details, which no one has known until now because the spiritual meaning of the Word has not been disclosed before. Who cannot see, even from a great distance, that Jehovah would not have placed

two trees in the garden, one of which was a stumbling block, if doing so did not have some spiritual significance? [The same goes for the fact that Adam and Eve] were cursed because they both ate from a particular tree; and that that curse remains in effect for every human being after them, which means that the whole human race was damned for the misdeed of a single individual[37]—and a misdeed in which there was no evil from a craving of the flesh or a wickedness of the heart. Does this square with divine justice? Why indeed did Jehovah, who was present and watching this happen, not distract Adam from eating? And why did he not throw the snake into the underworld before it exercised its persuasive powers?[38] [2] But, my friend, the reason God did not do all this is that he would have taken away human free choice by so doing, and yet freedom is what makes a human a human and not an animal.[39] Once this is known, it becomes obvious that the two trees, one for life and the other for death, represent human free choice in spiritual matters.

For another thing, hereditary evil is not from this source; it is from our parents instead. Parents pass on to their children a weakness for the evil they themselves have been involved in.[40] Anyone can see that this is the case by carefully examining the behavior, the minds, and the faces of children, and indeed of extended families, descended from the same ancestor. Nevertheless, it is up to each individual in the family whether he or she wishes to move toward that evil or away from it, since each one has his or her own free choice.

As for what the tree of life and the tree of the knowledge of good and evil mean in detail, see the memorable occurrence[41] related above in §48:16–19, where this has been fully explained.

We Are Not Life, but We Are Vessels for Receiving Life from God

There is a generally held belief that there is life in us, that it belongs to us, and that therefore we are not only vessels for receiving life but we ourselves are life. This common belief derives from the way things appear to be, because we are alive, that is, we sense, think, speak, and act completely as if we had autonomy. Therefore the statement that we are not life, but are vessels for receiving life, cannot help but seem like something completely unheard of before, or like a paradox that goes against our sense-oriented thinking[42] because it goes against the way things appear to be. I have blamed this misleading belief on the way things appear to

470

be—the belief that we are in fact life, and therefore that life has been created as part of us and grafted onto us from birth. But the real reason for this misleading belief (which is based on the way things appear to be) is that many people today are earthly, and few are spiritual. The earthly self makes judgments based on appearances and resulting false impressions, when in fact these run directly counter to the truth, which is that we are not life but are vessels for receiving life.

[2] The fact that we are not life but are vessels for receiving life from God is demonstrated by the following clear points of evidence: All things that have been created are intrinsically finite. Human beings, because they are finite, could only have been created from finite things.[43] Therefore in the Book of Creation[44] it says that Adam was made from the ground and its dust [Genesis 2:7; 3:19]. In fact, he was named for the ground, since "Adam" means the soil of the earth.[45] And every human being actually consists of nothing other than types of materials that are in the earth or are in the atmosphere from the earth.[46] The elements that are in the atmosphere from the earth we absorb through our lungs[47] and through the pores all over our bodies; we absorb the denser substances through foods made up of earthly elements.

[3] As for the human spirit, however, that too has been created from things that are finite. What is the human spirit but a vessel for the life that the mind possesses? The finite things of which it is made are spiritual substances. These substances exist in the spiritual world, but they have also been incorporated into our earth in a hidden way. If these spiritual substances were not present within material substances, seeds would not be loaded with hidden instructions and would not miraculously develop, without deviation, from the first shoot all the way to the production of fruit and new seeds. Worms would not be generated from emanations from the ground and from the gases exuded by plants with which the atmosphere is saturated.[48]

[4] It is unreasonable to think that the Infinite could create anything other than what is finite; and that human beings, because they are finite, are anything other than forms that the Infinite is able to bring to life from the life he has within himself. Indeed, this is what is meant by the following: "Jehovah God formed the human being, the dust from the earth, and breathed into his nostrils the breath of life" (Genesis 2:7). Because God is infinite, he is life in itself. This life is not something he can create and then transfer into a human being—that would make the human being God. The serpent or Devil,[49] and from him, Eve and

Adam, had the insane thought that this had actually happened. This is why the serpent said, "On the day you eat some of the fruit of this tree, your eyes will be opened and you will be like God" (Genesis 3:5).

[5] At the end of the earliest church,[50] when it came to its final close, people latched onto the dreadful conviction that God had transfused and transferred himself into human beings. I know so because I have heard it from their own mouths.[51] On account of their horrendous belief that they are gods, they remain profoundly hidden in an underground chamber.[52] No one can get near it without collapsing as a result of inner dizziness. (The fact that Adam and his wife mean and describe the earliest church was made known under the previous heading [§466].)

If we are capable of thinking with a faculty of reason that is lifted above the sense impressions of the body, surely we all see that life cannot be created. What is life except the inmost activity of the love and wisdom that come from God and are God? It could also be called the living force itself.[53] Someone who sees this can also see that life cannot be transferred into anyone unless it is transferred along with love and wisdom. Surely no one does deny or could deny that everything good that relates to love and everything true that relates to wisdom come solely from God; to the extent that we receive those qualities from God we are alive from God and are called "born of God" [John 1:13; 1 John 3:9; 5:4, 18], that is, regenerated. On the other hand, to the extent that we do not accept love and wisdom, or goodwill and faith (which are the same thing), we do not receive life from God (which is life in itself) but from hell, which is a completely inverted form of life called spiritual death.[54]

From the points just made we can see and conclude that the following things cannot be created:

1. The Infinite
2. Love and wisdom
3. Life
4. Light and heat[55]
5. The quality of being active, when regarded in its own right[56]

Nevertheless, organs that are able to receive the above can be and are created.

These points can be illustrated through analogies. Light cannot be created, but its organ, the eye, can. Sound, which is a motion in the atmosphere, cannot be created, but its organ, the ear, can. Likewise incapable of being created is heat, which is the primary active thing[57] that all objects in the three kingdoms of nature[58] have been created to receive; and as they receive it they do not act but are rather acted upon.

[2] A feature of creation is that where there are active entities, there are also passive entities; the two types of entities join together to become, in effect, one thing.[59] If the active entities were able to be created the way the passive entities are, there would be no need for the sun or for heat and light from it. All created things would subsist without them.[60] But in reality, if the sun and its heat and light were removed, the whole created universe would fall into chaos. [3] The sun of our world is made up of created substances whose activity produces fire.[61] These points have been made for the purpose of illustration.

It would be similar for us if spiritual light, which is essentially wisdom, and spiritual heat, which is essentially love, stopped flowing into us and being received by us.[62] An entire human being is nothing but a form organized in such a way as to receive those two qualities, from both the physical and the spiritual worlds, since the worlds correspond to each other. If you deny that we are forms for receiving love and wisdom from God, you have to rule out the existence of inflow[63] as well, along with the idea that everything good comes from God, and that a partnership[64] with God is possible. Then there would be no point to the statement that we are able to be a dwelling place and a temple for God.

473 Why do we not know this from any light of reason? Because that light is overshadowed by our mistaken ideas, which arise because we trust what our outer physical senses tell us. We have the sensation that our aliveness comes from a life within us, because what is instrumental feels what is principal as its own; it cannot distinguish itself from what is principal. The principal cause and the instrumental cause together behave as one cause, according to a theory known to the world of learning.[65] The principal cause is life; the instrumental cause is the human mind.

It also appears as though animals possess a life that has been created as part of them, but this is a similarly mistaken idea. Animals are organisms created to receive light and heat from the physical world and from the spiritual world at the same time. Every species is a form of some earthly love. It receives the light and heat of the spiritual world indirectly through heaven and hell—the gentle animals through heaven and the savage animals through hell.[66] The difference between us and them is that only human beings receive light and heat (that is, wisdom and love) directly from the Lord.

The Lord himself teaches in John that he is life in itself and therefore **474**
life itself:

> The Word was with God and the Word was God. In him was life and
> the life was the light of humankind. (John 1:1, 4)

> As the Father has life in himself, so he has given the Son to have life in
> himself. (John 5:26)

> I am the way, the truth, and the life. (John 14:6)

> Those who follow me will have the light of life. (John 8:12)

As Long as We Are Alive in This World, We Are Held Midway between Heaven and Hell and Kept in Spiritual Equilibrium There, Which Is Free Choice

In order to know what free choice is and what qualities it has, we need **475**
to know where it comes from. Once we have learned its origin, we recognize not only what it is but what qualities it has.

Free choice originates in the spiritual world, where our minds are
kept by the Lord. Our mind is the spirit within us that lives after death.
Our spirit is continually in contact with people in that world who are
similar to us. Our spirit is also present with people in the physical world
through the material body with which it is surrounded. The reason we
do not know that our minds are among spirits is that the spirits we are
associating with in the spiritual world think and speak in a spiritual way,
but our spirit, as long as it is in a physical body, thinks and speaks in an
earthly way; and spiritual thought and speech cannot be understood or
perceived by an earthly person, or the reverse. This is also why we cannot see them. But when our spirit is spending time with spirits in their
world, then it uses spiritual thought and speech to communicate with
them, because the inner mind is spiritual, but the outer mind is earthly.
Therefore we communicate with spirits through our inner faculties, but
we communicate with other people through our outer faculties. The former communication gives us perceptions and the ability to think ana-
lytically. If we did not have this inner communication, we would think
no more and no differently than an animal. And if all interaction with
spirits were taken away from us, we would die instantly.

[2] To make it possible to comprehend how we can be held midway between heaven and hell and kept as a result in spiritual equilibrium, which is the origin of our free choice, a few words will be said about this.

The spiritual world consists of heaven and hell. Heaven is above the head and hell there is below the feet. Hell is not, however, in the center of the earth that we inhabit. It is below the lands of the other world, which are spiritual in origin and therefore do not have extension,[67] although they appear to have it.

[3] Between heaven and hell there is a great gap, which, to those who are in it, appears like an entire globe.[68] Into this intervening area evil in great abundance exhales from hell, and on the other hand goodness, also in great abundance, flows in from heaven. This interspace is what Abraham was referring to when he said to the rich man in hell, "Between us and you a great gulf has been established, so that those who try to cross over from here to you cannot, and neither can those who are there cross toward us" (Luke 16:26).

The spirit of every human being is in the midst of this vast interspace for one reason: so that we will have free choice. [4] Because this interspace is so huge and looks to those who are there like a great globe, it is called "the *world* of spirits." It is also full of spirits, because every human being first comes there after death and is prepared there for either heaven or hell. There we are among spirits and in interaction with them, just the way we had previously been among people in our former world. (There is no purgatory there. Purgatory is a fable invented by Roman Catholics.)[69] That world is specifically dealt with in *Heaven and Hell* (published in London in 1758) §§421–535.

476   Every human being from infancy to old age is relocating and changing places in that world.[70] In *early childhood* we are kept in the eastern region there, on its north side. In *later childhood and youth,* as we acquire a foundation in our religion, we move in a series of stages away from the north and toward the south. In *early adulthood,* when we begin to think with our own minds, we are brought farther south. Later on, when we become independent and able to judge for ourselves and are growing in matters that inwardly relate to God and love for our neighbor, we move into the southern region, on its east side. But if we have a fondness for evil and indulge in it, we move toward the west.[71]

All who are in the spiritual world live in one region or another. People who are involved in goodness from the Lord live in the *east,* because that is where the sun that surrounds the Lord is.[72] People who are in ignorance live in the *north*. People who have good understanding live in the *south*. People who are involved in evil live in the *west*.

[2] Our body is not kept in that interspace or central area, but our spirit is. As its condition changes, by moving either toward what is good or toward what is evil, our spirit is moved to different places or locations in this or that region and comes into contact with the people who live there. It is important to know, however, that the Lord does not transfer us here or there. We relocate ourselves in various ways. If we choose what is good, then we together with the Lord relocate—or rather the Lord together with us relocates—our spirit farther east. If, however, we choose what is evil, then we together with the Devil relocate—or rather the Devil together with us relocates—our spirit farther west. And please note that when I say "heaven" I mean the Lord, because the Lord is everything to all of heaven, and when I say "the Devil" I mean hell, because all the people there are devils.

We are kept in this great interspace and are constantly held in the center of it for one reason only: to grant us free choice in spiritual matters. The equilibrium in question is spiritual, because it is an equilibrium between heaven and hell, and therefore between good and evil. All the people who are in that great interspace are inwardly in partnership either with angels in heaven or with devils in hell. (Today that partnership is either with Michael's angels or with the dragon's angels [Revelation 12:7].) All people after death travel toward their own kind in that interspace and associate with people who love similar things. This happens because love connects all individuals there with others like themselves and allows them to breathe freely and to be in the state of life they were in before. Then step by step they shed outer traits that are not in harmony with what is inside them. Once that process is complete, good people are lifted into heaven and evil people move to hell. In either case they gravitate toward people with the same dominant love[73] as their own.

This spiritual equilibrium or free choice can be illustrated by earthly examples of equilibrium. It is like the equilibrium experienced by a person tied around the waist or arms between two men of equal strength. The person in the middle is pulled by one man to the right and by the other to the left. In that situation the person in the middle is able freely to pull to one side or the other as if not constrained by any force at all. If that person lunges to the right, the man on the left is actually dragged in that direction so violently that he falls to the ground. A similar situation would occur if someone, even a weak person, were to be tied to three men on the right and three equally strong men on the left. In fact, it would be the same if someone were tied between camels or horses.

[2] This spiritual equilibrium or free choice can be compared to a pair of scales with equal weights on both sides; if even something small is then added to one side, the pointer above will wobble to and fro. The same responsiveness is true of a carrying pole, or a large beam balanced on its fulcrum.

Each and every thing inside us, such as our heart, lungs, stomach, liver, pancreas, kidney, intestines, and the rest, is in an equilibrium like this.[74] As a result, every part can perform its functions in a state of complete ease. The same is true of all our muscles; without the equilibrium that exists between them, all action and reaction would stop and we would no longer function as a human being. Given that all parts of our bodies are in an equilibrium like this, all parts of our brains have a similar state of equilibrium. As a result, so also do all the elements that are in our minds, which relate to our will and our intellect.[75]

[3] Animals, birds, fish, and insects also have freedom, although it is their physical senses that drive them, and their appetites and pleasures that point the way. It would be much the same for us, if we had the same freedom of action as we do of thought; in this condition the senses of the body would drive us as well, and our cravings and pleasures would point the way.

It is different for us if we absorb the spiritual teachings of the church and restrain our free choice accordingly. We are then led by the Lord away from cravings and evil pleasures and our native eagerness for them, and we strive for what is good and turn away from what is evil. The Lord then moves us closer to both the east and the south in the spiritual world, and we are brought into heavenly freedom, which is true freedom.[76]

The Fact That Evil Is an Option Available to Everyone's Inner Self Makes It Obvious That We Have Free Choice in Spiritual Matters

479 I will support the idea that we have free choice in spiritual things first by familiar arguments[77] and then by particular arguments. People will recognize the validity of these arguments as soon as they hear them.

The *familiar arguments* are these:

1. The wisest of people, Adam and his wife, let themselves be seduced by a serpent.[78]

2. Their firstborn son Cain killed his brother Abel, and Jehovah God did not dissuade Cain by speaking with him[79] but instead cursed him only after the fact.

3. The Israelite nation in the wilderness worshiped a golden calf, even though Jehovah saw this from Mount Sinai and did not protect the people from doing so.

4. David took a census of the people and because of it, a plague came upon them, which caused the death of many thousands, yet God did not act before but only after the fact, when he sent the prophet Gad to David and announced his punishment.

5. Solomon was allowed to institute forms of worship that were idolatrous. Many kings after him were allowed to desecrate the Temple and the holy practices of the church.

6. Later, that nation was allowed to crucify the Lord.

7. Muhammad was allowed to establish a widespread religious movement, which did not conform to Sacred Scripture.[80]

8. Christianity has split into many sects, and each sect has split into heresies.

9. In the Christian world there are many ungodly people and even people who boast about their godless actions. There are also plots and deceptions, even against godly, just, and honest people.

10. Injustice sometimes triumphs over justice in law courts and business proceedings.

11. The ungodly, too, are elevated to positions of honor and become leaders and heads of the church.

12. Wars are allowed to happen, which involve the killing of many people and the plundering of cities, nations, and households, not to mention many other atrocities.

Is it possible to attribute such things to anything but the free choice that exists in everyone? The concept of "permission" well known throughout this world is from no other source.[81]

On the point that the laws of permission are also the laws of divine providence, see *Divine Providence* (published in Amsterdam in 1764) §§234–274. The numbered points just above are explored there.

There are countless *particular arguments* that would show that we have just as much free choice in spiritual matters as in earthly matters.

If you wish, you could do an experiment on yourself. See if you are able to think about God, the Lord, the Holy Spirit, and the divine matters known as the spiritual concepts of the church seventy times a day

480

or three hundred times a week. And if it is some pleasure or even some craving that brings you to do it (whether you happen to have faith or not), do you feel any compulsion in doing so? Whatever state you are in, consider whether you could think at all if you did not have free choice. Surely, free choice is of supreme importance in what you say, in prayers to God, in preaching, and in listening. In fact, since you take a breath after each instance of speaking your thoughts, if your free choice did not extend to specific things even down to the most minute details, would you be able to breathe any more than a statue can?

I say "any more than a statue" rather than "any more than an animal," because an animal breathes as a result of its earthly free choice. We breathe as a result of our free choice in earthly matters and also our free choice in spiritual matters. We are born different from animals. From birth, animals and all the ideas they have, which are associated with their earthly love, are focused on food and reproduction. We, however, have no innate ideas at birth; we have only a faculty for knowing, understanding, and becoming wise, and an inclination to love ourselves and the world and also to love our neighbor and God.[82] This is why I said that if free choice were taken away in regard to the individual things we will and think, we would breathe no more than a *statue* does; I did not say we would breathe no more than an *animal* does.

481 People do not deny that we have free choice in earthly matters. Nevertheless, that free choice exists only because we have free choice in spiritual matters. The Lord flows into everyone from above or within with divine goodness and divine truth, as was previously shown [§§362–364]. Through this inflow he imparts a different life to us than the life animals receive. He also gives us the power and the desire to receive divine goodness and truth and to act on them. He never takes this away from anyone. It follows from this that the Lord perpetually wills that we receive what is true and do what is good and therefore become spiritual. That is what we were born for.

To become spiritual without having free choice in spiritual matters is as impossible as it is to shove a camel through the eye of a sewing needle [Matthew 19:24; Mark 10:25; Luke 18:25], or to touch some star in heaven with our hand.

[2] I was shown through living experience[83] that everyone—even every devil—has the capability of understanding and willing truth; this ability is never taken away.

One of the inhabitants of hell was once carried up into the world of spirits and was there asked by angels from heaven whether he was able to understand what was being said to him (the things being said were divine truths). He answered that he was indeed able to understand. He was then asked why he had not accepted similar truths. He said that he did not love them and therefore was not willing to accept them. He was told that he did, however, have the capacity to be willing. He was amazed by this but denied that he had the capacity. Therefore angels inspired his intellect with the glory of fame and the pleasures that go with it. Upon accepting that inspiration he did indeed become willing and even loved those truths. Soon, though, he was let back into his former state, in which he was a robber, an adulterer, and a slanderer of his neighbor. Then because he was no longer willing, he did not understand those truths anymore.

This shows that we are human because of our free choice in spiritual things. Without it, we would indeed be a log, a stone, or Lot's wife after she had become a statue.[84]

As for the point that if we had no free choice in spiritual matters, we would have no free choice in civic, moral, and earthly matters either, this stands to reason from the fact that the spiritual things that are called theological dwell in the highest region of the human mind, just as the soul dwells in the body. That is where such things live, because the door through which the Lord "comes in to us" [Revelation 3:20] is on that level. Beneath them are civic, moral, and earthly concerns, which in human beings receive all their life from the spiritual qualities that reside above. Because the life from the Lord flows in at the highest level and because our life consists of the power to freely think and will, and therefore speak and act, it follows that our free choice in politics and earthly matters comes exclusively from our spiritual freedom. Our sense of what is good and true and what is just and upright in civic matters comes from that spiritual freedom; and this sense is the very essence of true intellect.

[2] Our free choice in spiritual matters is like the air in our lungs, which we breathe in, hold inside, and breathe out in accordance with every change in our thoughts. Without spiritual free choice we would be worse off than those who have difficulty breathing because of a suffocating nightmare, angina, or asthma. It is also like the blood in our heart: as we begin to run out of blood, our heart first palpitates, then convulses and stops altogether. It would be like a body in motion, which moves as long as there is some force driving it; the body stops when the force stops. The same is true of the free choice that the human will possesses. Both our will and our free choice could be referred to as *living* forces,

because action stops when the will stops, and the will stops when free choice stops.

[3] Taking away human spiritual freedom would be like removing the wheels from coaches, the air-catching arms from windmills, the sails from ships. It would be like breathing out for the last time and dying. The life of our spirit consists of its free choice in spiritual matters. Angels groan when someone merely mentions that this type of free choice is denied by many ministers of the church today. The angels call that denial a madness beyond madness.

If We Had No Free Choice in Spiritual Matters, the Word Would Be Useless and Therefore the Church Would Be Nothing

483 It is recognized throughout the Christian world that broadly speaking the Word is the law, or the book of the laws we must live by in order to be blessed with eternal life. Surely, the statements in the Word to the effect that we should do good and not evil and should believe in God and not idols occur more often than any others.[85] The Word is full of commandments and exhortations of this kind, with blessings and promises of reward for those who follow them and curses and threats against those who do not. What would be the purpose of all these statements if we had no free choice in spiritual matters, that is, in areas that concern salvation and eternal life? They would be empty statements that serve no use. If we held fast to the idea that we have no power and no freedom in spiritual things, and thus were removed from any power of will in that respect, Sacred Scripture would seem to us like a blank piece of paper with no letters on it, or a sheet of paper on which a whole pot of ink had been spilled, or just serifs and dots without letters—a volume entirely without meaning.[86]

[2] There should be no need to confirm this from the Word; but the church of today has plunged into mindless folly in regard to spiritual matters and has cited a number of passages from the Word in support of its view (although the passages have been interpreted falsely). Therefore I feel obligated to quote some passages that command us to do and believe. They are the following.

> The kingdom of God will be taken away from you and given to a people that produces the fruits of it. (Matthew 21:43)

Produce fruits worthy of repentance. The axe is already lying against the root of the tree. Every tree, then, that does not produce good fruit is being cut down and thrown into the fire. (Luke 3:8, 9)

Jesus said, "Why do you call me 'Lord, Lord' and yet you do not do what I say? Everyone who comes to me and hears my words and does them is like someone who has built a house on the rock; but those who hear and do not do are like someone who has built a house on the ground without a foundation." (Luke 6:46–49)

Jesus said, "My mother and siblings are those who hear the Word of God and do it." (Luke 8:21)

We know that God does not hear sinners, but if people worship God and do his will, them he hears. (John 9:31)

If you know these things, you are happy if you do them. (John 13:17)

Those who have my commandments and do them are the ones who love me, and I will love them. (John 14:21)

In this my Father is glorified, that you bear much fruit. (John 15:8)

You are my friends if you do whatever I command you. I have chosen you so that you will bear fruit and your fruit will remain. (John 15:14, 16)

Make the tree good. A tree is recognized by its fruit. (Matthew 12:33)

Produce fruits worthy of repentance. (Matthew 3:8)

The one sown in good ground is one who hears the Word and bears fruit. (Matthew 13:23)

Those who are reaping a harvest receive their reward and gather fruit for eternal life. (John 4:36)

Wash yourselves; purify yourselves. Remove the evil of your doings; learn to do good. (Isaiah 1:16, 17)

The Son of Humankind[87] will come in the glory of his Father, and then he will render to all according to their deeds. (Matthew 16:27)

Those who have done good things will depart into a resurrection of life. (John 5:29)

Their works follow them. (Revelation [14:13;] 20:12, 13)

Behold, I am coming quickly and my reward is with me, so that I will give to all according to their work. (Revelation 22:12)

Jehovah, whose eyes are opened in order to give to all according to their ways. He treats us according to our works. ([Jeremiah 32:19;] Zechariah 1:6)

[3] The Lord also teaches the same thing in his parables, many of which involve the theme that those who do good things will be accepted and those who do evil things will be rejected. For example, the parable of the vinedressers in the vineyard (Matthew 21:33–44); and the parable of the talents and minas, with which people traded (Matthew 25:14–30; Luke 19:12–27).

Likewise about faith Jesus said, "Those who believe in me will not die to eternity" but will live (John 11:25, 26). "This is the will of the Father, that everyone who believes in the Son has eternal life" (John 6:40). "Those who believe in the Son have eternal life, but those who do not believe in the Son will not see life; instead God's wrath remains upon them" (John 3:36). "God so loved the world that he gave his only begotten Son so that everyone who believes in him would not perish but would have eternal life" (John 3:15, 16). And further, "You are to love the Lord your God with your whole heart and your whole soul and your whole mind. And you are to love your neighbor as yourself. The Law and the Prophets[88] depend on these two commandments" (Matthew 22:37–40). But these are only a handful of passages from the Word, like a few cups of water from an ocean.

484   After reading these quotations and others from one end of the Word to the other, who fails to see the emptiness (I would prefer not to say "idiocy") of the quotations given above in §464 from the ecclesiastical book called the *Formula of Concord*? Would we not think to ourselves, "If what we are taught there is true—that we have no free choice in spiritual matters—wouldn't that make religious practice, which is the doing of what is good, a meaningless expression? And without religious practice, what is the church except the bark from a piece of wood, which is only useful as kindling?" We would also think, "If the church does not really exist, because it has no religious practice, what then are heaven and hell but fables made up by the ministers and leaders of the church to captivate common people and to elevate themselves to high honors?" This is the source of that detestable popular phrase: "Who can do what is good

on their own? Who can acquire faith on their own?" Therefore people do not bother and live a hedonistic life.

[2] But, my friend, abstain from evil, and do what is good, and believe in the Lord with your whole heart and your whole soul; and the Lord will love you and give you love for what you do and faith in what you believe. Then you will do what is good because of love and you will believe because you have faith, which is confidence. And if you persevere like this, a reciprocal partnership [with the Lord] will develop and become permanent. This is salvation itself and eternal life.

If we did not use the powers that have been granted to us to do what is good, and we did not use our minds to believe in the Lord, what would we be except a wasteland or a desert, like ground that is so utterly dry that it repels rather than absorbs rain? We would be like a sandy field where there are sheep that have nothing to eat. We would be like a spring that has dried up, or like stagnant water around a spring that is blocked. We would be like a home where there is no harvest and no pond; unless we left there immediately and looked for an inhabitable spot elsewhere, we would die of hunger and thirst.

If We Had No Free Choice in Spiritual Matters, There Would Be Nothing in Us That Would Allow Us to Forge a Partnership with the Lord, and Therefore [There Would Be] No Ascribing [of Goodness to Us], Only Mere Predestination, Which Is Detestable

As was fully demonstrated in the chapter on faith [§§336–391], without free choice in spiritual matters no one would have any goodwill or faith, still less a partnership between those two things. From the points made there it follows that if we had no free choice in spiritual matters there would be nothing in us that would allow the Lord to form a bond with us. Without a reciprocal partnership [with the Lord] reformation and regeneration would be impossible, and therefore there would be no salvation.

An irrefutable result of this is that without a reciprocal partnership of the Lord with us and us with the Lord, there would be no ascribing [of goodness to us]. Convincing ourselves that [after death] there is no assigning of spiritual credit for goodness or blame for evil (because we lack free choice in spiritual matters) has many consequences, and they

485

are severe. They will have to be unveiled in the last part of this book,[89] where we will explore the heresies, absurdities, and contradictions that flow forth from today's belief that the merit and justice of the Lord God the Savior are assigned to us.

486   Predestination is an offspring of the faith of today's church. It is born from the belief that we are absolutely powerless and have no choice in spiritual matters. It arises from that belief and also from the notions that our conversion to God is more or less passive, that we are like a log, and that we have no awareness of whether grace has brought this log to life or not. [In other such teachings] it is said that we are chosen by the pure grace of God exclusive of any human action, whether that action is initiated by the powers of our nature or of our reason. We are told that our being chosen takes place where and when God wants—it is entirely up to him. In the sight of one who reflects, the good works that follow faith as signs of it are just like works of the flesh. The Spirit that produces those good works does not reveal what their origin is, but produces them as works of grace or good pleasure, just as it does with faith itself.

[2] From these teachings it is clear that the dogma of today's church regarding predestination has arisen from denial of free choice as a shoot arises from a seed. I can assert that it flows forth as a scarcely avoidable by-product of that belief.[90] A flowing forth like this first occurred among the Predestinarians; then another came from Gottschalk, and later on yet another from Calvin and his followers. Eventually the concept was firmly established by the Synod of Dort. From there it was imported by the Supralapsarians and the Infralapsarians as a sacred central effigy in their religion, or better yet, as the head of Medusa the Gorgon[91] carved into the shield of Pallas [Athena].[92]

[3] How could we attribute more harmfulness or cruelty to God than by believing that he predestines some members of the human race to hell? It would be believing in divine cruelty to think that the Lord, who is love itself and mercy itself, would want a multitude of people to be born for hell or millions to be born under a curse, that is, to be born devils and satans.[93] It would be believing in divine cruelty to think that even though the Lord has divine wisdom, which is infinite, he would neglect to ensure through providence and foresight that those who live good lives and acknowledge God are not thrown into eternal fire and torment.

The Lord is in fact the Creator and Savior of all. He alone leads all people. He wishes the death of no one. How could we attribute greater savagery to him than by thinking that the vast arrays of nations and populations under his divine guidance and watchful eye would just be handed over by predestination as prey to satiate the Devil's gaping jaws? This is the offspring of the faith of today's church; the belief of the new church, though, abhors it as something monstrous.

It used to seem incredible to me that any Christian could ever come to such a deranged conclusion, let alone spread it around by word of mouth or bring it to light by publication; and I refused to believe it even though such a conclusion was in fact drawn by a select group of clergy at the Synod of Dort in the Netherlands, and was afterward written out in a careful hand and distributed to the public. To convince me, some of those who participated[94] in the decisions of that Synod were brought to me.

487

When I noticed them standing near me I said, "How could someone whose reason is at all sound conclude that there is predestination? What else could this have led to except a flood of ideas that God is cruel and that religion is fraudulent? If people support predestination and engrave it on their hearts, how can they avoid seeing the teachings of the church and the Word as pointless? Can they think of God as anything but a tyrant, since he predestines hundreds of thousands to hell?"

[2] They stared at me with a satanic look[95] and said, "We were selected to participate in the Synod of Dort. At the time, and even more so since then, we convinced ourselves of many things concerning God, the Word, and religion that we didn't dare divulge. Instead, when we spoke about and taught those topics, we spun and wove a web of multicolored threads, and on it we spread peacock feathers."

Because the speakers were trying to do the same thing now, angels who were given power by the Lord closed the outer levels of their minds and opened the inner levels in them, and made them speak from those levels instead.[96]

They then said, "We based the faith that we had then and that we still have now on a series of conclusions. We believe the following: [3] (1) There is no such thing as the Word of Jehovah God; there is only some empty verbosity from the mouth of the prophets. (We came to this thought because the Word predestines all to heaven,[97] and people themselves are to blame if they don't walk on the paths that lead there.)[98] (2) Religion does and should exist, but it is no more than a strong wind that bears a [calming,] fragrant odor to the masses. Therefore religion should be taught by ministers to the small as well as the great,[99] and should be based on the Word, because the Word's teaching is well received. (We had these thoughts because predestination actually renders religion null and void.)

(3) The civil laws of justice are religion; but we are predestined not because of the lives we lived by those laws but exclusively because that is up to God, like the decision of an absolute monarch based on one look at our face. (4) With the exception of the one point that God exists, everything the church teaches ought to be regarded as nonsense that we should disapprove of and garbage that we should throw out. (5) The supposedly spiritual teachings that are paraded before us are actually nothing more than vapors of subsolar ether:[100] if they penetrate us deeply they cause dizziness and lethargy and turn us into a detestable monster in the sight of God."

(6) They were asked whether they believed that the faith on which they based the idea of predestination was spiritual or not. They answered that people are predestined based on their faith, but when faith is granted them, they are like logs. From that state they are indeed brought to life, but not spiritually.

[4] After uttering these horrible things, they wanted to leave, but I said to them, "Stay here a little longer, and I will read to you from Isaiah."

What I read them was this:

> Do not be happy, all Philistia, that the rod that was striking you is broken, because from the root of the serpent a basilisk has come out, and its fruit is a flying fire snake. (Isaiah 14:29)

I used the spiritual meaning of the passage to explain it: *Philistia* means the church that is separated from goodwill. The *basilisk that has come out from the root of the serpent* means the teaching of that church that there are three gods and that Christ's righteousness is assigned to every individual. *Its fruit,* which *is a flying fire snake,* means the idea that there is no credit for good actions or blame for evil actions; there is instant mercy, regardless of whether our lives have been good or evil.

[5] "Perhaps that is the meaning," they said. "But find us a passage on predestination in that volume that you call the Holy Word."

I opened it up and in the same prophet I came upon this passage, which agrees with what I had quoted them earlier:

> They were laying the eggs of a poisonous snake and weaving the webs of a spider. Whoever eats their eggs dies, and when someone crushes [one of those eggs], a viper is hatched. (Isaiah 59:5)

When they heard that, they did not wait around for the explanation. Five of the people who had been brought to me hurled themselves violently into a cave. Around it there appeared a dark glow—a sign that they had no faith or goodwill.

From all this it follows that the Synod's decree about predestination is not just an insane heresy but a cruel heresy as well. It has to be eradicated from the brain so thoroughly that not even a single jot of it remains.

The belief that God predestines people to hell is savage. It can be compared with the savagery of parents in some barbaric cultures who throw their nursing babies out into the streets.[101] It is like the savagery of some enemies who throw the bodies of people they have killed into the woods to be eaten by wild animals.[102] It is like the cruelty of a tyrant who divides the people under him into groups and sends some groups to the executioners, hurls some groups into the depths of the sea, and throws other groups into the fire. It is like the rage that drives some wild animals to eat their own young. It is also like the insanity of dogs that suddenly attack their own reflection in a mirror.

488

If We Had No Free Choice in Spiritual Matters, God Would Be the Cause of Evil, and We Could Not Be Credited [with Goodwill or Faith]

The notion that God is the cause of evil follows from the modern-day belief that was first hatched by those who participated in the Council of Nicaea.[103] At that event a heresy was thrown together and cooked up that still persists today, which is that there are three divine persons from eternity, each of which is a God on his own. Once that egg was hatched, the followers had no choice but to turn to each divine person as an individual god. The participants at Nicaea put together a belief that the merit or justice of the Lord God the Savior is assigned to us. Then, to prevent the idea that we actually acquire the Lord's merit, they took away any idea that we have free choice in spiritual matters, and brought in the notion that we are completely powerless in regard to that faith. Because they centered all the spiritual teaching of the church on that belief alone, they declared the existence of a similar spiritual powerlessness in regard to everything the church teaches about salvation. As a result, horrific heresies came into being, one after another, founded upon that faith and the notion of human powerlessness in spiritual matters, including predestination, that

489

most damaging of concepts, which was covered under the preceding heading [§§485–488]. All these teachings entail the idea that God is the cause of evil or that God created both good and evil.

My friend, do not put your trust in any council. Put your trust in the Lord's Word, which is high above councils. Look at all the notions hatched by Roman Catholic councils![104] Look at the egg the Synod of Dort laid from which the horrendous viper of predestination came forth!

[2] Now you might suppose that the free choice granted to human beings in spiritual matters is part of the chain of causes of evil, and therefore that if free choice of this kind had not been granted to us, we would not be able to sin. But, my friend, stop for a moment here and consider whether any human being could be created so as to be human without having free choice in spiritual matters. If this were taken away from us, we would be statues and no longer human. What is free choice except the power to will and do and think and speak to all appearances as if we did so on our own? Because this ability was granted to us so that we could live as human beings, two trees were placed in the Garden of Eden—the tree of life and the tree of the knowledge of good and evil. This means that from the freedom that has been granted to us we can eat fruit from the tree of life and we can eat fruit from the tree of the knowledge of good and evil.

490 Everything God created was good, as the first chapter in Genesis makes clear. As we read there in verses 10, 12, 18, 21, and 25, "God saw that it was good." Then in verse 31 we read, "God saw all that he had made, and yes, it was very good." This is also apparent from the fact that human beings were originally in paradise. Evil arose from humankind, as is evident from the state of Adam after or as the result of the Fall, namely, that he was expelled from paradise.

From these points it is clear that if we had *not* been given free choice in spiritual matters, God himself, not us, would have been the cause of evil, and therefore both good and evil would have been created by God. It is atrocious, though, to think that he created evil. God endowed us with free choice in spiritual matters, and therefore he was not the creator of evil. He never inspires anything evil within us. This is because he is goodness itself. God is omnipresent in goodness and constantly urges and demands that he be received. If he is not received, he still does not leave, because if he were to leave, we would instantly die; in fact, we would collapse into a nonentity. Our life and the subsistence of everything we are made of is from God.

[2] God did not create evil. It is something we ourselves introduced, because we turn what is good, which continually flows in from God, into what is evil, and by means of that evil we turn ourselves away from God and toward ourselves. When we do so, the delight connected with that goodness remains but becomes a delight in evil. (Without a seemingly similar delight remaining, we would no longer be alive, because delight produces the life of our love.) Nevertheless, these two kinds of delight are completely opposite to each other. We do not realize this as long as we are alive in this world, but after our death we will recognize it and sense it very clearly. There, the delight that accompanies a love for what is good turns into heavenly blessedness, but the delight that accompanies a love for what is evil turns into something horrible and hellish.

From all this it stands to reason that all of us are predestined to heaven and none of us is predestined to hell. We devote ourselves to hell by abusing our freedom in spiritual matters; then we embrace the types of things that emanate from hell. As was noted above [§§475–478], we are all kept in the central area between heaven and hell, so that we are in an equilibrium between good and evil and therefore have free choice in spiritual matters.

God granted freedom not just to human beings but also to every type of animal; he even granted to inanimate things something analogous to freedom. Each entity receives that gift in accordance with its own nature. He also provides them all with what is good, but the entities themselves turn it into evil. **491**

This can be illustrated by comparisons: The atmosphere gives every human being the ability to breathe, and does the same for every animal, whether domesticated or wild, and also for every bird, whether it is an owl or a dove; it also gives birds the ability to fly. Yet the atmosphere is not responsible for the fact that what it offers is taken up by creatures that are opposite to each other in nature and character.

The ocean offers itself to every type of fish as a place to live and also provides them all with food, yet the ocean is not responsible for the fact that one type of fish eats another, or that a crocodile turns the ocean's generosity into poison that it uses to kill people.[105]

The sun supplies light and heat to all things, but its objects, which are the various types of vegetation on earth, use them in different ways. A good kind of tree or bush uses that heat and light one way; a thorn or a bramble uses them another way. A harmless plant does something very different with them than a poisonous plant does.

[2] Rain from high up in the atmosphere falls everywhere on the ground. The ground then distributes that water to every bush, plant, and blade of grass, and each of them takes up as much of it as it needs. This is what I meant by something analogous to free choice, because these plants freely drink the water in through orifices, pores, and passageways that are open when it is warm. The earth does no more than offer moisture and nutrients; the plants take them in according to their thirst and hunger, so to speak.

It is similar with human beings. The Lord flows into every one of us with spiritual heat, which is essentially the goodness of love, and spiritual light, which is essentially the truth of wisdom. How open we are to these qualities depends on which way we are turned, either toward God or toward ourselves. Therefore in teaching us about loving our neighbor, the Lord says, "You are to be children of your Father, who makes the sun rise on the evil and on the good, and sends rain on the just and on the unjust" (Matthew 5:45). Elsewhere we read that "he wills the salvation of all" [1 Timothy 2:4; Ezekiel 18:23, 32].

492 To these points I will add the following memorable occurrence.

Several times I have heard words issuing forth from heaven about the good actions that come from goodwill. These words passed through the world of spirits and penetrated into hell, even to its greatest depth. Step by step the words turned into words that are directly opposed to the good actions that come from goodwill, and finally became expressions of hatred against the neighbor. This is an indication that everything that emanates from the Lord is good. It is the spirits in hell who turn that emanation into evil. A similar thing happened with some truths related to faith. As they went along they were turned into falsities opposed to those truths. The receiving form turns what is flowing in into something that harmonizes with itself.

Every Spiritual Gift the Church Has to Offer That Comes to Us
in Freedom and That We Freely Accept Stays with Us;
What Comes to Us in Other Ways Does Not

493 What we accept in freedom stays with us, because freedom relates to our will; and since freedom relates to our will it also relates to our love. The will is a vessel for love, as I have shown elsewhere [§§39, 263, 362:1].

Freedom is a characteristic of everything that belongs to love and everything that belongs to our will. Anyone can see this from the statement "I want to do this because I love it," and the other way around, "because I love this I also want to do it." Nevertheless, the will we have is dual. We have an inner will and an outer will; our inner self has a will and so does our outer self. This is what makes it possible for con artists to act and speak one way before the world and another way with their close friends. Before the world they act and speak from the will of their outer self, but with friends, from the will within, and here I mean the will of the inner self where their dominant love resides.

Just from these few points we can see that our inner will is our true self. It is the location of the underlying reality[106] and essence of our life. Our intellect is the form of that inner self. Through our intellect our will makes its love visible. Our freedom is a matter of everything we love and everything love leads us to want. Whatever comes forth from the love in our inner will is the delight of our life. And because the love in our inner will is the underlying reality of our life, it also truly belongs to us.

This is why something that the freedom of this will leads us to accept stays with us; it adds itself to what is our own. The opposite occurs if something is brought in apart from our freedom; that something is not accepted in the same way. But this is to be taken up in the ensuing discussion [§§496, 500].

It is essential, however, to understand that what stays with us are the spiritual matters related to the Word and the church that we drink in with love and support with our intellect. This does not happen to the same extent with civil and political matters. Spiritual matters ascend into the highest region of the mind and take shape there, because that is the level where the Lord enters us, bringing divine forms of truth and goodness. That level is like a temple that he inhabits. Civil and political matters, because they have to do with the world, occupy lower areas of the mind. Some of them are like smaller buildings outside the temple, and some are like points of entry into it.

494

The reason why spiritual matters related to the church dwell in the highest region of the mind is that they belong to our soul and exist to serve our eternal life. Our soul exists on the highest level and its nourishment comes exclusively from spiritual food. This is why the Lord refers to himself as bread. He says, "I am the living bread that comes down from heaven. Anyone who eats this bread will live forever" (John 6:51). Our love, which is the source of our blessedness after death, also dwells on that level; and our free choice in spiritual matters principally resides there.

All the freedom we enjoy in earthly matters comes down from this higher freedom; and because freedom originates there, it has a share in all the free choices we make in earthly matters. From among our earthly options, the love that is dominant in us on the highest level selects everything that is well suited to itself. That higher freedom is present the way a spring is present in all the water that flows from it, or the way the fertility of a seed is present in each and every part of the tree that results from it—especially the fruit, in which the seed renews itself.

All those who deny and reject free choice in spiritual matters, however, tap into another water source and give it an outlet in themselves. They turn spiritual freedom first into a freedom that is merely earthly, and finally into a freedom that is hellish. This freedom too is like the fertility of a seed, and it too passes freely through trunk and branches into fruits, but those fruits are rotten inside because of the source from which they sprang.

495 All the freedom that comes from the Lord is true freedom. The freedom in us that comes from hell is slavery. To someone in hellish freedom, however, spiritual freedom inevitably looks like slavery, because the two are opposites. Nevertheless, all people who are in spiritual freedom know and even sense that hellish freedom is slavery. To angels that freedom is therefore as repulsive as the stench of a corpse, but hellish spirits breathe it in like an intoxicating perfume.

As the Lord's Word makes clear, worship that takes place in a state of freedom is true worship, and what is spontaneous is pleasing to the Lord. This is why it says in David, "I will sacrifice to God willingly" (Psalms 54:6); and "The willing among the people have gathered, the people of the God of Abraham" (Psalms 47:9). This is why the children of Israel made freewill offerings[107] (their holy worship consisted principally in sacrifices). Because of God's pleasure in what is spontaneous they were commanded that "Every man whose heart impels him, and everyone whose willing spirit moves him, should bring a freewill offering to Jehovah for the work of the tent [of meeting]" (Exodus 35:5, 21, 29). And the Lord says, "If you remain in my Word you are truly my disciples. And you will know the truth and the truth will set you free. If therefore the Son makes you free, you will be truly free. Everyone who commits sin, though, is a slave of sin" (John 8:31–36).

What we accept in freedom stays with us because our will takes it in and makes it our own; it becomes part of our love, and our love recognizes it as its own and uses it to form itself. **496**

This will be illustrated by comparisons. Because they are based on earthly phenomena, heat will take the place of love.

We know that as a consequence of the presence of heat, and in proportion to its intensity, the pores that exist in every plant open up, and as they open, the plant is inwardly restored to a form that reflects its own nature. It willingly takes in elements that nourish it, it retains the elements that best suit it, and it grows.

A similar thing happens with an animal. Whatever an animal chooses to eat (driven by its love for being nourished—its "appetite") is incorporated into its body and remains a part of it. The animal is continually adding elements to its body that are well suited to it, because all its component parts are perpetually being rebuilt. Some [scholars], but not many, recognize that this is the case.[108]

[2] In animals also, heat opens up all parts of their body and allows their earthly love to run free. This is why in spring and summer animals come into (or return to) their reproductive instinct and an instinctive desire to raise their offspring. All this takes place in the context of the greatest freedom, because it is part of the dominant love that was instilled in them from creation, for the sake of preserving the universe in the state in which it was created.

[3] I use the freedom that heat brings about to illustrate the freedom that love brings about because love produces heat, as we can see from its effects. For example, as people's love is rising up into an intense state or as it goes into a rage, they are sparked, they heat up, and they become inflamed. The heat in our blood—our vital heat—and generally speaking, the heat in animals, comes from no other source. As a result of this correspondence, heat modifies the systems of the body so that they are readily receptive to the things for which love yearns.

[4] All the systems within a human being are in an equilibrium and therefore have a freedom like this. In a state of freedom, the heart pumps blood both upward and downward, the mesentery moves chyle,[109] the liver produces blood, the kidneys separate it, the glands filter it, and so on. If the equilibrium was compromised, that body part would become diseased and would fall into paralysis or loss of control. Equilibrium and

freedom are one. In the entire created universe no substance exists that does not seek its own equilibrium in order to be free.

Although Our Will and Intellect Exist in This State of Free Choice, the Doing of Evil Is Forbidden by Law in Both Worlds, the Spiritual and the Earthly, Since Otherwise Society in Both Realms Would Perish

497 The fact that everyone has free choice in spiritual matters is something that any of us can know just by observing our own thoughts. Who is not free to think about God, the Trinity, goodwill and the neighbor, faith and its activity, the Word and all that comes from it, and the fine points of theology (once one has learned what they are)? Who is unable to think, draw conclusions, teach, or write either for or against them? If this freedom of ours were to be taken away from us for one moment, our thought would stop, our tongue would become silent, and our hand would seize up. Therefore, my friend, just from observing your own thoughts you are in a position (if you so desire) to reject and condemn [the current view] as an absurd and damaging heresy in Christianity today, a heresy that has put the heavenly teaching on goodwill and faith, on salvation and eternal life, into a coma.

[2] The following are reasons why the will and the intellect are where this free choice dwells in us: (1) Because these two faculties must be instructed and reformed first; and then through them, the two faculties of the outer self that make us speak and act are to be instructed and reformed. (2) Because these two faculties of our inner self constitute the spirit within us that lives on after death. Our spirit lives under a form of law that is entirely divine, whose primary principle is that we think of the law, do the law, and obey the law [as if we did so] on our own, although we actually do so from the Lord. [3] (3) Because our spirit is midway between heaven and hell, and therefore midway between good and evil. As a result we are in equilibrium. This is what gives us free choice in spiritual matters. (On this type of equilibrium, see §§475–478.) Nevertheless, as long as we are alive in this world, our spirit is in an equilibrium between heaven and *the world*. At this point we scarcely realize that the more we turn away from heaven toward the world, the closer we move toward hell. The reason we are partly aware and partly unaware of

this is so that in this regard as well we may be free and may be reformed. [4] (4) Because these two faculties, the will and the intellect, are two vessels for the Lord. The will is a vessel to receive love and goodwill, and the intellect is a vessel to receive wisdom and faith; as the Lord brings each of these qualities about in us we are in a state of complete freedom, which allows us a partnership with him that is mutual and reciprocal and results in our salvation. (5) Because the entire judgment we undergo after death hinges on the use we made of free choice in spiritual matters.[110]

The culmination of the points just presented is that free choice in spiritual matters dwells in a state of complete perfection in our soul. Just as water wells up from underground to form a spring, free choice flows from our soul into our mind, into both its chambers (the will and the intellect), and flows through them into our bodily senses and our speech and actions.

498

There are three levels of life within us: the soul, the mind, and bodily sensation. Everything that exists on a higher level enjoys a greater perfection than the things that are on a lower level.

The Lord is present with us *through* our human freedom, *in* that freedom, and *with* that freedom, constantly urging us to receive him but at the same time never removing or taking away our freedom, since, as I mentioned above [§§493–496], no spiritual action that we have taken stays with us unless we freely chose to take it. Therefore you could say that our freedom is where the Lord dwells with us in our soul.

[2] Nevertheless, in both worlds—the spiritual and the earthly—the doing of evil is forbidden by law, since otherwise society would no longer exist anywhere. This is clear without explanation, but I will still illustrate it by the fact that without those external restraints not only would society cease to exist, but in fact the entire human race would perish. There are two loves that human beings find particularly enticing: love of dominating everyone, and love of possessing everyone's wealth. These loves will rush on to infinity if the reins on them are let loose. The hereditary evil we are born with arises primarily from these two loves. Adam's only problem was a desire to become like God; we read that the serpent inspired that desire in him [Genesis 3:4, 5]. Therefore when he is cursed he is told that the land is going to yield him thorns and thistles (Genesis 3:17, 18); these plants mean everything that is evil and consequently false. All people who are slaves to these loves view themselves alone as the only thing in which and for which all others exist. People like this have no compassion, no fear of God, no love for their neighbor.

Therefore they have mercilessness, savagery, and cruelty, and a hellish longing and eagerness for stealing and robbing and for the deceitfulness and trickery involved. The animals of the earth have no innate desires of this kind; when they kill and devour, the only love driving them is their desire to fill their stomachs or to protect themselves. Therefore, because they have these types of love, evil people are more savage, more ferocious, and worse than any animal.

[3] The behavior of a rioting crowd, when the restraints of the law break down, reveals that human beings are inwardly this way. This aspect of human nature is also visible in massacres and raids, when the sound [of the trumpet] gives the soldiers permission to unleash rage against the conquered or captured. Hardly anyone declines such an opportunity before the beat of the drum calls it off. This makes clear that if no fear of legal punishment held us back, not only society but the human race as a whole would be destroyed.

The only thing that removes all these traits is the proper exercise of our free choice in spiritual things, which is to focus our mind on the state of our life after death.

499 This point should also be illustrated through comparisons, as follows.

No creation could have taken place unless some free choice existed in all things that were created, both animate and inanimate. If animals lacked free choice in earthly matters, they would have no ability to choose the food that was the most nourishing for them, and would not be able to reproduce or protect their offspring; so there would be no animals.

If the fish in the sea or the crustaceans on the sea floor had no freedom, there would be no fish or crustaceans. Likewise, if every little insect had no freedom, there would be no silkworms producing silk, no bees producing honey or wax, no butterflies playing with their partners in the air, feeding on the nectar in flowers, and representing our blessed state in the breezes of heaven after we, like caterpillars, have shed our old skin.

[2] Unless there were something analogous to free choice in the soil of the ground, in the seed planted in it, in every part of the tree that germinates from that seed, in its fruits, and again in new seeds, there would be no plants. Unless there were something analogous to free choice in every type of metal and stone, whether noble or base,[111] there would be no metal, no stone, not even a grain of sand. Each of these things freely absorbs ether,[112] exhales its own natural emanation, casts off particles that have broken down, and integrates new particles into itself.[113] This activity results in the magnetic field that surrounds a magnet, the iron field that surrounds iron, the copper field that surrounds copper, the

silver field that surrounds silver, the golden field that surrounds gold, the stony field that surrounds stone, the nitrous field that surrounds niter, the sulfuric field that surrounds sulfur, and the fields of various kinds that surround each type of particulate matter on earth.[114] In the case of every seed, these fields penetrate its inmost parts and supply materials for its growth. Without exhalations from every little grain of dust in the earth, the seed would not begin or continue in the process of germination. How else could the earth penetrate into the very center of a seed that has been sown, bringing in water and solid particles, except through materials given off by what surrounds the seed? Take, for example, "a grain of mustard seed, which is the least of all seeds, but when it has grown, it is bigger than all other plants and becomes a large tree" (Matthew 13:32; Mark 4:30, 31, 32).

[3] If all created things have been endowed with freedom, then, each according to its own nature, why would we humans not have free choice according to our nature, which is that we are to become spiritual? This is why we have been granted free choice in spiritual matters from the womb even to our last moment in this world, and afterward to eternity.

If We Did Lack Free Choice in Spiritual Matters,
Then in a Single Day Everyone on the Whole Planet
Could Be Induced to Believe in the Lord;
but in Fact This Cannot Happen, Because What We Do Not
Accept through Our Free Choice Does Not Stay with Us

If free choice in spiritual matters had not been granted to us, then in a single day God could induce everyone on the planet to believe in him; but this is only taken as true when divine omnipotence is not well understood. People who do not understand divine omnipotence are able to reckon either that no divine design[115] exists, or that God can act just as easily against his design as with it. But in fact, without the divine design no creation would have been possible. The first element of the divine design is that we are an image of God, so that we can be perfected in love and wisdom and therefore become more and more of an image [of him]. God continually works toward this within us, but if we had no free choice in spiritual matters that would allow us to turn ourselves toward God and forge a partnership with him, his work would be pointless, because his goal would be impossible to achieve.

There is a design from which and according to which the whole world and each and everything in it was created. And because all creation was brought about from that design and according to it, therefore God is called the divine design itself. Therefore it is the same whether you say "to act against the divine design" or "to act against God." God could not act against his own divine design, since that would in fact be acting against himself. Therefore he leads every human being in a manner in keeping with his being that design. The wandering and the fallen he leads into that design; the resistant he leads toward it.

[2] If it would have been possible to create the human race without endowing it with free choice in spiritual matters, what then would have been easier for the omnipotent God than to induce everyone on the whole planet to believe in the Lord? Could he not have installed this faith in everyone, either directly or indirectly? He could have done so directly through his own absolute power and his constant, irresistible efforts to save us; or he could have done it indirectly through inflicting torment upon our consciences and devastating convulsions upon our bodies, and threatening us with death if we did not accept. He could have achieved the same result by opening hell to us and surrounding us with devils holding terrifying torches in their hands, or by calling up from hell dead people we once knew who now look like horrible specters. But to these arguments comes a response in the words of Abraham to the rich man in hell: "If they do not hear Moses and the prophets, they are not going to be persuaded even if someone were to rise from the dead" (Luke 16:31).

501　These days people are asking why miracles do not happen anymore the way they used to.[116] There is the belief that if they did happen, we would all acknowledge God from the depths of our hearts. The reason miracles are not happening today the way they used to is that miracles are coercive; they take away our free choice in spiritual matters. They make us more earthly than spiritual. Since the time of the Lord's Coming, everyone in the Christian world has had the capability of becoming spiritual. We become spiritual solely from the Lord through the agency of the Word. If miracles induced us to believe, we would actually lose this capability, because, as I just mentioned, they are coercive and take away our free choice in spiritual matters. And when it comes to spiritual things, everything that is forced on us intrudes into our earthly self and closes the door, so to speak, to the spiritual level in us that is our true inner self. It deprives our inner self of all ability to see anything true in the light. After that, our only thought about spiritual matters would be reasoning on the part of our earthly self, and our earthly self sees everything that is truly spiritual upside down.

[2] The reason why miracles did occur before the Lord's Coming was that then the people in the church were earthly in nature and were not open to the spiritual matters that belong to the inner church.[117] If spiritual matters had been opened up to them, they would have desecrated them. Therefore all their forms of worship were rituals that meant and represented the inner teachings of the church. The only way they could be induced to perform the rituals correctly was through miracles; and in fact [at times] not even miracles could persuade them, because there was something spiritual lying hidden within those representative acts of worship. This is clear from the fact that even though the children of Israel in the wilderness had witnessed so many miracles in Egypt and the greatest of miracles on Mount Sinai, Moses had not been absent for more than a month before they were dancing around the golden calf and shouting that it had led them out of Egypt. They engaged in similar acts once in the land of Canaan, even though they saw astounding miracles performed by Elijah and Elisha, and later on, the divine miracles performed by the Lord.[118]

[3] The main reason why miracles are not happening today is that the church has denied that we have any free choice in spiritual matters. It achieved this by sanctioning the notion that we are completely unable to contribute anything to our own acceptance of faith, and that we play no role whatever in our own conversion or our salvation in general (see §464 above). People who have these beliefs become more and more earthly, and the earthly self, as mentioned just above, looks at everything spiritual the wrong way up and therefore decides against it. In that circumstance, the higher region of the human mind—the primary location of our free choice in spiritual matters—would be closed; the spiritual teachings that were apparently corroborated by the miracles would inhabit the lower, merely earthly region of the mind, while false beliefs about faith, conversion, and salvation remained fixed in place on that higher level. The result would be that satans would live on the higher floor and angels on the lower floor, like vultures above hens. After a while, the satans would break the dead bolt and burst in with a fury on the spiritual teachings that were allotted a place below, and would not merely deny those teachings but would blaspheme and desecrate them. Therefore for such people the situation afterward would be much worse than it was before.

People who have become earthly because of false beliefs about the spiritual teachings of the church cannot help thinking that divine omnipotence is above and beyond the design [of the universe], and therefore that divine omnipotence exists outside that design. As a result they lapse into deranged thoughts such as the following.

502

"Why did the Lord come into the world and why was this a redemption, when God's omnipotence could have allowed him to accomplish the same thing from heaven as he did on earth? Why wouldn't he, through his redemption, have saved the entire human race down to the last person? After that point, why would the Devil be able to prevail against the Redeemer in us? Why does hell exist? Since God is omnipotent, why hasn't he destroyed hell, or why doesn't he do so now? Or else why doesn't he lead all the devils out of there and make them all angels of heaven? Why have a Last Judgment? Is he unable to move all the goats from the left to the right and make them sheep?[119] Why did he cast down from heaven the angels of the dragon and the dragon itself instead of changing them into angels of Michael? Why doesn't he grant faith to both groups, assign them the Son's justice, and so forgive their sins and justify and sanctify them? Why doesn't he give the animals of the earth, the birds in the sky, and the fish in the sea the ability to speak and gain understanding, and bring them into heaven along with people? Why either in the past or now hasn't he transformed our world into a paradise that has no tree of the knowledge of good and evil and no serpent, where all the hills are flowing with vintage wine, and yielding their own gold and silver, so that all would spend their lives as images of God there, singing and shouting and in everlasting celebrations and joy? Wouldn't these be fitting accomplishments for the omnipotent God?" And so on.

[2] But, my friend, all this is nonsense. Divine omnipotence is not outside the design. God himself is the design. Because all things were created by God, they were created by the design, in the design, and for the design. There is also a design into which humankind was created, which is that whether we are blessed or cursed depends on our own exercise of free choice in spiritual matters.

As mentioned above [§499:1], it would not be possible to create a human being, or even an animal, bird, or fish, that had no free choice; but animals have a form of free choice that is merely earthly, whereas people have both earthly free choice and spiritual free choice.

503 To these points I will add the following memorable occurrences.
The first memorable occurrence. I heard that an assembly had been called for and charged with discussing human free choice in spiritual matters.

The gathering took place in the spiritual world. There were scholars in attendance from every region who, in the physical world in which they had previously lived, had given thought to this subject.[120] It also included many of those who participated in the councils that occurred before or after the Council of Nicaea.

The participants gathered in a round temple much like the Pantheon in Rome, which was formerly devoted to the worship of all the gods, but was later dedicated by the papal seat to the worship of all the holy martyrs. In this spiritual temple, too, there were altars of a kind along the walls, but in this case there were benches at each altar. The participants were sitting on these benches and leaning their elbows on the altars as if they were tables. They had no designated chairperson to act as their leader; instead individuals, whenever they felt the urge, would burst forth into the center of the room and pour out their considered opinion. I found it astounding that everyone present at that assembly was convinced that human beings are completely powerless in regard to spiritual matters. They all ridiculed the notion of spiritual free choice.

[2] When the participants had gathered, one of them suddenly burst forth into the center of the room and blasted out the following in a loud voice: "We have no free choice in spiritual matters—no more freedom than Lot's wife had after she was turned into a pillar of salt. If any free choice had remained in us, surely we would have acted on our own and acquired for ourselves the faith of our church; but our faith is the belief that it is entirely God the Father's free choice and decision to grant this faith to whomever he wishes, whenever he wishes. God would not have this decision or this option at all, though, if we were able to acquire faith for ourselves through some freedom or decision of our own. In that case our faith, which is a star that shines before us day and night, would burn out like a shooting star hitting the atmosphere."

After that another person burst forth from his bench and said, "We have no more free choice in spiritual matters than an animal does—no more than a dog.[121] If we did possess it, we would do good things on our own; but in fact all goodness is from God and we cannot receive anything that is not given us from heaven [John 3:27]."

[3] After him, another person jumped up from his chair and lifted his voice from the center of the room and said, "Human beings have no more free choice in spiritual matters, or even sight of spiritual matters, than a barn owl has in the daytime or a chick has when it is still hidden

within its egg—both are as blind as a mole. If we were sharp-sighted enough to see things related to faith, salvation, and eternal life, we would believe that we were capable of regenerating and saving ourselves, and we might actually attempt it and desecrate both our thoughts and actions with a constant desire for reward."

Another person rushed to the center of the room and put forth this opinion: "Those who think they are able to will and understand anything related to spiritual matters since the fall of Adam are insane and become raving lunatics, because they believe they are a deity or demigod who owns a share of divine power outright."

[4] Then another person came breathlessly into the center of the room, carrying under his arm a book containing the orthodoxy, as he called it, that contemporary Evangelicals swear to observe, titled the *Formula of Concord*. He opened the book and read the following passage from it:

> We are utterly corrupt and dead to what is good, so that in our nature after the Fall but before our regeneration, not the least spark of spiritual power remains that would enable us to prepare ourselves for the grace of God, or to accept it once it was offered, or to make room for grace by ourselves and on our own, or to understand, believe, comprehend, think, will, start, finish, enact, work, or cooperate in spiritual matters, or to adapt or accommodate ourselves to grace, or to contribute anything to our own conversion, by half or to the least extent. In spiritual matters, which concern the salvation of our souls, we are like Lot's wife when she became a pillar of salt, and like a log or a stone, devoid of life, which has no functioning eyes, mouth, or senses. Nevertheless, we do retain locomotive power to control our outer parts, go to church, and hear the Word and the Gospel. [In the edition I own, these statements appear on pages 656, 658, 661, 662, 663, 671, 672, 673][122]

[5] After hearing these words, they all agreed with them and exclaimed in unison, "Yes, that is indeed the orthodox view."

I was standing nearby, listening intently to all this. Because I had grown intensely angry in my spirit, I asked in a loud voice, "If in regard to spiritual matters you view humans as pillars of salt, animals, and beings that are blind and insane, what then are your theological teachings? Surely they are spiritual, aren't they?"

After some silence they replied, "In our entire body of teaching there is absolutely nothing spiritual that reason can grasp. Our faith is the only spiritual thing in our theology, but we have sealed it off completely to keep anyone from looking into it; we have taken precautions to prevent even one spiritual ray from leaking out of it and appearing before our intellect. Furthermore, human beings do not contribute even a tiny amount to that faith as the result of their own free choice. We have also completely removed goodwill from the spiritual arena; we have turned it into something merely moral, just as we have done with the Ten Commandments. Nor would we say that justification,[123] forgiveness of sins, regeneration, or salvation were at all spiritual. We say that faith produces those results, but we have no idea how. In place of repentance we have substituted penitence. To prevent people from thinking of this penitence as spiritual, we have moved it entirely out of the reach of faith. The only ideas we have adopted about redemption are purely earthly: they are that God the Father locked the human race into damnation, but his Son took that damnation upon himself and allowed himself to be hung on the cross. By so doing he induced his Father to feel pity. And besides these, there are many similar teachings in which you are supposed to perceive something that is merely earthly and not at all spiritual."

[6] Still feeling the intense anger that had come upon me earlier, I continued the exchange. "If we had no free choice in regard to spiritual matters," I said, "what would we be but brute animals? Spiritual free choice is what distinguishes us from them. Without it, what is the church but a cleaner of clothes with a filthy face and blank, blind eyes?[124] Without it, what is the Word but a volume entirely without meaning?[125] What occurs more often in the Word than statements and commandments that we should love God and our neighbor and have faith? Or that our salvation and life depend on our level of love and faith? No one lacks the ability to understand and do the things that are prescribed in the Word and in the Ten Commandments. How could God order and command us to do such things if we had not been given the ability to do them? [7] Find some farm hand, whose mind is not clogged with theological fallacies, and tell him he has no more ability to understand or will things related to faith, goodwill, and salvation than a log or a stone. Tell him that he is incapable of applying and adapting himself to those things. He is going to laugh so hard that his whole body shakes. He is going to say, 'What could be more insane than that? Why do I bother with the preacher and his sermons then? What is the difference in that case between the church building and a barn? How is worship any different from plowing? What a mindless thing to say! It is the height of foolishness. Nobody denies, of course, that everything good comes from God. But haven't we been

granted the ability to do good things under our own initiative on God's behalf? And a similar ability to believe?'"

When the participants heard that, they yelled, "What we said was orthodox teaching, based on orthodox authorities. What you said was boorish and based on the authority of a farm hand!"

At that moment lightning suddenly crashed down from the heavens. To avoid being destroyed by it, they rushed out in a crowd and fled from there to their own homes.

504 *The second memorable occurrence.* At one point I was experiencing the inner spiritual sight enjoyed by the angels of the higher heaven, even though I was in the world of spirits. I saw two spirits, who were not far from me although they were quite far from each other. I could tell that one of them loved goodness and truth and was therefore connected to heaven, but the other loved evil and falsity and was therefore connected to hell. I came nearer and called them together. From the sounds and contents of their responses, I gathered that the one was every bit as able as the other to perceive truths and acknowledge them, to think with understanding, and to steer the faculties of his intellect as he pleased and the faculties of his will as he wished.[126] Therefore in the whole rational arena each one had the same level of free choice. Furthermore, I observed that as a result of that freedom in their minds, there was a light in them that extended from the first type of sight (the sight of perception)[127] to the lowest type of sight (the sight of the eye).

[2] Nevertheless, I observed that when the one who loved evil and falsity was left to his own thoughts, a kind of smoke from hell arose and extinguished the light that was above his memory; as a result, that level in him became as dark as midnight. I also noticed that the smoke caught fire and burned like a flame, illuminating the region of his mind below the memory.[128] This led him to think horrendous falsities that were derived from the evils of his self-love.

When the other person, though, who loved goodness and truth, was left to himself, I saw a kind of gentle flame flowing down from heaven, which illuminated the region of his mind above the memory, and the region below it as well, all the way to the eye. Because of this flame, the light in him began to shine more and more as his love for goodness led him to perceive and think truth.

This experience made it clear to me that everyone, whether good or evil, possesses spiritual free choice; but hell often extinguishes that freedom in those who are evil, whereas heaven kindles and exalts it in those who are good.

[3] Afterward I had a conversation with each of them. I spoke first with the one who loved evil and falsity. We talked a little about his situation; but when I mentioned free choice he went into a rage.

He said, "Ah, what insanity it is to believe that we have free choice in spiritual matters! Can any of us acquire faith for ourselves and do good on our own? Doesn't the priesthood today teach us from the Word that no one is able to receive anything unless it is given from heaven [John 3:27], and that Christ the Lord said to his disciples, 'Without me you cannot do anything' [John 15:5]? I might add that none can move their feet or hands to do anything good or make their tongues say anything true that arises from goodness. Therefore the great thinkers of our church have led us to conclude that we human beings are unable to will, understand, or think anything spiritual and cannot even accommodate ourselves to willing, understanding, or thinking anything spiritual, any more than a statue, a log, or a stone could. Therefore God, who alone possesses absolute freedom and limitless power, inspires us with faith as he pleases. By the activity of the Holy Spirit without any effort or power on our part, this faith produces every ability that ignorant people ascribe to us as our own."

[4] Then I spoke with the other person, the one who loved goodness and truth. After some conversation about his current situation, I mentioned free choice. He said, "What insanity it is to deny that we have free choice in spiritual matters! All have the ability to will and do what is good and to think and say what is true under their own initiative on behalf of the Word and of the Lord, who is the Word. The Word says, 'Produce good fruit,' and 'Believe in the Light'; 'Love one another,' and 'Love God.'[129] It also says, 'Those who hear and do my commandments are the ones who love me and I will love them' [John 14:21]—not to mention a thousand passages like this throughout the Word.[130] What would the point of the Word be if we had no ability to will and think and do and say what it commands us to do? If we lacked these powers, religion and the church would be like a shipwrecked vessel that has run aground, whose captain is standing on the top of its mast, shouting, 'There is nothing I can do,' even though he sees the other sailors hoisting sails and sailing off in the lifeboats.

"Surely, Adam was given freedom to eat from the tree of life and also from the tree of the knowledge of good and evil. Because he freely chose to eat from the latter tree, smoke from the serpent (meaning hell) entered his mind and he was thrown out of paradise and cursed. Yet even then he did not lose free choice: we read that the way to the tree of life was protected by an angel guardian,[131] which implies that if this action had not been taken, he could have tried to eat from that tree again."

[5] At this point the one who loved evil and falsity said, "I am going to take with me what I said myself, but leave behind what I just heard from you. Everyone knows that God alone is living and active and that of ourselves we are dead and merely passive. How could a being that is intrinsically dead and merely passive take into itself anything alive and active?"

"We are an organism that receives life," I responded. "God alone is life itself. God pours his own life into this organism and every part of it, just as the sun pours its heat into a tree and every part of it. God grants us to feel his life in ourselves as our own. God wants us to feel this so we can live according to the laws of the divine design (that is, the commandments in the Word) as if we did so under our own initiative, and arrange ourselves to receive God's love. Nevertheless, although God constantly keeps his finger on the pointer of the scales to keep us in check, he never violates our free choice by forcing us.

[6] "A tree cannot receive anything that the heat of the sun brings in through the roots unless each individual filament of the roots grows warm. Elements cannot rise up through the root system unless those individual filaments, having received that warmth, give off heat to help the elements pass through. It is similar with us in regard to the heat of life we receive from God; but unlike a tree, we sense this heat as our own, although it is not actually ours. To the extent that we believe this heat belongs to us and not to God, we receive from God the light of life but not the heat of love; instead, the heat of love we feel comes from hell. Because that heat is thick, it blocks and closes off the purer channels within us as an organism, just as impure blood blocks and closes off the capillaries in our bodies.[132] This is how we turn ourselves from spiritual people into merely earthly people.

[7] "Our free choice comes from our sense that we have life within us as if it were our own. God allows us to feel this way for the sake of our partnership [with him]. A partnership with God would not be possible if it were not reciprocal, and it becomes reciprocal when we act freely, and completely as if we were on our own. If we were not allowed by God to

feel this way, we would not be human and our life would not be eternal. Our reciprocal partnership with God is what makes us humans and not animals and enables us to live to eternity after death. What makes all this possible is our free choice in spiritual matters."

[8] Upon hearing this, the evil spirit moved off into the distance. I then saw a flying serpent of the type that is known as a prester[133] on a particular tree. It was offering a piece of fruit to someone there. I went in the spirit in that direction. There in place of the serpent I saw a human monster, whose face was so covered with a huge beard that only the nose protruded. In place of the tree there was a lit torch, next to which stood the person whose mind had filled with smoke and who had then rejected free choice in spiritual matters. Suddenly a similar smoke came out of the torch and poured out in all directions. Because those figures were taken out of my sight at that point, I left. But the other person, the one who loved goodness and truth and who asserted that human beings do have free choice in spiritual matters, remained with me on my journey home.[134]

The third memorable occurrence. On one occasion I heard a loud scraping sound like two millstones grinding against each other. As I moved in the direction of the sound, it stopped. I saw a narrow doorway that opened on a steep descent, which in turn led to a building with vaulted ceilings. The building contained a number of rooms divided into small compartments; each compartment contained two people, who were gathering support in the Word for justification by faith alone. One would do the searching, and the other would take notes; then they would switch. [505]

I went up to a compartment that was near the door and asked, "What are you gathering and writing down?"

They said, "Passages that concern the *act of justification* or the *activation of faith,* which is faith itself in the actual process of justifying us, bringing us to life, and saving us. In our Christianity, this is the primary teaching of the church."

I said to them, "Tell me some sign of that activation—the process through which that faith is introduced into our heart and soul."

One of them replied, "The sign of that activation occurs in a single moment, when we are struck with grief that we have been condemned. When we are having that penitent feeling, we think about Christ and the fact that he took away the damnation of the law. We take hold of this merit of his with confidence, and with this in our thoughts we turn to God the Father and pray."

[2] "So this is the activation," I said, "and this is the moment?

"So how," I asked, "am I to understand what is said about this activation, that nothing in us helps it along any more than we would help it along if we were a piece of dead wood or a stone; and that as far as that activation goes, we cannot begin it, will it, understand it, think it, work it, cooperate in it, or apply or adapt ourselves to it? Tell me how that squares with what you just said, that the activation occurs when we think about the burden of the law, about how the damnation it prescribes was taken away by Christ, and about the confidence with which we take hold of his merit; and that while having these thoughts we turn to God the Father and pray. Aren't we the ones who are doing all these things?"

"We don't do them actively," he said; "we do them passively."

[3] "How," I replied, "can anyone think, have confidence, and pray passively? Doesn't taking away our ability to be active and cooperative also take away our ability to be receptive, and everything else we have, including any activation of faith? What then is your 'activation' but something purely theoretical, which is called a figment of the imagination? (I hope you don't share the belief of those who think the activation of faith only occurs in the predestined, who are completely unaware of the infusion of faith within themselves! They could roll the dice to find out whether faith has been infused into them yet or not.) Therefore, my friend, believe that in regard to faith and goodwill we work under our own initiative on God's behalf. Without this work on our part, your 'activation of faith,' which you call the primary teaching of the church in Christianity, is nothing more than Lot's wife as a statue, pinging when touched with a scribe's quill or fingernail, because it is made of pure salt (Luke 17:32). I say this because you make yourselves like statues in regard to the activation of faith."

When I had said these things, he violently seized a lamp with his hand, intending to throw it in my face, but the lamp quickly went out and he hit the forehead of his companion instead. I left laughing.

506 *The fourth memorable occurrence.*[135] In the spiritual world I once saw two groups of animals: a herd of *goats* and a flock of *sheep*. I wondered who they were, because I knew that animals that are seen in the spiritual world are not animals but forms that correspond to the feelings and thoughts of people who are in that area. Therefore I went toward them. As I approached, the images of animals disappeared and in their place I saw people. It became obvious that the people who constituted the herd of goats were those who were adamantly devoted to the teaching that we are justified by faith alone. The people who constituted the flock of sheep were those who believed that goodwill and faith are one, just as goodness and truth are one.

[2] I then spoke with the people who had appeared to be goats. I said, "Why are you meeting together?"

Most of the people in that group were clergy, who boasted of their reputation for being highly educated because they knew the secrets of justification by faith alone. They said that they were gathered to sit in council because they had heard the following.[136]

> The statement of Paul that "we are justified by faith apart from the works of the Law" (Romans 3:28) has not been understood correctly, in that "faith" here does not mean the faith of the church today, which is a belief in three divine persons from eternity, but instead means faith in the Lord God the Savior Jesus Christ; and "the works of the Law" here does not mean the works of the law of the Ten Commandments but the works of the Mosaic Law given for Jews.[137]

> Therefore through a wrong interpretation of this mere handful of words you have come to two hugely false conclusions—that the phrase concerns (1) the faith of the church of today and (2) the works of the law of the Ten Commandments.

> That Paul did not mean those works but the works of the Mosaic Law, which were given for Jews to follow, is very clear from Paul's words to Peter, chiding him for making others follow Jewish religious practices, even though Peter himself should have known that "No one is justified by the works of the Law, but by the faith of Jesus Christ" (Galatians 2:14, 15, 16). [On the point that "the faith of Jesus Christ" means faith in him and from him, see §338.][138] And because "the works of the Law" mean "the works of the Mosaic Law," therefore Paul distinguishes between the law of faith and the law of works, and between Jews and non-Jews, and between the circumcised and the uncircumcised (by the "circumcised" there he means Judaism, as he does throughout). Paul closes that section with the following words: "Therefore are we doing away with the law through faith? By no means! We are establishing the law." Paul says all these things in a single series (Romans 3:27, 28, 29, 30, 31). Paul also says in the preceding chapter, "Hearers of the law are not going to be justified by God, but doers of the law will be justified" (Romans 2:13).

Also, "God renders to all according to their works" (Romans 2:6). Again, "It is right that all of us should appear before the tribunal of Christ, so that each of us will report what we did through our body, whether good or evil" (2 Corinthians 5:10). Paul makes many other such statements as well. From this it is clear that Paul rejected faith without good works every bit as much as James did (James 2:17–26).

[3] We have further established that Paul meant the works of the Mosaic Law intended for Jews from the fact that all the statutes for Jews that were given through Moses are called "the Law," and therefore are works of the Law, as we see in the following passages: "This is the law of the trespass offering" (Leviticus 7:1). ["This is the law of the peace offering"] (Leviticus 7:11 and following). "This is the law of the burnt offering, the grain offering, the sacrifices for sin and guilt, and the consecrations" (Leviticus 7:37). "This is the law of the animals and the birds" (Leviticus 11:46 and following). "This is the law for a woman who has given birth to a son or a daughter" (Leviticus 12:7). "This is the law of leprosy" (Leviticus 13:59; 14:2, 32, 54, 57). "This is the law for someone who has a discharge" (Leviticus 15:32). "This is the law of jealousy" (Numbers 5:29, 30). "This is the law of the Nazarite" (Numbers 6:13, 21). "This is the law of cleansing" (Numbers 19:14). "This is the law of the red heifer" (Numbers 19:2). "[This is] the law for a king" (Deuteronomy 17:15–19). In fact, the entire Book of Moses is called the Book of the Law (Deuteronomy 31:9, 11, 12, 26; see also Luke 2:22; 24:44; John 1:45; 7:22, 23; 8:5).

To these points [the writers of this piece] added that they see in Paul[139] that we must live by the law of the Ten Commandments and that those commandments are fulfilled by goodwill (Romans 13:8, 9, 10). And [the writers] further observed that Paul said, "There are three things: faith, hope, and goodwill. The greatest of these is goodwill" (1 Corinthians 13:13); therefore the greatest of the three is *not* faith.

[4] So this, the clergy said, was why they had convened. I left so as not to disturb them; and again from far away they looked like goats. They looked sometimes like they were lying down, and at other times like they were standing, but in either case they kept away from the flock of sheep. When they were debating they looked like they were lying down, and when they had come to a conclusion they looked like they were standing up. I fixed my gaze on their horns and was amazed to see that they seemed at one moment as if they extended forward and upward

from their foreheads, and at another as if they were curving toward their backs; eventually they seemed to be bent completely backward. Then suddenly [the priests] turned in the direction of the flock of sheep, although they themselves still looked like goats.

So I went toward them again and asked what was going on now. They said they had concluded that faith alone produces acts of goodwill the way a tree produces fruit. But at that point thunder occurred and lightning flashed overhead. Soon an angel appeared, standing between the herd and the flock.

He called out to the flock of sheep, "Don't listen to them. They have not left their former belief, which is that faith alone justifies and saves. They have absolutely no actual goodwill. For another thing, a tree does not represent faith; it represents a human being. Instead, go through the process of repentance and look to the Lord and you'll have faith. Faith before that is a faith without life."

Then the goats with the bent-back horns tried to come at the sheep, but the angel standing between them divided the sheep into two flocks. He said to the flock of sheep on the left, "Go ahead and join the goats, but I'm telling you, a wolf is coming that is going to snatch them away, and you along with them."

[5] Once the sheep had been divided into two flocks and the sheep on the left had heard the angel's warning, they looked at each other and said, "Let's have a discussion with our former colleagues."

The flock of sheep on the left then said to the flock of sheep on the right, "Why have you left our pastors?[140] Surely faith and goodwill are one, just as a tree and its fruit are one. A tree is extended through its branches into its fruit. Break off part of the branch through which the tree has a connection with the fruit, and the fruit is going to perish, and along with the fruit, all the seed of the new tree that has yet to come about. Ask our priests whether this is the case."

So the sheep on the right posed the question. They looked over at the sheep on the left, who were winking at the priests in the hope that they would endorse what they had said.

"What you said is indeed right, as far as it goes," the priests answered, "but the parallel between the extension of faith into good works and the extension of a tree into its fruit is something about which we know many further secrets, although this is not the place to reveal them to the public. In the thread that links faith and goodwill there are many little knots that only we priests are able to untie."

[6] Then a priest who was one of the sheep on the right stood up and said to the sheep on the left, "To you those priests replied that what you said is right; but among themselves they say it is not right, because in fact they have a different opinion."

So the sheep on the right asked the angel, "What are the priests thinking now? Does their thinking align with their teaching?"

"No," the angel said. "Their thinking is that every act of goodwill (called a good work) that people do for the sake of their salvation and eternal life is not in the least bit good, because human beings want to save themselves through their own effort, acquiring the justice and merit of the one Savior for themselves; this is how it is with every good work that people feel is of their own will. Therefore those priests believe that there is absolutely no connection between faith and goodwill. They would not even say that faith is retained or preserved through good works."

[7] "The accusations you are making against the priests are false," said the sheep on the left. "Don't they openly preach to us goodwill and its actions, which they call the works of faith?"

"You are not understanding what they are preaching," the angel replied. "The clergyman among you [sheep] is the only one who is paying attention and understands. Those priests are thinking of a goodwill that is only moral and of good works that are only civic and political. These they call works of faith, but they are not works of faith at all, because an atheist would be capable of doing them the same way and in the same form. Therefore the [goat] priests are in complete agreement with each other that no one is saved by any works that she or he performs, but by faith alone.

"I can illustrate their position by comparisons they make. An apple tree produces apples, but if we do good things for the sake of our salvation through an extension of ourselves the way an apple tree produces apples through an extension of itself, the apples we make are inwardly rotten and full of worms. They also say that a vine produces grapes, but if we were to aim to do good spiritual actions the way a vine produces grapes, the fruit we would make would be wild grapes."[141]

[8] The sheep on the left asked [the priest among the sheep on the right], "Then what do the priests mean by acts of goodwill or works that are the fruit of faith?"

"Perhaps they are invisible," [the priest] replied, "and somewhere near faith, although they are not joined to it. They are like the shadow that follows along behind us when we are facing the sun—a shadow we don't notice unless we turn around. In fact, I would venture that they are like horses' tails, which in many areas today are cut off, because people say, 'What do I need with this? It serves no purpose as long as it is still attached to the horse, and it easily gets dirty there.'"

At this, someone from the flock of sheep on the left became upset and said, "There has to be *some* connection between good works and our faith. Otherwise how could those works be called the works of faith? Perhaps good actions that come from goodwill are subtly introduced by God into the things we do willingly, through the agency of some inflow or other—through some feeling, for example, or influence, or inspiration, some stimulation or stirring of the will, some wordless awareness in thought—and then an urging, a penitence, a movement of conscience that results in an impulse to obey the Ten Commandments and the Word, whether felt in childhood or old age; or by some other means like these. How else could they be called the fruits of faith?"

To this the priest replied, "No, that's not it. If those priests do say it happens by some such method, they are just stringing words together for a sermon. The sum of their words, though, is that good works have no relationship to faith. Now, some priests do say good works are related to faith, but as the *signs of faith* rather than as *bonds that join faith and goodwill.* And some priests have come up with the idea that faith and goodwill are connected by the Word."

[The person among the sheep on the left] said, "But that *is* how the two are connected, isn't it?"

"Not the way those priests think of it," replied [the priest]. "They are thinking that the union takes place through our merely hearing the Word. They assert that in matters of faith, every part of our reason and every part of our will is impure and focused on earning merit, since in spiritual matters we are unable to understand, will, work, or cooperate any more than a piece of dead wood."

[9] When one of the sheep on the right heard that human beings are believed to be this way in all matters related to faith and salvation, he said, "I heard someone say, 'I have planted a vineyard. Now I will drink wine until I am drunk.' But someone else asked, 'Are you planning to drink this wine from your own drinking cup using your own right hand?' 'No,' the first one said. 'I'm planning to drink from an invisible cup using an invisible hand.' 'In that case,' the other person said, 'you will definitely not become intoxicated!'"

In a moment the same man said to the sheep on the left, "Please listen to me. I am telling you, drink wine from the Word with understanding. Don't you know that the Lord is the Word? Isn't the Word from the Lord? Isn't he therefore in it? If you do what is good because of the Word, then, you are following the Lord in doing what is good—following his edict, his will. If you look to the Lord, he himself will lead you and teach you, and you will do what is good under your own initiative on the Lord's behalf. When someone does something on behalf of his or her monarch, obeying a royal edict or command, is that person entitled to say, 'In doing this I am obeying my own edict or command, my own will'?"

At that point he turned toward the clergy and said, "Ministers of God, do not lead your flock astray."

[10] Most of the flock of sheep on the left then withdrew and rejoined the flock on the right.

Some of the clergy began saying, "We have heard things we never heard before. We are shepherds; we must not leave our sheep." And they too withdrew with them.

These clergy kept saying, "The word that that man spoke is true. If someone does something from the Word, and is therefore following the Lord's edict and will, is that person entitled to say, 'I am doing this on my own'? If someone does something by royal command, is that person entitled to say, 'I am doing this on my own'? We now see divine providence, and why we have been unable to identify the connection between that faith and good works, even though the church community holds that such a connection exists. It could not have been found because it could not exist. That faith was not a faith in the Lord, who is the Word; it was not based on the Word."

The rest of the priests in the herd of goats, however, went away, waving their hats back and forth and crying out, "Faith alone! Faith alone! It shall live on!"

507 *The fifth memorable occurrence.* Once I was having a conversation with angels. The conversation eventually turned to the craving for evil that every one of us is born with.

One angel said, "In the world where we are, people who are experiencing that craving appear to us angels as fools, although at the time they seem to themselves to be supremely wise. Therefore when they are undergoing the process of being brought out of their foolishness, they go back and forth between their foolishness and the rationality that in their case resides in their outer selves. When they are in the latter state they see, recognize, and admit to their own insanity, and yet they passionately long to return from their rational state to their state of insanity. Once back in it, they immerse themselves in it like someone finding freedom and delight again after a period of duress and unpleasantness. This shows that they take inward enjoyment in their own craving rather than in gaining perspective.

[2] "By creation every human being is composed of three universal loves: love for our neighbor, which is also a love of being useful (this love is related to the spirit); love for the world, which is also a love of possessing wealth (this love is related to matter); and love for ourselves, which is also a love of dominating other people (this love is related to the body).

"We are truly human when love for our neighbor or love of being useful plays the role of the head, love for the world or love of possessing wealth plays the role of the torso, and love for ourselves or love of dominating plays the role of the legs and feet. If, however, love for the world plays the role of the head, our humanity is hunchbacked. If love for ourselves plays the role of the head, our humanity is standing on its hands rather than its feet, with its head down and its buttocks in the air.

[3] "When our love of being useful plays the role of the head and the other two loves play the role of the torso and the legs, as they are designed to, in heaven our face looks angelic and we have a beautiful rainbow around our head. If our love for the world or of wealth plays the role of the head, from heaven's perspective our face looks gray like a corpse and we have a yellow ring around our head. If our love for ourselves or of dominating others plays the role of the head, from heaven's perspective our face looks burnt and dark and we have a white ring around our head."

"What does the ring around the head represent?" I asked.

"Intelligence," the angels replied. "The white ring surrounding a face that is burnt and dark represents that those people hold their intelligence outside or around themselves, but have insanity in their inner levels or within themselves. Such people are wise when they are in their bodies but insane when they are in their spirits. None of us is wise in spirit except with the help of the Lord; we become wise as he generates and creates us anew."

[4] As soon as they said this, the ground on the left opened up. Through the opening I saw a devil rising up, whose face was burnt and dark and who had a white ring around his head.

"Who are you?" I inquired.

"I am Lucifer, son of the dawn," he said. "I was thrown down because I made myself like the Highest. I am described in Isaiah 14:[14]."[142]

He was not actually Lucifer, although he believed he was.

"Since you have been thrown down," I said, "how are you able to rise up out of hell?"

"I am the Devil there," he replied, "but here I am an angel of light. Don't you see that my head is surrounded by a white ring? If you wish, you can also see that I am moral among the moral, rational among the rational, and spiritual among the spiritual. I also had preaching ability."

"What did you preach about?" I asked.

"I preached against people who commit fraud, against people who commit adultery, and against all the types of love that come from hell. In fact, I then called my 'Lucifer' self the Devil, and I invoked curses against that me. On that account I was lifted with praise to the heavens, and that is why I am called the son of the dawn. I myself have been amazed to notice that when I was in the pulpit I had no other thought but that I was speaking uprightly and correctly. I learned why this was: it was because I was in my outer self and that self was separated at the time from my inner self. But although this has been revealed to me, I have still not been able to change myself, because I set myself above the Highest and exalted myself against him."

[5] "How were you able to preach those things," I asked, "given that you yourself commit fraud and adultery?"

"I am one way," he replied, "when I am in my outer self or my body, and another way when I am in my inner self or my spirit. In my body I am an angel; in my spirit I am a devil. In my body I am in my intellect; in my spirit I am in my will. My intellect lifts me upward, but my will takes me down. When I am in my intellect, a white ring surrounds my head, but when my intellect becomes completely subservient to my will and becomes its property (which is the final outcome that awaits us), then the ring grows darker and disappears; and once it is gone I can no longer rise up into this light."

When he saw the angels with me, a sudden rage showed in his face and voice. He, as well as the ring around his head, turned dark, and he fell down into hell through the opening by which he had risen up.

Those who were present concluded from what they had heard and seen that our quality is the quality of our will, not the quality of our intellect, because the will easily moves the intellect to see things from its own perspective and makes the intellect subservient to itself.

[6] Then I asked the angels, "Where does the rationality of devils come from?"

"It comes from the glory of their love for themselves," they replied. "Self-love is surrounded by glory—glory supplies the brightness of its fire. This glory lifts the intellect virtually into the light of heaven. In all of us, in fact, the intellect is capable of being lifted up in accordance with the concepts we have; but our will can be lifted up only if we live according to the truths of the church and the truths of reason. This is how it comes about that atheists whose love for themselves leads them to glory in their reputation and take pride in their own intelligence have a more sublime rationality than many others, but only when they are involved in the thought of their intellect, not when they are involved in the love in their will. The love that resides in the will possesses the inner self; the thoughts in the intellect possess the outer self."

The angel also told me why we are composed of three kinds of love (love of being useful, love for the world, and love for ourselves): to enable our thinking to come from God, although it seems to come entirely from ourselves. "The highest areas of a person's mind," he said, "are turned upward toward God; the middle areas are turned outward toward the world; and the lowest areas are turned downward toward the body. Because the lowest things are turned downward, our thinking appears to occur under our own initiative, when in fact it comes from God."

The sixth memorable occurrence. One day there appeared to me a magnificent temple, square in form. The roof was shaped like a crown—it arched upward and was elevated all around. The walls were continuous windows of crystal clear glass.[143] The door was made of a pearly substance.[144] On the southwest side of the interior there was a large raised pulpit, on top of which, to the right, the Word lay open, surrounded by a sphere of light so bright that it engulfed the whole raised area of the pulpit and made it shine.[145] In the middle of the temple there was a sanctuary, with a veil at the front of it that was now lifted up. There an angel guardian, made out of gold, stood with a sword moving this way and that in its hand.

[2] Once I had looked carefully at all of these items, the meaning of each one flowed into my meditation. The temple means the new church. The door made of a pearly substance means our entry into the new church. The crystal clear windows mean the truths that enlighten the new church. The pulpit means its priesthood and preaching. The Word that lay open on the pulpit, lighting up the raised area of it, indicates that the Word's inner meaning, which is spiritual, has been revealed. The sanctuary in the middle of the temple means the partnership between the new church and the heaven of angels. The angel guardian made out of

508

gold, standing in the sanctuary, means the literal meaning of the Word. The sword moving back and forth in its hand means that the literal sense can be turned this way and that, provided the purpose is to apply it to some truth. The fact that the veil in front of the angel guardian was lifted up means that the Word has now been opened to view.

[3] Later on, as I came closer to the building, I saw an inscription above the door: *Now It Is Allowed,* which means that we are now allowed to use our intellect to explore the mysteries of faith.

Seeing this inscription brought to my mind how extremely dangerous it is to use our intellect to explore any dogma of faith that was constructed by a self-serving mindset and therefore consists of falsities. It is even worse to use statements from the Word to support such dogmas. Doing so shuts down our intellect at its highest level, and gradually shuts it down at lower levels as well, to the point where theological teachings become disgusting to us and are finally obliterated, the way writing on paper is eaten away by worms or wool clothing is consumed by moths. Then the only way in which our intellect still functions is in dealing with political issues that affect our life in the region where we live, with civic issues that affect our jobs, and with domestic issues that relate to our homes. In these arenas we continually embrace the material world and love it for the alluring pleasures it offers, the way idolaters carry their golden effigy close to their heart.

[4] The dogmas of the Christian churches of today have been constructed not from the Word but under a self-serving mindset; as a result they consist of falsities. These dogmas have also been supported by certain statements in the Word. Therefore in the Lord's divine providence the Word was taken away from the Roman Catholic laity;[146] and although the Word was opened up for Protestants, they closed it by their widespread assertion that the intellect has to be held under obedience to their faith.

[5] In the new church, however, the opposite happens. In this church, we are allowed to use our intellect to explore and penetrate all the church's mysteries and also to use the Word to support what we find. The reason this is allowed is that the teachings of the new church are continuous truths revealed by the Lord through the Word. Rational arguments that support these truths cause the intellect to open up more and more at its highest level and to be elevated into the light that the angels in heaven enjoy. That light is essentially truth. In that light, acknowledgment of the Lord as the God of heaven and earth shines in its glory. This

is the meaning of the inscription *Now It Is Allowed* over the door to the temple, and the meaning of the fact that the sanctuary veil in front of the angel guardian was lifted up. It is a principle of the new church, you see, that falsities shut down the intellect but truths open it up.

[6] Afterward I saw someone like a young child overhead, holding a piece of paper in his hand. As he came nearer to me, he grew into a person of medium height. He was an angel from the third heaven,[147] where all the inhabitants appear from a distance like little children. When he was in my presence, he handed me the piece of paper. Because it was written in the curved letters they use in that heaven,[148] however, I handed it back and asked that they[149] express the meaning of the message in words adapted to the ideas in my thinking. He replied, "What is written there is this: '*From now on, explore the mysteries of the Word, which was formerly closed up. All of its individual truths are mirrors that reflect the Lord.*'"

Chapter 9

Repentance

509 NOW that faith [§§336–391], goodwill [§§392–462], and free choice [§§463–508] have been treated, the related topic of repentance comes next, because without repentance there can be no true faith and no genuine goodwill, and no one could repent without free choice. Another reason why there is a treatment of repentance at this point is that the topic that follows is regeneration [§§571–625], and none of us can be regenerated before the more serious evils that make us detestable before God have been removed; repentance is what removes them.

What else are unregenerate people but impenitent? And what else are impenitent people but those who are in a drowsy state of apathy? They know nothing about sin and therefore cherish it deep within themselves and make love to it every day the way an adulterous man makes love to a promiscuous woman who shares his bed.

To make known what repentance is and what effect it has, this treatment of it will be divided into separate headings.

Repentance Is the Beginning of the Church within Us

510 The extended community that is known as the church consists of all the people who have the church within them. The church takes hold in us when we are regenerated, and we are all regenerated when we abstain from things that are evil and sinful and run away from them as we would run if we saw hordes of hellish spirits pursuing us with flaming torches, intending to attack us and throw us onto a bonfire.

As we go through the early stages of our lives, there are many things that prepare us for the church and introduce us into it; but acts of repentance are the things that actually produce the church within us. Acts of repentance include any and all actions that result in our not willing, and consequently not doing, evil things that are sins against God.

Before repentance, we stand outside regeneration. In that condition, if any thought of eternal salvation somehow makes its way into us, we at first turn toward it but soon turn away. That thought does not penetrate us any farther than the outer areas where we have ideas; it then goes out into our spoken words and perhaps into a few gestures that go along with those words. When the thought of eternal salvation penetrates our will, however, then it is truly inside us. The will is the real self, because it is where our love dwells; our thoughts are outside us, unless they come from our will, in which case our will and our thought act as one, and together make us who we are. From these points it follows that in order for repentance to be genuine and effective within us, it has to be done both by our will and by thinking that comes from our will. It cannot be done by thought alone. Therefore it has to be a matter of actions, and not of words alone.

[2] The Word makes it obvious that repentance is the beginning of the church. John the Baptist was sent out in advance to prepare people for the church that the Lord was about to establish. At the same time as he was baptizing people he was also preaching repentance; his baptism was therefore called a baptism of repentance.[150] Baptism means a spiritual washing, that is, being cleansed from sins. John baptized in the Jordan River because the Jordan means introduction into the church, since it was the first border of the land of Canaan, where the church was.[151] The Lord himself also preached that people should repent so that their sins would be forgiven. He taught, in effect, that repentance is the beginning of the church; that if we repent, the sins within us will be removed; and that if our sins are removed, they are also forgiven. Furthermore, when the Lord sent out his twelve apostles and also the seventy, he commanded them to preach repentance. From all this it is clear that repentance is the beginning of the church.

As for the point that the church does not exist within us until the sins inside us have been removed, this is something anyone can conclude through the use of reason.

511

It can also be illustrated through the following comparisons. No one can pasture flocks of sheep, goats, and lambs in fields or woodlands that are already occupied by all kinds of predatory animals, without first driving away the predators. No one can turn land that is full of thornbushes, brambles, and stinging nettles into a garden without first uprooting those harmful plants. No one can go into a city that is occupied by hostile enemy forces, set up a new administration devoted to justice and judgment, and make it a good place for citizens to live without first expelling the enemy. It is similar with the evils that are inside us. They are like predatory animals, brambles and thornbushes, and enemies. The church could no more live alongside them than we could live in a cage full of tigers and leopards; or lie down in a bed whose sheets were lined, and pillows stuffed, with poisonous plants; or sleep at night in a church building under whose stone floor there are tombs with dead bodies in them—would we not be harassed there by ghosts that were like the Furies?[152]

The "Contrition" That Is Nowadays Said to Precede Faith and to Be Followed by the Consolation of the Gospel Is Not Repentance

512 The Protestant Christian world holds that there is a certain type of anxiety, pain, and terror (which they call "contrition") that comes over people who are going to be regenerated. It comes on before they have faith and is followed by the consolation of the Gospel.[153]

They claim that this contrition arises in them as the result of fear of the justifiable anger of God, and therefore fear of the eternal damnation that clings to us all because of Adam's sin and because of our resulting inclination toward evil. They say that the faith that ascribes the merit and justice of the Lord our Savior to us is not granted us if we lack that feeling of contrition. Those who have acquired this faith are said to receive "the consolation of the Gospel," which means that they are justified, that is, renewed, regenerated, and sanctified, without any cooperation on their part. In this way they are moved from damnation to the eternal blessedness that is everlasting life.

Let us examine this "contrition": (1) Is it the same as repentance? (2) Is it of any value? (3) Does it in fact exist?

513 *Is this contrition the same as repentance or not?* The description of repentance in the sections below will enable you to conclude that repentance is not possible unless we know not only in a general way but also in specific detail that we are sinners. This is something we cannot know unless we examine ourselves, see the sins that are within us, and condemn ourselves on their account. The contrition that preachers say is necessary to our faith has nothing in common with the actions just listed. It is only a thought and a confession that we have been born into the sin of Adam and into an inclination toward the evils that spring from that sin, and that therefore the wrath of God is upon us and we deserve damnation, destruction, and eternal death. Clearly, then, this contrition is not the same as repentance.

The next step in these considerations is as follows. Since this contrition is not the same as repentance, *Is it of any value?* We are told that it contributes to our faith as a prerequisite to what follows, although it does not mix together with, join, or become part of that faith. But the faith that follows it is the belief that God the Father assigns us the justice acquired by his Son, and then (even though we are not actually aware that we have any sin) he declares us just, new, and holy, and puts a robe on us that has been washed and made white by the blood of the Lamb [Revelation 7:14]. When we walk in that robe, what are the evils that are in our lives but sulfurous stones thrown into the depths of the sea?[154] What then is Adam's sin but something that has been covered over, removed, or taken away by the assignment to us of Christ's justice? When we walk along holding our belief in the justice and also the innocence of God the Savior, what then is that feeling of contrition good for if not for giving us confidence that we are safe in Abraham's embrace [Luke 16:22] and can therefore regard those who do not yet feel contrition or have faith as wretched inhabitants of hell or as dead people? They say that there is no living faith in those who lack contrition. To that one could add that if they immersed themselves now and then in damnable evils, they would not feel them or pay them attention any more than piglets lying in a filthy gutter notice the stench. From these points it is clear that this contrition, as long as it is not repentance, is not actually anything.

The third step in these considerations is, *Apart from repentance does this contrition really exist?*

In the spiritual world I have approached a number of people who had convinced themselves that faith assigns us Christ's merit; I have asked them whether they had ever felt any contrition.

"Why should we feel contrition?" they replied. "Since our childhood we have believed as a certainty that Christ through his suffering took away all our sins. Feeling contrition is out of alignment with this belief. Feeling contrition is to throw ourselves into hell and torment our own consciences, when in fact we know that we have been redeemed and are therefore exempt from and immune to hell."

They added that the prescribed feeling of contrition is simply a figment of the imagination now accepted as a replacement for the repentance that is so often mentioned in the Word and in fact commanded there. Yes, perhaps there is some such emotion felt by people who are simple and ignorant of the Gospel, when they hear or think about the torments of hell.

They also said that the consolation of the Gospel, which had been impressed upon them from their earliest youth, so thoroughly took away that feeling of contrition that whenever it was mentioned they would laugh to themselves about it. They felt that hell had no more power to terrify them than the fires of Vesuvius and Etna[155] would have over people living in Warsaw and Vienna. It scared them no more than vipers and poisonous snakes in the deserts of Arabia or tigers and lions in the forests of Tartary[156] would scare people who live in some European city in safety, rest, and tranquillity. Indeed, the wrath of God had no more power to terrify or crush them than the wrath of the king of Persia would have over those who live in Pennsylvania.

[2] From these conversations and by my own reasoning about church traditions I have become convinced that this feeling of contrition—unless it is the type of repentance described in the following pages [§§528–531]— is a mere piece of imaginative theater. The Protestant churches substituted the feeling of contrition for repentance in order to move away from the Roman Catholics, who urge both repentance and goodwill. After the Protestants established their notion of justification by faith alone, they cited as a reason for this substitution the concern that both repentance and goodwill would introduce into their faith something that smacks of the desire to earn merit, which would defile it.

By Itself, an Oral Confession That We Are Sinners Is Not Repentance

516　The Protestant Reformers who signed the Augsburg Confession have this to say about oral confession:

> Not one of us can know our own sins; we are unable to list them. They are inward and hidden away. Therefore our confession of them would be false, inaccurate, maimed, and crippled. On the other hand, if we confess that we are nothing but sin, we include all our sins, leave none out, and forget about none. Although the listing of our sins is unnecessary, it should not be done away with, since it helps those with

sensitive and trembling consciences; but this type of confession is vulgar and childish—it is best suited to those who are relatively simple and unrefined. (*Formula of Concord,* pages 327, 331, 380)[157]

After they broke away from Roman Catholics, Protestants adopted this type of confession in place of active repentance because this confession is based on their belief in the assignment [of Christ's merit], which is said by itself to produce forgiveness of sins and to regenerate us, even if we lack goodwill and do not practice repentance. Another reason for this substitution is that inseparably attached to that belief is the view that we do not cooperate with the Holy Spirit at all in the moment of our justification. Yet another reason is the belief that we have no free choice in spiritual matters. And still another is the view that everything [spiritual] is the result of unmediated mercy—nothing is mediated by us or through us.

There are many reasons why an oral confession that we are sinners is not by itself repentance. Among them is this: Any and every human being, even godless people and devils, are capable of uttering an exclamation like this and making outward shows of devoutness, when they think about the clear and present danger of being tortured in hell. Surely everyone can see, though, that this outburst is not the result of any inner devoutness. It is an outward act of the imagination and the lungs, not an inward act of the will and the heart. The godless and the devils are still inwardly burning with love and desire for doing evil; this passion drives them the way windstorms drive a windmill. An outburst like this, then, is nothing more than a plot to fool God or to deceive ordinary people in order to be set free. How difficult is it to make our lips and our breath cry out, to raise our eyes and lift up our hands? As the Lord says in Mark, "Isaiah prophesied about you hypocrites correctly when he said, 'These people honor me with their lips, but their heart is far from me'" (Mark 7:6). And in Matthew, "Woe to you, scribes and Pharisees,[158] because you clean the outside of your cup and plate, but the insides are full of plundering and self-indulgence. Blind Pharisee! First clean the inside of your cup and plate, so that the outside may be clean as well" (Matthew 23:25, 26; that chapter includes more passages like this).

A similarly hypocritical form of worship is found among those who have convinced themselves of the modern-day belief that through his suffering on the cross, the Lord took away all the sins of the world, which they take to mean the sins of anyone who utters formulaic prayers about

517

518

appeasement and mediation. Some such people are indeed capable of standing in the pulpit and, with a loud voice as if they were ablaze with passion, pouring forth one holy thought after another about repentance and goodwill, even though they themselves view repentance and goodwill as having no value for our salvation. They take "repentance" to mean nothing more than oral confession, and "goodwill" to mean nothing more than acts of public charity. But they preach this way merely to win the favor of the crowd. These are the type to which the following words of the Lord refer:

> Many will say to me in that day, "Lord, Lord! Haven't we prophesied in
> your name, and haven't we done a number of miracles in your name?"
> But then I will declare to them, "I don't know you. Go away from me,
> you who practice wickedness." (Matthew 7:22, 23)

[2] On one occasion I heard someone in the spiritual world praying like this: "I am covered with skin disease. I am a leper. I have been disgusting from my mother's womb. There is nothing in me that is whole from my head to the sole of my foot. I am unworthy to lift my eyes toward God. I deserve death and eternal damnation. Have mercy on me for the sake of your Son. Purify me in his blood. The salvation of all is up to you. I beg for your mercy."

People standing nearby who had heard this asked him, "How do you know this is what you are like?"

"I know this," he replied, "because that is what I have been told."

Then he was sent to exploratory angels. In their presence he said similar things.

After conducting their investigation they gave their report: "Everything he said about himself is true. Nevertheless, he does not recognize a single evil in himself, because he has never examined himself. He had the belief that after making an oral confession, any evil he had done would no longer be evil in the sight of God, for two reasons: God would turn his eyes away from it, and he would be appeased. Therefore even though this person was a deliberate adulterer and robber, a lying slanderer, and an ardently vengeful person, he did not recover from any of his evils. This is what he was like in his will and his heart, and this is what he would have been like in word and deed if fear of the law and of losing his reputation had not held him back."

After the discovery that this was what he was like, he was judged and sent off to join other hypocrites in hell.

The nature of these people can be illustrated by various comparisons. **519**
They are like church buildings full of dragon spirits and people meant
by the locusts in the Book of Revelation.[159] They are like pulpits where
there is no copy of the Word, because it has been hidden under foot.

They are like [a building with] exterior walls covered in beautifully
colored plaster, but screech owls and dreadful night birds[160] are flying
around inside because the windows were left open. They are like white-
washed tombs in which lie the bones of the dead. They are like gilded coins
made out of dregs or dried dung. They are like bark and pith around a
core of rotted wood. They are like the vestments of the sons of Aaron[161]
worn on a leprous body. They are like wounds that are thought to have
been cured, but infecting pus remains just under a thin surface of skin.

Who does not know that outward holiness and inward profaneness
do not go together?

People like this are more afraid than others to examine themselves.
As a result they are no more aware of the vices that are inside them than
they are of the foul-smelling contents of their own intestinal tract before
they excrete them into the latrine.

Be careful, however, not to confuse the people I have just mentioned
with those who live good lives and have good beliefs. Also, do not confuse them with those who are practicing repentance from some sins and
who pray or quietly say an oral confession like [the one above] to themselves, perhaps during worship and especially in times of spiritual crisis.
It is common for a confession like this both to precede and to follow
reformation and regeneration.

From Birth We Have a Tendency toward Evils of Every Kind. Unless We at Least Partly Lay Them Aside through Repentance, We Remain in Them, and If We Remain in Them We Cannot Be Saved

We are all born with a tendency toward evils. As is recognized in the **520**
church, from our mother's womb we are nothing but evil.[162] Now, the
reason this is recognized is that the church councils and leaders have
passed down to us the notion that Adam's sin has been passed on to
all his descendants; in this view, this is the sole reason why Adam and
everyone since has been condemned; and this damnation clings to us all

from the day we are born. Many teachings of the church are based on these assertions. For example, [we are told that] the Lord instituted the washing of regeneration that is called baptism so that this sin would be removed. This sin was also the reason for the Lord's Coming. Faith in his merit is the means by which this sin is removed. The churches have many other teachings as well that are based on this notion.

[2] Nevertheless, the teachings that were brought forward above in §469 make it clear that there is no such thing as evil that we inherit from Adam. Adam was not the first human being. "Adam" and "his wife" are used symbolically to describe the first church on this planet. The Garden of Eden symbolizes the wisdom of the people in that church; the tree of life symbolizes their focus on the Lord who was to come; the tree of the knowledge of good and evil symbolizes their focus on themselves instead of the Lord. *Secrets of Heaven,* which was published in London, uses many parallel passages found elsewhere in the Word to demonstrate thoroughly that the first chapters of Genesis describe this church in symbolic terms.[163] Once people comprehend and absorb the teachings presented in that work, they experience a collapse of their formerly cherished opinion that the evil bred into us by our parents comes from [Adam's sin]; they realize that inherited evil comes not from Adam but from some other source.

As was amply demonstrated in the chapter on free choice [§§466–469], the tree of life and the tree of the knowledge of good and evil exist within every human being; and the fact that these trees are said to have been placed in a garden means that we have free choice to turn ourselves toward the Lord or to turn ourselves away from him.

521   My friend, the evil we inherit comes in fact from no other source than our own parents. What we inherit, though, is not evil that we ourselves actually commit but an inclination toward evil. All who reflect on their experience will acknowledge the truth of this. Surely everyone realizes that children are born with faces, habits, and temperaments that are like those of their parents. Grandchildren and great-grandchildren resemble their grandparents and great-grandparents. By these similarities we tell families apart. This applies to peoples and nations as well. We can tell Africans from Europeans, Neapolitans from Germans, the British from the French, and so on. Who is unable to tell whether people are Jewish by their faces, eyes, speech, and gestures?

If you were able to sense the sphere of life that emanates from people's native character,[164] you would be convinced that minds and personalities, too, carry family and national resemblances.

[2] We are not born with actual evils but only with a tendency toward them. We may have a greater or a lesser tendency to a specific evil. Therefore after death no one is judged on the basis of his or her inherited evil; we are judged only on the basis of our actual evils, the evils we ourselves have committed. This is clear from the following commandment of the Lord: "Parents will not be put to death for their children; children will not be put to death for their parents. Each will die for her or his own sins" (Deuteronomy 24:16). I have become certain of this from my experience in the spiritual world of little children who had died. They have an inclination toward evils and will them, but they do not do them, because they are brought up under the Lord's supervision and are saved.

[3] The only thing that breaks the inclination and tendency toward evil that is passed on by parents to their offspring and descendants is the new birth from the Lord that is called regeneration. In the absence of rebirth, this inclination not only remains uninterrupted but even grows from one generation to the next and becomes a stronger tendency toward evil until it encompasses evils of every kind.

This is why Jewish people today are still images of their father Judah, who took a Canaanite woman as his wife and through [her and] adultery with his daughter-in-law Tamar generated the three lineages of the Jewish people.[165] This heredity among Jewish people grew to such a degree that they were incapable of embracing the Christian religion with any heartfelt faith. The reason I say they were incapable is that the inner will within their mind was opposed to it, and this made it impossible.

The rest of the heading is self-evident: every evil remains inside us unless it is laid aside; and if we remain in our evils we cannot be saved. From what has gone before, it is evident that no evil can be laid aside except by the Lord, working in those who believe in him and who love their neighbor. See especially the section in the chapter on faith that teaches that the Lord, goodwill, and faith form a unity in the same way our life, our will, and our intellect form a unity; if we separate them, each one crumbles like a pearl that is crushed to powder [§§362–367]; and the section that teaches that the Lord is goodwill and faith within us, and we are goodwill and faith within the Lord [§§368–372].

How can we become part of that unity? We cannot unless we lay aside at least some of our evils through repentance. I say that *we* lay aside our evils, because the Lord does not lay them aside by himself without our cooperation. This too was fully shown in that same chapter and in the chapter on free choice that follows it.[166]

523   There is a saying that no one can fulfill the law, especially since someone who breaks one of the Ten Commandments breaks them all [James
2:10–11; Matthew 5:19]. But this formulaic saying does not mean what it
seems to. The proper way to understand it is that people who purposely
or deliberately behave in a way that is contrary to one commandment in
effect behave contrary to the rest, because doing something [against one
commandment] purposely and deliberately is the same as completely
denying that that behavior is sinful and rejecting any argument to the contrary. And people who thus deny and reject the very idea of sin do not care
whether *any* given act is labeled a sin or not.

This is the type of resolve developed by people who do not want to
hear anything about repentance. People who, through repentance, have
laid aside some evils that are sins, though, develop a resolve to believe in
the Lord and to love their neighbor. They are held by the Lord in a resolution to abstain from many other things as well. Therefore if it happens
that because they did not realize what was going on or because they were
overwhelmed by desire, they commit a sin, it is not held against them.
It was not something they had planned to do, and they do not support
what they did.

[2] I may reinforce this point as follows. In the spiritual world I have
come across many people who had shared a similar lifestyle when they were
in the physical world. They all dressed in fashionable clothing, enjoyed
fine dining, took profit from their business, went to the theater, told jokes
about lovers as if they themselves were lustful, and many other things of
the kind. Yet for some of these people the angels labeled their behaviors as
evil and sinful, whereas for others the angels did not. The angels declared
the former guilty and the latter innocent. Upon being asked why this was,
since the people had done the same things, the angels replied that they had
evaluated all the people on the basis of their plans, intentions, and purposes and distinguished them accordingly. Those whose intent excused
them, the angels excused, and those whose intent condemned them, the
angels condemned, since all who are in heaven have good intent, and all
who are in hell have evil intent.

524   These points may be illustrated with comparisons. The sins that we
retain when we do not practice repentance are like various diseases we
suffer that are fatal unless we are given medicine that takes away what
is causing harm. Such sins are especially like gangrene, which spreads (if
not caught in time) and inevitably leads to death. They are like boils and
abscesses that have not been lanced and opened—the accumulation of

pus will press into surrounding tissues, then into nearby internal organs, and finally into the heart, causing death.

[2] Sins that remain can also be compared with tigers, leopards, lions, wolves, and foxes. Unless these animals are kept in caves or are bound with ropes or chains, they will attack our flocks and herds, like a fox among the hens, and slaughter them. Such sins are like poisonous snakes— if the snakes are not held down with pegs and their fangs removed, they will inflict their deadly bite on us. If a whole flock of sheep is left in fields that have poisonous plants, they will die unless the shepherd moves them to safe pasture. A silkworm and therefore its silk will be destroyed if other grubs are not shaken from the leaves of its tree.

[3] Sins that remain can also be compared to grains kept in barns or houses, which become moldy, rancid, and therefore useless if they do not have enough air circulating around them to take away the harmful elements. If a fire is not extinguished when it first breaks out, it will destroy the whole city or the entire forest. If thistles and thornbushes are not uprooted, they will completely overrun a garden.

As experienced gardeners know, a trunk that comes from bad seed or a bad root sends its noxious sap into the branch of a good tree that has been grafted onto it, and the bad sap that creeps up that branch is then turned into good sap and produces useful fruit. Something similar occurs in us when evil is laid aside through the process of repentance; through repentance we are grafted onto the Lord like a branch onto a vine and we bear good fruit (John 15:4, 5, 6).[167]

Having a Concept of Sin and Then Looking for Sin in Ourselves Is the Beginning of Repentance

It is impossible for anyone in the Christian world to lack a concept of sin. Everyone in Christianity from early childhood on is taught what evil is, and from youth on is taught which evils are sinful. All adolescents learn this from their parents and teachers, and also from the Ten Commandments, which for all who grow up in Christianity is the first book they own.[168] As they get a little older, they are further taught this by the preaching they hear in church, by instruction they receive at home, and most thoroughly by [their own reading of] the Word. Beyond that, they are also exposed to it by the civil laws of justice, which teach much the same things as the Ten Commandments and the other injunctions in the Word.

525

The evil that is sinful is simply evil against our neighbor; and evil against our neighbor is also evil against God, which is what sin is.

Nevertheless, having a concept of sin does nothing for us unless we examine the actions we have taken in our lives and see whether we have either openly or secretly done any such thing.

Before we take this action, everything about sin is just an idea to us; what the preacher says about it is only a sound that comes in our left ear, goes out our right ear, and is gone. Eventually it becomes a subject relegated to vague thoughts and mumbled words in worship, and for many it comes to seem like something imaginary and mythical.

Something completely different occurs, however, if we examine ourselves in the light of our concepts of what is sinful, discover some such thing in ourselves, say to ourselves, "This evil is sinful," and then abstain from it out of fear of eternal punishment. Then for the first time we receive the instructive and eloquent preaching in church in *both* of our ears, take it to heart, and turn from a non-Christian into a Christian.

526   What could possibly be better known across the entire Christian world than the idea that we should examine ourselves? Everywhere in both Roman Catholic and Protestant empires and monarchies, as people approach the Holy Supper[169] they are given teachings and warnings that they must examine themselves, recognize and admit to their sins, and start a new life of a different nature. In British territories this is done with terrifying threats. During the prayer that precedes communion, the priest by the altar reads and proclaims the following:

> The way and means of becoming a worthy partaker in the Holy Supper is first to examine your life and your conversations by the rule of God's commandments. In whatever regard you notice that you have committed an offense of will, speech, or act, then bewail your own sinfulness and confess yourselves to Almighty God, with full purpose of amending your life. If you observe that your offenses are not only against God but also against your neighbors, you shall reconcile yourselves to them, being ready to make restitution and satisfaction to the utmost of your power for all injuries and wrongs done by you to any other, and being likewise ready to forgive others who have offended you, just as you wish to have forgiveness from God for your offenses. Otherwise receiving the Holy Supper does nothing but increase your damnation. Therefore if any of you is a blasphemer of God, or a hinderer or slanderer of his Word, or an adulterer, or someone taken with malice or ill will, or involved in any other grievous crime, repent of your sins. Or else do

not come to the Holy Supper; otherwise, after you take it the Devil may enter into you as he entered into Judas, fill you with all wickedness, and bring you to destruction of both body and soul.[170]

Nevertheless, there are some people who are incapable of examining themselves: for example, children and young men and women before they reach the age at which they can reflect upon themselves; simple people who lack the ability to reflect; all who have no fear of God; some who have a mental or physical illness; and also people who, entrenched in the teaching that justification comes solely through the faith that assigns us Christ's merit, have convinced themselves that if they practiced self-examination and repentance something of their own selves might intrude that would ruin their faith and divert or redirect their salvation from its sole focus.

527

For the types of people just listed, an oral confession is of benefit, although, as discussed earlier in this chapter [§§516–519], it is not the same as practicing repentance.

[2] People who know what sin is and especially those who know a lot about it from the Word and who teach about it, but who do not examine themselves and therefore see no sin within themselves, can be compared to people who scrape and save money, only to put it away in boxes and containers and make no other use of it than looking at it and counting it. They are like people who collect pieces of gold and silver jewelry and keep them in a safe in a storage room for no other purpose than to own them. They are like the businessman who hid his talent in the ground and the one who wrapped his mina in a handkerchief (Matthew 25:25; Luke 19:20). They are like the hardened pathways and rocks onto which the seed fell (Matthew 13:4, 5). They are like fig trees with abundant foliage that bear no fruit (Mark 11:13). They are like hearts of stone that have not turned to flesh ([Ezekiel 36:26]; Zechariah 7:12). They are "like partridges that nest but do not bear young. They amass riches, but without judgment. In the middle of their days they leave their riches behind and at the end of their [lives] they become fools" (Jeremiah 17:11). They are also like the five young women who had lamps but no oil (Matthew 25:1–12).

[3] People who take in many teachings from the Word about goodwill and repentance and who know all about the commandments and yet do not live by those things could be compared to gluttons who stuff food in chunks into their mouths and swallow it without chewing, so that it sits undigested in their stomach, and substances pressed from it pollute their chyle[171] and cause chronic diseases, from which they eventually die a wretched death.

No matter how much light they may have, people like this can be called winters, frozen lands, arctic climates, and indeed snow and ice, because they have no spiritual warmth.

Active Repentance Is Examining Ourselves, Recognizing and Admitting Our Sins, Praying to the Lord, and Beginning a New Life

528 Many passages in the Word and many unambiguous statements by the Lord there make it clear that we absolutely have to repent and that our salvation depends on it. For now I will give just the following examples. "John preached a baptism of repentance and said, 'Bear fruits worthy of repentance'" (Luke 3:3, 8; Mark 1:4). "Jesus began to preach and said, 'You must repent'" (Matthew 4:17). "Jesus said, 'Repent, because the kingdom of God has become closer'" (Mark 1:14, 15). "If you have not practiced repentance, you will all perish" (Luke 13:5). "Jesus preached to his disciples that in his name they should preach repentance and forgiveness of sins to all the nations" (Luke 24:47; Mark 6:12). Therefore "Peter preached repentance and baptism in the name of Jesus Christ for forgiveness of sins" (Acts 2:38). Peter also said, "Repent and turn yourselves around, so that your sins may be wiped out" (Acts 3:19). Paul "preached to all people everywhere that they should repent" (Acts 17:30). Paul "also proclaimed in Damascus, in Jerusalem, throughout the region of Judea, and to the nations, that they should repent, turn themselves to God, and do things that are in keeping with repentance" (Acts 26:20). Paul "also proclaimed to both Jews and Greeks repentance before God and faith in the Lord Jesus Christ" (Acts 20:21). To the church of Ephesus the Lord said, "I have something against you, that you have left behind the goodwill you had at first. Repent. Otherwise if you do not repent, I will remove your lampstand from its place" (Revelation 2:4, 5). To the church in Pergamos he said, "I know your works. Repent" (Revelation 2:13, 16). To the church in Thyatira he said, "I will hand you over to affliction if you have not repented of your works" (Revelation 2:19, 22, 23). To the church in Laodicea he said, "I know your works. Be zealous and repent" (Revelation 3:15, 19). "There is joy in heaven over one sinner who repents" (Luke 15:7). There are of course more passages as well.

From these teachings it is clear that we absolutely have to repent. What repentance involves, however, and how we go about it will be shown in what follows.

With the reasoning powers we have been given, surely we are all able to understand that repentance does not consist of a mere oral confession that we are a sinner and of listing a number of things about sin, like a hypocrite (see §518 above). What is easier for us, when we feel anguish and agony, than breathing out and emitting sighs and groans through our lips, beating our chests, and declaring ourselves guilty of sins of every kind, even if we are actually unaware of a single sin within ourselves? Does the Devil's gang, which lives inside our loves, go out of us along with our sighing? Surely they whistle contemptuously at our histrionics, and stay inside us as before, since we are their home.

These points serve to clarify that by "repentance" the Word does not mean mere confession; as I said before, it means a repentance from evil actions.

The question then is, How are we to repent? The answer is, we are to do so *actively*. That is, we are to examine ourselves, recognize and admit to our sins, pray to the Lord, and begin a new life.

The fact that repentance is not possible without examining ourselves was shown under the previous heading [§§526–527]. And what is the point of examining ourselves unless we recognize our sins? What is the point of that recognition unless we admit that those sins are in us? What is the point of all three of these steps unless we confess our sins before the Lord, pray for his help, and then begin a new life, which is the purpose of the whole exercise? This is active repentance.

[2] The fact that this is the sequence of actions to take is something we are all capable of realizing as we leave childhood and become more and more independent and able to reason for ourselves. We can see this from thinking of our baptism. The washing of baptism means regeneration; and during the ceremony our godparents promised on our behalf that we were going to reject the Devil and all his works.[172] Likewise thinking of the Holy Supper, we have all been warned that in order to approach it worthily we have to repent from our sins, turn ourselves to God, and start a new life.[173] We can also think of the Ten Commandments—the catechism that is in the hands of all Christians. Six of the ten simply command us not to do evil things.[174] If we do not remove these evils through repentance, we are unable to love our neighbor and even less able to love

God, even though the Law and the Prophets, that is, the Word and therefore salvation, hinge on these two commandments [Matthew 22:40].

[3] Repentance becomes effective if we practice it regularly—that is, every time we prepare ourselves to take the Communion of the Holy Supper. Afterward, if we abstain from one sin or another that we have discovered in ourselves, this is enough to make our repentance real. When we reach this point, we are on the pathway to heaven, because we then begin to turn from an earthly person into a spiritual person and to be born anew with the help of the Lord.

531 This change can be illustrated by the following comparison. Before repentance, we are like a desert, inhabited by terrifying wild creatures, dragons, eagle-owls, screech owls, vipers, and bloodletting snakes; in the clumps of bushes in that desert there are the owls and vultures [mentioned in the Bible], and satyrs are dancing [Isaiah 13:21].[175] After these creatures have been expelled by human work and effort, however, that desert can be plowed and cultivated into fields, and these can be planted with oats, beans, and flax, and later on with barley and wheat.

This can also be compared to the wickedness that is abundant and dominant in humankind. If evildoers were not chastised and punished with whippings and death, no city would survive; no nation would last. In effect, each one of us is society itself in its smallest form. If we do not treat ourselves in a spiritual way as evildoers are treated by the larger society in an earthly way, we are going to be chastised and punished after death; and this will continue until out of sheer fear of further punishment we stop doing evil, even if we can never be compelled to do what is good out of love for it.

True Repentance Is Examining Not Only the Actions of Our Life but Also the Intentions of Our Will

532 The reason why true repentance is to examine not only the actions of our life but also the intentions of our will is that our intellect and our will produce our actions. We speak from our thought and we act from our will; therefore our speech is our thought speaking, and our action is our will acting. Since this is the origin of what we say and do, it is clear without a doubt that it is these two faculties that commit the sin when our body sins.

It is in fact possible for us to repent of evil things we have done through our bodies but still think about evil and will it. This is like cutting down the trunk of a bad type of tree but leaving its root still in the ground; the same bad tree grows up from the root again and also spreads itself around. There is a different outcome when the root is pulled up, though; and this is what happens within us when we explore the intentions of our will and lay our evils aside through repentance.

[2] We explore the intentions of our will by exploring our thoughts. Our intentions reveal themselves in our thoughts—for example, when we contemplate, will, and intend acts of revenge, adultery, theft, or false witness, or entertain desires for those things. This applies as well to acts of blasphemy against God, against the holy Word, and against the church, and so on.

If we keep our minds focused on these issues, and explore whether we would do such things if no fear of the law or concern for our reputation stood in the way, and if after this exploration we decide that we do not will those things, because they are sins, then we are practicing a repentance that is true and deep. This is even more the case when we are feeling delight in those evils and are free to do them, but at that moment we resist and abstain. If we practice this over and over, then when our evils come back we sense our delight in them as something unpleasant, and in time we condemn them to hell. This is the meaning of these words of the Lord: "Any who try to find their soul will lose it, and any who lose their soul for my sake, will find it" (Matthew 10:39).

People who remove evils from their will through this type of repentance are like those who in time pulled up the weeds that had been sown by the Devil in their field, allowing seeds planted by the Lord God the Savior to gain free ground and to sprout for the harvest (Matthew 13:25–30).

There are two loves that have been deeply rooted in the human race for a long time now: love for dominating everyone, and love for possessing everyone's wealth. If the reins are let out on the first type of love, it rushes on until it wants to be the God of all heaven. If the reins are let out on the second type of love, it rushes on until it wants to be the God of the whole world. All other forms of love for evil are ranked below these two and serve as their army.

These two loves are extremely difficult to find by self-examination. They live at a deep level within us and hide themselves away. They are like vipers lurking in a craggy rock surface that save up their venom so that when someone falls asleep on the rock, they strike lethal blows and then slither back out of sight.

These loves are also like the sirens mentioned by ancient writers. The sirens would use their singing to lure people in and kill them.[176]

533

These two loves dress themselves up in robes and tunics just the way devils use magic to project images in order to appear well dressed before their own cronies and others they wish to deceive.

[2] It is important to note, however, that these two loves can be more prevalent among commoners than among the great; more prevalent among the poor than among the wealthy; more prevalent among subjects than among royalty. The latter in each case are born into power and wealth. Over time, the latter come to view their power and wealth much the way people at a somewhat lower level—commanders, governors, admirals, or even impoverished farm workers—view their own households and possessions. It is not the same, though, when monarchs wish to exercise power over nations that are not their own.

[3] The intentions of our will must be examined, because our love resides in our will. Our will is a vessel for our love, as shown above [§§39, 263, 362:1]. From its residence in our will, our whole love imparts its feelings of delight to the perceptions and thoughts in our intellect. Our perceptions and thoughts do nothing on their own; they serve our will. They are in harmony with our will and agree with and support everything that has to do with our love.

Our will, then, is the home in which we live. Our intellect is just the front hall through which we go in and out. This is why I said above that we must examine the intentions of our will. When these are examined and have been laid aside, we are lifted from our earthly will—where the evils we inherited and the evils we have actually committed are lodged—to our spiritual will. Through that higher will, the Lord reforms and regenerates our earthly will, and also works through it to reform and regenerate the sensory and voluntary faculties of our body, until the process has encompassed the whole of us.

534 People who do not examine themselves are like people with a sickness that closes off their capillaries and therefore corrupts their blood, causing their limbs to go to sleep and atrophy, and resulting in severe chronic diseases because their humors,[177] and therefore the blood that arises from them, are viscous, sticky, irritating, and acidic. People who do examine themselves, however, including the intentions of their will, are like people who are healed from these diseases and regain the vitality they felt when they were young.

People who examine themselves in the right way are like ships from Ophir[178] completely filled with gold, silver, and precious stones; before they examined themselves, though, they were like barges loaded down with unclean freight, carting away the filth and excrement from city streets.

People who examine themselves deeply become like mines, whose walls all shine with ores of precious metals; before they do so, however, they are like foul-smelling swamps inhabited by serpents and poisonous snakes with glittering scales, and harmful insects with shiny wings.

People who do not examine themselves are like the dry bones in the valley; but after people have explored themselves they become like those same bones after the Lord Jehovih[179] put sinews on them, brought flesh upon them, covered them with skin, and breathed spirit into them, and they came to life (Ezekiel 37:1–14).

Repentance Is Also Practiced
by Those Who Do Not Examine Themselves
but Nevertheless Stop Doing Evils Because Evils Are Sinful;
This Kind of Repentance Is Done by People Who Do
Acts of Goodwill as a Religious Practice

In the Protestant Christian world, active repentance, which is examining ourselves, recognizing and admitting to our sins, praying to the Lord, and starting a new life, is extremely difficult to practice, for a number of reasons that will be covered under the final heading in this chapter [§§564–566]. Therefore here is an easier kind of repentance: When we are considering doing something evil and are forming an intention to do it, we say to ourselves, "I am thinking about this and I am intending to do it, but because it is a sin, I am not going to do it." This counteracts the enticement that hell is injecting into us and keeps it from making further inroads.

535

It is amazing but true that it is easy for any of us to rebuke someone else who is intending to do something evil and say, "Don't do that— that's a sin!" And yet it is difficult for us to say the same thing to ourselves. The reason is that saying it to ourselves requires a movement of the will, but saying it to someone else requires only a low level of thought based on things we have heard.[180]

[2] There was an investigation in the spiritual world to see which people were capable of doing this second type of repentance. It was discovered that there are as few of such people as there are doves in a vast desert. Some people indicated that they were indeed capable of this second type of repentance, but that they were incapable of examining themselves and confessing their sins before God. Nevertheless, all people who do good actions

as a religious practice avoid actual evils. It is extremely rare, though, that people reflect on the inner realms that belong to their will. They suppose that because they are involved in good actions they are not involved in evil actions, and even that their goodness covers up their evil.

But, my friend, to abstain from evils is the first step in gaining goodwill. The Word teaches this. The Ten Commandments teach it. Baptism teaches it. The Holy Supper teaches it.

Reason, too, teaches it. How could any of us escape from our evils or drive them away without ever taking a look at ourselves? How can our goodness become truly good without being inwardly purified?

I know that all devout people and also all people of sound reason who read this will nod and see it as genuine truth; yet even so, only a few are going to do what it says.

536 Nevertheless, all people who do what is good as a religious practice— not only Christians but also non-Christians—are accepted and adopted by the Lord after they die. The Lord says, "'I was hungry and you gave me something to eat. I was thirsty and you gave me something to drink. I was a stranger and you took me in. I was naked and you clothed me. I was sick and you visited me. I was in prison and you came to me.' And he said, 'As much as you did this to one of the least of my people, you did it to me. Come, you who are blessed, and possess as your inheritance the kingdom prepared for you from the foundation of the world'" (Matthew 25:34–36, 40).

Here I will add something previously unknown: All people who do good things as a religious practice, after death reject the teaching of the church of today that there are three divine persons who have existed from eternity. They also reject the belief of today's church as it is applied to those three in sequence.[181] Instead they turn themselves to the Lord God the Savior and drink in the teachings of the new church with great pleasure.

[2] All others, however, who have not exercised goodwill as a religious practice, have hearts that are as hard as diamonds. At first they worship three gods, then the Father alone, and finally no God. They regard the Lord God the Savior as not the Son of God but only the son of Mary born from her having slept with Joseph.[182] Then they shake themselves free of all the good actions and true insights taught by the new church and soon join up with dragon spirits.[183] Along with these spirits they are driven off into deserts or caves that lie at the outer boundaries of the so-called Christian world.[184] After some time elapses, as a result of their separation from the new heaven[185] they rush into committing crimes and are therefore sent down into hell.

[3] This is the final outcome for those who do not do acts of goodwill as a religious practice. They believe that none of us can do anything good on our own unless we do it to earn merit; therefore they omit doing such things. They join up with the goats, who are condemned and thrown into the eternal fire prepared for the Devil and his angels, because they did not do the things that the sheep did. See Matthew 25:41 and following; and note that it does not say there that they did evil things; it just says that they did *not* do *good* things. People who do good things, but not as a religious practice, actually do evil things, since "No one can serve two lords without hating one and loving the other, and staying close to one and ignoring the other" (Matthew 6:24). Jehovah says through Isaiah, "Wash yourselves; purify yourselves. Remove the evil of your actions from before my eyes. Stop doing evil. Learn to do what is good. Then, if your sins have been like scarlet, they will become as white as snow. If they have been red as crimson, they will be like wool" (Isaiah 1:16, 17, 18). Jehovah says to Jeremiah, "Stand in the entrance to Jehovah's house and proclaim there this word. 'Thus spoke Jehovah Sabaoth,[186] the God of Israel: "Make your ways and your works good. Do not put your trust in the words of a lie, saying, 'The temple of Jehovah, the temple of Jehovah is here [that is, the church].'[187] When you steal, kill, [commit adultery,] and swear falsely, then do you come and stand before me in this house that carries my name? Do you say, 'We were carried away,' when you are committing all these abominations? Has this house become a den of thieves? Behold, I, even I, have seen it," says Jehovah'" (Jeremiah 7:2, 3, 4, 9, 10, 11).

It is important to realize that people who do what is good only because they possess a natural goodness and not because of their religion are not accepted [by the Lord] after they die. This is because the only goodness that was in their goodwill was earthly and not also spiritual; and spiritual goodness is what forges a partnership between the Lord and us, not earthly goodness without spiritual goodness. Earthly goodness is of the flesh alone, and is inherited at our birth from our parents. Spiritual goodness is goodness of the spirit and is born anew with the help of the Lord.

People who, as a religious practice, do good actions that have to do with goodwill and, as part of that same practice, do not do evil things, but who have not yet accepted the teaching of the new church about the Lord, can be compared to trees that bear good fruit, but only a few pieces of it. Such people are also like trees that bear pieces of fruit that are fine but small; the trees are nevertheless kept and taken care of in gardens. They can also be compared to olive trees and fig trees that grow

537

wild in the forest, and to fragrant herbs and balsam bushes that grow wild on hills. They are like little buildings that are houses of God in which devout worship occurs. They are the sheep on the right [Matthew 25:33], and are examples of the ram that was attacked by a goat in Daniel 8:2–14. In heaven their clothes are red. After they have been initiated into the good actions and attitudes taught by the new church, however, their clothes become purple and (if they also accept the truths of the new church) more and more beautifully radiant.

We Need to Make Our Confession before the Lord God the Savior, and Also to Beg for His Help and Power in Resisting Evils

538 It is the Lord God the Savior to whom we must turn, (1) because he is the God of heaven and earth, the Redeemer and Savior, who has omnipotence, omniscience, and omnipresence, who is both mercy and justice itself, and (2) because we are his creation and the church is his sheepfold, and we are commanded many times in the New Covenant[188] to turn to him and worship and adore him.

In the following words in John the Lord commands that we are to turn to him alone:

> Truly, truly I say to you, those who do not enter through the door to the sheepfold but instead climb up some other way are thieves and robbers. The person who goes in through the door is the shepherd of the sheep. I am the door. Anyone who enters through me will be saved and will find pasture. The thief does not come except to steal, slaughter, and destroy. I have come so that they may have life and abundance. I am the good shepherd. (John 10:1, 2, 9, 10, 11)

The "other way" that we are not to climb up is toward God the Father, because he cannot be seen, and is therefore inaccessible and unavailable for partnership. This is why he came into the world and made himself able to be seen, accessible, and available for partnership. He did this for only one reason: so that human beings could be saved. If we do not direct our thinking toward God *as a human being,* our whole mental sight of God is lost. It collapses like our eyesight when we send it out into the universe.[189] Instead of God we see empty nothingness, or nature as a whole, or certain objects within nature.

[2] The being who came into the world was God himself, who from eternity [has been and] is the One. This is very clear from the birth of the Lord and Savior. He was conceived by the power of the Highest through the Holy Spirit. As a result the Virgin Mary gave birth to his human manifestation. It follows then that his soul was the Divinity itself that is called the Father—God is, after all, indivisible—and the human being born as a result is the human manifestation of God the Father, which is called the Son of God (Luke 1:32, 34, 35). It follows from all this that when we turn to the Lord God the Savior, we are turning to God the Father as well. This is why he replied to Philip, when Philip asked him to show them the Father, "Those who see me see the Father. How then can you say, 'Show us the Father'? Do you not believe that I am in the Father and the Father is in me? Believe me that I am in the Father and the Father is in me" (John 14:6–11). For more on this, see many things that are stated in the chapters on God [§§6–7], the Lord [§§92–94], the Holy Spirit [§§139–141], and the Trinity [§§164–169].

There are two duties that we are obliged to perform after we have examined ourselves: prayer and confession. The *prayer* is to be a request that [the Lord] have mercy on us, give us the power to resist the evils that we have repented of, and provide us an inclination and desire to do what is good, since "without him we cannot do anything" (John 15:5). The *confession* is to be that we see, recognize, and admit to our evils and that we are discovering that we are miserable sinners.

There is no need for us to list our sins before the Lord and no need to beg that he forgive them. The reason we do not need to list our sins before the Lord is that we searched them out within ourselves and saw them, and therefore they are present before the Lord because they are present before us. The Lord was leading us in our self-examination; he disclosed our sins; he inspired our grief and, along with it, the motivation to stop doing them and to begin a new life.

[2] There are two reasons why we should not beg the Lord to forgive our sins. The first is that sins are not abolished, they are just relocated within us. They are laid aside when after repentance we stop doing them and start a new life. This is because there are countless yearnings that stick to each evil in a kind of cluster; these cannot be set aside in a moment, but they can be dealt with in stages as we allow ourselves to be reformed and regenerated.

The second reason is that the Lord is mercy itself. Therefore he forgives the sins of all people. He blames no one for any sin. He says, "They do not know what they are doing" [Luke 23:34] (but this does not mean our sins are taken away altogether). To Peter, who was asking how many times he should forgive a friend who was sinning against him—whether he should give forgiveness as many as seven times—the Lord answered, "I do not say as many as seven times, but as many as seventy times seven" (Matthew 18:21, 22). How forgiving, then, is the Lord?

It does no harm, though, for people who are weighed down by a heavy conscience to lighten their load by listing their sins before a minister of the church, for the sake of absolution. Doing so introduces them to the habit of examining themselves and reflecting on their daily evils. Nevertheless, this type of confession is earthly in nature, whereas the confession described above is spiritual.

560 190 Giving adoration to some vicar [of Christ] on earth as we would to God or calling on some saint as we would call on God has no more effect on heaven than worshiping the sun, the moon, and the stars, or seeking for a response from fortune-tellers and believing in their meaningless utterances. Doing this would be like worshiping a church building but not God, who is in that church. It would be like submitting a request for glorious honors not to the king himself but to a servant of the king who is carrying his scepter and crown. This would be pointless, like paying deference to a gleaming scarlet robe but not the person who is wearing it; like praising the glorious light and golden rays from the sun but not the sun itself; like saluting names but not people. The following statement in John is for people who do such things: "We must remain in truth in Jesus Christ. He is the true God and eternal life. Little children, beware of idols" (1 John 5:20, 21).

Active Repentance Is Easy
for People Who Have Done It a Few Times;
Those Who Have Not Done It, However,
Experience Tremendous Inner Resistance to It

561 Active repentance is examining ourselves, recognizing [and admitting to] our sins, confessing them before the Lord, and beginning a new life. This accords with the description of it under the preceding headings. People in the Protestant Christian world—by which I here mean all [Christians] who have separated from the Roman Catholic Church, and also people who belong to that church but have not practiced active repentance—experience tremendous inner resistance to such repentance, for various reasons. Some do not want to do it. Some are afraid. They are in the habit of not doing it, and this breeds first unwillingness, and then intellectual and rational support for not doing it, and in some cases, grief, dread, and terror of it.

[2] The primary reason for the tremendous resistance to active repentance among Protestant Christians is their belief that repentance and goodwill contribute nothing to their salvation. They believe that faith alone brings salvation; when faith is assigned to us, it comes with forgiveness of sins, justification, renewal, regeneration, sanctification, and eternal salvation, without our having to cooperate either actually on our own or even seemingly on our own. The teachers of their dogma call this cooperation of ours useless, and even a roadblock that is resistant and harmful to [our reception of] Christ's merit. Although the lay public is ignorant of the mysteries of this faith, its teaching has nevertheless been sown in them through just a few words: "Faith alone saves," and "Who among us can do anything good on our own?"

This has made repentance among Protestants like a nest of baby birds abandoned by parents who were caught and killed by a bird-catcher.

An additional cause of this resistance is that in spirit, so-called Reformed people are among spirits in the spiritual world who are no different than they are, who introduce these reactions into their thinking and steer them away from the first step of introspection and self-examination.

I have asked many Protestants in the spiritual world why they did not practice active repentance, even though in all their denominations they were commanded to do so in the Word and in baptism and also before coming to Holy Communion. They had various responses.

562

Some said that it is enough just to feel contrition and then to orally confess to being a sinner.

Some said that repentance of the type mentioned above, because it is something we have to do of our own will, is not in agreement with the faith that is universally received.

Some said, "Who could examine themselves when they know they are nothing but sin? It would be like casting a net into a lake that is full from top to bottom of bad-smelling muck that contains stinging worms!"

Some said, "Who would be able to look so deeply into themselves that they could see the sin of Adam inside, as the source of all their actual evils? Aren't their evils and the sin of Adam washed away by the waters of baptism, and wiped away or completely covered over by the merit of

Christ? What is repentance in that case but an imposition that seriously disturbs the conscientious? Surely, because of the Gospel we are under grace and not under the hard law of that repentance." And so on.

Some said that when they set out to examine themselves, they are seized with dread and terror as if they had seen a monster next to their bed at twilight.

These responses reveal why active repentance in the Protestant Christian world is, so to speak, neglected and moldy.

[2] In the presence of these same people I asked some Roman Catholics about their acts of confession before their ministers and whether they experienced inner resistance to confession. They answered that after they were initiated into it, they were not afraid to list their misdeeds before a confessor who was not severe. They even felt some pleasure in compiling their list, and would laugh when they said some of the lighter things out loud, although they would state the serious ones a little more timidly. Every year, at the time established by custom of years past, they would go back willingly again.[191] After absolution, they would celebrate. They also mentioned that they regarded as impure any people who were unwilling to disclose the uncleanness in their hearts.

When the Protestants who were present heard all this, they ran away. Some were laughing and guffawing; some were shocked but also gave the Catholics praise.

[3] Afterward some other people came along who were Catholic but had lived in Protestant areas. According to the customary practice there, they had gone before their priest and made not a specific confession like their companions from elsewhere in Catholicism but only a general confession. These people said that they were utterly unable to examine themselves, to investigate or divulge either the evils they had done or the secret evils in their thoughts. They felt as much resistance and terror as they would crossing through a ditch to climb ramparts where an armed soldier was shouting, "Stop! Go no farther."

This makes it clear that active repentance is easy for those who have done it a few times, but those who have not done it experience tremendous resistance to it.

563 It is well known that habits form a kind of second nature, and therefore what is easy for one person is difficult for another. This applies also to examining ourselves and confessing what we have found.

It is easy for manual laborers, porters, and farm workers to work with their arms from morning till evening, but a delicate person of the nobility cannot do the same work for half an hour without fatigue and sweating. It is easy for a forerunner[192] with a walking stick and comfortable shoes to ply the road for miles, whereas someone used to riding in a carriage has difficulty jogging slowly from one street to the next. [2] All artisans who are devoted to their craft pursue it easily and willingly, and when they are away from it they long to get back to it; but it is almost impossible to force a lazy person with the same skills to practice that craft. The same goes for everyone who has some occupation or pursuit.

What is easier for someone who is pursuing religious devotion than praying to God? And what is more difficult for someone who is enslaved to ungodliness?

All priests are afraid the first time they preach before royalty. But after they get used to it, they go on boldly.

What is easier for angelic people than lifting their eyes up to heaven? What is easier for devilish people than casting their eyes down to hell? (If they are hypocrites, however, they can look toward heaven in a similar way, but with aversion of heart.)

We are all saturated with the goal we have in mind and the habits that result from it.

Those Who Have Never Practiced Repentance or Looked at or Studied Themselves Eventually Do Not Even Know What Damnable Evil or Saving Goodness Is

Since only a few people in the Protestant Christian world practice repentance, it is important to add that those who have not looked at or studied themselves eventually do not even know what damnable evil or saving goodness is, because they lack the religious practice that would allow them to find out. The evil that we do not see, recognize, or admit to stays with us; and what stays with us becomes more and more firmly established until it blocks off the inner areas of our minds. As a result, we become first earthly, then sense-oriented, and finally bodily.[193] In these cases we do not know of any damnable evil or any saving goodness. We become like a tree on a hard rock that spreads its roots into the crevices in the rocks and eventually dries up because it has no moisture. **564**

[2] All people who were brought up properly are rational and moral. There are different ways of being rational, however: a worldly way and a

heavenly way. People who have become rational and moral in a worldly way but not also in a heavenly way are rational and moral only in word and gesture. Inwardly they are animals, and predatory animals at that, because they are in step with the inhabitants of hell, all of whom are like that. People who have become rational and moral in a heavenly way as well, however, are truly rational and truly moral, because they have these qualities in spirit as well as in word and deed. Something spiritual lies hidden within their words and actions like the soul that activates their earthly, sense-oriented, and bodily levels. Such people are in step with the inhabitants of heaven.

Therefore there is such a thing as a rational, moral person who is spiritual, and such a thing as a rational, moral person who is only earthly. In the world you cannot tell them apart, especially if their hypocrisy is well rehearsed. Angels in heaven can tell the two apart, however, as easily as telling doves from eagle-owls or sheep from tigers.

[3] Those who are only earthly can see good and evil qualities in others and criticize them, but because they have never looked at or studied themselves, they see no evil in themselves. If someone else discovers an evil in them, they use their rational faculty to hide it, as a snake hides its head in the dust; then they plunge themselves into that evil the way a hornet dives into dung.

Their delight in evil is what has this blinding effect. It surrounds them like a fog over a swamp, absorbing and suffocating rays of light. This is the nature of hellish delight. It radiates from hell and flows into every human being, but only into the soles of our feet, our back, and the back of our head. If we receive that inflow with our forehead and our chest, however, we are slaves to hell, because the human cerebrum serves the intellect and its wisdom, whereas the cerebellum serves the will and its love. This is why we have two brains.[194] The only thing that can amend, reform, and turn around hellish delight of the kind just mentioned is a rationality and morality that is spiritual.

565 Allow me to briefly describe people whose rationality and morality are merely earthly. Such people are truly sense-oriented. If they continue in this direction, they become bodily or carnal. The description that follows will be presented as a list of points in outline form.[195]

"Sensory" is a term for the lowest level of life within the human mind; it clings, and is closely joined, to the five senses of the human body.

"Sense-oriented people" are people who judge everything on the basis of their physical senses—people who will not believe anything unless they can see it with their eyes and touch it with their hands. What they can see and touch they call "something." Everything else they reject.

The inner levels of their mind, levels that see in heaven's light, are closed to the point where they see nothing true related to heaven or the church. Their thinking occurs on an outermost level and not inside, where the light is spiritual. Since the light they have is dull and earthly, people like this are inwardly opposed to things related to heaven and the church, although they are outwardly able to speak in favor of them. If they have hope of gaining ruling power or wealth by so doing, they are even capable of speaking ardently in favor of them.

The educated and the scholarly who are deeply convinced of falsities—especially people who oppose the truths in the Word—are more sense-oriented than others.

[2] Sense-oriented people are able to reason sharply and skillfully, because their thinking is so close to their speech as to be practically in it—almost inside their lips; and also because they attribute all intelligence solely to the ability to speak from memory. They also have great skill at defending things that are false. After they have defended falsities convincingly, they themselves believe those falsities are true. They base their reasoning and defense on mistaken impressions from the senses that the public finds captivating and convincing.

Sense-oriented people are more deceptive and ill intentioned than others.

Misers, adulterers, and deceitful people are especially sense-oriented, although before the world they appear smart.

The inner areas of their mind are disgusting and filthy; they use them to communicate with the hells. In the Word they are called the dead.

The inhabitants of hell are sense-oriented. The more sense-oriented they are, the deeper in hell they are. The sphere of hellish spirits is connected to the sensory level of our mind through a kind of back door.[196] In the light of heaven the backs of their heads look hollowed out.[197]

The ancients[198] had a term for people who debate on the basis of sense impressions alone: they called them serpents of the tree of the knowledge [of good and evil].

[3] Sense impressions ought to have the lowest priority, not the highest. For wise and intelligent people, sense impressions do have the lowest priority and are subservient to things that are deep inside. For unwise people, sense impressions have the highest priority and are in control.

If sense impressions have the lowest priority, they help open a pathway for the intellect. We then extrapolate truths by a method of extraction.

Sense impressions stand closest to the world and admit information that is coming in from it; they sift through that information.

We are in touch with the world by means of sense impressions and with heaven by means of impressions on our rationality.

Sense impressions supply things that serve the inner realms of the mind.

There are sense impressions that feed the intellect and sense impressions that feed the will.

Unless our thought is lifted above the level of our sense impressions, we have very little wisdom. When our thinking rises above sense impressions, it enters a clearer light and eventually comes into the light of heaven. From this light we become aware of things that are flowing down into us from heaven.

The outermost contents of our intellect are earthly information. The outermost contents of our will are sensory pleasures.

566 Our earthly self is like an animal. Over the course of our lives we take on the image of an animal. Because of this, sense-oriented people in the spiritual world appear surrounded by animals of every kind. These animals are correspondences. Regarded on its own, our earthly self is only an animal, but because a spiritual level has been added to it we are capable of becoming human. If we decline to undergo this transformation, even though we have the faculties that make it possible, we can still pretend to be human although we are then actually just animals that can talk. In that case our talking is based on earthly rationality, but our thinking is based on spiritual insanity; our actions are based on earthly morality, but our love is based on spiritual satyriasis. To someone else who has a rationality that is spiritual, our actions seem almost exactly like the frenzied dancing of someone bitten by a tarantula, called Saint Vitus's or Saint Guy's dance.[199]

[2] As we all know, a hypocrite can talk about God, a robber can talk about honesty, an adulterer can talk about being a faithful spouse, and so on. We have the ability to close and open the door that stands between what we think and what we say, and the door that stands between what we intend and what we do (the doorkeeper is prudence or else deceitfulness). Without the ability to close these doors, we would quickly fall into acts of wickedness and cruelty with greater savagery than any animal. That door is opened in us all after death, though, and then it becomes apparent what we truly are. Then the forces that keep us in check are punishment and imprisonment in hell.

Therefore, kind reader, take a look inside yourself, diligently search out one evil or another within yourself, and turn away from it for religious reasons. If you turn away from it for any other reason or purpose, you are only doing so so that it will no longer appear before the world.

To these points I will add the following memorable occurrences.

The first memorable occurrence. I was suddenly overcome with a deathly illness. My whole head felt worse and worse. A poisonous smoke was blowing in from the Jerusalem that is called Sodom and Egypt (Revelation 11:8).[200] I was half dead and in severe pain. I thought I was about to die. I lay in bed in that condition for three and a half days. My spirit developed this sickness, and then my body came down with it as well.

Then I heard voices around me saying, "Look, he is lying dead in the street of our city—the one who was preaching that we should repent so that our sins would be forgiven and [that we should worship] only Christ the human being."

They asked some of the clergy, "Is he worthy of burial?"

The clergy replied, "No. Let him lie there as a spectacle."

They kept going away and coming back to mock me.

And I am telling the truth when I say that this happened to me at the very time that I was explaining the eleventh chapter of the Book of Revelation.[201]

Then I heard more serious words from the people who had been mocking me—especially these: "How can repentance be practiced apart from faith? How can Christ the human being be adored as God? Given that we are saved for free without our deserving it at all, what then do we need except faith alone—the faith that God the Father sent the Son to take away the damnation of the law, to credit us with his own merit, to justify us before the Father, to absolve us from our sins (with the priest as his mouthpiece), and then to give us the Holy Spirit, who activates every good thing within us? Aren't these points in accordance with Scripture and also with reason?"

The crowd of bystanders applauded these statements.

[2] I heard all this but was unable to respond because I was lying there almost dead.

After three and a half days, however, my spirit regained its health. In the spirit I went from that street into the city, and I said again, "Practice repentance and believe in Christ, and your sins will be forgiven and you

567

will be saved. If you do not, you will perish. The Lord himself preached that we must repent in order for our sins to be forgiven, and that we must believe in him. He commanded the disciples to preach the same message.[202] Surely the dogma of your faith leads to utter complacency about the way you live!"

"What are you babbling about?" they replied. "The Son has made satisfaction. The Father has assigned us the Son's credit and has justified us for the reason that these are our beliefs. We are now led by the spirit of grace. What sin could there be within us? What death could there be among us? Do you grasp this Good News, you preacher of sin and repentance?"

Then a voice from heaven said, "Surely the faith of someone who has not practiced repentance is nothing but a dead faith. The end has come, the end has come upon you who are complacent, guiltless in your own eyes, justified by your own faith—satans!"

At that moment a chasm suddenly opened up in the middle of the city and spread outward. The houses were falling in on each other and the people were swallowed up. Soon water bubbled up from the great hole and flooded what was already devastated.

[3] After they sank to a lower level and were seemingly covered in water, I wanted to know what their situation was like in the depths. A voice from heaven told me, "You will see and hear."

Then the water that had seemingly flooded them disappeared from before my eyes. (Water in the spiritual world is a correspondence that appears around people who have false beliefs.) I saw the people in a sandy place at a great depth, where there were piles of stones. They were running between the piles of stones and loudly bemoaning their having been cast out of their great city. They were shouting and wailing, "Why has this happened to us? We are clean, pure, just, and holy because of our faith. Through our faith we have been cleansed, purified, justified, and sanctified."

Some among them were saying, "Hasn't our faith made it possible for us to appear before God the Father and be seen and esteemed by him and declared before angels as clean, pure, just, and holy? Haven't we been reconciled, atoned for, ritually purged, and therefore absolved, washed, and wiped free of our sins? Didn't Christ take away the damnation of the law? Why then have we been thrown down here like the damned? We did hear from a bold proclaimer of sin in our great city, 'Believe in Christ and practice repentance.' But didn't we believe in Christ when we believed in his merit? Didn't we practice repentance when we confessed that we were sinners? Why then has this happened to us?"

[4] A voice was then heard from the side: "Are you aware of any sin in yourselves? Have you ever examined yourselves, and then abstained from any evil because it is sinful against God? If you do not abstain from sin, then you are still in it; and sin is the Devil. You, then, are the people of whom the Lord spoke when he said, 'You will then begin to say, "We ate and drank with you. You taught in our streets." But he will say, "I tell you, I do not know you, where you are from. Depart from me, all you workers of wickedness"' (Luke 13:26, 27). Matthew 7:22, 23 is also about you. Therefore go away, each to your own place. Do you see the openings to those caves? Go in there, and each of you will be given your own work to do, and food in accordance with your work. If you don't go in, your hunger will drive you in."203

[5] After that a voice from heaven came to some people who were up at the level of the ground204 but were outside the city (see Revelation 11:13). The voice said loudly, "Beware! Beware of associating with people like that. Don't you understand that evils that are called sins and acts of wickedness make us unclean and impure? How can you be cleansed and purified from them except by active repentance and by faith in the Lord Jesus Christ? Active repentance is examining yourselves, recognizing and admitting to your sins, accepting that you are at fault, confessing them before the Lord, begging for his help and power in resisting them, stopping doing them, and living a new life. All this is to be done as if you were doing it on your own. Do this once or twice a year when you are about to take Holy Communion. Afterward, when the sins for which you are at fault recur, say to yourselves, 'We do not want these, because they are sins against God.' This is active repentance.

[6] "Surely you can all recognize that if you do not examine yourselves and see your sins, you remain in them. From birth you find all evils delightful. It feels good to take revenge, to be promiscuous, to cheat, to slander, and especially to dominate others out of love for yourselves. Because they feel good you overlook them. If someone happens to point out to you that they are sins, you make excuses for them because they feel good; you use false arguments to insist that they are not sins, and you stay in them. And afterward you do those evil things more than you did before, to the point where you no longer know what sin is or even whether there is such a thing.

"It is different, however, for people who actively go through a process of repentance. The evils that they recognize and admit to [in themselves] they call sins. They therefore begin to abstain and turn away from them. Eventually they begin to feel the pleasure of those evils as unpleasant.

The more this happens, the more they see and love what is good, and eventually even feel delight in it, which is the delight that the angels in heaven feel. Briefly put, the more we put the Devil behind us, the more we are adopted by the Lord and are taught, led, held back from what is evil, and kept in what is good by him. This is the pathway from hell to heaven; there is no other way."

[7] It is amazing that Protestants have such a deep-seated resistance, antipathy, and aversion to active repentance. Their reaction to it is so strong that they cannot force themselves to do self-examination, to see their sins, and to confess them before God. It is as if they are overcome by horror as soon as they form the intention to do it. I have asked many Protestants in the spiritual world about this, and they all said that it is completely beyond their strength. When they heard that Catholics practice this, that is, that they examine themselves and openly confess their sins to a monk, the Protestants were profoundly amazed, especially since the Protestants themselves could not do this even in secret before God, although they had been commanded, just as the Catholics had been, to do this when they were about to take the Holy Supper. Some people in the spiritual world investigated why this was, and discovered that faith alone was what had led to such an impenitent state and such an attitude of heart. Then those Protestants were allowed to see that Catholics who worship Christ and do not call on the saints are saved.[205]

[8] After that we heard a kind of thunder, and a voice speaking from heaven and saying, "We are amazed. Say to the gathering of Protestants, 'Believe in Christ and practice repentance, and you will be saved.'"

So I said it.

I added, "Clearly, *baptism* is a sacrament of repentance and therefore introduction into the church. What else do godparents promise for the child being baptized but that he or she will renounce the Devil and all his works? Clearly, *the Holy Supper* is a sacrament of repentance and therefore introduction into heaven. Doesn't the priest say to those about to take it that they absolutely have to practice repentance first? Clearly, *the catechism* is the universal teaching of the Christian church; it urges repentance. Isn't it true that the six commandments on the second tablet[206] say, 'You are *not* to do this and that thing that is evil,' not, 'You *are* to do this and that thing that is good'? Therefore you are capable of knowing that the more we renounce and turn away from what is evil, the more we desire and love what is good; and that before that, we do not know what good is, or even what evil is."

The second memorable occurrence. Most people who are devout or wise want to know what the outcome of their life will be after they die. I will reveal some generalities so that they will know.

568

After they die, all people become aware that they are still alive but are in another world. They hear that above them lies heaven where there are eternal joys, and below them lies hell where there is eternal suffering. Next, they are put back into the outer selves they had while they were still in the physical world. At that point they believe that they are definitely going to heaven. They speak intelligently and act prudently.

Some of them say, "We have lived moral lives. We have had honorable pursuits. We have not done evil deliberately."

Others say, "We have attended church regularly. We have heard Mass. We have kissed holy statues. We have poured forth prayers on our knees."

Some say, "We have given to the poor. We have helped the needy. We have read religious literature, including the Word," and more of that nature.

[2] Nevertheless, after they have said that, angels appear and say, "All the things you mentioned, you did in your outer selves, but you are still unaware of what you are like in your inner selves. You are now spirits in a substantial[207] body. Your spirit is your inner self. This is the part in you that thinks about what it wants and wants what it loves; what it loves is the delight of your life.

"From early childhood we all begin our lives in our outer selves. We learn to behave morally and speak intelligently. When we have formed some idea of heaven and its blessedness, we begin to pray, to go to church, and to attend the customary religious rituals. Meanwhile when evils rise up from their native source, we begin hiding them deep within our mind and also cleverly covering them with a veil of reasonings based on mistaken ideas, to the point where we do not know that evil is evil. Then, because those evils have been covered over and buried in the dirt, so to speak, we no longer reflect on them; we just take care that they do not appear before the world. We practice a moral life only in outward ways. Therefore we become a dual person—a sheep on the outside but a wolf on the inside. We are like a golden box that contains poison; like people with disgusting breath who keep something sweet-smelling in their mouths so that others nearby cannot tell; and like a rat's skin that smells of balsam.

[3] "You have asserted that you lived moral lives and pursued religious practices. Let me ask, however, did you ever examine your inner selves? Did you become aware of any desire for revenge, even to the point of

committing murder? Any desire to indulge lust, even to the point of committing adultery? Any desire to commit fraud, even to the point of committing theft? Any desire to lie, even to the point of bearing false witness? Four of the Ten Commandments say, 'You are not to do these things,' and the last two say, 'You are not to desire to do these things.' Is it your belief that your inner self was much like your outer self in these regards? If this is your belief, perhaps you are wrong."

[4] "What is our inner self?" they replied. "Isn't it the same as our outer self? We have heard from our ministers that our inner self is simply our faith, and that our devout words and moral lives are signs that we have faith, because they are our faith at work."

"Faith that truly has power to save does indeed reside in the inner self, along with goodwill," the angels replied, "and these do lead to Christian faithfulness and morality in the outer self. If, however, desires for revenge, for committing fraud and theft, and for lying remain in your inner self (meaning your will and your thinking) and inwardly you love those desires (no matter what you say or do outwardly), then evil takes precedence over goodness, and goodness is less important to you than evil. In this case, no matter how much you speak as if you had understanding or act as if you had love, there is evil within you, and your words and actions just cover it up. Then you are like clever chimpanzees who can mimic human actions, although their heart is far different.

[5] "You know nothing about your inner self, because you have not examined yourselves, and after self-examination have not practiced repentance. Soon, however, you will see exactly what it is like, when your outer self is taken off, and you are introduced into your inner self. When this happens, you will no longer be recognized by your companions or even by yourselves. I[208] have seen evil people, who had been moral, become like predatory animals, looking at their neighbor with hostile eyes, burning with murderous hatred, and uttering blasphemy against the God they had worshiped in their outer selves."

When they heard that, they walked away. The angels then said to them, "After this you are going to see the outcome of your life. Soon your outer self will be taken away, and you will come into your inner self, which is now your spirit."

569 *The third memorable occurrence.* Every type of love that is within us exudes a delight by which it makes itself felt. This delight is exuded first into our spirit and then into our body. The delight that comes from our love and the enjoyment that comes from our thinking go together to constitute our life.

As long as we are alive in our earthly bodies, this delight and this enjoyment register only in an obscure way, because our bodies absorb them and dull them. After death, though, when our physical body is taken away and therefore this covering or clothing of our spirit is removed, the delights associated with what we love and the enjoyment associated with what we think are fully felt and perceived. Amazing to say, they are sometimes experienced as odors. This is the mechanism whereby people in the spiritual world are all associated by what they love; this is how heavenly loves bring people together in heaven, and how hellish loves bring people together in hell.

[2] In heaven the feelings of delight that come from [angels'] loves are turned into odors like all the kinds of fragrances, sweet smells, pleasant breezes, and delicious sensations that we experience in vegetable gardens, flower gardens, fields, and forests on a morning in spring.

In hell the feelings of delight that come from [devils' and satans'] loves are turned into the kind of foul odors, rotten smells, and stenches given off by outhouses, dead bodies, and ponds full of garbage and sewage. It is astounding, but the devils and satans who are there sense these odors as fragrances, perfumes, and incense that are refreshing to their noses and their hearts.

In the physical world there does exist an association by odors among animals, birds, and crawling insects, but there is not the same association for people, until they have shed their material bodies as a kind of skin.

[3] As a result, heaven is most precisely arranged according to all the varieties of love for what is good, and hell, in exactly the opposite way, is arranged according to all the varieties of love for what is evil. This opposition is why there is a great gulf between heaven and hell that cannot be crossed [Luke 16:26]. The people who are in heaven cannot stand any of the odor from hell. It causes them nausea and vomiting, and threatens to render them unconscious if they breathe it in. The same thing happens to the people who are in hell, if they cross the midpoint of that great gulf.

[4] On one occasion I saw a devil who looked from a distance like a leopard. He had been seen several days earlier among angels of the lowest heaven. He had developed the skill of turning himself into an angel of light, crossing the gulf, standing between two olive trees, and avoiding sensing any odor that would be harmful to his life. He was able to do this because there were no angels present. But as soon as angels arrived, he started having convulsions, and fell down with all his limbs curled up. He looked at that point like a giant snake twisting itself in coils. Eventually he rolled himself down into the gulf. He was picked up by his people

and carried into a cave, where he was revived by the heavy stench of his own delight.

[5] On another occasion I saw a satan being punished by his own people. I asked why this was, and was told that by holding his nose he had been able to approach people who had the smell of heaven; he had then come back, but his clothes had brought back that smell with him.

It has happened to me several times that when some cave of hell opened up, the stench of a corpse assaulted my nostrils and made me vomit.

All this shows why it is that in the Word, "smell" means perception. It says quite frequently that from people's burnt offerings Jehovah would smell a pleasing aroma.[209] (The oil for anointing and the incense were prepared with fragrant spices [Exodus 30:22–25, 34–35].) On the other hand, the children of Israel were commanded to carry unclean things from their camp outside its borders, and they were to dig a hole for their fecal matter and cover it up (Deuteronomy 23:12, 13). The reason for this was that the camp of Israel represented heaven and the desert outside their camp represented hell.

570 *The fourth memorable occurrence.* On one occasion I had a conversation with a recently arrived spirit. While in the world, he had meditated a great deal on heaven and hell. ("Recently arrived spirits" mean people who have recently died. They are called spirits because they are then human beings who are spiritual [rather than physical] in nature.)

As soon as he came into the spiritual world he resumed meditating on heaven and hell. When he thought about heaven he felt happy; when he thought about hell he felt sad.

When he realized that he was actually in the spiritual world, he immediately asked, "Where is heaven and where is hell? What is heaven, what is hell, and how are they experienced?"

"Heaven is above your head," [the spirits] replied, "and hell is under your feet. You are now in the world of spirits, which is midway between heaven and hell. What heaven is, what hell is, and how they are experienced, however, is not something we can describe in a few words."

Because he had a burning desire to know, he threw himself to his knees and prayed devoutly to God to be taught.

An angel immediately appeared at his right hand. The angel lifted him up and said, "You have prayed to be taught about heaven and hell. *Investigate and find out what delight is, and you will know.*" Upon saying this, the angel was raised up out of sight.

[2] The recently arrived spirit then said to himself, "What is this? 'Investigate and find out what delight is, and you will know what heaven is, what hell is, and how they are experienced'?"

Soon he left there and traveled around. When he encountered people he asked them, "Tell me, if you would, please, what delight is."

Some said, "What kind of question is that? Who doesn't know what delight is? It is joy and happiness. Delight is delight—one is like another. We are not aware of any differences."

Others said, "Delight is the laughter of the mind. When our mind is laughing, our face is cheerful, our speech is full of jokes, our gestures are playful, and our whole self embodies delight."

Others said, "I'll tell you what delight is! It is dining and eating delicacies, drinking and getting drunk on vintage wine, and then chatting about various topics, especially the games of Venus and Cupid!"[210]

[3] Annoyed at this the new spirit said to himself, "These answers are crude and unsophisticated. The delights these spirits mentioned are not heaven and are not hell either. I wish I could meet some people with wisdom."

He left the people he was with and asked around to learn where he might find people with wisdom.

An angelic spirit[211] noticed him and said, "I can sense your burning desire to know what the universal attribute of heaven is and what the universal attribute of hell is. Since the answer is *delight,* I will take you up onto the hill. There is a meeting every day there between spirits who conduct research on results, spirits who survey means, and spirits who investigate purposes.[212] The spirits who conduct research on results are called spirits of the academic disciplines, or abstractly, Knowledges. The spirits who survey means are called spirits of intelligence, or abstractly, Intelligences. The spirits who investigate purposes are called spirits of wisdom, or abstractly, Wisdoms. Directly above them in heaven there are angels who see means in terms of the purposes behind them, and see results in terms of the means that lead to them. From these angels the three groups receive their enlightenment."

[4] The angelic spirit then took the newly arrived spirit by the hand and led him up the hill to the group of spirits who investigate purposes; they are called Wisdoms.

"Forgive me," the newly arrived spirit said to them, "for coming up to join you. The reason why I have done so is that since my childhood I have been meditating on heaven and hell. I have recently come into this world. Spirits who were assigned to me at the time of my transition told me that heaven was over my head and hell was beneath my feet, but they would not tell me what heaven is, what hell is, and how they are experienced. Because of my constant thought about heaven and hell I became anxious and prayed to God. An angel appeared beside me and said, 'Investigate and find out what delight is and you will know.' I did investigate, but have learned nothing. I ask you then, if you would, please, to teach me what delight is."

[5] "To all individuals in heaven," the Wisdoms replied, "delight is the most important thing in their lives; and to all individuals in hell, delight is the most important thing in their lives. Those in heaven take delight in what is good and what is true. Those in hell take delight in what is evil and what is false. Delight is always related to love, and love is the underlying reality of our lives. How human we are depends on what kind of love we have. Therefore how human we are also depends on what kind of delight we feel. When our love is active, it causes us to feel delight. A heavenly love becomes active with the help of wisdom; a hellish love becomes active with the help of insanity. In either case the activity causes the person to experience delight. The heavens and the hells have delights that are opposite to each other, however. The heavens love what is good and therefore take delight in benefiting others. The hells love what is evil and therefore take delight in harming others. If you know what delight is, you will indeed know what heaven is, what hell is, and how they are experienced. [6] But investigate and find out more about delight from the spirits who survey means; they are called Intelligences. As you go out, they are on your right."

So he left there and came to the next group. He stated the reason he had come and asked them to teach him what delight is. They greatly enjoyed being asked, and said, "It is true that those who know what delight is know what heaven is, what hell is, and how they are experienced. The will, which is the faculty that makes us human, is not moved an inch by anything other than delight. By definition, the will is simply the desire that belongs to some love and therefore some delight. There is something agreeable and therefore pleasing that causes us to will. Since the will is what drives the intellect to think, not a moment of thinking occurs unless there is some delight flowing in from the will.

"The reason why this is the case is that everything that happens in the soul and mind of angels, spirits, and human beings is set in motion by the Lord through an inflow that comes from him—an inflow of love and wisdom. This inflow is the movement that causes the whole experience of delight, which at its point of origin is called blessedness, good fortune, and happiness; and in its derivation is called delightful, pleasant, and pleasurable. In a universal sense it is what is known as *good*. The spirits of hell, however, turn all things upside down within themselves. They turn what is good into what is evil and what is true into what is false. The only thing they retain is the sense of delight, because if delight did not continue, they would have no will and no sensation, and therefore no life. This should clarify the nature, experience, and origin of the delight felt in hell, and the nature, experience, and origin of the delight felt in heaven."

[7] Upon hearing that, the newly arrived spirit was brought to the third group, the spirits who conduct research on results; they are called Knowledges. They said, "Go down into the lower earth[213] and go up into the higher realm. In them you will perceive and sense the delights of heaven and of hell."

At that point, however, the ground suddenly yawned wide at some distance from them. Up through the chasm came three devils, who were visibly lit up by the delight that comes from what they love. The angels who were accompanying the newly arrived spirit perceived that it was not by coincidence that the three devils had come up just then. The angels called out to the devils, "Don't come any closer, but from where you are, tell us something about what delights you."

"It is important to know," they replied, "that all people, whether labeled good or evil, have their own delight. The so-called good people have theirs and the so-called evil people have theirs."

"What do you take delight in?" the angels asked.

"What is delightful to us," they replied, "is whoring, taking revenge, cheating, and speaking blasphemy."

"What are those delights like for you, exactly?" the angels asked.

The devils replied that their delights were sensed by others as resembling the stench of excrement, the reek of dead bodies, and the smell of stagnant urine.

"Are those things actually delightful to you?" the angels asked.

"Very much so," the devils replied.

"Then you are like the filthy little creatures that live in those substances," said the angels.

"If we are, we are," the devils said, "but those things give our noses intense pleasure."

"Do you have anything further to add?" the angels asked.

"Yes," they replied. "Everyone is allowed to have her or his delight, even if it is of the 'most unclean' kind, as others call it, provided she or he does not attack good spirits and angels; but because our delight makes it absolutely impossible to resist attacking them, we are thrown into workhouses where we suffer many hard things. Being restrained and withdrawn from our delights causes the so-called torment of hell, which is profound inner pain."

"Why do you attack people who are good?" the angels asked.

"We can't help it," the devils said. "A kind of rage comes over us every time we see any angel and sense the Lord's divine sphere around that angel."[214]

"Then you are also like animals," we said.

Soon afterward, when they noticed the newly arrived spirit with the angels, a diabolical rage came over them, which looked like a burning fire of hate. Therefore to prevent their doing any harm, they were thrown back into hell.

After that, other angels appeared in a shining white light. They were the angels who see means in terms of the purposes behind them, and see results in terms of the means that lead to them—the angels in the heaven directly above the three groups. That shining light rolled downward through spiraling turns, carrying a ring of flowers and placing it gently on the head of the newly arrived spirit. Then a voice came to him from above: "This wreath of honor is given to you because you have meditated on heaven and hell since you were young."

Chapter 10

Reformation and Regeneration

NOW that repentance has been treated, the next topic in order is our reformation and regeneration. These two both follow our repentance and are moved forward by it.

There are two states that we all inevitably enter into and go through if we are to turn from an earthly person into a spiritual person. The first state is called *reformation,* the second is called *regeneration.* In the first state we look from our earthly self toward having a spiritual self; being spiritual is what we long for. In the second state we become someone who is both spiritual and earthly. The first state is brought about by truths (these have to be truths related to faith); through these truths we aim to develop goodwill. The second state is brought about by good actions that come from goodwill; through these actions we come [more deeply] into truths related to faith.

To put it another way, the first state is a state of thought that occurs in our intellect; the second state is a state of love that occurs in our will. As the second state begins and progresses, a change takes place in our minds. There is a reversal, because then the love in our will flows into our intellect and leads and drives it to think in agreement and harmony with what we love. As good actions that come from love take on a primary role, and the truths related to faith are relegated to a secondary role, we become spiritual and are a new creation [2 Corinthians 5:17; Galatians 6:15]. Then our actions come from goodwill and our words come from faith; we develop a sense of the goodness that comes from goodwill and a perception of the truth that is related to faith; and we are in the Lord and in a state of peace. In brief, we are reborn.

[2] If we begin the first state while we are in this world, we can be brought into the second state after we die. If we do not begin the first state while we are in this world, we cannot be brought into the second state or be reborn after we die.

These two states can be compared to the increase of light and heat that occurs as the day progresses in springtime. The first state is like the early light before dawn, when the rooster crows. The second state is like the dawn and the morning. The further development within the second state is like the increase of light and heat as the day progresses toward noon.

These two states can also be compared with the growth of grain crops. In the first stage they are like grass; after that they develop ears or fruiting spikes; and finally the grain itself grows within those structures.

These two states can also be compared with the growth of a tree. It begins as a sprout growing out of a seed in the ground. This then becomes a shoot. Then branches form and are adorned with leaves. Then the tree blossoms and fruit begins to grow in the heart of the flowers. As the fruit grows and develops, it produces new seeds, which are in effect the tree's offspring.

The first state, the state of reformation, can be compared to the state of a silkworm when it draws silky threads out of itself and wraps itself in them. After all its hard work [of transformation], it becomes able to fly in the air and feeds no longer on leaves as before but on the nectar of flowers.

Unless We Are Born Again and Created Anew, So to Speak, We Cannot Enter the Kingdom of God

572 The Lord teaches in John that if we are not born again we cannot enter the kingdom of God: "Jesus said to Nicodemus, 'Truly, truly I say to you, unless you are born again you cannot see the kingdom of God'" (John 3:3). And again, "Truly, truly I say to you, unless you have been born of water and the spirit you cannot enter the kingdom of God. That which is born of flesh is flesh, and that which is born of spirit is spirit" (John 3:5, 6). The *kingdom of God* here means both heaven and the church, because the church is the kingdom of God on earth. The same is true in other passages in the Word where the kingdom of God is mentioned; see, for example, Matthew 11:12; 12:28; 21:43; Luke 4:43; 6:20; 8:1, 10; 9:11, 60, 62; 17:21; and elsewhere. To be *born of water and the spirit* means to be born of truths related to faith and of a life lived by those truths. For truth as the meaning of *water*, see *Revelation Unveiled* 50, 614, 615, 685, 932.[215] The fact that *spirit* means living our lives by divine truths is clear from the Lord's words in John 6:63.[216] *Truly, truly* means that this is the truth. Because the Lord was truth itself, Scripture frequently says *Amen* [or *Truly*]. The Lord himself is called *Amen* (Revelation 3:14). In the Word, those who are regenerated are referred to as *children of God* and *those born of God;* and regeneration is expressed as our having a new heart and a new spirit.[217]

Since being created also means being regenerated, the heading above speaks of those who are "born again and created anew, so to speak." It is clear from the following passages that being *created* has this meaning in the Word.

573

> Create for me a clean heart, O God, and renew a firm spirit within me. (Psalms 51:10)

> You open your hand, and they are filled with goodness. You send forth your spirit, and they are created. (Psalms 104:28, 30)

> The people who are yet to be created will praise Jah.[218] (Psalms 102:18)

> Behold, I am going to create Jerusalem as a rejoicing. (Isaiah 65:18)

> Thus says Jehovah, the one who created you, O Jacob; the one who formed you, O Israel: "I have redeemed you. All who are called by my name I have created for my glory." (Isaiah 43:1, 7)

> . . . so that they may see, recognize, consider, and understand that the Holy One of Israel has created this. (Isaiah 41:20)

There are other such passages as well; and see also the places where the Lord is called Creator, Shaper, or Maker.[219]

This sheds some light on what the following words mean, which were spoken by the Lord to his disciples:

> Go into the whole world and preach the gospel to every creature. (Mark 16:15)

Creatures here mean all who are able to be regenerated. See also Revelation 3:14; 2 Corinthians 5:17.

Reason, too, makes it entirely clear that we have to be regenerated. We are born with evils of every kind from our parents. These evils reside in our earthly self, which left to itself is directly opposed to our spiritual self. Nevertheless, we are born for heaven.

574

We cannot come into heaven, then, unless we become spiritual, and that happens through regeneration alone. It follows inevitably from this that our earthly self and its desires have to be tamed, brought under control, and turned upside down. Otherwise we cannot take a single step in the direction of heaven; we slip instead farther and farther down into hell.

Surely any of us can see this provided we have the following concepts: we believe that human beings are born with evils of every kind; we acknowledge the existence of good and evil, and recognize that each of them is opposed to the other; we believe in life after death and in heaven and hell; and we see that evil constitutes hell and goodness constitutes heaven.

Left to its own devices, our earthly self is by nature not at all different from animals. That is, in regard to its will it is just like a wild beast. It differs from animals in its intellect, however. Its intellect can be lifted above the desires in its will and not only see those desires but even restrain them. This allows us to think with and speak from our intellect, which animals cannot do.

[2] By considering savage creatures of all kinds, we can see what we humans are like by birth, and what we will remain if we are not regenerated. We will be a tiger, a panther, a leopard, a wild boar, a scorpion, a tarantula, a viper, or a crocodile, and so on. Therefore unless regeneration transforms us into sheep, what else are we but a devil among the other devils in hell? Surely, then, if we were not held back by the law of the land from our own inborn ferocious nature, we would attack and butcher each other or rob each other of everything down to the breeches. Out of the whole human race, how many are there who are not born satyrs and priapuses or crawling reptiles?[220] Without regeneration, how many of these turn into anything better than a monkey?[221] And the only thing that allows them to rise that far is the outward morality they cultivate in order to hide the evils that are inside them.

575   The qualities of people who have not been regenerated are further described in the following comparisons and similes in Isaiah:

> The spoonbill and the vulture will possess it, and the owl and the raven will dwell there. He will stretch over it a line of pointlessness and plumb lines of devastation. Thornbushes will climb its altars; thistles and brambles will climb up on its fortifications. It will be a home for dragons, a courtyard for the daughters of an owl. Vultures will encounter shrieking

night birds, and the satyr will meet with its mate. The night creature will also rest there. The blackbird will nest there, and lay eggs, and brood, and hatch them in its shadows. Indeed, the hawks will gather there, each one with its mate. (Isaiah 34:11, 13, 14, 15)

The Lord Alone Generates or Creates Us Anew, Provided We Cooperate; He Uses Both Goodwill and Faith as Means

The chapters on goodwill and faith have already shown that the Lord carries out the process of regenerating us by means of goodwill and faith. See especially the point that the Lord, goodwill, and faith form a unity in the same way our life, our will, and our intellect form a unity; if we separate them, each one crumbles like a pearl that is crushed to powder [§§362–367].

576

Both of these things, goodwill and faith, I call *means* because they forge our partnership with the Lord. Together they ensure that our goodwill is real goodwill and that our faith is real faith. The process of our regeneration cannot occur without our having some part to play in it; for this reason, the heading reads "provided we cooperate."

In preceding chapters, our cooperation with the Lord has come up several times [§§48:5–6, 89, 99, 100, 110:4–6, 368–372]; it will be illustrated again here, however, because the human mind is by nature unable to rid itself of the sensation that it carries out this process under its own power.

[2] In every motion and every action there is an element that is active and another element that is responsive. The active element acts, and then the responsive element acts in response. As a result, a single action comes forth from the two elements. A mill is activated in this manner by a waterwheel; a carriage by a horse; a motion by a force; an effect by a cause; a dead force by a living force; and in general an instrumental cause by a principal cause. Everyone knows that each pair together completes a single action.

In the case of goodwill and faith, the Lord acts, and we act in response. There is an activity of the Lord that prompts our human response. The power to do good things comes from the Lord. As a result, there is a will to act that seems to be our own, because we have free choice. Either we can take action together with the Lord and by doing so, form a partnership with him; or else we can take action drawing on the power of hell, which is outside the Lord, and by doing so, separate ourselves from him. Actions of ours that are in harmony with the Lord's actions are what I mean here by "cooperation." To make this even clearer, it will be illustrated with comparisons below [§§577:2–3, 578].

577 It follows from this that the Lord is constantly active in regenerating us. He is constantly active in saving us, and no one can be saved without being regenerated, as the Lord himself says in John: "Those who are not born again cannot see the kingdom of God" (John 3:3, 5, 6). Regeneration is therefore the means of being saved; and goodwill and faith are the means of being regenerated.

The notion that we are regenerated as a consequence of simply having the faith that is preached by the church of today—a faith that involves no cooperation on our part—is the height of foolishness.[222]

[2] The kind of action and cooperation just described is visible in action and movement of all types. The interaction between the heart and all its arteries is an example. The heart acts and the arteries use their sheaths and linings to cooperate; this results in circulation.[223] A similar thing happens with the lungs. The air pressure, which depends on the height of the atmosphere above it, acts upon the lungs; the lungs work the ribs, which is immediately followed by the ribs working the lungs.[224] This breathing motion affects every membrane in the body. The meninges of the brain, the pleura, the peritoneum, the diaphragm, and all the other membranes that cover the internal organs and inwardly hold them together, act and react and cooperate in this way, because they are flexible.[225] Together these movements provide for our continued existence.

A similar thing happens in every fiber and nerve and in every muscle. In fact it even occurs in every piece of cartilage. It is well documented that in each of these there is an [initiating] action and then a cooperation.[226]

[3] Such cooperation also exists in all our bodily senses. Just like the motor organs, the sensory organs consist of fibers, membranes, and muscles; but there is no need to describe the cooperation of each one. It is well known that light acts upon the eye, sound upon the ear, odor upon the nose, taste upon the tongue; and that the organs adapt themselves to that input, which results in sensation.

Surely everyone can see from these examples that thought and will could not exist unless there was a similar action and cooperation between life as it inflows and the spiritual organic structure underlying our brain.[227] Life flows from the Lord into that organic structure. Because the organic structure cooperates, it perceives what it is thinking. Likewise it perceives what is under consideration there, what conclusion is formed, and what action it has decided to take. If the life force alone took action but we did not cooperate (seemingly on our own), our ability to think would not exceed a log's. We would have no more thought than a church building does when a minister is preaching; the church can indeed feel the reverberation of sound coming through the double doors as an echo, but it cannot appreciate anything about the sermon. We would be no different if we did not cooperate with the Lord in developing goodwill and faith.

What we would be like if we did not cooperate with the Lord can 578 be further illustrated with the following comparisons. If we perceived or sensed anything spiritual related to heaven or the church, it would strike us as something hostile or disagreeable flowing in, the way our nose would react to a rotten smell, our ear would react to a dissonant sound, our eye would react to a hideous sight, or our tongue would react to something disgusting.

If the delight associated with goodwill and the enjoyment associated with faith were to flow into the spiritual organic structure of the mind of people who take delight in evil and falsity, such people would feel terrible pain and torment until they eventually collapsed unconscious. The spiritual organic structure consists of long strands in helixes; under that circumstance in people of that type, it would wrap itself in coils and would be tormented like a snake on a swarm of ants.[228] The truth of this has been fully demonstrated to me in the spiritual world through an abundance of experiences.

Because We Are All Redeemed, We Are All Capable of Being Regenerated, Each of Us in a Way That Suits the State We Are In

To clarify the statement in the heading, I need first to say something 579 about redemption. The Lord came into the world for two main reasons: to move hell away from both angels and people; and to glorify his own human nature.[229] Before the Lord's Coming, hell had grown so much that it was assaulting the angels of heaven. By placing itself between heaven and the world, hell had also become able to intercept the communication between the Lord and human beings on earth; as a result, no divine truth or goodness from the Lord was able to get through to human beings. A total damnation threatened the entire human race, and the angels of heaven would not have been able to maintain their integrity for long either.

[2] In order to move hell out of the way and to remove the impending threat of total damnation, the Lord came into the world, relocated hell, brought it under control, and made heaven accessible again, so that he would be able to be present among people on earth and regenerate and save those who were living according to his commandments. All who are regenerated are saved. This is what is meant by the statement in the heading that because we are all redeemed, we are all capable of being regenerated. And because being regenerated is the same thing as being saved, we are all also capable of being saved.

Therefore the teaching of the church that without the Lord's Coming no one could have been saved[230] should be taken to mean that without the Lord's Coming no one could have been regenerated.

[3] As for the second purpose for which the Lord came into the world—to glorify his human manifestation—he did this in order to become the Redeemer, the Regenerator, and the Savior to eternity. There is a belief that because the Lord carried out a redemption while he was in the world, therefore we have all already been redeemed. We should not believe that. We should believe instead that forevermore he redeems people who believe in him and do what he says. On this topic, see further in the chapter on redemption [§§123:6, 126–133].

580 The reason why the heading asserts that we are capable of being regenerated in a way that suits the state we are in is that the uneducated, for example, are regenerated in a different way than the educated. People with different interests are regenerated in different ways. People who are in different lines of work are regenerated in different ways. People who study the outer meanings of the Word are regenerated in a different way than those who study its inner meanings. Those who inherited an earthly goodness from their parents are regenerated in a different way than those who inherited evil from their parents. People who have become heavily involved from an early age in the pointless pursuits of this world are regenerated in a different way than people who have discontinued those activities, whether they stopped them sooner or later in their lives. Briefly put, people who constitute the Lord's outer church are regenerated in a different way than people who constitute his inner church.[231] The variety is in fact infinite, just like the variety of faces and minds. Despite the variety, however, absolutely all of us are capable of being regenerated and saved in a way that suits the state we are in.

[2] The truth of this can be seen by considering the heavens, and the fact that all people who have been regenerated go there. There are three heavens: the highest, the middle, and the lowest. If we receive love for the Lord as a result of our regeneration, we come into the highest heaven. If we receive love for our neighbor, we come into the middle heaven. If we practice only an outer goodwill and acknowledge the Lord as God the Redeemer and Savior, we come into the lowest heaven. All such people are saved, but in different ways.

[3] The reason why all are capable of being regenerated and saved is that the Lord is present with, and brings his divine goodness and truth to, every human being. This is the source of everyone's life and everyone's faculty of understanding and will and also everyone's free choice in spiritual matters. No human being is lacking these attributes. Everyone has also been given means that teach commandments concerning good and evil and the idea that there is a God. Christians find these teachings in the Word; non-Christians find them in whichever religion they are in.

From this it follows that everyone is capable of being saved. It is our own fault, not the Lord's fault, if we are not saved. It is our fault because we have not cooperated.

The chapter on redemption showed that the Lord's redemption and his suffering on the cross were two distinct things, and they should not in any way be confused with each other [§§126–133]. That chapter also taught that both redemption and the suffering on the cross allowed the Lord to take on the power to regenerate and save people.[232]

The received faith in the church of today that claims the suffering on the cross *was* redemption itself has led to hordes of horrible falsities about God, faith, goodwill, and all the other teachings that hang like unbroken chains on these three. Take, for example, the belief that God locked the human race into damnation, but was willing to be brought back to a merciful outlook by the imposition of that damnation on his Son, or by the Son's taking that damnation upon himself. Or take the belief that the only people who are saved are those who, whether through God's foresight or predestination, are granted Christ's merit. Another concept hatched from the mistaken idea mentioned above is the belief that those people who have been gifted with that faith are simultaneously regenerated without any cooperation on their part; indeed, that those people have therefore been released from the damnation of the law and are no longer under the law but under grace.

Yet the Lord said that he would not take away even the tip of one letter[233] of the law (Matthew 5:18, 19; Luke 16:17); and said to his disciples that they should preach repentance for the forgiveness of sins (Luke 24:47; Mark 6:12). And he himself said, "The kingdom of God has come near. Repent and believe in the gospel" (Mark 1:15). The gospel here means the good news that we can be regenerated and therefore saved. This would not have been possible if the Lord had not brought about redemption, that is, if he had not taken power away from hell through battles against it and victories over it, and if he had not glorified his human manifestation, that is, made it divine.

582 Think about it rationally and tell me what the whole human race would be like if the faith of today's church were to persist—that is, the belief that the passion of the cross is the sole thing that has redeemed us; that we who have been granted the Lord's merit are not subject to the damnation of the law; that this faith itself forgives our sins and regenerates us (even though we have no way of knowing whether this faith is in us or not); and that if we were to cooperate at all in the activation of faith, which is the moment when faith is granted to us and becomes part of us, we would corrupt this faith and ruin our chances of salvation, since we would be entangling Christ's merit with our own.

I beg you, think about it rationally and tell me: Is this not the equivalent of rejecting the entire Word, since the principal teaching of the Word concerns our regeneration through spiritually washing away evils and exercising goodwill? How then are the Ten Commandments (the starting point of our reformation) more valuable than the paper in which shopkeepers roll up the spices they have sold?[234] What then is religious practice except wailing that we are sinners and begging God the Father to have mercy on us for the sake of his Son's suffering—a mere matter of words from the lungs and not of action from the heart? How then is redemption different from a papal indulgence?[235] How is redemption different from the punishing of a whole monastery by the flogging of a single monk, which is sometimes done?

[2] If this faith regenerates us all by itself, and we practice no repentance and develop no goodwill, how will our inner self (which is our spirit, the part of us that lives on after death) avoid being like a city that has burned to the ground? How will our outer self not be like rubble left over from that fire? How will our inner self not be like a field or a meadow laid waste by caterpillars and locusts?

From the angels' point of view, people who practice no repentance and develop no goodwill are like people who keep a pet snake hidden under their clothes close to their heart so it will not be seen. They are like a sheep that is asleep next to a wolf. They are like someone who is lying under a beautiful quilt but wearing a nightgown made of spiderwebs. What will their life be like after they die? Given that all in heaven are sorted by differences in their regeneration and all in hell are sorted by differences in their rejection of regeneration, will these people not have a life that is only bodily then, like the life of a fish or a crab?

Regeneration Progresses Analogously to the Way We Are Conceived, Carried in the Womb, Born, and Brought Up

For human beings, there is a constant correspondence between the stages a person goes through physically and the stages a person goes through spiritually, or developments in the body and developments in the spirit. The reason is that at the level of our souls we are born spiritual, but we are clothed with earthly material that constitutes our physical body. When our physical body is laid aside, our soul, which has its own spiritual body, enters a world in which all things are spiritual. There we associate with other spiritual beings like ourselves.

Our spiritual body has to be formed within our physical body. The spiritual body is made out of truth and goodness that flow into us from the Lord through the spiritual world. We find a home within ourselves for that goodness and truth in things that parallel them in the physical world, which are called civic and moral forms of goodness and truth. This makes clear, then, the nature of the process that forms our spiritual body.

Since there is a constant correspondence within human beings between the stages we go through physically and the stages we go through spiritually, it follows that we go through something analogous to being conceived, carried in the womb, born, and brought up.

This explains why the statements in the Word that relate to physical birth symbolize aspects of our spiritual birth that have to do with goodness and truth. In fact, every earthly reference in the literal sense of the Word embodies, contains, and symbolizes something spiritual. (In the chapter on Sacred Scripture [§§189–281] it is fully demonstrated that there is a spiritual meaning within each and every detail of the literal sense of the Word.)

[2] The earthly references to birth in the Word inwardly refer to our spiritual birth, as anyone can see from the following passages:

> We have conceived; we have gone into labor. We appeared to give birth, yet we have not accomplished salvation. (Isaiah 26:18)

> You are having birth pangs, O earth, in the presence of the Lord. (Psalms 114:7)

> Will the earth give birth in a single day? Will I break [waters] but not cause delivery? Will I cause delivery and then close [the womb]? (Isaiah 66:7–9)

> Sin is having birth pangs and No will be split open. (Ezekiel 30:16)[236]

> Pains like those of a woman in labor will come upon Ephraim. He is an unwise son, because he does not remain long in the womb for children. (Hosea 13:12, 13)

Many similar passages occur elsewhere.

Since physical birth in the Word symbolizes spiritual birth, and spiritual birth comes from the Lord, he is called our Maker and the one who delivered us from the womb, as is clear from the following passages.

> Jehovah, who made you and formed you in the womb . . . (Isaiah 44:2)

> You delivered me from the womb. (Psalms 22:9)

> On you I was laid from the womb. You delivered me from my mother's belly. (Psalms 71:6)

> Listen to me, you whom I carried from the womb, whom I bore from the womb. (Isaiah 46:3)

There are other such passages as well.

This is why the Lord is called the Father, as in Isaiah 9:6; 63:16; John 10:30; 14:8, 9. This is why people who have received things that are good and true from the Lord are called "children of God" and "those who are born of God,"[237] and why they are said to be siblings to each other (Matthew 23:8). This is also why the church is referred to as a mother (Hosea 2:2, 5; Ezekiel 16:45).

584   The above points make it clear that there is a correspondence between physical birth and spiritual birth. Because there is this correspondence, it follows that not only can we speak of this new birth as including stages of being conceived, being carried in the womb, being born, and being brought up, but those stages of our rebirth are actually real. What exactly the stages are, however, will be presented in proper sequence as this chapter on regeneration unfolds.

Here I will just mention that human seed is conceived inwardly within the intellect and takes shape within the will. From there it is transferred into the testicles, where it wraps itself in an earthly covering. Then it is delivered to the womb and finally enters the world.[238]

There is also a correspondence between human regeneration and every aspect of the plant kingdom. This is why the Word portrays us as *trees,* the truth we have as *seed,* and the goodness we have as *fruit.*

[2] A bad species of tree[239] can be born anew, so to speak, and afterward bear good fruit and good seed; this is clear from grafting. Even though the bad sap rises from the root through the stem all the way to the point where the graft was made, it nevertheless turns into good sap and makes the tree good. A similar thing happens with people who are grafted onto the Lord, as he teaches with the following words:

> I am the vine; you are the branches. Those who live in me and I in them bear much fruit. If any do not live in me, they are cast out as branches. Once dried they are thrown into the fire. (John 15:5, 6)

Many scholars have pointed out the parallels between human reproduction and the reproduction not just of trees but of all plants.[240] I will add something on the subject here to wrap up this discussion.

585

Among trees and all other members of the plant kingdom there are not two sexes—masculine and feminine. There is just one sex, which is masculine. The ground or earth alone is a mother to them all, and is therefore like a woman.[241] The ground receives the seeds of plants of all kinds. It opens those seeds, carries them as in a womb, nourishes them, and gives birth to them—that is, brings them forth into daylight. Afterward it clothes them and sustains them.

[2] Once the seed has opened in the earth, it first develops a root, which is like a heart. From the root it sends out sap, which is like blood. By so doing it makes a kind of body complete with limbs: the body is the trunk; its limbs are the branches and twigs. The leaves that the plant unfurls immediately after its birth play the role of the lungs. Just as the heart cannot produce motion or sensation without the help of the lungs,

but with their help brings us to life, the root cannot develop into a tree or a plant without the help of the leaves. The flowers, which are the first steps toward fruit, are a means of refining the sap (the "blood" of the plant) by separating the purer elements from elements that are impure, and then forming a new stem to allow the purer elements to flow into the center of the flowers. The purified sap then flows through this stem and begins to construct and then mature the fruit.[242] The fruit is like a testicle; the seeds mature within it.[243]

The plant soul (or to put it another way, the plant's prolific essence),[244] which is dominant at the inmost level within every drop of sap, comes from no other source than the heat of the spiritual world. Because this heat originates in the spiritual sun, its constant goal is to generate [new life] and therefore ensure that creation continues. Because this heat has the generation of new people as its essential aim, therefore whatever it generates bears some resemblance to humankind.

[3] In case you are surprised by my saying that all the inhabitants of the plant kingdom are masculine and that only the earth or the ground plays the role of woman or mother to all, I will use the illustration of a similar situation among bees. According to Swammerdam's eyewitness account, as presented in his *Book of Nature*,[245] there is only one common mother who produces all the offspring within a whole hive. If these little creatures have but one common mother, why should that not be the case with all plants?

[4] The idea that the earth is a mother to all can also be illustrated spiritually. The "earth" in the Word means the church, and the church is a mother to all, and is even called that in the Word [Galatians 4:26]. For evidence that *earth* means the church, see the discussion of this word in *Revelation Unveiled* 285, 902.

The reason why the earth or ground is able to infiltrate the center of a seed, including its prolific material, and bring this out and circulate it, is that every little grain of dirt or pollen exudes from its essence a subtle emanation, which penetrates the seed. This infiltration is a result of the active force of the heat from the spiritual world.[246]

586   We can be regenerated only gradually. Each and every thing that exists in the physical world serves as an illustration of this fact. A seedling does not grow up into a mature tree in a single day. First there is a seed, then a root, then a shoot, which develops into a trunk; then branches come out of that and develop leaves and finally flowers and fruit. Wheat and barley do not spring up ready for harvest in a single day. A home is not built in a single day. We do not become full grown in a single day; reaching wisdom takes us even longer. The church is not established—let alone perfected—in a single day. We will make no progress toward a goal unless we first make a start.

People who have a different conception than this of regeneration know nothing about goodwill or faith, or how each of these qualities grows as we cooperate with the Lord. All this makes clear that regeneration progresses analogously to the way we are conceived, carried in the womb, born, and brought up.

The First Phase in Our Being Generated Anew Is Called "Reformation"; It Has to Do with Our Intellect. The Second Phase Is Called "Regeneration"; It Has to Do with Our Will and Then Our Intellect

Because this heading and headings to follow concern reformation and regeneration, and reformation pertains to the intellect but regeneration pertains to the will, it is important for you to know the difference between the intellect and the will. The difference between them has been laid out above in §397. Therefore I recommend that you read that section first, and then read what is here.

587

The evils we are born with are in the will that is part of our earthly self; this earthly will pressures the intellect to agree with it and to have thoughts that harmonize with its desires. Therefore if we are to be regenerated, this has to happen by means of our intellect as an intermediate cause.[247]

This process draws on pieces of information that our intellect receives, first from our parents and teachers, and later from our reading the Word, listening to preaching, reading books, and having conversations. The things that our intellect receives as a result are called truths. Therefore to say that we are reformed by means of our intellect is the same as saying that we are reformed by means of truths that our intellect receives. Truths teach us who to believe in, what to believe, and also what to do and what to will. After all, whatever we do, we do from our will and in accordance with our understanding.

Since our will is evil from the day we are born, and since our intellect teaches us what is evil and what is good and that it is possible for us to will one and not the other, it follows that our intellect is the means by which we have to be reformed. During the phase called our reformation, we come to mentally see and admit that evil is evil and goodness is good, and make the decision to choose what is good. When we actually try to abstain from evil and do what is good, the phase called our regeneration begins.

588   For this purpose we have been granted the ability to lift our intellect almost all the way into the light enjoyed by the angels in heaven. This lifting allows us to see what we ought to will and what we ought to do in order to be successful during our time in this world and blessed with happiness after death to eternity. We become successful and blessed if we gain wisdom for ourselves and keep our will obedient to that wisdom. We become unsuccessful and unhappy, however, if we devote our intellect to obeying our will. The reason for this is that from the time we are born, our will has a tendency toward evils of various kinds, including evils that are horrendous. If our will was not restrained by our intellect and instead we let it run free, we would quickly fall into criminal behavior; because of our inborn savage animal nature, for purely selfish reasons we would wipe out and butcher everyone and anyone who failed to show us favor or indulge our lusts.

[2] For another thing, if our intellect were incapable of being perfected on its own and of then perfecting our will, we would not be human at all; we would be animals. If there were no separation between our will and our intellect and if the intellect could not rise above the will, we would be unable either to think or to say what we thought. We would only be able to make noises that expressed our feelings. We would not be able to act in reasonable ways, either; we would act on instinct alone. We would be completely incapable of knowing anything about God or seeing him through what we knew; as a result, we would be unable to form a partnership with him and live forever.

We have thoughts and we will things as if we did so on our own. This feeling that we think and will on our own is what allows for a reciprocal partnership [with the Lord]. No partnership can exist without reciprocation. For example, no partnership would exist between an active element and a responsive element if there were no adaptation or point of contact between them.

God alone is an active force. We allow ourselves to experience that active force and we cooperate with it to all appearances as if we were acting on our own, although inwardly we are actually acting from God.

From the statements just made, if you take them in the right way, you can see what human beings are like. You can see the quality of love the human will has if it is lifted up by means of the intellect; and you can see the quality of love the human will has if it is not lifted up.

It is important to know that the capacity to lift the intellect even to a level of understanding possessed by the angels in heaven has been created as a part of every human being, the evil as well as the good. In fact every devil in hell retains this ability, since all those who are in hell existed as human beings [in the physical world]. I have often been shown through living experience that this is the case.

589

Nonetheless, the reason the devils in hell are insane rather than intelligent in spiritual matters is that they will what is evil and not what is good. Knowing and understanding truths is repulsive to them, because truths favor what is good and oppose what is evil.

These points also make it clear that the first step in our being generated anew is to receive truths in our intellect. The second step is to intend to put those truths into practice; eventually it takes the form of actually putting them into practice.

No one can justifiably be called a "reformed" person solely on the basis of his or her knowledge of truth. By lifting our intellect above the love that resides in our will, we are all capable of grasping those truths, saying them, teaching them, and preaching them. A truly reformed person is someone who desires the truth because it is true. This desire attaches itself to our will, and if it persists, forges a partnership between our will and our intellect. Then our regeneration begins. (Later sections will deal with how our regeneration proceeds and is perfected after that [§§591–614].)

The following comparisons can illustrate what people are like when their intellect has been lifted up but the love in their will has not. They are like an eagle that soars on high, but as soon as it sees something to eat below, such as hens, cygnets, or even little lambs, it drops like a stone and devours them.

590

They are also like an adulterous husband who has a whore hidden in his basement. He keeps going back and forth to the top level of his house. Up there in the presence of his wife he says wise things to his guests about faithfulness in marriage, but now and then suddenly leaves to go downstairs and satisfy his lewd desires with his whore.

They are also like swamp flies that fly in a column above the head of a running horse. Once the horse stops, they plunge back into their swamp.

This is what we are like when our intellect is lifted up but the love in our will remains below, near our feet, immersed in the unclean desires of its nature and lusting for sensual gratification.

[2] Because people in this state shine intellectually as if they possessed wisdom and yet their will is contrary to wisdom, they are like snakes with scales that reflect the light, or like beetles that shine as if they were made of gold. They are also like the strange light over swamps at night, or from the glow of rotting wood, or from phosphorus.[248]

Some who are in this state can masquerade as angels of light, both among people in this world and, after they die, among angels of heaven. After a brief examination there, however, their clothes are removed and they are thrown out naked. They cannot be detected in this world, because here their spirit is not visible; it is covered over with a mask, like the one a comic actor wears on stage. The fact that they can use their faces and words to masquerade as angels of light is both a result and a sign of the fact that they can lift their intellect almost all the way into angelic wisdom, above the love in their will, as I mentioned before. Since our inner and our outer self can go in opposite directions like this, and because our body is cast off but our spirit remains, it is clear then that a dark spirit can live behind a bright face, and a raging spirit can lie behind soothing words.

Therefore, my friend, know people for what they are, not by their mouth but by their heart—that is, not from what they say but from what they do. The Lord says, "Beware of false prophets who come to you in sheep's clothing but are inwardly as predatory as wolves. Recognize them by their fruits" (Matthew 7:15, 16).

Our Inner Self Has to Be Reformed First;
Our Outer Self Is Then Reformed through Our Inner Self—
This Is How We Are Regenerated

591   It is a common saying in the church today that our inner self has to be reformed first and that our outer self is then reformed through our inner self.[249] The church, however, takes the "inner self" to mean faith and nothing else—specifically, the faith that God the Father assigns us the merit and justice of his Son and sends us the Holy Spirit. They believe that this faith constitutes our inner self, and that our outer self, which is our moral, earthly self, is derived from it. To them, our moral, earthly

self is an appendage to that faith, like the tail on a horse or a cow; or like the tail of a peacock or a bird of paradise, which is long and feathery, but is completely separate from the real wings. According to the church, some type of goodwill follows that faith, but if a goodwill that comes from our own volition ever becomes present it will destroy our faith.

[2] Since faith is the only inner self that is recognized by the church today, there is no inner self, because according to the church none of us know whether that faith has been granted to us or not. As I have shown above, this faith is not actually possible, and is therefore fictional [§§505, 582]. It follows, then, that for people today who have convinced themselves of that faith, the only "inner self" they have is their earthly self, which has been teeming since birth with evils in great abundance. To this view they have added the notion that regeneration and sanctification spontaneously result from this faith, and that any cooperation on our part is excluded (although in reality regeneration only happens through our cooperation). As a result, the regeneration taught by the church of today is unrecognizable, even though the Lord says that those who are not regenerated cannot see the kingdom of God [John 3:3].

The concepts of the inner and outer self taught by the new church are completely different, however. In this view, our inner self is our will. It is the source of the thoughts we have when we are left to ourselves, such as when we are at home. Our outer self is what we do and say in company or in public. Our inner self, then, is goodwill and faith—goodwill that belongs to our will, and faith that occupies our thoughts.

Before we undergo regeneration, goodwill and faith constitute our earthly self, which is divided into an inner and an outer level. This is clear from the fact that we are not allowed to act in company or in public the way we do when left to ourselves at home. What causes the split into an inner and outer level is that civil law prescribes punishments for those who do evil things and rewards for those who do good things. Since no one wants to be punished and everyone wants to be rewarded, we therefore force ourselves to create an outer self that is separate from our inner self. The reward takes the form of wealth or a good reputation; we achieve neither one unless we live according to the law. This is why morality and benevolence are practiced outwardly, even by people who have no morality or benevolence inwardly. This is the origin of all hypocrisy, flattery, and pretense.

As for the earthly self being split into two levels, this is an actual division of both will and thought. Every action that we take originates in our will; every word we say originates in our thought. Below our first earthly will, we ourselves create a second will and a second thought process, which also belong to our earthly self. The will that we create ourselves could be called our *bodily* will, because it drives the body to behave in moral ways. The thought process that we create ourselves could be called *lung-related* thought, because it drives our lips and tongue to say things that show a good understanding.

Taken together, this type of thought and this will can be compared to the inner bark that adheres to the outer bark of a tree; or it can be compared to the membrane that adheres to the shell of an egg. Behind this self-made thought and will lies the inner earthly self. If we are evil, our inner earthly self is like rotten heartwood within a tree whose outer and inner bark appears whole; or like a rotten egg inside a clean white shell.

[2] Now to the nature of the inner earthly self that we are born with. Its will has a tendency toward evils of every kind and therefore its thinking has a tendency toward falsities of every kind. This inner self, then, is what needs to be regenerated. If it is not regenerated, it harbors hatred toward everything related to goodwill and anger at everything related to faith.

It follows, then, that our inner earthly self must be regenerated first, and our outer self must then be regenerated through our inner self. This sequence follows the divine design. To regenerate our inner self through our outer self would go contrary to the divine design, because the inner self acts as the soul of the outer self, not only in a general way but in every detail. The inner self is present in everything we say, without our even realizing it. This is what allows angels to perceive the quality of our will from a single action of ours, and the quality of our thinking from a single thing we say—the "quality" meaning whether we are hellish or heavenly. As a result, they have complete knowledge of us. From our tone of voice they perceive the interests that drive our thinking; from a gesture of ours, or the form of one action, they perceive the love that resides in our will. They detect this no matter how good we are at presenting ourselves as a Christian and a moral citizen.

594 Our regeneration is portrayed in Ezekiel as the dry bones on which sinews were placed; then flesh, and skin, and spirit was breathed into them, and they came to life (Ezekiel 37:1–14). The following words in that story make it obvious that it represents regeneration: "These bones are the whole house of Israel" (Ezekiel 37:11). There is also a comparison there involving graves. We read that God will open graves and cause

bones to rise up out of them, and he will put spirit in them and place them in the land of Israel (Ezekiel 37:12, 13, 14). The land of Israel here and elsewhere means the church. Bones and graves were used to represent regeneration because people who have not been regenerated are called the dead, and people who have been regenerated are called the living. The former are spiritually dead, but the latter are spiritually alive.

Every created thing in the world, both animate and inanimate, has an inner level and an outer level. The one level does not exist in the absence of the other, any more than an effect can exist without a cause. Every created thing is considered valuable if it is inwardly good, and worthless if it is inwardly bad, even where inner badness lies within outer goodness. Every wise person in the world and every angel in heaven evaluates people and things in this way.

What a person who has not been regenerated is like and what a person who has been regenerated is like can be illustrated through comparisons. People who have not been regenerated but who present themselves as moral citizens and "good Christians" can be compared to a corpse that has been embalmed with fragrant oils but nevertheless gives off a reek that overpowers the fragrances, assaults your nose, and hurts your brain.

They can also be compared with a mummy that has been gilded and placed in a silver coffin; as you look inside, your eye is met with a deformed, blackened corpse.

[2] They can be compared with bones and skeletons in a tomb that has been decorated with lapis lazuli and other precious stones.

They can also be compared with the rich man clothed in purple and fine linen, whose inner level was nonetheless hellish (Luke 16:[19–25]).

They can be compared with poison that tastes sweet; with hemlock in bloom; with fruit that has gleaming skin but whose flesh has been eaten away by worms; and with a wound that is carefully bandaged and has recently developed a thin layer of new skin, but inside is still full of infectious pus.

In our world, of course, the inside is sometimes valued highly on the basis of what is outside, but only by people who themselves have no inner goodness and who therefore judge things by appearances. This is not how it works in heaven, however. The body that can be turned this way and that around the spirit and can be bent from evil to good is removed by death, and then only the inner self remains, which constitutes the spirit. Then even from far away such people look like a snake that has shed its skin, or rotten wood whose shiny bark has been removed. [3] It is different, though, for those who have been regenerated. Their inner level is good and their outer level, which appears to be like anyone else's, is actually as different from that of the people just mentioned as heaven is from hell, since it has a soul of goodness inside.

After death it means nothing anymore whether people in this world were of high rank and lived in a mansion and walked around with an entourage, or lived in a hut and were waited on by a child. It does not matter if they were an archbishop who wore a scarlet robe and a two-tiered tiara, or a shepherd tending a few sheep in the woods, who wore a loose-fitting country coat with a hood for his head.

[4] Gold is still gold whether it shines next to the fire or its surface is blackened with smoke. Gold is still gold whether it has been poured into a beautiful shape like that of a little child or an unpleasant shape like that of a rat. The rats made of gold and placed next to the ark were still found acceptable and pleasing (1 Samuel 6:3, 4, 5, and following), because gold symbolizes inner goodness. Diamonds and rubies that have been kept in their matrix of limestone or clay are just as valuable as diamonds and rubies set in a queen's necklace, because they are valued for their inner goodness. And so on.

This makes it clear that what is on the outside derives its value from what is on the inside and not the other way around.

Once Our Inner Self Is Reformed, a Battle Develops between It and Our Outer Self; Whichever Self Wins Will Control the Other Self

596 The reason why a battle develops at this point is that our inner self has been reformed through truths. These truths allow us to see what evil and falsity are; but we still have evil and falsity in our outer or earthly self. At first, therefore, a disagreement arises between our new will, which is above, and our old will, which is below. Because these two wills are in disagreement, what they delight in is incompatible as well.

As we know, the flesh is against the spirit and the spirit against the flesh; the flesh and its lusts have to be brought under control before the spirit can become active and we can be a new person [Romans 7:22–23; Galatians 5:16–17, 24–25; Ephesians 4:22–24; 1 Peter 2:11].

After this disagreement of wills occurs, a battle develops, which is what is known as a crisis of the spirit.[250] This inner conflict, this battle, is not between good and evil [directly], but between truths that defend what is good and falsities that defend what is evil. Goodness cannot do its own fighting; it fights through truths. Evil, too, cannot do its own fighting; it fights through falsities. Likewise, the will is unable to do its own fighting; it fights through its intellect, where its truths are kept.

[2] That battle is something we feel inside ourselves and nowhere else; we experience it as an attack of conscience. In reality, though, it is the Lord and the Devil (meaning hell) that are fighting inside us. They fight for control over us, or to see whose we will be. The Devil, or hell, attacks us and summons the evils that are inside us. The Lord protects us and summons the good things that are inside us.

Although this battle takes place in the spiritual world, it is also a battle inside ourselves between the truths that defend what is good and the falsities that defend what is evil within us. Therefore we have to join the fight as if we were acting completely on our own. We have free choice to act either on the Lord's behalf or on the Devil's behalf. We are on the Lord's side if we stay with the truths that defend what is good. We are on the Devil's side if we stay with the falsities that defend what is evil.

It follows from this that whichever self wins, whether it is our inner self or our outer self, it will control the other. It is entirely the same as two enemy monarchs who fight over which of them is going to rule the other's country; the one who wins gains control of the other's territory, and all who live there have to obey their new ruler.

In this case, if our inner self wins it rules and gains control of all the evils in our outer self; our regeneration then continues. If on the other hand our outer self wins, it rules and drives away all the good qualities in our inner self; our regeneration then ceases.

There is some recognition today that crises of the spirit exist, but hardly anyone knows what causes them, what they are like, or what good they do. What causes them and what they are like was just covered above; so was the good they do. That is, when our inner self wins, it gains control of our outer self. Once this is under control, our lusts are uprooted. Desires for goodness and truth are planted in their place, arranged in such a way that the good and true things we will and think about we also practice and speak about from the heart. In addition, through victory over our outer self we become spiritual and the Lord brings us into association with the angels of heaven, all of whom are spiritual.

597

[2] The reason why crises of the spirit have not been known until now, and why hardly anyone has realized what causes them, what they are like, and what good they do, is that until now the church has not had

truths. None of us have truths unless we turn directly to the Lord, reject our former faith, and embrace this new faith. This is why no one has been brought into a crisis of a [truly] spiritual sort since the fourth century, when the Council of Nicaea introduced a belief in three gods.[251] If people had been brought into this inner conflict, they would have given up immediately and plunged themselves even deeper into hell.

The feeling of contrition that is claimed to precede the faith of today is not a crisis of the spirit. I have asked many about it, and they said that it is a word and nothing more, unless it is perhaps some fearful thought on the part of ordinary people when they contemplate the fires of hell.[252]

598 Once the conflict is over, we are present in heaven in our inner self and present in the world through our outer self. Therefore crises of the spirit accomplish a joining of heaven and the world within us. Then the Lord within us rules our world from our heaven, following the divine design.

The opposite happens if we remain earthly. Then we greatly desire to rule heaven from our world. All who have a love for power that comes from loving themselves are like this. If we are examined inwardly, it is discovered that we do not believe in any god, but only in ourselves. After death, we believe that we *are* a god who has greater power than others. This is the kind of insanity that exists in hell. It falls to such a depth that some there say they are God the Father, some say they are God the Son, and others say they are God the Holy Spirit. Some Jews there say they are the Messiah. This makes it clear what we are like after death if our earthly self is not regenerated. It shows what we would imagine ourselves to be if a new church were not established, in which things that are genuinely true are taught. This is the topic of the following words of the Lord: "At the close of the age," meaning the end of the church of today, "there will be a great affliction such as has never existed since the world began until now and will never exist again. In fact, unless those days were cut short no flesh would be saved" (Matthew 24:3, 21, 22).

599 During the battles or conflicts within us, the Lord carries out an individual act of redemption, much like the all-encompassing redemption he brought about while he was in the world.

While he was in the world, the Lord glorified his human manifestation, that is, made it divine, through battles and inner conflict. In a similar way within us individually, the Lord fights for us while we are undergoing inner conflict and conquers the hellish spirits who are assaulting us. Afterward he "glorifies" us, that is, makes us spiritual.

After his universal redemption, the Lord restructured all things in heaven and in hell in accordance with the divine design. He does much the same thing in us after crises of the spirit—that is, he restructures all the things in us that relate to heaven and the world in accordance with the divine design.

After his redemption, the Lord established a new church. Likewise, he establishes the principles of the church in us and turns us into an individual church.

After redemption, the Lord granted peace to those who believed in him. He said, "I leave my peace with you; I give my peace to you. I do not give to you the way the world gives" (John 14:27). In much the same way, after we have undergone a crisis of the spirit he allows us to feel peace, that is, gladness of mind and consolation.

From all this it is clear that the Lord is the Redeemer to eternity.

If our inner self alone were regenerated and not our outer self at the same time, we could be compared to a bird flying in the air that can find no place to rest on dry ground but only in a swamp, where it is attacked by snakes and frogs, and it flies away and dies. **600**

Under that circumstance we could be compared to a swan swimming in the middle of the ocean, too far from shore to create a nest, so the eggs it lays sink into the water and are devoured by fish.

We could also be compared to a soldier who is standing on a wall that crumbles beneath his feet, causing him to fall and die in the rubble.

We could also be compared to a healthy tree transplanted into unhealthy ground, where an army of grubs consumes the root, causing the tree to wither and fade away.

We could also be compared to a house without a foundation, or a column without a footing to support it.

This is what we would be like if our inner self alone were reformed but not our outer self at the same time. We would have no outlet through which to do what is good.

When We Have Been Regenerated, We Have a New Will and a New Intellect

When we have been regenerated we are renewed, or new. This is something the church of today knows, both from *the Word* and from *reason*. **601**

We know this from the following teachings in *the Word*.

Make your heart new and your spirit new. Why should you die, O house of Israel? (Ezekiel 18:31)

I will give you a new heart and I will put a new spirit within you. I will remove the heart of stone from your flesh and give you a heart of flesh. I will put my spirit within you. (Ezekiel 36:26, 27)

From now on we regard no one on the basis of the flesh. Therefore if anyone is in Christ, she or he is a new creation. (2 Corinthians 5:16, 17)

The *new heart* in these passages means a new will and the *new spirit* means a new intellect, since "heart" in the Word means the will and "spirit," when it appears alongside "heart," means the intellect.

From *reason* as well we know about our renewal: the person who has been regenerated must have a new will and a new intellect, because these two faculties are what make us human. They are the parts of us that are regenerated. The quality of these two faculties determines the quality of the human being. People who have an evil will are evil; if their intellect supports that will, they are even more evil. The opposite is true of good people.

Only religion renews and regenerates us. It is allotted the highest place in the human mind. Below itself it sees civic concerns that relate to the world. In fact, it rises up through these concerns the way the purest sap rises up through a tree to its very top, and surveys from that height the earthly things that lie below, the way someone looks down from a tower or a high point of land onto the fields below.

602   It is important to note, however, that our intellect can rise up almost into the light that the angels of heaven have, but if our will does not rise along with it, we are still the old self, not the new self. (I have already shown how the intellect lifts the will up with itself, higher and higher [§§587–590].) For this reason, regeneration is primarily a matter of the will, and only secondarily a matter of the intellect. The intellect in us is like light in the world, and our will is like the heat here. Without heat, light brings nothing to life and makes nothing grow; as we know, light has to act in partnership with heat. The intellect that is in the lower part of the mind is actually in the light of this world; the intellect that is in the higher part of the mind is in the light of heaven. Therefore if our will is not lifted up from the lower region into the higher region to join the intellect, it remains at the level of the world. Then our intellect flies up and down, up and down. Every night, though, it flies down and sleeps

with our will below, and the two make love like a married man and a whore and bring forth two-headed offspring.[253]

Again, it is clear that if we do not have a new will and a new intellect, we have not been regenerated.

The human mind has three levels. The lowest is called the earthly level; the middle is called the spiritual level; the highest is called the heavenly level. As we are regenerated, we are lifted from the lowest level, which is earthly, onto the higher level that is spiritual, and from there onto the heavenly level. (The existence of three levels within the mind will be demonstrated under the next heading [§§608–609].)

As a result, someone who has not been regenerated is called earthly, but someone who has been regenerated is called spiritual. Clearly, then, the mind of someone who has been regenerated is lifted up to the spiritual level. From up there it sees what is going on in the earthly mind below.

By paying even slight attention to our own thoughts, any of us can see and admit that there is a lower level and a higher level within the human mind. After all, we can see what we are thinking. Therefore we say, "I was thinking this or that, and now I am thinking something else." We could never do this if there were not an inner level of thought, called perception, which can carefully examine our lower level of thought, called thinking.

[2] When judges hear or read arguments that a lawyer has laid out in a long chain, they bring them together into one view, one all-encompassing image, in the higher level of their mind. Then they direct their attention toward the lower level, where earthly thought occurs, and they arrange the arguments into a sequence and hand down a sentence or judgment based on their higher vision.

Surely everyone realizes that we are capable of having thoughts or making decisions in a moment or two that take half an hour to put into words through our lower thought.

I present these examples to make it known that the human mind has higher and lower levels.

As for the new will, it is above the old will, on the spiritual level. So is the new intellect. The intellect is with the will and the will is with the intellect. They come together on that level, and together they examine the old, earthly self and arrange all the things in it so that they obey what is higher.

Surely everyone can see what would happen if there were only one level to the human mind—evil traits and good traits would be brought together and mixed up with each other there, as well as false impressions and true impressions, and conflict would erupt. It would be like putting wolves and sheep, or tigers and calves, or hawks and doves together in the same cage. The inevitable outcome would be a cruel slaughter, in which the savage animals tore the gentle ones to pieces.

Therefore it has been provided that good things along with their truths are gathered on a higher level so that they can remain safe and ward off an attack, and can use chains and other means to bring evils under control and finally disperse them along with their falsities.

This is the point made in an earlier section, that the Lord through heaven rules the things of this world that are present in a regenerated person. The higher or spiritual level of the human mind is in fact a heaven in miniature form, and the lower or earthly level is the world in miniature form. This is why the ancients referred to the human being as a microcosm. We could also be called a microheaven.[254]

605   People who have been regenerated, that is, people who have been made anew in will and intellect, are in the heat of heaven; that is, they have the love that heaven has. They are also in the light of heaven; that is, they have the wisdom heaven has. On the other hand, people who have not been regenerated are in the heat of hell; that is, they have the love that hell has. They are also in the darkness of hell; that is, they have the insanities that hell has.

Nowadays this is well known, yet in other ways it is not known, because the church as it exists today has made regeneration an appendage to its faith. It says that reasoning should not be applied to the subject of faith, and should therefore not be applied to anything that is an appendage to faith, namely, regeneration and renewal.

To people [in the church today], regeneration and renewal, along with that faith itself, are like a house whose doors and windows have been boarded up. No one knows who or what is inside the house. It may be empty; it might be full of demons from hell, or angels from heaven.

In addition, confusion has been caused by a misunderstanding of the fact that we can rise up with our intellect almost into the light of heaven and therefore think and speak intelligently about spiritual matters, no matter what the love in our will is like.[255] Not knowing the truth of this situation has led to complete ignorance about what it is to be regenerated and made new.

606   From the above we can conclude that when we have not been regenerated, we see ghosts at night, so to speak, and think they are real people. When we are being regenerated, we become aware first thing in the morning that what was seen in the night was unreal. When we have been regenerated and are in broad daylight, we realize that our visions in the night were a form of madness.

People who have not been regenerated are dreaming; people who have been regenerated are awake. In fact, in the Word our earthly life is compared to a sleep and our spiritual life to wakefulness.[256]

People who have not been regenerated are meant by the foolish young women who had lamps but no oil. People who have been regenerated are meant by the prudent young women who had lamps and also oil [Matthew 25:4]. The lamps mean things that belong to our intellect; the oil means things that belong to our love.

People who have been regenerated are like the oil lamps on the lampstand in the tabernacle. They are also like the showbread and the incense on the table and the altar there.[257] They are the people in Daniel 12:3 who are as radiant as the brightness of the firmament and who shine like the stars for an age and forever.

[2] People who have not been regenerated are in the Garden of Eden, so to speak, but they eat from the tree of the knowledge of good and evil and are thrown out of the garden; in fact they *are* that tree. People who have been regenerated are also in that garden but they eat from the tree of life. The Book of Revelation makes clear that it is possible to eat from the tree of life: "To those who overcome I will give [food] to eat from the tree of life, which is in the middle of the paradise of God" (Revelation 2:7). The Garden of Eden means a spiritual understanding that arises from a love for truth; see *Revelation Unveiled* 90.

Briefly put, someone who has not been regenerated is a child of the evil one; someone who has been regenerated is a child of the kingdom (Matthew 13:38). A *child of the evil one* in this passage means a child of the Devil, and a *child of the kingdom* means a child of the Lord.

People Who Have Been Regenerated Are in Fellowship with the Angels of Heaven; People Who Have Not Been Regenerated Are in Fellowship with the Spirits of Hell

Every human being is in fellowship, that is, in close association, with either angels of heaven or spirits of hell, because we are born to become spiritual, and we cannot become spiritual unless we are associated with

607

others who are spiritual. In the work *Heaven and Hell* I have shown that our minds are in both worlds, the physical and the spiritual [§§432–444].

Nevertheless both the people and the angels or spirits are unaware of this connection, because as long as we remain alive in this world, we are in an earthly state, whereas the angels and spirits are in a spiritual state. Because of the differences between what is earthly and what is spiritual, neither one of us appears to the other. The nature of the differences is described in the memorable occurrence recorded in *Marriage Love* 326–329.[258] That passage makes it clear that it is not our thoughts but rather our feelings that form a connection between us. Yet hardly any of us reflect on our feelings, because they are not in the light of our intellect and thought; they are instead in the warmth of our will and of the emotions that relate to what we love. Nevertheless, the connection that is established by feelings of love held in common between people on the one hand and angels and spirits on the other is so tight that if it were broken and the angels and spirits were separated from us, we would immediately lose consciousness. If that relationship were not reestablished and angels and spirits were not reconnected to us, we would die.

[2] When I say that we become "spiritual" as a result of being regenerated, I do not mean that we [who are still in the physical world] become as fully spiritual as angels; I mean that we become both spiritual and earthly, meaning that within our earthly self there is a spiritual self, which is present in much the same way thought is present in speech or the will is present in action—if one stops, the other stops. Similarly, our spirit is present in the individual things our body does. The spirit is what drives the earthly component to do what it does. Viewed on its own, the earthly part of us is something passive; it is a dead force. The spiritual part of us is something active; it is a living force. Something passive, a dead force, cannot take action on its own. It must be driven by something active, a living force.

[3] Since we live constantly in fellowship with inhabitants of the spiritual world, as soon as we leave the physical world we are immediately placed among the spirits like ourselves whom we had been with while in the world. This is why all of us after we die seem to ourselves to be still alive in the world—we come into contact with people who have the same feelings as we do in our will. We claim these spirits as "our people," just as friends and neighbors in this world claim each other as "their people." This is what the Word means when it says that those who die are gathered to their people.[259]

These points establish the fact that people who have been regenerated are in fellowship with the angels of heaven, whereas people who have not been regenerated are in fellowship with the spirits of hell.

It is important to know that there are three heavens and that they are divided up according to three levels of love and wisdom. As we progress in our regeneration we come into fellowship with angels from those three heavens. Because this is the case, the human mind, too, has three levels or areas just like the heavens. (For more on the three heavens and their division according to the three levels of love and wisdom, see *Heaven and Hell* 29 and following; see also the little work *Soul-Body Interaction* 16, 17.)[260]   **608**

Here the nature of the three levels into which the heavens are divided will be illustrated only by a comparison. They are like the head, the upper body, and the lower body in a person. The highest heaven constitutes the head; the middle heaven, the upper body; and the lowest heaven, the lower body. In fact, the whole of heaven in the Lord's sight is like one human being. The truth of this has been disclosed to me through firsthand experience: I was given permission to see an entire community of heaven, which consisted of tens of thousands of angels, as one human being. Why would the whole of heaven not appear that way before the Lord? For more on this living experience, see *Heaven and Hell* 59 and following.

[2] This also clarifies how we should understand the well-known saying in the Christian world that the church constitutes the body of Christ, and that Christ is the life within this body.[261] It serves as well to illustrate the point that the Lord is everything to all heaven, since he is the life within that body. The Lord is also the life within the church that exists among people who acknowledge him alone as the God of heaven and earth and who believe in him. (He himself teaches, in Matthew 28:18, that he is the God of heaven and earth, and in John 3:15, 16, 36; 6:40; 11:25, 26, that we are to believe in him.)

The three levels on which the heavens exist, and therefore on which the human mind exists, can to some extent be illustrated by physical things in our world. The three levels are like the relative differences in value between gold, silver, and copper. (The statue of Nebuchadnezzar, Daniel 2:31 and following, is another analogy that uses these metals.) These three levels are as different from each other as a ruby, a sapphire, and an agate are different in purity and value. An olive tree, a grapevine, and a fig tree would be another set of examples; and so on. In fact, in the Word, gold, a ruby, and an olive tree symbolize goodness that is heavenly,   **609** the type of goodness found in the highest heaven; silver, a sapphire, and a grapevine symbolize goodness that is spiritual, the type of goodness found in the middle heaven; and copper, an agate, and a fig tree symbolize goodness that is earthly, the type of goodness found in the lowest heaven. (I have shown above that the three levels are the heavenly, the spiritual, and the earthly [§603].)

610   The following needs to be added to what has been stated so far: Our regeneration does not happen in a moment. It gradually unfolds from the beginning all the way to the end of our lives in this world; and after this life is over, it continues and is perfected.

Because we are reformed through battles and victories against the evils of our flesh, the Son of Humankind says to each of the seven churches that gifts will be given to those who overcome. That is, to the church in Ephesus he says, "To those who overcome I will give [food] to eat from the tree of life" (Revelation 2:7). To the church in Smyrna he says, "Those who overcome will suffer no harm from the second death" (Revelation 2:11). To the church in Pergamos he says, "To those who overcome I will give the hidden manna to eat" (Revelation 2:17). To the church in Thyatira he says, "To those who overcome I will give power over the nations" (Revelation 2:26). To the church in Sardis he says, "Those who overcome will be clothed in white garments" (Revelation 3:5). To the church in Philadelphia he says, "Those who overcome I will make pillars in the temple of God" (Revelation 3:12). To the church in Laodicea he says, "To those who overcome I will grant to sit with me on my throne" (Revelation 3:21).

Let me also add the following as a final note: The more we are reborn, that is, the more the process of regeneration is perfected in us, the less we attribute anything of goodness and truth, or goodwill and faith, to ourselves; we attribute it all to the Lord. We are taught this very clearly by the truths that we keep drinking in.

The More We Are Regenerated, the More Our Sins Are Laid Aside; This Relocating of Them Is the "Forgiving of Sins"

611   The more we are regenerated, the more our sins are laid aside, because the process of being regenerated is a matter of restraining our flesh so that it does not control us, and taming our old self and its cravings so that it does not rise up and destroy our intellectual faculty. Once our intellectual

faculty is destroyed we can no longer be reformed; this reformation cannot take place unless our spirit, which is above our flesh, is instructed and
perfected.

Surely everyone (whose intellect is still intact) can see from what was
just stated that this sort of process cannot be completed in a moment. It
happens in stages, much the way we are conceived, carried in the womb,
born, and brought up, as was presented above [§§583–586]. The traits of
the flesh or the old self are embedded in us from the day we are born. They
build the first home for our mind. Cravings live in that home like predatory animals in their dens. At first they live in the entryways. Then bit by
bit they move by stealth into levels of the house that are below ground.
Later on they go upstairs and make bedrooms for themselves there. This
takes place gradually as we grow up from our childhood through youth to
young adulthood, when we begin to have thoughts that come from our
own understanding and perform actions that come from our own will.

[2] Surely everyone can see that the home that has been established
in our mind to this point—a place where cravings join hands and dance
with each other like owls, vultures, and satyrs [Isaiah 13:21; 34:13–15]—
cannot be torn down in a single moment and a new home constructed
in its place. First the cravings that are holding hands and dancing have
to be set to one side, and new healthy desires for what is good and true
need to be brought in to replace our unhealthy desires for what is evil
and false.

All this cannot happen in a moment. Every wise person can see the
truth of this just from the fact that each evil is composed of countless cravings. Every evil is like a piece of fruit that under its skin is full of worms with
black heads and white bodies.[262] There are a great number of such evils and
they are joined to each other, like a spider's offspring when they first hatch
out of its belly. Therefore unless one evil after another is taken away until
their confederation is broken up, we cannot become a new person.

These things have been stated to support the point that the more we
are regenerated, the more our sins are laid aside.

From the day we are born we have an inclination toward evils of
every kind. Because of that inclination we yearn for these evils. If we
have the freedom, we also do them. From birth, we long to control other
people and to own what belongs to them. These two longings tear to
pieces any love we might have for our neighbor. They induce us to hate
anyone who opposes us; that hatred leads us to desire revenge; and that
desire for revenge inwardly cherishes the idea of our opponent's death.
The same forces also lead us to think it is perfectly acceptable to commit

612

adultery, to take things by secret acts of thievery, and to slander people, which is bearing false witness. People who think these things are acceptable are atheists at heart. This is the nature we are born with. Clearly then, we are born a hell in miniature.

Nevertheless, unlike animals, we are born with inner levels of mind that are spiritual. We are born for heaven. Because our earthly or outer self is a hell in miniature, as just noted, it follows that heaven cannot be planted in that hell; that hell must be moved out of the way.

613 People who know how heaven and hell differ from each other and how the one is located in relation to the other are able to know how we are regenerated and what we are like afterward. To make this better understood to those who do not have this knowledge, I will briefly reveal the following.

All those who are in heaven turn their faces toward the Lord. All who are in hell turn their faces away from the Lord. Therefore when you look at hell from heaven, you see only the backs of the people there and the backs of their heads; in fact they also look upside down (like people on the far side of the earth) with their feet up and their heads down, even though they walk on their feet and turn their faces this way and that. It is the fact that the inner levels of their minds are turned in the opposite direction that makes them look this way. This may sound hard to believe, but I have seen it myself.

[2] These experiences revealed to me how regeneration takes place. It happens in the same way that hell is relocated and sequestered from heaven. As I noted above, by our first nature—the nature we are born with—we are a hell in miniature. By our second nature, the nature we derive from our second birth, we are a heaven in miniature.

It follows from this that the evils within us are relocated and sequestered on an individual scale in the same way that hell is relocated and sequestered from heaven on a grand scale. As our evils are relocated, they turn away from the Lord and gradually turn themselves upside down. This happens step by step as heaven is implanted in us—that is, as we become a new person.

In the hope of shedding further light, I will add that every evil within us has a connection to people in hell who are involved in that same evil. On the other hand, every good thing within us has a connection to people in heaven who are involved in that same goodness.

614 From these points it can be seen that being forgiven for our sins is not a matter of their being completely washed away or eliminated from us, but of their being relocated and sequestered within us. It is also clear that every evil that we have actively made our own stays with us.

Because "forgiveness of sins" means that they are relocated and sequestered within us, it follows that we are withheld from our evil by the Lord and held in goodness. This is the benefit that regeneration gives us.

On one occasion I heard someone in the lowest heaven saying that he was free of sin because his sins had been washed away; he added that this had been done by the blood of Christ.[263] Because he was in heaven and had that mistaken belief through ignorance, he was plunged back into his sins. As they returned upon him, he owned up to them. As a result, he adopted a new belief, which was that every human being and every angel is held back by the Lord from what is evil inside them and kept in what is good.

[2] This experience also makes it clear that our sins are not instantly forgiven; they are forgiven in accordance with our regeneration and our progress in it.

The laying aside of our sins, which is called forgiveness of sins, can be compared with the dumping of waste from the camp of the children of Israel in the surrounding desert (their camp represented heaven; the desert represented hell).[264]

It can also be compared with the separation of the nations from the children of Israel in the land of Canaan, and of the Jebusites in Jerusalem [Joshua 15:63]; they were not cast out, they were just kept apart.

It can also be compared with Dagon, the god of the Philistines. When the ark was brought in, Dagon first lay on its face on the ground, and afterward lay with its head and its hands broken off on the threshold [1 Samuel 5:3, 4]. It was not cast out; it was just moved to a different place.

[3] It can also be compared with the demons that the Lord sent into the pigs, who then plunged into the sea [Matthew 8:31, 32]. The sea here and elsewhere in the Word means hell.

It can also be compared with the dragon's gang,[265] which was separated from heaven. It first invaded the earth and was then cast down to hell [Revelation 12:9; 20:2, 10].

It can also be compared with a forest full of predatory animals. Once the forest is cut down, the animals retreat into the surrounding bushes, and the land in the middle is leveled and cultivated as a field.

Regeneration Would Be Impossible without Free Choice in Spiritual Matters

Without free choice in spiritual matters we could not be regenerated— **615** surely no one is so stupid as to be unable to see that. Without free choice, would we be able to turn to the Lord and acknowledge him as the Redeemer and the Savior and as the God of heaven and earth, as he himself teaches in Matthew 28:18? Without that kind of free choice, how could we believe in him, that is, turn to him in faith, and worship him? How could we work on receiving the means and the benefits of salvation from him? How could we cooperate in receiving those things from him? Without free choice, how could we do anything good for our neighbors or practice goodwill toward them? How could we introduce teachings related to faith and goodwill into our thinking and willing, and bring them forth and put them into action?

Without free choice, regeneration would be nothing but a word the Lord once used (John 3),[266] which either sticks in our ear or moves down from our thought that is closest to speech into our mouth as the sound of a twelve-letter word—a sound that no meaning can lift into any higher region of the mind, so it falls into the air and is gone.

616   Tell me, if you can, whether any blinder stupidity about regeneration could possibly exist than the one exhibited by people who have convinced themselves of the modern-day faith. That belief holds that although we are like a log or a stone, that faith is poured into us. Once it is poured in, then our justification follows, which means that our sins are forgiven and we are regenerated (not to mention many other gifts we are given). Any work on our part must be strictly excluded from this process to prevent us from doing any violence to the merit of Christ. In order to establish this dogma with even greater solidity, they take away any notion that we have free choice in spiritual matters and replace it with the idea that we are completely powerless in those respects. Since God alone then does his part of the work, and no power has been granted to us to do our part in cooperating and therefore forming a partnership with God, how are we different in regard to regeneration from someone who is shackled hand and foot? We are like so-called galley slaves, who are chained inside ships. What happens to them if they take the chains off their hands and feet? Like them, [under this teaching] we too are punished and condemned to death if we exercise our free choice and do anything good for our neighbor or make any effort to believe in God for the sake of our salvation.

[2] Where does that leave people who are convinced of these views and yet feel a devout desire to go to heaven? What can they do but wait like a ghost in limbo, trying to guess whether that faith and all its benefits

have already been poured into them, or if not, whether they are being poured in now? "Has God the Father shown mercy? Has his Son interceded for me? Is the Holy Spirit tied up elsewhere or is it working on me yet?" After a while without any information to go on, they would stop posing these questions and just comfort themselves with these thoughts: "Perhaps that grace is present in the morality I am still practicing now just as much as I was before. Maybe morality is actually sacred in my case, although the same quality is admittedly profane in people who have not acquired this faith. To preserve the holiness present in my morality I will be careful from now on not to work on faith or goodwill at all on my own." And so on.

Everyone who thinks about regeneration but does not believe in free choice in spiritual matters is a ghost like this, or, if you prefer, a pillar of salt [Genesis 19:26].

People who believe that regeneration can exist in the absence of free choice in spiritual matters, that is, without any cooperation on their part, become as cold as a stone toward all the true teachings of the church. If they are warm, they are warm with cravings that are like pitch and tar burning in a torch lit from the fireplace.

617

They are like people who live in a mansion that has sunk into the ground all the way up to its roof and is flooded with muddy water; so they live on the bare roof and make themselves a rough shelter on it out of swamp reeds. In time, though, even the roof goes under and they are swallowed up.

They are also like a ship that contains precious cargo of all kinds taken from the treasury of the Word, but that cargo is either eaten away by rats and moths or thrown into the sea by the sailors, robbing the merchants of their goods.

The learned professors who are steeped in the mysteries of that faith are like shopkeepers in stalls who sell statues of idols, fruit and flowers made out of wax, seashells, snakes in glass bottles, and other merchandise of that sort.

People who do not even try to look upward because they have been told that the Lord has not granted human beings any spiritual ability are, in regard to their actions, like animals that keep their heads down and stay in the forests looking for food. If they stumble upon orchards, they are like caterpillars that consume the leaves of the trees. If they happen to lay their eyes on pieces of fruit, and even more so if they lay their hands on them, they fill the fruit with worm-laden [eggs]. Eventually they become like reptiles with scales—like those scales, their mistaken ideas rattle and glisten.[267] And so on.

Regeneration Is Not Possible without the Truths That Shape Faith and Are Joined with Goodwill

618 We are regenerated by three things: the Lord, faith, and goodwill. These three would lie hidden like extremely valuable gems buried underground if divine truths from the Word did not open them to view. In fact, they do lie hidden for people who deny that we can cooperate with the Lord, even though such people read the Word a hundred or a thousand times and those things stand forth in clear light there.

Take the Lord, for example. Do any who are convinced of the faith of today regard with open eyes the statements in the Word that the Lord and the Father are one, that the Lord is the God of heaven and earth, and that the will of the Father is that we believe in the Son, not to mention countless other similar teachings about the Lord that occur in both testaments?[268] The reason for this is that they do not have truths, and are therefore not in a light in which they could see things of this kind. Even if they were given such light, their false beliefs would extinguish it. Then they would pass over teachings like this as if the words had been erased or deleted, or as if they were covered gutters that people step on and cross over. The purpose of these analogies is to make it known that without truths we do not see this teaching about the Lord, even though it is a key component of our regeneration.

[2] What of faith? Without truths, faith cannot even exist. Faith and truth are one with each other. The goodness within faith constitutes its soul, so to speak, and truths constitute its body. Therefore saying that we believe or have faith and yet knowing no truths related to faith is like extracting the soul from a body and then trying to have a conversation with that soul, even though it is invisible. All the truths that constitute faith's body emit light; they shine on the face of faith and make it visible.

A similar thing is true of goodwill. It emits heat. The light of truth joins together with this heat, just as heat and light join together during springtime in this world and the two of them bring animals and plants on earth into a reproductive state again.

[3] The same thing happens with spiritual heat and light. They join together within us, when we are focused both on truths that relate to faith and on good actions that relate to goodwill. As indicated above in the chapter on faith,[269] each truth that relates to faith gives off a light that shines, and each good action that relates to goodwill gives off a heat that lights a fire within us. The point is also made there that spiritual light is essentially intelligence, and spiritual heat is essentially love; the Lord alone combines these two in us as he is regenerating us. As the Lord says, "The words that I speak are spirit and are life" (John 6:63). "Believe in the light, so that you may become children of the light. I have come into the world as a light" (John 12:36, 46).

The Lord is the sun of the spiritual world. All spiritual heat and light come from that sun. That light enlightens us; that heat kindles a fire within us. Through both of them working together in us, the Lord brings us to life and regenerates us.

From the points just made it is clear that without truths we cannot have an accurate concept of the Lord. Without truths there is also no faith and therefore no goodwill. This means that without truths, there is no theology, and where there is no theology there is no church. Yet the crowd of people who call themselves Christians today lack truths. They say they are in the light of the gospel, but in fact they are in thick darkness.

619

Today truths lie well hidden beneath falsities, like gold, silver, and precious stones buried among the bones in the valley of Hinnom.[270] The truth of this has been clearly revealed to me through the spheres in the spiritual world that flow forth from modern-day Christianity and spread themselves abroad.

[2] One such sphere, which affects one's thinking about the Lord, emanates and pours forth from the southern region, where learned clergy and well-educated laity reside. Wherever this sphere reaches, it subtly induces new mental images. For many people, it takes away their belief in the divinity of the Lord's human nature; for many others, it weakens their belief; and for many others, it makes their belief foolish. It does this by introducing a faith in three gods, which produces confusion.

[3] The second sphere, which concerns faith, is like a black cloud in winter that causes darkness, turns the rain to snow, strips leaves from the trees, freezes water, and robs sheep of their food. Working jointly with the first sphere mentioned above, this sphere induces a drowsy stupor regarding the oneness of God, the process of regeneration, and the means of being saved.

[4] The third sphere concerns the relationship between faith and good-will. It is so strong that it is irresistible, and today it is unspeakably horrible. Like a plague, it infects anyone who breathes it in. It takes away any con-nection between faith and goodwill, even though these two means of salva-tion have been established since the creation of the world and are brought together by the Lord. This sphere also overcomes people in the physical world and extinguishes the wedding torches at the marriage of truth and goodness.271 I have felt this sphere. Sometimes when I would think about the connection between faith and goodwill, this sphere would stand be-tween the two and make violent efforts to separate them.

[5] The angels complain about these spheres and pray to the Lord that they will be dissipated; but the answer they get is that these spheres can-not be dissipated as long as the dragon is still on earth, since that sphere comes from the dragon's gang.272 Scripture tells us that the dragon was cast down to the earth, and adds: "Rejoice because of this, O heavens, and woe to those who live on the earth" (Revelation 12:[9, 12]).

[6] These three spheres are like air masses, originating from the drag-on's nostrils, that are then driven far and wide by a windstorm; because they are spiritual they are able to infiltrate and influence minds.

There are only a few spheres of spiritual truths in the spiritual world today. They are found only in the new heaven and among the people who are beneath that heaven who have been separated from the dragon's gang. This is why these truths are as far out of sight to people in the world today as ships on the Baltic Sea are to admirals and ship captains who are sailing the North Sea.273

620 The fact that regeneration is not possible without the truths that shape our faith can be illustrated by the following comparisons. This is no more possible than a human mind without an intellect, since truths are what shape our intellect. Our intellect is what teaches us what to believe, what to do, what regeneration is, and how it happens.

Truths are equally as necessary to regeneration as the sun's light is to the life of animals and the growth of trees. If the sun did not give light along with heat, it would be like the sun that is described in the Book of Revelation as sackcloth of hair274 (Revelation 6:12), or like the blackened sun (Joel 2:31) that leads to thick darkness on the earth (Joel 2:2). A simi-lar thing would happen to us without truths that emit light.

The Lord in the spiritual world is the sun that radiates the light of truth. Without spiritual light flowing into human minds, the church is in thick darkness, like the shadow of an everlasting eclipse.

[2] Undergoing a process of regeneration, which is carried out by means of faith and goodwill, but without truths to teach and lead us, would be like sailing across a great ocean without a helm or without a compass and charts. It would be like riding a horse through a dark forest at night.

The inner mental vision of people who have falsities instead of truths, but believe them to be true, could be compared to the eyesight of people who have a blockage in their optic nerve; although they cannot see a thing through their eye, it still looks as though it is functioning and healthy. Physicians call this form of blindness amaurosis or "transparent blockage."[275] Their rational or intellectual faculty is closed at the top and open only at the bottom, which causes their rational light to be no better than the light they receive through their eyes. The judgments they come to are therefore all fabricated and are sewn together with mistaken impressions. They stand like astrologers on street corners with telescopes, uttering meaningless predictions. This will be the condition of all who are devoted to theology if the Lord does not open up genuine truths from the Word.

To these points I will add the following memorable occurrences.   **621**

The first memorable occurrence. On one occasion I saw a group of spirits who were all on their knees praying to God to send them angels so that they could speak with the angels face to face and open up to them the thoughts that were in their hearts.

When they got up from praying they saw three angels in fine linen standing nearby. The angels said, "The Lord Jesus Christ heard your prayers and sent us to you. Open up to us the thoughts that are in your hearts."

"Our priests have told us," they replied, "that in matters of theology the intellect is no help. Faith is what is needed. And an intellectual kind of faith is not well suited in these matters, they say, because it originates from, and smacks of, self rather than God.

[2] "We are British. We have heard many things from our own holy ministers and we believe them; but when we speak with others who also call themselves Protestants, and with others who call themselves Roman Catholics, and with Protestant Dissenters,[276] they all seem well informed and yet on many points they disagree with each other. Nevertheless they

all say, 'Believe us!' And some say, 'We are ministers of God—we know these things!'

"What we ourselves know is that the divine truths that are called the truths of faith—the truths of the church—do not come from one's native soil or by heredity; they come out of heaven from God. They show the way to heaven. Along with good actions that come from goodwill, these truths become part of our lives. They lead us to eternal life. [Because we had heard differing views of what is true,] we therefore became anxious and prayed to God on our knees."

[3] "Read the Word and believe in the Lord," the angels said, "and you will see the truths that are to be part of your faith and your life. The Word is the only common source from which all who are in the Christian world draw their teachings."

Two members of the group said, "We have read it but we didn't understand it."

"You did not turn to the Lord, who is the Word," the angels replied, "and you had already convinced yourselves of falsities.

"What is faith without light?" the angels went on. "What is thinking without understanding? It is not human. Ravens and magpies can learn to talk without understanding. This we can assure you: every single human being whose soul desires it has the capability to see the truths of the Word in light. All animals know, just by seeing it, what food will keep them alive. We human beings are animals that are rational and spiritual. We too see the food that will keep us alive—not the food for our body but the food for our soul, which is the truth that relates to faith—*if* we are hungry for it and ask the Lord for it. [4] The true substance of any information we take in without understanding will not remain in our memory; only the words will remain.

"For this reason, when we angels look down from heaven at the world [these days], we don't see anything. We just hear sounds, and most of them are discordant.

"Allow us, however, to list some teachings that learned clergy have taken out of the realm of the intellect, because they are unaware that there are two ways of understanding, a worldly way and a heavenly way. When the Lord enlightens people, he lifts up our worldly way of understanding. If we have closed our intellect for religious reasons, however, the heavenly way of understanding is closed, and then we see nothing more in the Word than a blind person would see. We have seen many people of this type fall into pits from which they did not rise again.

[5] "For the sake of illustration, let's take examples of such teachings. Surely you are able to understand what goodwill is and what faith is. Goodwill is treating our neighbor well, and faith is having accurate thoughts about God and about the essential teachings of the church. Therefore, people who treat others well and think properly, that is, who live a good life and believe the right things, are saved."

The British spirits replied that they did indeed understand those things.

[6] "In order to be saved," the angels went on, "you have to practice repentance from your sins. Those who do not practice repentance remain in the sins they were born with. The practice of repentance is to not will evils, because they are against God. It involves examining yourselves once or twice a year, seeing your evils, confessing them before the Lord, begging for his help, no longer doing them, and launching into a new life. More and more as you do this and believe in the Lord, your sins are forgiven."

Some from the group said, "We understand this, and this also tells us what 'forgiveness of sins' means."

[7] The group then asked the angels to tell them more, particularly on the subjects of God, the immortality of the soul, regeneration, and baptism.

"We will not say anything you don't understand," the angels replied, "since otherwise what we say might fall like rain on a sandy place and on seeds there that are bound to shrivel up and die no matter how much water they get from heaven."

On the subject of *God* the angels said, "All who come into heaven are allotted a place there, and experience eternal joy, on the basis of their idea of God. One's idea of God is what rules universally in everything having to do with worship. An idea of God as a spirit—if a spirit is believed to be like ether or wind—is a meaningless idea. An idea of God as a human being is a true idea. God is divine love and divine wisdom and all the attributes that go along with them. A human being has love and wisdom; ether and wind do not. The idea of God that we have in heaven is the idea of the Lord our Savior; he is the God of heaven and earth, as he himself taught [Matthew 28:18]. If your idea of God becomes like ours, then we will all be able to be together."

As the angels said these things the faces of the British spirits shone.

[8] On the subject of *the immortality of the soul* they said, "Human beings live to eternity because they are capable of forming a partnership

with God through love and faith—absolutely everyone is capable of forming a partnership like this. If you think a little more deeply about it, you can understand that this capability is what allows the soul to be immortal."

[9] On the subject of *regeneration* they said, "Who cannot see that everyone (at least everyone who has been taught that God exists) possesses the freedom either to think about God or not to think about God? All people, then, have just as much freedom in spiritual matters as they do in civic and earthly matters. The Lord constantly grants this freedom to everyone. Therefore we are at fault if we do not think about God. Our ability to have such thoughts is what makes us human; the inability of animals to have such thoughts is what makes them animals. Therefore we have the ability to reform and regenerate ourselves as if we are doing so on our own, provided that at heart we admit that the Lord is the one doing the work. Everyone who practices repentance and believes in the Lord is reformed and regenerated. We have to do both of these things as if we are acting on our own, even though the ability to act seemingly on our own comes from the Lord. Now, it is true that left to ourselves we would be able to contribute nothing to our regeneration—absolutely nothing. Nevertheless, you were not created as statues; you were created as human beings so that you would be able to do this with the help of the Lord but as if you were acting on your own. Developing love and faith as our response is the sole thing that the Lord truly wants us to do for him.

"To sum this up: Do these things on your own, but believe that you do them with the help of the Lord; then you will be doing them *as if* you were acting on your own."

[10] The group then asked, "Is this 'doing things as if one is acting on one's own' an attribute that human beings have had from creation?"

"It is not that kind of attribute," the angels replied, "because acting on one's own is actually something that belongs to God alone.[277] It is, however, granted to us continually; that is, it is always with us. If we do what is good and believe what is true as if we were doing so on our own, we are angels of heaven. If we do what is evil and therefore believe what is false, however—which is actually something that is also done as if we were acting on our own—we are spirits of hell. You are surprised to hear that this too is done as if we were acting on our own. But you see this, don't you, when you say that familiar prayer to be kept safe so that the Devil does not seduce you and take possession of you the way he took possession of Judas, fill you with all wickedness, and destroy both your soul and your body?[278]

"Regardless of whether our actions are good or evil, we all [necessarily] come into fault if we believe that what we do originates with ourselves, though the same is not true if we believe our actions only *seem* to originate with ourselves.[279] If we believe that some good deed comes from ourselves, we claim for ourselves something that actually belongs to God. If we believe that some evil deed comes from ourselves, we attribute to ourselves something that actually belongs to the Devil."

[11] On the topic of *baptism* the angels said, "Baptism is a spiritual washing, which is reformation and regeneration. The child is reformed and regenerated when, having become an adult, he or she does the things the godparents promised on his or her behalf. There are two such promises in baptism: repentance, and faith in God. The godparents promise first that the child will renounce the Devil and all his works, and second that the child will believe in God. All children in heaven are initiated into these two practices, although to them 'the Devil' is hell and 'God' is the Lord. For another thing, baptism is a sign to the angels that someone belongs to the church."

When they had heard all this, some from the group said, "We understand."

[12] A voice was heard off to the side, however, that shouted, "We don't understand."

Another voice shouted, "We don't want to understand."

Someone went to find out who those voices came from and learned that they came from people who had convinced themselves of false beliefs and who wanted to be trusted in as oracles and worshiped on that account.

"Don't be surprised at that," the angels said. "There are a tremendous number of people like that these days. From our point of view in heaven they look like sculptures skillfully made in such a way that the lips can move and they can make sounds as if they were alive.[280] They are unaware, however, of whether the breath that supports their sound comes from hell or heaven, because they don't know whether what they are saying is false or true. They reason and reason and provide one supporting argument after another, but cannot tell at all whether something is true or not. It is important to be aware that human ingenuity can provide arguments to support any assertion it wants, even to the point that the assertion appears to be true. Heretics have this ability; godless people, too; in fact, atheists are able to argue that there is no God except nature alone."[281]

[13] After that, the group of British spirits was stirred with a desire for wisdom. They said to the angels, "There is such a wide range of opinions on the *Holy Supper*. Tell us what the truth is."

"The truth is," the angels replied, "that through that most holy act, people who turn to the Lord and practice repentance form a partnership with the Lord and become part of heaven."

Some in the group said, "That is a mystery!"

"It is a mystery," the angels replied, "but one that can be understood nevertheless. Bread and wine do not produce this effect—there is nothing holy about them; but physical bread and spiritual bread have a mutual correspondence. So do physical wine and spiritual wine. Spiritual bread is holy love and spiritual wine is holy faith. Each is from the Lord, and each is the Lord. Therefore a partnership of the Lord with us, and of us with the Lord, comes about not through the bread and wine but through the love and faith in the individual who has practiced repentance. To join in a partnership with the Lord is also to become part of heaven."

After the angels taught them something about correspondences, some in the group said, "Now for the first time we can understand this, too!"

When they said that, to my surprise something flamelike from heaven came down with light[282] and united them with the angels, and the angels and the spirits felt love for each other.

622   *The second memorable occurrence.* People's preparation for heaven occurs in the world of spirits, which is midway between heaven and hell. Once the time of their preparation has come to an end, they are all seized with an intense longing for heaven. Soon their eyes are opened and they see a pathway to a community in heaven. They take this pathway and make their ascent. At the top they come to a gated entrance with a guard. The guard opens the gate and allows them in. Then someone stops them for questioning and passes on word from the governor that they are to go farther into the community and look around to see whether there are any homes there that they recognize as their own. (There is a new home for every newly arrived angel.) If they find their home, they stay there and send a report back to that effect. If they do not find a home there, they go back and say that they did not see one. In that case, a wise person explores whether the light they have agrees with the light in that community, and especially whether the heat they have is the same. In essence, the light in heaven is divine truth and the heat is divine goodness. Both of them emanate from the Lord, who is the sun there. If the new arrivals have a different light and heat than that community has, that is, if they have a different truth and goodness, they are not accepted there. They leave and travel along pathways that are open between communities in heaven until they find a community that is in complete harmony with the feelings in their hearts. That is their home forever, because there they are among their own people, who are like relatives and friends that they love with all their heart because they share the same passions. There they experience the happiness that makes them most alive and their heart fills with delight because their soul is at peace. The intense pleasure of the heat and light of heaven cannot be expressed in words. Angels share that joy with each other. This is what happens to people who become angels.

[2] People who are involved in evils and falsities are given permission to go up to heaven as well; but when they enter it they begin to gasp and struggle for breath. Soon their vision blurs, their intellect shuts down and their thinking comes to a stop, and they feel as though they are looking death in the face, so they stand there stock-still. Then they start to have heart palpitations and chest pains, and their mind is overcome with agony and an ever increasing torment. By that point they are writhing like a snake placed too close to a fire. They roll themselves away and hurl themselves over a cliff that appears at that moment; they do not stop moving until they are in hell among people like themselves where they can take a deep breath and where their heart can again beat at its own rhythm.

After that they hate heaven, they reject the truth, and they have a blasphemous ill will toward the Lord, because they believe that he was responsible for the torture and torment they suffered in heaven.

[3] From these few sentences you can see what outcome awaits people who regard the truths that relate to faith as worthless (even though those truths constitute the light that angels have in heaven) and who regard good actions that come from love and goodwill as worthless (even though those good actions constitute the vital heat that angels have in heaven).

You can also see how seriously mistaken it is to believe that everyone can enjoy the bliss of heaven once she or he is allowed in. Nevertheless there is a belief today that getting into heaven is just a matter of mercy; and that getting into heaven is just like going to a wedding reception in this world and experiencing joy and happiness there.

People need to know that in the spiritual world, whatever desires you feel as a result of what you love and whatever thoughts they lead to are shared with everyone, because you will then be spirits, and desires related to love and the thoughts that result are the life of the spirit. Compatible desires bring people together and incompatible desires drive them apart; and incompatibility of that kind causes torment. A devil experiences this torment in heaven and an angel experiences it in hell. Therefore spirits are appropriately separated from each other based on all the varieties and diversities and differences in the desires they have as a result of what they love.

623 *The third memorable occurrence.* On one occasion I was given the experience of seeing three hundred people (some clergy, some laypeople), all of whom were considered learned and well educated because they were skilled at supporting the idea of justification by faith alone.[283] (Some took faith alone even farther than that.) Because they had the belief that going to heaven is just a matter of being let in by grace, they were granted permission to go up into a community of heaven (although it was not one of the higher communities). As they went up, they looked from a distance like calves. When they entered heaven, they were treated with civility by the angels, but as they began to converse with each other, the people began to shake. They experienced dread and then almost deadly torture. They threw themselves down from there headfirst. As they fell they looked like dead horses.

The reason they looked like calves as they went up was that an earthly feeling of excitement about what one is about to see and find out appears [in heaven] like a calf, because there is a correspondence. The reason they looked like dead horses as they fell back down was that one's understanding of truth looks like a horse, again because there is a correspondence. A complete lack of understanding of the truth of the church looks like a dead horse.

[2] There were children below that place, who saw them coming down and looking like dead horses. The children turned their faces away and said to their teacher, who was with them at the time, "What kind of omen is that? At first we saw them as people, but now we see them as dead horses instead. We turned our faces away because we couldn't bear to look. Teacher, we don't want to stay here anymore. Can we leave?" So they all left.

As they were going along the road, the teacher told them what a dead horse means: "A horse means a person's understanding of truth from the Word. All those horses you saw had that meaning. When people are walking along and meditating on the Word, their meditation looks from a distance like a horse. The horse looks alive and of good breeding if their meditation is spiritual in nature; but it looks pitiful or even dead if their meditation is physical in nature."

[3] "What is the difference between a meditation on the Word that is spiritual in nature and a meditation on the Word that is physical in nature?" the children asked.

"I will illustrate this with examples," the teacher replied. "When people are reading the Word devoutly, surely they are all thinking to themselves about God, their neighbor, and heaven. All who think about God only on the basis of how he is portrayed and not how he is in his essence are thinking physically. Likewise, all who think about their neighbor only on the basis of how they look on the outside and not what their quality is on the inside are thinking physically. And all who think about heaven as just a place and do not consider the love and wisdom that make heaven heaven are thinking physically."

[4] "But we have thought about God on the basis of how he is portrayed," the children said. "We have thought about our neighbors on the basis of their form as human beings. We have thought about heaven as a place that is up above us. When we were reading the Word, did we look like dead horses to anyone?"

"No," the teacher said. "You are still children. You couldn't help thinking that way; but I perceive a desire in you to know and understand. Because that desire is spiritual, you have actually had thoughts that are spiritual. There is some spiritual thinking that lies behind your thoughts of a physical nature, although you are not aware of it.

"But let me go back to what I was saying, which is that people who think physically when they read the Word or reflect on it look at a distance like a dead horse; people who read and reflect spiritually, look like a living horse; and thinking about God only on the basis of how he is portrayed and not on the basis of his essence is thinking physically.

"There are many attributes of the divine essence, such as omnipotence, omniscience, omnipresence, eternity, love, wisdom, mercy, grace, and so on. There are also attributes that emanate from the divine essence, which are the functions of creating, conserving, redeeming, saving, enlightening, and instructing. All who think about God on the basis of how he is portrayed come up with three gods, because they say, 'One God is the Creator and Preserver, the second is the Redeemer and Savior, and the third is the Enlightener and Instructor.'[284] On the other hand, all who think about God on the basis of his essence come up with one God, because they say,

'God created us. God also redeems us and saves us, and he also enlightens and instructs us.'

"This is why people who think about the divine Trinity on the basis of how it is portrayed, and therefore think physically, cannot help coming up with three gods instead of one, based on the images in their physical kind of thinking. Nevertheless, contrary to their own thinking, they are constrained to say that there is a unity of the three through their essence; because they do in fact have at least a few vague thoughts about God's essence.

[5] "So, students, think of God in terms of his essence, and then consider how he is portrayed. Basing your thinking about his essence on how he is portrayed is thinking physically, even about his essence; whereas basing your thinking about how he is portrayed on what his essence is, is thinking spiritually, even about how he is portrayed.

"Because people in classical times thought physically about God and about his attributes, they came up with not just three gods but a great many, approaching a hundred. They turned each attribute into a god.[285]

"Keep in mind that what is physical does not influence what is spiritual, but what is spiritual does influence what is physical.

"Thinking of our neighbors in terms of their outward form and not their inner qualities is the same mistake. So is thinking of heaven as a place and not considering the love and wisdom that constitute heaven. The same goes for each and every detail in the Word. Therefore people who hold on to physical ideas of God, the neighbor, and heaven cannot understand anything in the Word. The Word to them is a dead letter. While they are reading it or meditating on it, from a distance they look like a dead horse.

[6] "The people you saw coming down from heaven, who turned into dead horses before your eyes, are people who closed their rational sight to the theological and spiritual teachings of the church, both for themselves and for others, through the strange dogma that the intellect has to be held under obedience to their faith.

"They failed to consider that closing off the intellect for religious reasons renders it as blind as a mole; it fills it with thick darkness, and a kind of darkness that actually rejects all spiritual light. It blocks that light from flowing in from the Lord and heaven, and throws a bolt against it all the way down on the level of the physical senses, far below the rationality that should be considering matters of faith. It puts that bolt in the side of the nose and fastens it in the nasal cartilage so that such people are prevented from even smelling things that are spiritual. As a result, some who become like this actually lose consciousness when they catch a whiff of something spiritual. By 'a whiff' I mean a perception.

"This is the type of person who turns God into three. Yes, they say that as far as essence is concerned, there is one God. Nevertheless, when they say prayers that are based on their faith, praying that God the Father have mercy for the sake of the Son and send the Holy Spirit, clearly they are making three gods. How could they not? They are praying to one to have mercy for the sake of another and to send a third."

Then their teacher taught them about the Lord, that he is the one God, and that the divine Trinity exists within him.

The fourth memorable occurrence. I woke up in the middle of the night and saw an angel quite high up toward the east. The angel was holding a piece of paper in his right hand that was shining brightly because of the sun.[286] On the middle of the page there were words in gold lettering; I saw the words *The Marriage of Goodness and Truth.* A glow shone from the writing that extended to form a large halo around the piece of paper. That halo or aura looked like the dawn of a morning in spring.

624

Then I saw the angel coming down, still carrying the piece of paper in his hand. As he came down, the piece of paper became less and less radiant, and the writing on it that said *The Marriage of Goodness and Truth* turned from gold to silver, then copper, then iron; it eventually became the color of rusty iron and tarnished copper. Then I saw the angel drop into a dark storm cloud and pass through it to the ground. There the piece of paper was no longer visible, although the angel was still holding it in his hand. This was in the world of spirits, the place where all of us first come together after we die.

[2] The angel addressed me and said, "Ask the people who are coming here whether they can see me or anything in my hand." Great throngs of people then arrived. One great crowd came from the east, another from the south, another from the west, and another from the north.

The new arrivals from the east and the south were people who during their lives in the world had been devoted to learning. I asked them whether they could see anyone here with me, and if so, was there anything in his hand. They all said that they could not see anything of the sort.

The new arrivals from the west and the north were people who during their lives in the world had believed what they were told by the educated. I asked them the same question. They said they too saw nothing. Nevertheless, after all the earlier people in their groups had moved on, the last people to arrive from the west and north said that they did see a man with a piece of paper. They were people who through goodwill during their lives in the world had come to have a simple faith, or who knew some truth because of their goodness. They said the man they saw was well dressed and the piece of paper had neatly written lettering on it. When they looked at it more closely they said they read the words, "The marriage of goodness and truth."

[3] They addressed the angel directly and asked him to tell them what this meant.

The angel said, "From creation, all things that are in the whole of heaven and all things that are in the whole world are nothing but a marriage of goodness and truth, since each and every thing, whether it lives and moves or does not, was created both *from* a marriage of goodness and truth and *for* that marriage. Nothing was created for truth alone, and nothing was created for goodness alone. Neither truth nor goodness is anything on its own, but when they marry each other they become something, and the nature of that something depends on the quality of their marriage.

"In the Lord God the Creator, divine goodness and divine truth exist in their essential quality. The divine goodness is the underlying reality within that essential quality; the divine truth is that quality's capacity to become manifest.[287] They also enjoy a complete union together, since in the Lord they become one in an infinite variety of ways. Since these two are one in God the Creator, they are also one in each and every thing that was created by him. As a result, there is also an eternal covenant, like a marriage, that joins the Creator to all that he created."

[4] The angel also noted that Sacred Scripture, which was dictated by the Lord, is as a whole and in every part a marriage of goodness and truth. (See above, §§248–253.)

"For Christians," he added, "Sacred Scripture is the sole source of the *church,* which is formed from true teachings, and *religious practice,* which is formed from good actions that follow those true teachings; therefore you can see that the church, too, is as a whole and in every part a marriage of goodness and truth.

"The same things that were just said about the marriage of goodness and truth also apply to *the marriage of goodwill and faith,* since goodness relates to goodwill and truth relates to faith."

After saying this, the angel rose up off the ground and flew up through the storm cloud into heaven. As he ascended, the piece of paper began shining again as it had before. To my astonishment, the halo that had looked like the dawn when I first saw it now came down and dispersed the storm cloud that had been darkening the land. The weather became warm and sunny.

The fifth memorable occurrence. On one occasion when I was meditating on the Lord's Second Coming, an intensely bright light suddenly appeared and shone right in my eyes. I looked up and was amazed to see that the whole heaven[288] above me was full of light. I heard praises upon praises in a long chain from the east to the west.

An angel appeared by me and said, "These praises are glorifying the Lord on account of his Coming. The praises are coming from angels of the eastern and western heavens."

All that was heard from the southern and northern heavens was a gentle murmur.

Because the angel was hearing it all, he first said to me, "The praises they are using to celebrate the Lord come from the Word."

Soon afterward he said, "Now they are specifically glorifying and celebrating the Lord with the following words in the prophet Daniel:

> You saw iron mixed with muddy clay, but they will not stick together. But in those days God will make a kingdom rise in the heavens, which will not pass away throughout the ages. It will grind down and consume all the [other] kingdoms, but it will stand throughout the ages. (Daniel 2:43, 44)

[2] After that I heard something like a voice singing, and farther to the east I saw a brilliant light that was even brighter than the one I had seen before. I asked the angel what the praises were there. He said they were praising the Lord with the following words in Daniel:

> I saw visions in the night, and behold, *the Son of Humankind* was coming with the clouds of heaven. He was given dominion and a kingdom. All peoples and nations will worship him. His dominion is a dominion of an age that will not pass, and his kingdom is one that will not perish. (Daniel 7:13, 14)

"They are also celebrating the Lord with the following words from the Book of Revelation.

> Jesus Christ has glory and strength. Behold, he is coming with the clouds. He is the Alpha and the Omega,[289] the Beginning and the End, the First and the Last, the One who is, who was, and who is to come,

625

the Almighty. I, John, heard this from *the Son of Humankind* among the seven lampstands. (Revelation 1:5, 6, 7, 10, 11, 12, 13; 22:8, 13; also Matthew 24:30, 31)

[3] I looked again at the eastern heaven, and it lit up to the right, and its brightness extended into the southern expanse. I heard a sweet sound. I asked the angel, "What are *their* praises for the Lord?"

The angel said, "They are using the following words in the Book of Revelation.

> I saw a new heaven and a new earth, and I saw the holy city, the new Jerusalem, coming down from God out of heaven, prepared like a *bride* for *her husband.* I heard a loud voice from heaven, saying, "Behold, the tabernacle of God is among *people,* and he will dwell with them." And the angel spoke with me saying, "Come, I will show you *the bride, the wife of the Lamb."* And [the angel] carried me away in the spirit to the top of a mountain great and high, and showed me the city, holy Jerusalem. (Revelation 21:1, 2, 3, 9, 10)[290]

"They are also using these words.

> "I, Jesus, am the bright and morning star." And the spirit and the *bride* say, "Come!" And he said, "*I am coming quickly."* Truly indeed, *come, Lord Jesus.* (Revelation 22:16, 17, 20)

[4] After these and many other praises, there was an overall praise that went from the east to the west of heaven and also from the south to the north.

I asked the angel, "What now?"

"These praises," the angel replied, "are using the following passages from the prophets.

> So that all flesh may know that I, *Jehovah, am your Savior and your Redeemer.* (Isaiah 49:26)

> Thus said Jehovah, the King of Israel and *its Redeemer, Jehovah Sabaoth:* "I am the First and *the Last, and there is no God except me."* (Isaiah 44:6)

> It will be said in that day, "*Behold, this is our God.* We have waited for him to free us. *This is Jehovah whom we have waited for."* (Isaiah 25:9)

> The voice of one crying in the desert, "Prepare a way for Jehovah. *Behold, the Lord Jehovih is coming with strength;* like *a shepherd* he will feed his flock." (Isaiah 40:3, 10, 11)

A Child is born to us; a Son is given to us. His name will be called Wonderful, Counselor, God, Hero, *Father of Eternity,* Prince of Peace. (Isaiah 9:6)

Behold, the days are coming when I will raise up for David a righteous offshoot who will reign as king; and this is his name: *Jehovah is our Justice.* (Jeremiah 23:5, 6; 33:15, 16)

Jehovah Sabaoth is his name, *your Redeemer, the Holy One of Israel. He will be called God of all the earth.* (Isaiah 54:5)

In that day, Jehovah will be king over the whole earth; in that day there will be one Jehovah, and his name will be one. (Zechariah 14:9)

Because I heard and understood these things, my heart rejoiced. Filled with joy, I went home, and there returned from the state of my spirit into the state of my body and wrote down the things that I had heard and seen.

Chapter 11

The Assignment of Spiritual Credit or Blame

The Faith of the Church of Today, Which Is Claimed to Be the Sole Thing That Makes Us Just, and the Belief That Christ's Merit Is Assigned to Us Amount to the Same Thing

626 THE faith of the church of today, which is claimed to be the sole basis of our justification,[291] *is* the belief that Christ's merit is assigned to us; that is, the two concepts amount to the same thing. This is because each belongs to the other or is a part of the other and supports the other's existence.

If you mention faith but you do not include the idea of an assigning, the word "faith" is just a meaningless sound. By the same token, if you mention an assigning but you forget to mention faith, that too is a meaningless sound. If the two are mentioned together, however, now the sounds start to form a phrase, although understanding will still not occur. To engage the intellect, it is necessary to add a third element: the merit of Christ. Now you have a sentence that can be uttered with some rationality, because the faith of the church of today is that God the Father assigns us the justice of his Son and sends the Holy Spirit to produce its effects.

627 Therefore in the church of today, these three—faith, the concept of assigning, and the merit of Christ—are one. They could be called a triune concept, because if any of the three is taken away, the theology of today becomes nothing. Like a long chain hanging on a carefully fastened hook, the theology of today hangs on those three points taken as a single doctrine. If faith or the concept of assigning or the merit of Christ were taken out of the equation, everything that the church says about how we are made just, how our sins are forgiven, and how we are brought to life, renewed, regenerated, and sanctified, and also everything it says about the gospel, free choice, goodwill and good works, and in fact eternal life—all this would be like an abandoned city, or rubble that was once a church building. That leading faith would be nothing and therefore the entire church would be deserted and uninhabited.

These points clarify what the pillars are that are supporting the house of God today. If these pillars were pulled down, the church would collapse like the house where the satraps of the Philistines and some three thousand other people were enjoying themselves. Samson pulled down the two pillars of that house at the same time, so that the Philistines died or were killed (Judges 16:29, 30). I say this because, as has been shown above and will be shown in the appendix below,[292] the faith in question is not Christian—it disagrees with what the Word teaches; and it is meaningless to speak of the concept of assigning in connection with that faith, since Christ's merit is not assignable.

The Concept of Assigning That Is Part of the Faith of Today Has a Doubleness to It: There Is an Assigning of Christ's Merit, and There Is an Assigning of Salvation as a Result

The entire Christian church holds that God the Father grants justification, and therefore salvation, by assigning the merit of Christ, his Son. This assigning is thought to take place by grace "whenever and wherever God wants." It is his choice. People who are assigned the merit of Christ are adopted and counted as children of God.

628

The leaders of the church have not taken a single step beyond this concept of the assignment of merit or lifted their minds above it. Because of their theory that God makes his choice arbitrarily, they have lapsed into wild and horrendous errors. They have eventually wandered even into the detestable notion of predestination and the abominable idea that God pays no attention to what we do in our lives; he only regards the faith that is inscribed on the deeper levels of our minds.

If this error about the assignment of merit is not destroyed, atheism is going to pervade all Christianity, and Christians will then be ruled by the king of the abyss, "whose name in Hebrew is Abaddon and who has the Greek name Apollyon" (Revelation 9:11). [2] Both "Abaddon" and

"Apollyon" mean one who destroys the church with falsities. The *abyss* means [the hell] in which these falsities exist. (See *Revelation Unveiled* 421, 440, 442.) It follows then that this false concept regarding the assignment of merit, and all the false beliefs that follow from it in an extended series, are the very things over which the Destroyer rules. As noted just above [§627], the entire Christian theological system depends on that concept of the assignment of merit like a long chain hanging on a carefully fastened hook; it also depends on it the way we and all our limbs depend on our head. This concept of the assignment of Christ's merit is dominant everywhere; therefore it is as Isaiah says: "The Lord will cut the head and the tail off Israel. The head is the person who is honored; the tail is the person who teaches lies" (Isaiah 9:14, 15).

629   The heading above states that the "assigning" that is included in the faith of today has a doubleness to it. I do not mean *double*[293] in the sense that God and his mercy toward all are two things, but *double* in the sense that God's mercy applies to some [and not others]. I do not mean *double* in the sense that parents and their abundant love toward all their children are two things, but *double* in the sense of parents who love one or two of their children but not the rest. I do not mean *double* in the sense that the divine law and its application to all are two things, but *double* in the sense that the divine law applies to just a few. The one kind of doubleness then is broad and applies in the same way to all; the other is restricted and divisive. The first possesses unity; the second double-dealing.

The teaching today is that Christ's merit is assigned by an arbitrary choice. Those who benefit from it have salvation assigned to them. Therefore some are adopted and the rest are rejected. This would be like God lifting some people into the safety of Abraham's embrace [Luke 16:22] but handing others off as scraps of food to the Devil.

The truth is that the Lord rejects no one and hands no one away. We do that to ourselves.

630   For another thing, the modern-day concept that Christ's merit is assigned to us takes away any notion whatsoever that we have the power of free choice in spiritual matters. It does not even leave us enough free choice to pat out a flame on our clothes and keep our body safe, or use water to extinguish a fire in our home and save our family. Yet the Word from beginning to end teaches that we must all abstain from things that are evil, because they belong to the Devil and come from the Devil; we must do things that are good, because they belong to God and come from God; and we must do these things under our own initiative, but with the help of the Lord.

The modern-day concept that Christ's merit is assigned to us, however, denies us the power to do these things, on the grounds that doing them would be deadly to our faith and salvation; it aims to prevent anything of ourselves from interfering with that assigning of Christ's merit.

Once that notion was established, it spawned the satanic concept that we are completely powerless in spiritual matters. This is like telling someone, "Walk, but you have no feet." "Wash yourselves, but both of your hands have been amputated." "Do what is good, but sleep now." "Eat something nutritious, but don't use your tongue."

It is the same as saying that we are endowed with a kind of will that is not actually a will. What is to stop us from saying the following? "I have no more capability than Lot's wife as a pillar of salt [Genesis 19:26]. I have no more power than Dagon, the god of the Philistines, when the ark of God was brought into Dagon's shrine. I am afraid that, like Dagon's, my head too will be pulled off and my hands will be broken off on the threshold (1 Samuel 5:4). I have no more power than Beelzebub, the god of Ekron. To judge by his name, his only power is to keep flies away."[294]

(For evidence that the church of today believes in extreme powerlessness in spiritual matters, see the quotes on free choice assembled above in §464.)

As regards the first of the two types of "assigning" that are said to contribute to our salvation—the arbitrary assigning of Christ's merit, which is followed by the assigning of salvation—theologians have differing views on this. Some say that this assigning takes place as the result of God's absolute power, which he can exercise at will; it occurs in people whose outer or inner form are pleasing to God. Others hold that this assigning is based on God's foreknowledge; it is granted to those who have been given grace and are going to be receptive to that faith.

631

Although these two opinions are coming from different angles, they nevertheless aim at the same target. They are like two eyes that are looking at the same stone or two ears that are listening to the same song. At first glance they may seem divergent, but they come to the same result.

Both sides maintain that we are completely powerless in spiritual matters, and everything we have to offer is excluded from faith. Therefore whether the grace that is receptive to faith is poured in at will or on the basis of foreknowledge, it amounts to the same thing: the notion that God chooses some but not others. If, on the other hand, that grace (which is called preexistent) were universal, our making some effort of our own to apply ourselves would be helpful; but both theories treat this thought like leprosy.

According to them, we know no more than a log or a stone about whether grace has granted us faith yet or not. If faith has been poured into us, we do not know what it is like. There is no real evidence that faith is present, since this position denies the human race any goodwill, godliness, or effort to start a new life, or even the freedom or faculty for doing anything good or evil.

The signs that supposedly do testify to the presence of faith in us are all laughable. They are no different from the augury the ancients practiced using the flight of birds.[295] They are no different from the choices astrologers make based on the stars or gamblers make based on a roll of the dice. Ideas this ridiculous and worse follow from the notion that the Lord's justice is assignable, and that his divine justice, together with faith (which they also refer to as justice), is actually integrated into the so-called elect.

The Concept of a Faith That Assigns Us the Merit and Justice of Christ the Redeemer First Surfaced in the Decrees of the Council of Nicaea Concerning Three Divine Persons from Eternity; from That Time to the Present This Faith Has Been Accepted by the Entire Christian World

632 The Council of Nicaea was hosted by the emperor Constantine the Great in his palace in Nicaea, a city in Bithynia. He had been persuaded to call the council by Alexander, bishop of Alexandria. All the bishops of Asia, Africa, and Europe were invited. Their charge was to challenge and condemn, using Sacred Scripture, the heresy of Arius, a presbyter in Alexandria who was denying that Jesus Christ was divine. The council occurred in the year of our Lord 325.[296]

The participants in the council came to the conclusion that three divine persons had existed from eternity: the Father, the Son, and the Holy Spirit. This is particularly easy to see from the two statements called the Nicene Creed and the Athanasian Creed.[297]

In the Nicene Creed we read the following:

> I believe in one God, the Father Almighty, Creator of heaven and earth. I believe in one Lord, Jesus Christ, the Son of God, the only

begotten of the Father, born before all the ages, God from God, who has the same substance as the Father, and who came down from the heavens and was incarnated by the Holy Spirit through the Virgin Mary. And I believe in the Holy Spirit, the Lord and Life-giver, who proceeds from the Father and the Son, and who along with the Father and the Son is worshiped and glorified.[298]

[2] The following statement appears in the Athanasian Creed.

The catholic[299] faith is this, that we venerate one God in a trinity, and the Trinity in unity, neither confusing the persons nor dividing the substance. Just as Christian truth compels us to confess each person individually as God and Lord, so the catholic religion forbids us to say that there are three gods or three lords.

That is, it is allowable to *confess* three gods and lords but not to *say* three gods and lords. We do not *say* three gods and lords because religion forbids it, but we *confess* three gods and lords because that is what the truth dictates.

The Athanasian Creed was composed immediately after the Council of Nicaea by one or more of the people who had attended that council. It was accepted as an ecumenical or catholic creed.

Clearly, then, that was when it was decreed that the church should acknowledge three divine persons from eternity, each of whom is individually God, although there should be no mention of three gods or lords but only of one.

After that time a belief in three divine persons was accepted, ratified, and proclaimed by all the bishops, prelates, church leaders, and elders in the Christian world right up to the present day, as we all know.

633

Because this belief led directly to a mental image of three gods, it could not help but result in a faith that is applied to these three persons in sequence. That is, we are to turn to God the Father and beg that he either assign us the justice of his Son or else have mercy on us because of the Son's suffering on the cross, and send us the Holy Spirit to produce the intermediate and final effects of our salvation.

[2] This belief is the offspring that was born from these two creeds. When the swaddling cloths are unraveled, however, what comes into view is not one child but three. At first the three are joined in a kind of embrace, but soon they are separated. People have decided that the three are joined by one essence but distinguished by various properties or activities: creating, redeeming, and working; or the assigning of justice, the justice assigned, and the carrying into effect, respectively. Although people made one God

out of these three, they did not make one Person out of these three persons; if they had, the idea of three gods would have been obliterated. As long as each person is individually recognized as a God, as the creed indicates, this trinitarian view remains in place. The danger was that if three persons were to have become one, the whole house built upon these three as its pillars would have collapsed into a heap.

[3] The Council of Nicaea introduced the idea of three divine persons from eternity for the reason that it had not properly examined the Word and had therefore found no other protection against the Arians. The reason why they then collated those three persons, each of whom is God all by himself, into one was out of fear. They were afraid that every rational, religious person on all three continents[300] would have accused them of believing in three gods and would have vilified them.

The reason why they handed down a belief that applied to those three in sequence was that no other belief would have been consistent with that starting point.

One might add to this that if one of the three were omitted, the third would not be sent out, and so all the workings of divine grace would be ineffectual.

634   The truth should be made public: When a faith in three gods was introduced into the Christian churches, which happened from the time of the Council of Nicaea, all the goodness related to goodwill and all the truth related to faith were sent into exile, because goodwill and faith are incompatible with mental worship of three gods mixed with oral worship of one God. The mind in that case denies what the mouth is saying, and the mouth denies what the mind is thinking. The result is that there is no real faith in three gods and no real faith in one God either.

Clearly, then, from that time on, the Christian temple did not just develop cracks; it collapsed into a pile of rubble. From that time on, the pit of the abyss was opened, and smoke arose from it like the smoke of a great furnace, darkening the sun and the air, and locusts came out of it onto the ground (Revelation 9:2, 3; see the explanation of these verses in *Revelation Unveiled* [§§422–425]). In fact, from that time on, the desolation foretold by Daniel [Daniel 9:2, 26, 27; 11:31; 12:11] began and increased (Matthew 24:15). The eagles gathered around that faith and its idea that merit can be assigned to us (Matthew 24:28); the *eagles* in that passage mean the sharp-sighted leaders of the church.

[2] If someone responds by pointing out that all the bishops and celebrated men at that council made this decision *by a unanimous vote,* I would

counter by asking whether we should have any faith in councils. Was it not also by a unanimous vote that the Roman Catholic councils decided the pope is the vicar of Christ, saints ought to be invoked, relics and bones should be venerated, and the elements in the Holy Eucharist should be separated?[301] Is this not how they came up with purgatory, indulgences, and so on?[302] Why should we have confidence in councils, when the Synod of Dort, again with a unanimous vote, decided on the detestable notion of predestination and erected it as a central religious icon?[303]

O reader of mine, put your trust in the holy Word rather than in councils, and turn to the Lord and you will be enlightened. The Lord *is* the Word. That is, the divine truth itself is there.

To round out this section, the following mystery will be disclosed. Seven chapters of the Book of Revelation,[304] in describing the end of the church of today, use language similar to that which Exodus uses to describe the devastation of Egypt. In both cases there are similar plagues, each of which has as its spiritual meaning some falsity that brought on this devastation even to the point of death. Therefore the church that is being destroyed today is called *Egypt,* understood spiritually (Revelation 11:8).

635

The plagues in Egypt were as follows. The water was turned into blood, causing the death of every fish, and the river stank (Exodus 7). Similar statements are made in Revelation 8:8; 16:3. *Blood* means divine truth that has been falsified; see *Revelation Unveiled* 379, 404, 681, 687, 688. The fish that then died mean truths in our earthly self (*Revelation Unveiled* 290, 405).

Frogs came up on the land of Egypt (Exodus 8). There is also a mention of frogs in Revelation 16:13. *Frogs* mean reasonings born of a desire to falsify truths; see *Revelation Unveiled* 702.

Painful sores came upon the people and animals in Egypt (Exodus 9). A similar thing occurs in Revelation 16:2. *Sores* mean inner evils and falsities that destroy the good qualities and true teachings of the church; see *Revelation Unveiled* 678.

Hail and fire fell on Egypt (Exodus 9). Something similar occurs in Revelation 8:7; 16:21. *Hail* means hellish falsity; see *Revelation Unveiled* 399, 714.

Locusts came up over Egypt (Exodus 10). A similar thing occurs in Revelation 9:1–11. *Locusts* mean falsities on the lowest level; see *Revelation Unveiled* 424, 430.

Thick darkness came upon Egypt (Exodus 10). A similar thing occurs in Revelation 8:12. *Darkness* means falsities that arise from ignorance, or from false religious beliefs, or from evils in our lives; see *Revelation Unveiled* 110, 413, 695.

Eventually, the Egyptians perished in the Reed Sea[305] (Exodus 14). In the Book of Revelation, though, the dragon and the false prophet perish in a lake of fire and sulfur (Revelation 19:20; 20:10). Both of these—the Reed Sea and the lake of fire and sulfur—mean hell.

The reason why similar things are said of Egypt and of the church whose close and end are described in the Book of Revelation is that *Egypt* means a church that at its outset was outstanding. This is why Egypt, before the devastation of its church, is compared to the Garden of Eden and the garden of Jehovah (Genesis 13:10; Ezekiel 31:8). It is also called the cornerstone of the tribes, and a child of the wise and of the ancient monarchs (Isaiah 19:11, 13). For more on Egypt in its original state and in its state of devastation, see *Revelation Unveiled* 503.

The Concept of a Faith That Assigns the Merit of Christ Was Completely Unknown in the Apostolic Church That Existed before the Council of Nicaea; and Nothing in the Word Conveys That Concept Either

636 The church that existed before the Council of Nicaea was called the apostolic church. The fact that this was an extensive church that had developed on three of the world's continents (Asia, Africa, and Europe) is clear from the empire of Constantine the Great, which included many countries in Europe (though they later separated from the empire), as well as nearby countries outside of Europe. Constantine was a Christian and a vigorous champion of his religion. Therefore, as mentioned above, he called together bishops from Asia, Africa, and Europe to his palace in the city of Nicaea in Bithynia in order to throw Arius's offences out of his empire.

This happened as a result of the Lord's divine providence, because a denial of the Lord's divinity would have killed the Christian church and made it like a tomb engraved with the epitaph "Here lies . . ."

[2] The church that existed before that time was called the apostolic church; its noteworthy writers were called the apostolic fathers, and other true Christians were called brothers and sisters. It is clear from the creed known as the Apostles' Creed (so named for the church at the time)[306]

that that church did not acknowledge three divine persons, and that it did acknowledge a Son of God born in time but not a Son of God from eternity:

> I believe in God, the Father Almighty, Creator of heaven and earth. I believe in Jesus Christ, his only begotten Son, our Lord, who was conceived of the Holy Spirit and born of the Virgin Mary. I believe in the Holy Spirit, the holy catholic church, and the communion of saints.[307]

Clearly, then, they acknowledged no other Son of God than the one who was conceived of the Holy Spirit and born of the Virgin Mary, which completely rules out any Son of God born from eternity. This creed, like the other two,[308] has been accepted as a true and universal creed by the entire Christian church right up to our time.

In those early times, all who were then part of the Christian world acknowledged that the Lord Jesus Christ was God and that he had all power in heaven and on earth and power over all flesh, as he himself says (Matthew 28:18; John 17:2). In obedience to his command from God the Father, they believed in him (John 3:15, 16, 36; 6:40; 11:25, 26). The truth of this is obvious from the fact that when Arius and his followers began denying the divinity of our Lord and Savior who was born from the Virgin Mary, the emperor Constantine the Great called together all the bishops in order to convict and condemn that position, using Sacred Scripture. The bishops did indeed accomplish this, but to avoid a wolf they stumbled onto a lion, or as the saying goes, the one who tried to avoid Charybdis fell upon Scylla:[309] They invented a Son of God from eternity, who descended and took on a human nature. They believed that by doing this they had rescued and restored the Lord's divinity. They did not realize that God himself, the Creator of the universe, had come down in order to become the Redeemer and therefore to be the Creator once again, according to the following clear statements in the Old Testament: Isaiah 25:9; 40:3, 5, 10, 11; 43:14; 44:6, 24; 47:4; 48:17; 49:7, 26; 60:16; 63:16; Jeremiah 50:34; Hosea 13:4; Psalms 19:14.[310]

637

The apostolic church, which worshiped the Lord God Jesus Christ, and at the same time God the Father in him, can be compared to the garden of God.[311] Arius, who arose then, is like the serpent sent in from hell. The Council of Nicaea is like Adam's wife, who offered fruit to her husband and persuaded him to eat it. After eating the fruit, they appeared naked to themselves, so they covered their nakedness with fig leaves. Their nakedness symbolizes the innocence they had before that

638

point. The fig leaves symbolize the truths belonging to their earthly self, which were falsified more and more.

That early church can also be compared to the twilight before dawn and the early morning, and on through the day until late afternoon.[312] Then dark clouds came up, lasting until evening and continuing into the night. During the night, some places saw the moon rise. Some of the people in those places saw something in the Word in the light of the moon, but the rest continued on into such thick darkness of night that they could no longer see anything of divinity in the Lord's humanity, even though Paul says that "all the fullness of divinity dwells physically in Jesus Christ" (Colossians 2:9), and John says that "the Son of God who was sent into the world is the true God and eternal life" (1 John 5:20).

[2] The early or apostolic church could never have guessed that a church was yet to come that would say there is one God but worship three gods at heart; separate goodwill from faith; separate forgiveness of sins from repentance and the effort to lead a new life; and conclude we are completely powerless in spiritual matters. Least of all would they have guessed that some Arius would raise his head, and once dead, would rise again and secretly rule the church to the bitter end.

639   Nothing in the Word conveys this concept of a faith that assigns us the merit of Christ. This is very clear from the fact that the church had no knowledge of such a faith before the Council of Nicaea introduced the idea of three divine persons from eternity. Once that belief was brought in and it pervaded the entire Christian world, every other concept of faith was sent away into the darkness.

Therefore any who read the Word now, and see anything resembling faith, the concept of assigning, or the merit of Christ, spontaneously fall into that concept and believe it to be the only interpretation. They are like someone who sees the writing on one page and stops there and never turns the page to see anything else in the book.

[2] They are like people who convince themselves that something is true even though it is actually false and who support that point alone. Such people come to see falsity as true and the truth as false. Eventually, when anyone speaks against that point of view, they clench their teeth and hiss, "You don't understand!" By then their whole mind is wrapped up in that belief and is covered with a callus so thick that it rejects as contradictory everything that is not in agreement with their so-called orthodox beliefs. Their memory is like a writing tablet covered with the words of that one dominant theological teaching; if any other thought comes

along, their memory has no room to take it in, so they spit it out like foam from their mouth.

[3] For that matter, find convinced materialists (whether they believe that nature created itself or that God came into existence after nature or that nature and God are the same thing)[313] and tell them that the truth is the opposite of what they think. Will they not look at you as someone deluded by the fables of the church elders, or else as a simplistic or thick-headed or demented person?

The same goes for all false concepts that persuasion and conviction have fixed in place. Such concepts eventually look like a painted rug fastened with an abundance of nails to a wall that was slapped together using old broken stones.

The Merit and Justice of Christ Cannot Be Assigned to Anyone Else

To recognize that the merit and justice of Jesus Christ cannot be assigned to anyone else, it is necessary to know what his merit and his justice are. The merit of our Lord and Savior is redemption. For the nature of redemption, see the material in the relevant chapter above, §§114–133. There you will see that redemption was a matter of gaining control of the hells and restructuring the heavens, and afterward establishing a church. Therefore redemption was something only the Divine could bring about. That material also shows that through his acts of redemption the Lord took on the power to regenerate and save people who believe in him and who do what he commands.[314] Without this redemption no flesh could have been saved [Matthew 24:22].

640

Since redemption was something only the Divine could bring about and was the work of the Lord alone, and since that redemption is his merit, it follows that that merit is no more applicable or attributable or assignable to anyone else than the functions of creating and preserving the universe. Redemption was in fact a kind of re-creation of the angelic heaven and also of the church.

[2] The church of today, however, attributes that merit of the Lord the Redeemer to people who acquire faith by grace, as is clear from its teachings. This idea is central. The leaders of that church and also their followers, both in the Roman Catholic church and in the Protestant churches, say that through the assignment of Christ's merit, people who

acquire faith are not only *considered* to be just and holy but actually *are* just and holy. Their sins are not sins before God, because those sins have been forgiven and they themselves have been justified, meaning reconciled, made new, regenerated, sanctified, and assigned to heaven.

From the Council of Trent, the Ausgburg Confession, and the commentaries on them[315] that have been widely accepted, it is abundantly clear that the entire Christian church today teaches this doctrine.

[3] The claim that all these benefits are transferred into that faith leads directly to the notion that possessing that faith is the same as having the Lord's own merit and justice. Therefore one who possesses that faith is Christ in an alternate form. After all, they say Christ himself is justice, and that faith is justice, and the assigning of merit, by which they mean its attribution or application, causes us not merely to be *considered* just and holy but actually to *be* just and holy. To this assigning, attributing, and applying of merit, just add an actual transfer of it and you too will be a pope, a vicar of Christ![316]

641 In reality, the Lord's merit and justice are purely divine. The nature of purely divine things is such that if they were to be applied or attributed to us, we would instantly die and would be so thoroughly consumed, like a stick thrown into the sun itself, that not even ashes would be left. Therefore when the Lord in all his divinity approaches angels and people, he does so through a light that is tempered and moderated to suit the nature and the faculties of each individual; he works through something fully suited and accommodated to that person. The same is true for the heat through which he makes his approach.

[2] In the spiritual world there is a sun. The Lord is in the center of that sun. From it he flows, through heat and light, into the whole spiritual world and into all the people there. All the light and heat there come from that sun. The Lord also flows from that sun, with the same heat and light, into the souls and minds of people [in the material world]. That heat, in its essence, is the Lord's divine love; that light, in its essence, is the Lord's divine wisdom. The Lord adapts that light and heat to the nature and faculties of the angels and people who are receiving him. This takes place through spiritual auras or atmospheres that convey and carry that heat and light.[317] The divine qualities that directly surround the Lord constitute that sun. It stands at a distance from angels, just as the sun in the physical world stands at a distance from people, so that it will not shine on them unprotectedly and directly, because if it did, they would be consumed, as I say, like a stick thrown into the sun itself.

[3] All this makes it clear that the Lord's merit and justice, purely divine as they are, could never, ever be brought through any process of assignment into any angel or any person. In fact, without the protections just mentioned, if only one undiluted drop of it were to touch us we would immediately be tormented as if we were fighting for our lives; we would thrash about, our eyes rolling in their sockets, and die. In the Israelite church the truth of this was clear from the statement that no one can see God and live [Exodus 33:20].

[4] In the following words in Isaiah, there is a description of what was to happen to the sun of the spiritual world after Jehovah God took on a human manifestation and added to it redemption and a new justice:

> The light of the sun will be seven times as strong, like the light of seven days, on the day when Jehovah will bind up the brokenness of his people. (Isaiah 30:26)

From beginning to end, that chapter is about the Lord's Coming.

In the following words in the Book of Revelation, there is a description of what would happen if the Lord were to come down and directly approach some godless person:

> They will hide themselves in caves and in the rocks on the mountains, and they will say to the mountains and the rocks, "Hide us from the face of the One sitting on the throne and from the anger of the Lamb." (Revelation 6:15, 16)

The phrase "the anger of the Lamb" is used here because their terror and torment at the approach of the Lord makes him seem angry to them.

[5] The point I am making becomes even clearer from the fact that when any godless people are brought into heaven, where goodwill and faith in the Lord are dominant, darkness comes over their eyes, dizziness and insanity assault their minds, pain and torment afflict their bodies, and they become like dead people. What would happen, then, if the Lord himself were to come into us with his divine merit (which is redemption) and his divine justice? Even the apostle John could not bear the presence of the Lord: we read that when he saw the Son of Humankind among seven lampstands, he fell at his feet as if dead (Revelation 1:13, 17).

In the decrees of the councils and the articles of the confessions that Protestants swear to observe, we read that through an infusion of Christ's merit God justifies the godless.[318] In fact, though, not even the goodness of an angel can be communicated to a godless person, much less joined

642

to that person, without either being rejected and bouncing back like a rubber ball thrown against a solid wall, or being swallowed up like a diamond thrown into a swamp. In fact, forcing something truly good on such a person would be like tying a pearl to the snout of a pig.[319]

Surely everyone realizes that you cannot inject mercy into ruthlessness, or innocence into revenge, or love into hatred, or harmony into discord. Doing so would be like mixing heaven and hell.

People who have not been reborn are, in spirit, like panthers and eagle-owls; they can be compared to brambles and stinging nettles. People who have been reborn are like sheep and doves, and they can be compared to olive trees and grapevines. Please consider, if you will, how panther-people could possibly be converted into sheep-people, or eagle-owls into doves, or brambles into olive trees, or stinging nettles into grapevines, through any assignment or attribution or application of divine justice. Would that process not sooner condemn them than justify them? In reality, in order for that conversion to take place the predatory nature of the panther and the eagle-owl and the damaging nature of the brambles and the stinging nettles must first be removed and something truly human and harmless implanted in their place. The Lord in fact teaches in John 15:1–7 how this transformation occurs.

There Is an Assigning of Spiritual Credit, but in Addition to Whether We Have Faith, It Also Takes into Account Whether Our Actions Have Been Good or Evil

643   We are assigned spiritual credit or blame [after death][320] depending on whether our actions have been good or evil. The Word teaches this in countless passages. Some such passages have indeed been quoted earlier [§376], but to show for certain that no other "assigning" than this is meant, some passages like this will also be given here, as follows.

> The Son of Humankind is going to come. Then he will repay all according to their deeds. (Matthew 16:27)

> Those who have done good things will depart into a resurrection of life; those who have done evil things will depart into a resurrection of judgment. (John 5:29)

> A book is opened, which is the book of life, and all are judged according to their works. (Revelation 20:12, 13)

> Behold, I am coming quickly, and my reward is with me to give to all according to their work. (Revelation 22:12)

> I will bring judgment upon them according to their ways and will reward them for their works. (Hosea 4:9; Zechariah 1:6; Jeremiah 25:14; 32:19)

> In the day of his anger and just judgment, God will repay all according to their works. (Romans 2:5, 6)

> It is right for us all to appear before Christ's judgment seat, so that each of us may carry away what we have done through our body in regard to those things, whether good or evil. (2 Corinthians 5:10)

[2] When the church first began, this was the only principle governing the assignment of spiritual credit or blame. When the church comes to an end, this will still be the only principle. We see from the story of Adam and his wife that this was the principle operative when the church first began. Adam and Eve were condemned because they did something evil: they ate from the tree of the knowledge of good and evil (Genesis 2, 3). We see from the following words of the Lord that exactly the same principle will still be in effect at the end of the church:

> When the Son of Humankind comes in the glory of his Father, then he will sit on the throne of his glory and say to the sheep on the right, "Come, you who are blessed, and possess as your inheritance the kingdom prepared for you since the founding of the world; because I was hungry and you gave me something to eat. I was thirsty and you gave me something to drink. I was a stranger and you took me in. I was naked and you clothed me. I was sick and you visited me. I was in prison and you came to me." But to the goats on the left, who had not done good things, he said, "Depart from me, you who are cursed, into the eternal fire prepared for the Devil and his angels." (Matthew 25:31 and following)

From this statement, anyone with open eyes can see that we are assigned spiritual credit or blame [after death] based on whether our actions were good or evil.

[3] We are indeed assigned credit for having faith, provided genuine goodwill and true faith work together in us to produce good actions. As we have seen, if our actions are not the result of both goodwill and faith, they are not actually good; see §§373–377 above. Therefore James says:

> Was not Abraham our father justified by works when he offered his son on the altar? Do you see that faith was working together with works,

and because of its works faith was recognized as perfect? And the Scripture was fulfilled, which says, "Abraham believed God, and it was credited to him as something just." (James 2:21, 22, 23)

644 We have seen, then, that the Word speaks of an assigning of spiritual credit or blame [after death]. Leaders and officials in the Christian churches have taken these passages to mean we are given spiritual credit if we have a faith that is inscribed with the justice and merit of Christ. Why? Because for fourteen centuries, from the time of the Council of Nicaea, they had not been willing to find out that faith meant anything other than this. Therefore this was the only faith that occupied their memory and became systematized in their mind. From that time on, this faith developed a light of its own that was like a bonfire at night. In that light, this faith looked like the profoundest of theological truths, a verity on which all other truths were leaning, one on top of the other. All other truths would have collapsed, they felt, if this chief truth, this central pillar were removed.

Therefore if they had given thought while reading the Word to any other meaning of faith than "the faith that assigns Christ's merit to us," that light and their entire theology would have been extinguished, and a darkness would have arisen and caused the entire Christian church to fade away. Therefore that concept of faith was left in place, "like the stump of a root in the ground, once the tree had been cut down and destroyed, until seven times would pass over it" (Daniel 4:23).

As for today, are there any leaders of the church devoted to this teaching who do not stuff their ears with cotton when that concept of faith comes into question? They do not want to hear it.

O reader of mine, unblock your ears and read the Word, and you will clearly perceive different concepts than the ones you have convinced yourself of until now—a different meaning of faith and a different sense of how spiritual credit or blame are assigned.

645 The Word from beginning to end is full of things that bear witness to and reinforce the idea that the basis upon which we are all assigned spiritual credit or blame [after death] is whether our actions were good or evil. Christian theologians must be blocking their ears with a kind of wax and smearing their eyes with a kind of ointment to prevent themselves from ever hearing or seeing anything but the idea that their faith is the basis of salvation.

Their faith is exactly like an eye disease; it is called "transparent blockage," and it deserves to be called that, because it is a total blindness caused by an obstruction in the optic nerve, and yet the eye appears fully able to see. In a similar way, those who are devoted to that concept of faith walk around with their eyes wide open, seeming as though they can see perfectly well, and yet they cannot see a thing. They say we know nothing about that faith when it enters us, for we are like a log at the time. When we have received it we supposedly have no idea whether that faith is in us, and whether it contains anything or not. Again, they claim to see clearly that that faith then conceives and gives birth to the noble offspring of being justified: namely, having sins forgiven, being brought to life, being renewed, being regenerated, and being sanctified—and yet they say they do not see, and would not be able to see, a single sign of any of those results.

All my experience of what happens to people as they cross from this world to the next has testified to me that after death we are assigned spiritual credit or blame based on whether our actions were loving and good or wicked and evil. After our first few days in that world, we are all examined to determine our quality—that is, the quality of our religious life in the physical world. The examiners then report their findings to heaven, and we are transferred to those like ourselves—to "our people," if you will. This is how the assigning is actually carried out. 646

The fact that good actions were what saved all who are in heaven, and evil actions were what condemned all who are in hell has become clear to me from observing the way each area is organized by the Lord. The entirety of heaven is arranged into communities according to all the varieties of love for doing what is good; the entirety of hell is arranged into hordes according to all the varieties of love for doing what is evil. The Lord arranges the church on earth in a similar way, because the church corresponds to heaven. The church's religious practice is the doing of what is good.

[2] In fact, choose any rational, religious people you wish from anywhere on the planet and ask them this: "What type of person goes to heaven and what type of person goes to hell?"

They will all answer the same way: "Those who do what is good will go to heaven. Those who do what is evil will go to hell."

As we all must surely know, the amount of love a true human being has for others, whether they are individuals, groups, cities, or even whole countries, depends on how good their actions are. The same applies to things that are outside of the human realm as well. We love animals and even inanimate things like houses, possessions, fields, gardens, trees, woods, lands, and even metals and types of stone based on how good and useful they are. (How *good* they are is exactly the same as how *useful* they are.) Why then would the Lord's love for people and the church not depend on how good their actions are?

There Is No Way in Which We Can Simultaneously Hold the Views of the New Church and the Views of the Former Church on Faith and the Assignment of Spiritual Credit; If We Did Hold Both These Views at Once, They Would Collide and Cause So Much Conflict That Everything Related to the Church Would Be Destroyed in Us

647 The views held by the new church regarding faith and the assignment of spiritual credit cannot coexist with the views of the former (and still persisting) church because the two positions do not overlap by a third or even a tenth.

The faith of the former church teaches that three divine persons have existed from eternity, each of whom is God individually or by himself, and all three are creators. The faith of the new church teaches that from eternity there has been only one divine person, and therefore one God; there is no other God except him. Therefore the faith of the former church says the divine Trinity has been divided into three persons, but the faith of the new church says the divine Trinity is united in one person.

[2] The faith of the former church was a belief in a God who cannot be seen, who is inaccessible, and with whom no partnership can be formed. Their idea of him was like their idea of a spirit, which is like their idea of ether or wind. The faith of the new church, however, is a belief in a God who can be seen, who is accessible, and with whom a partnership can be formed, inside whom, like a soul in a body, there exists a God who cannot be seen, who is inaccessible, and with whom no partnership can be formed. Their idea of him is that he is a human being, because the one God, who has existed from eternity, became a human being in time.

[3] The faith of the former church attributes all power to the God who cannot be seen and takes it away from the God who can be seen. It says that God the Father assigns faith to us, and through that faith gives us eternal life; the God who can be seen merely intercedes. Together each of them (or according to the Greek church,[321] just God the Father) gives

to the Holy Spirit—who by himself is the third God in the hierarchy—all power to produce the effects of that faith. The faith of the new church, however, attributes to the God who can be seen (in whom is [the God] who cannot be seen) all power to assign spiritual credit or blame and also to produce the effects of salvation.

[4] The faith of the former church is primarily a belief in God the Creator, and not also a belief in him as the Redeemer and Savior. The faith of the new church is a belief in one God who is the Creator, the Redeemer, and the Savior.

[5] The faith of the former church is that the faith we have been granted and assigned leads spontaneously to repentance, the forgiving of our sins, renewal, regeneration, sanctification, and salvation without anything of ourselves getting mixed up in or participating in these processes. The faith of the new church teaches that repentance, reformation, and regeneration, and therefore the forgiving of our sins, occur only with our cooperation.

[6] The faith of the former church says that Christ's merit is assigned to us and that that assigning is embraced by the faith we have been granted. The faith of the new church teaches that, in addition to whether we have faith, we are assigned spiritual credit or blame depending on whether our actions have been good or evil, and that this concept of assigning follows what is taught in Sacred Scripture, but the other goes against it.

[7] The former church says that a faith that contains the merit of Christ is granted to us when we are like a log or a stone; it also says we are completely powerless when it comes to spiritual matters. The new church, however, teaches a completely different kind of faith: it is not a faith in Christ's merit, but rather a faith in Jesus Christ himself as God the Redeemer and Savior. The new church also teaches that we have free choice, which allows us to adapt ourselves so that we are more receptive, and also allows us to cooperate [with the Lord].

[8] The former church attaches goodwill to its faith as a kind of appendage, but not as anything necessary for salvation; this is the nature of its religious practice. The new church unites faith in the Lord and goodwill toward our neighbor as two things that are inseparable; this is the nature of its religious practice.

There are also many other points of disagreement besides these.

This brief list of points of discord or disagreement makes it clear that there is no way in which we can simultaneously hold the views of

648

the new church and the views of the former, still-persisting church on faith and the assignment of spiritual credit or blame. Because there is such discord and disagreement between these two views on faith and the assignment of spiritual credit or blame, they are completely incompatible. Therefore if we did hold both these views in our mind at once, they would collide and cause so much conflict that everything related to the church would be destroyed in us, and we would fall into such a state of spiritual madness or else spiritual unconsciousness that we would not know what the church was or whether such a thing even existed. Would we then know anything about God, or about faith, or about goodwill?

[2] The faith of the former church, because it prevents light of any kind from entering its reasoning, can be likened to an owl. The faith of the new church can be likened to a dove that flies by day and sees things in the light of heaven. Therefore keeping these two ideas together in one mind would be like keeping an owl and a dove together in one nest. The owl would lay its eggs there, and the dove would lay its eggs. After incubation, both sets of chicks would hatch, and then the owl would tear apart the dove's chicks and feed them to its chicks. (Owls are voracious.)

[3] The faith of the former church is portrayed in Revelation 12 as a dragon, and the faith of the new church is portrayed as the woman clothed with the sun, who had a crown of twelve stars on her head. Therefore by analogy we can see what the state of our mind would be if we kept both these views in the same home, so to speak. The dragon would stand by the woman who was about to give birth with the intention of devouring her child; after she flew away into the desert, it would pursue her and cast water like a river out of its mouth to swallow her up.

649   A similar thing would happen to us if we were to embrace the faith of the new church but also hold onto the faith of the former church regarding the assignment of the Lord's merit and justice, since from the latter concept as from a root, all the dogmas of the former church rise up like shoots.

If this were to happen, it would be like people escaping from five of the dragon's horns but getting caught on the other five.[322] It would be like running away from a wolf but stumbling onto a tiger. It would be like climbing out of a dry pit only to fall into a pit full of water and drown.

In this circumstance, we could easily return to all the teachings of our former faith. (Their true nature is exposed above.) We could easily then succumb to the damaging belief that we are able to assign and apply the Lord's divine attributes to ourselves, namely, his redemption and his justice, which in actuality can only be adored by us but not applied as part of us. If we were to succeed in assigning or applying the Lord's redemption and justice to ourselves we would be consumed as if we had been thrown unprotected into the sun, even though the sun's light allows us to see and its warmth keeps our bodies alive. (I have shown above [§640] that the Lord's merit is redemption, and that his redemption and justice are two divine attributes that cannot be joined to us.)

We must all therefore take care not to write the former church's concept of assigning merit on top of the new church's concept of assigning spiritual credit or blame, since doing so would have tragic consequences that would stand in the way of our salvation.

The Lord Ascribes Goodness to Everyone; Hell Ascribes Evil to Everyone

It is a new concept for the church that the Lord ascribes goodness to us all and ascribes no evil to us, but the Devil (meaning hell) ascribes evil to us all and ascribes no goodness to us. The reason this is new is that in the Word it says many times that God is angry at people, takes revenge, hates them, condemns them, punishes them, throws them into hell, and tests them,[323] all of which actions actually come from evil and are therefore evil things to do. In the chapter on the Sacred Scripture, however, I showed that the literal meaning of the Word was written in what are called apparent truths and correspondences [§§215, 226, 254, 256–258]. It was written this way to allow for a partnership between the outer church and the inner church, and therefore between the world and heaven. There I also mentioned that when we read things like that in the Word, the apparent truths are turned into genuine truths as they pass over from us into heaven. In this case, the genuine truths are that the Lord is never angry, never takes revenge, never hates us, never condemns us, never punishes us, never throws us into hell, never tests us. He does evil to no one. In the spiritual world I have often witnessed this change and conversion of meaning.

650

Reason, too, affirms that the Lord is not capable of doing anything evil to anyone. This means that he cannot ascribe evil to people, either. He is love itself, mercy itself, goodness itself. These are the attributes of his divine essence. Therefore for evil or anything like it to be an attribute of the Lord would go against his divine essence and would be

651

inconsistent with himself. It would be as atrocious as combining the Lord and the Devil or heaven and hell, when nevertheless "There is a great gulf fixed between them, so that those who want to rise up from here to there cannot, and neither can those who want to cross from there to here" (Luke 16:26). Even the angels of heaven are unable to do anything evil to anyone, because of the essence of goodness they have from the Lord. On the other hand, spirits from hell cannot do anything *but* evil to others, because of the nature of evil they have from the Devil. (The essence or nature that each individual adopts in the world cannot be changed after death.)

[2] Ponder, if you would, what the Lord would be like if he regarded the evil with anger but the good with mercy. (There have been countless evil people and countless good people.) What if he saved the good because of his grace, but condemned the evil as an act of vengeance against them? What if he had one expression, a soft and lenient look, when he regarded the good, but another expression, a hard and ruthless look, when he regarded the evil? What sort of individual would the Lord God be?

Everyone who has heard sermons in church knows that everything intrinsically good comes from God and everything intrinsically evil comes from the Devil. If any one of us, then, were to accept both good and evil into ourselves willingly—good from the Lord and evil from the Devil— we would surely be neither cold nor hot but lukewarm, and would be spewed out, according to the Lord's words in Revelation 3:15, 16.

652   From the Lord's own words, we can see that he ascribes goodness to everyone and evil to no one, and therefore that he judges no one to hell but instead lifts us all toward heaven to the degree that we will follow along.

> Jesus said, "When I am raised up from the earth I will draw all people to myself." (John 12:32)

> God did not send his Son into the world in order to judge the world, but so that the world would be saved through him. Those who believe in him are not judged; but those who do not believe have already been judged. (John 3:17, 18)

> If any hear my words but do not believe, I do not judge them. I have not come to judge the world but to save the world. Those who reject me and do not accept my words have something that judges them: the

Word that I have spoken. This will judge them on the last day. (John 12:47, 48)

Jesus said, "I judge no one." (John 8:15)

Here and elsewhere in the Word "judgment" means judgment to hell, which is damnation. *Judgment* is not mentioned in connection with salvation; instead the term "resurrection of life" is used (John 5:24, 29; 3:18). [2] The "Word" that will judge us means the truth, and the truth is that all evil comes from hell, and evil and hell are one. When evil individuals are lifted by the Lord toward heaven, their evil drags them downward; and because they love that evil they follow it of their own accord. Another truth in the Word is that goodness is heaven. Therefore when good people are lifted by the Lord toward heaven, they go up seemingly of their own accord and are brought in. The latter people are said to be written in the book of life (Daniel 12:1; Revelation 13:8; 17:8; 21:27).

[3] In actual fact there is a kind of field that constantly emanates from the Lord, which pulls all toward heaven. It fills the entire spiritual world and the entire physical world. It is like a strong current in the ocean that secretly carries ships along. All people who believe in the Lord and live by his commandments come into that field or current and are lifted up. Those who do not believe, though, are not willing to enter it. They move themselves to the sides and are there caught in a flow that leads down into hell.

As everyone knows, a lamb can only behave like a lamb. A sheep can only behave like a sheep. By the same token, a wolf can only behave like a wolf, and a tiger can only behave like a tiger. If all these animals are put in the same space, surely the wolf will devour the lamb and the tiger will devour the sheep. That is why there are shepherds to guard the flock.

653

As everyone knows, a spring of sweet water is incapable of issuing bitter water from its source. A good kind of tree is incapable of bearing the fruit of a bad kind of tree. A grapevine cannot poke us the way a thornbush can; a lily cannot scrape us the way a bramble can; a hyacinth cannot pull at our clothes the way a thistle can; and neither can these bad plants do what these good plants do. Therefore we pull all those weeds out of fields, vineyards, and gardens, gather them into piles, and throw them in the fire. A similar thing happens to evil people as they arrive in the spiritual world, according to the Lord's words (Matthew 13:30; John 15:6). The Lord also said to some of the Jews,[324] "You offspring of vipers! How can you say good things when you yourselves are evil? Good people, from the good treasure of their heart, bring forth good things. Evil people, from the evil treasure of their heart, bring forth evil things" (Matthew 12:34, 35).

It Is What Our Faith Is United to That Determines the Verdict
We Receive. If We Have a True Faith That Is United
to Goodness, the Verdict Is Eternal Life; If We Have a Faith
That Is United to Evil, the Verdict Is Eternal Death

654   Deeds of goodwill appear similar in outward form regardless of whether they are done by Christians or non-Christians. Both kinds of people exercise civility and morality by doing good things for their companions, and these are at least somewhat like actions of love for their neighbor. Indeed, non-Christians give to the poor, help the needy, and hear sermons in places of worship. Who is in a position, though, to judge whether those acts, which are good in outward form, are also good in inward form—that those earthly good actions are also spiritually good? The only basis for such a conclusion is the faith that accompanies those actions. It is faith that reveals their quality. Faith brings God into those actions; faith also unites itself to those actions in the inner self, which causes deeds of earthly goodness to become inwardly spiritual.

    The truth of this can be fully seen in the chapter on faith, in the following points made there: Faith is not alive before it is united to goodwill. Goodwill becomes spiritual through faith, and faith becomes spiritual through goodwill. Faith without goodwill is not real faith, because it is not spiritual; goodwill without faith is not real goodwill, because it has no life. Faith and goodwill apply themselves to each other and are united mutually and reciprocally.[325] The Lord, goodwill, and faith form a unity in the same way our life, our will, and our intellect form a unity; if we separate them, each one crumbles like a pearl that is crushed to powder [§§362–367].

655   From the sections just referred to, it becomes clear that faith in the one and only true God is what makes our goodness truly good even in its inner form. Faith in a false God, on the other hand, makes our goodness good in outer form only. This type of goodness is not intrinsically good; for example, the faith the ancient non-Christians used to have in Jupiter, Juno, and Apollo; the faith the Philistines had in Dagon, and other

Canaanites had in Baal or else Baal of Peor; the faith Balaam the prophet had in his God, and the Egyptians had in theirs.³²⁶ These kinds of faith are completely different from faith in the Lord, who is the true God and eternal life, as John says in 1 John 5:20, and in whom all the fullness of divinity dwells physically, as Paul says in Colossians 2:9.

What is a faith in God but a looking toward him and experiencing his presence as a result, and also a sense of confidence that he is helping us? What is *true* faith but the things just mentioned, along with confidence that everything good comes from him and that he causes that goodness to be effective for our salvation? Therefore if faith of this kind is united to goodness, the verdict is eternal life. The outcome is markedly different, however, if faith is not united to goodness; it is even worse if faith is united to evil.

The nature of the relationship between goodwill and faith in people who believe in three gods, but say they believe in one God, was shown earlier [§634]. That is, their goodwill is united to their faith only in their outer, earthly self, for the reason that their mind has the idea of three gods while their mouth confesses one God. If at the moment of speaking, their mind were to come forth into what their mouth was saying, it would erase the mention of one God. Instead it would open their lips and unleash its concept of three gods. **656**

As everyone can see on the basis of reason, it is impossible for both evil and a faith in the one only true God to coexist in us. Evil is opposed to God, and faith is in favor of God. Evil belongs to our will and faith belongs to our thoughts. The will flows into the intellect and causes it to think. There is no flow in the other direction; the intellect merely teaches what should be willed and done. **657**

Therefore the good things an evil person does are intrinsically evil. They are like a shiny piece of bone with a rotten marrow. They are like an actor on a stage impersonating an important dignitary. They are like an attractive face on a worn-out prostitute. They are like a moth with silver wings that lays its eggs on the leaves of a good kind of tree, destroying its fruit. They are like fragrant smoke from a poisonous plant. In fact, they are like robbers who espouse morality, and con artists who are devout.

Therefore the goodness such people practice, which is actually intrinsically evil, is in the back bedroom, so to speak; their faith is pacing and pontificating in the front hall, but it is really just a fairy tale, a ghost, a bubble.

This makes evident the truth of the proposition stated in the heading, that our faith receives its verdict based on whether goodness or evil is united to it.

No Spiritual Credit or Blame Is Assigned to Us on the Basis of What We Think; It Is Assigned Only on the Basis of What We Will

658 Every educated person knows that there are two faculties or parts to the mind: the will and the intellect. Few are aware, however, of how to tell them apart, how to describe the properties of each, and how the two work together. People who do not know these things cannot develop anything beyond an extremely obscure idea of their own mind. Therefore, the point made in the heading—that no spiritual credit or blame is assigned to us on the basis of what we think; it is assigned only on the basis of what we will—cannot possibly be comprehended unless the attributes of thinking as opposed to willing are covered first. In a brief summary, the attributes of the two are as follows.

(1) Love itself and things related to love reside in our will. Knowledge, understanding, and wisdom reside in our intellect. Our will brings the influence of its love to bear on the contents of our intellect and induces them to show it favor and consent. As a result, our nature as a human being depends on the nature of our love and our understanding.

[2] (2) From this it follows that everything good and everything evil is a matter of the will. Whatever comes from love we call good, even if it is actually evil; the delight that constitutes the life of our love has this effect. Through this delight the will influences the intellect and secures its consent.

[3] (3) Our will is therefore both the underlying reality and the essence of our life; the intellect is both the capacity to become manifest and the actual manifestation of our life. Essence is nothing unless it takes shape in some form; likewise the will is nothing unless it takes shape in the intellect. Therefore the will gives itself a form in the intellect and brings itself to light.

[4] (4) The love that is in our will is our purpose. It uses the intellect to find and collect the means of bringing itself forth into results. Because our purpose is also our plan—something love intends to carry out—our plan, too, belongs to our will. Through the process of forming

an intention, our love enters our intellect and urges it to think of and reflect on means, and to come to decisions that lead in time to results.

[5] (5) Our entire sense of self resides in our will. The first time we are born, the self is evil. The second time we are born, the self becomes good. The first time, we are born of our parents; the second time, we are born of the Lord.

[6] From these few points it is clear that the will has one set of attributes and the intellect has another. They are created to be joined together, just as an underlying reality and its capacity to become manifest are joined together. Therefore we are who we are primarily because of our will, and only secondarily because of our intellect. This is why we are assigned spiritual credit or blame on the basis of what we will (and therefore whether our actions have been good or evil), not on the basis of what we think. Evil or goodness, as mentioned above, reside primarily in our will and only secondarily in our intellect.

Why are we not blamed for any evil thing we think about? Because we have been created with the ability to understand and think about both what is good and what is evil. What is good comes from the Lord and what is evil comes from hell. We are in the middle. We have the capacity to choose one or the other, because we have free choice in spiritual matters (see the treatment of this topic in its own chapter [§§463–508]). Because we have the capacity to choose in freedom, we are able either to will something or else not to will it. What we choose to will is taken on by our will and becomes part of it; what we choose not to will is not taken on and does not become part of our will.

[2] All the evils that we have a tendency toward from the day we are born are a lasting part of the will of our earthly self. When we allow ourselves to be influenced by these evils they flow into our thinking. Good things along with truths flow down into our thinking from above, from the Lord. In our thoughts the two are weighed against each other, like weights on a pair of scales. If we choose evil things, they are received by our old will and become part of it. If we choose good things along with truths, a new will and a new intellect are formed by the Lord above our old will and our old intellect. Gradually over time, the Lord uses the truths that are in our new intellect to implant new forms of good on that higher level. Through these truths he also gains control over the evils that are below, moves them out of the way, and sets everything in order.

[3] This also makes it clear that our thought process purifies and excretes, so to speak, the evils that are resident in us from our parents. If

659

we were assigned spiritual blame, then, for the evils we think about and consider, our reformation and regeneration could never take place.

660   Because goodness belongs to the will and truth to the intellect, and many things in the world, such as fruits and useful things of all kinds, correspond to goodness, and because the assignment of spiritual credit or blame corresponds to the setting of values and prices, it follows that what has been said here about the assignment of spiritual credit or blame could be compared with the way everything in creation is valued. As has been shown here and there so far in the work, everything in the universe relates to goodness and truth, or on the other hand to evil and falsity.

Therefore you could draw a comparison with the fact that a religion is valued for its goodwill and faith, not for the rituals that accompany them.

You could also make a comparison with the fact that ministers in a given religion are valued for their will and their love, and also their understanding of spiritual matters, not their affability or their clothing.

[2] There is a comparison too with worshiping and with the church building in which it occurs. The will worships; the intellect is its church building, so to speak. The building is esteemed as holy not on its own account but because of the divine things that are taught there.

A comparison also exists with an empire. We value an empire where goodness rules along with truth, but not an empire where there is truth but no goodness.

Who values monarchs for their attendants, horses, and carriages rather than for the regal quality that is recognized in the monarchs themselves, a regal quality that consists of love for, and prudence in, governing?

Surely everyone at a victory parade is looking at the people who were victorious and judges the parade by their accomplishments, not their accomplishments by the parade.

Everyone in general, therefore, assesses forms based on their essences and not the reverse. The will is the essence. Thought is the form. No one can assign any value to the form except the value it derives from its essence. The essence, then, is what is truly valued, and not the form.

661   To these points I will add the following memorable occurrences.

The first memorable occurrence. In the upper northern region of the spiritual world, on the eastern side of that region, there are separate places of instruction for teenagers, for young adults, for adults, and also for old people. All who die as little children and are brought up in heaven are taken to these places; so are all new arrivals from the physical world who want to learn about heaven and hell.

This area is situated toward the east so that all the people there can be instructed by an inflow from the Lord, since the Lord *is* the east because he is in the sun there. That sun is pure love from him. The heat from that sun, in its essence, is love; and the light from that sun, in its essence, is wisdom. Through that sun the Lord inspires the people who are there with this love and wisdom. The more they love becoming wise, the more receptive they are; and the more receptive they are, the more inspired they become.

After their period of instruction is over, those who have developed an understanding are called disciples of the Lord and are sent forth from there. They are sent first to the west. Those who do not stay in the west then move on to the south. Some move on through the south to the east and become part of communities there, where their homes will be.[327]

[2] On one occasion, when I was meditating on heaven and hell, I felt a growing desire to have a universal concept of the state of each one, because I know that someone with a universal understanding can make sense of details, because the details are part of that overall picture.

With this desire in my heart, I turned my attention toward the area on the eastern side of the northern region where those places of instruction are. A way there then opened up to me, and I went along it. I came into one college, where there were young adults. I went up to the senior faculty who taught there and asked them whether they know what the universal characteristics of heaven are, and what the universal characteristics of hell are.

They replied that they know very little about them, but added, "If we look toward the Lord in the east, we will be enlightened and will know the answer."

[3] They did so and said, "There are three universal characteristics of hell. They are the complete opposites of the universal characteristics of heaven. The universal characteristics of hell are the following three loves: a love for power that comes from loving ourselves; a love for possessing other people's wealth that comes from loving the world; and promiscuous love. The universal characteristics of heaven are the following three loves, which are the opposites of the loves just mentioned: a love for power that comes from loving to be useful; a love for possessing worldly wealth that comes from loving to do useful things with it; and true marriage love."

Once they had said that and I had wished them peace, I left there and went home.

When I was home again, a voice from heaven said to me, "Reflect on these three universal characteristics above and the three below, and then we will see them on your hand."

They said "on your hand" because everything that we reflect on with our intellect appears before the angels as if it was written on our hands. This is why the Book of Revelation says that people would receive a mark on their forehead or on their hand (Revelation 13:16; 14:9; 20:4).

[4] I then engaged in a reflection on the first universal love in hell, the love for power that comes from loving ourselves. Then I considered the universal love in heaven that is its opposite, the love for power that comes from loving to be useful. I was not allowed to consider the one love without considering the other, because the intellect does not accurately perceive the one love in the absence of the other, since they are opposites. Therefore in order to perceive them both, they have to be set side by side, one against the other. We have more appreciation for the beauty and symmetry of a nice face when we see it next to an ugly, misshapen face.

As I considered the love for power that comes from loving ourselves, I was given an awareness that this is the most profoundly hellish love and that it exists among those who are in the lowest hell. I could also see that a love for power that comes from loving to be useful is the most profoundly heavenly love and that it exists among those who are in the highest heaven.

[5] A love for power that comes from loving ourselves is profoundly hellish because of its origin: it arises from self-centeredness. From birth the self is utterly evil, and what is utterly evil is the complete opposite of the Lord. As a result, the further people progress into that evil love for power, the more they deny God and the holy teachings of the church and instead worship themselves and the material world. If you are involved in this evil, I urge you to examine it in yourself; you will see what I mean.

It is also in the nature of this love that the more the reins on it are let out, which happens when impossibilities no longer block the way, the more it rushes on, one step after another, all the way to the top. It does not end there, either; if there is no higher step, it groans with pain.

[6] In politicians this kind of love rises to the point where they want to be monarchs and emperors. If they could, they would rule over all parts

of the world and would be called kings of kings and emperors of emperors. The same kind of love in the clergy rises to the point where they want to be gods. If they could, they would rule over all parts of heaven and would be called gods. (Politicians and clergy of this type do not acknowledge any God at heart, as will be seen in what follows just below.)

On the other hand, people who want to be in charge because they love being useful actually want the Lord rather than themselves to be in charge, since the love of being useful comes from the Lord and is in fact the Lord himself. People of this type regard high positions as nothing more than means of being useful. They value being useful far more than they value the positions themselves. The people we discussed a moment ago value high positions far more than they value being useful.

[7] As I was meditating on these things, an angel said to me on behalf of the Lord, "In a moment you will see, and be visually convinced of, the hellish nature of that love."

Then suddenly the ground to the left opened up and I saw a devil rising up from hell. He had a square hat on his head that was pressed down over his forehead to his eyes.[328] His face was covered with a pustular rash as if he had a high fever. His eyes were fierce. His chest protruded misshapenly. He was belching smoke from his mouth as if he was a furnace. His groin was visibly on fire. Where his feet should have been, he had just ankles with bones but no flesh. His body gave off a rotten, filthy heat.

When I saw him I was terrified and shouted to him, "Stay where you are! But tell me, where are you from?"

"I am from below," he answered in a rasping voice. "I live there in a community of two hundred people. It is the single most important community of all. All of us there are emperors of emperors, kings of kings, dukes of dukes, and princes of princes. No one there is just an ordinary emperor, king, duke, or prince. We sit there on thrones above thrones and issue commands to the entire universe and beyond."

"Are you aware," I asked him, "that your fantasy about ruling the world has made you insane?"

"How can you say such a thing?" he replied. "This is exactly who we see we are, and our colleagues acknowledge it too."

[8] When I heard that, I no longer wanted to tell him, "You are insane," because his fantasy actually had driven him insane.

Then I was given the knowledge that back when this devil was alive in the world, he was only a caretaker in someone's house; but he had come into such pride in his spirit that he despised the entire human race in comparison with himself. He had also indulged in the fantasy that he was more than a king, and even more than an emperor. That pride had led him to deny God and to consider all the holy teachings of the church as worthless for him, although he did think they had some value for the stupid masses.

Eventually I asked him, "The two hundred of you there, how long are you going to keep up this boasting to each other?"

"Forever," he said. "Although those among us who torture anyone for denying their utter superiority do sink down. We are allowed to boast, but not to harm anyone."

"Do you know," I asked him, "what happens to the people who sink down?"

"They sink into a kind of prison," he said, "where they are called the lowest of the low, and they have to do work."

"Take care that you yourself do not sink down," I told him.

[9] After that the ground opened again, this time over to the right. I saw another devil rising up who had something like a bishop's miter on his head that had an imitation snake coiled around it with a menacing head protruding from the top. The skin of this devil's face was covered in leprous lesions from his forehead to his chin, as was the skin on both his hands. His genitals were exposed and were as black as soot, although a burning glow emanated from within them like dark coals in a fireplace. His ankles looked like a pair of vipers.

As soon as the first devil saw him, he got down on his knees and worshiped him.

I asked him why he did that.

"He is the God of heaven and earth," he said, "and he is omnipotent!"

"What do you say to that?" I asked the second devil.

"What should I say?" he replied. "I do have all power over heaven and hell, and the fate of all souls is in my hand."

I asked the second devil, "How can someone who is an emperor of emperors bow down like that before you, and how can you accept his adoration?"

"He is my servant," he replied. "What is an emperor compared to God? In my right hand I carry the thunderbolt of excommunication."

[10] Then I said to this second devil, "How can you be this insane? In the world you were only a low-level clergyman. Because you suffered from the fantasy that you had been given the keys, and therefore the

power of binding and loosing,[329] you let your spirit get carried away to such a height of madness that you now believe you are God himself."

Outraged at this, he swore and said, "I *am* God! The Lord no longer has any power in heaven because he transferred it all to us. We need only to say a word and heaven and hell worshipfully obey us. If we send people to hell, the devils immediately accept them. The angels respond the same way to the people we send to heaven."

"How many are there," I asked, "in your community?"

"Three hundred," he said. "We are all gods, but I am the god of gods."

[11] Then the ground opened beneath them both and they sank deep down into their hells.

I was allowed to see that beneath their hells there are workhouses. The devils that cause harm to others fall down into them. All who are in hell are allowed to have their fantasy and even to boast about it, but they are not allowed to harm others.

Why do the people there act this way? Because they are in the spirit, and once the spirit has been separated from its body, it comes into complete freedom to act according to its own feelings and the thoughts they give rise to.

[12] Afterward, I was given a chance to inspect their hells. The hell where there were emperors of emperors and kings of kings was full of filth of every kind. The devils there looked like predatory animals of various kinds, with savage looks in their eyes.

The other hell, where there were gods and the god of gods, was similar. In it, the dreadful, shrieking night birds[330] mentioned in the Word [Isaiah 13:21, 22; 34:14; Jeremiah 50:39] appeared to be flying around them. This is how the images of their fantasies looked to me.

These experiences made clear to me the form that a *political* type of love for ourselves takes and the form that an *ecclesiastical* type of it takes. The former induces people to want to be emperors, and the latter, to want to be gods. This is what they want and what they imagine themselves to be, to the extent that the reins on these loves are let out.

[13] After witnessing these depressing and distressing sights, I looked around and noticed two angels, who were standing not far from me, talking to each other. One was wearing a woolen robe of a radiant, flaming red, over a tunic of shining linen. The other was similarly dressed, but in scarlet, and with a miter that had rubies set in it on the right side.

I went up to them and greeted them by wishing them peace. I respectfully asked them, "Why are you down here?"

"We came down from heaven," they replied, "because we received a command from the Lord to tell you about the blissful outcome that awaits people who want to be in charge because they love being useful.

"We both worship the Lord. I am the leader of our community. The other angel here is the highest ranking priest in our community."

The leader then said that he was a servant of his community, in that he served it by doing useful things for it. The other angel said that he was a minister to the church there, in that by serving the members of the community he was administering holy things that were useful for their souls. They both said that they experienced lasting joys that came from an eternal happiness they felt from the Lord.

"Our community is gleaming and magnificent in every way," they said. "All the gold and precious stones make it gleam. The mansions and parks make it magnificent. Why? We love being in charge because we love being useful, not because we love ourselves. Love for being useful comes from the Lord. Because of the origin they have, all the good and useful things in the heavens have a gleam and a radiance to them. Since this is the type of love that all the members of our community have, the very atmosphere there looks golden, because the light there comes from the warm blaze of the sun, and that warm blaze corresponds to this love of ours."

[14] When they said that, I noticed a similar atmosphere around them; it smelled beautifully fragrant. I mentioned that to them, and also asked that they say some more about what it is to love being useful.

They went on to say, "We did indeed aspire to the high positions we now hold, but for the sole purpose of being more fully useful and expanding and broadening that usefulness. We are also inundated with honors, and we accept them not for our own sake but for the good of the community. Our friends and companions who make up the wider population of the community hardly realize that the honors that go along with the high positions we hold are not actually ours, or that the useful things we do are not coming from us. But we know. We can actually sense that the honors that accompany these high positions are outside of us. They are like clothing that has been put on us. The useful things we do, though, come from a love for those useful things that is planted in us by the Lord. This love finds its bliss in the shared experiences with others that happen in the course of those useful activities. We know from experience that as we carry out the useful activities we love, our love for them grows, and along with that love comes wisdom about how to involve others. If we hold this usefulness back and do not share it with others, our bliss disappears. Then that plan to be useful becomes like food lodged in our stomach that is not broken down and shared to nourish the body and all its parts but remains undigested and causes nausea.

"Briefly put, heaven in its entirety is nothing other than a framework to contain usefulness of every kind, from the highest to the lowest. What is usefulness if it is not love for our neighbor in action? What else holds the heavens together but that love?"

[15] "How can people know," I asked, "whether they are being useful because they love themselves or because they love being useful? Whether we are good or evil, we all do useful things, and we do useful things because of some love or other. Let's imagine that there is a community in the world that consists of nothing but devils and another community that consists of nothing but angels. I think that the devils would do just as many useful things for their community as the angels would do for theirs, because the devils are on fire with self-love and seek the splendor of their own glory. Who can tell, then, what love inspires our useful actions?"

The two angels answered my question as follows: "Devils do useful things for their own sake and for the sake of their reputation, either to gain a position of greater honor or to make more money. These are not the reasons why angels do useful things, however; angels do useful things because they are useful things to do and because the angels love doing them. People are unable to tell these types of usefulness apart, but the Lord knows the difference. All who believe in the Lord and abstain from evils because they are sins do useful things in response to the Lord. All who do not believe in the Lord and do not abstain from evils because they are sins do useful things in response to themselves and for their own sake. This is the difference between the useful things that devils do and the useful things that angels do."

After saying that, the angels went away. From a distance they looked like they were riding in a chariot of fire like Elijah [2 Kings 2:11] and were carried back up to their heaven.

The second memorable occurrence. After some interval of time, I went into a grove of trees and went for a walk, meditating on people who crave all worldly wealth and therefore fantasize that it is theirs. At some distance away I noticed two angels talking with each other and looking over at me now and then.

I started to walk toward them, and as I did they said to me, "We perceive within ourselves that you are meditating on the same thing we

662

are talking about, or else we are talking about the same thing you are meditating on; this is happening because we share the same interests and desires."

I asked what they were talking about. They said, "About fantasies and cravings and understanding. Just now we were talking about people who take delight in envisioning and imagining that they own everything in the world."

[2] I asked them to tell me their thinking on the three topics they mentioned: craving, fantasy, and understanding.

They began their response by saying, "All human beings are born with inner cravings. We come into outward understanding through our education. None of us have inward understanding (meaning understanding in our spirit), still less inward wisdom, except from the Lord. If we turn to the Lord and form a partnership with him, we are all held back from our cravings for evil and kept intent on understanding. Without this, we are nothing but cravings, although we have understanding on the outer, physical level as a result of our education.

"We crave honor and money, that is, high position and wealth. We do not achieve them, though, unless we appear to be moral and spiritual, and therefore intelligent and wise; so from our childhood on, we learn how to appear this way. This is why, as soon as we encounter other individuals or the public, we turn our spirit the other way up, moving it away from our cravings, and we speak and act in appealing and honorable ways around them, using skills we developed in childhood, which we have retained in our bodily memory. We take great care to prevent any of the insane cravings we have in our spirit from leaking out.

[3] "As a result, all people who are not inwardly led by the Lord are pretenders, flatterers, and hypocrites; they seem human, but they are not. In a manner of speaking, they are wise in the shell of their body, but insane in the kernel of their spirit. Their outer self is human and their inner self is a predatory animal. They keep the back of their head upward and their forehead down, walking along with their head hanging down and their face looking at the ground as if they were heavily burdened. When they lay aside their bodies and become spirits, and are set free, they become their own insane cravings.

"For example, those who are involved in self-love long for power over the universe; in fact, they wish they could extend the limits of the universe in order to expand their empire. They never see the end of it. Those who are involved in love for the world long to possess all the wealth of the world. They are pained and envious if anyone keeps treasures hidden from them.

"To prevent their becoming nothing but cravings and no longer human, such people are given the opportunity in the spiritual world to continue thinking fearfully about losing their reputations, and therefore their status and wealth, and also about incurring the penalties of the law. They are also encouraged to devote their minds to some study or work, which will keep them in their outer selves and in a state of intelligence, no matter how deranged and insane they are inside."

[4] Next I asked whether all who are involved in their cravings are also involved in fantasizing that they have what they want.

"People who develop the fantasy that they have what they are craving," they replied, "are people who think within themselves and talk to themselves and indulge their imagination too much. They virtually sever the connection between their spirit and their body. They flood their intellect with foolish self-indulgence, vividly imagining that everything belongs to them.

"People who remove their spirit from their body and are unwilling to give up the pleasure their madness gives them come fully into that madness after death. People like this may have a few thoughts about what is evil and false based on their religion, but they have virtually no thoughts of restraining their love for themselves (which destroys their love for the Lord) or their love for the world (which destroys their love for their neighbor)."

[5] After that a strong desire came upon the two angels and me to see people whose love for the world has brought them to a craving in visual form, or fantasy, that they possess all the wealth in the world. We perceived that we were inspired with this desire so that we would know more about this type of person.

Since their living quarters were not in hell itself but were above it, just under the ground below our feet, we looked at each other and said, "Let's go down there."

An opening appeared with steps leading down. We descended by them. We were told to make our approach from the east toward these people to avoid coming into the fog of their fantasies and experiencing its shadow both intellectually and visually.

We came upon a house that was made out of reeds; there were cracks in it everywhere. It was surrounded by a fog that constantly poured out through the cracks in three of the walls like smoke. We went inside and saw fifty people sitting on long benches on one side, and fifty on long benches on the other. They were turned away from the east and south and were facing west and north. They all had tables in front of them. There were bulging money sacks on the tables, and a great quantity of gold coins around the sacks.

[6] "Is that all the money in the world?" we asked.

"No," they said, "but it is all the money in the nation."

Their speech had a hissing sound to it. Their faces were round and as red as a snail's shell. The pupils of their eyes were gleaming and the rest of their eyes were green, an effect caused by the light of their fantasy.

We stood in their midst and asked, "Do you actually believe that all the money in the nation belongs to you?"

"It *does* belong to us," they answered.

"To which one of you?" we asked.

"Each of us," they said.

"How could it belong to each of you?" we said. "There are a lot of you."

They replied, "Each of us knows, 'All the money is mine.' We are not allowed to think and certainly not allowed to say, 'What is mine is not yours.' We are allowed, though, to think and say, 'What is yours is also mine.'"

Even to us the coins on the tables seemed to be made of pure gold. When we let in light from the east, though, they turned out to be just grains of gold that the group had enlarged through a united effort of visualization. They said that each person who joined the group had to bring in some gold. They would cut that into small pieces, and then cut the pieces into individual grains. Then through the single-minded power of their visualization, they would expand each grain into a larger coin.

[7] We then said to them, "You were born rational people. Where did you get this ridiculous fantasy?"

"We realize that it is imaginary," they answered, "and is just idle entertainment, but because deep in our minds it gives us such pleasure, we come in here and relish the feeling that we own it all. Mind you, we only stay here for a few hours and then leave, and our sanity comes back to us every time. Still, from time to time the thrill of visualizing it comes over us again. It drives us to keep coming back in here, then leaving, then coming back again. So we alternate between being sensible and being insane. We are very aware, too, that bad things happen to people who sneak off with others' belongings."

"What bad things?" we asked.

"Well, they are swallowed up and are thrust down naked into some hellish prison, where they have to work to get clothing and food. Later on they get paid with a few small coins, which they save up, and which are their heart's delight. If they do any harm to their companions, they have to pay some of their coins as a fine."

The third memorable occurrence. On one occasion I was among angels and was listening to their conversation. They were discussing intelligence and wisdom, and the fact that people sense and perceive these two entirely as if they were part of themselves; therefore they think that any wanting or thinking they do, they do on their own. Yet in fact there is not a scrap of intelligence or wisdom in people; there is only a faculty to receive them.   **663**

Among a number of things the angels were saying was this: The tree of the knowledge of good and evil in the Garden of Eden symbolized the belief that intelligence and wisdom come from ourselves. The tree of life symbolized the belief that intelligence and wisdom come from God. Because Adam, influenced by the serpent, ate from the former tree, and because he believed that he either was already or would become like God, he was expelled from the garden and condemned.

[2] As the angels were having this conversation, two priests came along, and also a man who had been an ambassador in the world. I related to them what I had just heard from the angels about intelligence and wisdom.

These three started to argue with each other about what they had just heard. They also brought up the topic of prudence, and whether it, too, comes from God or from ourselves. There was strong disagreement among them. Interestingly, the three of them actually shared the same belief, which was that prudence, intelligence, and wisdom come from ourselves; they believed this because our sensations and the awareness we get from them support this point of view. The two priests, however, who were feeling a kind of theological zeal at that moment, were insisting that we have no intelligence or wisdom, and therefore no prudence, from ourselves. They gave the following passage from the Word as support: "We cannot receive anything unless it is given to us from heaven" (John 3:27). They also cited what Jesus said to his disciples: "Without me you cannot do anything" (John 15:5).

[3] The angels perceived, however, that no matter what the priests were saying, at heart they had the same belief as the ambassador. Therefore the angels said to the priests, "Take off your robes, and put on the

clothing worn by representatives of the state, and believe that that is what you are."

They did so. Then their thinking came from their inner self, and they voiced the opinions they had held inwardly, namely, that all intelligence and all wisdom reside in human beings and belong to them.

"Who still feels nowadays that these things flow in from God?" they said, and looked in each other's direction and gave each other support.

A feature that is unique to the spiritual world is that spirits think they actually are whatever they are dressed to look like. This is because our understanding is what clothes us there.

[4] At that very moment a tree appeared beside them. They were told, "This is the tree of the knowledge of good and evil. Take care not to eat from it."

Because their idea that their intelligence came from themselves had made them foolish, despite the warning they felt a burning desire to eat from it, and were saying to each other, "Why not? Fruit is good." And they went up to the tree and ate.

When the ambassador noticed them doing this, he joined them. They all became close friends and traveled together hand in hand on the path of their own intelligence, which leads down into hell. A bit later I saw them coming back from there, though, because they were not quite ready for hell yet.

664   *The fourth memorable occurrence.* On one occasion I looked out into the spiritual world to my right and noticed some of *the elect* talking together.

I went up to them and said, "I saw you from a distance. Around you there is a sphere of heavenly light, which told me that you are the type of people the Word refers to as 'the elect.'[331] Therefore I came over, in the hope of hearing what heavenly topic you were talking to each other about."

"Why are you calling us 'the elect'?" they asked.

"Because in the world where I live physically," I replied, "people's only understanding is that 'the elect' in the Word mean people who were chosen by God and predestined for heaven, either before they were born or afterward. The thought is that these people alone are granted faith as a token of their having been chosen. The rest are rejected and left to themselves to wander whatever path they like toward hell.

"I know, though, that there is no 'choosing' that takes place like this, either before birth or after it. All are chosen and predestined to heaven, because all are called. After they die, the Lord chooses those who, upon being examined, turn out to have lived good lives and to have believed the right things. Much experience has taught me that this is the truth. Because I saw you with a sphere of heavenly light around your heads, I perceived that you were among 'the elect,' who are being prepared for heaven."

"The beliefs you just mentioned are things we have never heard of before," they said. "Surely everyone knows that every single human being who is born is called to heaven. Of these, the people who believed in the Lord and lived by his commandments are chosen after death. To recognize any other method of selection is to accuse the Lord not only of being unable to save but also of being unjust!"

Then we heard a voice from heaven, coming from the angels who were directly above us. The voice said, "Come up here and we will ask the one among you who is still physically in the material world to tell us what the world knows about *conscience*."

665

We went up. After we entered there, some wise people came to meet us. They asked me, "What is the current understanding of *conscience* in your world?"

"If you would like," I replied, "we will go down[332] and call together a number of lay people and clergy who are believed to be wise. We will meet with them directly below you. We will pose the question, and you will hear with your own ears what their responses are."

They agreed to this. One of the elect picked up a trumpet and sounded it toward the south, the north, the east, and the west. Within about half an hour so many people arrived that they filled about an eighth of a mile square.

The angels above arranged them all into four groups. The first group consisted of politicians; the second, of scholars; the third, of physicians; the fourth, of clergy.

Once they were in their groups, we said, "Forgive us for calling you together. The reason is that angels directly above us are longing to know what your thoughts were on the subject of conscience when you were in the physical world, where you previously lived. This will also indicate what you still think of conscience now, since you still retain the ideas you had before."

The angels had been told, you see, that knowledge regarding conscience was among the information that had been lost to the world.

[2] After that, we got underway. We turned first to the group that consisted of politicians and asked them to tell us from their heart, if they

would, what they had thought before and were therefore still thinking now about *conscience.*

One after the other, they gave their replies. Their answers added up to this: all they knew was that having *conscience* meant *knowing within* themselves, or being *conscious* of what they were intending, considering, doing, and saying.[333]

"We did not ask," we said, "what you know about the etymology of the word *conscience* but what you know about conscience itself!"

"What else is conscience," they replied, "but the pain that arises from fear and anticipation that we might lose honor or wealth, and our reputation might suffer? But that pain is easy to deal with through a good feast, a few glasses of fine wine, and chatting about the games of Venus and Cupid!"[334]

[3] "All right; you are joking around," we said. "But tell us, if you would, whether any of you ever felt any anxiety arising from any other source than the fears you just mentioned."

"What other source could there be?" they replied. "Isn't the whole world like a stage on which each of us plays our scene, like some actor in a comedy?[335] We have tricked and manipulated all kinds of people through their own particular weaknesses. We have used mockery on some, flattery on some, deceit on some, pretended friendship on some, supposed honesty on some, and various other political maneuvers and seductive ploys. None of that caused us any mental pain whatsoever! On the contrary, it cheered us up and made us happy; we practiced breathing deeply of that happiness without laughing out loud.

"Now, we *have* heard from some of our colleagues that they sometimes did suffer from anxiety and chest pains or heart pain, which would also inhibit their ability to think. But when they asked their doctors about it, they were told it was caused by a melancholy humor from undigested food in their stomach or from an unhealthy spleen. We heard that by taking medication some of them, at least, were brought back to enjoying life."

[4] After listening to that group, we turned to the group that consisted of scholars. Many in the group were experts in anatomy.

To them we said, "You who have devoted yourselves to academic study and are therefore trusted as oracles of wisdom, tell us, if you would, what conscience is."

"What an odd question!" they said. "Now, we have heard that some people experience a sadness, grief, or anxiety that affects not only the abdominal region of their body but also the dwelling place of the mind. We believe the mind inhabits the two brains.[336] Because the brains consist of a network of fibers, we believe there is some harsh fluid that pulls at, or bites and chews on, the fibers of the brains. This has the effect of constricting the range of thoughts in the mind so that it is no longer able to be spread out across an enjoyable variety of different topics. As a result the afflicted person focuses on a single issue. This destroys the flexibility and elasticity of the fibers and makes them stubborn and rigid instead.[337] This leads in turn to an irregular circulation of the animal spirits,[338] a condition that physicians refer to as ataxia; and to a loss of functionality in the fibers, called lipothymy.[339] Briefly put, the mind remains stuck, as if it were held by enemy troops, and can no longer turn in this or that direction any more than a wheel that has been nailed down or a ship that has run aground on a sandbank.

"Mental and physical anguish of this kind arises in people when their dominant love suffers a loss. When the dominant love is under attack, the fibers of the brain contract. This contraction prevents the mind from running free and finding pleasures of various kinds. When people are in a crisis like this, depending on what kind of temperament they have they are overcome by fantasies, dementia, and madness, and disturbances of the brain in regard to religious issues, which they call an attack of conscience."

[5] We turned next to the third group, which consisted of those trained in medicine. The group included doctors and apothecaries.

We said, "Perhaps you know what conscience is, and whether it is a sharp pain that attacks the head and the soft tissues of the heart, and also affects areas below those, specifically the epigastric and hypogastric regions;[340] or whether it is something else."

"Conscience," they said, "is nothing but a pain of the type you just mentioned.

"We know more than others do about the origins of that pain. It originates in contingent diseases that attack the organic structures of the body and the head, and therefore the mind as well, since the mind sits in the organic structures of the brain like a spider at the center of its web. The mind runs back and forth in the brain much as the spider runs back and forth along the threads of its web. We call these contingent diseases *organic;* if they recur, we call them *chronic.*

"What our patients describe as pangs of conscience is in fact a disease of the organs surrounding the epigastric region. This disease inhibits the normal functioning first of the spleen and then of the pancreas and mesentery. This leads to diseases of the stomach and to cacochymy.[341] There is increased pressure around the orifice of the stomach, known as heartburn. This leads in turn to humors that are saturated with black, yellow, or green bile, which causes a blockage of the smallest blood vessels, known as capillaries, that results in cachexia, atrophy, and symphysis, as well as pseudopneumonia from excessively thick mucus, and the presence of ichorous, acrid lymph throughout the blood supply.[342] Similar symptoms are also brought about from pus finding its way into the blood serum because of burst empyemas, abscesses, and apostemes[343] in the body. Once this blood rises through the carotid arteries into the head, it wears down and eats and gnaws away at the medullary, cortical, and meningeal substances in the brain, and causes the pains that are called pangs of conscience."

[6] Upon hearing this we said, "You are speaking the language of Hippocrates and Galen, but that is Greek to us.[344] We do not understand. We did not ask you, though, about those diseases, but about conscience, which affects the mind alone."

"The diseases of the mind and diseases of the head are the same, and diseases of the head rise up from the body," they replied. "The mind and the body are attached. They are like two levels of the same house, having a staircase between them that allows people to go up or down. We know that the state of the mind depends inevitably on the state of the body. We have had success in healing that sense of heaviness or headache that we gather you mean by conscience. Some cases we have healed with bandages coated with irritating ointment to cause blisters;[345] some cases with infusions of emulsion; some cases with herbal remedies or painkillers."

[7] Because we were hearing the same things from them as before, we turned away from them and toward the clergy.

We said, "You know what conscience is. State what it is, and instruct the rest who are present."

"In some ways we know what conscience is," they answered, "but in others we don't. We believe that it is the feeling of *contrition* that precedes being chosen—that is, the moment when we are granted the faith through which we gain a new heart and a new spirit and are regenerated. Our sense is that very few actually experience this feeling of contrition. Some experience trembling and anxiety about hellfire. Hardly any feel contrition regarding their sins and God's righteous anger. For the few who do, we who hear their confessions have been able to heal them through the good news that Christ took away damnation through his suffering on the cross. He extinguished the fires of hell and opened heaven to those who are blessed with the faith that carries with it the assignment of the merit of the Son of God.

"Various different religions, both the true and the fanatical, have conscientious adherents, who become scrupulous about salvation, not only in essential matters, but also in matters of form, and even in issues that make no difference at all.

"Therefore, as we said before, we know that there is such a thing as a conscience, but we don't know the exact nature of true conscience—although it must be something thoroughly spiritual."

The angels who were above them had listened carefully to what each group said. They said to each other, "We gather that no one in Christianity knows what conscience is. We will send one of our own down there to teach them what it is."

666

An angel in white clothing immediately appeared in the center of the groups. Around his head there was a shining halo with tiny stars in it. He addressed all four groups and said, "In heaven we heard you stating, one after the other, your opinions on conscience. You all expressed the thought that conscience is some mental pain with a heavy feeling that attacks first the head and then the body, or else first the body and then the head.

"Conscience itself is not, however, a pain of any kind. It is a spiritual willingness to follow religious and faithful practices. People who are blessed with conscience have peace, tranquillity, and inner bliss when they follow their conscience, and a lack of tranquillity when they go against their conscience.

"The mental pain you think is conscience is not actually conscience; it is an assault, which is a battle felt in either the spirit or the flesh. When the assault is spiritual in nature, it begins in the conscience; if the assault is only earthly in nature, it begins in the diseases the physicians just listed.

[2] "What conscience is can be illustrated with examples.

"Priests who have a spiritual willingness to teach truths so that their flock will be saved have conscience. Priests who teach truths for any other reason or purpose have no conscience.

"Judges who are single-mindedly focused on justice and who practice it with good judgment have conscience. Judges who are primarily seeking a reward, friendship, or favor have no conscience.

"For another example, when people have something that belongs to someone else, and the other person is not aware that they have it, and therefore they could simply keep it without any fear of the law or risk to their position or reputation, if they return it to the other person anyway, because it is not theirs, they have conscience. They are doing what is right because it is the right thing to do.

"Imagine people who have the opportunity to take a particular position, but who know that someone else, who is also seeking the position, would do a better job for the community. If they yield to the other candidate for the good of the community, they have a good conscience. And so on.

[3] "All who have a conscience say what they say from the heart and do what they do from the heart. They have a mind that is not divided. They speak and act on the basis of what they understand and believe to be good and true. It follows from this that people who have true beliefs and clear perception are able to have a better conscience than those who are not enlightened and have a hazy perception.

"Our true spiritual life lies in true conscience. In it, our faith and our goodwill come together. Following our conscience is acting on the basis of our true spiritual life; going against our conscience is acting against our true spiritual life.

"For another thing, surely everyone knows just from common speech what conscience is. When we say of someone, 'That person has a conscience,' don't we mean, 'That person is just'? And on the other hand, when we say, 'That person has no conscience,' don't we mean, 'That person is unjust'?"

[4] When the angel finished saying this, he was suddenly taken up into his heaven. The four groups broke up and mingled together as one large group. After they had spoken with each other for a while about what the angel had said, they divided again into four groups, but this time the groups were different than before. One group consisted of those who understood what the angel said and agreed with it. The second group consisted of those who did not fully comprehend what he said, but still felt favorable to it. The third group consisted of those who were unwilling to comprehend the angel's message. They said, "What does conscience have to do with us?" The fourth group consisted of people who were mocking the whole idea. They said, "Conscience is just gas pain!"

I saw the groups moving away from each other. The first two groups went off to the right; the last two went off to the left. The last two groups headed downward, but the first two headed upward.

Chapter 12

Baptism

Without Knowing That the Word Has a Spiritual Meaning, No One Can Know What the Two Sacraments (Baptism and the Holy Supper) Entail and What They Do for Us

THE chapter on Sacred Scripture showed that there is a spiritual meaning throughout the Word and in every part of it [§§189–192], and that this meaning has been unknown until now [§§193–209]. It also showed that this meaning is now disclosed for the sake of the new church that is being established by the Lord [§§207, 271]. The nature of the spiritual meaning can be seen not only in that chapter but also in the chapter on the Ten Commandments [§§291–328]; the spiritual meaning of the commandments is explained there.

667

If the spiritual meaning of the Word had not been disclosed, would people be able to think beyond the earthly meaning or literal sense of the two sacraments, baptism and the Holy Supper?[346] They might mutter and say to themselves, "What is baptism but pouring water on a baby's head? What does that do for the baby's salvation? What is the Holy Supper but taking bread and wine? What does that do for our salvation? For that matter, what is holy about these rituals, other than the fact that the ecclesiastical hierarchy has traditionally accepted them as sacred and divine and has commanded us to observe them? Although the churches claim that when the Word of God is brought near the elements[347] they become sacred, these rituals are essentially just ceremonial."

[2] I call on you, lay people and even clergy, to examine whether the sense you have in your heart or spirit concerning these two sacraments is any different from this. Have you practiced them as divine rituals for different reasons and with different thoughts in mind than these?

Yet from the point of view of their spiritual meaning, these two sacraments are the holiest acts of worship. The following pages, where the true functions of these sacraments are described, will make this clear.

None of us could ever understand the true functions of the sacraments unless the spiritual meaning uncovered and unfolded them for us. Therefore if we do not know their spiritual meaning, we are not in a position to realize that they are more than mere ceremonies established as holy only by the fact that we have been commanded to do them.

668 The fact that baptism has been commanded is abundantly clear from John's baptizing in the river Jordan—all Judea and Jerusalem came there to be baptized (Matthew 3:5, 6; Mark 1:4, 5). Even the Lord our Savior himself was baptized by John (Matthew 3:13–17). The Lord also commanded his disciples to baptize all the nations (Matthew 28:19).

Surely everyone who is willing to can see that there was some divine purpose in the establishment of this practice—a purpose that has been hidden until now because the Word's spiritual meaning has not been revealed before. Today, however, this spiritual meaning is being revealed because the Christian church in its true essence is now getting underway for the first time. The former church was Christian not in essence or in reality but in name only.

669 In Christianity the two sacraments, baptism and the Holy Supper, are actually like two royal insignia on a monarch's scepter. If we do not know what function these sacraments perform, however, they seem to us like two figures carved in ebony on someone's walking stick.

In Christianity the two sacraments can also be compared to two rubies or precious garnets on an emperor's robe. If we do not know what function they perform, however, they seem to us like a pair of cheap carnelians or pieces of cut glass on someone's overcoat.

If the functions of the two sacraments were not revealed through the spiritual meaning, guesses about them would spread, but those guesses would have no more value than the pronouncements of people who read the stars or people in ancient times who read omens in the flight of birds or in entrails.[348]

The functions of the two sacraments can be compared to a church building that because of its extreme age has sunk into the ground; even the roof is completely covered with debris. People young and old walk or ride in carriages or ride horses over it without any idea that hidden underfoot there is a beautiful church with altars of gold, interior walls of silver, and decorations of precious stones. The only way to dig these treasures up and bring them to light is through the spiritual meaning, which is being disclosed today for the new church and its worship of the Lord.

The sacraments can be compared to two temples, one of which is built on top of the other. In the lower temple someone is preaching the good news of the Lord's new coming, and also the good news that we are regenerated and saved by the Lord. From this temple, around its altar, there is a way to go up to the higher temple. There the Holy Supper is being celebrated and there is a passageway to heaven where the Lord is welcoming us.

The sacraments can also be compared to a tabernacle. After we enter it a table appears on which the showbread has been carefully arranged. That tabernacle also contains a golden incense altar, and in the middle, a lampstand with its lamps lit, allowing all these things to come into view. Eventually, if we allow ourselves to be enlightened, the veil to the most holy place opens, where in place of the ark that held the Ten Commandments, the Word is kept. Above it there is a mercy seat, protected by angel guardians that are made of gold.[349]

These are representations of the two sacraments and their functions.

The Washing Called Baptism Means a Spiritual Washing, Which Is the Process of Being Purified from Evils and Falsities and Therefore the Process of Being Regenerated

As we know from the statutes given through Moses, the children of Israel were commanded to wash. For example, Aaron had to wash before putting on his ministerial clothes (Leviticus 16:4, 24), and also before performing rituals at the altar (Exodus 30:18–21; 40:30, 31, 32). The Levites were commanded to do the same (Numbers 8:6, 7), and so were people whose sins had made them unclean. They were said to be sanctified by washing (Exodus 29:1, 4; 40:12; Leviticus 8:6). Therefore to give people a place to wash, there was a "sea" made of bronze and many washbasins placed around the Temple (1 Kings 7:23–39). People were also told to wash their vessels, furniture, and household items such as tables, saddles, beds, plates, and cups (Leviticus 11:32; 14:8, 9; 15:5–12; 17:15, 16; Matthew 23:25, 26).

[2] The washings just mentioned, and many other things like them, were commanded to and required of the children of Israel because the church that was established among them was symbolic in nature. It was

designed to prefigure the Christian church that was yet to come. There-fore when the Lord came into the world, he abolished these symbolic acts, all of which were external in nature, and established a church with practices that were all internal in nature. The Lord dispelled the allegories and revealed the true forms themselves, like someone who opens a veil or a door and allows what is behind it not only to be seen but also to be entered into.

Of all the rituals that had existed earlier the Lord carried over just two, although together they contain everything of the internal church. Baptism took the place of the washings, and the Holy Supper took the place of the lamb that was sacrificed every day and the lambs that were killed for the celebration of the Passover [Exodus 12:3–6; 29:38–41; Numbers 28:3–8].

671 It is clear from the following passages that the washings just men-tioned prefigured and foreshadowed, that is, symbolized, spiritual wash-ings that purify us from evils and falsities.

> When the Lord has washed excrement from the daughters of Zion, and has washed away blood, in the spirit of judgment and the spirit of cleansing . . . (Isaiah 4:4)

> Even if you wash yourself with lye and use much soap, the stains of your wickedness will remain. (Jeremiah 2:22; Job 9:30, 31)

> Wash me from my wickedness and I will be whiter than snow. (Psalms 51:7, 9)

> O Jerusalem, wash your heart from evil so that you will be saved. (Jeremiah 4:14)

> Wash yourselves; purify yourselves. Remove the evil of your actions from before my eyes. Stop doing evil. (Isaiah 1:16)

[2] As the following words of the Lord make very clear, the washing of our spirit is meant by the washing of our body, and the internal prac-tices of the [Christian] church were represented by the external rituals of the Israelite church.

> When the Pharisees and scribes saw that his disciples were eating bread with unwashed hands, they found fault, because the Pharisees and all the Jews do not eat unless they have thoroughly washed their hands. They had many other accepted practices as well, such as the washing of cups, clay vessels, copper vessels, and beds. The Lord said to them and

to the crowd, "All of you, hear me and understand. Nothing exists outside of you that can make you unclean by going into you. What makes
you unclean are the things that come out of you." (Mark 7:1, 2, 3, 4, 14,
15; Matthew 15:2, 11, 17, 18, 19, 20)

This is also clear elsewhere, as in the following passage.

> Woe to you, scribes and Pharisees, because you clean the outside of
> your cup and plate, but the insides are full of plundering and self-
> indulgence. Blind Pharisee! First clean the inside of your cup and plate,
> so that the outside may be clean as well. (Matthew 23:25, 26)

This makes it clear that the washing called baptism means a spiritual
washing, which is the process of being purified from evils and falsities.

Surely everyone of sound reason is capable of seeing that washing our **672**
face, hands, feet, and all our limbs—even washing our whole body in a
bathtub—does no more than wash away dirt so that we look clean and
properly human to others. Surely everyone can understand that there is
no physical act of washing that can reach our spirit and cleanse it as well.
[2] All criminals, robbers, and thieves have the ability to wash themselves
until they gleam; but that washing does not wipe away the characteristics
that make them criminals, robbers, and thieves.

The inner self flows into the outer self and produces the effects sought
by the will and the intellect. The outer self does not flow into the inner
self. A flow that goes inward is unnatural, because it goes against the
divine design; a flow that goes outward is natural, because it follows
the divine design.

From the points just made it follows that if our inner self is not puri- **673**
fied from evils and falsities, washings and baptisms have no more effect
than the Jewish practices of washing cups and dishes (Matthew 23:25–26).
As that passage goes on to suggest, they have no more effect than to make
us like tombs that appear beautiful from the outside but are inwardly full
of the bones of the dead and filthiness of every kind (Matthew 23:27–28).

This point is made clearer still by the fact that the hells are full of
satans who used to be people, many of whom had been baptized and
many of whom had not.

The functions that baptism performs are covered in what follows
[§§677–687]. Without the functions and benefits that are intended to
accompany baptism, the ceremony itself contributes no more to our salvation than the three-tiered tiara on the pope's head and the sign of the
cross on his shoes contribute to his papal supremacy; or than cardinals'

scarlet robes contribute to their position of power; or than bishops' cloaks contribute to the true effectiveness of their ministry; or than the throne, crown, scepter, and robe of monarchs contribute to their royal power; or than the silk caps of distinguished professors contribute to their intelligence; or than the standard carried before the cavalry contributes to the cavalry's bravery in battle.

It can even be fairly said that baptism does not purify us any more than the washing before shearing purifies a sheep or a lamb, because earthly people who have no spiritual self are no better than animals. In fact, as I have shown before [§§498:2, 566], they are more savage than the predatory animals in the forest.

Therefore no matter if you wash with rainwater, dew, and the purest possible springwater, or, as the prophets say, if you are cleansed with washing soda, hyssop,[350] detergent, and soap [Job 9:30; Psalms 51:7; Jeremiah 2:22] every day, you will still not be purified of your wickedness unless you avail yourself of the means of regeneration that were covered in the chapters on repentance [§§509–570] and on reformation and regeneration [§§571–625].

Baptism Was Instituted as a Replacement for Circumcision
Because Circumcision of the Foreskin Symbolized
Circumcision of the Heart; the Intent Was to Create
an Internal Church to Replace the External Church,
Which as a Whole and in Every Detail
Was an Allegory of That Internal Church

674 It is well known throughout Christianity that we have an inner self and an outer self, that our outer self is the same as our earthly self, and that our inner self is the same as our spiritual self, because it contains our spirit. It is also known that because the church consists of human beings, there is such a thing as a church that is internal in nature and such a thing as a church that is external in nature.[351]

If we conduct research on the succession of churches over time from ancient times to our own, we see that the former churches were external in nature. Their worship consisted of external actions that symbolized the internal practices taught by the Christian church, whose foundation the Lord laid when he was in the world, and which he is now building for the first time.

Circumcision was the main practice that differentiated the Israelite church from the other churches in the Middle East (and differentiated it later on from the Christian church as well).

Since, as mentioned before [§670:2], all the rituals of the Israelite church (which were external in nature) prefigured the practices of the Christian church (which are internal in nature), the primary sign that someone belonged to that church was inwardly similar to the primary sign that someone is Christian. Circumcision represented rejecting the cravings of the flesh, and therefore being purified from evils. Baptism means the same thing.

Clearly then, there are two reasons why baptism was commanded as a replacement for circumcision: (1) to differentiate the Christian church from the Jewish church;[352] and (2) to make it more easily recognizable that the Christian church is internal in nature, which is something the functions of baptism (soon to be covered here [§§677–687]) make clear.

Circumcision was instituted as a sign that the people of the Israelite church were descendants of Abraham, Isaac, and Jacob, as the following passages show:

> God said to Abraham, "This is a covenant with me that you will observe between me and you and your descendants after you. Circumcise every male among you. Circumcise the flesh of your foreskin as a sign of the covenant between me and you." (Genesis 17:9, 10, 11)

The practice of circumcision as a sign of the covenant was later reinforced by Moses (Leviticus 12:1, 2, 3).

Because this sign differentiated the Israelite church from other religions, before the children of Israel crossed the Jordan River they were commanded again to be circumcised (Joshua 5:[2]). The reason for this was that the land of Canaan symbolized the church and the Jordan River symbolized introduction into it.

For another thing, the children of Israel were given the following command to remind them of this sign once they were in the land of Canaan.

> When you have come into the land and have planted some tree for food, you are to circumcise the foreskin of its fruit. For three years it will be uncircumcised to you; it is not to be eaten. (Leviticus 19:23)

[2] The fact that circumcision symbolized and meant rejecting the cravings of the flesh and therefore being purified from evils (which is also

what baptism means) is clear from the passages in the Word where we read that the people were to circumcise their heart. For example, in the following passages:

> Moses said, "Circumcise the foreskin of your heart. Do not be stiff-necked any longer." (Deuteronomy 10:16)

> Jehovah God will circumcise your heart and the heart of your descendants so that you love Jehovah your God with your whole heart and your whole soul, and you will live. (Deuteronomy 30:6)

In Jeremiah:

> Circumcise yourselves for Jehovah so that he will remove the foreskins of your heart, O man of Judah and inhabitants of Jerusalem, to prevent my anger from going forth like a fire because of the wickedness of your doings. (Jeremiah 4:4)

In Paul:

> What counts with Jesus Christ is not our circumcision or lack of circumcision but faith working through goodwill and our being a new creation. (Galatians 5:6; 6:15)

[3] This makes it clear, then, that baptism was instituted to replace circumcision because circumcision of the flesh symbolizes circumcision of the heart. Circumcision of the heart also means being purified from evils, because evils of every kind rise up from the flesh; the foreskin means the filthy loves that belong to the flesh. Because circumcision and the washing of baptism have the same meaning, we read in Jeremiah: "Circumcise yourselves for Jehovah so that he will remove the foreskins of your heart" (Jeremiah 4:4); and soon after that we read, "Wash wickedness from your heart, O Jerusalem, so that you may be saved" (Jeremiah 4:14). The Lord teaches us in Matthew 15:18, 19 what circumcision and washing of the heart means.

676   There were many people among the children of Israel in the past, and there are many among Jews today, who believe they more than all others are the chosen people because they are circumcised. Likewise, there are many among Christians who believe they are the chosen people because they have been baptized. Yet both of these rituals, circumcision and baptism, were intended only as a sign and a reminder to be purified from evils. This purification is what truly makes people "chosen."

An outward change without an inward change is like a church build-ing with no worship inside; it is useless to everyone, except perhaps as a stable for animals.

An outward change without an inward change is like a field full of stalks and canes that have no grain. It is like a vine that has branches and leaves but no grapes. It is like the fig tree without fruit that the Lord cursed (Matthew 21:19). It is like the lamps in the hands of the foolish young women who had no oil (Matthew 25:3). In fact, it is like living in a mau-soleum with corpses under our feet, bones on the walls, and ghosts that fly near the ceiling at night. It is like a carriage drawn by leopards, with a wolf on top as the driver and an idiot sitting inside.

Our outer self is not human. It only looks human. (Our inner self, which is our capacity for wisdom from God, is what makes us human.) This, then, is also the nature of people who have been circumcised or baptized but have not circumcised or washed their heart.

The First Function of Baptism Is to Bring People into the Christian Church and at the Same Time to Bring Them into the Company of Christians in the Spiritual World

Many things establish the fact that baptism is what first brings us into the Christian church.

(1) Baptism was instituted as a replacement for circumcision. Just as circumcision was a sign that people belonged to the Israelite church, bap-tism is a sign that people belong to the Christian church, as was shown under the previous heading [§674]. This sign functions much like the ribbons of different colors tied to newborns of two mothers in order to tell them apart and not switch them by accident.

[2] (2) Baptism is only a sign that people belong to the church. This is clear from the fact that babies who are baptized have not yet developed the use of reason and are therefore no more capable of receiving any part of faith than new little branches on some tree would be.

[3] (3) Babies are not the only ones to be baptized; all who are con-verted to Christianity are also baptized, no matter how young or old they are. And they are baptized even before they receive instruction, based on nothing more than their declaring that they want to embrace Christian-ity. Baptism is what initiates them into the religion. This is the procedure

677

the apostles followed when the Lord told them to "make disciples of all the nations and baptize them" (Matthew 28:19).

[4] (4) "John baptized in the Jordan River all who came to him from Judea and Jerusalem" (Matthew 3:6; Mark 1:5). The reason why he baptized them in the Jordan River was that crossing that river brought people into the land of Canaan. The land of Canaan meant the church, because the church existed there. Therefore the Jordan meant the way people become part of the church (see *Revelation Unveiled* 367).

This is the earthly effect of baptism.

[5] In the heavens, baptism has the added effect of making the babies who are baptized [on earth] part of the Christian heaven. The Lord assigns angels from that heaven to take care of these babies. Therefore as soon as the babies are baptized, angels are put in charge of them to keep them in a state that is receptive to faith in the Lord. As the children grow up and become independent and able to reason for themselves, these protective angels of theirs leave them, and the now-grown children draw to themselves spirits who have the same life and faith as they do.

This makes it clear that baptism also brings us into the company of Christians in the *spiritual* world.

678   Not just babies but everyone who is baptized comes into the company of Christians in the spiritual world. This is because in that world peoples and nations are differentiated by their religion. Christians are in the center; Muslims are around them; idolatrous faiths of various kinds are behind them; and Jews are at the sides.[353]

In addition, all the people of a given religion are subdivided into communities there. In heaven they are arranged into separate communities according to specific desires that relate to loving God or loving their neighbor. In hell people are arranged into separate hordes according to specific desires that oppose the two loves just mentioned—therefore, according to specific cravings for evil.

[2] In the spiritual world, by which we mean both heaven and hell, all things have been arranged with great care to preserve distinctions in regard to both the larger aggregate groups and the individual components of those groups. The preservation of the entire universe hinges on this precise arrangement.

This precision would not be possible unless all of us, after we were born, were given some sign that identified which religious community we belonged to.

If there were no way to identify Christians (meaning baptism), some Muslim spirit or some idolatrous spirit would be able to attach to

Christians, either when they were newborn or later on in their child-hood, inspire them with an interest in Islam or idolatry, and turn them away and alienate them from Christianity, which would subvert and destroy the overall spiritual design.354

As anyone who traces effects back to their causes is in a position to know, the firm establishment of everything hinges on how it fits into the overall design. There are many different designs that are part of the overall design—there are designs of a general nature and there are specific designs within them; but one design is the most universal of them all. All the general designs and specific designs hang, if you will, from that overall design in an unbroken chain. The overarching design is present within all the individual designs in the same way that an essence is present in all the forms that share that essence—this is precisely how the individual elements are united within the overall design. It is this unity that allows for the preservation of the whole; otherwise it would collapse and go back not just to its primordial state of chaos but to nothingness.

What would the human body be like if all its large and small components were not precisely distinguished and arranged and their common existence was not dependent on one set of heart and lungs? What would the body be but mass confusion? Would the stomach perform its functions? Would the liver and pancreas perform their functions? Would the mesentery and mesocolon355 perform their functions? Would the kidneys and intestines perform their functions? The design of each organ and the design of how they all interact with each other is what allows them all to come together and seem like one thing to us.

[2] Without a precisely defined design, would the human mind or spirit be more than a confused, chaotic mush—that is, if the mind as a whole did not depend on the will and the intellect? Without the exact design it has, our mind would have no more ability to think or will than would a framed portrait of us or a bust of us in our home.

What would we ourselves be without a precisely differentiated inflow from heaven and without our receptivity to it? And what would that inflow be without the most universal inflow, which governs the whole and all its parts—without God, in other words? All things live, and move, and have their being in him and from him [Acts 17:28].

Countless things could serve to illustrate these points for the benefit of our earthly selves; let me pick just a few. Without a well-defined structure, what would an empire or a monarchy be but a gang of thugs? First, many of the thugs would band together and kill people by the thousands. Then a few of the thugs would kill all the other thugs.

What would a city be without a well-defined structure? For that matter, what would a household be? And what would a monarchy, a city, or a household be if each of them did not have one leader at the top?

680   To continue, what is a design without a hierarchy of elements? What is a hierarchy without levels? And what are levels without signs to make it known how high in the hierarchy a given level is? Without information about the various levels, a hierarchy is not recognizable as a hierarchy. In empires and monarchies, the signs or distinguishing indicators are the titles of the various positions and the administrative responsibilities they entail. These lead to chains of command through which all are coordinated as a single unit. This is how a monarch exercises royal power through a hierarchy of many subordinates; this allows the nation to function as a nation.

[2] The same is true of many other things. Take armies for example. How much power would they have if they were not precisely differentiated into battalions, and then into companies, and then into squads, so that every soldier has an immediate superior, and there is one supreme commander over all? What would that structure be without the signs that are called standards or colors, to show where each soldier ought to be? This organized structure allows all the soldiers in a battle to act as one. Without it, they would rush at the enemy like a pack of dogs with their mouths open, barking their ineffectual rage, only to be helplessly mowed down by a well-organized enemy arrayed in straight lines. What power do the divided have against the united?

These examples are intended to illustrate the first function of baptism: Baptism is a sign in the spiritual world that the individual in question belongs among Christians. All people in the Christian part of the spiritual world are integrated into a given community or horde depending on how genuinely Christian they are.

The Second Function of Baptism Is to Allow Christians to Know and Acknowledge the Lord Jesus Christ as Redeemer and Savior, and to Follow Him

681   This second function of baptism, that it allows those who have been baptized to know the Lord the Redeemer and Savior Jesus Christ, follows baptism's first function, which is to bring people into the Christian church and also to bring them into the company of Christians in the spiritual world.

What would the first function be if it were not followed by the second? Those who were baptized would be Christian in name alone. They would be like subjects who swore allegiance to their monarch but refused to accept the monarch's or the nation's laws and gave their loyalty and service to some barbaric foreign leader instead.

They would be like servants who promised to serve their master and received a uniform that indicated whom they served, but then ran away and served someone else while still wearing the same uniform.

They would be like a standard-bearer who ran off with the flag, cut it up, threw some of the pieces in the air, and tossed other pieces under the feet of soldiers marching by.

Having the name of being Christian (that is, being a disciple of Christ) but not acknowledging him and following him (that is, living by his commandments) is as featureless as a deep shadow, or smoke, or a painting all in black. The Lord says, "Why do you call me Lord but do not do what I say?" (Luke 6:46; see also the rest of the chapter). "Many will say to me in that day, 'Lord, Lord,' but I will then say to them, 'I do not know you.'" (Matthew 7:22, 23).

In the Word, the "name of the Lord Jesus Christ" means acknowledging him and living by his commandments. For the reason why his *name* has these meanings, see the explanation of the second of the Ten Commandments [§§297–300], "You are not to take the name of God in vain" [Exodus 20:7; Deuteronomy 5:11]. This is precisely what the *name of the Lord* means in the following passages.

682

Jesus said, "You will be hated by all nations for my name's sake." (Matthew 10:22; 24:9)

Where two or three are gathered in my name, I am there in the midst of them. (Matthew 18:20)

As many as received him, he gave them power to be children of God, if they believed in his name. (John 1:12)

Many believed in his name. (John 2:23)

Those who do not believe have already been judged because they have not believed in the name of the only begotten Son of God. (John 3:18)

Those who believe will have life in his name. (John 20:31)

You have labored for my name's sake and have not become worn out. (Revelation 2:3)

The phrase is used with the same meaning in other passages as well.

[2] Surely everyone can see that in these passages *the name of the Lord* does not mean just his name but also means acknowledging that he is the Redeemer and Savior, obeying him, and eventually coming to have faith in him.

In baptism babies receive the sign of the cross on their forehead and chest,[356] which is a sign that they are being initiated into acknowledging and worshiping the Lord.

Our *name* also means our quality, because in the spiritual world all are named for the qualities they have. Therefore the name of being Christian means our quality of having faith in Christ and having goodwill toward our neighbor from Christ. This is what "name" means in the following passage in the Book of Revelation:

> The Son of Humankind says, "You have a few names in Sardis who have not gotten their clothes dirty and who will walk in white clothes with me, because they are worthy." (Revelation 3:4)

Walking in white clothes with the Son of Humankind means following the Lord and living by the truths of his Word.

[3] "Name" has a similar meaning in John:

> Jesus said, "The sheep hear my voice and I call my sheep by name and lead them out. I walk in front of the sheep and they follow me, because they know my voice. They do not follow a stranger, however, because they do not know the voice of strangers." (John 10:3, 4, 5)

By name means by their quality as Christians; *following him* is hearing his voice, that is, obeying his commands. This is the "name" that all receive when they are baptized, in that it is part of the sign.

683 What is a name without the thing it stands for? It is pointless. It is the sound of an echo that bounces off the trees in the forest or off vaulted ceilings. It is the vague murmur people make sometimes when they are dreaming. It is the sound of the wind, the sea, or machines, which have nothing useful to say.

Would it be anything but a pointless exercise to be given the title of monarch, commander, mayor, bishop, abbot, or monk but not the position that goes with the title?

Our having the name of being Christian but living like a barbarian and breaking the commandments of Christ is like gazing at the sign of Satan instead of the sign of Christ, even though at our baptism Christ's name was woven into us with golden threads.

[2] Surely, people who receive the identifying mark of Christ but then laugh at the thought of worshiping him, snarl at every mention of his name, and declare him to be the son of Joseph rather than the Son of God are rebels and assassins of the king. Their words are blasphemies against the Holy Spirit, which cannot be forgiven in this age or in the age to come [Matthew 12:32]. Like dogs, they bite the Word with their jaws and tear it to pieces with their teeth. For those who are against Christ and against worshiping him, "All the tables are full of the vomit they cast forth" (Isaiah 28:8).

Yet the Lord Jesus Christ is the Son of God the Highest (Luke 1:32, 35), the only begotten (John 1:18; 3:16), the true God and eternal life (1 John 5:20); all the fullness of divinity dwells physically in him (Colossians 2:9). He is not the son of Joseph (Matthew 1:25). Not to mention thousands of other passages.

The Third Function of Baptism, and Its Ultimate Purpose, Is to Lead Us to Be Regenerated

This function is the ultimate reason why baptism exists; this is its goal. For one thing, true Christians know and acknowledge the Lord the Redeemer Jesus Christ, who, because he is the Redeemer, is also the Regenerator. (For the point that redemption and regeneration amount to the same thing, see under the third heading in the chapter on reformation and regeneration [§579].) **684**

For another thing, Christians have the Word. In it the means of being regenerated are set forth and described; those means are faith in the Lord and goodwill toward our neighbor.

This is the same as the point made about the Lord that "He baptizes with the Holy Spirit and with fire" (Matthew 3:11; Mark 1:8–11; Luke 3:16; John 1:33). The *Holy Spirit* here means divine truth that is related to faith; the *fire* means divine goodness that is related to love and goodwill. Both emanate from the Lord. (For more on the point that the *Holy Spirit* means divine truth that is related to faith, see the chapter on the Holy

Spirit [§§139–140]. For more on the point that *fire* means divine good-ness that is related to love, see *Revelation Unveiled* 395, 468.) It is through these two things that the Lord carries out the entire process of regenerat-ing us.

The Lord himself was baptized by John (Matthew 3:13–17; Mark 1:9; Luke 3:21, 22) not only so as to institute baptism for the future and set the example, but also because he glorified his human nature and made it divine in the same way that he regenerates us and makes us spiritual.

685   From all that has been said on this topic so far, it is possible to see that the three functions of baptism work together in unity as the first cause, the intermediate cause or means, and the last cause, which is the result and the ultimate purpose of all that went before.[357] The first function is to identify us as a Christian; the second function, which is a consequence of the first, is to allow us to know and acknowledge the Lord as the Redeemer, Regen-erator, and Savior; and the third function is to lead us to be regenerated by him. When that happens, we are redeemed and saved.

Since these three functions follow each other and come together in the last, and since angels see all three together as forming one thing, therefore when baptism is performed or read about in the Word or men-tioned in conversation, the angels who are present take it to mean regen-eration rather than baptism. For example, the Lord's words "Those who have believed and have been baptized will be saved, but those who have not believed will be condemned" (Mark 16:16) are taken by angels to mean that those who acknowledge the Lord and are regenerated are saved. [2] This is also why the Christian churches on earth refer to baptism as *the washing of regeneration*.

It is important therefore for Christians to know that people who do not believe in the Lord cannot be regenerated, even if they have been baptized. Being baptized but having no faith in the Lord does absolutely nothing for us (see the fourth section above under the second heading in this chapter [§673]).[358]

It should be very well known to every Christian that "baptism" includes being purified from evils and regenerated. When a baby is being baptized, the priest draws a cross, as a reminder of the Lord, with one finger on the baby's forehead and chest, and then turns to the godparents and asks, "Does this child renounce the Devil and all his works? Does this child accept the faith?" The godparents reply on behalf of the child, "Yes indeed."[359] Renouncing the Devil (meaning evils that come from hell) and having faith in the Lord are the elements that carry us through the process of being regenerated.

In the Word we read that the Lord God our Redeemer baptizes with **686** the Holy Spirit and with fire. This means the Lord regenerates us with divine truth that is related to faith and divine goodness that is related to love and goodwill; see above in the first section under this heading [§684].

In the heavens, those who have been regenerated by the *Holy Spirit,* that is, by divine truth that is related to faith, are differentiated from those who have been regenerated by *fire,* that is, by divine goodness that is related to love. The angels who have been regenerated by divine truth that is related to faith walk around in heaven in clothes of white linen and are called spiritual angels. Those who have been regenerated by divine goodness that is related to love walk around in red clothes and are called heavenly angels.

The following passages refer to the angels that walk around in white clothes: "Clothed in linen that is white and clean, they follow the Lamb" (Revelation 19:14). "They will walk with me in white" (Revelation 3:4; also 7:14). The angels seen at the Lord's tomb were wearing "white" and "shining" clothes (Matthew 28:3; Luke 24:4). All these angels were of this type. Linen means the just actions of those who are holy, as is openly stated in Revelation 19:8. (For the fact that the clothes mentioned in the Word mean truths, and clothes of white and linen mean divine truths, see *Revelation Unveiled* 379, where this is demonstrated.)

The angels who have been regenerated by divine goodness that is related to love have red clothing because red is the color of love. It is a color derived from the sun's fire and its redness, and the sun means love (see *Revelation Unveiled* 468, 725).

It is because clothes mean truths that the guest who was found not wearing a wedding garment was thrown out and hurled into outer darkness (Matthew 22:11, 12, 13).

Baptism as the process of being regenerated is represented by many **687** things both in heaven and in the world.

In *heaven,* it is represented by the clothes of white and clothes of red just mentioned. It is also represented by the marriage between the church and the Lord; by the new heaven and the new earth; and by the New Jerusalem coming down, about which the One sitting on the throne said, "Behold, I am making all things new" (Revelation 21:1–4, 5). It is represented by the river of living water coming forth from the throne of God and of the Lamb (Revelation 22:1). It is also meant by the five prudent young women who had both lamps and oil and who walked into the wedding with the bridegroom (Matthew 25:1, 2, 10). The person who has been baptized, that is, regenerated, is meant by the "creatures" [to whom the gospel is to be preached] (Mark 16:15) and by the "creation" (Romans 8:19, 20, 21), and the "new creation" (2 Corinthians 5:17; Galatians 6:15); "creature" comes from the verb "to be created," which means to be regenerated (see *Revelation Unveiled* 254).

[2] In *the world,* the process of being regenerated is represented by various things. For example, by the flowering of all things on earth in springtime and the ensuing stages of growth to the point of bearing fruit. Likewise, by the stages of development that every type of tree, bush, and flower goes through from the first to the last warm month.

The process of being regenerated is also represented by the development of fruits of all kinds from initial stem to ripe fruit. It is represented by the morning and evening rains and the falling dew that cause flowers to open, as they also close themselves to the darkness of night. It is represented by the fragrances of gardens and fields; and by the rainbow in the cloud (Genesis 9:14–17). It is also represented by the radiant colors of sunrise.

The process of being regenerated is also represented in a general way by the constant renewal of all things in the body by chyle and animal spirits[360] and then blood. Blood is constantly being purified of worn-out elements and renewed and in a sense regenerated.

[3] If we look even to the lowliest creatures on earth, we see an image of the process of regeneration in the miraculous transformation of silkworms, and of many other grubs and caterpillars into nymphs and butterflies, and of other creatures that in time are embellished with wings.

To these we might add a lighter example: the desire of some songbirds to splash in the water in order to wash and cleanse themselves before returning to their singing.

In brief, the whole world on every level of existence is full of symbols and emblems of regeneration.

The Baptism of John Prepared the Way So That Jehovah God Could Descend into the World and Bring about Redemption

688 In Malachi we read, "Behold, I am sending my messenger, who will prepare the way before me; and the Lord whom you seek and the messenger of the covenant whom you desire will suddenly come to his temple. Who can endure the day of his coming? Who can remain standing when he appears?" (Malachi 3:1, 2). The same book goes on to say, "Behold, I will send you Elijah the prophet before the great and dreadful day of Jehovah comes, so that I will not come and strike the earth with a curse" (Malachi 4:5, 6). When Zechariah the father is prophesying about his son John, he says, "You, child, will be called the prophet of the Highest. You will go before the face of the Lord to prepare his ways" (Luke 1:76). The Lord himself says about John, "This is he of whom it is written, 'Behold, I am sending my messenger before your face, who will prepare your way before you'" (Luke 7:27).

These passages make it clear that John was the prophet who was sent to prepare the way for Jehovah God, who was to come down into the world and bring about redemption. They also make it clear that how John prepared the way was through baptizing and also announcing the Coming of the Lord; and that if this preparation had not occurred, all people there would have been struck with a curse and would have perished.

John's baptism prepared the way because, as shown above [§§677–678], it brought the baptized people into the Lord's church that was to come, and brought them into the company of those in heaven who were awaiting and desiring the Messiah. Therefore angels protected them by preventing devils from breaking out of hell and destroying them. This is why we read in Malachi, "Who can endure the day of his coming?" (Malachi 3:2), and "so that Jehovah will not come and strike the earth with a curse" (Malachi 4:6).

There are similar statements in Isaiah: "Behold, the cruel day of Jehovah has come, a day of indignation and wrath and anger. I will shake heaven, and the earth will quake out of its place in the day of the wrath of his anger" (Isaiah 13:9, 13; see also Isaiah 13:6; 22:5, 12).

In Jeremiah that day is called a day of devastation, vengeance, and disaster (Jeremiah 4:9; 7:32; 46:10, 21; 47:4; 49:8, 26). In Ezekiel it is called a day of anger, cloud, and darkness (Ezekiel 13:5; 30:2, 3, 9; 34:11, 12; 38:14, 16, 18, 19). Amos, too, refers to it in similar terms (Amos 5:8, 18, 20; 8:3, 9, 13). We read in Joel: "Great and dreadful is the day of Jehovah. Who will endure it?" (Joel 2:11; see also Joel 2:1, 2, 29, 31). Also in Zephaniah: "In that day there will be the sound of a cry. The great day of Jehovah is near. That day will be a day of wrath, a day of distress and repression, a day of devastation and desolation. In the day of Jehovah's wrath the whole earth will be consumed, and he will make an end of all the inhabitants of the earth" (Zephaniah 1:7–18). There are similar statements in other passages as well.

[2] These passages make it clear that if baptism had not prepared the way for Jehovah as he was coming down into the world—a baptism that

had the effect in heaven of closing off the hells and protecting the Jews from total annihilation—[all people there, as stated above, would have been struck with a curse and would have perished].[361] Likewise Jehovah says to Moses, "If I rise up among you, I will consume the entire population in a single moment" (Exodus 33:5). This is further reinforced by what John said to the crowds that came out to be baptized by him: "Brood of vipers, who warned you to escape from the impending anger?" (Matthew 3:7; Luke 3:7). For references to John teaching about Christ and his Coming as he was baptizing, see Luke 3:16; John 1:25, 26, 27, 31, 32, 33; 3:23 and following. All the passages just given clarify how John prepared the way.

690　Now, the baptism of John represented a cleansing of the *outer* self, but the baptism that is practiced among Christians today represents a cleansing of the *inner* self, that is, our undergoing regeneration. This is why we read that John baptized with water but the Lord baptizes with the Holy Spirit and with fire; for this reason the baptism of John is called "a baptism of repentance" (Matthew 3:11; Mark 1:4 and following; Luke 3:3, 16; John 1:25, 26, 33; Acts 1:22; 10:37; [13:24]; 18:25; [19:4]).

The Jews who were baptized were purely external people; without faith in Christ, external people cannot become internal people. Those who were baptized with the baptism of John became internal people when they accepted faith in Christ and were baptized in the name of Jesus, as we see in Acts 19:3–6.

691　Moses said to Jehovah, "'Show me your glory.' Jehovah replied, 'You cannot see my face, because no one can see me and live.' And he said, 'Here is a place where you are to stand on the rock, and I will put you in a crevice in the rock and I will cover you with my hand until I have passed by. When I remove my hand, you will see my back, but my face will not be seen'" (Exodus 33:18–23).

The reason why we cannot see God and live is that God is love itself. In the spiritual world, love itself or divine love appears before the angels as a sun. It is at a distance from them just as the sun of our world is at a distance from us. If God, who is within that sun, were to come near the angels, they would perish, just as we would if the sun of our world came near us. The sun of that world is every bit as intense.

[2] Because of this there are continuous protective layers that modify and moderate the burning fire of that love and prevent it from flowing into heaven in its full strength, because the angels would be consumed by it. When the Lord makes himself more present in heaven, the godless spirits who are beneath heaven begin to wail, to be tormented, and to

lose consciousness, so they run away into caves and crevices in the mountains, crying, "Fall on us and hide us from the face of the One sitting on the throne!" (Revelation 6:16; Isaiah 2:19, 21).

In fact, it is not the Lord himself who comes down; it is an angel surrounded by a sphere of love from the Lord. Several times I have seen that godless spirits were terrified by an angel coming down like that, as if they had seen death itself right before their eyes. I have seen some of them hurl themselves headlong farther and farther down into hell; others were driven insane with rage.

[3] This explains why the children of Israel had to prepare themselves for three days before Jehovah the Lord came down on Mount Sinai; this is also why the mountain was fenced all around to prevent anyone from dying as a result of approaching it (Exodus 19).

Similar situations occurred in regard to the holiness of Jehovah the Lord that was captured in the Ten Commandments. They were delivered on that mountain, written by the finger of God on two tablets of stone, and stored away in the ark. The mercy seat was placed on top of the ark in the tabernacle, and the angel guardians were placed on top of the mercy seat, to keep anyone's eye or hand from directly contacting that holiness. Not even Aaron could draw near it except once a year, and only when he had ritually purged himself by offering sacrifices and burning incense.[362]

[4] This also explains why many thousands of people from Ekron and Beth-shemesh died for the sole reason that they saw the ark with their eyes (1 Samuel 5:11, 12; 6:19), and Uzzah died because he touched the ark (2 Samuel 6:6, 7).

Just these few examples illustrate the kind of curse and slaughter that would have befallen the Jews (a) if the baptism of John had not prepared them to accept the Messiah, who was Jehovah God in human form, and (b) if God had not taken on a human manifestation and revealed himself in this way. These examples also show that what prepared them was their being assigned to heaven and counted among those who were awaiting and desiring the Messiah; therefore angels were sent to protect them.

To these points I will add the following memorable occurrences.

The first memorable occurrence. As I returned home from the wisdom games [§48], I saw an angel in a blue robe along the way.

692

He came up and walked alongside me, and said, "I see that you have just left the wisdom games, and you are happy because of what you heard there. I sense that you are not fully in this world, though, because you are still in the physical world at the same time. Therefore you will not be aware of our Olympic halls,[363] where the ancient philosophers gather to determine from people newly arriving from your world what changes and developments wisdom has gone through and is going through now. If you wish, I will take you to the area where many of the ancient philosophers and their 'children' (meaning followers) live."

He took me to the border between the south and the east. From some high ground there I gained a view of where we were going. To my surprise I saw a city. To one side of it there were two hills; the hill nearer the city was not as high as the other.

He said to me, "This city is called New Athens; the smaller hill is New Parnassus, and the larger is New Helicon.[364] These are their names because the sages of ancient Greece stay here in the city and around it—Pythagoras, Socrates, Aristippus, Xenophon, and their followers and new recruits."[365]

I asked about Plato and Aristotle.

"They and their adherents live in another region," he said, "because their teachings were rational in nature and were focused more on the intellect, whereas the teachings of the philosophers here were moral in nature and were focused more on life."[366]

[2] He added that delegations of scholars from New Athens are frequently sent out to well-educated Christians to learn what people are thinking these days about God, the creation of the universe, the immortality of the soul, how a human being compares with an animal, and other topics that relate to inner wisdom.

"Just today a spokesperson announced a gathering," he said, "and indicated that our delegates had come across some people newly arrived from earth who told them some strange and interesting things."

We saw many people coming out of the city and the surrounding areas. Some had laurels on their heads; some were carrying palm fronds in their hands;[367] some were carrying books under their arms; some had pens tucked behind their left ears.

[3] We joined in with them and together we all climbed the hill. There on the top of the hill we came to a magnificent octagonal building, which they called the Palladium.[368] We went inside. There we saw eight hexagonal alcoves. Each alcove contained bookcases and a table. The people who were wearing laurel wreaths were seated at these tables.

In the main area of the Palladium there were carved stone benches; all the other people were seated on these.

A door opened to the left and the two people who had recently arrived from the earth were announced, brought in, and greeted. Then one of the people wearing laurel asked them, "*What are the latest developments on earth [in regard to wisdom]?*"

"One new development," they said, "is that people that are like animals, or animals that are like people, were found in the woods.[369] Their faces and bodies indicated that they had been born human, but they had been lost or left in the woods at the age of two or three. The people who reported this said that these feral children were unable to make noises that reflected thinking in any way; and even once found, they never learned to articulate sound into a single word of language. Unlike animals, they did not know what foods were suitable for them to eat, but put whatever they found in the woods into their mouths, whether it was clean or unclean; and there was more information like that.

"From this evidence, some of the scholars among us made conjectures and others drew numerous conclusions concerning how a human being compares with an animal."

[4] Some of the ancient philosophers asked what the conjectures and conclusions were.

"There were many of them," the two new arrivals said, "but they could all be boiled down to the following points.

"(1) Human beings by nature and by birth are stupider than any animal and are the lowliest of creatures. Without instruction that is what they remain as they grow up.

"(2) Human beings are capable of being instructed because they learn to make articulate sounds and to speak. By doing so they begin to reveal their thoughts. They do this progressively more and more until they are able to express the laws of society, although animals instinctively know many of these laws the day they are born.

"(3) Animals and human beings are equally rational.

"(4) If animals were able to speak, they would reason as skillfully as people on every topic. An indication of this is that animals think with just as much reason and prudence as people do.

"(5) Understanding is just a matter of variations of light from the sun, with the help of heat, as it passes through the ether. Therefore it is just an activity of our inner nature. It is capable of being raised up to the point where it becomes manifest as wisdom.

"(6) Therefore it is meaningless to believe that we live on after death any more than an animal does—except that for a few days after death some mist that looks like a ghost might be able to appear from the life that is leaving the body before it dissipates into nature, much the way a plant that has been resuscitated from its ashes appears in much the same form as it had had before.[370]

"(7) Therefore religion, which teaches life after death, is a fiction to keep commoners on an internal leash through the laws of religion, just as they are kept on an external leash by the laws of the state."

They added that those who are merely clever hold these opinions, but not those who are truly intelligent. When asked what the truly intelligent think, they answered that they had not actually heard, but they imagine that it must be different from this.

[5] Upon hearing this, all who were sitting at the tables said, "Oh, what sort of phase are the people on earth going through now? What reversal of fortune has wisdom undergone now? Has it turned into mindless fabrications? The sun has set. It has sunk beneath the earth to some point opposite the midday height where it should be.

"Surely everyone can know, based on the evidence of these people who have been abandoned and then found in the woods, that this is what people who have never been taught are like.

"Are we not what we have been taught to be? Are we not born in greater ignorance than the animals? Walking and talking are things we have to learn. If we do not learn to walk, will we ever stand up on our feet? If we do not learn to speak, will anything in our thinking ever change?

"Are we not all what we have been taught to be? If we have been taught falsities, then we are insane; if we have been taught truths, then we are wise. Nevertheless, those who have been driven insane by falsities are completely taken with the fantasy that they are wiser than those who have become wise through learning truths. Are there not idiotic and insane people who are no more human than the feral children found in the woods? Is it not true that people who have no memory are also much like feral children?

[6] "The conclusion *we* draw from all this is that without instruction people are not human, but they are not animals either. They are forms that have the capacity to receive and take in that which makes us human. Therefore we are not born human; we become human. The form in which we are born is that of an organism for receiving life from God, for

the purpose of being an entity into which God can bring all that is good and, through union with him, make that entity blissfully happy forever.

"From what you just told us we perceive that wisdom has either died or become so ridiculous that people know absolutely nothing about how the life that is in a human being compares to the life that is in an animal. As a result, people know nothing about the state of human life after death.

"The people who are in a position to know this but do not want to know it and who therefore deny it—as many from among you Christians do—are much like those who were found in the woods. The people found in the woods, however, were stupid only because they lacked instruction; these scholars have made themselves just as stupid through believing in the mistaken impressions they get from their own senses—impressions that cast darkness over truths."

[7] Then someone who was holding a palm branch stood up in the middle of the Palladium and said [to the sages], "Would you be so kind as to unravel a mystery? How is it that a human being, who was created as a form of God, can be changed into a form of the Devil? I know that the angels of heaven are forms of God and the angels of hell are forms of the Devil, and these two forms are opposite to each other. The latter are forms of insanity; the former are forms of wisdom. Would you tell us, therefore, how people who have been created as forms of God could possibly cross over from the light of day into a night so dark that they deny the existence of God and eternal life?"

One after the other in sequence, the teachers gave replies to this: first the Pythagoreans, then the Socratics, and afterward the rest. Among them there was one Platonist; he spoke last, and his opinion carried the day. It was as follows.

"In the Saturnian or Golden Age,[371] people knew and acknowledged that they were forms for receiving life from God. As a result, wisdom was engraved on their souls and hearts. They saw what was true in the light of truth. Truths also allowed them to identify a good course of action by the sense of love and delight they felt in taking it.

"In the ages that followed, however, the human race stepped back from acknowledging that all the truth of wisdom and all the goodness of love within them was flowing in continually from God. As a result, they stopped being dwelling places for God. Their speaking with God and their association with angels came to an end,[372] because the inner parts of their mind turned from the direction in which they had been facing.

Their minds had been turned upward by God toward God, but now they bent down more and more in another direction, outward toward the world. At that stage they were turned by God toward God but through the world. Later their minds turned upside down to face in the opposite direction, downward toward themselves. Because people cannot see God when they are inwardly upside down and turned away, they separated themselves from God and became forms of hell, or forms of the Devil.

[8] "It follows from this that in the first ages, people acknowledged with all their heart and soul that any goodness or love and any truth or wisdom they possessed came from God and were actually God's qualities within themselves. They saw themselves as nothing more than vessels to receive life from God. Therefore they were called images of God, children of God, and those who are born of God.

"In the subsequent ages, however, people no longer acknowledged this with all their heart and soul. They acknowledged it at first because someone convinced them to believe it; then because it was traditional to believe it. Eventually it became just a matter of empty words. Making an acknowledgment like this with words alone is no acknowledgment at all; in fact, it is a denial at heart.

"From this we can see what wisdom is like among Christians on earth today, who no longer know the difference between people and animals. (But they could have drawn inspiration from God through the written revelation they have.) Many Christians believe that if people live on after death, then animals do too; or else if animals do not live on after death, neither do people.

"Surely, then, the spiritual light we have, which enlightens the sight of the mind, has become a darkness to them; whereas the earthly light they have, which enlightens only the sight of the body, seems to them to shine brightly."

[9] After this was said, all who were gathered turned to the two new arrivals and thanked them for coming and speaking with them. They also asked the new arrivals to relay what they had heard here to their colleagues. The new arrivals said they intended to convince their colleagues of the truth that if we attribute all the goodness related to goodwill, and all the truth related to faith, to the Lord and none of it to ourselves, we are human and we become angels of heaven.

693   *The second memorable occurrence.* Several weeks later I heard a voice from heaven saying, "Another gathering is soon to take place on New Parnassus. Come; we will show you the way."

I went. As I was nearing the place, I saw someone on New Helicon with a trumpet, announcing and giving the signal for the gathering. I saw people from New Athens and the neighboring areas walking up the hill, as they had before. Among them were three people who had just arrived from the world. All three of them were Christians. The first was a priest, the second was a political leader, and the third was a philosopher. Along the way people were talking with them pleasantly on various topics—especially about ancient sages, whom they mentioned by name. The three asked whether they were actually going to see the people mentioned. The others replied that they would indeed see them and could even greet them if they wished, since the sages are approachable. The three asked in particular about Demosthenes, Diogenes, and Epicurus.[373]

"Demosthenes is not here," the locals replied. "He is with Plato. Diogenes and his students live at the foot of New Helicon, because they consider worldly things to have no value at all; they focus their minds on heavenly things alone. Epicurus lives on the border to the west. He does not come to see us, because we draw a distinction between good and evil desires; we see good desires as united to wisdom, but evil desires as contrary to wisdom."

[2] When they reached the top of the hill called New Parnassus, several attendants brought them water from the spring there in crystal goblets.

"This water," the attendants announced, "is from the spring that is mentioned by the ancient writers. That spring was said to have been dug out by the hoof of the horse Pegasus and was later dedicated to the nine maidens.[374] By the winged horse Pegasus the ancients actually meant the understanding of truth that leads to wisdom. By the hooves on its feet they meant experiential knowledge that leads to an earthly understanding. By the nine maidens they meant bodies of knowledge and academic disciplines of every kind. Today, stories like this are referred to as fables, but they were in fact correspondences that shaped the way the ancients communicated."

The locals then said to the three new arrivals, "Don't be too surprised at that—the attendants are instructed to say those things. We take drinking the water from that spring to mean (1) learning things that are true, (2) learning from those truths what goodness is, and (3) eventually becoming wise."

[3] The people then went into the Palladium, bringing with them the three new arrivals from the world: the priest, the politician, and the philosopher.

The people with laurel wreaths who were sitting at tables asked, "*What are the latest developments on earth [in regard to wisdom]?*"

"This is new," the three replied. "There is someone who says that he speaks with angels and sees the spiritual world as openly as he sees the physical world. The new discoveries he reports as a result are many. For some examples: After death we live on as human beings, just as we had lived in the physical world before. As we used to in the world, we see, hear, and speak. As we used to in the world, we wear clothes and accessories. As we used to in the world, we feel hunger and thirst and we eat and drink. As we used to in the world, we enjoy making love to our spouse. As we used to in the world, we go to sleep and wake up.

"In the spiritual world there are landmasses and bodies of water, mountains and hills, plains and valleys, springs and streams, gardens and woods. Just as in the physical world, there are also mansions and homes there, and cities and villages. There are also written documents and books; jobs and businesses; precious stones, gold, and silver.

"To put it briefly, every single thing that exists on earth exists in an infinitely more perfect form in the heavens. The only difference between the two is that everything in the spiritual world is spiritual because it has a spiritual origin. It all comes from the sun of that world, which is pure love. Everything in the physical world is physical and material because it has a physical origin. It all comes from the sun of that world, which is pure fire.

"After death, we are perfectly human. In fact, we are more perfectly human than we were before in the physical world, because the body we had in the physical world was material in nature, but the body we have in the spiritual world is spiritual in nature."

[4] The ancient sages asked them what the people on earth think of these things.

"For ourselves," the three replied, "we know for a fact that they are true, because we are here. We have examined and explored all these points. So let us tell you what people on earth are saying and reasoning in response."

The priest then said, "When the people in the ministry first heard these things, they called them visions, and then said they were made up. Later they said that the author had seen ghosts. Eventually they were at a loss to know how to respond, and just said, 'Go ahead and believe it if you want.' Until then we had all been teaching that before the day of the Last Judgment, people are not going to have bodies after they die."

"Are there no intelligent people among them," the sages asked, "who could make a case for these teachings and convince the others of the truth that human beings live on as human beings after death?"

[5] "There are people who make that case," the priest replied, "but they do not succeed in convincing the others. In making their case they use the following arguments.

"They say, 'It is against sound reason to believe that until the day of the Last Judgment we do not live on as human beings, but are just a soul without a body. In the meanwhile, what is the soul and where is it? Is it a breath? Is it some breeze flying around in the air? Or is it some entity hidden in the center of the earth? Is that where it finds its somewhere-or-other?[375] Tell me: Are the souls of Adam and Eve and everyone else who has lived over the past six thousand years or sixty centuries[376] really still flitting around in the universe or kept locked up in the center of the earth, waiting for the Last Judgment? What could be more anxiety-provoking and wretched than waiting around like that? Wouldn't they be like captives chained hand and foot in prison? If that were really the outcome that awaits us all after death, wouldn't it be better to be born a donkey than a human being?

"'Isn't it against reason to believe that the soul could be clothed again with the same body? Hasn't that body been completely consumed by worms, rats, or fish? Could new flesh really be attached to a skeleton that has been burned up by the sun or has disintegrated into dust? Could pieces of rotten corpses be reassembled and reunited with their souls?'

"But when the others hear arguments like these, they give no reasoned response. They simply stick to their faith, and say, 'We must hold our reason under obedience to faith.'

"About the gathering of all from the grave on the day of the Last Judgment they simply say, 'This is something omnipotence achieves.'

"As soon as they mention omnipotence and faith, reason goes out the window. I can tell you that by that point in the discussion, sound reason is of no value. To some of them it is like a ghost. If sound reason itself confronted them they would feel confident in telling it, 'You are insane!'"

[6] The ancient Greek sages said, "Surely unorthodox notions like theirs break down spontaneously through sheer incoherence. Yet in the world today, these ideas cannot be driven away by sound reason? Could there be a stranger notion than the things people are told about the Last Judgment? That the universe is going to perish then, and the stars of

heaven are going to fall onto a planet that is smaller than the stars?[377] That people's bodies—whether they were used as cadavers or were mummies that other people have since consumed[378] or that are now in shreds—are going to be put back together and reunited with their souls?

"When we were in the world we believed in the immortality of the human soul, based on an inductive process that reason took us through. We even assigned places for the blessed, which we called the Elysian fields.[379] We believed that our souls would be human in shape and appearance, but would be thin because they were spiritual."

[7] Having said that, the sages turned to the second new arrival, who during his life in the world had been a politician.

He confessed that he had not believed in a life after death. When he had heard these new things about it, he thought they were fabricated and made up. "As I reflected on these assertions, I said, 'How can souls have bodies? Surely everything that is human lies dead in the grave. If our eyes are in the grave, how can we see? If our ears are in the grave, how can we hear? What mouth would we have to speak with? If any part of us survives death, wouldn't it be like a ghost? How can a ghost eat and drink and make love to its spouse? Where does a ghost get clothing, a house, food, and so on? In fact, ghosts are just airy shapes; although they appear to exist, in reality they do not.'

"These are the sorts of thoughts I had in the world about human life after death. Now that I see everything, though, and have touched everything with my own hands, my own senses have convinced me that I am just as human as I was in the world. I cannot actually tell any difference between my being alive then and my being alive now, except that my reasoning is now sounder. When I have reflected on what I used to think, a number of times I have felt ashamed of myself."

[8] The philosopher too said similar things about his former point of view. In his case, though, he had labeled the new perspective he had heard about life after death as just another opinion and hypothesis like all the others he had gathered from writers old and new.

The wise were staggered by this. Those who were members of the Socratic school said, "On the basis of this news from earth we gather that the inner levels of the human mind have been closed off one after the other. Now in the world, a belief in what is false shines like the truth, and idiotic fabrication shines like wisdom. The light of wisdom that shone in our times has moved down from the inner parts of the brain to the outermost part of the mouth, below the nose. There it appears to others' eyes as gleaming lips, and the speech of the mouth seems to those others like wisdom."

Then one of the recruits that was there said, "How stupid the minds of earth-dwellers have become! I wish the followers of Democritus, who laugh at everything, and the followers of Heraclitus, who cry at everything,[380] were here; what a lot of laughing and crying we would hear then!"

After the session came to a close, they presented the new arrivals from earth with the insignia of that region—copper plates with hieroglyphics inscribed on them. With these in hand, the new arrivals departed.

The third memorable occurrence. A while later I looked in the direction of New Athens, a city that was introduced in an earlier account [§692:1], and I heard an unusual cry from there. It was a kind of laughter, but within the laughter there was a feeling of indignation, and within the indignation there was a sense of sadness. Yet it was not a cacophonous racket; it was harmonious, because the one sound was not competing with the others, but was within the others. (In the spiritual world, various emotions and the ways they combine are distinctly audible within a given sound.)

While still at a distance, I asked: "What is going on?"

"A messenger has come to us from the place where new arrivals from the Christian world first appear," the locals told me. "The messenger said he had heard from three people that in the world they had just left behind, they and everyone else believed those who are blessed and happy after death are going to experience complete rest from labor of all kinds. Since offices, jobs, and administrative positions are forms of labor, they thought there would be rest from these types of activity. Because the three people have been brought here by our emissary, and are standing at the gate and waiting, a great cry went up. A decision was immediately made to bring them not to the Palladium on New Parnassus as before but to the large auditorium, so that they can reveal the latest news from the Christian world. Delegates were sent out to them in order to give them a formal introduction to our assembly."

Because I was in the spirit, and spirits experience distances in accordance with their own desires,[381] and I desired to see and hear them, I seemed to myself to become present there. I saw them brought in, and I heard what they said.

[2] The "elders," meaning the wiser people, were sitting at the sides of the auditorium; the rest were sitting in the middle. Before them all there was a stage. The three new arrivals and the messenger were brought

694

in through the middle of the auditorium toward the stage in a formal procession accompanied by lesser dignitaries. After silence was obtained from the crowd, they were welcomed by an elder, and were asked, "*What are the latest developments on earth [in regard to wisdom]?*"

The new arrivals said, "There are many new developments. Could you kindly specify a topic?"

"*What is new in the thinking on earth regarding our world and heaven?*" the elder asked.

"When we came into this world not long ago," they replied, "we were told that here and in heaven there are administrative positions, ministries, functions, businesses, research in all the academic disciplines, and amazing works of art and creativity. We had believed, however, that after we migrated or were transferred from the physical world into the spiritual world we would come into eternal rest from our labors [Revelation 14:13]. What are jobs if not forms of labor?"

[3] "Did you take 'eternal rest from your labors' to mean never doing anything?" the elder asked. "Did you believe you would sit or lie down all the time, breathing in pleasures and swallowing joy?"

The three new arrivals smiled sheepishly and said that they had had some such thought.

"What do joy and pleasure and happiness have in common with doing nothing?" the elder continued. "When we are doing nothing, our mind does not develop; it collapses in on itself. Rather than bringing us to life, doing nothing is actually deadly for us.

"Imagine people who are sitting in a completely idle state with their hands hanging down and their eyes either looking at the floor or closed altogether; and then imagine that at that very moment an aura of exquisite happiness comes pouring down all around them. Despite it, their own listlessness would continue to control their head and body. Any lively, uplifted expression that tried to form on their face would immediately fall off. Eventually, as all their ligaments and tendons loosened through inactivity, they would sway back and forth until they fell over on the floor. What else but the stretching of our minds keeps our entire bodily system intent and ready for action? And what stretches our mind more than our work and other responsibilities, when we take delight in doing them?

"Therefore *I* will tell *you* some news from *heaven:* There are in fact administrative functions there, ministries, and higher and lower courts, as well as a variety of arts and skills that are practiced."

[4] Upon hearing that there were higher and lower courts in heaven, the three new arrivals asked, "Why are there courts? Surely all who are in heaven are inspired and led by God, and therefore know what the just and right thing to do is. Why then would they need judges?"

"In this world," the elder replied, "we are taught and we learn what is good and true, and also what is just and fair, much as we did in the phys- ical world. We do not learn these things directly from God, however; we learn them indirectly through other people. Just as people on earth do, all angels consider what is true and practice what is good as if they were doing so on their own. Depending on the state they are in, their success in doing so is mixed and not pure. For another thing, some angels are just simple folk, whereas others are wise. The wise angels need to adju- dicate when simple angels, because of their simplicity or ignorance, are unsure of what is right or depart from it.

[5] "But since you are still new arrivals in this world, why don't you follow me into our city, if that would suit you, and we will show you all there is to see."

They left the auditorium. Several of the elders accompanied them on a tour.

First they visited a huge library, which was subdivided into collec- tions for each of the various academic disciplines. The three new arrivals were dumbstruck to see the abundance of volumes. They said, "So there are books in this world too? Where do you get the paper and bindings, and the pens and the ink?"

"We get the sense," the elders said, "that as long as you were in that world, you believed that this world had nothing in it because it was spiri- tual. The reason you had this belief was that you conceived of what is spiritual as something nonphysical; and your idea of something non- physical was basically an idea of nothingness, like empty space.

"In fact, though, there is a fullness of all things here. All the things that are here are *substantial* rather than physical. Physical things actu- ally originate from substantial things.[382] We who are here are spiritual people because we are substantial rather than physical. Therefore all the things that exist in the physical world are present here in their perfection, including books and documents, and much more."

When the three new arrivals heard the idea of *substantial* things, it struck them as true, both because they had seen the written volumes and because they had just heard their hosts say that physical matter originates in what is substantial.

To reinforce these points, their hosts took them to visit the homes of scribes, who were copying original documents that had been written by the wise people of that city. The new arrivals inspected those products and were amazed at how precise and elegant the handwriting was.

[6] Then they were taken to see the various research institutes, schools, and colleges, and the places where literary games were held. Some of those games were called "the Games of the Maidens of Helicon"; some were called "the Games of the Maidens of Parnassus"; some were called "the Games of the Maidens of Athens"; and some were called "the Games of the Maidens of the Spring."383 The reason the locals gave for these names was that *maidens* mean feelings of love for the various academic disciplines. They said that everyone's degree of intelligence depends on how much she or he loves these disciplines. The so-called games were actually academic exercises and spiritual debates.

Then the new arrivals were taken around the city to see the government officials, and the administrators and their deputies. The deputies took them to see amazing works of art that artists had created using spiritual methods.

[7] After they had seen those things the elder spoke with them again on the subject of the eternal rest from labors that those who are blessed and happy come into after death.

"Eternal rest," he said, "is not idleness. Complete inactivity causes first mental and then physical lethargy, inertia, unresponsiveness, and loss of consciousness. These are death, not life. They are far from the eternal life that is enjoyed by the angels of heaven.

"Eternal rest, then, is a form of rest that keeps all those things at bay and makes us alive. What has this effect is something that lifts the mind; therefore it is some study or work that excites our mind, brings it to life, and gives it delight. This effect is produced by the usefulness that is the foundation, the context, and the purpose of our work. For this reason, the Lord regards the entirety of heaven as a context for usefulness. Each angel is an angel depending on how useful he or she is. The enjoyment we take in being useful carries us along as a helpful current carries a ship; it gives us everlasting peace and the rest that peace provides. This is what 'eternal rest from our labors' means.

"In fact, the marriage love that angels have, and all the vigor, ability, and pleasure that go along with it, depends on their level of devotion to being genuinely useful. Clearly then, the very level of aliveness that angels feel depends on the level of their mental devotion to usefulness."

[8] Once the three new arrivals were thoroughly convinced that eternal rest is not idleness, but is instead finding delight in some useful activity, several young women came forward with pieces of needlework and embroidery of their own making and gave them to the visitors. As the newly arrived spirits left, the young women sang them a song; through its angelic melody they expressed their love for useful activity and the pleasure it brings them.

The fourth memorable occurrence. Many people these days who believe in life after death think that in heaven all their thoughts will be of a devotional nature, and all their words will be prayers; and they will combine these thoughts and words with facial expressions and physical actions in pure, endless glorification of God. Their homes will therefore all be sacred buildings, houses of worship, and they will all be priests of God.

695

I can attest, however, that church-related sacred devotions take up no more space in angels' minds and homes than such activities do in our world, where God is celebrated in worship (although angels do achieve purer and deeper states of worship). In actuality, the heavens are highly developed in a variety of approaches to civic prudence, and a variety of approaches to rational development.

[2] One day I was carried up to heaven and led to a particular community. That community included philosophers of ancient times who were considered most outstanding because of their research and reflection on matters both rational and practical. They are now in heaven because they believed in God (and now believe in the Lord) and loved their neighbor as themselves.

I was then introduced at a meeting they were having. They asked where I was from.

"Bodily I am still in the physical world," I admitted, "but in spirit I am here in this spiritual world of yours."

The angels were elated to hear that. They asked, "In the world you still inhabit physically, what do people know and understand about *inflow?*"

I went over in my mind what I had gathered from the talks and written works of the best-known thinkers on earth.

"They do not yet recognize," I said, "any inflow from the spiritual world into the physical world. They do know, however, of an inflow of nature into physical objects. For example, they recognize that heat and light from the sun flow into animals and also into trees and bushes and bring them to life. Likewise, they recognize that cold flows into the same entities and causes them to die. They also recognize that light flows into our eyes and allows us to see; sound flows into our ears and allows us to hear; odors flow into our noses and allow us to smell things; and so on.

[3] "In addition, the greatest thinkers of our age have various thoughts about whether there is an inflow from the soul into the body or from the body into the soul. Three different lines of thought have developed: (1) Some posit that there is an inflow from the soul into the body. They call this *occasional inflow,* because it is thought to be occasioned when things impinge on our bodily senses. (2) Others posit instead that there is an inflow from the body into the soul. They call this *physical inflow,* because objects are thought to impinge on our senses and thereby on our souls. (3) The third group posits that there is an instantaneous inflow into the body and into the soul at the same time, which they call *a preestablished harmony.*[384] Yet all three camps consider these forms of inflow as occurring within nature. Some believe the soul is a particle or a drop of ether; some believe it is a tiny ball or point of heat and light;[385] some believe it is something deeply hidden in the brain.[386] Whichever theory they have, they do in fact refer to the soul as something spiritual; but by 'spiritual' they mean a purer form of physical matter, because they know nothing at all about the spiritual world or the existence of any inflow from it into the physical world. Therefore they stay within the realm of nature. They ascend and descend within nature, and lift themselves up into it like eagles taking to the air.

"People who spend all their time focused on nature are like people who have always lived on some little island out in the sea, who have no idea that any other land exists beyond their own. They are like fish in a river that have no idea there is air above the water in which they swim. For this reason if you mention to them that another world exists where angels and spirits live, and that all the inflow into human beings and even the inner inflow into trees[387] comes from there, they stand in utter disbelief as if they were hearing ghost stories or the babbling of some astrologer.

[4] "In actual fact, with the exception of our philosophers the people of the world in which I live bodily don't devote much thinking or talk to any other inflow than the inflow of wine into their cup, the inflow of food and drink into their stomach, and the inflow of pleasant tastes into their tongue. From time to time they think about the inflow of air into their lungs, and that sort of thing. But if they are told anything about the inflow of the spiritual world into the physical world, they say, 'Well then, let it flow in, if it is flowing in! But what difference does it

make and why is it useful to know about it?' And they leave, and afterward when they talk about what they had heard regarding that inflow, they fiddle around with it, like people who amuse themselves by rolling marbles around between their fingers."

[5] Afterward I spoke with those angels about the amazing things that come into being as a result of the inflow of the spiritual world into the physical world. For example, the way caterpillars turn into butterflies; the activities of bees and drones; the amazing ways of the silkworm, and even spiders.[388] Yet the inhabitants of earth attribute these things to the light and heat of the sun, and therefore to nature. I also mentioned that I have often been amazed at how people use these same phenomena to support a belief that nature is the source; through their support for nature they put their minds into the sleep of death and become atheists.

[6] After that, I told of the marvels of the plant kingdom, that all plants grow from one seed to the production of new seeds in just the right sequence, completely as if the ground itself knew how to adapt and accommodate its elements to serve the reproductive cycle of the seed. I spoke of how the ground seems to know how to develop a seed into a shoot, how to grow this into a trunk, how to make the trunk put forth branches and clothe them with leaves, how to decorate the plant with flowers and begin to develop a fruit at the heart of the flower, and generate seeds within the fruit as the plant's offspring so that it will be reborn. Because we see these events all the time and they recur every year, they become usual, customary, and commonplace to us, so that we see them as nothing more than "what nature does" rather than the miracles they truly are.

"The only reason people think this way," I went on, "is that they don't know that the spiritual world exists. They don't know that it works from within and activates each and every thing that comes into existence and takes shape in the world of nature and on the face of this planet. People don't know that this process echoes the way the human mind is present in the sensations and movements of the body. They don't know that every single thing in nature is like a membrane, a sheath, a piece of clothing that wraps around things that are spiritual and produces right next to us effects that reflect the ultimate goal of God the Creator himself."

The fifth memorable occurrence. On one occasion I prayed to the Lord to be allowed to speak to followers of Aristotle, followers of Descartes, and followers of Leibniz[389] all at once, so that I could learn what their thoughts were on the interaction between the soul and the body.

696

After I said this prayer, nine men were standing around me: three Aristotelians, three Cartesians, and three Leibnizians. The worshipers of Aristotle were to my left; the adherents of Descartes were to my right; and the supporters of Leibniz were behind me. At a great distance from me and quite far from each other, I saw three people wearing laurel. An inflow from heaven allowed me to perceive that they were the aforementioned masters and leaders themselves. One other person was standing behind Leibniz and holding the hem of his garment in his hand; I was told it was Wolff.[390]

[2] When the nine men noticed each other, they greeted and spoke to each other cordially at first. Soon, however, a spirit rose up from hell with a flaming torch in his right hand. He waved it back and forth before their faces. This made them become enemies with each other, three by three. They stared at the other groups with grim looks on their faces because they had all been overcome with a lust for arguing and disputation.

The Aristotelians, who were also Scholastics, went first.[391] They said, "Surely everyone sees that objects flow in through our senses to our souls, just as someone goes in through a doorway into a room. The soul experiences thought on the basis of that inflow. For example, when a man in love sees his beautiful bride, his eyes light up and bring his love for her to his soul. When misers see bags full of coins, all their senses feel a burning desire for the money; the senses bring this desire to their soul and stir up a longing to take it for themselves. When arrogant people hear someone praising them, their ears perk up and carry the praises to their soul. The bodily senses are entrances; they provide the only access to the soul. From these examples and countless others like them, the inescapable conclusion is that inflow comes from nature; it is physical."

[3] The adherents of Descartes responded to this by pointing their fingers at their foreheads and then retracting them. "Oh, you are just speaking from how things appear to be!" they said. "Don't you know that it is not the eye but the soul that loves the young bride? It is not the physical senses that feel their own longing for the money in the bags; it is the soul. It is not the ear that seizes on the praises of flatterers. Perception leads to sensation, and perception belongs not to the external organ but to the soul.

"Say, if you can, what causes the tongue and lips to speak if it is not thought? What causes the hands to do work if it is not the will? And thought and will belong to the soul. If not the soul, what causes the eye to see, the ears to hear, and the other organs to sense things and notice and pay attention to them? From these and countless other examples, all who have wisdom that transcends their bodily senses conclude that there is no inflow of the body into the soul. The only inflow is of the soul into the body. We refer to this as occasional inflow and also spiritual inflow."

[4] Upon hearing this the three men who were standing behind the other groups of three, the supporters of Leibniz, raised their voices and said, "We have heard these arguments from both sides and have compared them. In many regards the arguments of the latter group are stronger than those of the first group; but in many other respects, the arguments of the first group are stronger. Therefore, if we may, we are going to combine the two."

"How?" the others asked.

"There is no inflow from the soul into the body," they said, "and there is no inflow from the body into the soul. Instead, they both function side-by-side instantaneously and to the same effect. Our distinguished author gave this process a beautiful name: preestablished harmony."

[5] At this point the spirit from hell came up and appeared again with the flaming torch in his hand, but this time it was in his left hand. He waved it back and forth near the backs of their heads. As a result, the ideas they all had became confused. They exclaimed, "Neither our soul nor our body knows which position to take! We should settle this argument by drawing lots. We will accept whichever lot is drawn first."

They took three slips of paper, and wrote *physical inflow* on one, *spiritual inflow* on another, and *preestablished harmony* on the third. They placed all three in a deep hat, and chose someone to make the draw. He put in his hand and pulled out the slip that said *spiritual inflow*. Once they had seen it and read it, they all said, "We should adopt this, because it is what came up first." But some said this in a clear and steady voice, while others said it faintly and hesitantly.

An angel suddenly appeared standing next to them and said, "Don't think that the slip of paper that said *spiritual inflow* was drawn by chance; that was providence. Because your ideas are confused, you don't see the truth of it, but in fact the real truth offered itself to your hand as the correct answer so that you would come to favor it."

The sixth memorable occurrence. On one occasion I saw a strange aerial phenomenon not far from me. I saw a cloud that split into several little clouds, some of which were dark blue and some of which were black. I saw them apparently colliding with each other. Rays or bands of light shone through the clouds. At times these rays looked sharpened to

697

a point. At other times they looked blunted like broken swords. At times the rays came at each other, and at other times they retreated, just as if they were boxing. The little clouds of different colors, then, seemed as if they were doing battle with each other, but in fact they were just playing.

Because this strange sight was not far away, I was able to look at the area beneath it. There I discerned teenagers, young adults, and older adults entering a building of white stone above and red stone below. The phenomenon was occurring in the air directly above this building.

I addressed one of the people going into the building and asked, "What is this place?"

"It is a hall," the person replied, "where young adults are initiated into various issues related to wisdom."

[2] I then went in along with them. I was "in the spirit," that is, in the same state as the people of the spiritual world, who are known as spirits and angels.

In the hall I saw a lectern [on a stage] at the front of the room, benches in the middle of the room, seats all around at the sides, and a balcony above the entrance [at the back]. The lectern was for the young adults who would respond to the question for debate[392] that would be posed for that occasion. The benches were for the audience. The seats at the side were for people who had given wise responses at similar events in the past. The balcony was for the elders who were the arbiters and judges of the event. In the middle of the balcony there was a platform where a wise man was sitting, whom they referred to as the senior professor. He was the one who would propose the question to which the young adults would respond from the lectern.

After all were gathered, the man on the platform stood up and said, "Respond now, if you would, to the following question and resolve it if you can: *What is the soul and how do we experience it?*"[393]

[3] All were stunned to hear the question, and a murmur went through the crowd. Some members of the audience on the benches said, "From the Golden Age to our own, who among humans has ever been able to see and discern through rational thought what the soul is, let alone how we experience it? Isn't this beyond the reach of any intellect?"

The elders in the balcony responded, "This is not beyond the reach of the intellect but lies within its scope and purview. Just give your responses!"

Some young men stood up. They were the ones who had been selected that day to come up to the lectern and give their responses to whatever the question would be. There were five of them. An examination by the elders had identified them as particularly sharp-minded and capable. They sat down on padded chairs on either side of the lectern. Later on they got up in the same order in which they had sat down. When each speaker stood up to speak, he would first put on a silk vest that was opalescent in color, and over that a fine wool gown with flowers interwoven, and finally a hat, the top of which was covered in a floral wreath with a ringlet of tiny sapphires.

[4] I saw the first young man, clothed as just noted, going up to the lectern. He said, "What the soul is, and how we experience it, has not been revealed to anyone since the day of creation. It is a secret stored in the treasure-house of God alone. What has been disclosed is that the soul dwells within us like a queen. Where exactly she holds court is a topic on which learned authorities have made various conjectures. Some have thought that she sits in the little protuberance between the cerebrum and the cerebellum known as the pineal gland; they imagined this to be the seat of the soul because the entire person is governed through those two brains, and both brains are controlled by that little growth as it wishes; therefore it in effect controls the entire person from head to toe.

"This appeared either true," he added, "or at least plausible to many people in the world at the time, but in later times it was rejected as imaginary."

[5] After he had spoken, he took off the gown, the vest, and the hat. The second selected speaker put them on and went up to the lectern. His pronouncement on the soul was as follows.

"Throughout all of heaven and the whole world, no one knows what the soul is or how we experience it. All that is known is that it exists, and exists within us; but where it resides is a matter of conjecture. This much is certain, however: it dwells in the head, since that is where the intellect does its thinking and where the will does its intending. The front surface of the head contains organs for all five senses. The thing that gives life to the will, the intellect, and the senses is the soul, which resides within the head. Where exactly her court is I would not dare to say, but I see the point of those who assign the seat of the soul to the three ventricles of the brain; at other times, I side with those who locate it in the striated body in the brain; at other times, I side with those who locate it in the medullary substances of either brain; at other times, I side with those who locate it in the cortical substance; and at still other times I side with those who assign it to the dura mater. There is no lack of white pebbles to vote for each of these locations.[394]

"One could vote for the three ventricles of the brain because they are the vessels that hold the animal spirits and all the cerebral fluids. One could vote for the striated body because this forms the medulla out of which the nerves come forth and through which each brain is extended to form the spinal cord; the fibers that are woven together to form the entire body come out of the medulla and the spinal cord. One could vote for the medullary substance of each brain because this substance is a gathering place for, and a mass of, all the fibers that constitute the points of origin of the entire person. One could vote for the cortical substance because it contains the first and last ends and therefore the origins of all the fibers, both the sensory fibers and the motor fibers. One could vote for the dura mater because it is a common covering that surrounds both brains and through extensions covers the heart and the internal organs of the body. As for me, I'm not choosing any one of these over the other. I leave it to you to choose and decide, if you would, which theory you prefer."

[6] After he had finished speaking he stepped down from the lectern and passed the vest, gown, and hat to the third speaker.

The third speaker stepped up behind the lectern and said the following.

"Who am I as a young man to tackle so sublime a proposition? I challenge the learned persons sitting here at the sides of the room, I challenge you, the wise who sit in the balcony, indeed I challenge the angels of the highest heaven to answer me this: Can any human beings ever from their own rational light form for themselves any idea of the soul?

"As for where the soul's seat is within us, I, like anyone else, can offer a conjecture. My opinion is that the soul is in the heart and the blood. This is my conjecture because the heart rules both the head and the body through the agency of the blood. The heart extends its largest blood vessel, known as the aorta, to transmit blood to the entire body, and the vessels called the carotid arteries to transmit blood to the entire head. There is universal consensus on the point that the soul acts from the heart through the blood to sustain, nourish, and give life to the entire organic system of both the head and the body. You will find further support for your confidence in what I'm saying in the fact that Sacred Scripture mentions the soul and the heart many times. For example, you are to love God with all your soul and with all your heart; and God creates in us a new soul and a new heart. See Deuteronomy 6:5; 10:12; 11:13; 26:16; Jeremiah 32:41; Matthew 22:37; Mark 12:30, 33; Luke 10:27; and elsewhere. We are openly told in Leviticus 17:11, 14 that the blood is the soul of the flesh."

When he had finished, several shouted "Learned! Learned!" They were ministers.

[7] Then the fourth person put on the garments and stepped up to the lectern. "I too suspect that there is no one with mental faculties that are so fine-tuned and sharp as to be able to discern what the soul is and how we experience it. Therefore I am of the opinion that those who try to investigate the soul will find their mental edge worn down by years of fruitless research.

"Since I was young I have always shared the belief of the ancients that our soul is in everything throughout us; it is in every part. It is in the head, and everything it contains, and in the body, and everything it contains.³⁹⁵ It was a foolish invention on the part of recent writers to designate a seat for the soul in one particular area, rather than everywhere. For one thing, the soul is a spiritual substance; it fills us and dwells in us, but it cannot be said to have either extension or place. For another thing, surely when we say 'soul' we mean 'life'; and life is in the whole and in every part of us."

Many in the auditorium agreed with what he said.

[8] Then the fifth speaker stood up. Wearing the same apparel as the others, he expressed from the lectern the following opinion.

"I shall not spend time discussing where the soul is, and whether it is in this or that part or everywhere within the whole. Instead, drawing from my own storehouse and treasure I will reveal my thinking on the topic of what the soul is and how we experience it. Everyone thinks of the soul as something pure that can be compared to ether, air, or wind, but possesses some of the rational life that distinguishes us from animals. I base this opinion on the fact that when we expire, we are said to breathe out or exhale our soul or spirit. As a result, the soul that lives on after death is believed to be a kind of breath with some type of life that is capable of thinking, and this life is called the soul. What else could the soul be? Nevertheless, I did hear those in the balcony who said that the question of what the soul is and how we experience it is not beyond the reach of the intellect, but lies within its scope and purview. I ask and pray therefore that you yourselves unveil this eternal mystery!"

[9] The elders in the balcony looked toward the senior professor who had originally proposed the question. He gathered from their nodding that they wanted him to go down and teach.

He immediately came down from his platform, passed through the auditorium, and stepped up to the lectern. Stretching out his hand, he said, "Listen, if you would, please. Surely everyone believes the soul is the inmost and subtlest essence within us; but what is an essence without a form? It is a figment of the imagination. Therefore the soul is a form. Let me say what *kind* of form it is: It is the form of all the components of love and all the components of wisdom. All the components of love are called desires; all the components of wisdom are called perceptions. These perceptions come from these desires; therefore they come together as a single form. Within that form there are countless individual things, but the design, arrangement, and close interaction of them allow them to be referred to as one thing. They can be called one thing because nothing can be taken away and nothing can be added without turning the whole into something different than it is.

"What else is the human soul but a form like this? All the components of love and all the components of wisdom are the essential elements of this form. In human beings, these components are present in the soul, and the soul makes them present in the head and the body.

[10] "You are called spirits and angels. In the world, you believed that spirits and angels were like pieces of wind or ether, and were therefore just higher or lower minds. Now, of course, you see clearly that you are truly, really, and actually human beings, who used to live and think inside a physical body in the material world. You knew then that the physical body has no life or thought; there was a spiritual substance that lived and thought within the body. You called this the soul. You did not know what form it took, however; but now you have seen your soul, and you are seeing it right now. You yourselves are all souls! You yourselves are the souls about whose immortality you have heard and thought and said and written such a great deal. Because you are forms of love and wisdom from God, to eternity you can never die. Therefore the soul is the human form; nothing can be taken away from it and nothing can be added to it. The soul is the inmost form of all the forms throughout the entire body. And because the forms that lie outside draw both their essence and their form from what lies within, therefore you are souls just the way you appear to yourselves and to us right now.

"Briefly put, the soul is the real person, because it is the deepest self. Therefore its form is fully and perfectly human. It is not, however, life; it is a nearby vessel that receives life from God, and is therefore a dwelling place for God."

[11] Many applauded this statement of his; but some said, "We'll have to think about that."

I then went home. To my surprise I saw that over the hall, where that strange aerial phenomenon had appeared earlier, there now appeared a white cloud that had no rays or bands of light fighting with each other. That cloud then came down through the roof of the hall itself and lit up the walls. I heard that the people there saw passages of Scripture on the walls, among which was this: "Jehovah God breathed *the breath of lives* into the human being's nostrils, and the human being turned into a *living soul*" (Genesis 2:7).

Chapter 13

The Holy Supper

Without Knowing about the Correspondences of Physical Things with Spiritual Things, No One Can Know the Functions and Benefits of the Holy Supper

698 THE assertion in this heading has already been partly explained in the chapter on baptism, where the point was made that without knowing that the Word has a spiritual meaning, no one can know what the two sacraments—baptism and the Holy Supper—entail and what they do for us (§§667–669). The heading just above says "without knowing about the correspondences of physical things with spiritual things"; this is the same thing, because correspondences turn the earthly meaning of the Word into a spiritual meaning in heaven. As a result, these two layers of meaning correspond to each other. Someone who knows correspondences, then, is in a position to know the spiritual meaning of the Word.

For a further definition and description of correspondences, see the chapter on Sacred Scripture from beginning to end [§§189–281]. See also the exposition of the Ten Commandments from first to last [§§282–335], and the individual correspondences that are explained throughout *Revelation Unveiled*.

699 Every true Christian acknowledges that these two sacraments are holy, and are in fact the holiest acts of worship in Christianity; but who knows where their holiness comes from or where it resides?

The only thing we know from the earthly meaning of Scripture about the establishment of the Holy Supper is that people were given Christ's flesh to eat and his blood to drink in the form of bread and wine. Why was this a holy thing to do? People could not help but conclude that it was holy simply because the Lord commanded it to be done. Therefore the best minds in the church came up with the claim that when the Word is added to the elements, they become sacramental. But this story of where the holiness comes from is just something that people are told to keep in mind; it does not actually make any sense and is not visibly reflected in the elements or their symbolism.

Therefore some people take the Holy Supper with a feeling of confidence that their sins are forgiven by the ceremony; some take it because they believe it sanctifies them; some take it because they believe it strengthens their faith and promotes their salvation. People who do not take the ceremony seriously, however, only continue taking it because they developed the habit as young adults; and some who see nothing rational about it do not take it at all. Godless people have an outright aversion to it. They say to themselves, "It is just a ritual that the clergy have told us is sacred. What is it but bread and wine? What is this nonsense that the body of Christ, which hung on the cross, and the blood that he shed at the time, are shared with the participants along with the bread and wine?" and other arguments like that.[396]

The one and only reason why these types of ideas about this most holy sacrament are entertained throughout the Christian world today is that they accord with the literal meaning of the Word. Meanwhile its spiritual meaning lies hidden away and has not been disclosed until now. Yet the spiritual meaning alone reveals the true function and benefit of the Holy Supper.

700

This meaning is being revealed now for the first time because Christianity did not exist before, except in name only (some people, though, did have at least a shadow of it). Until now people have not turned directly to or worshiped the Savior himself as the only God, the One in whom the divine Trinity exists. People have approached him only indirectly, which is not turning to him and worshiping him, but merely showing him respect on the grounds that he is why we have salvation. He is seen then not as the essential cause but merely as an intermediate cause that is below and outside the essential cause.[397]

Now, however, Christianity itself is arising for the first time. The Lord is now establishing the new church that is meant by the New Jerusalem in the Book of Revelation. In it, God the Father, the Son, and the Holy Spirit are acknowledged as one, because they are together in one person. Therefore the Lord is pleased to reveal the spiritual sense of the Word now, so that this new church will be able to come into the true benefit of the sacraments of baptism and the Holy Supper. This will happen as people come to see with the eyes of their spirit (meaning with understanding) the true holiness that lies hidden within the sacraments, and will embrace that holiness through the means that the Lord has taught in his Word.

701   If the spiritual meaning of the Word were not opened—or to put it another way, if the correspondences of earthly things to spiritual things were not revealed—the holiness of the sacrament we are currently focusing on would be as impossible to recognize as the true value of a field that contains hidden treasure. Such a field is at first considered no more valuable than any other field; but when someone finds that there is treasure in the field, it is valued at a much higher price, and the person who buys it becomes the owner of that wealth. This happens to an even greater degree when it is discovered that the treasure in the field is more valuable than all the gold in the world.

[2] If we do not know about the spiritual meaning, this sacrament is like a house that is locked and shuttered, but full of treasure chests that contain valuables. People pass by the house like any other on the street. The clergy decorate its outside walls with a surface of marble and cover its roof with gold plate; as a result, the eyes of passers-by are drawn to the house and they compliment it and consider it more valuable. The situation is very different, however, when the house is opened up and all are allowed in, and a guard inside loans treasures to some and gives treasures to others, depending on each person's worthiness. I mention that some of the wealth is given away, because the valuables there never run out, since they are constantly restocked. This is how it is for the spiritual riches within the Word and the heavenly riches within the sacraments.

[3] Before the hidden inner holiness of the sacrament that is our topic here is revealed to us, the sacrament looks like river sand that invisibly harbors gold particles in great quantities. When that holiness is revealed, it is like collecting those gold particles, melting them together into a mass, and forming them into beautiful shapes.

Before the holiness of this sacrament has been disclosed and is seen, this sacrament is like a box or case made out of beech or poplar wood. Inside, however, it contains diamonds, rubies, and many other precious stones laid out in an orderly way in little compartments. Obviously, we see this box or case as more valuable when we hear what is hidden inside it; and we see it as still more valuable when we actually see for ourselves what is inside and are given its contents for free.

Before this sacrament's correspondences with heaven have been revealed and we have actually seen the heavenly things to which it corresponds, this sacrament is like angels seen in the world wearing everyday clothing. People at first accord them no more honor than their clothes would suggest they were due. People treat the angels completely differently, however, when they recognize that they are angels, hear them saying angelic things, and see them performing miracles.

[4] A situation I experienced in the spiritual world illustrates the difference between holiness that is merely said to be present and holiness that is actually experienced. Someone read out loud an epistle that had been written by Paul while he was traveling in the world but had never been made public, so no one knew that it was by Paul. The people who heard the letter considered it worthless to begin with; but when they were told it actually belonged among the Pauline Epistles, they found tremendous joy in it and adored every single thing about it.

This experience suggests that when leaders of the clergy assert that the Word and the sacraments are holy, they do succeed in conveying some sense of holiness; but it is nothing like the experience we have when the true holiness is unveiled and is visibly presented before our eyes, which occurs when the spiritual meaning is revealed. Then an outer sense of holiness becomes an inner sense of holiness, and being told something turns into acknowledging it for ourselves. This is true of the holiness within the sacrament of the Holy Supper.

> When We Know Correspondences, We Realize What
> "the Lord's Flesh" and "the Lord's Blood" Mean; We See
> That They Mean the Same Thing as "Bread" and "Wine" Do.
> That Is, "the Lord's Flesh" and "Bread" Mean
> the Divine Goodness That Comes from His Love and Also
> All the Goodness Related to Goodwill, and "the Lord's Blood"
> and "Wine" Mean the Divine Truth That Comes
> from His Wisdom and Also All the Truth Related to Faith;
> "Eating" Them Means Making Them Our Own

Because the spiritual meaning of the Word has been disclosed today, and correspondences have been disclosed as well, since they are what convey that meaning, all that is required here is to quote passages from the Word that allow us to see clearly what "flesh" and "blood" and the bread and the wine in the Holy Supper mean. First, however, I will present passages

702

that show how this sacrament was originally instituted by the Lord, and passages in which the Lord himself teaches about his flesh and blood and about bread and wine.

703 *How the Lord instituted the Holy Supper:*

Jesus prepared the Passover with his disciples. When evening had come, he reclined to dine with them. As they were eating, Jesus took *the bread,* blessed it, broke it, and gave it to the disciples. He said, "Take, eat; this is *my body."* And taking *the cup* and giving thanks, he gave it to them, saying, "Drink from it, all of you; this is *my blood* of the new testament, which is shed for many." (Matthew 26:26, 27, 28; Mark 14:22, 23, 24; Luke 22:19, 20)

[2] *What the Lord taught about his own flesh and his own blood, and about bread and wine:*

Work for food—not for the food that perishes but for the food that lasts to eternal life, which the Son of Humankind will give you. Truly, truly I say to you, Moses did not give you bread from heaven, but my Father gives you the true bread from heaven. The bread of God is the one who comes down from heaven and gives life to the world. I am the bread of life. Those who come to me will never be hungry, and those who believe in me will never be thirsty. I am the bread that came down from heaven. Truly, truly I say to you, those who believe in me have eternal life. I am the bread of life. Your ancestors ate manna in the desert and died. This is the bread that comes down from heaven so that anyone who eats of it will live and not die. I am the living bread that came down from heaven. Anyone who eats this bread will live forever. The bread that I will give is my flesh, which I am giving for the life of the world. Truly, truly I say to you, unless you eat the flesh of the Son of Humankind and drink his blood, you will not have life within you. Those who eat my flesh and drink my blood have eternal life; I will revive them on the last day. My flesh is true food and my blood is true drink. Those who eat my flesh and drink my blood live in me and I in them. (John 6:27, 32, 33, 35, 41, 47, 48, 49, 50, 51, 53, 54, 55, 56)

704 In these passages, *flesh* does not mean flesh, and *blood* does not mean blood, as all who are enlightened from heaven can sense within themselves. Both terms in their *earthly meaning* relate to the Lord's suffering on the cross, which people were to remember. This is why the Lord said, as he simultaneously celebrated the supper of the last Jewish Passover and instituted the supper of the first Christian Passover, "Do this in remembrance of me" (Luke 22:19; 1 Corinthians 11:24, 25).

Likewise, the *bread* does not mean bread or the *wine* wine. In their *earthly meaning*, these terms have the same import as flesh and blood—that is, the Lord's suffering on the cross. We read that "Jesus broke bread and gave it to his disciples and said, 'This is my body'; and he took the cup and gave it to them and said, 'This is my blood'" (Matthew 26:[26–28]; Mark 14:[22–24]; Luke 22:[19–20]). For this reason he referred to his impending suffering on the cross as a "cup" (Matthew 26:39, 42, 44; Mark 14:36; John 18:11).

Passages in the Word that mention these four things—flesh, blood, bread, and wine—show that they mean the spiritual and heavenly things to which they correspond.

705

For example, we can see from the following passages that *flesh* in the Word means something spiritual and heavenly.[398]

> Come and gather for *the feast of the great God,* that you may eat the flesh of kings and the flesh of commanders, the flesh of the mighty, the flesh of horses and those who ride on them, and the flesh of all people, free and slaves, small and great. (Revelation 19:17, 18)

And in Ezekiel,

> Gather yourselves from all sides to *my sacrificial meal,* which I will sacrifice for you, *a great sacrificial meal* on the mountains of Israel, so that you will eat flesh and drink blood. You will eat the flesh of the mighty and drink the blood of the leaders of the earth. At my sacrificial meal, you will eat fat until you are full and you will drink blood until you are drunk.[399] You will be filled at my table with horses and chariots, with the mighty and all the men of war. This is how I will present my glory among the nations. (Ezekiel 39:17–21)

Surely everyone sees that in the passages just quoted *flesh* does not mean flesh and *blood* does not mean blood; they mean things that are spiritual and heavenly that correspond to them. Otherwise what else would these be but astoundingly nonsensical statements? Are people really going to eat the flesh of kings and commanders, the flesh of the mighty, and the flesh of horses and those who ride on them? Are they really going to be filled up at the table by eating horses, chariots, the mighty, and all the men of war? Are they really going to drink the blood of the leaders of the earth, and drink blood until they are drunk? Clearly, these statements concern the Lord's Holy Supper, as we can tell because of the mention of "the feast of the great God" and "a great sacrificial meal."

[2] Since all things that are spiritual and heavenly relate exclusively to goodness and truth, it follows that *flesh* means good action that relates to goodwill and *blood* means truth that relates to faith. On the highest level, these words mean the divine goodness of the Lord's love and the divine truth of the Lord's wisdom.

In the following passage in Ezekiel, *flesh* again means spiritual goodness.

> I will give them one heart, and I will create a new spirit within you. I will remove their heart of stone and give them a heart of flesh. (Ezekiel 11:19; 36:26)

In the Word, "heart" means love. Therefore *a heart of flesh* means a love for what is good.

The passages cited below on the meaning of bread and wine [§§707–708] make it clearer still that *flesh* and *blood* mean spiritual goodness and spiritual truth, since the Lord indicates that his flesh is bread and his blood is wine that we drink from a cup.

706 "The Lord's blood" means the divine truth that belongs to him and to the Word, because the spiritual meaning of his *flesh* is the divine goodness of his love; these two are united in the Lord.

It is well known that the Lord is the Word. There are two things to which all the details in the Word relate: divine goodness and divine truth. Therefore if we substitute "the Word" for "the Lord," it is clear that his *flesh* and *blood* mean divine goodness and divine truth.

There are many passages that establish that *blood* means the divine truth that belongs to the Lord or the Word. For example, his blood is called "the blood of the covenant," and a covenant means a partnership. It is by means of his divine truth that the Lord forges a partnership with us. See, for example, Zechariah: "By *the blood* of your *covenant* I will release the prisoners from the pit" (Zechariah 9:11). In Moses, "After Moses had read the Book of the Law in the hearing of the people, he sprinkled half the blood upon the people and said, '*Behold, the blood of the covenant* that Jehovah has forged with you through all these words'" (Exodus 24:3–8). "And Jesus took the cup and gave it to them and said, 'This is my blood of the new covenant'" (Matthew 26:27, 28; Mark 14:24; Luke 22:20). [2] The "blood of the new covenant" or "testament" means the Word, which is called a Covenant and a Testament, both the Old and the New; therefore it means the divine truth that is there. Because blood has this meaning, the Lord gave his disciples wine and said, "This is my blood" [Matthew 26:28; Mark 14:24]; wine means divine truth. Therefore wine is also called "the blood of grapes" (Genesis 49:11; Deuteronomy 32:14).

The Lord's words make this clearer still:

> Truly, truly I say to you, unless you eat the flesh of the Son of Human-kind and drink his blood, you will not have life within you. My flesh is true food and my blood is true drink. Those who eat my flesh and drink my blood live in me and I in them. (John 6:50–58)

Blood here means the divine truth of the Word, as is very clear because it says that those who drink it have life within them and live in the Lord and he lives in them. As people within the church are capable of knowing, divine truth and a life according to it are what allow the Lord to be in us and us in the Lord; the Holy Supper strengthens these effects.

[3] Since blood means the Lord's divine truth, which is also the divine truth of the Word, and this is the Old and New Covenant or Testament itself, therefore blood was the holiest symbolic substance in the church that existed among the children of Israel—a church whose every detail was a correspondence of something earthly with something spiritual. For example, they took the blood of the Passover lamb and put it on the doorposts and the lintel of their houses, to keep the plague from coming upon them (Exodus 12:7, 13, 22). The blood of the burnt offering was sprinkled on the altar, on its base, and on Aaron and his sons and on their garments (Exodus 29:12, 16, 20, 21; Leviticus 1:5, 11, 15; 3:2, 8, 13; 4:25, 30, 34; 8:15, 24; 17:6; Numbers 18:17; Deuteronomy 12:27). Blood was also sprinkled in front of the veil that was before the ark, on the mercy seat there, and on the horns of the altar of incense (Leviticus 4:6, 7, 17, 18; 16:12, 13, 14, 15).

The "blood of the Lamb" mentioned in the Book of Revelation has the same meaning: "They washed their robes and made them white in the blood of the Lamb" (Revelation 7:14). So does the following statement in the same book: "War broke out in heaven. Michael and his angels fought against the dragon, and conquered it by the blood of the Lamb and by the Word of their testimony" (Revelation 12:7, 11). [4] There is no basis for thinking that Michael and his angels were able to conquer the dragon through anything other than the Lord's divine truth in the Word.

The angels in heaven are unable to think about any blood or about the Lord's suffering; they think instead about the divine truth and about his resurrection. When we think about the Lord's blood, angels think instead about the divine truth of the Lord's Word; when we think about the Lord's suffering, they think instead about the Lord's glorification, focusing exclusively on his resurrection. A great deal of experience has allowed me to know that this is the case.

[5] The fact that blood means divine truth is also clear from the following statements in David: "God will save the souls of the needy; their blood will be precious in his sight. And they will live; and he will give them some of the gold of Sheba" (Psalms 72:13, 14, 15). *The blood that is precious in the sight of God* stands for the divine truth that is among the people [meant by "the needy"]; *the gold of Sheba* is the wisdom they develop as a result.

In Ezekiel: "Gather yourselves to a great sacrificial meal on the mountains of Israel, so that you will eat flesh and drink blood. You will drink the blood of the leaders of the earth, and drink blood until you are drunk. This is how I will present my glory among the nations" (Ezekiel 39:17–21). This passage deals with the church that the Lord is going to establish among the nations. (On the point that the word "blood" here cannot mean blood, but must mean the truth from the Word that exists among them, see just above [§705].)

707   The Lord's words make it very clear that *bread* means the same thing as *flesh:* "Jesus took *the bread,* broke it and gave it [to the disciples] and said, 'This is my body'" (Matthew 26:[26]; Mark 14:[22]; Luke 22:[19]). Also, "*the bread* that I will give is my flesh, which I am giving for the life of the world" (John 6:51). The Lord also says that he is "*the bread of life.* Anyone who eats this *bread will live forever*" (John 6:48, 51, 58).

The same "bread" is also what is meant by the sacrificial animals, which are called *bread* in the following passages:

> The priest will burn them on the altar as *the bread of an offering made by fire to Jehovah.* (Leviticus 3:11, 16)

> The sons of Aaron will be holy before their God. They are not to profane the name of their God, because they make *offerings by fire to Jehovah as the bread of their God.* You will consecrate him, because he offers *the bread of your God.* A man of the seed of Aaron in whom there is any defect is not to come forward and offer *the bread of his God.* (Leviticus 21:6, 8, 17, 21)

> Command the children of Israel and say to them, "You are to observe my offering, *my bread for the offerings made by fire that exude an aroma of rest.* You are to offer them to me at the appointed time." (Numbers 28:2)

> One who has touched something unclean is not to eat of the consecrated offerings; he is to wash his flesh in water. Afterward he may eat of the consecrated offerings, *because that is his bread.* (Leviticus 22:6, 7)

The food to eat from the consecrated offerings was the flesh of the sacrificial animals, which is here also called *bread.* See also Malachi 1:7.

[2] The *food offerings* that were part of certain sacrifices were likewise made of grain, and were therefore a kind of bread; they, too, have the same meaning (Leviticus 2:1–11; 6:14–21; 7:9–13; and elsewhere). So does the *bread* that was on a table inside the tabernacle; it was called the showbread or the bread set before Jehovah (see Exodus 25:30; 40:23; Leviticus 24:5–9).

As the following quotations make clear, *bread* in the Word means heavenly bread, not physical bread.

> Humankind does not live by bread alone; humankind lives by everything that comes from the mouth of Jehovah. (Deuteronomy 8:3)

> I will strike the earth with hunger—not hunger for bread or thirst for water but for hearing the words of Jehovah. (Amos 8:11)

Furthermore the term "bread" is used to mean food of every kind (see Leviticus 24:5–9; Exodus 25:30; 40:23; Numbers 4:7; 1 Kings 7:48). And in fact the word "food" itself means spiritual food, as the Lord's words make clear in the following passage:

> Work for food—not for the food that perishes but for the food that lasts to eternal life, which the Son of Humankind will give you. (John 6:27)

The Lord's words also make it very clear that *wine* means the same thing as *blood:* "Jesus took *the cup* and said, 'This is my blood'" (Matthew 26:[27–28]; Mark 14:[23–24]; Luke 22:[20]). This correlation is also clear from the following statement: "He washes his garments in *wine,* and his clothes in the blood of grapes" (Genesis 49:11); this is said of the Lord. "Jehovah Sabaoth will make a feast of fat things for all peoples, a feast of lees or of *sweet wine*" (Isaiah 25:6); this is said of the sacrament of the Holy Supper that the Lord would establish in the future. Also in Isaiah, "All who are thirsty, go to the waters. Even you who have no money, go, buy, and eat; and even though you have no money, buy *wine*" (Isaiah 55:1). *The fruit of the vine* that people will drink anew in the heavenly kingdom (Matthew 26:29; Mark 14:25; Luke 22:18) has no other meaning than the truth that belongs to the new church and heaven. This is

708

why many passages in the Word refer to the church as *a vineyard* (for example, Isaiah 5:1, 2, 4; Matthew 20:1–16), and the Lord calls himself *the true vine* and calls people who are grafted onto him *branches* (John 15:1, 5). There are many more passages like these.

709 From all that has just been said, you can see what the Lord's flesh and blood and the bread and the wine symbolize in their threefold meaning— their earthly, spiritual, and heavenly meaning.

All people within Christianity who are at all involved in their religion should know, and if they do not know, should find out, that in addition to physical nourishment, there is such a thing as spiritual nourishment. Physical nourishment affects the body; spiritual nourishment affects the soul. For instance, Jehovah the Lord says in Moses, "Humankind does not live by bread alone, but by everything that comes from the mouth of Jehovah" (Deuteronomy 8:3).

Now, since the body dies and the soul lives on after death, it follows that spiritual nourishment exists to serve our eternal well-being. Surely everyone can see, then, that these two types of nourishment should not in any way be confused with each other. [2] If we do confuse the two, the ideas we form about the Lord's flesh and blood and the [sacramental] bread and wine will inevitably be earthly, sensory, and even materialistic, bodily, and carnal; and these types of ideas suffocate any appropriately spiritual idea we might have of this most holy sacrament.

If some people are so extremely simple that they are incapable of developing any mental concept beyond what they can see with their own eyes, I urge them, when they take the bread and the wine and hear the Lord's flesh and blood mentioned, to think of the Holy Supper as the most holy act of worship and remember Christ's suffering and the love that drove him to save humankind. As he says, "Do this in remembrance of me" (Luke 22:19). "The Son of Humankind came to give his life as a ransom for many" (Matthew 20:28; Mark 10:45). "I lay down my life for the sheep" (John 10:15, 17; 15:13).

710 This last point can also be illustrated with comparisons. Surely we all love and remember people who were moved by a passionate love of country to fight against its enemies even to their death in order to free it from the yoke of slavery. Surely we all love and remember people who saw their fellow citizens in extreme poverty, starving to death before their eyes, and were moved by compassion and took all the silver and gold out of their houses and distributed it expecting nothing in return. Surely we all love and remember people who were moved by love and friendship and took their last lamb and butchered it and prepared it as a feast for their guests. And so on.

Understanding What Has Just Been Presented Makes It Possible to See That the Holy Supper Includes All the Qualities of the Church and All the Qualities of Heaven, Both Generally and Specifically

The material under the previous heading showed that the Lord himself is in the Holy Supper, that the divine goodness that comes from his love is the flesh and the bread, and that the divine truth that comes from his wisdom is the blood and the wine. Therefore the Holy Supper has three things within it: the Lord, his divine goodness, and his divine truth. Since these are the three things that the Holy Supper includes and contains, it follows that it contains the characteristics that are found universally throughout all of heaven and the church; and because all the individual qualities depend on these universal characteristics the way contents depend on their context, it also follows that the Holy Supper includes and contains all the individual qualities found in heaven and the church. **711**

Therefore the first conclusion to be drawn from this is that since the Lord's flesh and blood and likewise the bread and wine mean divine goodness and divine truth, each of which comes from the Lord and in fact is the Lord, the Holy Supper contains, then, all the qualities of heaven and all the qualities of the church both generally and specifically.

It is well known that three things are essential to the church—God, goodwill, and faith—and that all the specific teachings and practices go back to these three essentials as the universal qualities that underlie them. **712**

These three are actually the same as the three mentioned just above. In the Holy Supper, the Lord is God; divine goodness is goodwill, and divine truth is faith. What else is goodwill but something good that we do with the help of the Lord? What else is faith but something true that we believe with the help of the Lord?

From these come the three grand faculties within our inner self: the soul or mind as a whole, the will, and the intellect. These three are vessels for receiving the three universal qualities mentioned just above. The soul or mind is a vessel for receiving the Lord (its life comes from him); the will is a vessel for receiving love or goodness; and the intellect is a vessel for receiving wisdom or truth. As a result, each and every attribute of our soul or mind does not merely relate to the three universal qualities of heaven and the church but actually emanates from them. Name something that human beings accomplish without using the mind, the will, or the intellect. If even one of these three were removed, would we be more than some soulless creature?

[2] Likewise there are three vital systems in our outer self: the body as a whole, the heart, and the lungs. Each and every subsystem within our bodies is part of and is dependent on these three vital systems. In fact, these three vital systems of our bodies correspond to the three grand faculties within our minds. The heart corresponds to the will, and the lungs (or breathing) correspond to the intellect. (The existence of correspondences like these has been fully covered earlier in the work.)

Therefore each and every part of us has been formed in a general way and also in specific to be a vessel for the three universal qualities of heaven and the church. The reason for this is that we have been created to be an image and likeness of God, so that we can be in the Lord and the Lord can be in us.

713   The universal qualities mentioned above also have three opponents: the Devil, evil, and falsity. The Devil (which means hell) is against the Lord; evil is against goodness; and falsity is against truth. These three negative qualities work together. Wherever the Devil is, there you also have evil and falsity.

The three negative characteristics apply, on large and small scales, to all the qualities of hell and also all the qualities of the world that are against heaven and the church. Because they are opposites, they have had to be completely separated [from their positive counterparts]; nevertheless they are kept in some connection through the amazing way in which all parts of hell are placed beneath and subjected to heaven, evil is under the control of goodness, and falsity is under the control of truth. (For more on this arrangement see *Heaven and Hell* [§§589–596].)

714   To keep all the individual components in their proper arrangement and connection there need to be universal categories that allow those components to come into being and within which they find continued existence. It is also necessary that the individual components bear some resemblance to their universal category. Otherwise the whole would perish and so would all its parts.

This interrelationship has allowed all things in the universe to be preserved in their integrity from the first day of creation until now and to remain so into the future.

As we know, everything in the universe has a relationship to goodness and truth. The reason why this is the case is that everything was created by God out of the divine goodness of love by means of the divine truth of wisdom. Take anything whatever—an animal, a bush, a rock: these three universal qualities are in some way inscribed on it.

The reason why Melchizedek (who represented the Lord) brought bread and wine out to Abram and gave him a blessing is that divine goodness and divine truth are the most universal qualities throughout heaven and the church. We read the following about Melchizedek: **715**

> Melchizedek, king of Salem, brought bread and wine to Abram. He was a priest to God the Highest. He gave him a blessing. (Genesis 14:18, 19)

The following passage in David makes it clear that Melchizedek represented the Lord:

> You are a priest forever of the kind Melchizedek was. (Psalms 110:4)

For more proof that these things are said of the Lord, see Hebrews 5:6, 10; 6:20; 7:1, 10, 11, 15, 17, 21. Melchizedek brought out bread and wine because these two elements include all the qualities of heaven and of the church, and therefore all that is a blessing. The bread and wine in the Holy Supper perform the same function.

The Lord Himself and His Redemption Are Fully Present in the Holy Supper

The Lord's own words show that he is fully present in the Holy Supper—that both his glorified humanity and his divinity, which was the source of his humanity, are present in it. **716**

The following passages show that his humanity is present in the Holy Supper: "Jesus took the bread, broke it, gave it to the disciples, and said, 'This is my body.' And he took the cup, gave it to them, and said, 'This is my blood'" (Matthew 26:[26–28]; Mark 14:[22–24]; Luke 22:[17–20]). Similarly in John, "I am the bread of life. Anyone who eats this bread will live forever. The bread that I will give is my flesh. Truly, truly I say to you, those who eat my flesh and drink my blood live in me and I in them, and they will live forever" (John 6:[48, 51, 56, 58]). These passages clearly show that the Lord is present in the Holy Supper in his glorified humanity.

[2] The following passages make it clear that the Lord is also wholly present in the Holy Supper in his divinity, which was the source of his humanity: He is the bread that came down from heaven (John 6:[51]). He in fact came down from heaven with all that divinity; we read that "The Word was with God, and the Word was God. All things were made by it. And the Word became flesh" (John 1:1, 3, 14). This point is also supported by the statements to the effect that the Father and he are one (John 10:30); that all things that belong to the Father are his (John 3:35; 16:15); and that he is in the Father and the Father is in him (John 14:10, 11, and so on).

For another thing, his divinity could not have been separated from his humanity any more than a soul can be separated from its body. Therefore the statement just above that the Lord is fully present in the Holy Supper in his glorified humanity leads to the fact that his divinity, which was the source of his humanity, is also present in the Holy Supper.

Given that his flesh means the divine goodness of his love, and his blood means the divine truth of his wisdom, it is clear that both the Lord's divinity and his glorified humanity are fully and infinitely present in the Holy Supper. As a result, it is a meal that is spiritual in nature.

717 The fact that the Lord's redemption is also fully present in the Holy Supper is a direct consequence of what was just stated. Where the Lord is fully present, his redemption is also fully present. In his humanity he is the Redeemer; therefore he is redemption itself. Where he is fully present, no part of redemption can be absent. Therefore all who approach the Holy Supper worthily become his redeemed.

Being redeemed means being liberated from hell, forming a partnership with the Lord, and being saved (see below in this chapter [§§719–730] and the more extended treatment in the chapter on redemption [§§114–133]). These then are the fruits that are given to us in the Holy Supper. They are not given us to the full extent that the Lord would like, however. Moved as he is by his divine love, he would prefer to give us all of these gifts [at once]. Instead we are given them in accordance with our own receptivity; however receptive we are, that is how far the process of redemption takes us. This makes it clear that those who go to the Holy Supper worthily come away with effects and fruits of the Lord's redemption.

All who are of sound mind have an endless capacity for receiving wisdom from the Lord, that is, for increasing the number of truths that constitute their wisdom. They also have a similarly endless capacity for receiving love, that is, of bearing more fruit in the form of good feelings and actions that constitute their love. This perpetual bearing of more good fruit and therefore of love, and this perpetual increase of truths and therefore of wisdom, is something that is experienced by angels, and also by people who are becoming angels.

The Lord is love itself and wisdom itself; therefore we are endowed with an endless capacity for uniting ourselves to the Lord and the Lord to ourselves. Nevertheless, because we are finite, his actual divinity cannot become an integral part of us; it can only make contact with us and affect us. For an example by way of illustration, the light of the sun cannot become part of the substance of our eye, and a sound in the air cannot become part of the substance of our ear. The light and sound can only impinge on our eyes and ears and give us the ability to see and hear. We are not life itself the way the Lord was, even in his humanity (John 5:26); we are vessels for receiving life. Life itself cannot become an integral part of us, but it can have contact with us and affect us. I have added these points to help you understand in exactly what way the Lord and his redemption are fully present in the Holy Supper.

The Lord Is Present and Opens Heaven to Those Who Approach
the Holy Supper Worthily; He Is Also Present with Those Who
Approach It Unworthily, but He Does Not Open Heaven
to Them. Therefore As Baptism Brings Us into the Church,
So the Holy Supper Brings Us into Heaven

What it is to approach the Holy Supper worthily and what it is to approach it unworthily will be covered under the two headings following this one, since the approach that we should have to the Holy Supper will make it easier to recognize the approach that is its opposite [§§722–724, 725–727].

The reason why the Lord is present with both the worthy and the unworthy is that he is omnipresent in heaven and in hell and also in the world; therefore he is equally present with the evil and the good. With the good (the regenerated), though, he is present both generally and personally. The Lord is in them and they are in the Lord; and where the Lord is, there heaven is as well. In fact, heaven constitutes the body of the Lord; therefore being in his body is the same as being in heaven.

[2] The presence of the Lord with those who approach the Holy Supper unworthily, on the other hand, is general but not personal. To put it another way, it is an external presence but not an internal presence. The Lord's general or external presence allows us to live as human beings and enjoy the capacity to know, to understand, and to speak from our intellect in a rational way. (Since we are born for heaven and are therefore born to be spiritual, we are not like animals, which are merely earthly.) We also enjoy the capacity to will and do the things that our intellect is able to know, understand, and articulate in a rational way. If our will refuses to go along with the truly rational insights in our intellect, which are also intrinsically spiritual, we become an external person.

The Lord's presence with people who go no further than understanding what is true and good is general and external in nature; but his presence with people who go further and actually will and do what is true and good is both general and personal, or both internal and external.

[3] People who go no further than understanding and saying things that are true and good are like the foolish young women who had lamps but no oil. People who not only understand and say things that are true and good but also will them and do them are like the prudent young women, who were let in to attend the wedding while the others stood at the door and knocked but were not allowed in (Matthew 25:1–12).

These statements show, then, that the Lord is present and opens heaven to those who approach the Holy Supper worthily, and that he is also present with those who approach it unworthily, but he does not open heaven to them.

720   It is important that we not believe the Lord *closes* heaven to those who approach the Holy Supper unworthily. The Lord does not do this to any people, even to the final hour of their lives in this world. We ourselves close heaven to ourselves [while we are in this world], by rejecting faith and living an evil life. But even if we do this, we are still constantly kept in a state that leaves open the possibility of repentance and turning our lives around. The Lord is always present and exerting pressure on us

to accept him. As he says, "I am standing at the door and knocking. If any hear my voice and open the door, I will come in and *will dine with them and they with me*" (Revelation 3:20). We ourselves are at fault if we do not open the door.

After death, though, heaven is closed to those who continued to approach the Holy Table unworthily to the end of their lives. Heaven can no longer be opened to them because the inner regions of their minds have by then become fixed and established.

Baptism brings us into the church, as I have shown in the chapter on baptism [§§677–680]; and if you have understood what I have just presented above, it should be clear that the Holy Supper brings us into heaven.

These two sacraments, baptism and the Holy Supper, function as the two gateways to eternal life. Baptism, which is the first gateway, gives admittance and introduces every Christian into all that the church teaches from the Word about the other life. All these teachings are means by which we can be prepared for heaven and led toward it. The second gateway is the Holy Supper. Through it, all who have allowed themselves to be prepared and led by the Lord are given admittance to and brought into heaven. There are no other universal gateways.

These two phases can be compared to those experienced by an heir to the throne: During the first phase she or he is initiated into all forms of knowledge related to governing; in the second phase, she or he is crowned and takes the throne.

[2] They can also be compared to the phases experienced by children who are born with a sizeable inheritance. During the first phase, they learn and become steeped in how best to handle wealth and possessions; in the second phase, they receive and begin to manage their inheritance.

These phases can also be compared with first building a house and then living in it; and with our education from childhood to the age at which we become independent and able to judge things for ourselves, and then our rational and spiritual life after that.

In each case the one phase has to come first before we can come into the second, because the second would be impossible if we had not undergone the first.

These comparisons serve to illustrate that baptism and the Holy Supper are like two gateways that bring us to eternal life. Beyond the first gateway there is a field we have to cross in order to reach our goal of the second gateway, where stands the prize that we have been aiming for.

721

Prizes are not awarded until the contest is over; medals are not given out until the competition has come to an end.

We Come Forward Worthily to Take the Holy Supper When We Have Faith in the Lord and Goodwill toward Our Neighbor—That Is, When We Have Been Regenerated

722 Every Christian who studies the Word knows, acknowledges, and perceives that the three universal elements of the church are God, goodwill, and faith. These are universal elements because they are the universal means of being saved.

Before we can be said to be religious and before anything of the church can be established in us *we have to acknowledge the existence of God;* any reasoning that has anything spiritual within it affirms the necessity of this. Therefore if we come forward to take the Holy Supper but do not acknowledge the existence of God, we desecrate the Holy Supper. We see the bread and wine with our eyes and we taste them with our tongue, but our mind is thinking, "This ritual is pointless. How do these elements differ from what I have on my table at home? I am only going through this to avoid the shame of being accused of being an atheist, first by the priest and then by everyone else."

[2] Once we have come to acknowledge the existence of God, *goodwill is the second means* that allows us to take the Holy Supper worthily. This is clear both from the Word and from the statements that are read throughout the Christian world before people come forward for the Holy Supper.

As for *the Word,* it teaches that the first commandment and rule is to love God above all and to love our neighbor as ourselves (Matthew 22:35–40; Luke 10:25–28). Paul teaches that there are three things that contribute to our salvation, and the greatest of these is goodwill (1 Corinthians 13:13). "We know that God does not hear sinners, but if people worship God and do his will, he hears them" (John 9:31). "Every tree that does not bear good fruit is cut down and thrown into the fire" (Matthew 7:19, 20; Luke 3:8, 9).

[3] As for *the statements that are read throughout the Christian world before people come forward for the Holy Supper,* these statements sternly

warn people to find goodwill through reconciliation and repentance first. The only example that I will copy out here is the statement read in England to people about to partake of the Holy Supper:

> The way and means of becoming a worthy partaker in the Holy Supper is first to examine your life and your conversations by the rule of God's commandments. In whatever regard you notice that you have committed an offense of will, speech, or act, then bewail your own sinfulness and confess yourselves to Almighty God, with full purpose of amending your life. If you observe that your offenses are not only against God but also against your neighbors, you shall reconcile yourselves to them, being ready to make restitution and satisfaction to the utmost of your power for all injuries and wrongs done by you to any other, and being likewise ready to forgive others who have offended you, just as you wish to have forgiveness from God for your offenses. Otherwise receiving the Holy Supper does nothing but increase your damnation. Therefore if any of you is a blasphemer of God, or a hinderer or slanderer of his Word, [or an adulterer,] or someone taken with malice or ill will, or involved in any other grievous crime, repent of your sins. Or else do not come to the Holy Supper; otherwise, after you take it the Devil may enter into you as he entered into Judas, fill you with all wickedness, and bring you to destruction of both body and soul.[400]

[4] *Faith in the Lord is the third means* of worthily enjoying the Holy Supper, because goodwill and faith act as one, like heat and light in spring; every type of tree comes back to life when heat and light work together. Likewise, it is spiritual heat (goodwill) and spiritual light (truth related to faith) that bring us all to life.

The following passages make it clear that faith in the Lord has this effect:

> Those who believe in me will never die; they will live. (John 11:25, 26)

> This is the will of the Father, that all who believe in the Son should have eternal life. (John 6:40)

> God so loved the world that he gave his only begotten Son so that everyone who believes in him would have eternal life. (John 3:16)

> Those who believe in the Son have eternal life. Those who do not believe in the Son will not see life; instead God's anger will remain upon them. (John 3:36)

We are in the truth in Jesus Christ, the Son of God. He is the true God
and eternal life. (1 John 5:20)

723   As has been clearly shown in the chapter on reformation and regeneration [§§571–625], we are regenerated by these three—the Lord, goodwill, and faith—working together as one; and if we are not regenerated,
we cannot come into heaven. Therefore the Lord can open heaven only
to those who have been regenerated, and not to others; and after their
earthly death, he can incorporate only them and not others into heaven.

The "regenerated" who come forward worthily mean those who have
these three essentials of heaven and the church within themselves. The
term does not refer, however, to people who have these essentials only
outwardly. The latter confess the Lord not with their soul but only with
their tongue; they practice goodwill toward their neighbor not with their
heart but only with their body. This is the nature of all those whom the
Lord calls "workers of wickedness":

You will then begin to say, "Lord, we ate and drank with you," but I
will say to you, "I do not know where you are from. Depart from me,
all you workers of wickedness." (Luke 13:26, 27)

724   As with earlier points, these points too can be illustrated by various
things that align well and also things that correspond. For example: The
only people who are allowed to share a meal at the table of an emperor
or monarch are people of the highest office and rank. Before such people
come to such a dinner, they put on their best clothes and their badges of
office in order to be allowed in and be well received. Why should we not
have to prepare for the table of the Lord, who is the Lord of Lords and
the King of Kings (Revelation 17:14)? All have been called and invited to
his table, but after they rise from it, only those who are spiritually worthy
and suitably dressed are brought into the palaces of heaven to experience
the joys that are there; only people like these are honored as members of
the royal family because they are children of the Highest King. Afterward
they sit down every day with Abraham, Isaac, and Jacob (Matthew 8:11),
meaning the Lord's divine heavenly quality, his divine spiritual quality,
and his divine earthly quality.

The points made above can also be compared to wedding celebrations on earth, to which only relatives, neighbors, and friends of the
bride and groom are invited. If others come, they are of course allowed
in, but because there is no seat for them at the table, they leave. The situation is similar with those who are invited to the wedding celebrations of

the Lord as the bridegroom and the church as the bride; the people who are invited are the neighbors, relatives, and friends who have acquired a new family tree through being regenerated by the Lord.

For another thing, in our world who else do we develop a deep friendship with except people who are good-hearted and who trust us and do things in accordance with our wishes? We count them and no others as our own people and trust them with everything we own.

When We Come Forward Worthily to Take the Holy Supper, We Are in the Lord and the Lord Is in Us; Therefore through the Holy Supper We Enter into a Partnership with the Lord

Many chapters above contain proof that we come forward to take the Holy Supper worthily when we have faith in the Lord and goodwill toward our neighbor, and that truths related to faith bring a presence of the Lord and good actions related to goodwill work together with faith to form a partnership between us and the Lord. 725

It follows from this that when we come forward worthily to take the Holy Supper, we form a partnership with the Lord; and when we have a partnership with the Lord, we are in the Lord and the Lord is in us. The Lord himself declares in John that this is what happens to us when we take the Holy Supper worthily: "Those who eat my flesh and drink my blood live in me and I in them" (John 6:56). In the same gospel, the Lord also teaches that this is a partnership with him: "Live in me and I [shall live] in you. Those who live in me, and in whom I live, bear much fruit" (John 15:4, 5; Revelation 3:20). What else is having a partnership with the Lord but being among those who constitute his body? Those who constitute his body are those who believe in him and do his will; and his will is for us to practice goodwill in accordance with the truths that relate to faith.

Eternal life and salvation are not possible without a partnership with the Lord, because he himself is eternal life and salvation. The following statement in John, as well as other passages in the Word, make it very clear that he is eternal life: "Jesus Christ is the true God and eternal life" (1 John 5:20). He is also salvation, because this is the same thing as eternal life. In fact his name, *Jesus,* means salvation;[401] therefore throughout the entire Christian world he is known as *the Savior.* 726

Nevertheless, the only people who come forward worthily to take the Holy Supper are people who have an inward partnership with the Lord; and the only people who have an inward partnership with him are the people who have been regenerated. (Who the "regenerated" are has been shown in the chapter on reformation and regeneration [§§571–625].)

[2] Now, there are of course many people who confess the Lord and do good things for their neighbor. If they do not do these things out of love for their neighbor and faith in the Lord, however, they have not been regenerated. Such people do good things for their neighbor solely for reasons that focus on the world and themselves, and not on their neighbor as their neighbor. The things that such people do are merely earthly and do not conceal anything spiritual inside them. The people who do them confess the Lord, but only with their mouth and lips, while their heart is far away.

Genuine love for our neighbor and genuine faith come solely from the Lord. Both of these qualities are granted to us when we use our free choice to do good things for our neighbor in an earthly way, believe truths in a rational way, and turn to the Lord, doing all three because we have been commanded to in the Word. Then the Lord plants goodwill and faith in our core, and makes them both spiritual. In this way, the Lord unites himself to us and we unite ourselves to the Lord—there is no partnership if it is not reciprocal. But these points have been more fully demonstrated in the chapters on goodwill [§§392–462], faith [§§336–391], free choice [§§463–508], and regeneration [§§571–625].

727 As we all know, in our world dinner invitations and banquets are used as a way to form partnerships and make connections. The one sending out invitations has the intention and hope of moving toward some goal that relates to consensus or friendship. This is even more the case with dinner invitations that are intended to serve a spiritual goal. The feasts that were held in the early churches were feasts of goodwill. There were similar events in the early Christian church, in which people would support and strengthen each other in maintaining their worship of the Lord with a good heart. The children of Israel would eat meals of the sacrificed animals next to the tabernacle; these events, too, meant unanimity in the worship of Jehovah. Therefore they would refer to the flesh that they were eating as holy (Jeremiah 11:15; Haggai 2:12). The same language is used many times in other passages, because that food came from a sacrifice. Why would this not be true of the bread and wine and the Passover

flesh at the supper of the Lord, who offered himself as a sacrifice for the sins of the whole world?

[2] The connection that we form with the Lord through the Holy Supper can be illustrated by the connection felt by families of a common ancestor. The first generation consists of siblings; later generations include a variety of relations, all of whom are connected in some way to the original ancestor. What binds them all together is not so much the shared flesh and blood but a similar soul and similar interests that they inherit through that flesh and blood. The fact that they are all related is generally visible in their faces and also their mannerisms. Therefore they are called "one flesh," as in Genesis 29:14; 37:27; 2 Samuel 5:1; 19:11, 12; and elsewhere.

[3] Our relationship with the Lord is similar; he is the Father of all the faithful and the blessed. Our partnership with him is brought about through love and faith. Because we have these two characteristics in common, we are called "one flesh." This is why the Lord says, "Those who eat my flesh and drink my blood live in me and I in them" [John 6:56].

Surely everyone can see that it is not the bread and wine that have this effect, but rather the good we do from love, which is meant by the bread, and the truth we believe, which is meant by the wine. These qualities belong exclusively to the Lord; they emanate from and are distributed by him alone. Every partnership is formed by love, and love is not love without trust.

People who believe that the bread really is flesh and the wine really is blood, however, and who cannot lift their thinking any higher than that, should keep thinking that way, but include the thought that the holiest thing in the ceremony—the factor that brings us into a partnership with the Lord—is a certain something that we are allowed to take in and incorporate into ourselves as if it belonged to us, although it actually still belongs to the Lord.

When We Come Forward Worthily to Take It, the Holy Supper Functions as [God's] Signature and Seal Confirming That We Have Been Adopted as His Children

Provided we take it worthily, the Holy Supper is able to function as [God's] signature and seal confirming that we have been adopted as his

728

children, because the Lord is present at that time, as was indicated above [§§719–721], and brings into heaven those who are born of him, that is, who have been regenerated by him. The Holy Supper has this effect because the Lord is present at it in his human manifestation; as was mentioned above, the Lord himself and his redemption are fully present in the Holy Supper [§§716–718]. He says of the bread, "This is my body," and of the wine, "This is my blood." Therefore he then makes us part of his body, and both heaven and the church constitute that body.

Earlier, while we are still undergoing the process of being regenerated, the Lord is of course present as well; through the work that he is doing in us, he is preparing us for heaven. In order for us to become an actual part of heaven, though, we need to present ourselves to the Lord in an active way. Because the Lord is also actively presenting himself to us [in the Holy Supper], we actively receive him—not as he was when he was hanging on the cross but as he is in his human manifestation after it was glorified, which is present in the Holy Supper. The "body" of his human manifestation is divine goodness, and the "blood" is divine truth. These qualities are given to us; through them we are regenerated and then we are in the Lord and the Lord is in us. As mentioned above [§716], the meal that is put on in the Holy Supper is spiritual in nature.

A proper understanding of all this shows that the Holy Supper is like a signature and seal that testify that the people who come forward worthily to take it are children of God.

729   Now, people who die as children and teenagers and do not reach the age at which they could come forward worthily to take the Holy Supper are made a part of heaven by the Lord through their baptism instead. The chapter on baptism has shown that *baptism brings people into the Christian church and at the same time brings them into the company of Christians in the spiritual world* [§§677–680]. In that world, the church and heaven are one. Therefore making these young ones a part of the church is also making them a part of heaven. Because they are raised under the Lord's supervision, they are regenerated more and more and become his children; they do not recognize anyone else as their parent.

As for children and teenagers who were born outside the Christian church, once they develop faith in the Lord, they are made part of the heaven that is designated for their religion, but they come there through a different means than baptism. They do not mix with people who are in the Christian heaven.

There is no such thing as a race of people anywhere on the entire planet who cannot be saved if they acknowledge God and live good lives. The Lord redeems all such people. We are all born spiritual by nature and therefore we all have a capacity for receiving the gift of redemption.

People who accept the Lord, that is, who have faith in him and do not practice evil in their lives, are called "children of God" and "those born of God" (John 1:12, 13; 11:52). They are also called "children of the kingdom" (Matthew 13:38) and "heirs" (Matthew 19:29; 25:34). The Lord's disciples are also called "children" (John 13:33), and so are all the angels (Job 1:6; 2:1).

The Holy Supper is similar to a covenant; after the terms are agreed upon, it is signed and sealed. The Lord's blood is the covenant, as he himself teaches. When he lifted the cup and gave it to the disciples he said, "Drink from it, all of you; this is my blood of the new testament" (Matthew 26:27, 28; Mark 14:23, 24; Luke 22:20). The *new testament* means the new covenant. Therefore the Word that was written through the prophets before the Lord's Coming is called the Old Testament or Old Covenant, and the Word written through the Gospel writers and apostles after his Coming is called the New Testament or New Covenant. On the point that blood and also the wine in the Holy Supper mean the divine truth contained in the Word, see the fifth and seventh sections under the second heading of this chapter [§§706, 708]. The covenant that the Lord has made with us and we have made with the Lord is the Word. The Lord came down as the Word, that is, divine truth. Because his blood is divine truth, the blood in the Israelite church (a church that represented the Christian church to come) was called *the blood of the covenant* (Exodus 24:8; Zechariah 9:11), and the Lord was called *a covenant to the people* (Isaiah 42:6; 49:8; Jeremiah 31:31–34; Psalms 111:9).

730

[2] According to the orderly sequence practiced in the world, a signature is absolutely necessary in order to finalize an agreement—a step that comes only after the terms have been worked out. What good is a will or a bequest without a signature? What good is a judicial statement without a signed opinion at the bottom to confirm the judgment? What good is it to be granted national authority if you have no charter to prove it? What good is a verbal offer of a promotion if there is no accompanying letter of confirmation? What good is taking possession of a house if you have no signed agreement of sale with the previous owner? What good does it do to run toward a goal or race for a finish line and a prize

if there is no goal or finish line where the prizes will be handed out, and the official has given you no firm indication that he will make good on his promises if you win?

These last analogies have been added solely for the sake of illustration, however, so that everyone including the uneducated will perceive that taking the Holy Supper is like receiving [God's] signature, seal, certificate, or evidentiary letter to prove even to the angels that we have been adopted as God's children; and also that taking the Holy Supper is like being given the key to our home in heaven where we will live forever.

731   On one occasion I saw an angel flying below the eastern heaven. He had a trumpet in his hand and held it to his mouth, sounding to the north, to the west, and to the south. He had a mantle that was flowing behind him as he flew, and was wearing a belt studded with rubies and sapphires that radiated a flame-colored light. His body was facing the ground as he flew parallel to it. He landed softly on the ground not far from where I was. As he touched the ground, he stood upright on his feet and walked here and there. When he noticed me he walked straight in my direction. I was in the spirit and was standing on top of a hill in the southern region. When he was close enough I greeted him and said, "What is going on just now? I heard the sound of your trumpet and saw you come down through the air."

"I have been sent," the angel said, "to summon the most famous scholars, the best researchers, and the most distinguished thinkers from the nations of the Christian world that are on this continent to meet on this hill where you are currently standing. They are to express their minds freely on the following question: When they were in the world, what had they thought and understood and what wisdom had they gained concerning *heavenly joy* and *eternal happiness?*

[2] "The reason behind this mission of mine is that several people who had recently arrived from the world came to our heavenly community, which is in the east. Once they had been allowed in, they told us that not a single person in the entire Christian world knows what heavenly joy is or what eternal happiness is; therefore people have no idea what heaven is. My companions and colleagues were profoundly shocked to hear this, and said to me, 'Go down, summon and call together the wisest people in the world of spirits, where all mortals are first gathered

after they leave the physical world, for the purpose of verifying from many mouths whether it is in fact true that Christians have this deep a darkness or this blind an ignorance about their future lives.'"

"Wait a little while," he added, "and you will see groups of the wise coming here. The Lord is going to prepare a place for them to meet."

[3] I did wait. About half an hour later I saw two groups of people coming from the north, two groups from the west, and two groups from the south. As they arrived, the angel with the trumpet ushered them into the building that had been prepared for the occasion, and they took up places that had been designated for them according to the regions they came from.

There were six groups. There was also a seventh group to the east, but the other groups did not see it because the light was in their eyes.

After all were gathered, the angel revealed the reason for the gathering. He asked that the groups come forward in sequence and express their wisdom concerning *heavenly joy* and *eternal happiness*. Upon hearing the topic, each group turned inward and formed a circle face to face in order first to call to mind what ideas they had formed on these subjects in the physical world, where they used to live; then to discuss the ideas with each other; and finally after discussion and consultation, to express the opinion of their group to the others present.

After consulting with each other, *the first group,* which was from the north, said, "Heavenly joy and eternal happiness are the same thing as living in heaven. Therefore all who become part of heaven come into the experience of its festivities, much as people do who attend a wedding. Surely heaven is before our eyes; it is above us, and is therefore a place. In that place and nowhere else there is tremendous bliss and extraordinary pleasure. When we come into heaven, our whole mind and our whole body come into this bliss and pleasure, because of the fullness of joys that is there. Therefore heavenly happiness, which is the same thing as eternal happiness, is simply a matter of being allowed into heaven; and it is divine grace that lets us in."

[2] After they finished speaking, *the second group* from the north brought forth their wisdom in the form of the following conjecture: "Surely heavenly joy and eternal happiness consist in extremely enjoyable interactions and delicious conversations with angels. Everyone's faces are smiling broadly and happily all the time; everyone is laughing with pleasure at the wonderful and incredibly clever things that are being said. What else are the joys of heaven but variations on this scene that go on to eternity?"

732

[3] *The third group,* which was the first group of wise people from the western region, presented the following as the result of what they had felt and thought: "Surely the height of heavenly joy and eternal happiness consists in dining with Abraham, Isaac, and Jacob. At their tables there will be the finest and most sumptuous foods and excellent vintage wine. After the meal there will be games, and young men and women dancing together to the sound of musicians on various instruments, with a break now and then for us to hear the singing of incredibly sweet songs. When the evening comes, there will be stage plays. The next day there will be yet another great feast; and it will continue like this every day to eternity."

[4] After they had said this, *the fourth group,* which was the second from the western region, announced their opinion: "We have had many ideas about heavenly joy and eternal happiness. Just now, we considered various joys and compared them with each other. The conclusion of our group is that heavenly joys are the joys of a garden paradise. Surely heaven is a garden paradise that extends all the way from the east to the west and from the south to the north. In it there are fruit trees and gorgeous flowers. At the center of them all there stands a magnificent tree of life. The blessed will sit by this tree and eat exquisitely flavorful fruit and wear wonderfully fragrant garlands of flowers. Because of the perpetual springtime there, these fruits and flowers are being born and reborn every day in unending variety; and because such things are constantly sprouting and flowering, and because the warmth of spring is everlasting there, the minds of the blessed, too, are continually being renewed and cannot help coming upon new joys every day and drinking them in. As a result, they return to the age at which their youth first blossomed; they are brought back into the primordial state that Adam and Eve experienced when they were first created; and they are restored to Adam and Eve's paradise, only relocated from earth to heaven."

[5] *The fifth group,* which was the first group of clever minds from the southern region, gave the following statement: "Surely heavenly joys and eternal happiness consist in the possession of great power and tremendous wealth, and the more-than-regal magnificence and shining splendor that come with them. These are the source of the joys of heaven and of our ongoing enjoyment of them, which is eternal happiness, as we have noticed from observing people in our former world who had such power and wealth. We have also gathered this from [the statements in the Word] that those who are happy in heaven are going to reign with

the Lord, and will be kings and princes, because they are children of the King of Kings and Lord of Lords; and that they are going to sit on thrones and angels will minister to them.⁴⁰² We have realized how magnificent heaven will be from the fact that the New Jerusalem—which is a way of describing the glories of heaven—will have glorious doors, each of which is a pearl, and streets of pure gold, and outside walls built on precious stones. Therefore all who are accepted into heaven will have their own royal palace gleaming with gold and precious stones, and power that rotates in sequence from one person to the next. Because we recognize that there is inherent joy and intrinsic happiness in such situations, and that God's promises cannot be broken, we could not attribute the happiest aspect of heavenly life to any other factor."

[6] After that, *the sixth group,* which was the second from the southern region, raised their voices and said, "The joy of heaven and the eternal happiness that goes with it come from perpetually glorifying God, in a celebration that goes on forever, and blissful worship with songs and shouting. It is a constant lifting of the heart toward God, with complete trust that he accepts our prayers and praise because we experience his divine showering of abundant blessings upon us."

Some in the same group added, "We will glorify him with gorgeous lamps full of wonderfully fragrant incense, and with impressive parades led by the pope holding a great horn, followed next by church leaders and priests of every rank, and then men holding palm branches and women carrying golden images in their hands."

The seventh group, which was not seen by the others because the light was in the others' eyes, was from the eastern part of heaven. Its members were angels from the same community as the angel with the trumpet. After hearing that not a single person in the entire Christian world knows what heavenly joy is or what eternal happiness is, they had said to each other, "This cannot possibly be true. Christians could never be that far in the dark or experience that degree of mental collapse. We should go down ourselves and hear if this is true or not; if it does turn out to be true, it is surely an omen of something."

At this point in the event, these angels said to the angel with the trumpet, "As you know, all people who have had a desire to go to heaven and have formed any particular conception of the joys heaven has in store for them are brought after they die to experience the joys they have been picturing. After they have explored the nature of their joys, and have experienced that their concepts of joy were based on empty ideas and

733

insane fantasies, they are brought up out of those concepts and taught better ones. This is what happens in the world of spirits for most people who have meditated on heaven during their life on earth and who have come to some conclusion about the joys of heaven to the point where they desire to experience them."

Upon hearing this, the angel with the trumpet said to the six groups of wise people from the Christian world who had been summoned, "Follow me, and I will bring you into your joys and therefore into heaven."

734   The angel then led the way. The first to go with him were the people who had convinced themselves that heavenly joys were extremely enjoyable interactions and delicious conversations with angels.[403] The angel brought them into a gathering of people in the northern region who had shared the same view of heavenly joys when they were in the physical world.

The people of this kind had been brought together to a very large house there. The house had more than fifty rooms, and the rooms had each been assigned a particular topic of conversation. In several rooms over here, people were discussing what they had heard and seen in the town square and in the streets. In several rooms over there, people were talking about love and relationships, and some were interjecting hilarious comments until all present were laughing hard with big smiles on their faces. In other rooms people were discussing the latest news about the royal family, the government ministers, the political state of the nation, and various points that had been leaked by members of secret committees, as well as their own projections and conjectures about what would happen next. In other rooms, people were discussing business; in other rooms, literature; in others, topics related to civic prudence and moral life; in others, matters related to the church and its various sects; and so on.

I was given permission to look around the house. I saw people rushing from room to room, looking for an exchange that would be close to their heart and joyful for them. I noticed that there were three types of people in these conversations: people who were desperate to speak; people who were eager to ask questions; and people who were avidly listening.

[2] There were four entrances to the house, one toward each point of the compass. I noticed that many people were leaving the conversations and hurrying to leave the building. I followed some to the east door. There I saw a number of people sitting by the door, looking depressed.

I went up to them and asked, "Why are you sitting here and looking so sad?"

"The doors to this house," they replied, "are kept locked to people who are trying to exit. It is now three days since we came in here. All the life has gone out of our desire to be in conversation. We are so worn out from the endless talking that we can hardly bear to hear even the buzz of it in the distance anymore. We are so fed up that we came to this door and have been banging on it to be let out, but the response we get is, 'The doors to this house do not open to let people *out;* they only open to let people *in.* Stay there and relish the joys of heaven!' Hearing that, we realized we are stuck here forever. We are feeling utterly depressed and are starting to have chest pains and rising anxiety."

[3] The angel then spoke to them and said, "The state you are in now is actually the *death* of your joys—yet you recently thought these activities were the only joys in heaven! In fact, they are only an adjunct to true heavenly joys."

"So what *is* heavenly joy, then?" they asked the angel.

His brief response was this: "It is the delight found in doing something useful for ourselves or for others. The delight that we feel in being useful derives its essence from love and takes its shape through wisdom. The delight in being useful that arises from love through wisdom is the soul and life of all heavenly joys."

"In the heavens," he added, "angels have very enjoyable conversations; these interactions are exhilarating to their higher minds, bring satisfaction to their lower minds, create pleasurable feelings in their chests, and refresh their bodies. These conversations only happen among them, though, after they have done useful things as a part of their jobs and their work. Their work puts soul and life into all the other things that make them happy and give them pleasure. If you take away that soul, that life, these ancillary joys gradually cease to be joyful; at first they become trivial, then completely pointless, and eventually depressing and anxiety-provoking."

Once he had said that, the door opened up. The people who had been sitting there jumped up and ran back to their homes, to their jobs and their work, and came back to life.

Afterward the angel addressed the people who had convinced themselves that heavenly joys and eternal happiness consist in dining with Abraham, Isaac, and Jacob, and then playing games and watching shows after the meal, then having another feast the next day, and so on to eternity.[404]

"Follow me," the angel said to them, "and I will bring you into the happiness of your joys."

735

He led them through a wooded area to a clearing with a large, low platform of wooden boards that had tables on it—fifteen on one side, and fifteen on the other.

"Why are there so many tables?" they asked.

"The first table is for Abram, the second for Isaac, the third for Jacob, and next to them is a row of twelve tables for the twelve apostles. On the other side, there are the same number of tables for their wives. The first three tables are for Sarai, Abram's wife; Rebecca, Isaac's wife; and Leah and Rachel, Jacob's wives. The other twelve tables are for the wives of the twelve apostles."

[2] Not too long afterward, the tables were loaded with dishes of food, and little pyramids with desserts[405] were neatly placed in the spaces between the dishes. The dinner guests stood next to the tables, excited to see the distinguished people who would be sitting at the heads of the tables. After a brief delay, they saw their honorable dinner companions entering in a procession, beginning with Abram and ending with the last of the apostles. Soon the patriarchs were seated on padded chairs at the heads of the tables. They addressed the visitors, who were still standing, and said, "We invite you to sit down with us."

The men sat down with the patriarchs and the women sat down with their wives. They all ate and drank together in a joyful yet reverent state of mind. After the meal was over, the famous figures left. Then there were games to play, and young men and women giving a dance performance, and afterward several stage plays. At the end of the evening, all were invited to another festival the next day, but with the following stipulation: "You will dine with Abram on the first day, Isaac on the second, Jacob on the third, Peter on the fourth, James on the fifth, John on the sixth, Paul on the seventh, and with the rest in sequence up to the fifteenth day, at which time the dinner cycle will repeat, although you will be sitting in different places. This cycle will go on forever."

[3] At that point the angel called together the people from his group, and said to them, "All the other guests you dined with were people who had formed mental images similar to your own about the joys of heaven and therefore eternal happiness. These banquets and shows were established with the Lord's permission for the purpose of allowing people to see that their ideas are foolish so that they can let go of them.

"The famous men that you saw at the heads of the tables were actually older actors with beards; many of them are country folk whose relative wealth compared to their neighbors has given them enough of a superior attitude for the part. They agreed to pretend that they were the ancient patriarchs. [4] But follow me now to the pathways that lead out of this arena."

They followed, and came upon fifty people here and fifty there who had crammed their stomachs full of food to the point of nausea and were longing for their usual routine at home—some for their professional duties, some for their businesses, and some for the work they did with their hands. Many of them, though, had been detained by the guards of that wooded area and questioned about which day of feasting they were on, and whether they had eaten with Peter or Paul yet. They were told that leaving before doing so was highly improper and would cause them great shame.

Many of the people said to the guards in response, "We are fed up with our joys! We can't even taste the food or the drink anymore—our sense of taste is burned out. Our stomach can't take it anymore, and we can no longer stand to put anything in our mouths. This ridiculous indulgence has gone on for whole days and nights on end. Please, we beg you, let us go!"

They were allowed out and ran home breathlessly.

[5] The angel called his group together again, and as they walked away together he taught them the following things about heaven.

"In heaven as on earth there is food and drink, and there are dinners and parties, and the tables of leading figures are laden with glorious spreads including special delicacies you don't find elsewhere; these things rejuvenate and refresh the mind. There are also sports and shows and concerts of vocal and instrumental music, all at the height of perfection. All these things are a joy to the angels, but they don't constitute their true happiness. Their happiness has to be present for these things to bring them joy. The happiness that is present within them during the joyful events is what makes the events joyful, enriches them, and keeps them from becoming meaningless and tedious. And the only source of anyone's true happiness is doing something useful through his or her work.

[6] "Hidden deep within the desires of every angel's heart there is a kind of current that draws her or his mind to do something. In that activity the mind finds its peace and satisfaction. This peace and satisfaction then condition the mind to be receptive to the love of being useful that flows in from the Lord. Receiving this love leads to the true heavenly happiness that gives life to the joys that I mentioned a moment ago.

"At the level of its essence, heavenly food is in fact love, wisdom, and usefulness working together; or to put it another way, usefulness that draws on wisdom and comes from love. For all of us in heaven, the type of food we are given for our bodies therefore depends on how useful a function we perform. People who perform the highest-level functions are given magnificent food; people who perform mid-level functions are given more moderate kinds of food, but still very good-tasting; people who perform low-level functions are given humble food. Those who do nothing get no food at all."

736   Next, the angel summoned the group of so-called wise people who considered heavenly joys, and the eternal happiness that results from them, to consist in the possession of great power and tremendous wealth, and the more-than-regal magnificence and shining splendor that come with them.[406] (They based their view on statements in the Word to the effect that we are going to be kings and princes and reign with Christ to eternity and angels will minister to us, and many more things of that nature.)[407]

The angel said to them, "Follow me, and I will bring you into your joys."

He took them into a portico with pillars and obelisks. At the front of it there was a low entryway that led into the portico itself. The angel brought them through this entrance. They came upon [twenty men here and] twenty there who were waiting around. Suddenly an actor who was pretending to be an angel appeared and said to them, "This portico is the entrance to heaven itself. Stay here for a while and prepare yourselves, because the older among you are going to become kings and the younger are going to become princes."

[2] After the actor said that, next to each pillar a throne appeared; a mantle of silk was laid out on it and a scepter and a crown were sitting on top of the mantle. Next to each obelisk a seat appeared that was raised about four and a half feet off the ground. On the seat there was a gold chain and a sash of the order of the knighthood, which was gathered and held at each end by a ring of diamonds.

Then the supposed angel cried out, "Go now and put on this finery; then take your seats and wait."

The older men immediately ran to the thrones and the younger men to the seats. They put on their royal trappings and sat down. A dense fog rose up from below. As they breathed it in, their heads began to swell and they straightened up on their thrones and seats and came fully to believe that they were now kings and princes. That fog was the aura of the fantasy that now inspired them.

Suddenly a number of young people appeared, flying down as if from heaven. Two of them took up positions behind each throne and one behind each seat in order to minister to the seated royalty.

Then a herald periodically proclaimed, "You, O kings and princes, wait here a little longer. Your royal courts are now being prepared in heaven. Soon, courtiers and attendants will come to escort you there." And they waited and waited until their spirits were exhausted and worn out by desire.

[3] After three hours heaven opened above their heads and angels looked down and felt sorry for them. The angels said, "Why are you sitting there like idiots and buffoons? These people played a trick on you and managed to turn you from people into statues. They were able to do this because you had taken it to heart that you were going to reign with Christ as kings and princes, and that angels would be ministering to you. Have you forgotten what the Lord said, that in heaven those who want to be great must be servants [Matthew 20:26, 27; Mark 10:43, 44]?

"You need to learn what 'kings' and 'princes' mean and what 'reigning with Christ' means. They mean becoming wise and performing a useful function. Christ's kingdom, which is heaven, is a kingdom of useful functions. The Lord loves everyone, and wants us all to have what is good. What is good is being useful. Because the Lord does good and useful things indirectly, here through angels and in the world through people, he gives those who are performing useful functions a love for being useful, and also a reward for being useful, which is inner bliss; and this inner bliss is eternal happiness.

[4] "As there is on earth, in heaven as well there is great power and tremendous wealth. There are governments and governmental responsibilities; therefore there are positions of greater and lesser power and status. Those who occupy the top positions have courts and palaces that are of greater magnificence and splendor than the courts and palaces of emperors and monarchs on earth. Because of the sheer number of courtiers, ministers, and attendants, and the finery they all wear, these leaders are surrounded with honor and glory. The people who occupy these top positions, though, are selected from among those whose hearts are devoted to the well-being of all and who are not affected beyond their bodily senses by the grandeur and magnificence that surrounds them in order to establish authority.

"Because it is crucial to the well-being of all that each person has some function in the community (and the community is in effect a body of the whole), and because all usefulness comes from the Lord and is carried out through the agency of angels and people as if they were acting on their own, clearly this is what it means to 'reign with the Lord.'"

Upon hearing this statement from heaven, the supposed kings and princes came down from their thrones and seats and laid down their scepters, crowns, and mantles. The dense fog that held the aura of their fantasy receded from them, and a bright cloud enveloped them that held an aura of wisdom; it restored their minds to sanity.

737 After that, the angel went back to the house where the wise from the Christian world were gathered. He next summoned the group that had taken on the belief that heavenly joys and eternal happiness were delightful experiences in a garden paradise.[408]

The angel said to them, "Follow me, and I will bring you to paradise, to your heaven, so that you can begin having the blissful experiences of your eternal happiness."

He led them through a tall gateway made of interwoven shoots and branches from excellent species of trees.[409] Beyond the entrance he led them along a meandering path from one area to another.

This was in fact a garden paradise at the first point of entry to heaven. This is where people are sent who had believed when they were in the world that heaven consists entirely of one garden paradise, because it is called paradise. It is also used for people who had latched onto the idea that after death there is complete rest from labors, and that this rest takes the form of breathing in delightful experiences, walking among beds of roses, being cheered up by the finest of wines, and enjoying drinking parties; they think that this life is only possible in a heavenly garden paradise.

[2] The group that was led along by the angel then saw a huge crowd of people—both male and female, of all ages. They were in groups of three here, three there; ten here, ten there. Some groups were sitting among rose gardens, weaving garlands for the heads of the older people and the arms of the young, and braiding flower sashes to go around the children's chests. Other groups were making fruit juice, squeezing grapes, cherries, and berries into cups and enjoying sipping from them. Other groups were inhaling the air, which was redolent with the fragrances of flowers, fruits, and sweet-smelling leaves. Some groups were singing, caressing the ears of their listeners with beautiful songs. Some groups were sitting by fountains, making different patterns with the

water that was squirting in the air. Other groups were going into gazebos to lie around on couches. They were all enjoying these and many other paradisal pastimes.

[3] After the angel's group had seen all this, he brought them along a path that wound here and there, until he finally stopped next to a group of people sitting in a gorgeous rose garden, bordered by olive trees, orange trees, and lemon trees. The people were rocking back and forth holding their heads in their hands, grief-stricken and weeping.

The people in the angel's group greeted them and asked "What's wrong?"

"It has been seven days now," they replied, "since we arrived in this paradise. When we first arrived, we felt as though our minds had been lifted into heaven itself and we had gained access to its inmost joys and pleasures. After three days, though, the fun began to wear off. These things became less and less pleasant to our minds; we eventually became numb to them and found no pleasure in them at all. When things we had thought would be such joys became no fun anymore, we started to fear that we were losing every delight of our life. We began to doubt there was even such a thing as eternal happiness. So then we began wandering along the pathways and through different areas, looking for that gateway through which we had come in. We walked around and around in great circles, and asked directions from the people we met. Some of them said, 'That gateway cannot be found. This garden paradise is a massive labyrinth. Those who try to leave go deeper and deeper into it. You have no choice but to stay here for eternity. You are in the heart of it now, the most central of all delights!'"

The sufferers went on, "For the last day and a half we have been sitting here. Because we lost all hope of ever finding the way out, we stayed in this rose garden. We look around at all the olives, grapes, oranges, and lemons; but the more we look at them, the more tired we get of everything we can see with our eyes, smell with our noses, and taste with our tongues. So this is why you see us crushed with sorrow, grief-stricken, and crying."

[4] The angel with the visiting group said to them, "This labyrinth of a garden paradise is actually just an entrance on the outskirts of heaven. I know the way out and I'll take you there."

At this the people sitting on the ground jumped up and gave the angel a hug. They joined the angel and his group. As they walked along, the angel taught them what heavenly joy and eternal happiness really are.

"They are not in fact the external pleasures of paradise," he said, "unless the internal pleasures of paradise are felt at the same time. External pleasures of paradise are just things that delight our bodily senses. Internal pleasures of paradise are things that satisfy the desires of our soul. If these inner pleasures are not present within these outer pleasures, the outer pleasures have no heavenly life, because they have no soul. Every delight that is lacking its corresponding soul fades and wears out over time; eventually it fatigues the mind more than work does.

"All throughout the heavens there are garden paradises, which are a source of great joy to the angels. The more of the soul's delight the angels have, the more truly joyful these joys become to them."

[5] At that point they all asked, "What is the soul's delight and where does it come from?"

"The soul's delight," the angel answered, "comes from love and wisdom from the Lord. Love is what produces this delight, and wisdom is how it produces it. Both love and wisdom find a home in the effect they have, and that effect is usefulness. This delight flows from the Lord into our soul and comes down through the higher and lower levels of our mind into all our bodily senses and finds its fulfillment in them. This is what makes a joy joyful and also makes it everlasting, because it comes from the eternal Source.

"You have now seen the features of a heavenly garden paradise, and I tell you the truth: there is not a single thing there, not even the least little leaf, that does not come from the marriage of love and wisdom in usefulness. Therefore if we have that marriage within ourselves, then we are in a heavenly paradise, and therefore in heaven itself."

738   After that, the angel guide returned to the first building, to the people who had firmly convinced themselves that heavenly joy and eternal happiness consisted in perpetually glorifying God in a celebration that would go on forever.[410] In the world, they had believed that they were going to see God and that the reason people referred to the life of heaven as "a perpetual Sabbath" was that it consisted entirely in worshiping God.

To this group the angel said, "Follow me and I will bring you into your joy."

He led them to a small town with a church building in the middle of it. All the houses there were referred to as sacred buildings. In that town the group saw crowds of people coming in from the territory surrounding it on every side. In among the crowd there were a number of priests, greeting and welcoming people and leading them by the hand to the gateways of the church, and through them to several of the buildings surrounding the church; they introduced the people to the everlasting worship of God.

"This town is a point of entry to heaven," the priests said. "The church building here is an entrance to a magnificent, enormous church that is in heaven. The angels glorify God there with prayers and praises forever. It is a rule both here and there that you first have to come into this church building and spend three days and nights here. After this period of initiation, you will walk around to the other houses in this town, all of which we consider to be sacred; you will go from one building to the next. Along with the rest of the congregations there, you will pray, shout, and have sermons read to you. Take great care that you do not think anything within yourselves, or say anything to anyone else, that is not holy, devout, and religious."

[2] Then the angel led his group to the church building. It was packed beyond capacity. There were many people there who had been of high rank and position in the world, and also many who had been ordinary people. There were groups of guards posted at each entrance to the church to prevent anyone from leaving before the three days had passed.

"Today is the second day since these people came in," said the angel. Look at them carefully and you will see how they are glorifying God."

The angel's group looked around. They saw that many of the worshipers were fast asleep. The people who were still awake were yawning and yawning. Because they were constantly lifting their thoughts toward God and never allowing those thoughts to come back down into their bodies, some of them had the feeling that they were faces disconnected from their bodies, and that was also how they appeared from the outside. Some of them, whose eyes were rolled back into their heads as a result of looking upward all the time, looked insane. Briefly put, the hearts of all were depressed and their spirits were fatigued with boredom. They turned away from the pulpit and began shouting, "Our ears are going deaf. Stop preaching! We're not listening to you anymore—the sound of your voice is making us sick."

They stood up and rushed en masse toward the doors, broke them open, pushed up against the guards, and shoved them out of the way. [3] The priests pursued them and clung on to them, teaching and teaching, praying and sighing. They were saying, "Celebrate the festival! Glorify God! Sanctify yourselves! This is a point of entry to heaven where we will be inaugurating you into the everlasting glorification of God that takes place in the magnificent, enormous church that is in heaven—this is your initiation into the enjoyment of eternal happiness!"

The worshipers did not understand these statements, though, and barely even heard them, because their minds had been dulled by this two-day suspension from their usual activity at home and at work.

When they tried to tear themselves away from the priests, however, the priests grabbed them by the arms or the clothes, pulling them toward the buildings where the sermons were being read, but without success. The people shouted, "Leave us alone! We are about to lose consciousness altogether."

[4] At that moment four men appeared, dressed in shining white, with caps on their heads. One of them had been an archbishop in the world; the other three had been bishops; they had since become angels. They called the priests together. After greeting them, they said, "We have been watching from heaven how you interact with these sheep. You have been feeding and feeding them to the point where they are having a mental breakdown. You evidently don't know what it means to glorify God. It means bearing the fruits of love—that is, performing our work faithfully, honestly, and diligently. Doing this is loving God; doing this is also loving our neighbor. It is the glue that holds society together, and it is what is best for the community. God is glorified by our doing this, and then also by our having worship at particular times. Have you not read what the Lord said? '*My Father is glorified* by this, that you bear much fruit; and you will become my disciples' (John 15:8).

[5] "Because it is your job, it is possible for you priests to keep going in a worship service of glorification. It brings you honor, glory, and financial reward. But if this were not your job, and you did not get honor, glory, and money from it, you would not be able to keep glorifying indefinitely any more than these people were able to."

The bishops then commanded the guards to open the doors and let everyone come in or go out as he or she wished, since there is a great multitude of people, ignorant of the true nature of heaven, who cannot conceive of heavenly joy in any other form than perpetual worship of God.

739 After that, the angel returned with his group to the original place of meeting. The groups of the wise had not left yet. The angel next summoned the people who believed that heavenly joy and eternal happiness were just a matter of being allowed into heaven by divine grace; and that the joy people then have was much like the joy people have in the world just by showing up when they are invited to a royal palace for the days of a festival or are invited to a wedding.⁴¹¹

To this group the angel said, "Wait here a while longer, if you would; I am going to sound the trumpet and summon some people who were famous for their wisdom regarding the spiritual teachings of the church."

Several hours later nine men arrived. As an indication of their distinguished reputations, they were all wearing laurel wreaths. The angel brought them into the building where all the others were who had previously been summoned.

Before the entire assembly, the angel welcomed the nine distinguished guests and said, "I know that because of the idea you had had of heaven, you fervently desired to go there, and it was granted. You went up to heaven; you then came back to this lower region beneath heaven with full knowledge of what heaven is like. Please tell us, therefore, if you would, how heaven seemed to you."

[2] The nine distinguished theologians gave their responses in sequence.

The *first* theologian said, "The idea that I had had of heaven from the time I was a child right through to the end of my life in the world was that it was a place—a place that contained all bliss, all good fortune, all delight, all satisfaction, and all pleasure imaginable. I thought that if I were simply to be allowed in, I would be surrounded by an aura of all that happiness, and would drink it in with every fiber of my being, like a bridegroom when he is getting married and when he enters the bridal suite with his bride.

"With this idea in mind, I went up into heaven. I got past the first guard post and the second. When I came to the third, the chief officer stopped me and said, 'Who are you, my friend?' I replied, 'Isn't this heaven here? I have come up here because I have longed and prayed to be in heaven. Please let me in.'

"He did let me in. I saw angels in white clothes. They gathered around me and were looking me over and murmuring, 'Look at this. A new guest who is not wearing the clothes of heaven!'

"I heard that and thought to myself, 'This reminds me of the person whom the Lord says came to the wedding without a wedding garment.' I said to them, 'Give me clothes like that.' But they just laughed.

"Then someone came running from the palace with these orders: 'Strip him naked, throw him out, and throw his clothes after him.' And in just that manner I was thrown out."

[3] The *second* theologian said, "I had the same beliefs he did, that if I was just allowed into heaven, which is above my head, joys would flow all around me and I would breathe them in forever. Well, my wish was granted. But when the angels saw me they ran away and said to each other, 'What is this strange omen? How did this night bird get here?' And in fact, I felt as though I had changed into something nonhuman, although in reality I had not; it was just the effect of breathing the atmosphere of heaven. Soon someone from the palace ran up with orders for two servants to lead me back down by the way I had come, and take me all the way to my home. When I was back at home again, I looked human again to myself and to others."

[4] The *third* theologian said, "My idea of heaven was always an idea of a place and not an idea of love. Therefore when I arrived in this world, I felt a tremendous longing for heaven. I saw people going up in that direction, so I followed them. I was let in, but not more than a few feet. Because of the idea I had of the joys and blessings there, when I tried to feel that delight in my mind it went blank instead and I lost my vision and began to lose my mind. That was the effect of the light of heaven, which was as bright and white as snow, and is essentially wisdom, so I'm told. Soon I was having heart palpitations and tremendous anxiety, due to the heat of heaven, which is just as intense as the light is bright and which I now understand is essentially love. I was attacked with inner pain. I threw myself down on my back on the ground there. While I was lying there, an attendant from the palace came with an order to carry me slowly back to my own light and heat. When I was in my own light and heat again, my spirit and my heart were restored."

[5] The *fourth* theologian said, "In my case also I had been thinking of heaven in terms of a place and not in terms of love. As soon as I arrived in the spiritual world I asked wise people whether I was allowed to go up to heaven. They told me, 'Everyone is allowed to go up; just take care not to be thrown back down.' I laughed when they said that, and up I went, believing as these others did that everyone in the entire world is capable of receiving those joys in all their fullness. In actual fact, though, when I was in heaven, I was almost knocked unconscious by it. Because I felt pain and torment in both my head and my body, I threw myself to the ground and rolled and writhed like a snake next to the fire. I crawled all the way to a cliff-edge and threw myself over it. I was picked up by people who were standing below and carried to an inn; there I recovered."

[6] The *other five* theologians told similarly astounding stories about their journeys up to heaven. They compared the state of their life in heaven to a fish that is lifted out of the water into the air and birds that are lifted up into the ether. They said that after those extremely difficult experiences, they no longer desired to go to heaven; they wanted no more than a life shared with other people who were like them, wherever such people happened to be.

They said, "We now know that in the world of spirits, where we are now, we all first undergo a preparation. The good are prepared for heaven, and the evil are prepared for hell. Once we are prepared, we see pathways that open up for us, leading to communities of people like ourselves; we will remain with these people to eternity. We find delight in following these paths, because they are the paths of our own love."

All the people in the first group heard this and admitted that they had had exactly the same ideas about heaven—that it was a place where they would forever drink in the joys that surrounded them.

[7] The angel with the trumpet then said to them, "Now you see that heavenly joys and eternal happiness are not a matter of where you are, but of what your state of life is. A heavenly state of life comes from love and wisdom. Because usefulness is what contains love and wisdom, a heavenly state of life is a matter of the partnership between love and wisdom in usefulness. You can also use the terms goodwill, faith, and good works. These are equivalent, because goodwill is love, faith is the truth that leads to wisdom, and good works are useful.

"Now, there are in fact locations in our spiritual world, as there are in the physical world. Otherwise there would be no places to live and no separate homes. Nevertheless, the nature of a location here is not physical; it is where something appears to be, based on its state of love and wisdom or of goodwill and faith.

[8] "All who become angels carry their own heaven deep within themselves, because their love is the love that constitutes their heaven. We were all created to be a miniature form, an image, and an emblem of the heaven that exists on a grand scale. That is what the human form is. Therefore all who are miniature forms of heaven come into some actual community of heaven. When they enter that community, they are entering a form that corresponds to themselves. Therefore it is as if they are going from themselves into a community that is already actually inside them, forming a connection between the community outside and the community within, and making the community's life their own

and giving their life to the community. Every community of heaven is like an aggregate whole, and the angels of that community are like individual yet similar parts that together make up that whole.

"It follows then that people who are entrenched in evils and falsities have created a model of hell in themselves. When they are in heaven, that model of hell is tormented by the inflow and the violent activity of one opposite against another. Hellish love is opposite to heavenly love. Therefore when the delights of these two loves encounter each other, they clash like enemies and kill each other."

740 When all that came to an end, a voice was heard from heaven saying to the angel with the trumpet, "Out of all who are gathered there, choose ten and bring them up to us. We have heard from the Lord that he will prepare them in such a way that for three days the heat and light or love and wisdom of our heaven will not bring them harm."

Ten were chosen to follow the angel. They climbed up along a steep trail to the top of a hill, and then from there up a mountain. The heaven of those angels was on the top of that mountain. From a distance it had previously appeared to them as a kind of expanse in the clouds. The gates were opened for them. After they had passed through the third set of gates, the angel who was bringing them in hurried to the prince of that community,[412] that heaven, and announced their arrival.

The prince said, "Take some of the members of my entourage and inform them that these visitors are here with my permission. Bring them into my outer court. Give them each a suite with a bedroom. Have some of my court attendants and some of my servants minister to the visitors and see to their wants." This was done.

When the angel was bringing them in, they asked whether it would be allowable for them to meet and visit with the prince of the community. The angel answered, "It is morning now; there will not be a chance before noon. Until then the angels are all performing their functions and doing their work. You are invited to a luncheon, however, and you will be seated at the head table with the prince. In the meantime I will take you into the palace, where you will see some magnificent and astounding things."

[2] When they were brought to the palace they first surveyed it from the outside. It was very large. The main structure was built out of porphyry and was sitting on a foundation made of jasper. In front of the entrance there were six tall pillars made of lapis lazuli. The roof was covered with a layer of gold. The palace had tall windows of completely clear glass, with gilded trim.

Then the ten visitors were led inside the palace and taken from room to room. They saw indescribably beautiful ornamentation there, beneath ceilings decorated with exquisite reliefs. Along the walls there were tables made of a gold and silver alloy; on them were utensils of various kinds made out of precious stones and whole gems shaped into heavenly forms.[413] There was more besides that as well, but they were things that no eyes on earth have ever seen, and therefore there would be no way for people to believe that such things exist in heaven.

[3] As the visitors were feeling stunned by the magnificent things they had seen, the angel said, "Don't be surprised. The things you have seen here were not made or crafted by any angelic hand. They were fashioned by the same Artist who made the universe and were given as gifts to the prince of our community. The art of architecture exists in heaven in its highest state. All the principles of architecture on earth come from here.

"Now, you might suppose," the angel added, "that things like this would bewitch our eyes and overwhelm us so that we would think of them as the very joys of our heaven; but in fact our hearts are not set on them. They are just accessories to the joy that is in our hearts. When we contemplate them as accessories and as the handiwork of God, then we behold the divine omnipresence and mercy that are present within them."

After that, the angel said to them, "It is almost noon. Come with me into the garden of our prince, which is next to the palace."

741

They went to the garden. At the entrance to it the angel said, "Enjoy this, the most magnificent of all the gardens in this heavenly community."

"What are you saying?" was their reply. "There is no garden here. We see just a single tree. On its branches and on its top we see something like pieces of fruit made of gold and leaves made of silver with emeralds along their edges, and under the tree there are little children with their caregivers."

The angel replied in an inspired voice: "The tree you mention is at the center of the garden. We call it 'the tree of our heaven'; others refer to it as the tree of life. Keep going forward, though, and get closer to it, and your eyes will be opened and you will see the garden."

They did so, and their eyes were opened. They saw trees bearing abundant edible fruit, with grapevines wrapped around their limbs. The fruit-laden tops of the trees were bowing inward toward the tree of life at the center.

[2] These trees were laid out in a long curving row that extended and came around to form the arcing arm of a grand spiral. It was a perfect

spiral of trees, in which one species followed another according to the relative excellence of its kind of fruit.⁴¹⁴ A large interspace separated the beginning of the spiral from the tree at the center; this open space was sparkling with a gleaming light, which lit the trees in such a way that each tree seemed to pass the glow on to the next, from the first trees all the way to the last.

The trees toward the center were the most excellent of all. They were covered in rich, sumptuous fruit. Called paradise trees, they were unlike anything that has ever been or could ever be witnessed on earth or anywhere in the physical universe. The trees next to them were various kinds of trees that yield oil; then came various kinds of trees that yield wines; then trees that give off beautiful fragrances; and finally trees whose wood is used for making things.

Here and there along this long, spiraling line of trees there were living benches that had been crafted by bending and weaving together the branches of the tree just behind them; these were decorated with an abundance of the tree's fruits. Along the continuous arcing line of trees there were openings that led into flower gardens, and these led to lawns that were divided into grassy areas and flower beds.

Seeing all this, the people accompanying the angel said, "It is heaven itself laid out before us! Wherever we turn our eyes, we encounter something of heaven, something of paradise, that is beyond description."

The angel rejoiced to hear this, and said, "All the gardens in our heaven are representative forms or models of the origins of heavenly blessings. The reason why you exclaimed, 'It is heaven itself laid out before us,' is that an actual inflow of these blessings lifted your minds. People who are not open to that inflow only see these garden paradises as a forest. People who love being useful are receptive to this inflow; people who love glory apart from usefulness are not."

Then the angel explained to them and taught them the meaning and representation of all the individual features of the garden.

742 While they were still engaged in that, a messenger came from the prince with an invitation to them to break bread with him. Two court attendants with the messenger were carrying clothes of fine linen. They said, "Please put these on, because none are allowed at the table of our prince if they are not wearing the clothes of heaven."

They put on the clothes and went with their angel. They were brought into a large walled area where people from the palace could take walks. There they waited for the prince to arrive. The angel introduced them to dignitaries and governors who were also awaiting the prince's arrival.

After a little while the doors opened. They saw the prince coming through the wider door to the west in a formal and splendid procession. First came his privy councilors, then the members of his cabinet, and then the highest officials in his court. In among the officials was the prince himself. After him came other distinguished members of the court, and then less distinguished members, and last of all the attendants. There were around a hundred and twenty in the procession all told.

[2] The angel was standing in front of the ten newcomers, who now looked like visiting dignitaries in their fine clothes. Then the angel stepped forward toward the prince, bringing them along, and respectfully presented them. The prince, without stopping, said to them, "Come break bread with me."

They followed him into a dining room. There they saw a table magnificently laid out. In the middle of the table there was a tall pyramid made of gold with a hundred small dishes held on three different tiers of its structure. These dishes held sweet breads and wine jellies, and other delicacies made with bread and wine. A wine that was like nectar was bubbling up through the center of the pyramid like a fountain; from the top of the pyramid the wine split into many flowing streams and filled goblets below. To the sides of the tall pyramid there were various heavenly forms made out of gold; these held large and small plates that were full of foods of all kinds. The heavenly forms that held these large and small plates were forms made with a wisdom and technique that no drawing or words in the physical world could possibly capture. The large and small plates were made of silver; forms were embossed on their edges that were similar to the forms on the stands that held them, only flatter. Each cup was made out of a translucent gem. This was what the table setting was like.

As for what the prince and the members of his government were wearing: The prince had on a purple robe, decorated with embroidered silver stars. Under the robe he was wearing a vest of shiny blue silk. The vest was open at the chest; underneath you could see the front of his shirt, which bore the insignia of his community. The insignia was an eagle brooding over her chicks at the top of a tree. This image was made with gleaming gold and was surrounded with diamonds. The privy councilors were dressed similarly, although without the insignia. In its place, they wore a braided gold chain around their neck with carved sapphires

743

hanging from it. The courtiers wore robes of light brown, with a decoration of young eagles surrounded by flowers. Their vests, breeches, and stockings were opalescent in color. So these were the kinds of clothes they were wearing.

744 The privy councilors, the members of the cabinet, and the governors were now standing by the table. At the prince's request, they joined hands and together softly spoke words of prayer and praise to the Lord. Then the prince gave a nod, and the dignitaries sat down on padded chairs at the table. The prince then said to the ten newcomers, "You too are to sit down with me. These are your places here." So they sat down. The court attendants whom the prince had originally assigned to them took up positions behind them.

The prince then said to them, "You are each invited to take a plate from its circular stand and also a dish from the pyramid."

They did so, and immediately fresh plates and dishes appeared and filled the empty spaces. Their goblets were filled with wine from the fountain leaping up from the grand pyramid. They ate and drank.

[2] When they were satisfied but not overly so, the prince spoke to his ten guests and said, "I have heard that down on the plain beneath this heaven you were called on to reveal your thoughts on the joys of heaven and eternal happiness. I understand that you gave various responses on this topic, depending on what particular things your bodily senses took delight in.

"But what delight do the bodily senses feel when the delights of the soul are not present? It is the soul that makes those delights enjoyable. In and of themselves, the delights of the soul are states of blessedness that are beyond our perception; but they become more and more perceptible as they descend into the thoughts of the mind and through these into the sensations of the body. In the thoughts of the mind they are perceived as blissful; in the sensations of the body they are perceived as delightful, and in the body itself they are perceived as pleasurable. These three kinds of joy combine to form eternal happiness. The happiness that comes from the latter feelings alone, however, is not eternal. It is temporary, because it comes to an end and passes away. Sometimes it even becomes unhappiness.

"You have now seen that all the things you listed as joys are in fact joys in heaven, and are superior to anything you could have imagined. Nevertheless these things do not affect our minds all that deeply.

[3] "There are three things that flow as one from the Lord into our souls. These three-in-one, or this trinity, if you will, are love, wisdom,

and usefulness. Love and wisdom do not actually take shape, except in some conceptual form, because they reside solely in the feelings and thoughts within our minds; but in usefulness they become real, because then they come together in some activity and work on the part of the body. Where these two come forth into reality, there they also remain. Because love and wisdom take form and find continued existence in usefulness, usefulness itself is what moves us. Usefulness is faithfully, honestly, and diligently carrying out the work involved in our jobs.

"Love of being useful and pursuit of usefulness keep our minds focused so they don't get distracted and wander off and partake of all the lusts and enticements that flow in from the body and the world through our senses, which would drive away to the four winds all religious and moral truths along with the good actions they enjoin. The mind's pursuit of usefulness harnesses these true insights and good impulses and turns the mind into a form that is receptive to the wisdom that comes from them. This pursuit also pushes aside the distortions and absurdities that arise from false and idle thoughts.

"On this topic, however, you will hear more from wise people from our community; I am going to send them to you this afternoon."

Having said this, the prince stood up from the table (and all the others stood up as well). He wished them all peace. He told the angel who was guiding the guests to take them back to their rooms and show them every honor and civility. He also told the angel to summon some sophisticated and affable people to entertain the guests with conversation about the various modes of recreation enjoyed in that community.

When the angel's group returned to their rooms, what the prince had just ordered was done. People from the city arrived who had been summoned to entertain the guests with conversation about the various modes of recreation in that community. After they met and greeted the newcomers, they all went for a walk together, enjoying a good conversation.

The angel guide then said [to the people from the city], "These ten people were invited to this heaven to see the nature of our joys here and to develop a new concept of eternal happiness. Tell them, if you would, some of the activities here that are rejuvenating for our bodily senses. Later on, we will be visiting with wise people, who are to inform them of some of the inward qualities that make these modes of recreation truly happy and joyful."

In response to this the people from the city provided the following examples.

745

"First: There are festival days here, which are scheduled by the prince in order to relieve our minds of the stress and fatigue that tends to affect us if we become overly competitive. On festival days there is music and singing in the streets, and there are sporting events and shows outside the city. In the public squares stages are set up, framed by screens of latticework that have grapevines interwoven in them and bunches of grapes hanging down. Between these the musicians sit on three tiers. They have all kinds of stringed instruments and wind instruments that cover the spectrum from treble to bass, with timbres ranging from soft to sharp. On either side of the musicians there are male and female vocalists, who entertain the audience with excellent songs and praises, in solos and as a choir. Now and then during the performance they will shift to a different type of music. On festival days, entertainments like this will start early and go all morning; then after a break for lunch they will continue through the afternoon into the evening.

[2] "Second: As another example, every morning from the houses around the public squares you hear girls and young women singing songs of great sweetness. The sound fills the entire city. Each morning the song embodies one particular feeling related to spiritual love. That is, the way the voices sound and the mode the song is in convey a given feeling so well that we experience the song as that feeling itself. The song flows into our souls as we listen and stirs in us the feeling it corresponds to. This is the nature of songs in heaven. The singers tell us that as those listening become more receptive, the sound of the song becomes more inspired, inwardly alive, and beautiful.

"When the song is over, the windows of the houses around the central square and also on the side streets are closed, and then so are the doors. Silence fills the entire city. No noise is heard anywhere, and no one is seen out of doors. All are then focused on doing the work that their jobs entail.

[3] "Third: At midday the doors are opened. A little later, some of the windows are opened as well. Then you see boys and girls playing in the streets, under the supervision of their caregivers and teachers, who sit on the porches of their houses.

[4] "Fourth: On the outskirts of the city there are various sporting activities for teenagers and young adults. There are games that involve a lot of running, games with balls, games with rackets. There are also contests in the arena for teenagers in order to see who is quicker or slower at speaking, taking action, and perceiving. Those who are quicker are

awarded a laurel wreath as their prize. There are also many other activities designed to bring out the young people's hidden talents.

[5] "Fifth: For yet another example, outside the city comedies are performed on stage. The players in them represent the various honorable and virtuous attitudes that go to make up a moral life. For the sake of contrast, some of the actors will play buffoons."

At this point one of the ten newcomers asked, "Why for contrast?"

"No virtue, or the honorable and appropriate actions that go with it, can be brought out in a living way without showing different levels of it from greatest to least. The buffoons represent the least level of that moral quality, just on the edge of no morality at all. It is actually forbidden by law, however, to portray the opposite of that moral quality—to depict behavior that is blatantly dishonorable or shows bad taste; that can only be implied or shown in some remote and indirect way. The reason for this prohibition is that there is no continuum that includes both behavior that is honorable and good, arising out of some virtue, and behavior that is dishonorable and evil. What is good and honorable diminishes to the least amount of it, and then comes to an end. Its opposite only starts up beyond the point at which that virtue has completely ceased to exist. Therefore heaven, where all things are honorable and good, has absolutely nothing in common with hell, where all things are dishonorable and evil."

As this conversation was still going on, a servant ran up and announced that the eight wise people who had been requested by the prince were present and were asking if they could come in. The angel immediately left to get them and brought them in.

After formal and gracious greetings all around, the wise began by addressing the group on the first beginnings and subsequent stages in the development of wisdom. They also mixed in some points about later stages. They said that among the angels, wisdom never has an end or comes to a stop; it grows and increases forever.

The angel who was in charge of the group said to the wise, "At the table earlier on, our prince told the group where wisdom resides, namely, in usefulness. If you would, could you tell them some more about that?"

The wise responded: "Humankind, as it was first created, was steeped in wisdom and in a love for wisdom, not for their own sake but for the sake of sharing it with others. As a result, an integral part of the wisdom of the wise was the recognition that none are wise for their own sakes alone and none are alive except for the sake of others. This led to the development of society, which would otherwise not have existed.

746

"Living for others is the same as doing things that are useful. Useful activities are what hold the community together. The community has as many bonds within it as there are good and useful things that are accomplished in it. The number of useful things to do is infinite.

"First, there are useful activities that are *spiritual* in nature; they relate to loving God and loving our neighbor. Second, there are useful activities that are *moral* and *civic* in nature; they relate to loving the society and community in which we live, and also loving our colleagues and fellow citizens, who constitute the community. Third, there are useful activities that are *earthly* in nature; they relate to loving the world and the things we need in order to continue to exist in it. Fourth, there are useful activities that are *bodily* in nature; they relate to loving to maintain ourselves for the sake of the higher forms of usefulness.

[2] "All these types of usefulness are built into us; they follow in this sequence, one after the other, and when they occur together, the one is inside the other.

"People who are involved in the first type of usefulness just mentioned, the spiritual forms of usefulness, are also involved in the rest as well. They are the wise.

"People who are not involved in the first type of usefulness, but are involved in the second, third, and fourth types, are not actually as wise, although they seem wise as a result of their external morality and civility alone.

"People who are not involved in either the first or the second type of usefulness, but are involved in the third and fourth types, are not wise.[415] They are satans; the only thing they love is the world. They love themselves because they love the world.

"People who limit themselves to the fourth type of usefulness are the least wise of all. They are devils, because they live for themselves alone. If they do anything for others, it is only for their own selfish benefit.

[3] "For another thing, every love has its own delight. The delight is what gives life to the love. The delight that belongs to the love of being useful is a heavenly kind of delight. It becomes integrated into the next delights in sequence, lifts them up according to their place in the sequence, and makes them eternal."

Then the wise listed some heavenly pleasures that result from loving to be useful. They said that in all, there are billions of them, and that people who become a part of heaven partake of them.

They spent the rest of the day and on into the evening engaged in a profound conversation about the love of being useful.

[4] Around the time of evening, a courier dressed in linen came to the ten newcomers who were with the angel and invited them to attend a wedding celebration on the following day. The newcomers were thrilled at the idea that they would be attending a wedding in heaven.

They were then brought to one of the privy councilors, and enjoyed an evening meal with him. After the meal they went back to their shared quarters, said good-night to each other, retired to their own rooms, and slept through until morning.

They awoke to hear the girls and young women singing from the houses surrounding the public square. That morning, the feeling embodied in the song was the desire for marriage love. The guests were intensely moved and affected by the sweetness of the song. Deep within their joyful response they became aware of a profoundly satisfying sense of bliss, which elevated and refreshed their joy.

When the time had come, the angel said, "Get dressed in the clothes from heaven that our prince sent you earlier."

They put them on, and were surprised to see that they were now radiant with a flame-colored light. They asked the angel what caused this. He said, "It is because you are going to attend a wedding today. On such days our clothes shine and become wedding garments."

Then the angel led them to the home where the wedding was to occur. A doorkeeper opened the door. Just beyond the entrance they were greeted and welcomed by an angel who had been posted there by the bridegroom. They were introduced and taken to seats reserved for them.

747

Soon they were invited to come into a large room that adjoined the wedding bedroom. They saw a table in the middle of the large room, which had a magnificent candelabra on it with seven golden branches and cups. Suspended along the walls there were lamps made of silver. Once the lamps were lit, the light they cast gave the whole atmosphere a golden tinge. The guests also noticed two tables on either side of the candelabra, which were laid out with little loaves of bread in three rows. In the four corners of the room there were tables with crystal goblets.

[2] As they were looking over all these things, a door opened from a room next to the wedding bedroom. Six young women[416] came out, followed by the bridegroom and the bride holding hands and leading each other to a love seat that was set up near the candelabra. The couple sat

down on it, the bridegroom on the left, and the bride on his right. The six young women stood beside the bride's side of the love seat.

The bridegroom was wearing a robe of gleaming purple and a tunic of shining linen. He was also wearing an ephod[417] with a golden brooch edged in diamonds. On the brooch was carved a young eagle, the wedding insignia of that community of heaven. The bridegroom's head was covered with a turban.

The bride was wearing a red robe over an embroidered gown that was all of one piece from her neck to her feet. Around her waist she had a golden sash, and on her head a crown of gold with rubies in it.

[3] When the couple had taken their seats, the bridegroom turned to the bride and placed a gold ring on her finger. Then he brought out bracelets and a necklace of pearls. He fastened the bracelets on her wrists and the necklace around her neck, and said, "Please accept these gifts as tokens of my love." When she accepted them, he kissed her and said, "Now you are my own," and referred to her as his wife.[418]

At that, the wedding guests cried out, "Let there be a blessing!" Each one cried it individually at first, and then all said it together. A delegate sent by the prince cried out the same thing when it was his turn. At that very moment the room was filled with sweet-smelling smoke, which was a sign of a blessing from heaven.

Then servants picked up the little loaves of bread from the two tables by the candelabra, and took the crystal goblets, which were now full of wine, from the tables in the corners. They gave each guest her or his own little loaf of bread and goblet of wine, and they all ate and drank.

Then the husband and wife stood up to leave. The six young women followed them, carrying in their hands little silver lamps, which were now lit; they went just as far as the threshold. The married pair went on into the wedding bedroom and closed the door.

748 After that, the angel guide spoke to some of the other guests about the ten newcomers who were with him. He told them that he had been commanded to bring the newcomers up to this community and show them the magnificent and miraculous things in the prince's palace. "They also dined with the prince at his table," he said, "and afterward had a chance to converse with some of the wise minds in our community."

The angel then asked the guests, "Would it be possible for the newcomers to have a conversation with you as well?"

They agreed and struck up a conversation. One of the men in attendance at the wedding, a wise person, said to the newcomers, "Do you understand the meaning of what you saw just now?"

The newcomers said, "A little." They asked the wise person, "Why was the bridegroom (now the husband) wearing those particular clothes?"

"The bridegroom (now the husband) was representing the Lord," he replied, "and the bride (now the wife) was representing the church, because weddings in heaven represent the marriage between the Lord and the church. This is why he had a turban on his head, and why he was wearing a robe, a tunic, and an ephod like Aaron [Exodus 28; Leviticus 8:7–9]. This is also why the bride (now the wife) had a crown on her head and was wearing a robe like that of a queen. Tomorrow they will dress differently, because this representation lasts only for today."

[2] The newcomers had another question: "Given that he represented the Lord and she the church, why was she sitting to his right?"

"Because there are two things," the wise guest replied, "that make a marriage between the Lord and the church: love and wisdom. The Lord is love and the church is wisdom. Wisdom is at love's right hand. All who are in the church become wise as if they were doing so on their own, and as they become wise, they receive love from the Lord. The right hand means power, and it is through wisdom that love has power.

"As I say, though, after the wedding day is over the representation changes. Then the husband represents wisdom and the wife represents the love of that wisdom; but this latter love is not the love I mentioned a moment ago. It is a second kind of love, which the wife has from the Lord in response to her husband's wisdom. The kind of love from the Lord mentioned earlier is the love for becoming wise that the husband has.[419] Therefore after the wedding day, both together, the husband and the wife, represent the church."

[3] The newcomers had yet another question: "Why were none of you men standing beside the groom (now the husband) the way the six young women were standing beside the bride (now the wife)?"

"The reason is that on this day," the wise person replied, "we ourselves are counted as virginal young women, and the number six means wholeness and completeness."

"We don't understand," the newcomers said.

"Virginal young women mean the church," the wise man said, "and both sexes constitute the church. In this sense, where the church is concerned we men too are considered to be virginal young women. This is made clear by the following statement in the Book of Revelation: 'These are the ones who were not defiled with women, for they themselves are *virgins,* and they follow the Lamb wherever he goes' (Revelation 14:4). Because young women mean the church, therefore the Lord compared the church to ten *young women* who were invited to a wedding (Matthew 25:1 and following). Because Israel, Zion, and Jerusalem mean the church, therefore the Word often speaks of *a virgin* or *daughter of Israel, of Zion,* or *of Jerusalem.*[420] In fact, the Lord describes his marriage with the church in the following terms in David: '*The queen stands at your right hand* in the best gold from Ophir; her clothing is interwoven with gold. In *embroidered clothes* she will be brought to her king; *young women behind her* as her friends will come into the palace of the king' (Psalms 45:9–15)."

[4] Then the newcomers asked, "Wouldn't it be more appropriate for a priest to be present and administer the ceremony?"

"That is appropriate on earth," the wise man responded, "but not in the heavens, because the ceremony here represents the Lord himself and the church. People on earth are not aware that weddings have this symbolic meaning. Still, among us here priests do indeed perform betrothal ceremonies; they hear, accept, confirm, and consecrate the couple's consent to be married. Consent is the essential ingredient in a marriage; all the other aspects of marriage that follow from consent are just the various forms that that consent takes."

749   After that, the angel guide went over to the six young women and told them, too, about his group of visitors. He asked if they would be willing to visit with his group.

The young women agreed and started in the direction of the group, but when they came close they suddenly turned around and walked off instead into a sitting room for women, where their female friends were spending time. The angel guide saw this unfold and went after them. He asked them, "Why did you suddenly leave without even speaking to my group?"

"We couldn't go near them," they replied.

"Why not?" the angel asked.

"We don't know; but we sensed something that refused to let us go further and turned us instead in the opposite direction. We hope they can forgive us."

The angel went over to his group and told them what the young women had said. He added, "My guess is that your love for the opposite sex is not chaste.[421] In heaven we love young women for their beauty and moral refinement; we love them intensely, but chastely."

The group laughed and said, "Your guess is entirely correct! Who can see women who are that beautiful just a few feet away and not feel any desire?"

After the celebrations came to an end, the wedding guests left, includ-   **750**
ing the ten newcomers with their angel guide. It was late evening, so they
went home to bed.

In the early light before dawn they heard a proclamation: "Today is
the Sabbath!"

They got up and asked the angel, "What does this mean?"

"It is a day for worshiping God," he replied. "Days like this recur at
regular intervals and are proclaimed by the priests. The worship service
takes place in our churches and lasts about two hours. If you want, you
can come with me and I'll take you there."

They got dressed and went with the angel. When they came into the
church, they saw that it was a very large semicircle with a seating capacity
of about three thousand. The seating took the form of extended, curved
pews that followed the lines of the church. The pulpit in front of the
pews was set back slightly from the focal point of the seating. There was
a door behind the pulpit on the left.

The ten newcomers came in with their angel guide. The angel
directed them to the places where they should sit. "All who come into
the church," he explained, "know their own place; they know it by a
kind of instinct and cannot sit anywhere else. If they do sit elsewhere,
they cannot hear or understand anything; in fact, they disrupt the proper
arrangement within the congregation, and once that is disrupted, the
priest's inspiration is lost."

After people were settled into their places, the priest went up into the   **751**
pulpit and preached a sermon that was full of the spirit of wisdom. The
topic was the holiness of Sacred Scripture and the Lord's union with both
worlds, the spiritual and the physical, that the Word provides. Because of
the enlightenment the preacher had, the sermon convinced the listeners
that that holy book was dictated by Jehovah the Lord, and that therefore
he is in it to such a degree that he *is* the wisdom it contains. Nevertheless
that wisdom, which is the Lord himself, lies hidden beneath the literal
meaning and is accessible only to people who are interested in theological truth and are engaged in living rightly as well; these are the people
who are in the Lord and whom the Lord is in.[422]

After the sermon, he finished with a heartfelt prayer, and came down
from the pulpit.

As the congregation was leaving, the angel asked the priest to greet
the ten newcomers. The priest joined their group. Their conversation
lasted for about half an hour. The priest talked about the divine Trinity
and said that it exists within Jesus Christ, since according to the apostle

Paul, all the fullness of divinity dwells physically in him [Colossians 2:9]. Then they talked about the union of goodwill and faith; but the preacher spoke of it as the union of goodwill and *truth,* because faith is truth.

752 After they expressed their gratitude to the preacher, they went back to their rooms. There the angel said to them, "Today is the third day since you came up into this community of heaven. You were prepared by the Lord to be able to be here for three days. Therefore the time has come for us to part. Take off the clothes that were sent to you by the prince, and put on your own clothes."

When the newcomers were back in their own clothes, they were inspired with a strong desire to leave; so they left and went back down. The angel came with them all the way to the place of the original meeting. There they humbly gave thanks to the Lord for blessing them with knowledge and understanding concerning heavenly joys and eternal happiness.

Chapter 14

The Close of the Age; the Coming of the Lord; and the New Heaven and the New Church

The "Close of the Age" Means the End of the Church, When Its Time Is Over

DURING the history of this planet there have been many churches. In the course of time each church has come to an end. After one church is finished, then a new church comes into existence. This cyclical pattern has continued up to the present time.   **753**

A church comes to an end when there is no divine truth left in it that has not been either falsified or rejected; and where there is no genuine truth, there can be no genuine goodness either, since every quality of goodness is shaped by truths. Goodness is the essence of truth; truth is the form of goodness. What has no form can have no quality. Goodness and truth are no more separable than the will and the intellect, or (to say the same thing in another way) than a feeling that relates to some love and the thinking that goes with that feeling. Therefore when the truth in a church comes to an end, the goodness in that church also comes to an end; and when this happens, that church itself draws to a close and comes to an end.

There are various factors that cause the demise of a church. A primary factor is things that make what is false appear to be true. When what is false is taken to be true, then goodness that is truly and intrinsically good—which is called *spiritual* goodness—no longer exists. In that state, what we believe to be good is merely the earthly goodness that results from a moral life. The factors that cause the loss of truth, and therefore of goodness as well, are the two earthly kinds of love that are completely opposite to the two spiritual kinds of love. These two earthly kinds of   **754**

331

love are known as love for ourselves and love for the world. When love for ourselves is dominant, it becomes the opposite of loving God. When love for the world is dominant, it becomes the opposite of loving our neighbor. Loving ourselves is wanting what is best for ourselves alone and not for anyone else unless we ourselves will benefit. Loving the world is similarly self-centered. When these types of love are deeply embedded in us they spread, like gangrene does through the body, and progressively destroy everything within us.

The biblical descriptions of Babylon[423] make it very clear that a love like this has invaded the churches (Genesis 11:1–9; Isaiah 13; 14; 47; Jeremiah 50; Daniel 2:31–47; 3:1–7 and following; 5; 6:8 to the end; 7:1–14; and Revelation 17 and 18 from beginning to end). Babylon eventually developed such an exalted idea of itself that it not only transferred all the Lord's divine power to itself but also put tremendous effort into steering all the wealth in the world toward itself.

[2] There is also fairly substantial evidence that many of the leaders of the churches that separated from Babylon[424] would themselves have developed loves that were similar if their power had not been restrained and curtailed. Where else does this path lead but to viewing oneself as God and the world as heaven? And yet taking this view corrupts every true teaching of the church. People who are exclusively earthly are incapable of recognizing or acknowledging truth that is actually and genuinely true; such people are incapable of being given such truth by God, because it rapidly turns into its opposite inside them and becomes false.

Besides these two kinds of love there are many other factors that bring truth and goodness to an end and cause the demise of the church, but they are only secondary and subordinate to the loves just mentioned.

755 The fact that the "close of the age" means *when the church comes to an end* can be seen from passages in the Word that contain phrases like this. For example,

> I have heard from Jehovah about *the end and the cutting down* that will fall upon the entire land. (Isaiah 28:22)

> *The end* has been established, and justice has been submerged, because the Lord Jehovih Sabaoth is bringing *the end and the cutting down* upon the whole land. (Isaiah 10:22, 23)

> The whole land will be consumed in the fire of Jehovah's passion, because he will quickly bring *an end* to all those who dwell in the land. (Zephaniah 1:18)

In these passages *the land* means the church, because it refers to the land of Canaan, where the church was. (For further confirmation, from a great abundance of scriptural passages, that *the land* means the church, see *Revelation Unveiled* 285, 902.)

> In the end *desolation* [will fly in] on a bird of abominations; even to *the close and the cutting down,* it will drip steadily upon *the devastation.* (Daniel 9:27)

For evidence that the material just quoted from Daniel is actually about the end of the Christian church, which is happening now, see Matthew 24:15.

> There will be *devastation* in all the land, but I will not bring on *the end.* (Jeremiah 4:27)

> The wickedness of the Amorites has not yet come to *a close.* (Genesis 15:16)

> Jehovah said, "I will go down and see whether they are making *an end,* as the cry that has come to me indicates." (Genesis 18:21, on the subject of Sodom)

[2] In the following passages, the Lord himself uses the phrase "the close of the age" to mean the time when the Christian church of today is at an end:

> The disciples asked Jesus, "What will a sign of your Coming and of *the close of the age* be?" (Matthew 24:3)

> At the time of harvest, I will say to the harvesters, "First gather the weeds to be burned; then gather the wheat into the barn. So it will be at *the close of the age.*" (Matthew 13:[30,] 40)

> At *the close of the age,* angels will go forth and separate the evil from among the just. (Matthew 13:49)

> Jesus said to his disciples, "Behold, I am with you even until *the close of the age.*" (Matthew 28:20)

It is important to realize that *devastation, desolation,* and *the cutting down* have much the same meaning as *the close of the age. Desolation* specifically means the end of truth; *devastation* means the end of goodness; and *the cutting down* means the complete end of both. The *fullness of time,* when the Lord came into the world [Galatians 4:4] and when he will come [Ephesians 1:10], has the same meaning as *the end* in this sense.

756 Various things in the physical world can serve to illustrate the close of the age. Each and every thing on earth grows old and becomes worn out through patterns that recur, which are called cycles; both long and short spans of time go through these cycles. In a longer cycle, the year goes from spring to summer and on into fall, and comes to an end in winter. After winter, spring comes again. This cycle relates to heat. In a shorter cycle, the day goes from morning to afternoon and on into evening, and comes to an end in the night. After night, morning comes again. This cycle relates to light.

We ourselves also go through a natural cycle like this. We begin our lives as a child; we come into youth and adulthood, and move on into old age. Then we die. Every bird in the sky and every animal on earth goes through the same kind of cycle as well.

Every tree begins as a shoot, grows up to its full height, and then weakens progressively until it falls over. Every bush and shrub goes through a similar cycle; in fact, every leaf and every flower blossom goes through one as well. Even the ground itself goes through something similar; in time it becomes unproductive. Water, too, that is not moving becomes more and more stagnant.

These are all examples of end times that recur. They are physical and time-bound, and yet the cycle comes around again. When the cycle comes to an end, it begins again. Every type of thing, then, is being born, and is dying, and is being born again. The purpose of all this is to ensure that creation continues.

The same thing happens with a church, for the reason that humankind *is* the church and constitutes it in a multigenerational way. One generation follows another. Human minds are always changing and different. Once wickedness is rooted in one generation, it is passed on to the next in the form of a tendency toward that wickedness. It is not uprooted except through the process of regeneration, which is something only the Lord can do for us.

Today the Christian Church Is at Its End; the Lord Foretold and Described This Event in the Gospels and in the Book of Revelation

757 The sections under the preceding heading showed that "the close of the age" means the time when the church is at an end. From this we can see what the Lord meant when he spoke of the close of the age in the Gospels (Matthew 24; Mark 13; Luke 21).

> As Jesus was sitting on the Mount of Olives, his disciples came to him privately and said, "What will the sign of your Coming and the close of the age be?" (Matthew 24:3)

Then the Lord foretold and described what the progressive stages would be like at the end, leading up to his Coming. He said, among other things, that he would come in the clouds of heaven with power and glory and gather his elect (Matthew 24:30, 31), which never happened during the actual destruction of Jerusalem.[425] The Lord described these events in the prophetic mode;[426] in that mode, each expression is pregnant with meaning. (What each phrase there[427] entails has been explained in *Secrets of Heaven* 3353–3356; 3486–3489; 3650–3655; 3751–3757; 3897–3901; 4056–4060; 4229–4231; 4332–4335; 4422–4424.)

The fact that everything the Lord said then to his disciples was about the time when the Christian church would come to an end is very clear from the Book of Revelation, which contains similar predictions about the close of the age and the Lord's Coming. Each verse of the Book of Revelation is explained in *Revelation Unveiled* (published in 1766). Since the points that the Lord made to his disciples about the close of the age and his Coming align with the points regarding the same events that he later revealed through John in the Book of Revelation, it is abundantly clear that the Lord was not referring to any other end than the end of the Christian church that exists today. There are also prophecies about the end of this church in Daniel; this is why the Lord says, "When you see that the abomination of desolation foretold by the prophet Daniel is standing in the holy place, let those who read note it well" (Matthew 24:15; Daniel 9:27). There are similar passages in the other prophets.

[2] The appendix[428] will show further that the abomination of desolation exists today within the Christian church. It will demonstrate that there is not one single genuine truth left in the church, and that if a new church were not raised up to take the place of the church that exists today, "No flesh would be saved," as the Lord says in Matthew 24:22.

Strange to say, though, the fact that the Christian church of today is severely devastated and is at its end is not at all apparent to those on earth who have become adamantly devoted to the church's false teachings. The reason for this is that becoming adamantly devoted to a teaching that is false is the same as denying a teaching that is true. Such people place a

758

heavy tarpaulin over the doorway to their intellect to prevent anything from sneaking into their mind and pulling down the tent poles and ropes that they have used to shape and reinforce their theological system.

If our rational faculty is earthly in nature, it is capable of supporting any notion it wishes to. It is capable of giving support equally to something false and to something true. Once a given idea has been reinforced in us, truth and falsity appear in the same light. We lose the ability to tell the difference between the dim, deceptive light we experience in a dream and the true light of day.

If our rational faculty is spiritual in nature, though, it is quite the opposite. How do we develop spiritual rationality? We turn to the Lord and he gives us a love for what is true.

759 Every church that is established by people who see the world through their own convictions appears to them to be the only church with any light; all other churches, which disagree, are in darkness. People who see the world through their own convictions are not much different from owls, which see light in the dark of night, but during the day see the sun and its rays as thick darkness. This is the nature of every church, both in the past and now, whose beliefs are false because its founders, who seemed to themselves entirely sharp-sighted, saw their own understanding as the morning light, and the Word as the shadows of approaching night.

Surely, when the Jewish church was in utter ruin, which it was when our Lord came into the world, its scribes and scholars were still loudly proclaiming that because it had the Word, their church alone was in the true light of heaven. Yet they crucified the Messiah, the Christ,[429] who was the Word itself and was every detail in it.

The church that the prophets and the Book of Revelation call Babylon proclaimed itself to be the queen and mother of all other churches, and held that the churches that separated from it were illegitimate children from which it should dissociate itself.[430] Yet it pushed the Lord our Savior off his throne and away from his altar, and set itself there instead.

[2] Every church, even the most heretical, once it is well established fills the towns and countryside with cries that it alone is orthodox and ecumenical and possesses the true gospel that was announced by the angel flying in the midst of heaven (Revelation 14:6). Then we all hear an echo of that voice coming back from the general population, saying, "That is the truth!"

Did the worldwide Synod of Dort see the concept of predestination as anything other than a shining star that had fallen from heaven into their heads? Did they not treasure that teaching as the Philistines treasured the idol of Dagon in the temple of Ebenezer in Ashdod, or as the Greeks treasured the Palladium in the temple of Minerva?[431] In fact, [Calvinists] hailed predestination as the sacred central effigy of their religion. They did not realize, though, that their star is a mere shooting star. It is just a transient phenomenon that emits a dim, deceptive light. When predestination falls into the brain, the distorting effect it has can lend support to any and every false teaching. Over time its light is taken to be the truth and it is declared a permanent star. Eventually people swear that it is the most important star in the sky.

[3] Do any people express notions with more conviction than materialistic atheists, even though their notions are things they dreamed up themselves? Yet the same people heartily ridicule the divinity of God, the heavenliness of heaven, and the spiritual teachings of the church.

All lunatics believe that their foolish thoughts are wise and that wisdom is folly. Just by looking with the naked eye, can anyone tell the difference between the phosphorescent glow of rotting wood and a splash of real moonlight? Some people are actually averse to pleasant fragrances (as some women are when they have hysteria);[432] they push such things away from their noses and prefer something rank. And so on.

I mention these illustrative examples to make it known that before the truth shines out from heaven in its own genuine light, when we are still in light that is merely earthly, we do not recognize that the church has come to an end—that is, that its teachings are all false. What is false does not see what is true; but what is true sees what is false. All of us have it in our nature to be able to recognize and understand truth when we hear it. But if we are convinced of falsities, we cannot import that truth into our intellect in such a way that it remains with us. We have no room for it inside. If it does happen to become part of us, a great throng of falsities gathers around and ejects it as a foreign object.

This, the Christian Church's Final Hour, Is the Same Kind of Night in Which the Former Churches Came to an End

Since creation first took place, there have been four churches on this planet, one after the other. Both the historical and the prophetic Word[433] make this clear. It is especially clear in Daniel, where these four churches are described in the form of the statue that Nebuchadnezzar saw in a

760

dream (Daniel 2); later on they are portrayed as the four beasts that rose up from the sea (Daniel 7).

   The first church, which should be called the earliest church, existed before the Flood; the Flood itself symbolically depicts the end and demise of that church. The second church, which should be called the early church, existed in the Middle East and also in parts of North Africa; it came to a close and perished as the result of various forms of idolatry. The third church was the Israelite church. It began with the issuing of the Ten Commandments on Mount Sinai and was further established through the Word that was written by Moses and the prophets. It came to a close and was brought to an end by people's desecration of the Word, which desecration reached a peak at the time that the Lord came into the world. Because of it, the people crucified the One who was the Word. The fourth church is the Christian church that was established by the Lord through the Gospel writers and the apostles. There were two phases of this church: the first lasted from the time of the Lord until the Council of Nicaea; the second lasted from then until the present day. Along the way, however, the church split into three main parts: the Greek, the Roman Catholic, and the Protestant; nevertheless, all three are referred to as Christian. Within each of these parts, there were also many individual movements that broke away and yet retained the name of the parent body; they became heresies within the Christian church.

761   As for the Christian church's final hour being the same kind of night in which the former churches came to an end, this is made clear by what the Lord foretold about the Christian church in the Gospels and in Daniel.

   In the Gospels it is clear from this statement:

> They will see the abomination of desolation. Then there will be a great affliction such as has never existed since the world began until now and will never exist again. In fact, unless those days were cut short no flesh would be saved. At the end, the sun will be darkened, the moon will not give its light, and the stars will fall from heaven. (Matthew 24:15, 21, 22, 29)

This time is also called *night* elsewhere in the Gospels; for example, in Luke: "During that night, two will be upon one bed. One will be taken; the other will be left" (Luke 17:34). Also in John, "I have to do the work of the one who sent me. Night is coming, when no one can work" (John 9:4).

   [2] Since all light departs in the middle of the night, and the Lord is the true light (John 1:4 and following; 8:12; 12:35, 36, 46), he said to his disciples

as he rose up into heaven, "I am with you even until the close of the age" (Matthew 28:20). After that he leaves them and goes to the new church.

Daniel, too, shows that the Christian church's final hour is the same kind of night in which the former churches came to an end:

> In the end desolation [will fly in] on a bird of abominations; even to the close and the cutting down, it will drip steadily upon the devastation. (Daniel 9:27)

The fact that this was a prediction of the end of the *Christian* church is made clear by the Lord's words in Matthew 24:15. It is also clear from Daniel's words about the fourth kingdom or the fourth church as depicted in Nebuchadnezzar's statue:

> As you saw iron mixed with muddy clay, they will mingle with the seed of humankind, but the two will not stick together, just as iron and clay do not stick together. (Daniel 2:43)

The *seed of humankind* means truth from the Word. [3] The same thing is also clear from the fourth church that was represented as the fourth beast to rise up from the sea:

> I saw visions in the night; behold, a fourth beast, dreadful and terrible, will devour the entire earth, trample it, and break it to pieces. (Daniel 7:7, 23)

These expressions mean that all the truth in the church is going to come to an end. Then there will be night, because truth is what provides daylight to the church.

Many similar prophecies regarding the Christian church occur in the Book of Revelation, especially in chapter 16, where we read about the bowls of God's anger that are poured out on the earth; these symbolize false teachings that will then flood the church and destroy it.

There are many similar passages in the prophets. For example, "Isn't the day of Jehovah a day of darkness and not light, a day of thick darkness and no brightness?" (Amos 5:18, 20; Zephaniah 1:15). "In that day, Jehovah will look down on the land, and behold, darkness; and the light will grow dark over its ruins" (Isaiah 5:30; 8:22). The *day of Jehovah* means the day of the Coming of the Lord.

The existence of four [successive] churches on this planet since the world was created accords with the divine design, which is that there is a beginning and an end of one thing before a new beginning arises. This is why every day begins with the morning, progresses [through the afternoon

762

to the evening], and comes to an end in the night; and after that, the cycle begins anew. Likewise, every year begins in spring, progresses through summer to fall, and comes to an end in winter; after winter, the cycle begins anew. In order to maintain these cycles, the sun starts out in the east, moves through the south into the west, and ends up in the north; from the north it returns to start the cycle again.[434]

The same is true of churches. The first church, which was the earliest church, was like the morning, spring, and the east. The second, or early church, was like the day, summer, and the south. The third church was like evening, fall, and the west. The fourth is like night, winter, and the north.

[2] From these orderly progressions, the ancient philosophers concluded that the world would have four ages.[435] They called the first the Golden Age; the second, the Silver Age; the third, the Bronze Age; and the fourth, the Iron Age. In the statue seen by Nebuchadnezzar, the churches were represented by these same metals [Daniel 2:31–45].

In the Lord's sight the church appears as a single individual. Just as we do as individuals, this universal human will go through its own life stages. It goes from childhood to youth, and on into adulthood and finally old age. When it dies, it rises again. The Lord says, "Unless a grain of wheat falls into the ground and dies, it stays the way it is; but if it dies, it bears much fruit" (John 12:24).

763   It is part of the divine design that things proceed from beginning to end; this is both a pattern overall and a pattern in smaller increments within the overall pattern. This design allows for the variety of all things, and this variety allows there to be qualities of all kinds. The quality of anything is more perfectly assessed through its contrast to things that are somewhat its opposite and things that are very much its opposite.

Darkness allows us to appreciate what a wonderful thing light is, and coldness allows us to appreciate what a wonderful thing heat is. Likewise (as everyone surely recognizes), falsity allows us to appreciate what a wonderful thing truth is, and evil allows us to appreciate what a wonderful thing goodness is.

What would color be if only white existed, and black did not?[436] The quality of the other colors would be poorer if there were no way to darken them.

What is sensation without contrast? And what is contrast without the existence of things that are opposites? Our eyesight is dimmed by whiteness alone, but is brought to life by colors—such as green, for example—that are darkened by a measure of blackness. Our ear grows deaf to a single note that constantly assaults our organs of hearing; the ear is stimulated, though, by notes in various different harmonic relationships.

[2] What is beauty if there is no ugliness to serve as a contrast? This is why some paintings highlight and bring to life the beauty of a young woman by including an ugly image beside her.[437]

What are joy and delight apart from their contrast with what is miserable and unpleasant?

Surely we all become deranged if we constantly think the same idea and never interrupt it with a variety of other notions that tend in different and even opposite directions.

The same is true of the spiritual qualities offered by the church. The opposites of these qualities relate to evil and falsity. Evil and falsity are not from the Lord, though; they come from us. We have free choice, and we can exercise that choice to serve either a good purpose or an evil purpose. Falsity and evil are like the dark and the cold. The sun does not cause the dark or the cold; it is the earth's turning away that causes them. And yet without that turning away, there would be no day, there would be no year, and therefore there would be nothing and no one on this planet.

I have been told that the churches and all their varying approaches to goodness and truth—provided their goodness has something to do with loving the Lord and their truths have something to do with faith in him—are like all the different gems on a monarch's crown.

After This Night Comes the Morning, Which Is the Lord's Coming

Since the successive stages of the church on both a large and a small scale are described in the Word as the four seasons of the year (spring, summer, fall, and winter) and as the four times of day (morning, afternoon, evening, and night),[438] and since the modern-day church, which is Christianity, is the night, it follows that now the morning is at hand. The morning is the beginning of a new church.

764

The following passages make it clear that the Word describes the successive stages of the church as the four parts of the day, which are determined by light.

Through *the evening and the morning,* for two thousand three hundred [days], what is holy will be made just. The vision of *the evening and the morning* is the truth. (Daniel 8:14, 26)

> Someone was crying out to me from Seir, "Watchman, watchman, what of *the night?*" The watchman replied, "*Morning* is coming, but so is *the night.*" (Isaiah 21:11, 12)

> The end has come. *The morning* is upon you, O you who dwell in the land. Behold, *the day* has come; *the morning* is over. (Ezekiel 7:6, 7, 10)

> In *the morning,* in *the morning* Jehovah will bring his judgment to light; it will not be lacking. (Zephaniah 3:5)

> God is in her midst. God will help her when she looks for *the morning.* (Psalms 46:5)

> I have been waiting for Jehovah. My soul waits for the Lord like those who watch for *the morning.* They watch for *the morning* because with him there is the most redemption. He will redeem Israel. (Psalms 130:5–8)

[2] In the passages just quoted *evening* and *night* mean the time when the church is at an end; *morning* means the time when the church is just beginning.

The Lord himself is also called the Morning, as we see in the following passages:

> The God of Israel spoke, the Rock of Israel said to me, "He was like *the morning light, a morning* without clouds." (2 Samuel 23:3, 4)

> I am the Root and the Offspring of David, the shining *morning star.* (Revelation 22:16)

> From the womb of your *dawn* comes the dew of your youth. (Psalms 110:3)

These quotations are about the Lord. Since the Lord is the Morning, he rose from the tomb first thing in the morning, in order to begin a new church (Mark 16:2, 9).

[3] What the Lord says about his Coming makes it obvious that we are to await it:

> As Jesus was sitting on the Mount of Olives, his disciples came to him and said, "Tell us what the *sign of your Coming* and of the close of the age will be." (Matthew 24:3)

> Immediately after the affliction of those days the sun will be darkened and the moon will not give its light; the stars will fall from heaven and the powers of the heavens will be shaken. Then *the sign of the Son of*

Humankind will appear, and they will see *the Son of Humankind coming in the clouds of heaven with power and glory.* (Matthew 24:29, 30; Mark 13:26; Luke 21:27)

Like the days of Noah, so will *the Coming of the Son of Humankind* be. Therefore be prepared, because you do not know at what hour *the Son of Humankind will come.* (Matthew 24:37, 39, 44)

In Luke:

When *the Son of Humankind comes,* will he find faith on the earth? (Luke 18:8)

In John:

Jesus said of John, "If I want him to remain *until I come . . ."* (John 21:22, 23)

[4] In the Acts of the Apostles:

When they saw Jesus taken up into heaven, two men were standing near them in white clothes. They said, "Jesus, who was taken up from you into heaven *will come in the same way you saw him go up to heaven."* (Acts 1:9, 10, 11)

In the Book of Revelation:

The Lord God of the holy prophets sent his angel to show his servants what must happen. "Behold, I am coming. Blessed are those who keep the commandments of this book. *Behold, I am coming,* and my reward is with me, to give to all according to their works." (Revelation 22:6, 7, 12)

And from the same chapter:

I, *Jesus,* have sent my angel to testify to you these things in the churches. I am the Root and the Offspring of David, a shining morning star. The spirit and the bride say, "*Come.*" And those who hear, say, "*Come.*" And those who are thirsty, *come.* Those who wish to, take the water of life freely. (Revelation 22:16, 17)

And again in the same chapter:

He who testifies to these things says, "I am indeed coming." Amen. Do indeed come, Lord Jesus! The grace of our Lord Jesus Christ be with you all. (Revelation 22:20, 21)

766 ⁴³⁹ The Lord is present with each and every human being. He exerts insistent pressure on us to receive him. When we do receive him, which occurs when we acknowledge him as our own God, Creator, Redeemer, and Savior, his First Coming occurs [in us], which is the twilight before dawn. From then on, we begin to be enlightened intellectually in spiritual matters and to grow into deeper and deeper wisdom. As we receive this wisdom from the Lord, we move through the morning into midday. The day continues into our old age until we die. Then we come to the Lord himself in heaven. There, although we died old, we are brought back into the morning of our lives, and the rudiments of wisdom that were planted in us while we were in the physical world grow and thrive to eternity.

767 If we have faith in the Lord and goodwill toward our neighbor, we are a church in miniature. The church as a whole is composed of such churches-in-miniature.

Here is an astounding fact: All angels see the Lord in front of them no matter which way they turn their bodies or faces. The Lord is the sun of the angelic heaven. When the angels are in a spiritual meditation he appears before their eyes. People in the world who have the church within them go through something similar as far as the sight of their spirit is concerned; but because the sight of their spirit is hidden behind the veil of their physical sight, and the bodily and worldly preoccupations of their other senses supply further distractions, people do not realize that this is the state their spirit is in.

The reason why angels see the Lord before them, no matter where they turn, is that he is the source of every truth that leads to wisdom and faith, and the source of every good action that comes from love and goodwill. These two types of things in them actually belong to the Lord. Therefore every truth that leads to wisdom is like a mirror in which they see the Lord, and every good action that comes from love is an actual image of the Lord. This then explains the cause of this surprising phenomenon.

[2] Evil spirits, on the other hand, continually turn themselves away from the Lord and are constantly focusing on their own love. This, too, occurs no matter where they turn their bodies or faces. The cause of this is the same, although the other way around. In some form or other, every evil act they do is an image of their dominant love, and every false thought they have makes that image visible in a kind of mirror.

[3] Nature, too, exhibits some phenomena like this. We can see it in plants that sprout up through thick grass; they strive to grow taller than the surrounding blades so they can catch the sun. Some plants also turn

to follow the sun from sunrise to sunset, in order to mature under its watchful eye. I do not doubt that all the twigs and branches of every tree have the same tendency and make some effort to do the same, and it is only because they lack the flexibility to turn that they remain still. Someone who looks carefully into the matter will observe that all whirlpools in water and even sandbars in the ocean spontaneously rotate according to the general progression of the sun.[440]

[4] Why then would human beings, who were created images of God, not turn to face him, unless they exercised the gift of free choice to redirect elsewhere that force and effort instilled in them by the Creator?

Another analogy would be a bride, who constantly holds some image of her bridegroom in the sight of her spirit. She sees him in the gifts he has given her as if these were mirrors. She longs for him to arrive, and when he does, love leaps up in her heart as she welcomes him with joy.

The Lord's Coming Is Not His Coming to Destroy the Visible Heaven and the Inhabitable Earth and to Create a New Heaven and a New Earth, As Many Have Supposed Because They Have Not Understood the Word's Spiritual Meaning

In the churches in existence today, there is a strongly held opinion about the Second Coming. They believe that when the Lord comes for the Last Judgment, he will appear in the clouds of heaven with angels and the sound of trumpets.[441] He will gather together all the people who are living on the earth and also the people who have died. He will separate the evil among them from the good, as a shepherd separates the goats from the sheep. Then he will cast the evil (the goats) into hell, and lift the good (the sheep) into heaven. At the same time he will create a new visible heaven and a new inhabitable earth. He will send a city down onto this new earth, which will be called the New Jerusalem. Its structure will follow the description given in Revelation 21. That is, it will be made of jasper and gold. The foundations of its walls will be made of precious stones of every kind. Its height, breadth, and length will be equal, at twelve thousand stadia[442] each. All the elect will be brought together into this city, including people who were still alive and also people who had died at any time since the world began. The elect will then return to their bodies and experience everlasting joy in that magnificent city, their heaven.

768

This is the belief concerning the Lord's Coming and the Last Judgment that is dominant in the Christian churches of today.

769 As for the state of human souls after death, there are some universally held opinions and some more narrowly held opinions today. They are as follows.[443]

People think that human souls after death are *breaths;* they like to think of these breaths as puffs of wind. These puffs of wind that are awaiting the day of the Last Judgment are kept either in the middle of the earth, where their somewhere-or-other is, or in the "limbo of the fathers";[444] but there is a difference of opinion on this point. Some think that breaths are forms made of ether or air, and are therefore like ghosts or phantoms; some of them live in the air, some in the woods, some in lakes and streams. Other people think that the souls of the dead are transferred to other planets or stars, and are given places to live there. Some think that souls return to their bodies after a thousand years. Most people think that souls are kept in some kind of storage[445] until the time when the entire firmament and the whole planet are going to be destroyed by fire—either by fire erupting from the center of the earth or by fire in the form of an all-encompassing thunderbolt cast down from the sky. Then the graves will be opened, and the stored souls will be put back into their bodies and taken to the holy city Jerusalem. On another planet, then, they will live together in enlightened bodies. Some there will live lower down, some higher up, since the city is going to be twelve thousand stadia high—as high as it is wide and long (Revelation 21:16).

770 I have asked the clergy and the laity whether they truly believe all that. Do they really believe that all those souls—the people who lived before the Flood, including Adam and Eve, and the people who lived after the Flood, including Noah and his children, as well as Abraham, Isaac, and Jacob, and all the prophets and apostles, and all other human souls—are still being stored in the center of the earth or are flitting around in the air or the ether? Do they really believe that all those souls are going to wear their bodies again and be reunited to them, even if their bodies were corpses that have been eaten by worms, rats, or fish, or were Egyptian mummies that people have taken as medicine, or were mere skeletons baked under the sun until they crumbled to dust?[446] Do they really believe that the stars of heaven are going to fall onto the earth, even though the earth is much smaller than the stars?[447] Surely all these thoughts are absurdities that reason rejects, just as it rejects any other thought that does not make sense.

To these questions some have no response at all. Others say that these are matters of faith, and that we need to hold our intellect under obedience to faith. Others say that these and many other things that transcend reason are accomplished by the divine omnipotence.

When they say the words "faith" and "omnipotence," reason is banished; by that point in the conversation sound reason either disappears and seems nonexistent or turns into a kind of ghostly apparition and is called insanity. To this they add, "Aren't our beliefs in strict accordance with the Word? Aren't we supposed to think and speak on the basis of what the Word says?"

As the chapter on the Sacred Scripture has shown, the Word's literal meaning was written in apparent truths and correspondences [§§193–209, 215, 226, 254–260]. As a result, there is a spiritual meaning within every detail. In that spiritual meaning, truth stands forth in its own light. The literal meaning is in the dark.

771

To prevent people in the new church from wandering off into the darkness of the Word's literal meaning the way the people of the old church have done—especially on the topics of heaven and hell, their own life after death, and the Lord's Coming—the Lord has chosen to open my spiritual sight and bring me into the spiritual world. He has allowed me not only to speak with spirits and angels, with friends and relatives, and even with monarchs and other political leaders, whose lives in the physical world had come to an end, but also to see the amazing conditions in heaven and the wretched conditions in hell. I have learned for a fact that after we die we do not spend time in some somewhere-or-other underground; and we do not fly around blind and mute in midair or deep space. We live on in a substantial body. If we come into the company of the blessed, we have a much better quality of life than we had while we were living in a physical body.

[2] Humankind now has the belief that the visible heaven and the habitable earth are going to be destroyed, and this affects people's thinking about the spiritual world. This belief is based on ignorance. In this state of ignorance, materialism and even atheism have begun to be rooted in the inner rational minds of the educated. The Lord wishes to prevent the human race from plunging still further into these views and to keep materialistic atheism from spreading further (like necrosis in flesh) among educated people; otherwise the outer minds of the educated and their statements before the public will be infected by it as well. Therefore he has commanded me to publish various things that I have heard and seen, both concerning *heaven and hell* and concerning *the Last Judgment,*

and to explain *the Book of Revelation*.[448] That book speaks of the Lord's Coming, the former heaven, the new heaven, and the holy Jerusalem. Anyone who reads and understands these works can see the true meaning of the Lord's Coming, the new heaven, and the New Jerusalem.

The Purpose of This Coming of the Lord—
His Second Coming—Is to Separate the Evil from the Good,
to Save Those Both Past and Present Who Believe in Him,
and to Form Them into a New Angelic Heaven
and a New Church on Earth; If He Did Not Do This,
"No Flesh Would Be Saved" (Matthew 24:22)

772   The purpose of the Lord's Second Coming is *not* to destroy the visible heaven and the inhabitable earth, as the sections under the previous heading have shown [§§768–771]. The Lord's own words make it clear that the purpose of the new church is not to destroy anything but to build something; therefore it is not to condemn anyone but to save those people ever since his First Coming who have believed in him, and those in the future who are going to believe in him.

> God did not send his Son into the world to judge the world but to save the world through him. Those who believe in him are not judged; but those who do not believe have already been judged because they have not believed in the name of the only begotten Son of God. (John 3:17, 18)

> If any hear my words but do not believe, I do not judge them. I did not come to judge the world but to save the world. Those who despise me and do not accept my words already have something that judges them. The Word that I have spoken—that will judge them. (John 12:47, 48)

The Last Judgment occurred in the spiritual world in 1757. The small work titled *Last Judgment* (published in London in 1758) and a later addition, *Supplement to the Last Judgment* (published in Amsterdam in 1763), made this information public.[449] I testify that it is the truth. I saw it with my own eyes in a state of full wakefulness.

773   The purpose of the Lord's Coming is to form a new heaven made up of people who have believed in him, and to establish a new church made up of people from now on who believe in him. These are the two goals

of his Coming. His ultimate purpose in creating the universe was exactly this: to form an angelic heaven made up of people. In this heaven, all who believe in God will live in eternal bliss. The divine love that God has, and that is his essence, cannot intend anything other than this, and the divine wisdom that God has, and that is God, cannot produce any other outcome than this.

The universe was created for the purpose of having an angelic heaven made up of members of the human race, and also for the purpose of having a church in the world, since the church gives the human race access to heaven. In addition, saving people, which requires that they be born in the world, is itself an ongoing act of creation. For this reason the Word sometimes uses the word "create," and means by it "forming people for heaven." See, for example, the following passages.

[2] *Create* for me a clean heart, O God, and renew a firm spirit within me. (Psalms 51:10)

You open your hand, and they are filled with goodness. You send forth your spirit, and *they are created*. (Psalms 104:28, 30)

The people who are *yet to be created* will praise Jah. (Psalms 102:18)

Thus says Jehovah, *the one who created* you, O Jacob; *the one who formed* you, O Israel: "I have redeemed you. I have called you by my name;[450] you [are mine]. All who are called by my name I have *created* for my glory." (Isaiah 43:1, 7)

They were prepared [for you] on the day *you were created*. You were perfect in your ways on the day *you were created*, until perverseness was found in you. (Ezekiel 28:13, 15)

This statement concerns the king of Tyre.

. . . so that they may see, recognize, consider, and understand that the hand of Jehovah has done this and the Holy One of Israel *has created* it. (Isaiah 41:20)

From the passages just quoted, it becomes clear what *creating* means in the following passages.

Jehovah is the one who *creates* the heavens, stretches out the earth, and gives life to the people upon it, and spirit to those who walk on it. (Isaiah 42:5; 45:12, 18)

Behold, I am *creating a new heaven and a new earth.* Enjoy forever what I am *creating.* Behold, I am *going to create Jerusalem* as a rejoicing. (Isaiah 65:17, 18)

774   The Lord is constantly present with every human being, the evil as well as the good. No one would be alive if the Lord were not present. Only when we let him in, however—that is, believe in him and do what he commands—does he come in.

The Lord's constant presence is what makes us rational, and what gives us the capacity to become spiritual. The light that emanates from the Lord as the sun of the spiritual world is what has this effect. We receive this light in our intellect; this light is the truth, and the truth is the source of our rationality.

When we add heat to this light, that is, when we add love to this truth, then the Lord comes in to us. The heat in question emanates from the same sun in the spiritual world; it takes the form of love for God and for our neighbor.

The situation in which the Lord is merely present with us, enlightening our intellect, is like the presence of the sun's light in the world. Unless heat is added to this light, everything on earth remains desolate. When, however, the Lord actually comes in to us, it is like the heat that comes into everything in the spring. Since heat and light work together at that time of year, the ground becomes workable, and the seeds sprout and grow up to bear fruit. (This also illustrates the parallel between the spiritual circumstances that affect our spirits and the earthly circumstances that affect our bodies.)

775   What is true of the individual as a church is also true of the human collective or aggregate known as the church. The church is a human collective or aggregate that is made up of many individuals; the human individual is the church as it exists within each of the many people who constitute it.

The divine design always includes overall systems and individual components. Everything that exists has both of these elements. Without the overall systems, the individual components would not take shape or be able to sustain continued existence, just as the individual parts of the body could not exist without belonging to some broader system within it. In the human body, the individual parts are the organs and the parts within those organs; connective tissue not only envelops the body as a whole but also wraps and separates the individual organs, and even the parts within them. The same complex structure is found in every animal, bird, and insect. In fact it is also found in every tree, shrub, and seed.

Strings and wind instruments would give no sound at all if there were not some underlying ability to vibrate that they shared in common. That vibration is shaped into the sound of each instrument and the sound of each instrument is in turn shaped into a range of individual notes.

Our entire physical sensitivity is like this, too, in its relationship with our five individual senses of sight, hearing, smell, taste, and touch. The relationship between our entire mental sensitivity and individual mental sensations is similar as well.

[2] These examples have been presented for the sake of illustration. They aim to show that the church as well is divided into grand ages and individual movements over time, and these all together form part of one overall history; each of the four churches, one after the other, formed a part of it. The overall history was shaped by these ecclesiastical epochs; and the epochs were shaped by the general and the individual movements within them.

In the human race, also, there are universal factors—two of them—that shape all the systems and individual parts within us. In our body these two universal factors are our heart and our lungs; in our spirit they are our will and our intellect. All that is alive within us, both on a general and on a particular level, depends on these two physical and these two spiritual factors. Without them, everything within us would fall apart and die.

The same thing would happen to the entire angelic heaven and the whole human race—in fact, all of creation—if all that existed within them both collectively and individually were not dependent on God, on his love and wisdom.

This Second Coming of the Lord Is Not Taking Place in Person but in the Word, Since the Word Is from Him and He Is the Word

Many passages say that the Lord is coming in the clouds of heaven; see, for example, Matthew 17:5; 24:30; 26:64; Mark 14:62; Luke 9:34, 35; 21:27; Revelation 1:7; 14:14; Daniel 7:13. Until now no one has known, however, what the *clouds of heaven* mean. People think the Lord is going to appear in person in the actual clouds in the sky.   **776**

The *clouds of heaven* stand for the Word's literal meaning, and the *glory* and *power* with which the Lord is going to come (Matthew 24:30) stand for the Word's spiritual meaning. The reason this has escaped everyone's notice until now is that no one yet, even in a theoretical flight of fancy, has guessed that there is any spiritual meaning within the Word of the type it actually contains.

Because the Lord has opened up the Word's spiritual meaning to me and has also allowed me to be with angels and spirits in their world as one of them, I have discovered that a *cloud of heaven* stands for the Word's earthly meaning, *glory* stands for the Word's spiritual meaning, and *power* stands for the power the Lord has through the Word.

Readers can see from the following passages in the Word that a *cloud of heaven* has this meaning.

> No one is like the God of Jeshurun, who is riding a horse in heaven, and in magnificence on *the clouds.* (Deuteronomy 33:26)

> Sing to God; praise his name. Celebrate the horse rider on *the clouds.* (Psalms 68:4)

> Jehovah is riding a horse on *a fast-moving cloud.* (Isaiah 19:1)

[2] To *ride a horse* means to equip us with divine truths from the Word, since a *horse* means our understanding of the Word (see *Revelation Unveiled* 298). Surely everyone can see that God does not literally ride a horse on the clouds. For another passage,

> God rode upon angel guardians and made *the clouds of the heavens* his tent. (Psalms 18:10–12)

Angel guardians, too, mean the Word (see *Revelation Unveiled* 239, 672).

> Jehovah binds the waters in his clouds and spreads *his cloud* over his throne. (Job 26:8, 9)

> Give strength to Jehovah, strength upon *the clouds.* (Psalms 68:34)

> Jehovah created *a cloud* by day over every dwelling place in Zion; he placed a cover over all glory. (Isaiah 4:5)

The Word in its literal meaning was also represented by the *cloud* in which Jehovah came down onto Mount Sinai when he proclaimed the law. The commandments of the law that were proclaimed at that time were and are the primary principles of the Word.

[3] The following things I have witnessed can be added to lend further support. In the spiritual world there are clouds, just as there are in the physical world, although spiritual clouds have a different origin than physical clouds do. In the spiritual world there are sometimes shining clouds over the angelic heavens and dark clouds over the hells. The shining clouds over the angelic heavens symbolize a lack of clarity that the angels there are experiencing because of the Word's literal meaning. When those clouds are breaking up, they symbolize the fact that the angels are coming into goodwill[451] as a result of the Word's spiritual meaning. The dark clouds over the hells symbolize that the Word is being falsified and desecrated there.

The fact that clouds have these symbolic meanings in the spiritual world is the origin [of their meanings in the Word]. The light that emanates from the Lord as the sun of the spiritual world symbolizes divine truth. Therefore the Lord himself is called the Light (John 1:9; 12:35). As a result, the Word itself, which is kept in the sanctuaries of the church buildings in the spiritual world, appears surrounded with shining light. Clouds dim that light.

The Lord is the Word, as is very clear from the following statement in John:

777

> In the beginning was the Word, and the Word was with God, and the Word was God. And the Word became flesh. (John 1:1, 14)

In this passage *the Word* means divine truth, because the Word is the only source of divine truth for Christians. The Word is the spring from which all the churches named for Christ draw living water in all its fullness. Admittedly, the church is in a cloud when it focuses on the Word's earthly meaning; but it is in glory and power when it focuses on the Word's spiritual and heavenly meaning. (The fact that the Word contains three levels of meaning, the earthly meaning, the spiritual meaning inside that earthly meaning, and the heavenly meaning inside that spiritual meaning, has been demonstrated in the chapter on the Sacred Scripture and in the chapter on the Ten Commandments or the catechism.)

This makes it clear that "the Word" in John means divine truth. John gives further testimony to the same effect in his first Epistle:

> We know that the Son of God has come and has given us *an understanding,* so that we may know *the truth.* And we are in *the truth* in his Son Jesus Christ. (1 John 5:20)

This is also why the Lord often says, "*Amen* I say to you." "Amen" in Hebrew means "the truth."[452] In fact, the Lord is "the Amen" (see Revelation 3:14) and "the Truth" (John 14:6).

When you ask church scholars of today what "the Word" means in John 1:1, they say it means "the supreme power of the Word." What else gives the Word supreme power but its divine truth?

[2] All this makes it clear that the Lord is now going to appear in the Word.

The reason he will not be appearing in person is that ever since he ascended into heaven, he has been in his glorified human manifestation. In this he cannot appear before any human beings unless he has first opened the eyes of their spirit. The eyes of the spirit cannot be opened in people who are engaged in evils and falsities—in any of the goats, whom he placed on his left [Matthew 25:33]. Therefore whenever he showed himself to his disciples, he first opened their eyes. We read, "And their eyes were opened and they recognized him, but he became invisible to them" (Luke 24:31). A similar thing happened with the women who were by his tomb after he had risen; this is why they were able to see angels sitting in the tomb and hear them speaking with them. No one can see angels through physical eyes.

Even before the Lord rose, it was not the apostles' physical eyes but their spiritual eyes that saw the Lord in his glorified human manifestation; after they came out of that state, they appeared to themselves to have been asleep. This is clear from the Lord's transfiguration in the presence of Peter, James, and John and the fact that they were then "heavy with sleep" (Luke 9:32). Therefore it is foolish to believe that the Lord is going to appear in person in a cloud of heaven; instead he is going to appear in the Word, since the Word is from him, and he is the Word.

778 All individuals are their own love and their own understanding. Whatever they say and whatever they do carries with it an essence that is drawn from these two essential properties of their life. Therefore angels can recognize the nature of our unique essence on the basis of nothing more than a brief conversation with us. From hearing the tone of our voice angels sense what we love; and from hearing what we say, angels sense our level of understanding.

What makes this possible is that all people have two grand faculties of life within them: their will and their intellect. Their will is a vessel and a dwelling place for their love, and their intellect is a vessel and a dwelling place for their understanding. Therefore all that comes forth from people, whether in the form of actions or words, constitutes the people themselves; their words and actions *are* the people themselves.

[2] In a similar way, but on a much higher level, the Lord is divine love and divine wisdom, or divine goodness and divine truth. His will belongs to divine love, and his divine love belongs to his will; his intellect is divine wisdom, and divine wisdom is his intellect. The human form is a container for these qualities. These points enable us to see how the Lord is the Word.

On the other hand, people who are against the Word, that is, those who oppose the divine truth it contains and therefore oppose the Lord and his church, are their own evil and their own falsity. Both within their minds and in the manifestation of their minds in their bodies, meaning the things they say and do, this is their nature.

This Second Coming of the Lord Is Taking Place by Means
of Someone to Whom the Lord Has Manifested Himself in Person
and Whom He Has Filled with His Spirit So That
That Individual Can Present the Teachings of the New Church
on the Lord's Behalf through the Agency of the Word

The Lord cannot manifest himself to everyone in person, as has been shown just above [§§776–778], and yet he foretold that he would come and build a new church, which is the New Jerusalem. Therefore it follows that he is going to accomplish this through the agency of a human being who can not only accept these teachings intellectually but also publish them in printed form.

779

I testify in truth that the Lord manifested himself to me, his servant,[453] and assigned me to this task; after doing so, he opened the sight of my spirit and brought me into the spiritual world; and he has allowed me to see the heavens and the hells and to have conversations with angels and spirits on a continual basis for many years now.[454] I also testify that ever since the first day of this calling, I have accepted nothing regarding the teachings of this church from any angel; what I have received has come from the Lord alone while I was reading the Word.[455]

780 For the purpose of being constantly present with me, the Lord has disclosed the spiritual meaning of his Word to me; in that meaning, divine truth stands forth in its own light, and the Lord is forever present in that light. His presence in the Word comes exclusively through its spiritual meaning. Through the light of the spiritual meaning, the Lord passes into the shadows in which the literal meaning stands, much the way the sun's light during the daytime passes through an intervening cloud. (I have shown above [§776] that the Word's literal meaning is like a cloud and its spiritual meaning is its glory; and the Lord himself is the sun from which that light comes; therefore the Lord is the Word.)

The glory with which the Lord is going to come (Matthew 24:30) means the divine truth in its own light; the Word's spiritual meaning exists in this light. This is clearly shown in the following passages.

> The voice of one crying in the desert, "Prepare a way for Jehovah. *The glory of Jehovah* will be revealed, and all flesh will see it." (Isaiah 40:3, 5)

> Shine, because *your light* has come and *the glory of Jehovah* has risen upon you. (Isaiah 60:1 to the end)

> I will give you as a covenant to the people, as *a light for the nations.* I will not give *my glory* to another. (Isaiah 42:6, 8; 48:11)

> *Your light* will break forth like the dawn. *The glory of Jehovah* will gather you in. (Isaiah 58:8)

> The whole earth will be filled with *the glory of Jehovah.* (Numbers 14:21; Isaiah 6:1, 2, 3; 66:18)

> In the beginning was the Word. In it there was life, and that life was *the light for humankind.* He was *the true light.* And the Word became flesh, and we saw *his glory, glory like that of the only begotten child of the Father.* (John 1:1, 4, 9, 14)

> The heavens will tell *the glory of God.* (Psalms 19:1)

> *The glory of God* will enlighten the holy Jerusalem. Its lamp is the Lamb. The nations that are being saved will walk in *his light.* (Revelation 21:23, 24)

Not to mention many other passages.

Glory means divine truth in all its fullness, because every magnificent thing that exists in heaven comes from the light that emanates from the Lord, and in its essence that light, which emanates from the Lord as the sun of the spiritual world, is divine truth.

"The New Heaven" and "the New Earth" and "the New Jerusalem Coming Down from Heaven" in the Book of Revelation Mean This [Second Coming of the Lord]

In the Book of Revelation we read:

781

> I saw a new heaven and a new earth, because the former heaven and the former earth had passed away. And I, John, saw the holy city, the new Jerusalem, coming down from God out of heaven, prepared as a bride adorned for her husband. (Revelation 21:1, 2)

We read something similar in Isaiah:

> Behold, I am creating a new heaven and a new earth. Be glad and rejoice forever. Behold, I am going to make Jerusalem a rejoicing and its people a joy. (Isaiah 65:17, 18)

As I have shown earlier in this chapter [§773], the Lord is at this time forming a new heaven. It consists of Christians who did acknowledge while they were in the world, and Christians who were able to acknowledge after they left the world, that the Lord is the God of heaven and earth, as he himself says in Matthew 28:18.

The New Jerusalem coming down from God out of heaven (Revelation 21) means the new church. For one thing, Jerusalem was the largest city in the land of Canaan. The Temple was there. The altar was there. The sacrifices were performed there. It was a center for divine worship. Three times a year every male in the entire country was commanded to come worship there.

782

Another reason is that the Lord was in Jerusalem and taught in its Temple; it was there that he glorified his human manifestation. For these reasons *Jerusalem* means the church.

The fact that Jerusalem means the church is abundantly clear in what the prophets of the Old Testament say about the new church that the

Lord is going to establish, which they refer to as Jerusalem. [2] I will present only passages in which the fact that *Jerusalem* means the church is easy to see for anyone who has the ability to reason inwardly. We will limit ourselves, then, to just the following.

> Behold, I am creating *a new heaven and a new earth,* and the earlier heaven and earth will not be remembered. Behold, I am *going to make Jerusalem* a rejoicing and its people a joy, so that I will rejoice over *Jerusalem* and take joy in my people. Then the wolf and the lamb will feed together; they will not do evil anywhere on my holy mountain. (Isaiah 65:17, 18, 19, 25)

> For Zion's sake I will not be quiet, for *Jerusalem's* sake I will not rest, until its justice goes forth as brightness, and its salvation is like a burning lamp. Then the nations will see your justice and every monarch will see your glory. You will be called by a new name that the mouth of Jehovah will announce. You will also be a beautiful crown and a royal miter in the hand of your God. Jehovah will be pleased with you, and your land will be married. Behold, your salvation is coming, and his reward is with him. They will call them "a holy people" and "those redeemed by Jehovah." You will be called a sought-after city, and not a deserted city. (Isaiah 62:1–4, 11, 12)

> [3] Awake, awake! Put on your strength, O Zion. Put on your beautiful clothes, *O Jerusalem,* holy city. The uncircumcised and the unclean will not come to you anymore. Shake yourself from the dust; arise. Sit down, *O Jerusalem.* The people will recognize my name in that day; I am the one who is saying, "Behold, it is I." Jehovah has comforted his people. He has redeemed *Jerusalem.* (Isaiah 52:1, 2, 6, 9)

> Shout, O daughter of Zion. Be joyful with all your heart, O daughter of *Jerusalem.* The king of Israel is in your midst. Do not fear evil anymore. He will be glad and joyful about you. He will rest in your[456] love. He will rejoice over you with shouting. I will give you a name and praise among all the peoples of the earth. (Zephaniah 3:14–17, 20)

> Thus said Jehovah, your Redeemer, speaking to *Jerusalem:* "You shall be inhabited." (Isaiah 44:24, 26)

> Thus said Jehovah, "I will turn back to Zion and I will live in the center of *Jerusalem.* Therefore *Jerusalem* will be called the city of truth, and the mountain of Jehovah Sabaoth will be called a holy mountain." (Zechariah 8:3, 20–23)

Then you will know that I am Jehovah your God, living on Zion, the holy mountain, and *Jerusalem* will be holy. And on that day it will happen that the mountains will drip with new wine and the hills will flow with milk. And *Jerusalem* shall remain from generation to generation. (Joel 3:17–21)

[4] On that day the branch of Jehovah will be beautiful and glorious. And it will happen that the people left behind in Zion and remaining in *Jerusalem* will be called holy—everyone who is written down as alive in *Jerusalem*. (Isaiah 4:2, 3)

At the end of days the mountain of Jehovah's house will be established on the top of the mountains. Teaching will go forth from Zion and the Word of Jehovah from *Jerusalem*. (Micah 4:1, 2, 8)

At that time they will call *Jerusalem* the throne of Jehovah, and all the nations will be gathered together to the name of Jehovah, to *Jerusalem*. No longer will they go toward the obstinacy of their evil heart. (Jeremiah 3:17)

Look toward Zion, the city of our appointed feasts. Your eyes will see *Jerusalem,* a peaceful dwelling place, a tabernacle that will not be taken down. Its stakes will never be removed and its ropes will not be broken. (Isaiah 33:20)

Not to mention other passages, such as Isaiah 24:23; 37:32; 66:10–14; Zechariah 12:3, 6–10; 14:8, 11, 12, 21; Malachi 3:4; Psalms 122:1–7; 137:5, 6.

[5] *Jerusalem* in the passages just quoted does not mean the Jerusalem where Jews once lived,[457] but the church of the Lord to come. This is clear from every detail of the description in the passages: for example, the point that Jehovah God is going to create a new heaven and a new earth, including a Jerusalem; that this Jerusalem is going to be a beautiful crown and a royal miter; that it is going to be called "holy," "the city of truth," "the throne of Jehovah," "a peaceful dwelling place," "a tabernacle that will not be taken down"; that the wolf and the lamb will feed together there; and we are told that the mountains there will drip with new wine, the hills will flow with milk, and it will remain from generation to generation. This is also clear from what we are told of the people there, that they are holy, they have all been written down as alive, and they are to be called "those redeemed by Jehovah."

What is more, all these passages indicate that only at the time of the Lord's Coming, especially his Second Coming, [but not before,] will

"Jerusalem" be the way these passages describe it. Before that, Jerusalem is not married; that is, it has not yet become the bride and wife of the Lamb, which is how the New Jerusalem is described in the Book of Revelation.

[6] In Daniel, *Jerusalem* means the church of today, the former [Christian] church. The beginning of this church is described in the following words.

> Know and understand that from the going forth of the Word even to the restoration and building of *Jerusalem,* to the time of the Messiah's rule, is seven weeks. After sixty-two weeks the street and the moat will be rebuilt and restored, but in troublesome times. (Daniel 9:25)

The end of the church of today is described in the following words from the same chapter:

> In the end desolation [will fly in] on a bird of abominations; even to the close and the cutting down, it will drip steadily upon the devastation. (Daniel 9:27)

The final stages of the church of today are also what the following words of the Lord in Matthew are referring to:

> When you see that the abomination of desolation foretold by the prophet Daniel is standing in the holy place, let those who read note it well. (Matthew 24:15)

Evidence that *Jerusalem* in the passages above does not mean the Jerusalem where Jews once lived is found in the passages in the Word in which we are told that Jerusalem has already been completely destroyed or is going to be in the future. See Jeremiah 5:1; 6:6, 7; 7:17, 18, and following; 8:5, 6, 7, and following; 9:11, 12, 13, 14, and following; 13:9, 10, 14; 14:16; Lamentations 1:8, 9, 17; Ezekiel 4:1 to the end; 5:9 to the end; 12:18, 19; 15:6, 7, 8; 16:1–63; 23:1–49; Matthew 23:37, 38; Luke 19:41–44; 21:20, 21, 22; 23:28, 29, 30; besides many other passages. See also the passages where Jerusalem is referred to as Sodom (Isaiah 3:9; Jeremiah 23:14; Ezekiel 16:46, 48; and elsewhere).

783 The church belongs with the Lord. Because of the spiritual marriage between what is good and what is true, the Lord is called the Bridegroom and Husband and the church is called the bride and wife. Christians know this from the Word, especially from the following passages in it.

> John said of the Lord, "The one who has *the bride* is *the groom.* The friend of *the groom,* though, who stands and hears him, rejoices at the voice of *the groom.* " (John 3:29)

Jesus said, "As long as *the bridegroom* is with them, *the children of the wedding* cannot fast." (Matthew 9:15; Mark 2:19, 20; Luke 5:35)

I saw the holy city, the new Jerusalem, coming down from God out of heaven, prepared as *a bride adorned for her husband.* (Revelation 21:2)

The angel said to John, "Come. I will show you *the bride, the wife of the Lamb,* " and from a mountain he showed him the holy city Jerusalem. (Revelation 21:9, 10)

The time for *the Lamb's wedding* has come; *his wife* has prepared herself. Blessed are those who are called to the *marriage supper of the Lamb.* (Revelation 19:7, 9)

"I am the Root and the Offspring of David, a shining morning star." *The spirit and the bride* say, "Come!" And those who are thirsty, come. Those who wish to, take the water of life freely. (Revelation 22:16, 17)

It is in accordance with the divine design that the new heaven is to **784** be formed first before the new church develops on earth. There is an inner level and an outer level to the church. Its inner level is united to the church in heaven, meaning heaven itself. This inner level has to be formed before the outer level; then the outer level is formed by means of the inner level. The clergy in the world today know that this is how it works.[458]

The new heaven is what creates the inner level of the church within us. The more that heaven grows, the more the New Jerusalem (that is, the new church) comes down from that heaven. This cannot take place in a moment. It comes about as the falsities of the former church are removed. What is new cannot take hold where people have been born into false beliefs, unless those beliefs are first uprooted. This uprooting has to be done with the clergy first, and then the laity. The Lord said, "No one puts new wine into old wineskins, or else the wineskins would burst and the wine would pour out. They put new wine into new wineskins, and both are preserved together" (Matthew 9:17; Mark 2:22; Luke 5:37, 38).

[2] The Lord's own words make it clear that these things do not occur until "the close of the age," meaning the end of the church.

Jesus said, "The kingdom of the heavens is like a person who sowed good seed in his field; but while people slept, his enemy came and sowed weeds and then went away. When the true crop sprouted, then the weeds appeared as well. The servants came to him and said, 'Do you want us to go and pull up the weeds?' He said, 'No. In pulling up the weeds, you might also uproot the wheat. Let them both grow together until the harvest. At the time of harvest, I will say to the harvesters, "First pull up the weeds and tie them into bundles to be burned; then gather the wheat into my barn."' The harvest is the close of the age. As the weeds are tied together and burned in the fire, so it will be at the close of the age." (Matthew 13:24–30, 39, 40)

The *wheat* here means the true teachings and good actions that belong to the new church; the *weeds* mean the false teachings and evil actions that belong to the former church. (The fact that "the close of the age" means the end of the church was shown under the first heading in this chapter [§§753–756].)

785

As for the point that everything has both an inner and an outer level, and that the outer level is dependent on the inner level as a body is dependent on its soul, many things in our world serve to illustrate this, when they are thought about in the right way.

This is obvious in the case of humankind. Our entire body serves our mind. Therefore there is an inner and an outer aspect to everything we do and say. The part of our mind called the will is present in every action we take, and the part of our mind called the intellect is present in every word we say. Our awareness, too, has two levels.

Every type of bird and animal and even every type of worm and insect has an inner and an outer level. So does every type of tree, plant, and sprout and even every type of stone and dirt in the ground.

A brief comment about silkworms, bees, and the dirt in the ground will be enough to illustrate this. The inner level in a silkworm is what drives its outer level to make silk and then to take to the air as a moth. The inner level in a bee is what drives its outer level to drink in the ingredients for honey from flowers and to build cells into amazing structures. The inner level of the dirt in the ground is what drives its outer level to support the germination of seeds by exhaling something from the center of each little piece of dirt, which penetrates into the center of the seed, causes it to sprout, and supports the growth of the plant even to the production of new seeds.[459]

The same is also true of their opposites. These, too, have an inner and an outer level. Take, for example, a spider. It has an inner level that drives its outer level; its inner level is its faculty and inclination to make a clever web and sit in the middle of it in order to capture and eat the flies that get caught in it. The same two levels exist in every harmful insect, every type of snake, and every predatory animal in the forest.[460] The same is also true of every godless, insidious, and deceitful human being.

This New Church Is the Crown of All the Churches That Have Ever Existed on This Planet

As I have shown above [§760], to speak in general terms there have been four churches on this planet since the beginning: there was one before the Flood, a second after the Flood; the Israelite church was the third, and the church called Christian was the fourth.   **786**

All churches depend on the recognition and acknowledgment of the one only God, with whom the individual in the church is able to form a partnership. Yet all four churches so far on this earth have lacked this truth. Therefore it follows that after these four will come a church that *will* recognize and acknowledge the one only God. God's divine love had no other purpose in creating the world than to unite humankind to himself, unite himself to humankind, and live with us in a partnership like this.

The former churches lacked this truth, because the earliest church, which existed before the Flood, worshiped a God who could not be seen.[461] No partnership is possible with a God like that. The early church, which existed after the Flood, did the same. The Israelite church worshiped Jehovah, who was essentially unable to be seen (Exodus 33:18–23), although Jehovah God did appear in a human form that he took on through an angel. In this form he appeared to Moses, Abraham, Sarah, Hagar, Gideon, Joshua, and sometimes the prophets.[462] That human form was a symbolic representation of the Lord who was yet to come. Because that form was symbolic, everything else in that church became symbolic as well. (It is well known[463] that the sacrifices and other rituals of their worship symbolized the Lord who was to come, and that these symbolic acts were done away with when he came.)

[2] Now, the fourth church, which was called Christian, did indeed orally acknowledge one God, but a God in three persons, each of whom is individually a god in his own right. Therefore their Trinity was divided; it was not united in one Person. As a result, even though their lips would speak of one God, the picture of three gods was stuck fast in their minds. In fact, after the Council of Nicaea the church's theologians came up with a new teaching of their own. They said that we ought to believe in

God the Father, God the Son, and God the Holy Spirit, none of whom can be seen, because all three came into being with the same divine essence before the world began. And yet, as mentioned just above, it is not possible to form a partnership with a God who cannot be seen. People are therefore still unaware that the one only God, who cannot be seen, came into the world and took on a human manifestation, not only for the purpose of redeeming humankind but also in order to become someone we could see and form a partnership with. We read, "The Word was with God, and *the Word was God,* and *the Word became flesh"* (John 1:1, 14). And in Isaiah, "A Child is born to us; a Son is given to us. His name will be called *God,* Hero, *Father of Eternity"* (Isaiah 9:6). The prophets also say many times that Jehovah himself is going to come into the world and become the Redeemer.[464] This took place through the human manifestation he took on.

787   This new church is the crown of all the churches that have ever existed on this planet because it will worship the one God, who can be seen, within whom is the God that cannot be seen, like a soul in a body. This is the only way we can form a partnership with God, because we are earthly and we think in earthly ways; and such a partnership must be formed in our thinking and then in the desires that belong to our love. This occurs when we think of God as a human being.

Establishing contact with a God we cannot see is like trying to make eye contact with the limitless vastness of outer space, or like being on the lookout in mid-ocean but not being able to see anything but endless sky and sea.

Establishing contact with a God we *can* see is like making eye contact with a person in the air or on the sea, whose arms then reach out, inviting us into an embrace.

Any partnership between God and us must also be reciprocated as a partnership between us and God, and this second aspect of the partnership is not possible unless we can see God.

[2] The fact that we were unable to see God before he took on a human manifestation is something the Lord himself teaches in John: "You have never heard the voice of the Father or seen what he looks like" (John 5:37). And in Moses we read that no one can see God and live (Exodus 33:20). In John we read that God's human manifestation allows him to be seen: "No one has ever seen God. The only begotten Son, who is close to the Father's heart, has made him visible" (John 1:18).

In the same gospel, "Jesus said, 'I am the way, the truth, and the life. No one comes to the Father except through me. Those who know me also know the Father, and those who see me also see the Father'" (John 14:6, 7, 9).

As for the point that we form a partnership with the God that cannot be seen through the aspect of him that can be seen, that is, through the Lord—this is something the Lord himself teaches in the following passages:

> Jesus said, "Live in me and I [shall live] in you. Those who live in me and I in them bear much fruit." (John 15:4, 5)

> On that day you will know that I am in my Father, and you are in me and I am in you. (John 14:20)

> The glory that you gave me, I have given them so that they may be one as we are one—I in them and you in me, so that the love with which you loved me may be in them, and I may be in them. (John 17:22, 23, 26; see also John 6:56)

See also the teachings that the Father and the Lord are one, and that we have to believe in him in order to have eternal life.[465]

Many times already in this work I have demonstrated that our salvation depends on our forming a partnership with God.

Daniel prophesied that this church is going to supersede the churches that have existed since the world began, that it is going to last for ages of ages, and that it is going to be the crown of all the churches that have existed until now. The first time Daniel makes this prophecy is when he recounts and explains Nebuchadnezzar's dream to him. It concerned four kingdoms, which meant the four churches; these were represented in the form of the statue Nebuchadnezzar saw. The text says, "In the days of these [kings], the God of the heavens will cause a kingdom to arise, which will never be destroyed. It will consume all the other kingdoms, and it shall stand forever" (Daniel 2:44). Daniel says that this will be caused by "a stone that becomes a great rock and fills the whole earth" (Daniel 2:35). A *rock* in the Word means the Lord's divine truth.

The same prophet writes elsewhere:

> I saw visions in the night, and behold, there was someone coming with the clouds of the heavens—someone like *the Son of Humankind.* He was given dominion, glory, and a kingdom. All peoples, nations, and tongues

788

will worship him. His dominion is a dominion of an age that will not pass, and his kingdom is one that will not perish. (Daniel 7:13, 14)

Daniel says this after having seen the four great beasts coming up out of the sea (Daniel 7:3). These beasts, too, represented the four former churches.

Both Daniel's own words (Daniel 7:4) and the Lord's (Matthew 24:15, 30) make it clear that Daniel's prophecies foretold what is happening at this very moment in time. Similar things are also said in the Book of Revelation:

> The seventh angel sounded. Then great voices came from heaven saying, "The kingdoms of the world have become kingdoms of our Lord and of his Christ, and he will reign for ages of ages." (Revelation 11:15)

789 As for what this church is going to be like, the other prophets gave predictions about it in many passages. I will present just a few here. In Zechariah,

> There will be a day, which is known to Jehovah—it will not be day or night, but around the time of evening there will be light. In that day living waters will go forth from Jerusalem, and Jehovah will become king over the whole earth. In that day there will be one Jehovah, and his name will be one. (Zechariah 14:7, 8, 9)

In Joel,

> And on that day it will happen that the mountains will drip with new wine and the hills will flow with milk. And Jerusalem shall remain from generation to generation. (Joel 3:18–20)

In Jeremiah,

> At that time they will call Jerusalem the throne of Jehovah, and all the nations will be gathered together to the name of Jehovah, to Jerusalem. No longer will they go toward the obstinacy of their evil heart. (Jeremiah 3:17; Revelation 21:24, 26)

In Isaiah,

> Your eyes will see Jerusalem, a peaceful dwelling place, a tabernacle that will not be taken down. Its stakes will never be removed and its ropes will not be broken. (Isaiah 33:20)

[2] In these passages, *Jerusalem* means the holy New Jerusalem, which is described in Revelation 21 and means the new church. Again, in Isaiah,

> A branch will come out of the trunk of Jesse. Justice will be his loincloth, and the truth will wrap his thighs. Then the wolf will live with the lamb, and the leopard [will lie down] with the goat. The young ox and the young lion and the fatted calf will be together, and a little child will lead them. The bull calf and the bear will graze; their offspring will lie down together. A nursing child will play over a cobra's hole, and a weaned child will reach a hand over the den of a poisonous snake. They will not do evil and they will not defile themselves anywhere on my holy mountain, because the earth will be full of the knowledge of Jehovah. In that day the nations will seek the root of Jesse, who stands as a banner for the peoples, and glory will be his rest. (Isaiah 11:1, 5–10)

As we all know, these conditions do not yet exist in the churches, least of all in the most recent church. In Jeremiah,

> Behold, the days are coming when I will make a new covenant. This will be the covenant. I will put my law inside them. I will write it on their hearts. I will be their God and they will be my people. They will all know me, from the least of them to the greatest of them. (Jeremiah 31:31–34; Revelation 21:3)

[3] Again, it is a well-known fact that conditions like these have not come about yet in the churches. The reason is that we have not turned to the God who can be seen—the God we "will all know." Yet he himself is the Word or the law that he will put inside us and write on our heart. In Isaiah,

> For Jerusalem's sake I will not rest until its justice goes forth as brightness and its salvation burns like a lamp. You will be called by a new name that the mouth of Jehovah will announce. You will also be *a beautiful crown and a royal miter* in the hand of your God. Jehovah will be pleased with you, and your land will be *married.* Behold, your salvation is coming, and his reward is with him. They will call them "a holy people" and "those redeemed by Jehovah." You will be called a sought-after city, and not a deserted city. [Isaiah 62:1–4, 11, 12]

What this church is going to be like is amply described in the Book of Revelation. That book is about the end of the former church and the

790

rise of the new church. The New Jerusalem, all the magnificent things about it, and its future as the bride and wife of the Lamb (Revelation 19:7; 21:2, 9) are a portrayal of the new church.

From the Book of Revelation I will quote just the following words, when the New Jerusalem is seen, coming down from heaven. We read,

> Behold, the tabernacle of God is with people, and he will dwell with them. They will be his people. He will be with them as their God. The nations that are being saved will walk in his light, and there will be no night there. I, Jesus, have sent my angel to testify to you these things in the churches. I am the Root and the Offspring of David, a shining morning star. The spirit and the bride say, 'Come.' And those who hear, say, 'Come.' And those who are thirsty, *come.* Those who wish to, take the water of life freely. Do indeed come, Lord Jesus! Amen. (Revelation 21:3, 24, 25; 22:16, 17, 20)

Postscript

791 After this work was finished,[466] the Lord called together the twelve disciples who followed him in the world. The next day he sent all of them out to the entire *spiritual world* to preach *the gospel* that *the Lord God Jesus Christ* reigns and that his kingdom will last for ages of ages, as foretold by Daniel (Daniel 7:13, 14) and by the Book of Revelation (Revelation 11:15); also that "people who come to the wedding feast of the Lamb are blessed" (Revelation 19:9). This occurred on June 19, 1770. This is what the Lord was referring to when he said, "He will send out his angels, and they will gather his chosen people from one end of the heavens to the other" (Matthew 24:31).

[Author's Additional Material]

792 The work *Heaven and Hell* is a treatise on the spiritual world.[467] That work describes many things about that world; and because every human being comes into that world after death, that work also covers the states people go through there.[468]

Surely everyone knows, or is at least capable of knowing, that we live on after death, because we are born human, created in the image of God, and because the Lord teaches us this in his Word. What exactly our life is going to be like there, though, has been a complete mystery until now. People have thought that we will then be a soul, which they like to think of as a piece of ether or air—a breath that we breathe out as we are dying, which retains our vital essence, but has no eyesight, no hearing, and no ability to speak.

In fact, though, we are still human beings after we die—so much so that we do not realize we are not still in the physical world. As we used to in the world, we see, hear, and speak. As we used to in the world, we walk, run, and sit. As we used to in the world, we lie down, sleep, and wake up. As we used to in the world, we eat and drink. As we used to in the world, we enjoy making love to our spouse. Briefly put, we are still human in every way.

This makes it clear that our death is not the extinction of our life but a continuation of it. Death is just a transition.

We are still human beings after we die, even though we are no longer visible to the physical eyes of people still in the world. This is clear from the angels that were seen by Abraham, Hagar, Gideon, Daniel, and some of the prophets. This is also clear from the angels that were seen in the Lord's tomb, and from the angels that were seen a number of times by John, as he says in the Book of Revelation.[469] It is especially clear from the Lord himself, who showed that he was still human by touching people and eating things; yet he also disappeared from before their eyes. But who could be so deranged as to think that the Lord stopped being human just because he disappeared?

People were able to see the Lord because the eyes of their spirit were opened at the time. When the eyes of our spirit are opened, things that are in the spiritual world appear to us just as clearly as things that are in the physical world. The difference between people in the physical world and people in the spiritual world is that people in the spiritual world are clothed in a substantial body, whereas people in the physical world are clothed in a material body that has a substantial body inside it. Substantial people see other substantial people just as clearly as physical people see other physical people. Because of the difference between what is physical and what is substantial, however, substantial people cannot see physical people and physical people cannot see substantial people. I could describe the nature of the difference between the two, but it would take too many words.

793

794. From eyewitness experience of many years now, I can pass on to you that, just as in the physical world, in the spiritual world there are landmasses, plains and valleys, mountains and hills, springs and streams; there are parks and gardens, woods and forests. There are cities there, with mansions and homes. There are also written documents and books; jobs and businesses; gold, silver, and precious stones.

To put it briefly, that world contains every single thing that exists in the physical world, although in heaven those things are immensely more perfect. The main difference, though, is that everything that comes into view in the spiritual world, such as houses, gardens, food, and so on, is created in a moment by the Lord. The things in that world are created to correspond with what is inside the angels and spirits, namely, their feelings and thoughts. The [living] things that come into view in the physical world, on the other hand, come forth from some kind of seed and grow.

795. Since this is how it is there, I have conversations every day with the races and peoples of this world. I have interaction not only with people in Europe but also people in Asia and Africa. I talk to people of a variety of religions. Therefore by way of an epilogue to this work I will add a brief description of the state of some of them.

Keep in mind that in the spiritual world, the state of every race and people in general and of each individual in particular depends on their acknowledgment and worship of God. All those who acknowledge God at heart, and from now on, who acknowledge the Lord Jesus Christ as God the Redeemer and Savior, are in heaven. People who do not acknowledge him are beneath heaven and are given instruction there. Those who accept the instruction are lifted up into heaven. Those who do not accept it are cast down into hell. In this second group are people like the Socinians, who turn to God the Father alone, and people like the Arians, who have denied that the Lord's human manifestation was divine.[470] The Lord himself said, "*I am the way, the truth, and the life. No one comes to the Father except through me*" (John 14:6); and when Philip asked to see the Father, the Lord said to him, "*Those who see and recognize me, see and recognize the Father*" (John 14:7 and following).

Luther, Melanchthon, and Calvin in the Spiritual World

796 I have often had conversations with these three leading reformers of the Christian church. I have learned what the state of their life has been from the beginning up to the present day.

As for *Luther,*[471] from the moment he arrived in the spiritual world he was an ardent evangelist for and defender of his own theological teachings. As the number of people from earth who agreed and favored his position grew, his impassioned championing of those teachings only increased.

He was given a home like the one he had had in the world, at Eisleben. In the middle of that home he set up a chair on a low platform. He would sit there, and his door was open to people who came to hear him. He would line them up in rows, placing those who were most favorable to his views closest to himself and situating the less favorable behind them. Then he would follow a routine of holding forth for a while, and breaking now and then for questions, but always with a view to using the questions as a way to get back to the main point of his lecture.

[2] Over time, because of the widespread approval he was receiving he adopted a particular style of persuasive speaking that is so effective in the spiritual world that no one can resist it or take up a contrary position to what is being said. Because this technique was in fact a type of incantation that had been practiced in ancient times, however, he was strictly forbidden to use it. He went back to appealing to people's memory and understanding instead.

The type of persuasion (actually a form of incantation) that he had been practicing draws its power from self-love. Eventually that self-love leads the style of discourse to become such that when anyone contradicts what you are saying, you attack not only the point being made but also the person who is making it.

[3] This was the state of Luther's life all the way up to the time of the Last Judgment, which occurred in the spiritual world in 1757. Then a year after that, Luther was relocated from that first house of his to another; at the same time he was brought into a different state of life as well.

He came to hear about my situation—that although I was still in the physical world, I was having conversations with people in the spiritual world. Therefore he (and many others) sought me out. After a lot of questions and answers back and forth with me, he came to understand that this day is the end of the former church, and the beginning of the new church that Daniel had foretold and that the Lord himself prophesied in the Gospels. Luther also understood the idea that this new church is what is meant by the New Jerusalem in the Book of Revelation and by the everlasting gospel proclaimed by the angel, flying in the midst of heaven, to the people who dwell on the earth (Revelation 14:6).

At that point in the conversation, though, he became extremely upset and protested loudly against what I was saying. Nevertheless, as he gradually came to see that the new church has been and is being constituted of people who acknowledge the Lord alone as the God of heaven and earth (as the Lord himself says in Matthew 28:18), and as he noticed that the group that gathered around him daily was becoming smaller, his protestations came to an end.

We then developed a closer relationship and he began confiding in me. Once he had become thoroughly convinced that he had based his central doctrine of justification by faith alone on his own ideas and not on the Word, he allowed himself to be taught about the Lord, goodwill, true faith, free choice, and even redemption; and all this teaching was based exclusively on the Word.

[4] After being convinced, he began to prefer the truths that are foundational to the new church, and to become stronger in them. During this period he was spending time with me every day. Then whenever these truths would come to his mind, he would start to laugh at his own prior teachings, because they went directly against what the Word says.

I once heard him saying, "It is not all that surprising, though, that I latched onto faith alone as what justifies us, and cut goodwill off from its own spiritual essence, and took away the notion of any human free choice in spiritual things, not to mention the many other things that faith alone, once that is accepted, leads to, like one link after another in a chain. It was all because my goal was to separate from the Roman Catholics, and the notion of faith alone was the only way to pursue and achieve that. Therefore I am not surprised that I wandered off into error. But I am surprised that one deranged person can produce so many other deranged people." Luther then looked over in the direction of some famous theological authors who were much read in their day, who were loyal adherents to his teachings.

"It does surprise me," he continued, "that people like these did not notice the statements in Sacred Scripture that contradict my teachings, even though such statements are standing there in plain sight."

[5] The angels who examine people informed me that this leader, more than many others who had convinced themselves that we are justified by faith alone, was in a state of openness to change, because since his youth, before he ever began the Protestant Reformation, he had taken to heart the teaching that goodwill has the highest priority; this is why in both his writings and his sermons he had taught so beautifully about goodwill.

It became clear from this that the idea of justification by faith alone had taken root in his outer, earthly self, but not in his inner, spiritual self. The outcome is very different for people who become convinced in their youth that goodwill is not spiritual; this spontaneously occurs in listeners when a teacher uses supporting evidence to establish that we are justified by faith alone.

[6] I have had a conversation with the person who was the prince of Saxony when Luther was in the world.[472] He told me that he had often raised objections to Luther, particularly on the point that Luther had separated goodwill from faith and declared that faith contributes to our salvation but goodwill does not, even though Sacred Scripture not only unites these two as the universal means of salvation, but Paul actually gives precedence to goodwill over faith when he says, "There are three things: faith, hope, and goodwill. The greatest of these is goodwill" (1 Corinthians 13:13). The prince noted, however, that Luther would give the same response every time—that he had no choice but to do so, because of the Roman Catholics. This prince is among the blessed.

As for *Melanchthon*,[473] I have been allowed to learn a number of things about the kind of life he had when he first arrived in the spiritual world and how his circumstances changed later on. I learned this not only from angels but also from some interactions of my own with him. I have spoken with him a number of times, but not as often or as intimately as with Luther. The reason the communication was not as often or as intimate was that he was not in a position to have as much access to me, because in his studies he was fixated on justification by faith alone; he was not focusing on goodwill, and I was surrounded by angelic spirits who were devoted to goodwill, and they blocked his access to me.

797

[2] I have been told that as soon as he arrived in the spiritual world, there was a house prepared for him that was much like the house where he had lived in the world. In fact, this is done for most newly arrived spirits, with the result that they do not realize they are no longer in the physical world. The time just after they died seems to them in retrospect as if they had merely been asleep.

Everything in his apartment was the same as it had been—the same table, the same writing desk with pigeonholes, the same bookcase. Therefore as soon as he arrived there, he sat down at his table as if he had just woken up from a night's sleep. He continued writing, as he had been, on the subject of justification by faith alone. He wrote on this topic for a number of days without making even the slightest mention of goodwill.

The angels noticed this and asked him through messengers why he was not also writing about goodwill.

"Goodwill has nothing to do with the church," he replied. "If it were made out to be some essential attribute of the church, people would take credit for being justified and saved, and this would deprive faith of its spiritual essence."

[3] When the angels who were above his head sensed his answer, and when the angels who were associated with him whenever he left home heard about it, they withdrew from him. (Every new arrival is accompanied by angels to begin with.)

Several weeks after that, the furnishings and supplies in his apartment began to fade away gradually until they disappeared. Eventually, there was nothing left there but a table, some pieces of paper, a pen, and some ink. The walls of his apartment were by then simply plastered with lime, and his floor was made of yellowish bricks. He found himself wearing humble clothing. He was very surprised by this, and asked around to find out why this was. He was told that it was because he was removing goodwill from the church when in fact goodwill is the very heart of the church. Every time it came up, however, he strongly disagreed.

He continued to write about faith as the church's only essential ingredient and the only means of being saved, and he kept creating a greater and greater distance between goodwill and the church. Because he did so, he one day suddenly found himself underground in a workhouse where there were others like him. He wanted to leave, but was prevented from doing so. He was informed that this and nothing else was the final outcome for people who threw goodwill and good works out the church door.

Nevertheless, because he had been one of the leaders of the Protestant Reformation, he was released from there by command of the Lord and brought back to his old apartment, where there was nothing but a table, some paper, a pen, and some ink.

Because his ideas were set, he once again filled that paper with the same theological error. Therefore there was no way to prevent him from going down again to his friends in confinement and then coming back up again. When he came back up, he was dressed in hairy animal skins, because faith that lacks goodwill is freezing cold.

[4] He told me firsthand that there was another room off his apartment at the back, where people like him who had likewise banished goodwill were sitting at three tables. A fourth table would sometimes

appear there as well, with various kinds of monsters on it, but he and the others were for some reason not frightened away by them. He said he was having conversations with the other people, and every day they were giving him further support for his views.

Quite a while later, fear did take hold of him, and he began writing something about goodwill, but what he would write on a piece of paper one day would no longer be visible the next day. (Actually, this can happen to anyone in that world. What the outer self writes without the compliance of the inner self at the same time—therefore what is written under coercion rather than in freedom—spontaneously deletes itself.)

[5] Then the new heaven began to be established by the Lord. In the light from that heaven, Melanchthon began to think that he might actually be in error. He started to feel anxiety about what his final outcome was going to be. He became aware of some deep ideas that had been impressed on him earlier about goodwill. In that state of mind he did some research in the Word. His eyes were opened and he saw that the Word was completely full of *loving God and loving our neighbor*. He came to see that what the Lord said was true—that all the Law and the Prophets, that is, the Word as a whole, did indeed hinge on these two commandments [Matthew 22:40].

He was then moved to another house much deeper to the south on the western side. He had a conversation with me there, and told me that now his writing about goodwill was not disappearing the way it used to; it would fade somewhat, but it was still legible the following day.

[6] I was surprised by the fact that when he walked, his footsteps made a clanking sound, like someone walking across cobblestones in iron shoes.

To these points I might add that once, when some spirits who had recently arrived from earth came to his apartment to see him and speak with him, he called on one of the magic spirits who had the ability to project images to look like furniture and accessories. That spirit decorated his apartment with apparent wall-hangings, carpets with a rose pattern, and a bookcase in the middle of the room. As soon as the visitors left, all that disappeared, though, and the apartment returned to its bare lime-plastered walls and its stark emptiness. But this happened when he was in that first state.

As regards *Calvin,*[474] I have been told the following. (1) When he first arrived in the spiritual world, he firmly believed that he was still in the world where he was born. Despite the fact that he had been told by

798

the angels who were associated with him in the beginning that he was no longer in his own world but was now part of theirs, he said, "My body is the same; my hands are the same. I have the same sensations."

The angels informed him that he was now in a substantial body. Before this, they said, he had been in this same substantial body, but it had been wrapped up inside a material body. Now that material body has been cast off, but he still has his substantial body, which is what makes him human. At first he understood this, but the next day he went back to believing that he was still in the world where he was born.

The reason for this was that he was a sense-oriented person; he believed nothing that he could not experience himself with his own bodily senses. This is why all the teachings of his faith were ideas of his own that he had hatched up himself; they did not come from the Word. He did indeed quote the Word [in his writing], but that was just for the sake of getting the common people to agree with him.

[2] (2) After that first period of time, the angels left him and he wandered here and there. He made inquiries about where the people were who since ancient times had believed in *predestination*.[475] He was told, "They are a great distance from here. They are kept locked up underground. The only way to reach them is through an underground passageway on the far side. The followers of Gottschalk[476] are still free to move around, however. Sometimes they have meetings in a place that in the spiritual language is called Pyris."[477]

Because he was longing to be with those people, he was taken to an assembly where some of them were staying. When he joined them, he was in his heart's delight. He formed a deep friendship with them.

[3] (3) When the followers of Gottschalk were taken away, however, to join their fellow [predestinarians] in that cave, he became bored. He went looking for a safe place to stay. He was finally accepted in a community exclusively made up of simple folk, some of whom were religious. When he became aware that they knew nothing about predestination and were incapable of understanding it even when they were told, he went into a remote corner of that community and dropped out of sight for a long time. He never opened his mouth on any subject related to the church.

This was providential, both because it allowed him an opportunity to withdraw from his erroneous belief in predestination, and also because it capped the size of the groups who ever since the Synod of Dort had been attached to that detestable heresy. In the course of time all such people were relegated to their companions in that cave.

[4] (4) Eventually, when modern-day predestinarians were asking, "Where is Calvin?" and an investigation uncovered that he was living on the outskirts of a community that consisted entirely of simple folk, he was summoned from there and taken to a governor who was caught up in the same garbage. The governor welcomed Calvin into his home and took care of him, right up until the time when the Lord began to establish the new heaven. Then, because the governor who had been taking care of him was himself thrown out along with a crowd of the governor's followers, Calvin moved into a whorehouse and lived there for some time.

[5] (5) Since he then enjoyed a freedom to go here and there, including visiting the area where I was living, I had an opportunity to speak with him. I first mentioned the new heaven, which the Lord is building up today among people who acknowledge the Lord alone as the God of heaven and earth, according to his own words in Matthew 28:18. I told him that the people in the new heaven believe that the Lord and the Father are one (John 10:30); that he is in the Father and the Father is in him; that those who see and recognize him, see and recognize the Father (John 14:6–11); and that therefore there is one God in the church, just as there is in heaven.

[6] After I said that, he at first, as usual, had absolutely nothing to say. After about half an hour, though, he did finally break his silence.

"Wasn't Christ a human being, the son of Mary who was married to Joseph?" he said. "How can a human being be worshiped as God?"

I said, "Isn't Jesus Christ, our Redeemer and Savior, both God and a human being?"

"He is both God and a human being," he replied, "but his divinity belongs to his Father, not to him."

"Where is Christ, then?" I asked.

"He is in the lowest parts of heaven," he said. He supported this with the fact that the Lord humbled himself before his Father and allowed himself to be crucified. Calvin then added some phrases that ridiculed the worship of the Lord, which suddenly popped into his mind from his time in this world. The gist of them was that worshiping the Lord is just another form of idolatry. He wanted to add some truly heinous statements about that worship, but the angels who were with me sealed his lips.

[7] I felt a passionate desire to convert him. I said, "It is not only that the Lord our Savior is both God and a human being, but in fact in him God is a human being and a human being is God."

I supported this point by quoting Paul's statement that all the fullness of divinity dwells physically in the Lord (Colossians 2:9), and John's statement that the Lord is the true God and eternal life (1 John 5:20). I also quoted the Lord's own words to the effect that the will of the Father is that everyone who believes in the Son has eternal life, and that those who do not believe in the Son will not see life; instead the anger of God remains on them (John 3:36; 6:40). I also said that the statement known as the Athanasian Creed indicates that in Christ, God and a human being are not two but one; they are in one person like the soul and the body of one human being.

[8] To that he replied, "All those things you just quoted from the Word are pointless. Surely the Word is the book of all heresies. It is like the weather vane on rooftops or on ships that can turn in any direction depending on the weather conditions. *Predestination alone* is what brings together all facets of religion. This concept is the dwelling place and tent of meeting at the center of every other aspect of religion. The faith that justifies and saves is the shrine and the sanctuary there. Does any human being have free choice in spiritual matters? Isn't everything related to salvation a free gift? Therefore arguments against all this, and against predestination, sound and smell to me like nothing more than stomach rumblings and belching.

"Because this is how it is, I have actually thought to myself that a church building where a congregation gathers to hear topics taught and the Word quoted is really a kind of zoo that holds both sheep and wolves. The laws of civil justice are a halter that keeps the wolves from attacking the sheep. (By 'the sheep' I mean those who are predestined [for salvation].) All the eloquent preaching that ministers provide has no more effect than if they were to stand there sobbing incoherently.

"I will give you my statement of faith. It is this: 'There is a God. He is omnipotent. The only people who are saved are those whom God the Father has chosen and predestined for salvation. All others are assigned their own final outcome or fate.'"

[9] Upon hearing that I was outraged. My retort was, "What you are saying is unspeakably heinous. Get away, you evil spirit! Being in the spiritual world as you are, surely you realize that there is a heaven and a hell. Predestination involves the assignment of some to heaven and of others to hell. How could you escape the idea, then, that God is like some tyrant who lets his cronies into the city and sends all the rest off to the executioner? You should be ashamed of yourself!"

[10] Then I read him sections in the *Formula of Concord*[478] that declare certain Calvinist teachings concerning the worship of the Lord and predestination to be erroneous. The following Calvinist teaching on *the worship of the Lord* is an example: "It is a damnable form of idolatry to place our confidence and faith of heart not only in Christ's divine nature but also in his human nature, and direct our honor and adoration toward both natures." The following Calvinist teaching on *predestination* is another example: "Christ did not die for all people but only for the elect. God created the majority of human beings for eternal damnation; he does not want those people to be converted and come to life. The elect and the reborn are incapable of losing faith or losing the Holy Spirit even if they commit all kinds of horrendous sins and crimes. People who are not among the elect, on the other hand, are inevitably damned; they cannot achieve salvation even if they are baptized a thousand times over, take the Eucharist every day, and lead the most holy, guiltless life imaginable" (*Formula of Concord,* Leipzig 1756, pages 837, 838).[479]

After I read these passages to him, I asked, "Are the statements written in this book something you really taught or not?"

"They are," he replied, "but I don't remember whether I wrote those words myself, or whether I just spoke them [and someone else wrote them down]."

[11] All the servants of the Lord who heard this went away from Calvin. He then hurried off to the road that led to the cave of people who had adamantly espoused the accursed concept of predestination.

Later on I had a chance to speak to several of the people held in that cave. I asked what their life was like there. They said that in order to get food they were forced to do work, and that all the people in the cave treated each other like enemies. Each one looked for occasions to do harm to the next, and would actually do so on the slightest provocation. Doing harm is the greatest delight of their lives. (For more about predestination and those who believe in it, see §§485–488 above.)

I have had conversations with many others as well—both with followers of these three and with various heretics. From visiting with all of them I was able to conclude that whoever among them had practiced a life of goodwill, and especially those who had loved the truth because it was true, were open to being instructed in the spiritual world and were receptive to the teachings of the new church.

People who have become adamantly devoted to theological falsities, however, and also people who have lived evil lives, are not open to being

799

instructed. Bit by bit, they distance themselves from the new heaven and come into association with people like themselves who are in hell. Once in hell, they become even more stubbornly and adamantly opposed to the worship of the Lord, even to the point where they cannot stand to hear the name Jesus. The complete opposite happens in heaven, where all are of one mind in acknowledging the Lord as the God of heaven.

The Dutch in the Spiritual World

800 In *Heaven and Hell*[480] I reported that Christian populations where the Word is read and where the Lord is known and acknowledged as the Redeemer and Savior are at the center of all the nations and peoples in the entire spiritual world. The reason for this is that the greatest spiritual light exists among them. That light radiates out from the center into all outlying regions, even the very farthest, as was shown above in §§267–272 in the chapter on the Sacred Scripture.

Within this Christian central region, Protestants are assigned particular places depending on how receptive they are to spiritual light from the Lord. Among the Dutch, that spiritual light is more deeply and fully joined to their earthly light, and they are therefore more receptive than others to what is reasonable and rational. As a result, they are given homes within that Christian central region that are in the eastern and southern parts of it. They are in the east to the extent that they have a capacity for receiving spiritual heat, and in the south to the extent that they have a capacity for receiving spiritual light.

(For the points that the regions of the spiritual world are not like the regions in the physical world, that people live in this or that region in accordance with their receptivity to faith and love, and that people who have an exceptionally great amount of love live in the east and people who have an exceptionally great level of understanding live in the south, see *Heaven and Hell* 141–153.)

801 Another reason why Dutch people live in these particular parts of the Christian central region is that their highest love and goal is doing business, and they love money only as a means that serves that higher goal. This is a spiritual kind of love to have.

If money is the ultimate goal people love, however, and doing business is loved only as a means that serves that ultimate goal—a situation found among Jews[481]—this is an earthly kind of love to have; it leads to insatiable desire for wealth.

The reason why loving to do business is spiritual when it is the ultimate goal is that business is useful and serves the common good. Yes, their own benefit is also part of the equation; when we are thinking from our earthly selves it may even appear more important than the common good. Nevertheless, when being in business is the goal, it is also what is loved the most; and the goal that we love the most is what is considered most important in heaven. The goal we love the most is like the leader of a country or the head of a household; all the other loves are like that leader's subjects and servants. The goal we love dwells in the highest and inmost regions of our mind. The intermediate loves we have are below and outside that highest love; they follow its commands.

The Dutch, more than other people, have this spiritual type of love. Jews have an inverted version of it; therefore their love of doing business is merely earthly in nature. What lies deep within it is not the common good but their own benefit.

The Dutch stick more strongly than others do to the core principles in their religion. They will not be moved. If someone tries to convince them that this or that teaching is out of step with the other things they believe, they will not accept it. They turn away and remain exactly where they were before. Even if they have an inner vision of truth, they will keep it at bay. They hold their rational faculty under tight obedience [to faith].

802

Since this is their nature, when they come into the spiritual world after death they are prepared in an unusual way to accept spiritual teachings from heaven (which are divine truths). They are not *taught* them, because they are not open to such teaching. Instead, what heaven is like is *described* for them. Then they are given an opportunity to go there and see it for themselves; up there they are bathed in whatever heavenly qualities are in harmony with their nature. They then return to their own people feeling a great desire for heaven.

[2] Then they are *taught* the truth, that God is one, not only in essence but also in person;[482] that the Lord, our Redeemer and Savior, is that God; and that the divine Trinity exists within him; and also this truth, that knowing and talking about faith and goodwill do nothing for us if we do not also put them to work in our lives, and that the Lord grants us faith and goodwill after we examine ourselves and practice repentance.

If they reject this teaching and persist in thinking of God as three persons and of religion as something merely theoretical rather than also practical, they are driven into wretched poverty and their business is taken away from them until they realize they are completely out of options.

Then they are taken to see people who have divine truths and who are therefore abundantly wealthy and have thriving businesses. While they are seeing these people, thoughts come into their minds from heaven regarding why these people are so well off, along with reflections on what kind of faith and what kind of life they have. They notice in particular that these people abstain from evils on the grounds that evils are sins. They also make a few inquiries, and verify that their thoughts and conjectures about the successful people are accurate.

They then go back and forth, back and forth, between being in their own poverty and being in the company of these successful people. Eventually they decide on their own that to escape their poverty they need to embrace the same beliefs and the same practices as the successful people. As they actually do embrace that faith and live that life of goodwill, their financial situation improves markedly and they begin enjoying life again.

[3] Through this method, [Dutch] people who had had at least some practice of goodwill in their lives are led to make further changes in themselves and are prepared for heaven.

After these experiences, people like this become steadier than others, so that they could be called steadiness itself. They will not allow themselves to be swayed by any faulty rationale, any mistaken impression, any confusion brought on by subtly deceptive reasoning, or any wrongheaded vision, no matter how many supporting arguments it has. They become more clear-sighted than they were before.

803   The professors who teach in their schools—especially the ones known as Cocceians[483]—devote intense study to the mystical teachings of the modern-day faith. These mystical teachings lead inevitably to the dogma of predestination, a dogma that was well established by the Synod of Dort. They sow and implant that teaching in their students, as if they were farmers who do not care from what kind of fruit they take seed to plant in their field.

As a result, the lay people from that country talk to each other a lot about predestination. They are of different opinions about it, however. Some embrace it with both hands. Some pick it up with just one hand and laugh at it. Others throw it away from themselves like a snake or a lizard.

Lay people there do not know the mystical teachings of faith that gave birth to that viper, because they focus on their businesses. The mystical teachings of that faith do indeed reach their intellect, but they do not sink in.

The dogma of predestination among the laity and also among the clergy of that nation is like a statue of a person, built upon a rock jutting out into the sea, with a great golden conch shell in its hand. When the ship captains who are sailing by see that statue, some of them lower the mainsail as a sign of honor and veneration, some just wink and salute at it, and others hiss at it as something ludicrous.

To them, predestination is also like some unknown bird from India situated atop a high tower. Some swear it is a turtledove, some guess that it is a rooster, and others curse at it and cry out, "It's a screech owl!"

In the spiritual world, the Dutch are easily told apart from other nationalities because they wear much the same clothing as they did in the physical world, with the difference that the ones who receive faith and a spiritual life dress more nicely than they used to. The reason they appear to wear the same kind of clothes is that they remain steadfast in the principles of their religion, and all the people in the spiritual world are clothed according to their religious principles. This is why people who are devoted to divine truths wear white clothes and linen garments.

804

The cities where the Dutch live are protected in an unusual way. All the streets are covered, and the ends of the streets have doors, so that the people cannot be seen from the surrounding rocks and hills. This comes about because of a deep-seated prudent desire they have to hide their plans and not divulge their intentions. (In the spiritual world people can see such things in you just by looking.)

805

Curious visitors sometimes come there in order to find out what life is like in those cities. When it is time for such people to leave, they are taken to the locked doors at the ends of the streets, then taken back to another locked door somewhere else, then to many others here and there, to the point where the visitors feel highly annoyed. Then they are finally released. This is to ensure that those visitors never come back.

[2] [Recently arrived] *wives* there who want complete control over their husbands live on one side of the city and are allowed to meet up with their husbands only when the husbands have invited them to do so; these invitations are polite and formal in nature. The wives are then also taken to homes where married partners live together without either partner dominating the other. The wives are shown how well decorated and clean these couples' homes are and how much fun they have in their lives. The wives also see that these conditions are the result of these couples'

mutual marriage love for each other. The wives who pay attention to this and take it to heart give up the thought of control. They are then allowed to move in with their husbands. The couples are then given a home closer to the center of town and are called angels. The reason for this is that true marriage love is a love that is heavenly in nature; it does not wish for control.

The British in the Spiritual World

806 There are two states of thought within us—an external state and an internal state. In our outer thinking we are in the physical world, but in our inner thinking we are in the spiritual world. In good people, these two states act as a unit; in evil people they do not.

What we are truly like inwardly is seldom obvious in the world, since we learn from early childhood to be moral and rational and we love to seem that way. In the spiritual world, though, what we are truly like is abundantly clear, because we are then a spirit, and our spirit *is* our inner self.

Because I have been allowed to be in the spiritual world and see there what people from various nations are truly like inwardly, I have a duty to reveal this information, since it is important.[484]

807 As for *the British,* the better people among them are at the center of all Christians, because they have a profound intellectual light. This does not appear to anyone in the physical world, but it is blatantly obvious in the spiritual world. They owe this light to their freedom of speech and freedom of the press, and their consequent freedom of thought.[485] (Among other peoples who do not have the same freedoms, that light is stifled because it does not have an outlet.) That light is not automatically activated in them, however; rather it is stimulated by others—particularly by people who are famous or powerful. As soon as they hear the latter make some statement, this light dawns in them. For this reason they are assigned governors in the spiritual world and are given preachers of great reputation and skill. Because of the native character they have, the British go along with the judgments of their governors and preachers.

808 There is a similarity of mind among the British. As a result, they form close ties with friends from their own country and rarely with others. They give each other aid and love honesty. They are highly patriotic and devote themselves passionately to the glory of their country. Their attitude toward people not born in Britain is much like someone on the roof of a palace looking through a telescope at those who live

and wander about outside the city. The politics in their nation occupies their minds and possesses their hearts, sometimes to such a degree that it distracts their spirits from the pursuit of a more refined judgment that would bring them to greater intelligence. As young people and students in the schools they do indeed eagerly tackle such pursuits, but their interest burns out in time like a shooting star. Nevertheless, their rationality is given life by those earlier studies; it sparkles with a light that they shape into beautiful forms, the way a prism placed in the sunlight sends out rainbows and adorns an otherwise plain surface with brilliant colors.

There are actually two great cities like London in the spiritual world. **809** Most British people come into one or the other of them after they die. I have had the opportunity to see and walk around one of the two. The center of that city is where [the earthly] London has its meeting place for traders called "the Exchange."[486] That is where their governors live. Above that city center is the eastern quarter of the city; below it is the western quarter; on its right side is the southern quarter, and on its left is the northern quarter. In the eastern quarter live people who were more devoted than others to living a life of goodwill; there are magnificent mansions there. The wise live in the southern quarter; they have many splendid possessions. In the northern quarter live people who had a greater love than others for free speech and freedom of the press. In the western quarter live people who proclaim justification by faith alone. On the right-hand side of that district there is an entrance to the city and also an exit from it. Those who live evil lives are sent away through this exit. The ministers who live in the west and teach faith alone do not dare to come into the city by the main streets, so they use narrower lanes instead, because no one is allowed to live in the city except people whose faith includes goodwill. I have heard complaints about the preachers from the west, that they fashion their sermons with great skill and eloquence and bring in a concept of justification by faith that is foreign to their listeners in such a way that the listeners no longer know whether one is supposed to do what is good or not. The preachers proclaim that faith itself is intrinsically good, and they separate this from good actions related to goodwill, which they say is a type of good that is done just to earn merit and is not therefore acceptable to God. When the people who live in the eastern and southern quarters hear sermons like that, though, they leave the church building and those preachers are soon deprived of their priestly status.

I have heard several reasons why those preachers are deprived of **810** their priestly status. People gave me the following as the primary reason.

"They shape their sermons to conform with their own earthly light and therefore their own spirit rather than with the Word and therefore the spirit of God. Yes, they do begin their sermons by quoting the Word, but they merely touch these quotes to their lips, and go no further because the quotes do not taste good to them. Instead they soon select some tasty idea of their own; like a piece of exquisite sugar candy, they swirl it around in their mouth and roll it back and forth over their tongue. This is how they teach.

"As a result there is no more spiritual content in their talks than there is in the tweeting of a songbird. The allegories with which they decorate their sermons are like a beautifully curled, flour-dusted wig on a great bald head. The mystical content in their sermons, which concerns justification by faith alone, we would liken to the quails that were blown from the sea into the camp of the children of Israel, which led to the death of thousands of people (Numbers 11:[31–34]). Theological teachings concerning goodwill and faith working together, though, we liken to manna from heaven."

On one occasion I heard some of their ministers talking to each other about faith alone and saw a kind of statue they had made to represent their faith alone. In the light of their own imagination it looked like a huge giant. When light from heaven was let in, however, the top half of the statue looked deformed and the bottom half looked like a snake. Once the ministers saw that, they left, and bystanders threw the image into a pond.

811　The other large city, also named London, is not in the Christian center at all, but is far away from it to the north. British people who were inwardly evil come into that London after they die. In the center of it there is open access to hell. Hell swallows these people up from time to time.

812　From the people from Britain in the spiritual world I have gathered that the British have two approaches to theology. One centers on their teachings regarding faith; the other centers on their teachings regarding goodwill. The people who are ordained into the priesthood embrace a theology of faith. Many of the laity, especially people who live in or near Scotland, embrace a theology of goodwill. Those in faith alone are afraid to tangle with these lay people, because the latter argue with them on the basis of both the Word and reason.

The theology centered on goodwill is visible in the statement the British read out loud every Sunday before people come forward to take the Holy Supper.[487] That statement plainly says that if people are not devoted to goodwill and do not abstain from evils on the grounds that they are sinful, they are hurling themselves into everlasting damnation. If they do not come forward to take the holy communion worthily, the Devil is going to enter into them as he entered into Judas.

Germans in the Spiritual World

As everyone knows, in any country that is divided into a number of regions there are different kinds of people that live in the different regions. Local populations can be as different from each other as the people who live in all the various climates on earth. Yet there is a commonality among people who live under the same monarch and the same set of laws. **813**

The subdivisions are more distinct in Germany than they are in the other countries that surround it. There is indeed a German empire, and all in the nation are subject to its authority. Nevertheless, the leaders of each province have a great deal of power in their own territories.

Germany contains larger and smaller states. The leader of each is like a monarch there. Religion, too, is divided in Germany. Some states are Lutheran; some are Calvinist; some are Roman Catholic. Given such diversity in both leadership and religious affiliation, Germans and their minds, inclinations, and lives are more difficult to generalize about from eyewitness experience in the spiritual world than other peoples and nationalities. Because a commonality exists wherever people speak the same language, though, the nature of Germans can to some extent be seen and described if various different concepts are brought together.

Since in each of its states Germans are under a strong individual leader, they do not have the free speech and freedom of the press that the Dutch and the British enjoy; and when free speech and freedom of the press are curtailed, freedom of thought, that is, of examining matters in a full and complete way, suffers as well. **814**

An analogy to this might be a fountain with a basin of such high sides that the water level in the basin is actually above the point at which the stream of water comes out, so that what should be a jet of water leaping up in the air does not even break the surface of the water standing in the basin. In this analogy, the stream of water symbolizes what people think, and the basin of standing water symbolizes what they say.

Briefly put, what flows in adapts itself to fit what flows out. Our higher understanding, then, adapts itself to fit the amount of freedom there is to say and do what we are considering.

For this reason, the members of this noble nation devote themselves more to memorization than to forming their own opinions. This explains why they are especially fixated on literary history and tend to give so much credit in their books to the people among them who are especially well known and highly educated. They cite the various opinions of these people copiously, and then pick one of them to endorse.

This attitude of theirs is represented in the spiritual world by a man who is carrying a number of books under his arm. When anyone confronts him and asks his opinion on something, he says, "I'll give you an answer," and immediately pulls a book from under his arm and reads a quote from it.

815 This condition of theirs affects them in many different ways. One of them is this: They hold the spiritual teachings of the church in their memory. They seldom lift them up into the higher level of their intellect; they just set them before the lower level of their intellect and reason about them on that level.

This is very different from the way thinking occurs in the nations that have freedom. When it comes to the spiritual or theological teachings of the church, the nations that have freedom are like eagles that can soar aloft to any height; the nations that have no freedom are like swans swimming on the surface of a river. Nations that have freedom are like majestic deer with great racks of antlers, running wherever they wish through fields, woods, and forests; nations that have no freedom are like deer kept in a game preserve for the royal family's amusement. People who have freedom are like the flying horses known to the ancients as Pegasuses, which fly not only over oceans but also over hills that are called Parnassian, and even over the Muses themselves below.[488] People who have not been set free intellectually are like well-bred horses in beautifully studded halters, standing in the royal stables. [2] These similes represent different degrees of judgment in regard to theological mysteries.

The clergy there, back at the time when they were students, would copy out material dictated by their teachers. They keep their notebooks as evidence of their scholarship. When they are ordained into the priesthood or established as lecturers in the schools, the talks they give from the pulpit or from the lectern are largely based on the quotations they wrote down.

The priests there who are outside the orthodoxy tend to preach about the Holy Spirit, and its miraculous way of working and stirring up holy feelings in our hearts.

German priests who support the modern-day orthodox position on faith appear to the angels as though they are wearing a wreath of horse-chestnut leaves. German priests who teach from the Word about good-will and its practical application, however, appear to the angels in wreaths of fragrant laurel leaves.

When the Lutherans there are disputing matters of truth with the Calvinists, they look like they are tearing at each other's clothes, because clothes mean truths.

I asked where the people from Hamburg live in the spiritual world. **816** I was told that they are not gathered together into any particular community, let alone a whole city. They are scattered and live among other Germans in various different areas. When I asked why, I was told that people from Hamburg are constantly focused elsewhere, and mentally, if not physically, traveling outside their city; they pay little attention to the city itself.

Whatever our state of mind is like in the physical world determines our outward conditions in the spiritual world. Our mind is our spirit; it is the part of us that survives death and lives on after being withdrawn from the physical body.

Roman Catholics in the Spiritual World

The Roman Catholics[489] in the spiritual world appear both around and **817** below the Protestants. The two groups are kept separate from each other by intervening areas that they are forbidden to pass through. There are monks, though, who use secret methods to communicate [with Protestants] and also send emissaries along uncharted paths to lure people into Catholicism, but the emissaries are discovered, punished, and either sent back to their people or cast down.

After the Last Judgment, which occurred in the spiritual world in **818** the year 1757, the circumstances of all people, including the Catholics, changed significantly. Newly arrived people are now no longer allowed to congregate in large groups the way they used to. Now instead there are pathways set aside for every type of love, whether good or evil. People who arrive from the world are immediately put on these pathways. They go along them to communities that correspond to their own loves. Evil people are drawn in the direction of communities that are in hell and good people are drawn in the direction of communities that are in heaven. This new arrangement prevents people from forming artificial heavens for themselves, which is something that used to happen in the past.[490]

In the world of spirits, which is midway between heaven and hell, there are many different communities. There are, in fact, as many of them as there are genera and species of desires that stem from either good or evil kinds of love.

Before these spirits are lifted up into heaven or cast down into hell, they have a spiritual partnership with people in the world, because people in the world, too, are midway between heaven and hell.

819 The Roman Catholics have a kind of council that meets in the southern quarter [of the world of spirits] on the east side of it. Catholic leaders meet there to discuss various issues related to their religion. They are particularly concerned with how to keep the general population in a state of blind obedience and how to expand their own dominion. No one who had actually been a pope in the world is allowed on the council, because a sense of their own divine authority still remains in their minds; as a result, they transfer the Lord's power in the world to themselves.[491] No cardinals are allowed on the council either, because of their sense of supremacy. The recently deceased cardinals and popes gather instead in a large room beneath the council chamber, but after a few days they are taken away; I was not allowed to find out where they are taken to.

[2] There is another place of meeting in the southern quarter on the east side. The business that is transacted there is to bring gullible commoners into [what they think is] heaven. The people in charge there have arranged a number of communities around themselves that are devoted to various different outward pleasures. In some communities there is dancing, in some there are musical performances, in some there are parades, in some there are stage plays, in some there are people who know how to generate images that convey various kinds of magnificence, in some there is just joking and laughter all the time. In some communities they have friendly conversations, discussing religion in one place, politics in another, lascivious topics in another, and so on.

The locals take the gullible commoners to one or another of these places, depending on what these people have thought is most pleasurable. They tell them that this is heaven itself. All of the people, though, after just a day or two of being there get tired of it and leave, because these are outward pleasures, not inward pleasures. In this way, many are disabused of frivolously believing that just being let into heaven accomplishes anything.

As for the Catholic forms of worship in that area, they are much like they are in the world. They consist of masses, which are conducted in a language that is not the usual language of spirits, but something cooked up with profound sounding words, by which the people are struck with a sense of external holiness and with trembling, although they have no idea what the words mean.

All who come into the spiritual world from our earth, including Roman Catholics, are kept at first in the confessional faith and religion of their country. Therefore the Catholics always have some representative pope over them, to whom they give the same type of ritual adoration they did in the world. It is very rare for any person who was actually a pope in the world to be placed among them, however. One exception is the person who filled the papal office thirty or forty years ago.[492] He is allowed authority over them because he believed at heart that the Word is holier than people generally think and that the one who should be worshiped is the Lord.

820

I was given an opportunity to speak with him. He said that he adores the Lord alone, because the Lord is God, and all power in heaven and on earth has been given to the Lord, as he himself says in Matthew 28:18. The pope also said that calling on the saints was a pointless exercise; and that when he was in the world he had intended to bring the church back to the worship of the Lord, but had been unable to do so, for reasons that he explained to me.

When the great northern city that had been home to both Catholics and Calvinists was destroyed at the time of the Last Judgment, I saw this pope being carried in a sedan chair and transferred to a safe place.

[2] On the outskirts of that vast community where he acts as pope, schools have been established for people to attend who are stuck in a state of doubt about their religion. There are converted monks there who teach people about God the Savior Christ and about the holiness of the Word. These monks leave it up to the individuals to decide to change their minds about the sacred practices introduced into the Roman Catholic church. Those who are receptive to their message are brought into a large community of people who have abandoned the practices of venerating the pope and the saints. When people come into this community, they feel as if they have arisen from sleep into wakefulness, or as if they have left behind the harsh conditions of winter for the pleasures of early spring. They feel like sailors who have found safe harbor.

The newcomers receive invitations from the people who live there to attend parties and are given crystal goblets of excellent wine to drink. I have been told that angels from heaven send to the hosts of these welcome parties a plate of manna that looks and tastes just like the manna that descended on the camps of the children of Israel in the desert. That plate is then passed around at the gathering, and each person there has a chance to taste real manna.

821　There are people from the Catholic nations of the world who had turned their thoughts more toward God than toward the pope and had done works of goodwill with a simple heart during their lives. When they realize that they are still alive after death, and are taught that in the spiritual world the Lord himself, the Savior of the world, rules, they are all easily brought out of the superstitious aspects of their religion. They find the transition from Catholicism to true Christianity as easy as walking into a church building through open doors; or as easy as walking by guards in a hallway to enter the royal court itself when commanded to do so by the monarch; or as easy as lifting up their face and eyes toward heaven when they hear voices up there.

[2] There are, on the other hand, Catholics who over the course of their lives in the world had rarely if ever given thought to God and who had loved the worship rituals solely because they were spectacular. It is difficult to lead these people away from the superstitious aspects of their religion—as difficult as getting into a church building whose doors are locked; or as difficult as walking by guards in a hallway to enter the royal court when the monarch has forbidden you to do so; or as difficult as it is for a snake lying on the grass to lift its eyes toward heaven.

A surprising thing is that none of the people of the Catholic religion who arrive in the spiritual world have the ability to see heaven, where the angels are. Heaven to them looks like a dark cloud over their heads in which they can see nothing. As soon as a Catholic who has been converted to the true Christianity comes among other converted Catholics, however, heaven is revealed to her or him. After that, from time to time they see angels in white clothes up there; and after their time of preparation comes to an end, they are lifted up to be with those angels.

Roman Catholic Saints in the Spiritual World

822　It is widely known that we all have innate, that is, inherited, evil from our parents; few know, however, what a fully developed version of that evil is like. The full version is found in the love of possessing everyone else's wealth and the love of having complete control. The nature of the second of these loves is that the more the reins are let out, the more that love bursts forth, until it becomes a burning desire to dominate everyone.[493] It eventually becomes a desire to be prayed to and worshiped as God. This love is the serpent that deceived Eve and Adam; it said to the woman, "God knows that on the day when you eat some of the fruit of that tree, your eyes will be opened and *you will be like God*" (Genesis 3:4, 5). The more the reins are let out, then, and we rush on into this love, the more we turn away from God and toward ourselves, and become a worshiper of self. In that state, we are indeed able to call on God because our love for ourselves warms our mouths, but our heart is cold because we actually despise God. In that state, the divine truths of the church are able to serve us as means, but because our goal is control, we do not love the means beyond their ability to serve us. In that state, if we are lifted up into the highest positions of honor, we imagine ourselves to be like Atlas carrying the world on his shoulders or like Apollo using his horses to steer the sun around the world.[494]

Since all human beings inherit this tendency, the people who are saints, according to papal bulls,[495] are removed in the spiritual world from the sight of others. They are hidden away and forbidden to have any interaction with people who worship them. The reason for this is to prevent that root, which is the most productive of evil, from becoming activated in them, giving them the deranged imagination that demons have. An insanity of this kind does take hold of people who, while they are still alive in the world, eagerly vie to become a saint after they die, so that people will pray to them. `823`

When they come to the spiritual world, many Catholics, particularly the monks, look for the saints, especially the patron saint of their order. They are very surprised when they are unable to find them. Later on, however, they are instructed that the saints live as ordinary people among others—either among those who are in heaven or among those who are in the lower earth. In either location, the saints are completely unaware that anyone is worshiping them or praying to them. (Some, who do realize this and actually want to be prayed to, slip into insanity and begin babbling.) `824`

In heaven, the worship of saints is considered to be a complete abomination. The angels shudder at the mere mention of it, because the more our worship is directed toward any human being, the less it is directed toward the Lord. In that circumstance the Lord is never the sole object of worship; and if the Lord is not the sole object of worship, then our worshipfulness is divided, which robs us of our communion with the Lord and the happiness of life that comes to us as a result.

[2] In order for me to learn what the Catholic saints are like, so that I could pass on the information, a hundred or so of them who knew they had been canonized were brought up from the lower earth. Most of them rose up behind me, and only a few in front. I had a conversation with one of them; I was told he was Xavier.496 When he was speaking with me, he was behaving very foolishly. He was able to tell me that in his own place where he is kept with others, he does not behave foolishly; he becomes an idiot, though, whenever he reflects that he is a saint and feels a desire to be prayed to. I heard a sympathetic murmur from the people behind me.

The situation is different, however, with the so-called saints who are in heaven. They have no awareness whatever of what is going on on earth, and they are not allowed to speak to any Catholics who are still hanging on to that superstition. This serves to protect them from the least idea of that sort.

825　　Anyone is in a position to conclude from the state these "saints" are in that praying to the saints is a meaningless activity. Indeed, I can testify that they do not hear prayers that are said to them on earth any more than the statues of them along the roadsides, or the walls of the church, or the birds building their nests in the steeple hear such prayers.

Those on earth who are devoted to the saints say that the saints share in the ruling power of the Lord Jesus Christ in heaven, but this is a fiction; it is completely untrue. They have no greater share in the Lord's power than a stable hand has with a monarch, or a doorkeeper has with a high ranking official, or a courier has with a leader of the church. John the Baptist himself says of the Lord, "I am not worthy to undo the strap of his sandal" (Mark 1:7; John 1:27). How much power can the saints have, then?

826　　Sometimes to the people in a Parisian community in the spiritual world, a woman appears in midair, wearing radiant clothes and having a saintly face. She says that she is *Geneviève*.497 When people begin to worship her, however, her face and clothes immediately change; she becomes like an ordinary woman. She criticizes the people for wanting to worship a woman who is no more esteemed among her friends than a servant girl would be. She expresses amazement that people in the world are taken with such nonsense.

827　　Here I will add something very much worth noting. On one occasion *Mary, the mother of the Lord* happened past. I saw her over my head in white clothing. Then, stopping for a while, she said that she had been the Lord's mother in the sense that he was born from her, but by the time he became God he had put off everything human that came from her. Therefore she now adores him as her God and does not want anyone to see him as her son, because everything in him is divine.

Muslims in the Spiritual World

The Muslims in the spiritual world appear behind the Roman Catholics **828** in the west; they form a kind of circle around them. The reason why they appear close behind the Christians is that they acknowledge our Lord as the greatest prophet and the wisest of people, who was sent into the world to teach people; some even acknowledge him as the Son of God.[498]

In that world, the distance between where people live and the center, where Christians are, depends on the extent to which they believe in the Lord and in one God. This belief unites people's minds to heaven and determines their proximity to the eastern region, the region closest to the Lord.

Since religion dwells in the highest levels within us, and our lower **829** levels draw their life and light from those highest levels, and because the idea of Muhammad is always uppermost in Muslim minds along with their religion, there is always some Muhammad who is set visibly before Muslims in the spiritual world. To get them to turn their faces toward the east, the region closest to the Lord, this Muhammad is placed below the center of the Christian region. This is not, however, Muhammad himself, who wrote down the Qur'an, but someone else who plays the role of Muhammad. It is not always the same person either; it changes. One of the Muhammads had come from Saxony but had been taken captive by Algerians and had become a Muslim.[499] Because he had originally been Christian, he was encouraged a number of times to tell the Muslims that the Lord was not the son of Joseph but rather the Son of God himself. Later on, other Muhammads took over from this one.

In the place where that representative Muhammad is to be found there appears a fire like that of a burning torch, so that people will recognize who he is. That fire is visible only to Muslims, however, and not to others.

The real Muhammad, who wrote the Qur'an, is not seen in public **830** these days. I have been told that in the beginning he was in charge of the Muslim population in the spiritual world, but because he wanted to exercise control over every aspect of their religious life as if he himself were God, he was removed from his home, which was next to the Catholic region, and sent down and to the right, near the southern region.

Some years ago, ill-intentioned people managed to convince one community of Muslims to acknowledge Muhammad as God. In order to put a stop to this development, Muhammad was brought up from the lower earth and shown to people. I, too, saw him at that time. He looked much like the bodily spirits who have no inner consciousness. His face was almost pitch black. I heard him say, "I am your Muhammad"; then he sank back down again.[500]

831   The main reason why Muslims are averse to Christians is that Christians believe in three divine Persons and therefore worship three gods, three creators. Muslims especially dislike Roman Catholics because they bow down before statues. Muslims call Catholics idolaters and call Protestants religious fanatics. They criticize Christians for creating a three-headed God and for saying "one" out loud but mumbling "three" under their breath. They accuse Christians of splitting omnipotence and making three powers out of and from the one power. Muslims compare Christians to animals with three horns, one for each god. Christians, they say, substitute three gods for one in their prayers, their liturgical music, and their sermons.

832   There is a heaven for Muslims, just as there is a heaven for all peoples who acknowledge one God, who love what is just, and who do what is good as a religious practice. The Muslim heaven is separate from the Christian heaven.

The Muslim heaven is actually divided into two heavens. In the lower of the two, Muslim men live honorable lives with multiple wives. The only Muslims, though, that are lifted up into the higher heaven are those who give up a plurality of wives and acknowledge our Lord and Savior and his authority over heaven and hell. I have been told that it is impossible for them to think that God the Father and our Lord are one, but they can believe that the Lord rules over the heavens and the hells because he is the Son of God the Father. This belief among them is what enables them to be lifted by the Lord into the higher heaven.

833   Christians who think in terms of divine providence but believe that only people who were born Christian can be saved may be disturbed by the fact that Islam is practiced in more countries than Christianity. This same fact does not bother people, however, who realize that everything comes about as a result of divine providence; the latter people look for divine providence in a given situation and find it.

In this case, the divine providence is operative in the fact that Islam recognizes the Lord as the greatest prophet, the wisest of all people, and even as the Son of God. On the other hand, though, Muslims limit their sacred literature to the Qur'an, and therefore Muhammad, who wrote it, often occupies their thoughts. They feel a certain reverence for him and do not give much thought to our Lord.

To make it abundantly clear that the Lord's divine providence was behind the rise of Islam and that its purpose was to wipe out the idolatry of many nations, I will give a few observations about this in an orderly sequence, the first of which concerns the origins of idolatry.

[2] Before Islam, idolatry had spread to many nations of the world. The underlying cause for this was that the churches that existed before the Lord's Coming were all symbolic in nature. The Israelite church was like that. Its tabernacle, Aaron's priestly garments, the sacrifices, all the features of the Temple in Jerusalem, and even that church's laws were symbolic.

The study of correspondences, which includes the study of symbolism, existed among ancient peoples. That study was particularly well developed in Egypt; the hieroglyphics there were based on it.[501] From that study they knew the symbolic meaning of living creatures of all kinds, of trees of all kinds, as well as what mountains, hills, rivers, and springs, and the sun, moon, and stars meant. As a result of their study of correspondences they came into spiritual knowledge, since the spiritual things being symbolically represented were in fact the origins of those [earthly] correspondences. The kinds of spiritual things they were learning were also the kinds of things that constitute the spiritual wisdom of angels in heaven.

[3] Now, because everything in ancient rituals of worship was symbolic and consisted of nothing but correspondences, they would worship on mountains and hills and also in groves and gardens. Springs of water were considered holy for the same reason. These people made sculptures of horses, cows, calves, lambs, and even birds, fish, and snakes, and placed these in and around their places of worship and also their homes, in a particular configuration depending on what spiritual quality of the church each figure corresponded to, or what it symbolically represented and therefore meant.

Later on, after the study of correspondences was lost, their descendants began to worship the sculptures themselves as something intrinsically holy. These people were not aware that their ancestors of long ago had not regarded the sculptures themselves as being the least bit holy, but instead had only seen them as symbolizing something holy because of what they corresponded to. This was the origin of the idolatrous practices that filled many nations of the world.

[4] In order to uproot these idolatrous practices, the Lord's divine providence arranged for the creation of a new religion that was well suited to the Middle Eastern way of thinking. This religion included material from both the Old and New Testaments of the Word. It taught that the Lord came into the world, and that he was the greatest prophet, the wisest of people, and the Son of God. This was all brought about through Muhammad, for whom the religion was named.[502]

All this makes it clear that the Lord's divine providence arranged for the creation of Islam (a religion well suited to the Middle Eastern way of thinking, as just mentioned) in order to wipe out the idolatrous practices of many nations and to give people instead some concept of the Lord before they died and arrived in the spiritual world. That religion would not have been accepted by so many nations and could not have uprooted idolatry if it did not harmonize with ideas they already had. That religion also had to allow polygamy, because if it had not, the Middle Easterners would have been even more vulnerable than Europeans to falling into flagrant adulteries of the filthiest kinds, and would have destroyed themselves.

834 On one occasion I was allowed to experience the heat of their polygamous love. I was in a conversation with one of the people who took turns acting as their Muhammad. After I had spoken with him for a while from a certain distance away, he sent me an ivory spoon[503] and some other objects that identified him as the sender. At that same time, a communication was opened up to me from various places devoted to the heat of their polygamous love.

The heat from some of these places felt and smelled like a bathhouse after people have bathed; from others it was like a kitchen where someone is boiling meat; from others, like hole-in-the-wall shops that are selling hot food that smells rank; from others, like an apothecary's basement where medicinal emulsions and other remedies are being prepared; from others, like brothels and whorehouses; from others, like a shop where hides, leather, and shoes are sold. In that heat there was a sense of rottenness, bitterness, and burning jealousy.

The heat in the Christian heavens, though, when the delight of the angels' love there comes across as a smell, has the fragrance of gardens and vineyards and beds of roses. In some places, it smells like a perfumer's shop; in others, like a wine press or a winemaker's cellar.

(I have shown a number of times in the memorable occurrences after chapters that in the spiritual world the delightful feelings associated with various kinds of love often come across as aromas.)[504]

Africans, and Non-Christians in General, in the Spiritual World

In the spiritual world, the peoples who did not know anything about the Lord appear farther from the center than those who did know something about him. The people on the farthest outskirts are those who were utterly devoted to idolatry or worshiped the sun and the moon while they were in this world. The members of those populations who acknowledge one God, however, and follow principles such as those embodied in the Ten Commandments in their religious practices and lives have direct communication with the Christians who are at the center; that communication is not intercepted by the Muslims or the Catholics. 835

Those populations are also subdivided according to their disposition and their capacity for receiving light through the heavens from the Lord. Some among them are relatively shallow in nature and some are deep. How deep or shallow they are is attributable partly to climate, partly to their inherited nature, partly to their upbringing, and partly to the particular religion they practice. The Africans are by nature deeper than the rest.

All non-Christians who acknowledge and worship one God as the Creator of the universe think of God as a human being. They say that no one could have any other idea of God. When they are told that many people think of God as ether or a cloud, they ask, "Where are there people like that?" 836

When they are told that some Christians are like that, they say, "That can't be right!"

They are told that some Christians get this idea from the fact that the Word refers to God as a spirit [John 4:24], and the only concept they have of a spirit is that it is like the material that ether is made of, or like some sort of cloud. These Christians do not know that every spirit and every angel is a human being. They are examined, however, to see whether the *spiritual* idea they have of God is the same as their *earthly* idea of him; it has been discovered that people who inwardly acknowledge the Lord our Savior as the God of heaven and earth have a spiritual idea of God that differs from their earthly idea of him.

I once heard a Christian minister saying that no one was capable of having the idea of a divine human being. I saw him taken around to various groups of non-Christians, each one of a deeper nature than the last, until he reached their heavens, and then eventually came to the Christian heaven; at every stage he was allowed to sense their inner awareness of God. To his surprise, all of them shared the view that God is a divine human being, and that we could not have been created by any other kind of God, since we are in his image and likeness.

837 Since Africans have a more highly developed inner judgment than other non-Christians, I have enjoyed a number of discussions with them on topics that require deep reflection. We recently had conversations about God, about the Lord the Redeemer, and about the differences between internal and external people. Because they took great pleasure in these discussions, I will pass along some of the perceptions they had on these topics as a result of their inner sight.

On the topic of God, they said, "It is definitely true that God came down and set himself before people in a visible form. He is our Creator, Protector, and Leader; the human race belongs to him. He sees, considers, and provides each and every thing both in heaven and on earth. He sees the good things and people in both worlds as being in himself and sees himself as being in them. This is because he is the sun of the angelic heaven, which appears as high above the spiritual world as the earth's sun does above the physical world. He who is the sun sees, considers, and provides each and every thing that exists below. Because it is his divine love that appears as a sun, it follows that he provides *things* from the largest to the smallest with the elements of life, and he provides *people* with the elements of love and wisdom. He provides the elements of love through the heat in the spiritual world, and the elements of wisdom through the light in the spiritual world. Therefore if you form an idea for yourselves of God as the sun of the universe, this idea will definitely lead you to see and acknowledge God's omnipresence, omniscience, and omnipotence."

838 Later on I had *a conversation with them about the Lord the Savior.* I said, "At the level of his essence, God is divine love. The divine love is like the purest fire. Love, by definition, has just one intention, which is to become one with someone else whom it loves. The divine love has just one intention, which is to unite himself to us and us to himself to such a degree that he is in us and we are in him. Yet because divine love is like the purest fire, clearly it would be entirely impossible for God in this form to be in us and cause us to be in him—everything we are would be reduced to a wisp of smoke!

"Because God at the level of his essence is burning with a love for uniting himself with us, it was necessary for him to wrap himself in a body that was adapted in such a way that we could receive it and enter into a partnership with him. Therefore God came down and took on a human manifestation according to the divine design that he himself established at the creation of the world. His conception occurred through an offshoot of his own power; he was carried in the womb, was born, grew in wisdom and love, and came closer and closer to his divine origin until he was fully united to it. In this way God became a human being and a human being became God. The Scripture about him, which the Christians have and which is called the Word, clearly teaches and testifies that this is the truth. God himself, whose human manifestation is called Jesus Christ, says that the Father is in him and he is in the Father, and that someone who sees him sees the Father. There are many other statements to the same effect.

[2] "Reason sees that there is no other way in which God, whose love is like the purest fire, could unite himself to people and people to himself. Could the fire of the sun as it truly is even touch us, let alone come into us, if it did not wrap its rays in the atmospheres, so that it could present itself in an adapted state as a moderate warmth? Pure ether could not surround us and would certainly be unable to flow into the bronchial tubes of our lungs if it had not adapted itself by being thickened with air.[505] A fish cannot stay alive in the air; it has to be in an element that is suited to its life. For that matter, no kings or queens on earth would orchestrate each and every thing in their countries directly or in their own person; they use officials in higher and lower positions who in effect constitute their royal body.

"The soul of someone could not present itself in visible form to another person, interact with that other, or communicate evidence of its love if it did not do so through a body. How then could God do this except through his own human manifestation?"

The Africans could see what I was saying better than the rest could, because the Africans have an inner rationality. In each of them, their agreement with what was said depended on the kind of perception they had.

839   The last topic we took up was *the differences between internal and external people.* I said, "People who have an inner perception about things are in the light of truth, which is the light of heaven. People who have an outer perception about things are not in the light of truth, because the light in which they consider things is only the light of the world. Internal people have intelligence and wisdom; external people have insanity and reversed vision.[506] Internal people are spiritual, because they think with their spirit when it is lifted out of their body, and this is how they are able to see truths in light. External people are earthly and sense-oriented, because they think on the basis of mistaken impressions they receive through their bodily senses; therefore they see truths as being in a kind of fog, and when they ponder them inwardly, they take for truth things that are actually false.

"Internal people are like people who are standing in a clearing on the top of a mountain, or standing at the top of a tower in a city, or standing at the top of a lighthouse by the sea. External people are like people who are standing in a valley at the foot of a mountain, or in an underground vault below a tower, or in a rowboat moored by the lighthouse—they only see what is close at hand.

[2] "Internal people are like people who live on the second or third floor of a large home with walls that consist entirely of windows of clear glass;[507] they have a sweeping view of the city in all directions and they recognize every building in it. External people are like people who live on the bottom floor with windows made of pieces of paper glued together. They cannot see even part of the street outside their own house; the only things they can see are inside their home, and the light there is as dim as if it came from a candle or a fireplace.

"Internal people are like eagles flying high, which can see everything that lies beneath them for miles in every direction. External people are like roosters who climb up on a little footbridge to crow loudly at hens that are walking around on the ground.

"Internal people realize that what they know compared to what they don't is like the amount of water in a jar compared to the amount of water in a lake. External people are quite sure they know everything there is to know."

The Africans enjoyed hearing all this because, as a result of their highly developed inner sight, they recognized the truth of it.

840   Since Africans are this way, a revelation is occurring among them today. It began in one place and then spread outward from there, but it has not yet reached the sea coasts.[508] The Africans have no use for new arrivals from Europe who believe that people are saved by faith alone, and therefore just by thinking and speaking, not by willing and doing. The Africans say that none have a worshipful attitude if they are not living by their religion. If we do not live by our religion, they say, there is no way to avoid becoming evil and stupid, because in that circumstance we are not receiving anything from heaven. Even very clever forms of wickedness they characterize as "stupidity" because such acts contain death rather than life.

I have spoken a number of times with Augustine,[509] who was the bishop of Hippo in Africa during the fourth century. He said he still lives in that area [in the spiritual world] and inspires people to worship the Lord; there is a good chance, he said, that this new gospel will spread from there into neighboring regions.

I have heard angels rejoicing about the revelation among Africans that I just mentioned. They are excited because it will open up a communication between them and the human rational faculty. This faculty has until recently been closed to angels as a result of the universal teaching that we have to hold our intellect under obedience to "faith," as defined by church authorities.

Jews in the Spiritual World

Before the Last Judgment, which took place in the year 1757, Jews appeared to the left side of the Christian center in a valley there. After the Last Judgment, however, they were transferred to the north and forbidden to interact with Christians unless those Christians were traveling and were not in their own cities.   **841**

In that area there are two large cities to which Jews are brought after they die. Before the Last Judgment both of these cities were referred to as Jerusalem, but after it they were given new names, since *Jerusalem* now refers to the teachings of the church that regards the Lord as the sole object of worship.

The governors overseeing these cities are converted Jews who warn the local populations not to say harsh and insulting things about Christ. The governors punish people who violate this rule.

The streets of these cities are ankle-deep in filth. The houses have so much foul-smelling garbage everywhere that it is difficult to get near them.[510]

Later on, though, I did find out that many from these Jewish populations have been given places to stay in the southern region. When I asked what type of people were relocating, I was told that they were Jews who had found little value in the worship practices followed by other Jews, and who had come to question whether the Messiah would ever come. There were also Jews there who had given rational thought to a variety of topics while they were in the world and who had lived rational lives as well; a majority of this last group were so-called Portuguese Jews.

842 From time to time Jews see an angel in midair above them carrying a rod in his hand. He leads them to believe that he is Moses. He urges them to give up waiting for the Messiah (which is an insane thing to do even there), since the true Messiah is Christ, who rules over them and all others. This Moses tells them that he himself knows Christ is the Messiah, and says he had even known about Christ when Christ was in the world.

After hearing this, people leave. Most of them forget this information, but a few of them hold on to it. Those who do take this to heart are sent to synagogues of converted Jews, where they receive further instruction. When they have been taught, they are given new clothes to replace their old rags, a neatly written copy of the Word, and a new home in a decent city.

The unreceptive are cast down. Many end up in forests or deserts and steal from each other.

843 In the spiritual world Jews trade in various commodities, just as they do in this world—especially in precious stones. In ways that I do not know about, they acquire gems from heaven, where precious stones exist in great abundance. The reason why they deal in precious stones is that they read the Word in its original language and consider its literal meaning holy. Precious stones correspond to the literal meaning. (I have shown above in the chapter on Sacred Scripture, §§217, 218, that the spiritual origin of precious stones is the Word's literal meaning and that as a result those stones and that meaning correspond to each other.) They also possess the skill to make fake gems and fool buyers, but if they actually commit this fraud they are severely punished by the governors.

844 More than others, Jews are unaware that they are in the spiritual world; they think they are still in the physical world. The reason for this is that they are thoroughly external people who do not think about religion in an inward way. Therefore they still say the same things about the Messiah that they used to say in the world.

Some say the Messiah is going to come with David and, glittering with gems, will go before the Jewish people and bring them into the land of Canaan. Along the way he will lift his rod and dry up the rivers they will cross. Christians (in private communication Jews refer to them as gentiles) will seize the hems of their garments, begging to be allowed to come with them. Others who are rich enough will also be allowed to join them as their servants.

They convince themselves that this is how it will be because of Zechariah 8:23 and Isaiah 66:20, and because of the statements in Jeremiah 30:9 and Ezekiel 34:23–25; 37:23–26 that David will come and be their king and shepherd. They are not at all open to hearing that *David* in these passages means our Lord Jesus Christ and that *Jews* here mean people who will belong to the Lord's church.

When they are asked whether they are completely convinced that all of them are going to come into the land of Canaan, they reply, "Yes. All will be included in this. And Jews who have died will be resurrected and will leave their graves; they too will come into the land of Canaan."

When they are told that it is impossible for the dead to come out of their graves, because those who have died are living now after death, they reply, "They will come down from where they are now and reenter their bodies. That's how they will come back to life."

When they are told that the land of Canaan is not large enough to hold them all, they reply, "It will be enlarged."

When they are told that the kingdom of the Messiah, because he is the Son of God, is going to be in heaven, not on earth, they reply, "The land of Canaan is going to be heaven."

When it is pointed out that they do not know the location of Bethlehem of Ephrata, where the Messiah will be born according to the prophecies in Micah (Micah 5:2) and David (Psalms 132:6), they reply, "The Messiah's mother will nevertheless give birth there." Some say, "Wherever she gives birth, that will be Bethlehem."

[2] When they are asked how the Messiah could dwell with such evil people, and this charge is backed up by citing many passages in Jeremiah and especially the song of Moses, which indicates that they are very wicked (Deuteronomy 32), they reply, "Among Jews some are good and some are evil; those passages refer to the Jews who are evil."

845

When they are told that they were originally descended from a Canaan-ite woman and also from Judah's whoring with his own daughter-in-law (Genesis 38), they reply, "That was not an act of whoring."

When they hear the retort that Judah commanded her to be brought out and burned because of her whoring [Genesis 38:24], they go off and consult with each other. After their consultation they say, "That was only the fulfillment of the brother-in-law's obligation that Judah's second son Onan and his third son Shelah had failed to perform."[511]

They add, "Most of us are descended not from the tribe of Judah but from the tribe of Levi, which was charged with the priestly respon-sibilities; but the important thing is that we have all descended from Abraham."

When they are told that there is a spiritual meaning existing within the Word that has much to say about Christ or the Messiah, they reply, "That is not true." Some of them say, "Inwardly in the Word, in its depths, there is nothing but gold." And many other statements to the same effect.

846 On one occasion I was carried up in my spirit to the angelic heaven, to a particular community there.[512] Some of the wise people of that com-munity met with me and asked, "*What are the latest developments on earth [in regard to wisdom]?*"

"This is new," I said: "The Lord has recently revealed secrets that are more excellent than any that have ever been revealed since the church first came into existence."[513]

"What are they?" they asked.

"They are as follows," I said.

(1) "In the Word, within each and every detail of it, there is a *spiritual meaning* that corresponds to its earthly meaning. Because it has this inner meaning, the Word allows the people of the church to form a partner-ship with the Lord; it also allows people to associate with angels. What makes the Word holy is that it contains this spiritual meaning.

[2] (2) "The *correspondences* that the spiritual meaning consists of have also been disclosed."

"Didn't the people living on earth already know about correspon-dences?" the angels asked.

"Not at all," I said. "This knowledge has lain hidden for thousands of years now—ever since the time of Job.[514] To the people alive then and the people who had lived before, the study of correspondences was the supreme field of study. Their wisdom was based on it, because it gave them knowledge of spiritual things that relate to heaven and the church. The study of correspondences was later twisted into a form of idolatry. Therefore in the Lord's divine providence it was so thoroughly wiped out and destroyed that no one could see a trace of it anymore. Nevertheless, the Lord is now disclosing it to allow the people of the church to form a partnership with him and be associated with angels. The Word is what brings this about, because everything that is in it is a correspondence."

The angels were thrilled to hear that the Lord had chosen to reveal this great secret, which had lain deeply hidden for thousands of years. They said that the purpose of his doing so was to bring the Christian church, which is founded on the Word but is now at its end, back to life and allow it to breathe in a new spirit through heaven from the Lord.

The angels asked whether the study of correspondences had uncovered yet what *baptism* and *the Holy Supper* mean—topics on which people have had so many different theories.

"Yes, this has been uncovered," I said.

[3] (3) "Today," I went on, "the Lord has also revealed *what our lives are like after we die.*"

"Why life after death?" the angels asked. "Surely everyone realizes that we live on after we die."

"In some ways yes, in some ways no." I replied. "People say that human beings do not survive death, but their souls do; the soul lives on as a spirit. They think of a spirit as a piece of wind or ether. These do not live as people until the day of the Last Judgment comes. Then the bodily elements they had left behind in the world are gathered together again (even if their bodies have been consumed by worms, rats, or fish) and are once more shaped into a body; in this way the soul will be resurrected as a person."

"What kind of theory is that?" the angels asked. "Surely everyone knows that people live on as people after death, with only one difference, which is that we then live as *substantial* people, and no longer the *physical* people we used to be. Just as physical people can see other physical people, substantial people can see other substantial people. We cannot tell any difference between being physical and being substantial, except that we are in a more perfect state."

[4] (4) The angels asked me, "What do people on earth know about our world [in general] and about *heaven* and *hell* [in particular]?"

"Nothing," I said. "Nevertheless the Lord is disclosing at this time what kind of world angels and spirits live in, which includes what heaven is like and what hell is like; and that angels and spirits have a partnership with people on earth. Many surprising facts about angels and spirits have been revealed as well."

The angels were thrilled to find out that the Lord had chosen to reveal such things to people, to prevent ignorance from keeping them in uncertainty regarding their own immortality.

[5] (5) I went on to say, "The Lord has also revealed today that your world has a different *sun* than ours. The sun in your world is pure love; the sun in our world is pure fire. Therefore, because your sun is pure love, everything that emanates from it is alive; because our sun is pure fire, nothing that emanates from it is alive. This is the most important difference between *what is spiritual* and *what is earthly*. This difference, which was previously unknown, has been made known now. As a result, the origin of the light that enlightens the human intellect with wisdom and the origin of the heat that ignites the human will with love have also been made known.

[6] (6) "It has also been disclosed that there are three levels of life. As a result there are three heavens. The human mind has these same three levels. As a result, we ourselves correspond to the three heavens."

"Didn't people know that already?" the angels asked.

"They knew about levels that range from more to less," I said, "but not at all about the levels that are prior as opposed to the levels that are subsequent."[515]

[7] (7) "Besides what you have just mentioned, has anything more been revealed?" the angels asked.

"Yes," I said. "There is information about *the Last Judgment;* about the fact that *the Lord* is the God of heaven and earth; about God being not only one essence but also one person, in whom the divine Trinity exists, and that the Lord is that person. Also information about *the new church* that the Lord is establishing, about its *teachings,* and about *the holiness of Sacred Scripture. The Book of Revelation* has been unveiled. There is also information about *the inhabitants of other planets* and about *the worlds in the universe.* Not to mention accounts of memorable occurrences and amazing things witnessed in the spiritual world; through these accounts much that relates to heavenly wisdom has been made known."[516]

After that I also told the angels that the Lord has revealed something still further to the world.   **847**

"What?" they asked.

"*True marriage love,*" I replied, "and its spiritual delights."[517]

"Surely everyone knows," the angels said, "that the delights involved in marriage love are greater than the delights of any other type of love. Everyone is capable of realizing that all the blessings, joys, and delights that the Lord could ever give us are brought together in one love, a love that corresponds to the love between the Lord and the church. The home for these blessings, joys, and delights is true marriage love; this love is sensitive to these pleasures and is able to receive and perceive them fully."

"People do not in fact know this," I said, "and the reason is that they have not turned to the Lord. They have not abstained from the lusts of the flesh and therefore are not in a position to be regenerated. True marriage love comes solely from the Lord. He gives it to people who allow him to regenerate them; these are also the people who are accepted into the Lord's new church that is meant by the New Jerusalem in the Book of Revelation.

"I have my doubts," I added, "that people in the world today are willing to believe that this love is intrinsically spiritual and is a result of their religious practice. They are likely to be resistant to this idea because they think of marriage love as something that relates to the body alone. Because the quality of this love depends on our religious practice, it is spiritual among spiritual people, earthly among earthly people, and merely carnal among adulterous people."

The angels were overjoyed to hear all this; yet they sensed a great sadness in me. "Where is your sadness coming from?" they asked me.   **848**

"Although the secrets that the Lord has revealed at this time are of higher quality and greater worth than any other concepts that have been published before," I said, "nevertheless on earth they are thought to have no value at all."

The angels were astounded to hear this. They asked the Lord for permission to look down into the world. They looked down and behold, there was nothing but darkness there.

The angels were told to write these secrets on a piece of paper and send it down to the earth, and they would see a sign of things to come.

They did so. The piece of paper that had these secrets written on it was sent down from heaven. As it descended, but while it was still in the spiritual world, it was shining like a star. When it passed down into the physical world, however, the light went out; on its way down the piece of paper grew darker and darker.

When the angels sent the piece of paper to conferences of well-educated clergy and laity, a murmur was heard from many of them. They were saying, "What is this? Does it have any value? What difference does it make whether we know these things or not? This is just a figment of someone's imagination." It looked like some of them were taking the piece of paper, folding it, and continually rolling and unrolling it in their fingers. Others looked like they were tearing at it and trying to stomp on it with their feet, but the Lord restrained them from committing that outrage. The angels were ordered to take it back and keep it safe.

Because the angels then became sad and were thinking, "How long will it be like this?" they were told, *"For a time and times and half a time"* (Revelation 12:14).[518]

849   Afterward I heard a hostile murmur from the lower regions, including the following words: *"Perform miracles and we will believe!"*

"Surely those secrets are miracles," I replied.

"No, they aren't," was their response.

"Then what are miracles?" I asked.

"Disclose and reveal events yet to come, and we will believe," they said.

"The Lord does not allow that," I said. "When we know what is going to happen, our reason, intellect, prudence, and wisdom stop working; they collapse and shut down."

I asked them again, "What other miracles should I perform?"

They shouted, "Do things like the ones Moses did in Egypt!"

"But what if in response to them you harden your hearts like Pharaoh and the Egyptians did?" I asked.[519]

"We won't!" they said.

I said again, "Tell me for certain that you are not going to dance around a golden calf and worship it, like Jacob's descendants did within a mere month of seeing the whole of Mount Sinai burning and hearing Jehovah himself speak from the fire[520]—in other words, seeing and hearing the greatest miracle of them all!" (In the spiritual meaning, a golden calf is the pleasure of the flesh.)[521]

The response from the lower regions was, "We will not be like the descendants of Jacob."

Then I heard a voice from heaven saying to them, "If you do not believe Moses and the prophets, that is, the Lord's Word, you are not going to believe on the basis of miracles any more than Jacob's descendants did in the desert, or any more than they did when they saw with their own eyes the miracles performed by the Lord himself when he was in the world."

After that, I saw some spirits coming up from the lower regions where I had heard those voices. They addressed me in a serious tone and said, "Those secrets that you enumerated in a long list a moment ago—why has your Lord revealed them to you, a lay person, and not to someone in the clergy?"

850

"That was entirely up to the Lord," I said. "He prepared me for this assignment from the time when I first came of age. But let me ask you a question in return. When the Lord was in the world, why did he choose fishermen to be his disciples? Why did he not choose anyone from among the lawyers, scribes, priests, or rabbis? Discuss this among yourselves and use judgment in coming to your conclusion, and you will discover the reason."

When I said that, there was another murmur, and then silence.

I foresee that many people who read the accounts of memorable occurrences that follow the chapters are going to believe that I fabricated them out of my own imagination, but I assert in truth that they were not made up. I truly saw and heard those things. And I did not hear or see them when my mind was in some sleepy state; I was in a state of full wakefulness.

851

The Lord chose to manifest himself to me and assign me the task of presenting the teachings that will be a part of his new church, which is meant by the New Jerusalem in the Book of Revelation. For this purpose he opened the inner levels of my mind or spirit, which allowed me to be in the spiritual world with angels and at the same time in the physical world with people. This has gone on for twenty-seven years now.[522] Who in the Christian world would have known anything about *heaven* or *hell* if the Lord had not chosen to open the sight of someone's spirit and show and teach that person about them?

[2] The types of things described in *the accounts of memorable occurrences* are indeed the types of things that appear in heaven, as is very obvious from the types of things seen and described by *John* in the Book of Revelation, and also the types of things seen and described by *the prophets* in the Word of the Old Testament.

In *the Book of Revelation*, the following examples occur. John saw *the Son of Humankind* in the middle of seven lampstands. He saw a tabernacle, a temple, an ark, and an altar in heaven. He saw a book that was sealed with seven seals. He saw the book opened, and horses that came out of it. He saw four creatures around a throne; twelve thousand people who had been chosen from each tribe; locusts rising up from an abyss; a woman giving birth to a male child and running away into a desert to avoid a dragon; two beasts, one rising up out of the sea, and another out of the land; an angel flying in the midst of heaven who had the everlasting gospel; a sea of glass mingled with fire; seven angels who had the seven last plagues; bowls that these angels poured out onto the earth, into the sea, into the rivers, into the sun, onto the throne of the beast, into the Euphrates, and into the air; a woman sitting on a scarlet beast; a dragon thrown into a lake of fire and sulfur; a white horse; a great supper; a new heaven and a new earth; the holy city Jerusalem coming down from heaven, with details of its entrances, its wall, and the wall's foundations. He also saw a river of living water, and trees of life producing different types of fruit every month. These and many other things were all seen by *John* when his spirit was in the spiritual world and in heaven.[523]

Similar things were also seen by the apostles after the resurrection of the Lord; for example, the visions that *Peter* had (Acts 11), and the things that were heard and seen by *Paul.*

Similar things were also seen by *the prophets* and recorded in the Old Testament. For example, *Ezekiel* saw four creatures that were angel guardians (Ezekiel 1 and 10); a new temple and a new earth, and an angel measuring them (Ezekiel 40–48). Ezekiel was brought to Jerusalem and saw abominations there; he was also brought to Chaldea (Ezekiel 8 and 11).

[3] Something similar happened to *Zechariah.* He saw a man riding among the myrtle trees (Zechariah 1:8 and following). He saw four horns and then a man who had a string in his hand for measuring (Zechariah 2). He saw a flying scroll and a measuring container (Zechariah 5:1, 6). He saw four chariots between two mountains, and saw horses as well (Zechariah 6:1 and following).

In the case of *Daniel,* he saw four beasts rising up out of the sea (Daniel 7:1 and following). He saw the Son of Humankind coming in the clouds of heaven, whose dominion will not pass, and whose kingdom will not perish (Daniel 7:13, 14). He saw battles between a ram and a goat (Daniel 8:1 and following). He saw the angel Gabriel and spoke with him (Daniel 9).

Elisha's servant saw chariots and horses of fire around Elisha; he saw them when his eyes were opened (2 Kings 6:17).

From these and many other passages in the Word it is clear that things of this nature in the spiritual world have appeared to many people both before and after the Lord's Coming. Why be surprised that this is also happening now, when a church is beginning, when the New Jerusalem is coming down from heaven?

[Author's] Table of Contents

The Faith of the New Heaven and the New Church in Both Universal and Specific Forms / §§1–3

Chapter 1: God the Creator

The Oneness of God

The Underlying Divine Reality or Jehovah

The Infinity of God: His Immensity and Eternity

6. Every created thing is finite. The Infinite is in finite objects the way something is present in a vessel that receives it; the Infinite is in people the way something is present in an image of itself. / §§33, 34

The Essence of God: Divine Love and Wisdom

1. God is love itself and wisdom itself. These two constitute his essence. / §37

2. Because goodness comes from love and truth comes from wisdom, God is goodness itself and truth itself. / §38

3. Because God is love itself and wisdom itself, he is life itself in its essence. / §§39, 40

4. Love and wisdom are united in God. / §§41, 42

5. The essence of love is loving others who are outside of oneself, wanting to be one with them, and blessing them from oneself. / §§43, 44, 45

6. These essential characteristics of divine love were the reason the universe was created, and they are the reason it is maintained. / §§46, 47

God's Omnipotence, Omniscience, and Omnipresence

1. It is divine wisdom, acting on behalf of divine love, that has omnipotence, omniscience, and omnipresence. / §§50, 51

2. We cannot comprehend God's omnipotence, omniscience, and omnipresence unless we know what the divine design is, and unless we learn that God is the divine design, and that he imposed that design on the universe as a whole and on everything in it as he created it. / §§52–55

3. In the universe and everything in it, God's omnipotence follows and works through the laws of its design. / §§56, 57, 58

4. God is omniscient; that is, he is aware of, sees, and knows everything down to the least detail that happens in keeping with the divine design, and by contrast is aware of, sees, and knows what goes against the divine design. / §§59–62

8. When he was being emptied out he was in a state of progress toward union; when he was being glorified he was in a state of union itself. / §§104, 105, 106

9. From now on, no Christians will go to heaven unless they believe in the Lord God the Savior. / §§107, 108

10. A supplement about the state of the church before and after the Lord's Coming / §109

Redemption

1. Redemption was actually a matter of gaining control of the hells, restructuring the heavens, and by so doing preparing for a new spiritual church. / §§115, 116, 117

2. Without that redemption no human being could have been saved and no angels could have continued to exist in their state of integrity. / §§118, 119, 120

3. The Lord therefore redeemed not only people but also angels. / §§121, 122

4. Redemption was something only the Divine could bring about. / §123

5. This true redemption could not have happened if God had not come in the flesh. / §§124, 125

6. Suffering on the cross was the final trial the Lord underwent as the greatest prophet. It was a means of glorifying his human nature. It was not redemption. / §§126–131

7. Believing that the Lord's suffering on the cross was redemption itself is a fundamental error on the part of the church. That error, along with the error about three divine Persons from eternity, has ruined the whole church to the point that there is nothing spiritual left in it anymore. / §§132, 133

Chapter 3: The Holy Spirit and the Divine Action

1. The Holy Spirit is the divine truth and also the divine action and effect that radiate from the one God, in whom the divine Trinity exists: the Lord God the Savior. / §§139, 140, 141

5. The apostolic church knew no trinity of persons. The idea was first developed by the Council of Nicaea. The council introduced the idea into the Roman Catholic church; and it in turn introduced the idea into the churches that have since separated from it. / §§174–176

6. The Nicene and Athanasian views of the Trinity led to a faith in three gods that has perverted the whole Christian church. / §§177, 178

7. The result is the abomination of desolation and the affliction such as will never exist again, which the Lord foretold in Daniel, the Gospels, and the Book of Revelation. / §§179, 180, 181

8. In fact, if the Lord were not building a new heaven and a new church, the human race would not be preserved. / §182

9. Many absurd, alien, imaginary, and misshapen ideas of God have come into existence from the Athanasian Creed's assertion of a trinity of persons, each of whom is individually God. / §§183, 184

Chapter 4: Sacred Scripture, the Word of the Lord

1. Sacred Scripture, the Word, is divine truth itself. / §§189–192

2. The Word has a spiritual meaning that has not been known until now. / §193

   (1) What the spiritual meaning is / §194

   There is a heavenly divine influence, a spiritual divine influence, and an earthly divine influence that emanate from the Lord. / §195

   (2) A demonstration that there is a spiritual meaning throughout the Word and in every part of it / §§196, 197, 198

   The Lord spoke in correspondences when he was in the world. While he was talking in an earthly way, he was also talking in a spiritual way. / §199

   (3) It is the spiritual meaning that makes the Word divinely inspired and holy in every word. / §200

(2) [A body of teaching has to be drawn from the Word's literal meaning and supported by it. / §§229, 230]

(3) The genuine truth in the Word's literal meaning, the truth that is needed for a body of teaching, becomes manifest only to those who have enlightenment from the Lord. / §§231, 232, 233

6. The Word's literal meaning provides a connection to the Lord and association with angels. / §§234–239

7. The Word exists throughout the heavens; it is the source of angelic wisdom. / §§240, 241, 242

8. The church is based on the Word; the nature of the church in individuals depends on their understanding of the Word. / §§243–247

9. There is a marriage between the Lord and the church, and therefore a marriage between goodness and truth, in the individual details in the Word. / §§248–253

10. We may derive heretical ideas from the Word's literal meaning, but we are condemned only if we become adamant about those ideas. / §§254–260

Many things in the Word are apparent truths; real truths lie hidden inside them. / §257

Becoming adamant about apparent truths leads to false ideas. / §258

The Word's literal meaning is a protection for the genuine truths that lie inside it. / §260

Angel guardians mean the Word's literal meaning; that is what they stand for in the Word. / §260

11. While in the world, the Lord fulfilled everything in the Word; by doing so he became the Word or divine truth even on the last or outermost level. / §§261, 262, 263

12. Before the Word that exists in the world today, there was a Word that has been lost. / §§264, 265, 266

13. Because of the Word, even people who are outside the church and who do not have the Word have light. / §§267–272

servant or his maid or his ox or his donkey or anything that is your neighbor's. / §§325–328

12. The Ten Commandments contain everything about how to love God and how to love our neighbor. / §§329–331

Chapter 6: Faith

Prefatory remarks: From the standpoint of time, faith is primary, but from the standpoint of purpose, goodwill is primary. / §336

1. The faith that saves us is faith in the Lord God our Savior Jesus Christ, / §§337–339

   because he is a God who can be seen, in whom is what cannot be seen. / §339

2. Briefly put, faith is believing that people who live good lives and believe the right things are saved by the Lord. / §§340–342

   The first step toward faith in him is acknowledging that he is *the Son of God.* / §342

3. The way we receive faith is by turning to the Lord, learning truths from the Word, and living by those truths. / §§343–348

   The underlying reality of this faith; the essence of this faith; the states of this faith; the form this faith takes / §344

   Merely earthly faith is actually a persuasion that pretends to be faith. / §§345–348

4. Having a quantity of truths that are bound together like strands in a cable elevates and improves our faith. / §§349–354

   The truths of faith can be multiplied to infinity. / §350

   Truths of faith come together to form structures that are like fascicles of nerves. / §351

   Our faith improves depending on the quantity of truths we have and how well they fit together. / §§352, 353

   However numerous these truths of faith are and however divergent they appear, they are united by the Lord. / §354

9. Acts of kindness related to goodwill consist in giving to the poor and helping the needy, although with prudence. / §§425–428

10. There are obligations that are related to goodwill. [Some of them are public]; some relate to the household; and some are personal. / §§429–432

11. The recreations related to goodwill are lunches, dinners, and parties. / §§433, 434

12. The first step toward goodwill is removing evils; the second step is doing good things that are useful to our neighbor. / §§435–438

13. As long as we believe that everything good comes from the Lord, we do not take credit for the things we do as we practice goodwill. / §§439–442

14. A life of goodwill is a moral life that is also spiritual. / §§443, 444, 445

15. A bond of love that we form with others without considering their spiritual nature is damaging after death. / §§446–449

16. There are such things as illegitimate goodwill, hypocritical goodwill, and dead goodwill. / §§450–453

17. The bond of love between evil people is actually a deep mutual hatred. / §§454, 455a, 455b

18. The connection between loving God and loving our neighbor. / §§456, 457, 458

Chapter 8: Free Choice

1. The precepts and dogmas of the church of today regarding human free choice / §§463, 464, 465

2. The fact that two trees—the tree of life, and the tree of the knowledge of good and evil [Genesis 2:9]—were placed in the Garden of Eden means that free choice in spiritual matters has been granted to humankind. / §§466–469

3. We are not life, but we are vessels for receiving life from God. / §§470–474

Chapter 9: Repentance

3. By itself, an oral confession that we are sinners is not repentance. / §§516–519

4. From birth we have a tendency toward evils of every kind. Unless we at least partly remove them through repentance, we remain in them, and if we remain in them we cannot be saved. / §§520–524

  What "fulfilling the law" really means / §§523, 524

5. Having a concept of sin and then looking for sin in ourselves is the beginning of repentance. / §§525, 526, 527

6. Active repentance is examining ourselves, recognizing and admitting our sins, praying to the Lord, and beginning a new life. / §§528–531

7. True repentance is examining not only the actions of our life but also the intentions of our will. / §§532, 533, 534

8. Repentance is also practiced by those who do not examine themselves but nevertheless stop doing evils because evils are sinful; this kind of repentance is done by people who do acts of goodwill as a religious practice. / §§535, 536, 537

9. We need to make our confession before the Lord God the Savior, and also to beg for his help and power in resisting evils. / §§538, 539, 560

10. Active repentance is easy for people who have done it a few times; those who have not done it, however, experience inner resistance to it. / §§561, 562, 563

11. Those who have never practiced repentance or looked at or studied themselves eventually do not even know what damnable evil or saving goodness is. / §§564, 565, 566

Chapter 10: Reformation and Regeneration

1. Unless we are born again and created anew, so to speak, we cannot enter the kingdom of God. / §§572–575

2. The Lord alone generates or creates us anew, provided we cooperate; he uses both goodwill and faith as means. / §§576, 577, 578

3. Because we have all been redeemed, we are all capable of being regenerated, each of us in a way that suits the state we are in. / §§579–582

Chapter 11: The Assignment of Spiritual Credit or Blame

concerning three divine persons from eternity; from that time to the present this faith has been accepted by the entire Christian world. / §§632–635

4. The concept of a faith that assigns the merit of Christ was completely unknown in the apostolic church that existed before the Council of Nicaea; and nothing in the Word conveys that concept either. / §§636–639

5. The merit and justice of Christ cannot be assigned to anyone else. / §§640, 641, 642

6. There is an assigning of spiritual credit, but it is based on whether our actions have been good or evil. / §§643–646

7. There is no way in which we can simultaneously hold the views of the new church and the views of the former church on faith and the assignment of spiritual credit; if we did hold both these views at once, they would collide and cause so much conflict that everything related to the church would be destroyed in us. / §§647, 648, 649

8. The Lord ascribes goodness to everyone; hell ascribes evil to everyone. / §§650–653

9. It is what our faith is united to that determines the verdict we receive. If we have a true faith that is united to goodness, the verdict is eternal life; if we have a faith that is united to evil, the verdict is eternal death. / §§654–657

10. No spiritual credit or blame is assigned to us on the basis of what we think; it is assigned only on the basis of what we will. / §§658, 659, 660

Chapter 12: Baptism

1. Without knowing that the Word has a spiritual meaning, no one can know what the two sacraments (baptism and the Holy Supper) entail and what they do for us. / §§667, 668, 669

2. The washing called baptism means a spiritual washing, which is the process of being purified from evils [and falsities] and therefore the process of being regenerated. / §§670–673

Chapter 13: The Holy Supper

3. Understanding what has just been presented makes it possible to see that the Holy Supper includes all the qualities of the church and all the qualities of heaven, both generally and specifically. / §§711–715

4. The Lord himself and his redemption are fully present in the Holy Supper. / §§716, 717, 718

5. The Lord is present and opens heaven to those who approach the Holy Supper worthily; he is also present with those who approach it unworthily, but he does not open heaven to them. Therefore as baptism brings us into the church, so the Holy Supper brings us into heaven. / §§719, 720, 721

6. We come forward worthily to take the Holy Supper when we have faith in the Lord and goodwill toward our neighbor—that is, when we have been regenerated. / §§722–724

7. When we come forward worthily to take the Holy Supper, we are in the Lord and the Lord is in us; therefore through the Holy Supper we enter into a partnership with the Lord. / §§725, 726, 727

8. When we come forward worthily to take it, the Holy Supper functions as [God's] signature and seal confirming that we have been adopted as his children. / §§728, 729, 730

Chapter 14: The Close of the Age; the Coming of the Lord; and the New Church

1. The "close of the age" means the end of the church, when its time is over. / §§753–756

2. Today the church is at its end; the Lord foretold and described this event in the Gospels and in the Book of Revelation. / §§757, 758, 759

3. This, the Christian church's final hour, is the same kind of night in which the former churches came to an end. / §§760–763

4. After this night comes the morning, which is the Lord's Coming. / §§764–767

5. The Lord's Coming is not his coming to destroy the visible heaven and the inhabitable earth and to create a new heaven and a new earth,

as many have supposed because they have not understood the Word's spiritual meaning. / §§768–771

6. The purpose of this coming of the Lord—his Second Coming—is to separate the evil from the good, to save those both past and present who believe in him, and to form them into a new angelic heaven and a new church on earth; if he did not do this, "no flesh would be saved" (Matthew 24:22). / §§772–775

7. This Second Coming of the Lord is not taking place in person but in the Word, since the Word is from him and therefore he is the Word. / §§776, 777, 778

8. This Second Coming of the Lord is taking place by means of someone to whom the Lord has manifested himself in person and whom he has filled with his spirit so that that individual can present the teachings of the new church on the Lord's behalf through the agency of the Word. / §§779, 780

9. "The new heaven" and "the new Jerusalem" in the Book of Revelation chapter 21 mean this [Second Coming of the Lord]. / §§781–785

10. This new church is the crown of all the churches that have ever existed on this planet. / §§786–791

Additional Material

[Author's] Index of the Accounts
of Memorable Occurrences

§§16–17: I heard some people who had recently arrived in the spiritual world talking among themselves about *three divine persons from eternity.* Then one of them who had been in a leadership position in the church during his life in the physical world proudly presented the views he had formed of that great mystery. He said that his opinion had been and still was that the three divine persons sit on exalted thrones in heaven. God the Father sits on a throne made of pure gold and has a scepter in his hand. God the Son sits to his right on a throne of pure silver and has a crown on his head. And God the Holy Spirit sits on a throne of dazzling crystal and holds a dove in his hand—the same form he took when Christ was baptized. Surrounding them are three tiers of hanging lamps glittering with precious stones. At quite a distance from this inner circle stand countless angels, all adoring and glorifying them. The church leader also spoke of how the Holy Spirit enacts faith, purification, and justification in people. He said that many of his colleagues in the clergy agreed with his take on this subject; he believed that because I was a layman, I too would put my faith in his views.

When I was given the opportunity to reply, however, I said that ever since I was a little child I had cherished the idea of one God. I explained to him what the Trinity truly is and what the Word really means when it speaks of God's throne, scepter, and crown. I added that believing in three divine persons from eternity inevitably leads to believing in three gods. Yet in reality the divine essence is indivisible.

§§25–26: A conversation among angels about *God,* to the effect that his divine essence is the underlying divine reality in itself, not from itself, and is united, uniform, absolute, and undivided. The angels also said that God has no specific location, although he is with those who are in specific locations, and that his divine love is visible to angels as a sun. The essence of the heat from that sun is love, and the essence of the light from that sun is wisdom.

The three emanating divine activities of creating, redeeming, and regenerating are activities of the one only God, not activities of three separate gods.

§35: At one point I was struck to think of the vast number of people who are convinced that nature is the source of all things and therefore that nature created the universe. In a lecture hall that contained people like this, an ingenious person and I debated three topics: (1) *whether nature comes from life or life comes from nature;* (2) *whether the center comes from the expanse or the expanse comes from the center;* and (3) *the center and the expanse of nature and of life.* "The center of nature" meant the sun in the physical world; "the expanse of nature" meant the physical world as a whole. "The center of life" meant the sun in the spiritual world, and "the expanse of life" meant the spiritual world as a whole. We vigorously debated the two sides of these questions; eventually it became clear which was the truth.

§48: I was taken to an outdoor arena used for discussing issues of wisdom. Angelic spirits from all four directions who had gathered there were told by angels to discuss three mysteries of wisdom: (1) *What is the image of God and what is the likeness of God?* (2) *Why are human beings born without any knowledge that relates to any love they have? Why are animals and birds born with knowledge related to every love they have?* (3) *What does the tree of life mean and what does the tree of the knowledge of good and evil mean?* The spirits were told to connect their responses into a single statement and give it to the angels from heaven. The group did so, and the angels approved of the resulting statement.

§71: I heard a sound like ocean waves coming from evil spirits just above hell. It was a riot on the part of people who had heard from above that God Almighty restricted himself to following the *divine design.* One spirit came up from below and sharply challenged me regarding this topic. He said that because God is omnipotent he is not restricted to following some divine design. He asked me to tell him more about this divine design, so I said that (1) God is the divine design itself; (2) he created humankind on the basis of his design and in keeping with it, and built that design into us; (3) he created our rational minds in imitation of the divine design in the whole spiritual world, and our bodies in imitation of the divine design in the whole physical world; (4) as a result, it is a law of the divine design that we are to rule our microcosm or physical-world-in-miniature from our microheaven or spiritual-world-in-miniature, just as God rules the macrocosm or physical world from his macroheaven or spiritual world; (5) there are many laws of the divine design that follow from this, and I mentioned a few of them to him. The account includes a description of what happened to those spirits afterward.

§72: A debate among some people from the Netherlands and England in the spiritual world concerning *predestination* and the *assignment of Christ's merit.* One side asked why God in his omnipotence does not assign his Son's justice to all people and redeem them all. Since he is omnipotent, he certainly has the power to turn all satans of hell into angels of heaven. He could turn Lucifer, the dragon, and all the goats into archangels if he wanted to. What would it take except a little word to that effect? The other side maintained that God is the divine design itself. God cannot act against the laws of his own design, because acting against them would be acting against himself. The account includes a number of lively points from the debate.

§73: Afterward I spoke with others who believed in predestination, who came to that view through their notion of God's omnipotence or absolute power. Otherwise, they felt, God's power would be less than the power of monarchs on worldly thrones, who can turn the laws of justice in another direction as easily as they turn the palms of their hands and who have the absolute power of an Octavian Augustus and also the absolute power of a Nero. My answer to them was that God created the world and everything in it from himself as the divine design. Therefore he endowed everything with its own design. There are as many laws of his design as there are truths in the Word. Then I listed several laws of the divine design and mentioned what God does as his part and what we do as ours. Those laws cannot be changed, because God is the divine design itself. We have been created as an image of his divine design.

§74: I talked with a gathering of clergy and lay people about *divine omnipotence.* They said that omnipotence was limitless and that the idea of a limited omnipotence makes no sense. I responded that it makes perfect sense for God to act all-powerfully in following the laws of justice and judgment in his actions. In fact, we read in David, "Justice and judgment are the support of your throne" (Psalms 89:14). It makes perfect sense for

God to act all-powerfully in following the laws of love and wisdom.[525] What makes no sense is to think that God could act against the laws of justice and love, which would not be acting with judgment or with wisdom. Yet the faith that the church is teaching nowadays entails such nonsense; for example, the notion that God could justify unjust people and bestow on godless people all the gifts of salvation and all the rewards of life. The account includes further details about the faith of today and about omnipotence.

§76: One day when I was meditating on *how God created the universe,* I was taken up in the spirit and brought to some wise people. They expressed to me their frustration with stubbornly persistent ideas they had formed while in the physical world. One idea was that the universe had been created out of chaos. Another was that the universe had been created out of nothing. Yet these ideas obscure, twist, and interfere with one's ability to meditate on how God created the universe. They asked for my perspective on this topic. I explained that it is impossible to draw any conclusions (other than fantasies) about the creation of the universe without knowing certain facts: There are two worlds, a spiritual world and a physical world, and each world has its own sun. The sun in the spiritual world is pure love; God is within that sun. All things that are spiritual, and are therefore substantial in essence, come from that sun. The sun in the physical world is pure fire. All things that are physical, and are therefore material in essence, come from this sun. Knowing these things allows us to conclude that God created the universe and to learn how he did it. I gave them a very general sketch of the stages of creation.

§77: Some satans from hell longed to talk with angels from heaven in order to convince them that *everything comes from nature* and that *God is only a word,* unless it means nature. They were given permission to ascend. Some angels came down from heaven into the world of spirits to hear what they had to say. Once they spotted the angels, the satans hurried furiously toward them and said, "You are called angels because you believe there is a God and that nature is nothing in comparison. Yet what you believe runs contrary to all the evidence of the senses. Have any of your own five senses ever detected anything other than nature?" The satans said these and many other harsh things.

The angels then brought back to the satans' remembrance that they were now alive after their own death, although they had not believed such a thing was possible. The angels showed them the magnificent and dazzling things that exist in heaven, and pointed out that such things exist in heaven because all the people there believe in God. Then they showed them the hideous and filthy things that exist in hell, and pointed out that such things exist in hell because all the people there believe in nature [alone]. By seeing the contrast, the satans were convinced for the time being that there is a God and that he created nature. Nevertheless, as they sank back down, their love for evil returned and closed off their intellect at the top. As a result they came back into their original belief that everything comes from nature and nothing comes from God.

§78: Through a living experience of a particular instance of creation, I was shown by angels *how the whole universe was created.* Taken up into heaven, I had the opportunity to see things of every kind from the animal kingdom, things of every kind from the plant kingdom, and things of every kind from the mineral kingdom; all these were exactly the same as their counterparts from those three kingdoms in the physical world. Yet the angels said that all the things I had seen were created by God instantaneously. I was also told that what is created persists as long as the angels' thinking is occurring in an inward state of love and faith. This instantaneous creation bears witness to the fact that similar things were created in a similar way in the physical world. The sole difference is that in the physical world, spiritual things are covered over with material substances; this covering has been provided by God for the sake of having one generation follow another, in order to perpetuate what was created. Therefore the creation of the physical universe was similar to what happens at every moment in heaven. Harmful and disgusting things in the three kingdoms of nature (the account gives specific examples) were not created by God but came into existence along with hell.

§79: A conversation with some people who had been well-respected philosophers when they were in the world. The topic was *how the universe was created.* They expressed the ideas they had formed during their earthly lives. One said that nature created itself. Another said that nature combined its elements to form vortices. The earth was the result of collisions between these vortices. A third countered that nature created itself out of a chaos that occupied a large portion of the universe. First, purer elements broke out of the chaos to form the sun and the stars; then less pure elements formed the atmospheres, and the densest elements formed the globe of the earth. When the philosophers were asked where human souls came from, they replied, "Ether divides itself into little separate balls. These balls pour into people who are about to be born and become their souls. After people die, these souls fly back to the aggregate mass in the ether where they started out. Then they come down into other people, as we know from the ancient concept of reincarnation." Then a priest, who used solid reasoning to argue that God created the universe, pounded all their arguments to a pulp and put them to shame. They nevertheless held on to the ridiculous ideas they had had to begin with.

§80: A conversation with a satan about *God, the angelic heaven,* and *religion.* Because he had no idea he was not still in the physical world, he said (among a number of other foolish things) that God is the universe; the angelic heaven is the ethereal firmament; and religion is an evil spell cast on the multitudes. When it was brought to his remembrance that he was in fact now alive after death himself (even though he had not formerly believed in life after death), for a brief moment he confessed that he was insane, but as soon as he turned homeward and left, his former insanity returned.

§110: In the night I saw a strange light falling to the earth. Many refer to it as "the dragon." I made a note of the place where it landed. The ground there was a mixture of sulfur and iron filings. In the morning I saw two tents there. Soon afterward I saw a spirit falling down from heaven. I went over to him and asked why he had fallen out of heaven like that. He answered that Michael's angels had thrown him down, because he had said that God the Father and his Son are two, not one. He said that the entire angelic heaven believes that *God the Father and his Son are one as a soul and a body are one*—a point the angels support with many passages from the Word. They also use rational argumentation as support: they say the Son's soul came from nowhere else but the Father; therefore that soul was an image of the Father, and the body that came from it contained that image. He added that when he was in heaven he of course spoke of one God, just as he used to do on earth; but because his verbal statements to this effect did not match what he was thinking, the angels said he did not believe in any God, because the two views cancel each other out. He said this was why he was thrown out of heaven.

The next day when I went back to the same spot, in place of the tents I saw two statues that were made of the same materials as the ground there, which, as I say, was a mixture of sulfur and iron. One statue represented the role of faith in the modern-day church; the other represented the role of goodwill. Both were beautifully dressed, but the clothes were just projected images. Because of the materials the statues were made of, however, when a rain shower fell from heaven they both began to fizz and burn.

§111: In the spiritual world, no one is able to say anything except what he or she truly thinks; if they do otherwise, their hypocrisy is plainly audible. As a result, no one in hell can say the name Jesus, because "Jesus" means salvation. This is how those in the other world can find out how many people in the Christian world today actually believe that Christ even in his human nature is God. Therefore there was a conference involving many clergy and lay people; they were asked to say "*divine-human.*" Scarcely any of the participants were able to think these two words together at the same time and say them. Many passages from the Word were read out loud to them to the effect that even the Lord's human manifestation was God, such as Matthew 28:18; John 1:1, 2, 14; 17:2; Colossians 2:9; 1 John 5:20; and others. The participants remained still unable to utter the words "divine-human." People were amazed to find that Lutherans were unable to say this, despite the fact that their orthodox writings teach that in Christ God is human and a human is God. It was even more surprising to find that Catholic monks who had celebrated with the utmost reverence the body of Christ in their Eucharist were unable to say this. These experiments showed that the vast majority of Christians today are inwardly either Arians or Socinians and that any adoration they pay to Christ as God is merely hypocritical.

§112: A dispute broke out concerning *Survey of Teachings of the New Church,* a little volume I published in Amsterdam.[526] People were particularly concerned about the teaching in it that we should *turn to and worship the Lord God the Redeemer rather than God the Father.* They countered that the Lord's prayer says, "Our Father, you who are in the heavens, your name must be kept holy; your kingdom must come"; therefore we should turn to God the Father. Summoned to settle this dispute, I demonstrated that it is impossible for us to turn to God the Father in his divinity, but we can turn to him in his humanity. Because the divine nature and the human nature together constitute one person, the Lord is the *Father* mentioned in the Lord's prayer. I backed this up with statements from the Word of the Old Testament, where the Son of God is called the Father of Eternity, and with many passages there that speak of Jehovah the Redeemer, Jehovah our Justice, and the God of Israel. I also cited many passages from the New Testament. Therefore when we turn to the Lord God the Redeemer, we are turning to the Father; then his name is kept holy, then his kingdom comes, and so on.

§113: I saw an army on red horses and black horses. The riders were all turned around with their faces toward the horses' tails and their backs toward the horses' heads. They were shouting battle cries against some riders on white horses. This ludicrous army had burst forth from the place called Armageddon (Revelation 16:16). The army consisted of people who in early adulthood had absorbed the dogmas of *justification by faith alone.* When they were promoted later on to high-ranking positions in the church, they rejected the teachings about faith and religion from the inner realms of their mind and moved them into the outer realms related to their body, where those teachings eventually disappeared altogether. The account includes a description of how they appeared in Armageddon.

There was a report from there that they wanted to meet with Michael's angels. This was granted, although the groups were to remain a certain distance apart. The two groups then battled over the meaning of the following words in the Lord's prayer: "Our Father, you who are in the heavens, your name must be kept holy; your kingdom must come" [Matthew 6:9–10]. Michael's angels said that the Lord the Redeemer and Savior is the Father of all who are in the heavens; he himself teaches that the Father and he are one; that the Father is in him and he is in the Father; that those who see him see the Father; that all things belonging to the Father are his; also that it is the will of the Father that people should believe in the Son, and that those who do not believe the Son will not see life; instead the anger of God will remain on them; also that all power in heaven and on earth belongs to him and that he has power over all flesh; and that no one has seen or could see God the Father except the Son alone, who is close to the Father's heart; and much more. After the

Armageddonites were thoroughly conquered as a result of this battle, one part of their group was thrown into the great pit mentioned in Revelation 9; the other part was sent out into a desert.

§134: I was in a church that was without windows, but had a large opening in the roof. The people who were gathered there were talking about *redemption.* They were of one mind in saying that redemption was accomplished through Christ's suffering on the cross. While they were discussing this, a dark cloud came and covered the opening in the roof, causing total darkness in the church. Soon the cloud was driven away by angels who came down from heaven.

The angels sent one of their own down to the church to teach the congregation about redemption. This angel said that the suffering on the cross was not redemption. Redemption was a matter of gaining control over the hells, restructuring the heavens, and restoring all things that had lapsed in both the spiritual and the physical world. Without these achievements, no flesh could have been saved [Matthew 24:22]. He said that the Lord's suffering on the cross was the last step in achieving union with the Father at the deepest level. He also said that confusing the suffering on the cross with redemption entails thinking many unworthy and in fact horrendous things about God—that God locked the whole human race into damnation, but the Son took that damnation on himself, which appeased the Father; then the Son's intercession restored the Father to his divine essence, which is love and mercy; not to mention many other qualities that are very wrong to ascribe to God.

§135: I saw the sun in the spiritual world, which surrounds Jehovah God in his human manifestation. Then from heaven I heard, *There is one God.* As this statement came down into the world of spirits, it changed as it was adapted to the form of the minds there. It eventually turned into a notion of three gods. One person added an argument in support of three gods, saying that there is one who created all things, a second who redeemed all people, and a third who puts everything into effect. Again, there is one who assigns spiritual credit or blame, a second who mediates for us, and a third who gives us our assigned and mediated credit. This, he argued, is how we receive the faith that makes us just. In reality, however, that belief in three gods has corrupted the entire Christian church.

With a perception that was given to me then, I revealed what mediation, intercession, appeasement, and ritual purging mean in the context of one God. These are actually four attributes of the human manifestation of Jehovah God, because without that manifestation, Jehovah God could not have gotten close to us nor we to him. *Mediation* refers to God's human manifestation as the intermediary. *Intercession* refers to his mediating as ongoing. *Appeasement* refers to God's human manifestation as providing every human being with welcome access to God. *Ritual purging* refers to this access as available even to those who have committed sins. All these [blessings] come to us through God's human manifestation.

§136: I entered a hall where people were discussing how one should interpret the statement that the Son of God *sits at the right hand of the Father.* They expressed various opinions of what this means, but they all agreed that he does literally do this. They discussed possible reasons for it. Some believed it was because he was the Redeemer; some believed it was because of love; some believed it allowed him to act as an adviser; some believed it was so the angels could honor him; some believed it allowed him to rule in place of the Father; some believed it was so that the Father could hear with his right ear the list of people for whom Jesus was interceding. The people also debated whether it was the Son of God from eternity who sits there, or the Son of God born in the world.

When they had finished, I raised my hand and asked if I might be allowed to say something and explain what sitting at the right hand of God means. I said that it means the omnipotence of God that is exercised through the human manifestation that he took on. It was through this manifestation that he achieved redemption, meaning that he gained control of the hells, created a new angelic heaven, and established a new church. To support that this is what sitting at the right hand of God means, I cited a number of passages from the Word in which the right hand means power. Afterward, there was further confirmation from heaven when a right hand appeared above them that had such power and so terrified them that they almost lost consciousness.

§137: In the spiritual world I was taken to attend a council. The participants included famous people who had lived before the time of the Council of Nicaea, called the apostolic fathers, and well-known people from after the time of that council. I noticed that some in the latter group were clean-shaven and wore curled wigs of women's hair, but all in the former group were bearded and wore no wigs. Before them all stood a man who had been a judge and critic of the writers of this century.

He began his remarks with the following lament: "Some layperson has risen up and pulled our faith down from its sanctuary. Yet that faith is a star that shines before us day and night. He did so because he is completely blind to the mysteries of our faith. He does not see that it contains the justice of Christ. He does not see that it contains the miracle of *justification by faith.* Yet our faith believes in *three divine persons* and therefore in the whole of God. Instead, he has redirected belief toward the second Person—in fact, not even the whole second Person, but just his human manifestation. How can his perspective do anything but spew materialist philosophy?" The group that had lived after the Council of Nicaea applauded his statement. They said that it was impossible for faith to be different or to come from any other source.

The apostolic fathers, who had lived before the century [of the Council of Nicaea], were upset, however. They related a number of things that people in heaven have to say about the Nicene and the Athanasian faith; the reader may review these in the account.

Because the chairman of the council was associated in spirit with an author in Leipzig, I addressed him and demonstrated from the Word that Christ is God even in regard to his human manifestation. I showed from the *Formula of Concord,* the dogmatic volume adhered to by Lutherans, that in Christ, God is human and a human is God. Among a number of other things, I also showed that the Augsburg Confession completely supports the worship of Christ. In response to all this he just looked away in silence.

After that I spoke with a spirit who was associated with an eminent man in Göteborg who had befouled the worship of the Lord with an even greater insult. By the end, these assaults of theirs were declared to be lies invented by treachery, aimed at turning and deterring the human will from the holy worship of the Lord.

§159: Smoke appeared, rising up from the lower earth. I commented that smoke simply means a mass of false beliefs. Some angels were then seized with a desire to explore which false beliefs were causing that smoke. They went down and came upon four sets of spirits in ranks. Two sets consisted of clergy: one group of these was of learned clergy; the other, regular clergy. Two sets consisted of laypeople: one group of these was educated laypeople; the other, uneducated laypeople. They were all convinced that people should *worship the God who cannot be seen.* That type of worship provides worshipers with holiness. God hears worship like that, which is not the case when worship is directed to a God who can be seen. They used various arguments to support the notion that holiness and God's hearing result from worshiping a God who cannot be seen. This is why they acknowledge the existence of three gods from eternity, none of whom can be seen.

They were shown, however, that worshiping a God who cannot be seen is no kind of worship at all; it is even worse to worship *three* gods who cannot be seen. As support for this point, Socinus and Arius were brought up from below, along with a number of their followers, all of whom worshiped a divinity that could not be seen. When Socinus, Arius, and their followers spoke from the earthly or outer level of their mind, they said that even though God cannot be seen, he does exist. When their outer mind was closed, however, and their inner mind was opened, and they were compelled to state their real beliefs about God, they said, "What is God? We haven't seen the way he looks or heard his voice. What then is God except nature, or else a figment of the imagination?" They were then taught that it pleased God to come down and take on a human manifestation so that we could see what he looks like and hear his voice. But to their ears, this was a pointless teaching.

§160: The first part of the account concerns the possibility that there are the same number of stars in the physical world as there are angelic communities in heaven, since every community in heaven sometimes shines like a star.

Next, I spoke with angels about a certain road that is crowded with countless spirits. It is the road by which all who die in the physical world cross over into the spiritual world. The angels and I went to that road. We took aside twelve people from the road and asked them what they believed about *heaven and hell* and *life after death*. Because they were just arriving from the physical world, they did not realize they were not still in that world. As a result they gave us the ideas they were bringing with them from that world. The first said that people who live moral lives go to heaven; therefore no one goes to hell, because everyone lives a moral life. The second said that God rules heaven, and the Devil rules hell. Because they are opposed to each other, one calls good what the other calls evil. Human beings are phonies who can take either side; therefore they are equally capable of living under either leader. The third said that heaven does not exist, and neither does hell. Who has come back to tell us about them? The fourth explained the reason why no one can come back and tell us about them, which is that when we die we become either a ghost or blowing air. The fifth said we need to wait for the day of the Last Judgment. Then they will tell all, and you will know all. But when he said that, he was laughing to himself. The sixth asked how a human soul that was no more than air blowing around could come back into a body that had been consumed by worms, and reclaim a skeleton that had either burned up or crumbled to dust. The seventh said people cannot live after death any more than animals and birds can—animals and birds are just as rational as human beings. The eighth said, "I believe in heaven, but I don't believe in hell. God is omnipotent. He can save everyone." The ninth said that God is too gracious to throw anyone into eternal fire. The tenth said that no one can go to hell, because God sent his Son to bear the sins of all people and purge them. What is the Devil capable of doing against that? The eleventh, who was a priest, said that the only people who are saved are those who have acquired faith. It is up to the Almighty to choose who is worthy. The twelfth, who was in politics, said, "I will not say anything about heaven or hell. It is good for the priests to preach about them, though, so that commoners are held mentally bound to laws and to leaders by an invisible chain."

The angels were stunned to hear these points of view. They woke the people up by teaching them that they were now alive after their own death. The angels brought them to heaven, but the people were unable to stay there long because it was discovered that they were not at all spiritual, and as a result the backs of their heads were hollowed out. At the end of the account, there is a discussion about that hollowing out and what causes it.

§161: I heard the sound of a mill. As I followed the sound I came to a building that was full of cracks. The entrance went down underground. Inside I saw a man who was collecting [on slips of paper] a number of passages from the Word and other books concerning *justification by faith alone.* Copyists in the next room were writing out on a full sheet the passages he had found. When I asked him the topic of the passages he was collecting now, he said, "The point that God the Father lapsed from an attitude of grace toward the human race, and therefore sent his Son to make atonement and appease the Father." By way of response, I said that it goes against Scripture and sound reason to think that God could lapse from an attitude of grace; that would be lapsing from his own essence, and that would mean he was no longer God. When I thoroughly demonstrated this, he became angry and ordered his copyists to throw me out. As I was walking out on my own, he picked up a book that happened to be at hand and threw it at me. The book was the Word.

§162: There was a dispute among spirits about *whether any of us can see any genuine truth in the Word without help from the Lord,* who is the Word. Because there was a strong difference of opinion, we conducted an experiment. The people who turned to God the Father did not see a single truth, but all who turned to the Lord saw things that were true.

As this debate went on, some spirits came up from the abyss mentioned in Revelation 9, a place where they discuss and explore the secrets of justification by faith alone. These spirits claimed that they turn to God the Father and see their mysteries in a perfectly clear light. They were told, however, that they are seeing those mysteries in faint, deceptive light, and that in reality, not a single thing they believe is true. Angered by this, they quoted many sayings from the Word. The angels' response was that those sayings are intrinsically true, but have been falsified by those spirits; the truth of this was shown by taking them to a place with a table onto which light flows straight from heaven. The spirits were instructed to write the truths they had taken from the Word on a piece of paper and place it on the table. They did so. The piece of paper with their truths written on it shone like a star. Nevertheless, when the spirits approached the table and fixed their gaze on the piece of paper, the paper came to look as if it had been blackened with soot.

Then the spirits were taken to another table of the same kind. On it was the Word, surrounded by a rainbow. One of the people present had been a leading author, while in the world, on the doctrine that we are justified by faith alone. When he confidently touched the Word with his hand, there was an explosion as if a gun had gone off. He was thrown into the corner of the room and lay there as if he were dead for about half an hour. The spirits were shown convincingly by this that the truths they knew from the Word were intrinsically true, but they had falsified them.

§185: The spiritual world has climatic zones just like the physical world, including northern zones with snow and ice. On one occasion I was led in spirit to that northern area. I went into a church that was buried in snow; inside, it was lit with lanterns. Behind the altar there was a plaque with an inscription: *The divine Trinity, the Father, Son, and Holy Spirit,* *who are essentially one God but personally three.* I heard a priest give a sermon on four mysteries of faith (see details in the account), saying that in regard to them we should hold our intellect under obedience to faith. After church, members of the congregation thanked the priest for a sermon that was rich in wisdom. I asked them whether they understood any of it. They answered, "We took it all in with open ears. Why do you ask whether we understood it? Isn't the intellect too stupid to understand these topics?"

The priest, who was still present, added, "Because you heard and did not understand, you are blessed, since you have salvation as a result." And so on.

§186: The *human mind* is differentiated into three levels, as is heaven, where angels live. In people who love truth because it is true, theological issues dwell on the highest level of the mind; moral issues are located on the middle level, below theological issues; and political issues dwell on the lowest level, below moral issues. Academic subjects of various kinds form a doorway to all the higher issues. In people who do not love truth, however, theological issues occupy the lowest level and become intertwined with their own self-interest and with lies told by their five senses. This is why some people are completely incapable of taking in theological truths.

§187: I was taken to the place where there are people meant by the *false prophet* in the Book of Revelation. They invited me to come and see their shrine. I went and saw it. In the shrine there was a statue of a woman dressed in scarlet clothes, holding a gold coin in her right hand and a chain of pearls in her left. These were projected images, however. When the Lord opened the inner levels of my mind, instead of the shrine I saw a house that was full of cracks, and instead of the woman, I saw a beast like the one described in Revelation 13:2. Under the floor there was a swamp; in the swamp the Word lay deeply hidden.

Soon, however, the east wind blew away the shrine and dried up the swamp, allowing the Word to appear. In the light of heaven a *tent* came into view, like the one Abraham had when three angels came to him to announce that Isaac was going to be born. As light was let in from the second heaven, instead of the tent I saw a temple like the Temple in Jerusalem. After that, light from the third heaven shone down. Then the temple disappeared, and I saw *the Lord alone,* standing on the foundation stone, where the Word was. Because an overpowering sense of holiness then filled our minds, that light was withdrawn, and instead the channel of light from the second heaven was reopened. As a result, the earlier appearance of a temple returned, with a tent in the middle of it.

§188: I saw a magnificent palace that had a chapel in its center. In the chapel there were three rows of chairs. A council had been called by the Lord there. The participants were to discuss *the Lord the Savior* and *the Holy Spirit.* When as many clergy had arrived as there were chairs, the council began.

Since the first topic was the Lord, the first issue to be discussed was, *Who took on a human manifestation in the Virgin Mary?* An angel standing by the table read to them what the angel Gabriel said to Mary: "*The Holy Spirit will descend upon you, and the power of the Highest will cover you; therefore the Holy One that will be born from you will be called the Son of God*" (Luke 1:35; see also Matthew 1:20, 25). The angel also read a number of statements in the prophets to the effect that Jehovah himself would come into the world and that Jehovah himself is called the Savior, the Redeemer, and Justice. This led the group to conclude that it was Jehovah himself who took on a human manifestation.

The second discussion on the topic of the Lord was, *Are the Father and the Lord Jesus Christ one as the soul and the body are one?* Many passages both from the Word and from a creed of the modern-day church were quoted in support of this point. The group concluded that the Lord's soul came from God the Father and therefore his human manifestation was divine. They also concluded that when we seek help from the Father, we must turn to the Lord's divine human manifestation. That is how Jehovah God sent himself into the world and made himself visible to human eyes, and accessible.

The third discussion took up the topic of *the Holy Spirit.* The first thing to be discussed was the issue of three divine persons from eternity. Passages from the Word were used to show that the holy quality that radiates from God, which is called the Holy Spirit, emanates from the Lord on behalf of the Father.

At the end, the council brought all its discussions together into a single conclusion: The divine Trinity exists within the Lord the Savior; the Trinity is made up of the divine nature as an origin called "the Father," the divine human manifestation called "the Son," and the emanating divine influence called "the Holy Spirit"; therefore there is one God in the church. After the council came to an end, the participants were given shining clothing and were led to the new heaven.

§277: In a manger, I saw large purses, which contained a significant quantity of silver. Young men were standing guard over them. In the next room, there were some modest young women and a faithful wife. In yet another room there were two little children. Last of all, I saw a whore and dead horses. Afterward I was told what each of these things meant. They were all depicting and describing the Word, either as it is in its essence, or the way it is understood nowadays.

§278: I saw an example of the writing used in the highest or third heaven. It consists of curved letters with little horns that turn upward. I was informed that these letters are somewhat similar to the Hebrew letters of earliest times, when they were more curved than they are today. The letter *h,* which was added to Abram and Sarai's names, means infinity and eternity. I was given an explanation of the meaning of a number of words in Psalms 32:2 on the basis of the letters alone. The meaning is that *the Lord is also compassionate to those who do evil.*

§279: Before the Israelite Word there was a Word whose prophetical portion was called *The Pronouncements,* and whose historical portion was called *The Wars of Jehovah.* It also included a work called the *Book of Jasher.* These three titles are mentioned in the Word we have now. That ancient Word existed in the land of Canaan, Syria, Mesopotamia, Arabia, Assyria, Chaldea, and Egypt; and in Tyre, Sidon, and Nineveh. That Word was full of a type of correspondences that presented heavenly and spiritual things remotely. This left it vulnerable to [misinterpretation by] idolaters. Therefore by divine providence it disappeared. I have heard that Moses took from that Word the things he wrote about creation, Adam and Eve, and the Flood, and what he mentioned about Noah and his three sons; but nothing after that. I have been told in the spiritual world by angels who had lived in Great Tartary that that same Word still exists among the peoples there; those peoples base the principles of their faith and life on it.

§280: People who are in the spiritual world cannot appear to people who are in the physical world, and neither can people in the physical world appear to people in the spiritual world. Therefore spirits and angels cannot appear to people, and people cannot appear to spirits and angels. This is due to *the difference between what is spiritual and what is earthly,* or, to put it another way, the difference between what is substantial and what is material. It is because of this that spirits and angels have completely different language, different writing, and different thinking than people do.

This was revealed to me through a living experience. Several times, spirits went home to their own group, then came back to me, and we made comparisons. We learned that spiritual language and earthly language have not even a single word in common. In addition, each of the letters in their writing contains a meaning relative to the topic at hand. They also think things that are beyond an earthly person's comprehension. The reason behind these differences is that spirits and angels are at the level of primary structures, whereas people in the world are in derivations from them. To put it another way, spirits and angels live among primary things that act as causes of secondary things; people live among those secondary things. A voice said that a similar difference exists between the language, writing, and thinking of angels of the third heaven compared to the language, writing, and thinking of angels of the second heaven.

§281: On *the states people go through after they die*—what happens generally, and what happens in particular to people who have convinced themselves of theological falsities. About both of these groups I have observed the following: (1) For the most part people come back to their own life spiritually on the third day after they die. At that point they have no idea they are not still alive in the former world. (2) All arrive at a world that is midway between heaven and hell; it is called the world of spirits. (3) They are transferred to various different communities as a way of finding out what their true quality is. (4) In that world, those who are good and faithful are prepared for heaven, and those who are evil and unfaithful are prepared for hell. (5) After this preparation, which lasts for several years, a road opens up for good people, leading to a particular community in heaven where they will live forever; a road into hell opens up for evil people. And so on. Afterward the account describes what hell is like. The spirits there called satans are people who were adamantly devoted to falsities; the spirits called devils are people who lived evil lives.

§332: From the lower earth, which is the next level up from hell, I heard people shouting, *"They are so just! They are so learned! They are so wise!"*

Because I was struck by the thought that there might be just, learned, and wise people in hell, I went down. First I went to the place where people were shouting, "*They are so just!*" I saw a courtroom of sorts. The judges in it were actually unjust and ingenious in their methods of bending the law and handing down favorable sentences to whomever they chose. They saw it as entirely up to their own whim to decide which side their adjudications would support. When they handed down sentences that favored their friends and supporters, these people went all the way down a long road shouting, "They are so just!" Angels later commented on these judges, saying that they are actually incapable of seeing what is just. Some time later, those judges were thrown into hell. Their law books turned into playing cards. Then, instead of being judges they were given the task of preparing makeup and applying it to the faces of promiscuous women to make them beautiful.

§333: Next I went to the place where people were shouting, "*They are so learned!*" I saw a large group of people who dispute about *whether a given thing exists or not.* They never come to a definite yes; therefore in considering any topic, they never get beyond the first step. They only touch on issues from the outside; they never go deeply into them. Their consideration of God stops at whether he exists or not.

In order to confirm that this was indeed their nature, I posed a question to them: "What does a religion need to be like in order to save people?" Their response was that they would need to debate the following related questions. (1) Is religion anything? (2) Is one religion more effective than another? (3) Is there such a thing as eternal life, and therefore is there such a thing as salvation? (4) Do heaven and hell exist? They began to discuss the first issue: "Is religion anything?" They said this question needed so much investigation that they could not finish within a year. One of them said it could not be finished within a hundred years. I replied, "Meanwhile you have no religion."

Nevertheless, they discussed this first question with such consummate skill that the crowd standing around them exclaimed, "They are so learned!" Angels told me that [in heaven's light] these kinds of people look like statues. Eventually they are sent out into desert places and blather to each other and utter nothing but nonsense.

§334: I went to the third group, where I had heard people shouting, "*They are so wise!*" I learned that the people who were gathered there were incapable of seeing whether a truth is true or not, yet they can take anything they want and make it appear to be true. Therefore they are called *providers of arguments.* From the sheer variety of responses they gave to questions posed to them, I observed that this was indeed their nature. For example, they were able to make it seem entirely true that faith is the most important thing in the church. Soon afterward, they were able to make it seem entirely true that goodwill is the most important thing in the church. They did the same for the point that goodwill and faith together are the most important thing in the church. Because they argued every point with consummate skill and draped it in compelling illustrations until it glowed like genuine truth, the crowd standing around them exclaimed, "They are so wise!"

When they said that nothing is true except what people make out to be true, someone proposed a few ridiculous points for them to argue as true: That light is darkness, and darkness is light; and also that crows are white, not black. They did indeed manage to make these points seem absolutely true. (For the arguments they used, see the account itself.)

Angels told me that people like this do not possess even a speck of understanding. Everything above their rational faculty is closed off; only what is below it is opened up. The nature of this lower area is that it can provide arguments to support whatever it wants, but cannot see any real truth for what it is. Being able to provide arguments to support whatever you want is not intelligence; intelligence is being able to see that what is true is true and what is false is false and to provide arguments to support that.

§335: I spoke with spirits who had been famous scholars during their lives in the physical world. They were having a sharp dispute about *innate ideas.* At issue was whether people are born with innate ideas the way animals are. An angelic spirit interrupted their conversation and said, "What you are fighting about is goat's wool. Neither people nor animals have any innate ideas." The spirits were all outraged by this.

When the angelic spirit was given the floor, the first point he made was that animals have no innate ideas, because they have no thought process. They operate entirely on the instincts that come from the earthly type of love they have. These function like a faculty of will in them. Their instincts flow directly into their bodily senses; they also drive the animals to do whatever agrees with and benefits their love. Ideas come into play only where there is thought. Animals have no thought; they have only sensation.

The angelic spirit supported this point with a number of illustrations—especially the remarkable facts known about spiders, bees, and silkworms. He said, "When a spider is weaving its web, is it thinking in its tiny head that it should weave its web this or that way to serve this or that purpose? When a bee is extracting [the raw materials for] honey from some flowers and wax from others, is it thinking in its tiny head, 'With this wax I will build adjacent cells one after the other; in them I will put enough honey to last all winter,' and other plans like that? Is a silkworm thinking in its tiny head, 'Now I will spend time spinning silk. When I have finished, I will fly off and play with my friends and ensure that I have offspring'? Similar arguments could be made about animals and birds."

Concerning human beings he said that any mother or wet nurse, or even any father, knows that newborn babies have no innate ideas whatsoever. They have no ideas before they learn to think. Then for the first time ideas develop in them. Their ideas form entirely in accordance with the quality of thought they have developed as a result of their education. The reason for this is that we have nothing innate except a faculty for knowing, understanding, and becoming wise, as well as a tendency to love not only ourselves and the world but also our neighbor and God.

Leibniz and Wolff heard this from a distance. Leibniz agreed, but Wolff felt otherwise.

§385: Once, an angelic spirit illustrated for me *what faith and goodwill are* and what their union accomplishes, through an analogy with light and heat. They come together to form a third entity. In essence, the light in heaven is truth that has to do with faith. In essence, the heat in heaven is goodness that has to do with goodwill. Light without heat, which is what is experienced on earth during winter, strips trees of their leaves and fruits. Faith without goodwill has a similar effect. Light united to heat, which is what is experienced on earth during spring, brings all things to life. Faith united to goodwill has a similar effect.

§386: Two angels came down. One was from the eastern part of heaven, where love is the primary focus; the other was from the southern part of heaven, where wisdom is the primary focus. They discussed *whether the essence of the heavens was love or whether it was wisdom.* They came to agree that love is the essence, and wisdom is derived from it. Therefore God created the heavens from love by means of wisdom.

§387: After that, I went into a large garden. A spirit showed me around. We came to a magnificent building called *the Temple of Wisdom.* It was square; its walls were made of crystal; its roof was made of jasper; its foundation was made of different types of precious stone. The spirit told me that none were allowed in it unless they believe that what they know, understand, and are wise about is so relatively small as to be almost non-existent compared to what they do not know, do not understand, and are not wise about. Because this was my belief, I was allowed to go in. I saw that the whole temple was built to be a form of light. In the temple, I related what I had just heard from the two angels concerning love and wisdom; [the spirits there] asked whether the angels had mentioned the third element, which is usefulness. [The spirits] said that without usefulness love and wisdom are mere conceptual entities; only in usefulness do they become real. The same is true for goodwill, faith, and good actions.

§388: One of the dragon spirits invited me to see the types of entertainment they love. He took me to something like *an amphitheater* with satyrs and whores in the seats. He said, "Now you are going to see our form of entertainment." He opened a gate and let in what looked like bull calves, rams, goats, and lambs. Soon, through another gate, he let in lions, panthers, tigers, and wolves. These animals attacked the herd of other animals and tore them to pieces and slaughtered them. The whole spectacle had been conjured up, though, through the use of projected images.

I then said to the dragon, "It won't be long before you see this amphitheater turned into a lake of fire and sulfur."

Once the entertainment was over, the dragon left, surrounded by his satyrs and whores. Seeing a flock of sheep, he realized that one of the many Jerusalem cities was nearby. When he saw the city he was overcome by a desire to capture it and drive out its inhabitants, but because there was a wall around it, he planned instead to use deceit to capture it. He sent in someone skilled in incantation. Once he was in the city, that person spoke skillfully to its citizens about faith and goodwill, raising the issue of which of the two was primary, and questioning whether goodwill contributes anything to salvation. Irritated at the response he received, the dragon left the city, gathered many of his people, and began to lay siege to the city; but while he was working on capturing and invading the city, fire from heaven devoured them, just as Revelation 20:8, 9 predicted it would.

§389: On one occasion a document was sent down from heaven. It strongly urged people [of a community in the world of spirits] to *acknowledge the Lord the Savior as the God of heaven and earth,* as he himself taught (Matthew 28:18). The people sought advice from two bishops in that community regarding what they should do. The bishops told them to send the document back to the heaven where it came from. When they did so, the community sank down, but not very far.

The next day some of them came up from there and recounted what had happened to them after they sank down. They mentioned that they had gone back to the bishops and confronted them about the outcome of their advice. They then had a long interchange with the bishops concerning the state of the modern-day church. They rebuked the bishops for their doctrinal positions on the Trinity, goodwill, and justification by faith, and for other elements of their orthodoxy. They asked the bishops to abandon those positions because they are contrary to the Word; but it was pointless. When they said that according to the Epistle of James the bishops' faith was dead and even diabolical [James 2:14–26; 3:13–15], one of the bishops took off his miter and put it on the table, saying that he would not put it back on until he had taken his revenge for these insults to his faith. Just then, however, a monster appeared rising up from below that looked like the beast described in Revelation 13:1, 2. The monster took the bishop's miter and carried it away.

§390: I came to a house where people were discussing the good things that people do in *an ongoing state of being justified* by their faith. At issue was whether that good is or is not *religious* good. There was consensus that "religious good" means good that contributes to salvation. The group that prevailed had the opinion that no good thing we do contributes anything to our salvation. Their argument for this was that any good that people do voluntarily cannot be united to something they get for free, and salvation is had for free. How could any good that people do be united to the merit of Christ? The merit of Christ is the sole source of salvation. How could the work that people do be united to the work that the Holy Spirit does? It does everything without the help of humankind. For these reasons they concluded that even when we are being justified by our faith, faith alone saves us; our good works contribute nothing to our salvation. Two non-Christians standing in the front hall said to each other, "These people have no religion. Clearly, religion is doing good to our neighbor for the sake of God and therefore with God and from God."

§391: I heard angels complaining about the *spiritual poverty* in the church today. It is so pervasive, they said, that people know only that there are three divine persons and that faith alone saves. Of the Lord they know only some historical facts. They are completely unaware of the statements in the Word that concern the Lord, his unity with the Father, and his divinity and power.

The angels told me that one angel went down to investigate whether there really was such spiritual poverty among Christians today. That angel asked someone what his religion was. He answered, "Faith." The angel asked him his point of view on redemption, regeneration, and salvation. He answered that they all had to do with faith. Asked about goodwill, he said it exists in that faith; we cannot do anything good on our own.

The angel then said to him, "You give answers like someone playing the same note again and again on a flute. I am not hearing anything but faith. If you don't know anything except faith, you don't know anything." He took him to join his companions in a part of the desert where there was not even any grass. There is more to the account as well.

§459: I saw five halls surrounded with different kinds of light. I joined a large group of people entering the first hall, which was surrounded with a fiery light. There was a huge crowd inside. The chairperson proposed that people give their opinions of *goodwill.*

As the event got underway, the *first* person said that goodwill is morality inspired by faith. The *second* defined it as religious devotion combined with compassion. The *third* defined it as doing good to everyone, whether honest or dishonest. The *fourth* defined it as doing everything you can for your relatives and friends. The *fifth* defined it as giving donations to the poor and helping the needy. The *sixth* defined it as building hospices, hospitals, and orphanages. The *seventh* defined it as providing church buildings with an endowment and benefiting its ministers. The *eighth* defined it as the ancient Christian family feeling. The *ninth* defined it as forgiving anyone's wrongs. They all gave ample support for their own definition; because there was a great deal of this supporting material, it cannot be copied here—see the account itself.

I was then given permission to express my own opinion. I said that goodwill is to act in all our work, and in every role we have, with judgment based on a love for justice—but only if that love comes solely from the Lord the Savior. After giving supporting arguments for my definition, I added that the actions described by the nine distinguished participants are outstanding examples of the practice of goodwill, provided they are done with judgment in accordance with justice; and because the sole source of true justice and judgment is the Lord our Savior, these are actions we need to take on his behalf. Many felt approval in their inner selves for what I had said, but their outer selves did not yet approve.

§460: Off in the distance I heard a sound like teeth grinding together and a hammering sound mixed in with it. I went in the direction of the sounds and saw a hut made of rushes plastered together. Instead of the sounds of hammering and teeth grinding together that I had heard before, I now heard inside the hut an argument about *faith and goodwill,* and which of these two was the essence of the church. The side that favored faith put forward its arguments. They said that faith is spiritual, because it comes from God; but goodwill is earthly, because it comes from human beings. The side that favored goodwill said that goodwill is spiritual, but faith is merely earthly unless it is united to goodwill. A syncretist who was trying to resolve the dispute provided additional support for the view that faith is spiritual and goodwill is only earthly. In response, people said to him that a moral life comes in two types: there is a moral life that is spiritual, and there is a moral life that is merely earthly. People who live for the Lord have a life that is moral in a spiritual way; people who do not live for the Lord have a life that is moral in an earthly way. The latter type of life is practiced by evil people and sometimes even by the spirits in hell.

§461: I was led in the spirit to a certain garden in the southern part. There I saw people sitting under a laurel tree eating figs. I asked them *how it is that we can do something good on God's behalf and nevertheless do it completely as if we were acting on our own.* They replied that God produces goodness inside us, but if we do something good of our own volition and understanding, we pollute that goodness to such an extent that it is no longer good. My response to that was that we are only organs that receive life. If we believe in the Lord, we do good things under our own initiative on the Lord's behalf. If we do not believe in the Lord, and still more so if we do not believe in God at all, we do good things under our own initiative on hell's behalf. The Lord has given us free choice to do one or the other of these. To show that the Lord gives us this freedom, I quoted passages from the Word that command us to love God and our neighbor, to produce good, loving actions as a tree bears fruit, and to do what the Lord commands so that we will be saved; and passages showing that we will all be judged according to our works. We would not have been commanded to do all this if we were incapable of doing good things under our own initiative on the Lord's behalf. After I said this, I gave them branches from a grapevine; in their hands, the branches suddenly produced grapes. The account contains more as well.

§462: I saw a magnificent harbor with large and small vessels. Boys and girls were sitting in them, waiting for *sea turtles,* which would rise up out of the sea. When the turtles emerged, I saw that they had two heads. Whenever they wanted to, they would retract one head into the shell that covered their body. The other head looked human; with it they spoke to the boys and girls. In exchange for the turtles' elegant words, the children would stroke them and give them gifts.

An angel explained the meaning of what I had seen. The turtles are [clergy] in the world (and therefore also the spirits of clergy after they die) who say that once we have acquired faith, God does not look at anything we think or anything we do; the only thing he cares about is the faith that lies hidden deep within our minds. In front of the congregations assembled in their churches, these clergy utter sacred teachings from the Word just as much as other clergy do, but they do so from the larger head, which looks human. They insert the smaller head into the larger head or else retract it into their body.

I later saw the same members of the clergy flying through the air in a boat with seven sails. They were wearing laurel wreaths and purple robes and were shouting that they are the wisest of all clergy. These visions were images of their pride, flowing forth from the pictures in their minds. When they were back on land, I argued with them first on the basis of reason and then on the basis of Sacred Scripture. I put forward many arguments to show that their teaching was insane and came from hell, as one can tell because it goes contrary to Sacred Scripture. (The arguments I used were too extensive to copy here; see the account itself.)

Afterward, I saw them in a sandy place in clothes made out of rags, with something like fishnets wrapped around their waists that still showed their nakedness. They were eventually sent down to a community near the Machiavellians.

§503: An assembly had been called for. It met in a round temple with altars along the walls. The participants were sitting at these altars. There was no leader there, so individuals would burst forth into the center of the room whenever they felt so inclined and proclaim their views. The topic of conversation concerned *free choice in spiritual matters.* The *first* person to burst into the center of the room said that people have no more free choice in spiritual matters than Lot's wife had when she was turned into a pillar of salt. A *second* said that people have no more free choice than an animal like a dog. A *third* said that people's free choice is no better than a mole's or a barn owl's eyesight in broad daylight. A *fourth* said that if people were to have free choice in spiritual matters, they would become raving lunatics and believe that they, like gods, could regenerate and save themselves. A *fifth* read quotations from the Lutheran book called the *Formula of Concord* to the effect that in spiritual matters human beings have no more free choice than a log or a stone and cannot understand, think, or will such things at all, or adapt or accommodate themselves to receive anything spiritual. (More such teachings from that book are given in §464.)

After these speakers had finished, I was given permission to speak. I said, "If we had no free choice in regard to spiritual matters, what would we be but brute animals? If there is no free choice, what is the point of any theological teachings?"

Their reply was this: "Read our theology. You will not find anything spiritual in it. The spiritual aspect lies so deeply hidden within it that not even its shadow appears. Read what our theology has to say about justification, that is, about the forgiving of sins, regeneration, sanctification, and salvation. You will not see anything spiritual there. What is spiritual flows in through faith without our being in the least bit aware of it." The speaker also indicated that goodwill was far removed from anything spiritual, and that repentance, too, was not within reach of anything spiritual. In regard to redemption, the speaker assigned merely human, earthly attributes to God: for example, that he locked the human race into universal damnation; but the Son took that damnation upon himself and appeased his Father. "What else was the Son's intercession and mediation with the Father if it was not that?" he asked. "Clearly then, there is nothing spiritual anywhere in our theology; there is not even anything rational. It is below what is spiritual and rational, and consists entirely of what is merely earthly." Suddenly they heard a thunderbolt crashing down from heaven. The participants were terrified; they rushed out and fled to their homes.

§504: I spoke with two spirits, one of whom loved goodness and truth, and the other of whom loved evil and falsity. I gathered that each of them had the same ability to think rationally. When the one who loved evil and falsity was left to himself, however, I saw a kind of smoke rise up from hell and extinguish the light that was above his memory. When the one who loved goodness and truth was left to himself, I saw a kind of gentle flame flow down from heaven and illuminate the region of his mind above the memory, as well as the region below it.

Afterward I had a conversation about *free choice in spiritual matters* with the one who loved evil and falsity. When I merely mentioned free choice he went into a rage. He proclaimed that none can move their hands or feet to do anything that is spiritually good; none can move their tongue or lips to say anything that is spiritually true. "Therefore we are not even able to adapt or accommodate ourselves to receive anything spiritual," he continued. "Surely we are all dead and merely passive in all such matters. How can something that is dead and merely passive do anything good or think anything true on its own? Is this not in accordance with what our church says?"

The other person, the one who loved goodness and truth, had this to say about free choice in spiritual matters: "If there is no spiritual free choice, what is the point of everything in the Word? What is the point of the church? What is the point of religion? What is the point in worshiping God? If there is no spiritual free choice, why have ministers? Because of the light in my intellect, I know that without spiritual freedom humans would be animals, not humans. It is that freedom that makes us human and not animals. For another thing, if there were no free choice in spiritual matters, we would not live on after death. There would be no eternal life, because we could have no partnership with God. Denying spiritual free choice, then, is something that could only be done by people who are spiritually insane."

Afterward we saw a flying serpent in a tree. It was offering a piece of fruit to the one who denied that we have free choice in spiritual matters. As he took the fruit and ate it, smoke rose up from hell and extinguished any light that existed in the higher part of his rational mind.

§505: I heard a loud scraping sound like two millstones grinding against each other. As I moved in the direction of the sound, I came to a building with many small compartments in it; it housed the great thinkers of recent times. They were finding support for justification by faith alone.

I went up to one compartment and asked the person there what he was studying now. He said, "I am studying the *act of justification,* which is the primary teaching in our Christianity." I asked whether he knew of any sign that indicates when that justifying faith has begun to enter us and when it has finished. He replied that faith enters us passively, not actively.

To that I said, "If you take away our ability to be active in respect to our faith, aren't you also taking away our ability to be receptive to it? Doesn't that make your 'activation of faith' something purely theoretical, a figment of the imagination? Isn't it no more than Lot's wife as a statue, pinging when touched with a scribe's quill or fingernail, because it consisted of nothing but salt?" He became very angry and grabbed a lamp to throw at me, but the lamp went out and he hit his companion instead.

§506: I saw two groups of animals: a herd of *goats* and a flock of *sheep*. When I saw them closer at hand, however, in place of the goats and sheep I saw people. I perceived that the herd of goats consisted of people who had made faith the only thing that saves us. The flock of sheep consisted of people who believed that goodwill together with faith [is what saves us]. When asked why they were there, the people who had looked like goats said they had convened a council because they had been told that Paul's statement in Romans 3:28 that "we are justified by faith apart from the works of the Law" had not been understood correctly. "Faith" in that passage, they were told, does not mean the faith of [the church of] today; it means faith in the Lord the Savior. The "works of the Law" do not mean the works of the law of the Ten Commandments; they mean the works of the Mosaic Law, which were rituals. Passages were included that show this. The members of the council said their conclusion was that faith produces good works the way a tree produces fruit. The members of the flock of sheep agreed with this last point.

Then an angel stood between the herd and the flock and told the sheep not to listen to the goats. "They have not left their former belief," the angel said, and divided the sheep into two flocks. To the sheep on the left, the angel said, "Go ahead and join the goats, but I'm telling you, a wolf is coming that is going to snatch them away, and you along with them." There was an investigation to find out what the goats meant when they said that faith produces good works the way a tree produces fruit. It was discovered that their actual understanding of the relationship between faith and goodwill was quite the opposite of what they had said; their statement was misleading.

Once both groups of sheep learned this, they reunited. Some of the goats even joined them, saying that goodwill is the essence of faith and that when faith is separated from goodwill it is only earthly, but when it is united to goodwill it becomes spiritual.

§507: A conversation with angels about the three types of love that are universal and therefore exist in every human being: *love for our neighbor, or love of being useful* (in its essence this love is related to the spirit); *love for the world, or a love of possessing wealth* (in its essence this love is related to matter); *and love for ourselves, or love of dominating other people* (in its essence this love is related to the body). When these three loves are prioritized in the right way within us, we become truly human. They are rightly prioritized when love for our neighbor plays the role of the head, love for the world plays the role of the torso, and love for ourselves plays the role of the legs and feet. Our condition is entirely different when these loves are situated in us in a way that goes against the divine design. There was a demonstration of what human beings are like when love for the world plays the role of the head, and what they are like when love for themselves plays the role of the head. Under either of these conditions, they are upside-down people. At the level of their inner minds, they are predatory animals; at the level of their outer minds and bodies, they are clowns.

Then we saw a devil rising up from below. He had a dusky face and a white ring around his head. He said he was Lucifer (although in actual fact he was not). He said he was inwardly a devil, but outwardly an angel of light. He related that when he is in his outer self, he is moral among the moral, rational among the rational, and spiritual among the spiritual. When he was in the world, he was a preacher; he would rail against evildoers of every kind. At that time he was called a son of the dawn [Isaiah 14:12]. He himself was amazed to note that when he was in the pulpit he had no awareness that he was not as he said he was. Yet he was completely different when he was no longer in church. He even told us why. It was because in church he was in his outer self and in his intellect alone; when he left church he was in his inner self and in his will. His intellect lifted him up into heaven; his will dragged him down into hell. But the will rules the intellect; it turns the intellect to favor and agree with what it wants. Afterward this devil, who passed himself off as Lucifer, sank down into hell.

§508: I saw a round[527] temple, whose roof was shaped like a crown. Its walls were continuous windows of crystal clear glass. Its door was made of a pearly substance. In it there was a large raised pulpit, on top of which lay the Word, surrounded by a sphere of light. In the middle of the temple there was a sanctuary, with a veil at the front of it, but the veil was now lifted. In the shrine stood an angel guardian [made out of gold] with a sword moving this way and that in its hand.

After I saw all this, the meaning of each detail was explained to me (see the account itself). Above the door there was an inscription: *Now It Is Allowed,* which means that we are now allowed to use our intellect to explore the mysteries of faith. It came to mind how extremely dangerous it is to use our intellect to explore any dogma of faith that was constructed by a self-serving mindset and therefore consists of falsities. It is even worse to use statements from the Word to support such dogmas. This is why the Word was taken away from Roman Catholics and why Protestants [were allowed to] close the Word by their widespread assertion that the intellect has to be held under obedience to their faith. The dogmas of the new church, however, are all from the Word. We are allowed to use our intellect to explore them, because they are continuous truths from the Word; in fact, they shine in the intellect. This is the meaning of the inscription *Now It Is Allowed* over the door, and the meaning of the fact that the sanctuary veil in front of the angel guardian was lifted up.

Then a young child (who was actually an angel in the third heaven) brought me a piece of paper. The writing on it said, *"From now on, explore the mysteries of the Word, which was formerly closed up. All of its individual truths are mirrors that reflect the Lord."*

§567: I was suddenly overcome with a deadly illness from smoke that was blowing in from the Jerusalem that is called Sodom and Egypt (Revelation 11:8). To people in that city I looked as though I actually was dead. They said to each other that I was not worthy of burial, much like what happened to the two witnesses in that same chapter of the Book of Revelation. Meanwhile I was hearing abundant blasphemies from the city-dwellers because I had been preaching repentance and faith in the Lord Jesus Christ. A judgment on them began. I saw the whole city sink down to a lower level and become flooded with water. Afterward I saw them running between piles of stones and loudly bemoaning what had happened to them even though, according to the faith of their church, they believed they had been reborn and had become just. They were told, however, that they were nothing of the kind, because they had never practiced any kind of repentance and therefore did not know of a single damnable evil in themselves. Then a voice from heaven told them that faith in the Lord and repentance are the two means of being regenerated and saved; the whole Word, the Ten Commandments, and the sacraments of baptism and the Holy Supper all make this abundantly clear. For details, see the account itself.

§568: All people come into the spiritual world after death and are at first kept outwardly in the state they had been in during their lives in the world. Because most people in this outward state live moral lives and go to church and pray to God, they believe they are definitely bound for heaven. For this reason they are taught that after we die, we all gradually put off that *outer self,* and our *inner self* is opened up. Then we come to know what we are truly like inside. After all, what makes us human is not only our action and our speech but our will and our intellect. This is what allows us to appear outwardly as a sheep when we are inwardly a wolf. A wolf is in fact what our inner self is like if we have not examined the evils we have willed and intended, and have not practiced repentance from those evils. And so on.

§569: Every type of love exudes a delight, but in the physical world *these delights that come from what we love* are not often detectable with our senses. In the spiritual world, however, they are very plainly sensed; in fact, they sometimes turn into odors. Then the quality of those delights and the nature of the love they come from is easily perceptible. The delights that come from loving what is good—the types of delight found in the heavens—come across as the fragrances that belong to vegetable gardens and flower gardens. On the other hand, the delights that come from loving what is evil—the types of delight found in the hells—come across as the foul odors and stenches given off by outhouses and [fetid] ponds. Because the two kinds of delight are opposites, devils are tormented when they smell some sweet aroma coming from heaven, and angels are tormented when they smell some reeking stench from hell. The account uses two of my own experiences to lend support to this point. This is why the oil for anointing was prepared with fragrant spices, and why we read [in the Word] that Jehovah smelled a pleasing aroma from burnt offerings. On the other hand, this is also why the children of Israel were commanded to carry unclean things from the camp outside its borders and to dig a hole for their fecal matter. Their camp represented heaven and the desert outside the camp represented hell.

§570: A recently arrived spirit who, during his life in the world, had meditated a great deal on heaven and hell, desired to know how the one and the other are experienced. A message for him from heaven said, *"Investigate what delight is, and you will know."* He went off on his investigation, but asking spirits who were merely earthly yielded pointless answers. Then he was taken to three groups in sequence. One group investigates purposes; its members are called Wisdoms. The second group surveys means; its members are called Intelligences. The third group conducts research on results; its members are called Knowledges. The recently arrived spirit was taught by these three groups that no angel, no spirit, and no human being would have any life if they did not experience delight from some love. In the absence of delight coming from some love, the will cannot take a single step, and neither can the thought process. What anyone calls good is what that person loves and takes delight in. The delight of heaven is delight in doing good; the delight of hell is delight in doing evil.

As further instruction for the newly arrived spirit and not by mere coincidence, a devil rose up and described for him the delights of hell. They were delights in taking revenge, whoring, stealing, and blaspheming. When those delights are sensed as odors [by those] in hell, they are experienced as intoxicating scents; therefore this devil referred to them as the delights of their nostrils.

§621: I saw a group of spirits praying to God to send angels who could teach them about various points of faith. In many areas they were feeling unsure, because the churches disagree with each other and yet all the ministers say, "Believe us! We are ministers of God—we know these things." Angels did appear to them, so the spirits asked them about *goodwill and faith, repentance, regeneration, God, the immortality of the soul,* and *baptism and the Holy Supper.* On each topic the angels gave answers that were understandable to the spirits. The angels added that an incomprehensible teaching is like a seed sown in sand; no matter how much rain falls on it, it still shrivels up. The angels also said that if people close their intellect for religious reasons, they no longer see anything in the Word in the light that the Lord provides there; in fact, the more they read the Word, the blinder they become regarding its teachings on faith and salvation.

§622: *How we come into heaven after we have been prepared for it:* After preparation, we see a pathway to a community in heaven where we will live forever. We take that pathway. At the outskirts of the community there is a gate, which is opened for us. Once we are inside, there is an investigation to see if our light and heat (meaning our truth and goodness) is the same as the light and heat of the angels of that community. Once that is established, we look around to find out where our home is. For every new angel there is a new home. Once we find our home, we are accepted and counted as one of them. If we have no light and heat (meaning no truth or goodness of heaven) within us, though, it is a very hard experience for us to be there. When we enter that community we are miserably tormented. Because we feel tortured we throw ourselves down from there headfirst. We feel such torment in that case because the sphere of light and heat in heaven is the opposite of our own light and heat. After that, we no longer long for heaven; instead we associate with people like ourselves in hell.

All this shows the pointlessness of thinking that going to heaven is just a matter of being let in as a result of grace, and that once we are let in we too will experience joys there, as people on earth do when they are allowed into a home where a wedding is taking place.

§623: Many people who believed that *going to heaven is just a matter of being let in by grace,* and that once they were there they would experience heavenly joy, were granted permission to go up into heaven. They were not able, however, to stand the light and the heat there, that is, the faith and the love; therefore they threw themselves down from there headfirst. As they were falling, they looked like dead horses to people who were standing below.

Among the people standing below and seeing them that way were some children and their teacher. The teacher taught the children what the vision of dead horses meant, and also what sort of people would appear that way from a distance: they were people whose reading of the Word entails thoughts of God, their neighbor, and heaven that are physical rather than spiritual in nature. It is materialistic thinking to judge God's essence on the basis of how he is portrayed, to judge our neighbors' quality on the basis of how they look and sound, and to judge heaven's state of love on the basis of its location. It is spiritual thinking, on the other hand, to judge God primarily by his essence and only secondarily by how he is portrayed; to judge our neighbors primarily by their quality and only secondarily by how they look and sound; and to judge heaven primarily as a state of love and only secondarily as a location.

Afterward the teacher told the students that a *horse* means a person's understanding of the Word. When people have spiritual thoughts as they read the Word, it is a living text to them. Therefore from a distance they look like living horses. When people have materialistic thoughts as they read the Word, it is a dead text to them. Therefore from a distance they look like dead horses.

§624: I saw an angel with a piece of paper in his hand. On it were written the words *The Marriage of Goodness and Truth.* The angel descended from heaven into the world. I saw that in heaven the piece of paper shone, but bit by bit as the angel descended, the paper shone less and less. Eventually both the piece of paper and the angel became invisible to all but some uneducated people who were simple at heart. The angel explained to these people what the marriage of goodness and truth involves: each and every thing in the whole heaven and each and every thing in the whole world contains both together, because goodness and truth are united in the Lord God the Creator. Therefore nowhere does there exist anything that consists solely of goodness or solely of truth. In absolutely everything there is a marriage of goodness and truth. In the church there is a marriage of goodwill and faith, because goodwill relates to goodness and faith relates to truth.

§625: When I was thinking deeply about the Lord's Second Coming, I saw heaven full of light from east to west and heard angels *glorifying and celebrating the Lord using passages from the Word*—both from portions of the Old Testament written by the prophets and portions of the New Testament written by the apostles. For the actual passages from the Word that were used in this glorification, see the account itself.

§661: In the northeastern region there are *places of instruction.* People who take to heart the instruction offered there are called disciples of the Lord.

On one occasion when I was in the spirit, I asked teachers there whether they knew what the universal characteristics of heaven are and what the universal characteristics of hell are. They replied that the universal characteristics of heaven are three loves: a love of being useful; a love for possessing worldly wealth that comes from loving to do useful things with it; and true marriage love. The universal characteristics of hell are three loves that are the opposite of the three heavenly loves: a love for power that comes from loving ourselves; a love for possessing other people's wealth that comes from loving the world; and promiscuous love.

The account continues with a description of the *first hellish love, which is love for power that comes from loving ourselves.* The more the reins on this love are let out, the more laypeople with this love want to rule the world; clergy with this love, though, want to rule heaven. Having contact with people like this in hell confirmed for me that people who are caught up in this type of love experience fantasies. In hell, people like this are together in a particular valley. Their minds' highest delight is to imagine that they are emperors of emperors and kings of kings. People in another community there believe themselves to be gods. I witnessed the fact that when people from the first community see people from the second, they are so overcome that they fall on their knees and worship them.

Afterward I spoke with two angels, one of whom was the leader of a community in heaven, and the other was the highest ranking priest in that community. They told me that there are magnificent, gleaming things in their community; these things have their origin in the primary love felt by the people there, which is love of being useful rather than love for themselves. These leaders are inundated with honors, but they accept them not for their own sake but for the benefit to the authority of their office.

I then asked them how people can know whether it is loving themselves or loving the world or loving being useful that motivates their useful activities, since all three motivations make people useful. "Imagine a community," I said, "consisting of nothing but satans and another community consisting of nothing but angels. I would bet that the satans, driven by love for themselves and love for the world, are going to do just as many useful things for their community as the angels are going to do for theirs. Who can tell, then, what love inspires our useful actions?" The leader and the priest replied that satans do useful things in order to benefit their own reputations, to be raised to positions of honor, or to gain wealth. Angels, however, do useful things because they are useful. The main distinction between the satans and the angels is that all who believe in the Lord and abstain from evils because they are sins do useful things in response to the Lord, and therefore do what they do because they love being useful. All who do not believe in the Lord and do not abstain from evils because they are sins do useful things in response to themselves and for their own sake. They do what they do out of love for themselves or love for the world.

§662: I went into a grove of trees and saw two angels talking to each other. I joined them. They were talking about what it is *to crave all the wealth in the world.* They said that many people who seem moral from the point of view of their actions and rational from the point of view of their conversation are actually devoted to that insane craving for wealth. When people indulge themselves in thoughts related to that craving, the craving takes the form of fantasies.

Because all who are in the spiritual world are allowed to indulge their fantasies, provided they do no evil to others, there are gatherings in the lower earth for people with similar fantasies. The location of these gatherings is widely known, so we went down and joined a group of people with this craving. We saw them sitting at tables on which there were massive piles of gold coins. They told us it was all the money in the nation. It was in fact, though, only a vision they created through their imagination—a fantasy. When we said they were insane, they stepped away from their tables and confessed that what we had said was true; but because that visualizing was tremendously pleasurable to them, they could not help going back to it from time to time and indulging in it again; it was extremely enticing to their senses. They added that if any of them sneak off with another's belongings or do evil to another, the perpetrators fall into a prison farther below and have to work to get food, clothing, and a few small coins. If they do evil there, they are punished and their coins are taken away.

§663: I was listening to an argument between an ambassador and two priests concerning *whether intelligence and wisdom, and therefore also prudence, come from God or from ourselves.* The ambassador was adamant that they come from ourselves; the priests were arguing that they come from God. Some angels perceived, however, that the priests inwardly had the same beliefs as the ambassador—that intelligence and wisdom and therefore prudence come from ourselves. To make this clear, the angels asked the ambassador to take off his official robes and put on priestly vestments instead. When he did so, the ambassador put forward a series of arguments to show that all intelligence and prudence come from God. Then the priests were asked to take off their vestments and put on the robes of political office. Once they had done so, the priests spoke from their inner selves and said that all intelligence and prudence come from ourselves. The reason they made these statements was that spirits think they actually are whatever they are dressed to look like. After this exchange, the three became friends at heart and talked together as they traveled along a descending path. A bit later I saw them coming back, however.

§664: The account treats first of the people whom the Word refers to as *the elect*. They are people who are discovered after death to have lived a life of goodwill and faith. They are separated from people who had not lived that life. In that sense they are *chosen* and prepared for heaven. [The truth is that] all are called; therefore to believe that only some but not all are specially chosen and predestined for heaven (either before birth or after it) is to accuse God of being unable to save and also of being unjust.

§§665–666: A newly arrived spirit told people in heaven that no one in Christianity knows what *conscience* is. Because angels could not believe that, they told some spirit to sound a trumpet and gather intelligent people so he could assess whether people know what conscience is. This was done. Among the people who came were politicians, scholars, physicians, and clergy.

The *politicians* were the first to be asked what conscience is. Their response was that it is a pain that arises from fear (either before or after the fact) of losing honor or wealth, or that it is the result of a melancholy humor caused by undigested food in the stomach, and so on.

Then the *scholars* were questioned to find out what they knew about conscience. Their response was that it is grief or anxiety that either moves from the body into the head or from the head into the body. It has various causes; it especially arises when people focus their minds on just one single issue. This is prone to happen when people's dominant love suffers a loss, leading sometimes to fantasies or madness. In some, it takes the form of disturbances of the brain in regard to religious issues, which people call an attack of conscience.

Next the *physicians* were asked what conscience is. They said that it is just a pain that arises from a number of pathological conditions, which they enumerated at great length. Many cases have responded well to drugs. (For the list of diseases thought to cause the pains that are called pangs of conscience, see the account itself.)

Finally the *priests* were asked what conscience is. They said it is the same as the feeling of contrition that precedes faith. They have found the gospel works to cure these attacks. They added that conscientious adherents in all religions, both the true and the fanatical, become scrupulous about salvation, even in issues that actually make no difference at all.

When the angels had heard all this, they could see that it was true—no one knows what conscience is. Therefore they sent down an angel from their community to teach the people. This angel stood in the middle of them and said, "Conscience is not some pain, as you all suppose. It is a life according to religious principles. This kind of life is practiced especially by people who are devoted both to faith and to goodwill. People who have a conscience say what they say from the heart and do what they do from the heart." (The angel gave several examples.) "Therefore when we say, 'That person has a conscience,' we mean, 'That person is just.' And the reverse."

Upon hearing this, the participants fell into four groups. One group understood what the angel said and agreed with it. A second group did not fully comprehend it, but still felt favorable. A third group were unwilling to comprehend; they said, "What does conscience have to do with us?" A fourth group mocked the whole idea; they said, "Conscience is just gas pain!" The last two groups then went off to the left, but the first two groups went off to the right.

§692: I was taken to a place where ancient Greek philosophers live. They call that place New Parnassus. I was told that now and then they send out delegates to summon some new arrivals from the world and find out from them what quality of wisdom exists on earth today. The delegates had recently come across two newcomers from the Christian world and had brought them to New Parnassus.

Shortly after arriving there the newcomers were asked, *"What are the latest developments on earth [in regard to wisdom]?"*

They replied, "One new development is that people have been found in the woods. Perhaps they were lost there in early childhood. Their faces look human, but they were not actually human. As a result, people in the world have concluded that human beings are nothing more than animals; the only major difference is that humans can articulate sounds and speak. Animals could be just as wise as humans if they were given the ability to articulate sounds." And so on.

Based on this information the philosophers were able to determine what changes wisdom had undergone since their own times [on earth]. Especially telling to them was the fact that people no longer recognize the fundamental distinction between humans and animals, and do not realize that people are born with no more than the form of a human being. Through instruction they become human, and their degree of humanness depends on how receptive they are to that instruction. Truths lead us into wisdom; falsities lead us into insanity. Our doing evil turns us into predatory animals inside. All we have at birth is a faculty for knowing, understanding, and becoming wise. The purpose of our being born this way is that it allows us to be something[528] to which God can impart more and more wisdom, from the first steps of it to the highest heights.

The philosophers added something they had come to understand from the newcomers' report: wisdom, which had been in the east when they were alive on earth, was now in the west. Afterward they taught the newcomers how it is that human beings, who have been created in the form of God, could be turned upside-down into the form of a devil. For details, see the account itself.

§693: Another gathering was announced in the place where the ancient philosophers live. The reason for it was that their emissaries had come across three new arrivals from the world. The first was a priest, the second was a politician, and the third was a philosopher.

Once they were brought there, the new arrivals were asked, "*What are the latest developments on earth [in regard to wisdom]?*"

"This is new," they replied: They had heard that someone on earth says he speaks with angels and spirits; that person has related many things about the state angels and spirits are in. Some of what he says is as follows: Human beings are just as human after death. The only difference is that after death we are clothed with a spiritual body, whereas before death we are in a physical body.

The philosophers then asked the *priest* what he had thought of those teachings while he was still on earth. His reply was that he had believed we would not live again as human beings until the day of the Last Judgment. Therefore he and his colleagues in the ministry thought of those teachings first as visions, then as something made up; eventually they did not know what to think of them. The ancient philosophers asked the priest whether people on earth had the rational capacity to see that human beings are still human after death, which would allow them to dismiss absurd notions of how souls spend their time—for example, the idea that souls flit around in the universe like breezes, or that they are constantly waiting for the Last Judgment to occur so that they can be reunited with their bodies. (In that case, our fate would be worse than any animal's.) The priest replied that some may make those arguments, but they fail to convince others. People see the coming together or reuniting of souls with their corpses and skeletons in the grave as something achieved by the omnipotence of God. And as soon as people mention omnipotence and faith, reason goes out the window.

Next, the ancient philosophers asked the *politician* what he thought about the new teachings just mentioned. His answer was that in the world he had been unable to believe that human beings are going to live on as humans after death, since everything that makes us human lies dead in the grave. He believed that the person presenting these new teachings was seeing ghosts but mistaking them for angels and spirits. The politician added, however, that he was now for the first time convinced by his own senses that he is just as human as he was before. Consequently he is ashamed of his former point of view.

The newly arrived *philosopher* said that he, too, had had much the same point of view, and so had other members of his school. The things that that writer had heard and seen, the philosopher labeled as just another opinion and hypothesis, like all the others he had gathered from other writers old and new.

The ancient philosophers were staggered to hear this. They were especially struck that Christians, whose revelation should give them more light than others have, are in such thick darkness concerning their own life after death. They said, "[While we were still alive in the physical world,] we knew about life after death and believed in it, and so did the sages of our day." They added their observation that the light of wisdom that had been in the inner parts of the brain during their times on earth had now moved down below the nose to the mouth. There it appears to others like gleaming lips, and the speech of the mouth seems like wisdom.

Then one of the recruits at the event said, "How stupid the minds of earth-dwellers have become! I wish the followers of Democritus, who laugh at everything, and the followers of Heraclitus, who cry at everything, were here; what a lot of laughing and crying we would hear then!" The new arrivals were then given gifts of copper plates with hieroglyphics inscribed on them, and they departed.

§694: Some new arrivals from the world were discovered, brought to the city below New Parnassus, and asked, "*What are the latest developments on earth [in regard to wisdom]?*" They replied that in the world they had believed there would be complete rest from labors after death. Yet when they arrived in the spiritual world they were told that there are similar administrative positions, functions, and types of work as there are in the world. This means that it is not a rest.

Wise people who were in attendance said, "Did you really believe that at this stage you were going to live in complete idleness, even though idleness causes both mental and physical lethargy, inertia, unresponsiveness, and loss of consciousness? These are death, not life."

The new arrivals were taken around the city and saw administrators and artists at work. The newcomers were amazed at what they saw, because they had believed their souls would be living in some void until the new heaven and the new earth came about. They were taught that everything they were seeing was substantial and was called spiritual, whereas everything in their former world was material and was called earthly. Then they were told that this distinction exists because the two have different origins. Everything in the spiritual world takes shape from and is sustained by a sun that is pure love, whereas everything in the physical world takes shape from and is sustained by a sun that is pure fire. They were also taught that in the spiritual world there are not just administrative positions; there is also research of all kinds and also writing and books.

The newcomers were overjoyed to learn all this. As they were leaving, some young women came with pieces of needlework and embroidery of their own making and gave them to the visitors. They also sang the newcomers a song, whose angelic melody expressed their love for useful activity and the pleasure it brings.

§695: I was brought to a meeting that was attended by some ancient philosophers. I was asked what people in my world know about *inflow*. My answer was this: The only inflow they know about is the inflow of their sun's heat and light into the objects in nature, both living and inanimate. They have no idea there is such a thing as an inflow from the spiritual world into the physical world, even though that inflow is what actually causes all the amazing things they see in the animal kingdom and the plant kingdom. (I listed some examples.) Because they do not recognize the existence of this inflow, they convince themselves that nature is the source. They become materialists and eventually atheists.

§696: I spoke with followers of Aristotle, Descartes, and Leibniz about [their theories called] *physical inflow, occasional inflow,* and *preestablished harmony* and heard the arguments they used to support their own hypothesis. Because they were limited to the supporting arguments and were unable to rise above them and examine the issue with their intellect, they decided to draw lots in order to see which theory was correct. Spiritual inflow was the answer they drew, which is closer to occasional inflow than to the other theories.

§697: I was led to a hall where young adults were being initiated into various issues related to wisdom. This was accomplished through a discussion of a topic proposed by a leader there. On that occasion the topic for discussion was, *What is the soul and how do we experience it?* There was a lectern. The respondents would stand at it to give their answers.

The *first* speaker stood up and said that no one since the world was created has been able to determine what the soul is and how we experience it. Because people have known, however, that there is a soul inside us, they have pondered where it is. Some thinkers conjectured that it is in the pineal gland, which sits between the cerebrum and the cerebellum in our heads. The speaker said he had originally espoused this view, but when many later rejected it, he too had moved away from that opinion.

The *second* speaker stood up and said he believed the seat of the soul was in the head, since that is where the intellect is; but because he was unsure, at different times he followed different authorities with regard to where it is in the brain—those who believe it is in the three ventricles of the brain, those who say the striated body, those the medullary, those the cortical substances, and those the dura mater. He left it up to the individual to decide.

The *third* speaker stood up and said that the seat of the soul is in the heart and extends to the blood. He supported this view with passages from the Word that mention the heart and the soul.

The *fourth* speaker stood up and said that since childhood he had sided with the ancients in believing that the soul is not in one part of the body, but is throughout it, because it is a spiritual substance, which can be said to fill the body but cannot be said to occupy this or that place within it. He added that "soul" means life, and life is present throughout the body.

The *fifth* speaker stood up and said that in his view the soul was something pure that could be compared to ether or air. This was his belief because people think the soul will be something like this after it leaves the body.

When the speakers had finished, the wise people in the balcony concluded that none of the speakers knew what the soul is. Therefore they asked the leader, who had proposed the question, to come down and teach. After coming down [from his platform], he said that the soul is the essence itself within a human being. And because an essence is nothing without a form, the soul is the purest human form. It is the truly human form; in every part of it wisdom and love dwell together, along with all their perceptions and desires. "When you were in the physical world," he said, "you believed that you would be souls after death. [You have in fact died]; therefore you yourselves are now souls." And so on. His statement was supported by the following passage in the Book of Creation (Genesis 2:7): "Jehovah God breathed *the breath of lives* into Adam's nostrils, and the human being turned into a *living soul.*"

§§731–752: I saw an angel with a trumpet. With it he called together the most celebrated Christian thinkers. The topic was what they had believed in the world about the *joys of heaven and eternal happiness.* The reason for the event was that someone had told people in heaven that no one in Christianity knows anything about these joys and this happiness. About half an hour later we saw six groups of well-educated Christians arrive. When the question was posed to them regarding what they had known about the joys of heaven and eternal happiness, the *first group* said that they believed it was simply a matter of being allowed into heaven and all its accompanying celebratory joys, as if they were merely being allowed into a home where a wedding and its accompanying festivities were taking place. The *second group* said they believed that that joy and happiness consists in extremely enjoyable interactions and delicious conversations with angels. The *third group* said they believed that that joy and happiness consists in dining with Abraham, Isaac, and Jacob. The *fourth group* said they believed that that joy and happiness consists in the delight of a garden paradise. The *fifth group* said they believed that that joy and happiness consists in the possession of great power, tremendous wealth, and more-than-regal magnificence. The *sixth group* said they believed that that joy and happiness consists in glorifying God in a celebration that goes on forever. So that these well-educated thinkers could find out whether the things they mentioned truly were the joys of heaven, they had an opportunity to experience their joys. Each group had this experience separately. The purpose was for them to learn by living experience whether they had merely imagined these activities would be joyful or whether these activities actually were joyful. Most people go through this when they cross over from the physical world to the spiritual world (§§731, 732, 733).

Soon afterward, the group that thought heavenly joy would take the form of extremely enjoyable interactions and delicious conversations with angels was allowed to experience what it imagined to be joy. Because these were external joys, however, and were not internal, the enjoyment wore off after a few days and they left (§734).

Then the group that believed heavenly joys would consist in dining with Abraham, Isaac, and Jacob were allowed to have that experience. They, too, came to feel that those joys were only external and not internal, and became tired of them and left (§735).

A similar thing happened to the group that believed heavenly joy and eternal happiness consisted in great power, tremendous wealth, and more-than-regal magnificence (§736).

A similar thing also happened to the group that believed heavenly joy and eternal happiness consisted in the joys of a garden paradise (§737).

A similar thing also happened to the group that believed heavenly joy and eternal happiness consisted in perpetually glorifying God in a celebration that goes on forever. Eventually this group was taught what *glorifying God* truly means in the Word (§738).

Finally, a similar thing also happened to the group that believed they would come into heavenly joy and happiness if they were simply allowed into heaven, and that the joys they would experience there would be much like those we experience when we go into a home where a wedding is occurring and take part in its festivities. They were shown by living experience, however, that the only people who experience joys in heaven are people who have lived the life of heaven—that is, a life of goodwill and faith. For people who have lived the opposite kind of life, heaven is actually a place of torment. Therefore people like this leave heaven and associate with others like themselves (§739).

Since the angels had gathered from this that no one in the physical world nowadays knows what the joys of heaven are like and what eternal happiness is like, they instructed the angel with the trumpet to choose ten of the participants and bring them to a community in heaven. In this way they could see with their own eyes and perceive in their own minds what heaven is and what the joys there are like. The angel did so. After the ten were brought in, they started with a tour of the magnificent palace of the leader of that community (§740). Then they toured the gardens next to the palace (§741). Afterward they saw the leader himself and his dignitaries in all their finery (§742). Invited to dine with the leader, they saw a table setting with amazing accoutrements unlike anything that eyes on earth have ever seen. At the table the leader taught them about heavenly joys and eternal happiness. He said that in essence these consist of inner bliss, which leads in turn to outward delight. The very essence of inner bliss is a desire to be of use (§§743, 744). After dinner, the leader ordered some of the wisest members of the community to be summoned. These people talked with the visitors at length about what exactly the inner bliss that constitutes eternal happiness is, where it comes from, how it turns external delights into joys, and so on (§§745–746). After that the ten had the opportunity to see a wedding in that heaven, which is described (§§747–749); and lastly, to hear preaching (§§750–751). Having seen and heard all this, being full of newfound knowledge of heaven, and feeling happy at heart, the ten went back down (§752).

§§846–851: This account deals with *this revelation*. The Lord chose to manifest himself to me and open the inner levels of my mind, allowing me to see what is in heaven and what is in hell. By so doing, he revealed secrets that are of greater excellence and importance than any other secrets that have been disclosed before. They are as follows: (1) In each and every detail of the Word there is a *spiritual meaning,* which is not apparent in its literal meaning. Therefore the writing in the Word consists of correspondences between spiritual things and earthly things. (2) What those *correspondences* are like has been made clear. (3) *Human beings live on after they die.* (4) What *heaven* and *hell* are like. Also teachings regarding *baptism* and *the Holy Supper.* (5) There is a *sun* in the spiritual world that is pure love from the Lord, who is surrounded by that sun. The light that emanates from that sun is wisdom and the heat that emanates from it is love. It is also the source of faith and goodwill. All things that emanate from that sun are spiritual and alive. The sun of the physical world, on the other hand, is pure fire. All things that emanate from this sun are earthly and dead. (6) There are three levels [of life]. They have been unknown until now. (7) There is information about the *Last Judgment. The Lord the Savior is the God of heaven and earth.* There is information about the *new church* and its *teachings;* about *the inhabitants of other planets* and about *the worlds in the universe* (§846). (8) There is also information about *marriage love.* This love is spiritual among spiritual people, earthly among earthly people, and merely carnal among adulterous people (§847). Angels learned through eyewitness experience that although these secrets are more excellent than any other secrets disclosed before, many today think of them as having no value at all (§848).[529] I heard some people in the lower earth murmuring that if

I performed *miracles,* they would believe [what I had written]. I replied that they would not be convinced by miracles any more than Pharaoh and the Egyptians were, or any more than Jacob's descendants were when they danced around the golden calf in the wilderness, or any more than Jews were when they saw miracles performed by the Lord himself (§849). Finally, why the Lord revealed these secrets to me instead of to someone in the clergy (§850).

The things that are in the accounts of *memorable occurrences* that come after the chapters are true. Before the Lord's Coming, similar things were seen and heard by the prophets; after the Lord's Coming, similar things were seen and heard by the apostles—Peter, Paul, and especially John in the Book of Revelation. The account lists examples (§851).

A Proposition Put Forward by a Certain Duke-Elector in Germany, Who Had Also Held the Highest Ecclesiastical Office in His Province

On one occasion I saw in the spiritual world a certain duke-elector in Germany who had also held the highest position among the church leaders in his province.[530] Next to him there were two bishops and two ministers. From a distance I heard what they were saying to each other. The duke-elector was asking the other four whether they knew what constitutes the theological pinnacle of Christianity.

[852]

The bishops replied, "The theological pinnacle of Christianity is the teaching *that faith alone justifies and saves.*"

The duke-elector then asked them a further question: "Do you know what lies inwardly hidden in that faith? Remove the lid from it, look inside, and tell me what you see."

"The only thing that lies hidden inside it," they said, "is *the merit and justice of the Lord our Savior.*"

"Isn't it true, then," the duke-elector said, "that what lies hidden inside it is the Lord our Savior in his human manifestation, whose name is *Jesus Christ?* In his human manifestation he alone was Justice."

"Yes, this clearly and definitely follows," they said.

The duke-elector pressed on by saying, "Open up that faith and look inside it further and search well to see whether there is anything else in there."

The ministers said, "*The grace of God the Father* also lies hidden within it."

The duke-elector said, "If your conception and perception is accurate, you will see *that it is the grace of the Son with the Father.* It is the Son who petitions and intercedes.

"Therefore I say to you, since you confess, venerate, and embrace that *faith alone* of yours, you must in every way confess, venerate, and embrace *the Lord alone*—the Lord our Savior in his human manifestation.

"As we noted before, in his human manifestation the Lord himself was and is *Justice.* In the following passages from the sacred pages I observe that in his human manifestation he himself is also *Jehovah* and *God:* 'Behold, the days are coming when I will raise up for David a righteous offshoot who will reign as king and will prosper. And they will call him by this name: *Jehovah is our Justice'* (Jeremiah 33:15, 16). In Paul, '*All the fullness of divinity* dwells physically in Jesus Christ' (Colossians 2:9). In John, 'Jesus Christ is *the true God* and eternal life' (1 John 5:20). Therefore he is also called '*the God of faith'* (Philippians 3:9)."[531]

Notes & Indexes

Notes

Notes to Chapter 8, §§463–508

1 (in §463). Swedenborg uses the term "church" (Latin *ecclesia*) in several different ways; see volume 1, pages 675–676 note 3. Here he is using it historically to mean the core religious approach of a given age or era through which heaven was connected with humankind, of which he asserts there have been five major instances, in the following sequence: the earliest (or "most ancient") church, the early (or "ancient") church, the Jewish church, the Christian church, and the "new church," whose teachings are presented in this and his other theological works. [KK, JSR]

2 (in §463). "The Word" here means the Bible. For further discussion of the term as Swedenborg uses it, see volume 1, page 679 note 17. [JSR]

3 (in §463). The phrase "new creatures" here is a biblical allusion. In §687:1 below Swedenborg points out the scriptural derivation of the noun "creature" (Latin *creatura*) from the verb "to be created" (Latin *creari*), and cites Mark 16:15; Romans 8:19–21; 2 Corinthians 5:17; Galatians 6:15, some or all of which he may have in mind here. [Editors]

4 (in §463). Throughout *True Christianity,* following a practice of his times, Swedenborg uses the term *Formula of Concord* to refer to the authoritative compilation of Lutheran doctrinal statements, originally titled *Concordia Pia* (see *Concordia* 1756), and now known as the *Book of Concord* (see Kolb and Wengert 2000). Swedenborg's use of the title *Formula of Concord* may cause some confusion, since the "Formula of Concord" is one of the doctrinal statements contained in the *Book of Concord* as a whole (see Kolb and Wengert 2000, 486–660). For more on the *Book of Concord* and Swedenborg's use of it, see the introduction to volume 1, pages 84–85; and pages 717–718 note 258, also in volume 1. [JSR]

5 (in §463). "Reformed" here means Calvinist. The mention of "religious treatises" probably refers to a work by John Calvin (1509–1564), the *Institutes of the Christian Religion* (= Calvin 1960), which was a foundational document for the Protestant Reformation. For Calvin's arguments concerning free choice, see *Institutes* 2:2:2–4. [JSR]

6 (in §464:1). The Augsburg Confession (1530) was the earliest and most important of the Lutheran statements of faith; as such it was given a prominent place in the *Book of Concord* (= *Concordia* 1580). See Kolb and Wengert 2000, 30–105. [RGE, JSR]

7 (in §464:1). The term "first parents" here refers to Adam and Eve; see Genesis 2–3. [Editors]

8 (in §464:1). The page numbers given parenthetically by Swedenborg in this section refer to the 1756 Leipzig edition of the *Book of Concord* or to its lengthy appendix, which was created by the volume's editor, Adam Rechenberg (1642–1721); see *Concordia* 1756. (Swedenborg cites page numbers alone without numbered paragraph divisions because in the 1700s those divisions had not yet been made; they were first introduced in the edition of 1827 by Karl August von Hase [1800–1890]: see *Libri* 1827.) Where

possible, the present edition gives parallel page-and-paragraph-number references from Kolb and Wengert 2000; Rechenberg's appendix, however, is not included in that or any other recent English translation of the *Book of Concord*. In the case of this particular page, the parallel reference in Kolb and Wengert 2000 is 544.5. Readers should be warned that Swedenborg is no more exacting in his quoting of the *Book of Concord* than in his quoting of the Bible; see pages 13–14. [JSR]

9 (in §464:2). The parallel in the modern edition of Kolb and Wengert 2000 is found at 544.6–7. [Editors]

10 (in §464:3). The likening of people's spiritual state to a log or a stone recalls Jeremiah 2:27, which rebukes Israel for turning its back and not its face to God, and for claiming instead a tree as its father and a stone as its mother. In Genesis 19:15–26, Lot's wife similarly disobeys God, turning her face to look back toward the burning city instead of forward, and becoming thereby a pillar of salt. [KK]

11 (in §464:3). The parallel in the modern edition of Kolb and Wengert 2000 is found at 547.20–548.20. [Editors]

12 (in §464:4). The parallel in the modern edition of Kolb and Wengert 2000 is found at 549.24. [Editors]

13 (in §464:5). The parallels in the modern edition of Kolb and Wengert 2000 are found at 555.59 and 555.61–556.62. [Editors]

14 (in §464:6). The parallel in the modern edition of Kolb and Wengert 2000 is found at 561.89. [Editors]

15 (in §464:7). "Church fathers" is a traditional collective term for the most prominent theologians, teachers, and ecclesiastical leaders of the first centuries of Christianity. The phrase "God draws, but he draws the willing" is attributed to John Chrysostom (around 347–407); see Chrysostom 1843, 56. [JSR]

16 (in §464:7). The Latin phrase here translated "sacred words" is the reading found in Swedenborg's first edition: *Sacrorum verborum*. Although it is presented as part of a quotation, this reading differs slightly from the words used in *Concordia* 1756, 582: *sanorum verborum*, literally, "sound words," presumably meaning "sound teachings." [JSR]

17 (in §464:7). The parallel in the modern edition of Kolb and Wengert 2000 is found at 493.16–494.16. [JSR]

18 (in §464:8). On this hereditary "disease," see subsection 10 immediately below, where it is clear that original sin is meant. [Editors]

19 (in §464:8). The parallel in the modern edition of Kolb and Wengert 2000 is found at 534.12. [Editors]

20 (in §464:9). In the modern edition of Kolb and Wengert 2000 the parallel for *Concordia* 1756, 219, is found at 234.6–235.10; for *Concordia* 1756, 579 and following, at 492.4–494.19; for *Concordia* 1756, 663 and following, at 548.21–549.26. The appendix to *Concordia* 1756 (see note 8) is not included in recent English translations, and so no modern parallel for that reference is provided here. [Editors]

21 (in §464:9). The parallel in the modern edition of Kolb and Wengert 2000 is found at 556.65–557.66. [Editors]

22 (in §464:10). The parallel in the modern edition of Kolb and Wengert 2000 is found at 490.21. [Editors]

23 (in §464:10). The parallel in the modern edition of Kolb and Wengert 2000 is found at 533.5. In *Concordia* 1756 the pagination in the part of the volume cited here

runs as follows: 638, 639, 640, 639, 640, 641. The present edition refers to these as pages 638, 639[a], 640[a], 639[b], 640[b], 641. [Editors]

24 (in §464:10). The parallel in the modern edition of Kolb and Wengert 2000 is found at 533.6. [Editors]

25 (in §464:10). The parallel in the modern edition of Kolb and Wengert 2000 is found at 533.11–534.11. [Editors]

26 (in §465). Which particular paintings Swedenborg was thinking of are not known, but examples of paintings juxtaposing beauty and ugliness from before his time are: (1) *The Ill-Matched Lovers,* a work of 1520–1525 by the Flemish artist Quentin Matsys (1466–1530), now in the National Gallery of Art, Washington, D.C.; (2) a series of works on the theme of death and the maiden by the German Hans Baldung Grien (1480–1545), of which one, a version from 1510, is in the Kunsthistorisches Museum, Vienna. [JSR, SS]

27 (in §466). The term "Book of Moses" here refers to the Book of Genesis. As was the custom in his day, Swedenborg refers to the Pentateuch (Genesis, Exodus, Leviticus, Numbers, and Deuteronomy) as books of Moses. [JSR]

28 (in §466). In the context of Christian belief, the theory that people existed before Adam and Eve is called pre-Adamism. A passage in *Spiritual Experiences* (= Swedenborg 1998–2002) §3390 makes clear that Swedenborg did accept at least some form of this theory. Pre-Adamism has a long history that includes such notable or notorious adherents as Julian the Apostate (331–363 C.E.) and Giordano Bruno (1548–1600); it was opposed implicitly by Augustine (354–430) in such passages as *City of God* 15:16–17, and more explicitly by Martin Luther (1483–1546) and Calvin (Duncan 1972, 107). Its most conspicuous adherent in the 1600s was the Calvinist Isaac La Peyrère (1596–1676), whose works *Prae-Adamitae* (Pre-Adamites) and *Systema Theologicum ex Prae-Adamitarum Hypothesi* (Theological System Based on the Theory of the Pre-Adamites) were published in 1655. He mentions the same arguments referred to by Swedenborg in *True Christianity,* among others (see La Peyrère 1655b, proem). His thesis was highly controversial, to say the least: more than thirty refutations were published within the next fifty years, and he himself was said to have been forced to recant through imprisonment (Duncan 1972, 110). The intense interest in the question can be seen as typical of a period in which revelation was being increasingly challenged by the demand that the Bible accord strictly with reason and in which theories about evolution were gradually taking shape. It is significant that Swedenborg, while accepting pre-Adamism, stands above the question in this passage and advocates a symbolic reading of the Adamic story. For brief summaries of pre-Adamism and related matters up to the end of the 1600s, see Almond 1999, 49–60; Duncan 1972, 101–111; Popkin 1998, 413–414; for a fuller study, see Popkin 1987. [SS, FLS]

29 (in §466). The name Jehovah is a rendering of the tetragrammaton, יהוה *(yhvh)*, "YHWH," the four-letter name of God in the Hebrew Scriptures. Swedenborg uses it frequently, in keeping with Christian practice. For more on the name Jehovah, see volume 1, page 677 note 9. [GFD, JSR]

30 (in §466). For more on Swedenborg's use of the term *church,* see note 1. The qualifier "earliest" limits the term to the era before the Flood; see *Secrets of Heaven* 286. [SS]

31 (in §466). *Secrets of Heaven* was published by Swedenborg in eight volumes between 1749 and 1756. For passages in the work that illustrate in various ways how

Adam and his wife represent the earliest church, see §§64, 277, 286–291, 469–480, 1013. [JSR, LSW]

32 (in §466). Throughout his published theological works, Swedenborg uses the term "the Lord" to refer to Jesus Christ as God. For more on Swedenborg's view of the undivided divinity of the Lord God Jesus Christ, see volume 1, pages 676–677 note 8. [JSR]

33 (in §466). *Secrets of Heaven* 305 and 4447:2 discuss the particular inner meaning of the Garden of Eden mentioned in this section; compare also *Secrets of Heaven* 98. The precise symbolism of the tree of life given here is not stated in *Secrets of Heaven* in so many words, but there are related interpretations in §§105, 2187:3, 3427:3. Likewise in the case of the tree of the knowledge of good and evil; see *Secrets of Heaven* 126–128, 198. On the eating of the latter tree meaning incorporating evil into ourselves, see *Secrets of Heaven* 202. For further discussion of both these trees and what eating from them means, see *True Christianity* 48:16–20. For general discussion of the inner meaning inherent in Scripture, see *True Christianity* 193–209. [SS, LSW]

34 (in §467:4). In Swedenborg's theological cosmology there are two worlds or universes, one physical and one spiritual, which are related to each other through "symbolic representations," or correspondences (see volume 1, page 682 note 35). Swedenborg uses the term *spiritual world* as an umbrella term that includes heaven, hell, and the intermediate "world of spirits" to which people first go after they die, before going to either heaven or hell. For the distinction between the spiritual world and the world of spirits, see *Divine Love and Wisdom* 140; for more on the world of spirits, see *Heaven and Hell* 421–431. [JSR]

35 (in §468). In Swedenborg's theology the word *heavenly* often has a special meaning, and is frequently contrasted with what is "spiritual," which is of somewhat lower value, and what is "earthly," which is lower still. (For more on "higher" and "lower" or "inner" and "outer" in Swedenborg's theology, see volume 1, page 676 note 6.) The term *heavenly* is associated with love for the Lord, and with an approach to life in which goodness and love are the predominant values. The term *spiritual* is associated with love for one's neighbor, and with an approach to life in which truth and wisdom are the predominant values. See *Heaven and Hell* 20–28. The term *heavenly church,* then, applies to the type of church, or the level within a church, that is "highest," in the sense of being closest to the Lord; and a person of the heavenly church is someone who possesses these heavenly characteristics. (For Swedenborg's special uses of the term *church,* see volume 1, pages 675–676 note 3.) The terms *heavenly church* and *heavenly type of church* appear frequently in *Secrets of Heaven;* see, for instance, §886:2. [JSR]

36 (in §468). As was the custom in his day, Swedenborg refers to Psalms as a book of David. [Editors]

37 (in §469:1). Swedenborg, in ascribing the actual misdeed to "a single individual," may have been following a tendency among theologians of the early modern period to assign the fault for original sin to Adam alone; see Almond 1999, 195–196. But Adam is here likely being used androcentrically to represent both Adam and Eve, as was customary in Christian theology. Contrast *Divine Providence* 236, 241, in which both Adam and Eve are said to have been "led astray by the serpent." (Passages of *Divine Providence* in these notes are from the translation by George F. Dole.) [SS]

38 (in §469:1). These details of the story of the fall of Adam and Eve are given in Genesis 2–3. Very early commentators, including Philo Judaeus (around 15 B.C.E.–50 C.E.)

and Origen (around 185–around 254) had analyzed the Fall as allegorical (for a summary, see Duncan 1972, 42–46), but most scholars took the story quite literally and exercised their ingenuity in devising answers to the challenges it presented. By the beginning of the eighteenth century, however, "the difficulties inherent in the text" of the story were "no longer being seen as catalysts for inquiry but as grounds for scepticism" (Almond 1999, 214). Swedenborg here repeats some of the standard reservations about the story expressed by critics (though he puts them to his own use). For example, the article on original sin in the *Philosophical Dictionary* (1764) of Voltaire (1694–1778) mocks the notion "that [God] created all the generation of [humans] in order to torment them with eternal tortures, on the pretext that their first father ate a fruit in a garden" (Voltaire [1764] 1962, 416). The tendency to trivialize Adam and Eve's transgression was apparently of long standing; the church father Augustine cautions against it in *City of God* 14:12 (= Augustine 1952, 387): "[One] ought not to think the sin was a small and light one because it was committed about food." For more on this subject, see *Divine Providence* 241. [SS]

39 (in §469:2). In Swedenborg's view, the freedom to choose between evil and good, arising as it does from the faculties of will (or volition) and intellect (or discernment), is characteristically human. Because mere animals lack these qualities, they can never rise above or fall below their natural state. For more on Swedenborg's view of the will and intellect, see volume 1, page 683 note 39; on how he departs from eighteenth-century views of human nature, see volume 1, page 688 note 67. [KK]

40 (in §469:2). Swedenborg's concept of hereditary evil is based on the notion that an *inclination to evil* is inherited from one's parents, whereas the traditional concept of original sin, to which Swedenborg refers obliquely here, is based on the notion that all humans inherit *actual sin* from Adam and Eve. In Swedenborg's view, humans are born inclined to evils of every kind, and more so to those evils that one's parents have committed, but every human is perpetually in freedom to choose between good and evil. For more on Swedenborg's concept of hereditary evil, see §§520–521. [KK]

41 (in §469:2). In his last five published theological works (*Revelation Unveiled* [1766], *Marriage Love* [1768], *Survey, Soul-Body Interaction,* [both published in 1769], and the present work), Swedenborg uses the term "memorable occurrence" (Latin *memorabile,* plural *memorabilia,* traditionally translated "memorable relation") as a technical term for an extended narrative account of one of his spiritual experiences. [JSR]

42 (in §470:1). For further discussion of the nature of sense-oriented or sense-based thinking, see §565. [Editors]

43 (in §470:2). On the notion that humans could have been created only from finite things, compare *Divine Love and Wisdom* 4, 52–53. [SS]

44 (in §470:2). The term *Book of Creation,* though it can logically be used to refer to Genesis as the Bible book in which the narrative of creation is given, was in Swedenborg's time generally used to refer to nature as opposed to the Bible; by redefining the term here as the Book of Genesis, Swedenborg seems to be taking issue with two groups: Deists, who advocated learning about God by "reading in the Book of Creation" (that is, the natural world) rather than in the book of revelation (the Bible); and Naturalists, who believed the world arose strictly from natural causes. A similar use occurs at §20. For a discussion of Swedenborg's relationship with Deist thought, see Kirven 1965. For more on the Naturalists and Swedenborg's antipathy to them, see *Secrets of Heaven* volume 1 (= Swedenborg [1749–1756] 2008), page 616 note 157. [SS]

45 (in §470:2). For the connection in Hebrew between "Adam" and "soil," see volume 1, page 705 note 163. [JSR]

46 (in §470:2). The phrase "the atmosphere from the earth" reflects Swedenborg's theories of cosmogony. In his 1734 work of scientific theory, *Basic Principles of Nature,* Swedenborg hypothesizes that the earth was formed from heavy solids thrown off by the sun and that the lighter atmospheric matter was formed in turn from the material of the earth (*Basic Principles of Nature,* part 3, chapter 5, §§1–2 [= Swedenborg [1734] 1988a, 2:276–278]). According to the vortex theory of planetary motion to which Swedenborg subscribed, heavy objects tended to move toward the center and lighter objects away from the center, so the lighter atmospheric elements would tend to work their way out of the heavier material and accumulate around the body of the planet. See *Basic Principles of Nature,* part 3, chapter 11, §1 (= Swedenborg [1734] 1988a, 2:344–346). In *Divine Love and Wisdom* 302, Swedenborg expresses this idea in reverse, saying that the atmosphere "terminates" in the material substances of earth. The point here is that even the lighter atmospheric substances that are part of our bodies, such as the air that fills our lungs, can be said to have derived from the earth. On the vortex theory, compare also note 440. [SS]

47 (in §470:2). Although at the time of the writing of *True Christianity* oxygen had not been identified per se as the substance taken up by the blood, it had long been obvious that the human body did require the intake of some constituent of the atmosphere in order to survive. In one of his anatomical works, Swedenborg refers to the lungs as "a single stomach . . . feeding on aërial food, just as the stomach properly so called feeds upon terrestrial food prepared out of every kind of edible substance" (*Dynamics of the Soul's Domain* [= Swedenborg [1740–1741] 1955], part 1, §51). [SS]

48 (in §470:3). In this passage, the term "substance" is used in a philosophical sense that has much in common with Aristotelian, Scholastic, and Enlightenment usage but remains uniquely Swedenborgian. Swedenborg conceived of substance as originating from God through a process of God's "finiting," or delimiting, his infinity (*True Christianity* 29:3, 33, 76:3; *Divine Love and Wisdom* 282–357). In Swedenborg's philosophic system, in distinction from that of many of his contemporaries, the resulting substance is not a "simple"—an indivisible, single foundation of other material—but instead contains innumerable things that are in a form more perfect than material things because they are closer in degree to the infinite God (*Divine Love and Wisdom* 229; *Marriage Love* 329). As substance proceeds outward from the Godhead it shares less and less with the Divine, and yet it still possesses some image of the Divine even when it finally becomes matter (*Divine Love and Wisdom* 317–318; *Divine Providence* 6). As the underlying basis of the material world, spiritual substance functions by forming a vessel or receptacle for divine inflow (*True Christianity* 33); the inflow then renders matter capable, as Swedenborg says here, of growing seeds and spontaneously generating worms from earth and plant exhalations or gases. Anything made of spiritual substance is alive in the sense that it is in the Divine and the Divine is in it (*Divine Love and Wisdom* 53). On the generation of seeds from the image of the infinite God contained in all things, see specifically *Divine Love and Wisdom* 318; on spontaneous generation, see *True Christianity* volume 1, page 754 note 580. [SS, FLS]

49 (in §470:4). Although Swedenborg here follows a long-standing Christian identification of the serpent in the Garden of Eden with the Devil (compare Revelation

12:9; 20:2), his theology maintains that there is no single supreme spirit of evil or ruler of hell. Just below in the text he explains: "Please note that . . . when I say 'the Devil' I mean hell, because all the people there are devils" (§476:2); see also volume 1, page 679 note 18. [JSR]

50 (in §470:5). For the term "earliest church" here, see the definition in note 30. For a description of the people who lived specifically at the end of this "church" period, see *Secrets of Heaven* 1265–1272; *Spiritual Experiences* (= Swedenborg 1998–2002) §§3353–3355, 3358–3374. [SS]

51 (in §470:5). For Swedenborg's brief report of a conversation with the people of the earliest church concerning their religious beliefs, see *Secrets of Heaven* 1268. [SS]

52 (in §470:5). The location of these people is also described in *Spiritual Experiences* (= Swedenborg 1998–2002) §3358 as "under a great rock midway in the deep," somewhere "beneath the buttocks [of the universal human]." In *Secrets of Heaven* 1266–1268 they are said to be "under the heel of the left foot," covered by "a kind of foggy crag." (Passages of *Secrets of Heaven* in these notes were translated by Lisa Hyatt Cooper.) On the universal human, a single human being formed by the angelic heaven and the church on earth, see *True Christianity* 119:1. [SS]

53 (in §471). For Swedenborg's identification of God's essence as divine love and wisdom, see §37. For background on the use of the term "living force" (Latin *vis viva*) in the physical science of the Enlightenment period, see *Divine Love and Wisdom* (= Swedenborg [1763] 2003a), page 276 note 93. [Editors]

54 (in §471). In §369:3, Swedenborg defines spiritual death as "earthly life without spiritual life." See also Romans 8:13. [JSR]

55 (in §472:1). It may puzzle today's readers that Swedenborg here states that light and heat cannot be created; some grasp of the physical model he is using is necessary to an understanding of these statements. Swedenborg here follows the majority of early modern philosophers in accepting as a basic principle that matter needs a source of motion outside of itself; that is, matter cannot serve as the original source of motion. Though each of these philosophers had a different way of explaining exactly how God instilled motion in matter, they were united and unwavering in their view that God was necessary to motion (Mercer and Sleigh 1995, 73–74, with note 17). In *Basic Principles of Nature*, part 3, chapter 5, §21 (= Swedenborg [1734] 1988a, 2:296), Swedenborg defines light and heat as different motions of particles of the ether, a superfine substance that interpenetrates the entire universe. (On heat, see also part 3, chapter 8, §10 [= 2:322]; for more information on ether in Swedenborg, see *True Christianity* volume 1, pages 696–697 note 116.) The motion of light and heat results from the efflux of ether from the substance of hard bodies through a submicroscopic tremulation, and it is this tremulation that cannot be "created"; the ether is always *inherently* in motion because it has been made so by God. According to this view, heat may be released by friction, but cannot strictly speaking be created by it. A similar logic apparently applies when Swedenborg goes on in the following paragraph to say the same of sound, which he understands to be a motion of air. By contrast, as he adds below, the eye and ear, which are passive receivers of the motion of light and sound, can in some sense be said to be creatable. This physical model is derived closely from that of René Descartes (1596–1650), who asserted: "Light is nothing other than a certain movement or action by which luminous bodies impel this very fine material [a material similar to that which Swedenborg terms the

ether] in straight lines in all directions around them" (Descartes 2001, 265 [= *Meteorology*, first discourse]; compare also Descartes 2001, 67–68 [= *Optics*, first discourse]). Likewise Descartes describes heat as the agitation of matter caused by contact with the inherent activity of particles of ether (Descartes 2001, 266 [= *Meteorology*, first discourse]). For Descartes's assertion that God created motion and that God continually conserves an equal quantity of motion in all created things, see Descartes [1644] 1983, 57–58 (= *Principles of Philosophy* 2:36). For a previous discussion that amplifies ideas in this passage, see *True Christianity* 40. [SS, FLS]

56 (in §472:1). By "the quality of being active," Swedenborg is referring to the Aristotelian principle of activity; that is, the principle of activity as opposed to passivity. Activity is that which acts on and causes changes in what is passive. (See below in subsection 2, with note 59, and compare *Secrets of Heaven* 7754.) The understanding of the German philosopher Gottfried Wilhelm Leibniz (1646–1716) was similar: "Activity is a quality of one phenomenon in virtue of which it tends to cause another" (as restated by Russell [1900] 2008, 45; see also 217–218, and Mercer and Sleigh 1995, 73–74). The Greek philosopher Aristotle (384–322 B.C.E.) implies that activity is fully inherent in an object in *On Generation and Corruption* 326b 29–327a 29 (= Aristotle 1984, 534–535), and many of the philosophic systems in the early modern period accordingly assumed that since only God could have created matter, it follows that only God could have endowed matter with the quality of activeness. Leibniz, for example, maintains that the Divine confers "an inherent law" on created things from which proceeds both action and reception of actions (Leibniz [1698] 1989, §5). Compare Swedenborg's statement in the 1742 work *Draft on Action:* "There is no action, even natural, which does not descend from [God]; for in God we live and move and have our being" (= Swedenborg 1984a, 139 [= chapter 27]; alluding to Acts 17:28). [SS, FLS]

57 (in §472:1). On heat as active, see note 55. See further note 56 above. [Editors]

58 (in §472:1). The phrase "the three kingdoms of nature" refers to the animal kingdom, the plant kingdom, and the mineral kingdom. [JSR]

59 (in §472:2). In Swedenborg's earlier physical theories, active components (called "actives") join with passive components (called "finites") to make up the material structure of the entire universe. See *Basic Principles of Nature,* part 1, chapter 6 (= Swedenborg [1734] 1988a, 1:140): "Before . . . anything elementary can exist, it is necessary that in the world there should be two principles, one active and the other passive: one which is perpetually in local motion, another which is not in local motion. Without these two principles no third can be produced which shall partake of the active and of the passive; in a word, nothing natural can come into being. For nature is that force which bodies possess of acting and suffering [that is, being acted upon]. . . . Unless the active were a something separate, the passive a something separate, and both together constituted one body, nothing could be obtained which would be in agreement with nature." For more in Swedenborg's works on the importance of the concept of active and passive, see *True Christianity* 607:2, as well as *Secrets of Heaven* 718, 7754; *Soul-Body Interaction* 11; and for discussion, see *Secrets of Heaven* volume 1 (= Swedenborg [1749–1756] 2008), pages 639–640 note 395. [SS]

60 (in §472:2). Here Swedenborg may be contrasting active physical forces such as light and heat to organs such as the human eye and ear mentioned just above. According to his physical theory, light and heat, being an activity or motion, cannot be produced

as can an eye or ear; if they could, they would render the sun unnecessary. (On the uncreatable nature of light and heat, see note 55 above.) Another reading would be that Swedenborg is referring to the active and passive particles of his physical theory (called "actives" and "finites," respectively; see note 59 above). Such an interpretation would be more problematic, as in Swedenborg's theory both active and passive particles may arise from modifications or recombinations of matter originally created by God, and Swedenborg here says that the active entities in question cannot be created the way passive entities are. [SS]

61 (in §472:3). According to the theory Swedenborg advances in *Basic Principles of Nature*, part 1, chapter 10, §1 (= Swedenborg [1734] 1988a, 1:203), the primitive sun originally consisted "of no other than actives," which were inevitably joined to passive particles. (On these active and passive particles, see note 59 above.) This combination of actives and passives formed a third entity, an elementary particle of which the matter of the sun is now composed. This elementary particle may be what Swedenborg means here by "created substances." Furthermore, according to Swedenborg there are two types of fire: common fire and "subtle, elementary fire," such as the sun emits. Common fire consists of the motion of air expanded violently by contact with actives of various types; in the case of elementary fire, ether expands instead of air. Common fire is fed by the release of air and actives from combustible material; elementary fire is fed by the release of actives from the breakdown of elementary particles in the sun. It is this elementary fire to which Swedenborg refers here. For more on the creation of the sun, see *Basic Principles of Nature*, part 1, chapter 10 (= Swedenborg [1734] 1988a, 1:203–208). For more on the nature of fire, see *Basic Principles of Nature*, part 3, chapter 8 (= Swedenborg [1734] 1988a, 2:311–329). [SS]

62 (in §472:3). For more on the correspondences of light with wisdom and heat with love, see volume 1, page 676 note 7. On the spiritual sun, which gives off the spiritual light spoken of here, see §24:1 and the references given in volume 1, page 694 note 104, as well as *Divine Love and Wisdom* 5. [Editors]

63 (in §472:3). "Inflow" (Latin *influxus*, traditionally translated "influx") is a philosophical term denoting a one-way influence of one level or entity on another; see volume 1, page 682 note 32. [JSR]

64 (in §472:3). For more on the use of the term "partnership" (Latin *conjunctio*) in Swedenborg's works, see volume 1, page 678 note 14. For more on the nature of this partnership with God, see §§368–372. [Editors]

65 (in §473). Compare *Secrets of Heaven* 2021. This is a striking example of Swedenborg's common practice of importing Aristotelian/Scholastic concepts into his theology, despite the general discrediting of Scholastic thought by secular thinkers during the period. In Scholastic use, a principal cause is "a cause which works by the power of its own form and makes the effect in some way like itself"; an instrumental cause is "an instrument or tool serving as a subordinate cause; a cause without initiative in the start of action, but applied and directed as a help to its efforts and purpose by a principal agent, and influencing the product chiefly according to the form and intention of the principal" (Wuellner 1956, 19; compare the discussion by the great Catholic theologian Aquinas [1224 or 1225–1274] in his *Summa Theologiae* 3:62:1 [= Aquinas 1952, 2:859]). Swedenborg's point is that the mind, though merely an instrument of life, assumes that the principle of life inheres in itself autonomously. The effect of these causes, in

Swedenborg's analogy, would be that an entire human being is nothing but a form organized in such a way as to receive love and wisdom (see above, §472). Swedenborg uses this terminology in other contexts as well; for example, in *Secrets of Heaven* 10738:4 he refers to the body as the instrumental cause and to the will as the principal. He also emphasizes the apparent but misleading unity of principal and instrumental in other passages (for example, *Soul-Body Interaction* 11:2). On the related tendency among some Enlightenment philosophers to invoke a "corrected" Aristotelian philosophy ("eclectic Aristotelianism"), see Mercer and Sleigh 1995, 69–70. [SS, FLS]

66 (in §473). In §66 Swedenborg says that animals in the spiritual world "are likenesses of the feelings of love and the resulting thoughts that angels have" (compare §506:1; *Divine Love and Wisdom* 52). Here he parallels that statement by saying that animals in the physical world correspond to forms of "earthly love." In *Secrets of Heaven* 10042:2 he explains that this phenomenon in the material world is actually caused by the phenomenon in the spiritual world: "The fact that animals of different kinds symbolize these things traces its cause to representations in the other world, where animals of many general and countless specific types appear. Such otherworldly sights are appearances— completely lifelike ones—that correspond to feelings and thoughts in the spirits and angels." For related passages, see *Secrets of Heaven* 2179, 3218, 3786:1, 9331; *Heaven and Hell* 110; *Divine Love and Wisdom* 338–341; *Revelation Explained* (= Swedenborg 1994– 1997a) §§1199–1201; *Draft on Divine Love* (= Swedenborg 1994–1997b, 451) §21 [heading] = §61 [Mongredien's numbering]. On the inflow from the spiritual world into animals, see *True Christianity* 335:6. It should be noted that in other passages in his works (for example, *True Christianity* 78:5), Swedenborg goes beyond the assertion that some animals are guided by the influence of hell and maintains that they were actually created by that influence—that is, by the influence of humans who have succumbed to evil. For references on that topic, see *True Christianity* volume 1, page 698 note 129. [SS]

67 (in §475:2). The concept of extension, as understood in the eighteenth century, refers to three-dimensionality, or the occupation of physical space. For more on the term, see volume 1, page 696 note 115. [Editors]

68 (in §475:3). The gap separating heaven from hell is described just below in this section as a "vast interspace" and as "the world of spirits." See note 34 above. [Editors]

69 (in §475:4). In Roman Catholic doctrine, purgatory is a place or state of purification involving temporary suffering, through which the souls of those who die in God's grace may make satisfaction for past forgivable sins and so become fit for heaven; for a history of the concept, see le Goff 1981. Swedenborg's dismissal of the concept of purgatory here is one of a number of criticisms of Roman Catholic teachings and practices expressed in his theological works. Many of these are typical of eighteenth-century Protestant views of Roman Catholicism: criticisms of the veneration of the pope as the vicar of Christ (§§177:4, 560, 634:2; see also note 301); of the abuse of power by Catholic leaders (§819); of indulgences as a means of absolving sins (§§177:4, 426, 582:1, 634:2; see also volume 1, page 734 note 406); of the invocation of saints (§§177:4, 634:2, 823–826; see also note 301); of the veneration of relics and bones (§634:2; see also volume 1, page 725 note 326); of the near rejection of Scripture (§270; see also volume 1, page 743 note 486); of barring the laity from partaking of one of the two elements (bread and wine) of the Eucharist, or Holy Supper (§§177:4, 634:2; see also volume 1, page 734 note 406); and of the use of a language unknown to most in the Mass

(§§159:4, 634:2, 819:2). These views are not surprising from a writer of theology who grew up in the late seventeenth and early eighteenth century in a Lutheran nation. Other criticisms Swedenborg makes are somewhat more surprising, in that he levels them at tenets espoused by both Roman Catholics and Protestants: the belief in a trinity of persons (§174); the position that Christ's merit can be assigned to people on the basis of their faith (§640:2); and the view that Mary is the source of Jesus' soul and is to be venerated (§§82:3, 94; see also §102:3 = §827, and volume 1, page 716 note 244). (Similar and even harsher statements appear in Swedenborg's other works, including *Heaven and Hell* 508:3; *New Jerusalem* 8; *Last Judgment* 55; *Divine Providence* 257; *Revelation Unveiled* 770, 796:2.) In other passages, however, Swedenborg sets Roman Catholicism in a positive light and even privileges it over Protestantism, particularly in regard to the practice of confession and other steps of active repentance (§§515:2, 562:2, 567:7). He asserts that these attitudes and practices of goodwill toward others make it easier for Catholics than for Protestants to let go of beliefs and actions that are not those of heaven (namely, those listed just above in this note) and adopt those that are (§§820:1, 821:1; see also *Survey* 105–108). Indeed, passages later in this text indicate that in the world of spirits there is a large community of good Catholics who are in touch with heaven and are in time saved and lifted into heaven itself (§§567:7, 820:2, 821; see also *Survey* 108). [KK, JSR]

70 (in §476:1). Farther on in §476 Swedenborg describes the maturation process that occurs as the spirit of each human being living in the physical world takes up residence in various sectors of the world of spirits, according to the quality of the person's beliefs and actions. As Swedenborg notes, our body is not in those areas, but our spirit is. [KK]

71 (in §476:1). Swedenborg gives some explanation of the meaning of these regions below. For more on direction and location in the spiritual world, see *Heaven and Hell* 141–153. [Editors]

72 (in §476:1). Swedenborg mentions in §24:1 that God is within the spiritual sun. For further references to the topic of the spiritual sun in Swedenborg's works, see note 104 there (volume 1, page 694). [Editors]

73 (in §477). On Swedenborg's concept of a dominant love, see §399. [Editors]

74 (in §478:2). In his anatomical works, Swedenborg over a hundred times refers to this notion that in a healthy, properly functioning body, the vital fluids (as well as the organs) are kept in "equilibrium" or "equation," constantly attempting to return to their baseline or balanced state. See, for example, *Dynamics of the Soul's Domain* (= Swedenborg [1740–1741] 1955), part 1, §§227, 521, and *The Soul's Domain* (= Swedenborg [1744–1745] 1960) §203 and note z. The concept is similar to the modern theory of physiological equilibrium or homeostasis. [SS, FLS]

75 (in §478:2). On Swedenborg's use of the concepts of "will" (Latin *voluntas,* elsewhere in this edition rendered "volition") and "intellect" (Latin *intellectus,* traditionally translated "understanding," and elsewhere in this edition, "discernment"), see volume 1, page 683 note 39. [JSR]

76 (in §478:3). Swedenborg here acknowledges the apparent paradox in his concept of freedom: "If we . . . restrain our free choice . . . we are brought into heavenly freedom, which is true freedom." Although Swedenborg gives further clarification below in §495, the most thorough explanation of the psychology of this apparent contradiction can be found in *Divine Providence* 145–149; in both places Swedenborg also cites John

8:31–36 as a proof text. The resolution of the difficulty lies in the fact that Swedenborg uses the same term, "freedom," for two opposite types: "hellish freedom" and "heavenly freedom." In *Secrets of Heaven* 2870, Swedenborg defines hellish freedom as the pursuit of love for one's self and the world and the pleasures pertaining to these loves; while heavenly freedom is love for the Lord and one's neighbor, and thus the love of what is good and what is true. Although both are called freedom, an adherent of one freedom sees the other form as slavery. See also *Secrets of Heaven* 2873–2874, 5428:3, 5763, 9589–9590; *New Jerusalem* 144, 148 (with extensive cross-references to *Secrets of Heaven*); *Divine Providence* 43–44, 97. As Swedenborg was aware, many other thinkers have similarly distinguished between true and apparent good or freedom, from Plato (427–347 B.C.E.) through the Christian fathers; compare, for example, what Augustine calls our "lesser freedom" *(libertas minor),* which is the simple freedom to choose, as opposed to our "greater freedom" *(libertas major),* which is the freedom to choose rightly. Augustine also defines these, respectively, as "being able not to sin" *(posse non peccare)* and "not being able to sin" *(non posse peccare;* see *On Rebuke and Grace* 33 [= Augustine 1997, 485]). For Swedenborg, angels are similarly not able to sin, insofar as their will belongs to the Lord; for this reason they "are in abject sorrow and in pain if allowed to think or will for themselves" *(Secrets of Heaven* 5428:3). [FLS, SS, JSR]

77 (in §479). Swedenborg refers to the arguments as "familiar" because they were part of the widespread criticism of the Bible by Deists and others during the Enlightenment. On this criticism, compare note 38; on Deism, see note 44. [SS]

78 (in §479). As noted at the end of this section, the twelve points listed here are taken up at some length in *Divine Providence* 234–274. The first six refer to episodes in the Bible; for references, see *Divine Providence* (= Swedenborg [1764] 2003b) §236 and page 376 notes 207 and 208. [JSR]

79 (in §479). The original Latin text here reads *non abduxerit illos loquendo cum illis,* "did not dissuade them by speaking with them," apparently in error; compare *Divine Providence* 236, 242. [JSR]

80 (in §479). Contrast Swedenborg's analysis of the advent of Islam in §833. On Swedenborg's attitude toward Islam, see note 354 below. [Editors]

81 (in §479). The concept that God permits evil so that humans may have free will has been approved, qualified, or rejected by many Christian theologians over the millennia. See, for example, Calvin's *Institutes of the Christian Religion* (= Calvin 1960) 2:4:3, where the validity of the notion is denied. [SS, FLS]

82 (in §480). On Swedenborg's views concerning the theory of innate knowledge, see volume 1, page 704 note 160; pages 750–751 note 549. [Editors]

83 (in §481:2). On the importance Swedenborg assigned to experiential knowledge in the corroboration of his theology, see volume 1, page 757 note 596. [Editors]

84 (in §481:2). Concerning the imagery of a log, a stone, and Lot's wife after she has become a statue, see §464:3 and note 10. [JSR]

85 (in §483:1). For passages in the Bible saying that we should do good, see §376; *Life* 2. For passages saying that we should not do evil, see §536:3; *Life* 113; *Divine Providence* 114. For passages saying we should believe in God, see §§107, 337–338. For passages saying that we should not believe in idols, see *Revelation Unveiled* 459–460; *Revelation Explained* (= Swedenborg 1994–1997a) §§587, 827:2. [LSW]

86 (in §483:1). The Latin phrase here translated "just serifs and dots without letters" is *soli apices aut jothae absque literis*. Elsewhere when Swedenborg uses the word *apex* (literally, "tip" or "top") in the context of biblical writing he means the small upward-pointing stroke that forms the tip of each letter in Hebrew "square" script. Elsewhere when he uses the word *jotha* (literally "jot," "iota," or "yod") in the context of biblical writing he is referring to either the smallest letter in Greek or the smallest letter in Hebrew. And elsewhere when he uses these words together he is alluding to Jesus' statement in Matthew 5:18 that "not one little letter or the tip of one letter will pass from the law until all of it is fulfilled." Here, however, it appears that by *jothae* Swedenborg means something even less than entire letters, since he says they are "without letters." The Latin phrase here translated "a volume entirely without meaning" is *codex inanis*, literally, "codex empty." This Latin pair of words, *codex inanis*, is reminiscent of the way ancient biblical manuscripts (and other documents, such as codes of law) have traditionally been named by the Latin word "codex" followed by an adjective; examples are the Codex Argenteus (the silver codex), the Codex Gigas (the giant codex), and the Codex Vaticanus (the Vatican codex). [JSR, GFD]

87 (in §483:2). The Latin phrase *Filius Hominis*, here translated "the Son of Humankind," is traditionally rendered "the Son of Man." On this term, see volume 1, page 675 note 1. [Editors]

88 (in §483:3). In §287 Swedenborg asserts that the term "the Law and the Prophets," used in such passages as the one from Matthew quoted here, means the entire Word. Generally, the phrase "the Law and the Prophets" refers to two main sections of the Hebrew Scriptures: the Law or Torah, comprising the five books of Moses: Genesis, Exodus, Leviticus, Numbers, and Deuteronomy; and the Prophets or Nevi'im, including the "Former Prophets," namely, Joshua, Judges, Samuel, and Kings, and the "Latter Prophets," namely, Isaiah, Jeremiah, Ezekiel, and the twelve minor prophets. [JSR]

89 (in §485). The promise made here for further exploration in "the last part of this book" was apparently never fulfilled. The material in question may have been intended as part of the promised appendix (see volume 1, page 689 note 71), which appears to have been abandoned to accelerate the date of publication (see the translator's preface to volume 1, page 29). [JSR]

90 (in §486:2). There are many "flowing forths" of predestinarian thought in Christian theology, beginning with the comments by Paul in Romans 8:29–30 and Ephesians 1:5, 11; see also Romans 9:14–29. The selected streams mentioned by Swedenborg in the text below can be described as follows. (1) By Predestinarians (Latin *Praedestinatiani*) here Swedenborg presumably means the earliest Christians to favor predestination, such as the monks of Adrumetum in north Africa who interpreted certain statements of Augustine (354–430) as teaching predestination, and the anonymous author of part 2 of the *Praedestinatus*, which is now dated to the fifth century c.e.; see *Concordia* 1756, appendix page 244 (for more on this appendix see note 8). (2) Gottschalk of Orbais (around 804–around 869) was a Roman Catholic monk who taught that Christ's ability to save was limited to the elect, and thus that all were predestined either to salvation or to damnation (so-called double predestination). His beliefs caused great controversy and were condemned as heresy by the church. They did, however, contribute to the "flowing" of predestinarian thought described here. For translations of his more important

works and of responses to him, see Genke and Gumerlock 2010. (3) The Protestant Reformer John Calvin (1509–1564), too, taught a double predestination, most notably in a chapter in his influential work *Institutes of the Christian Religion* (= Calvin 1960) 3:21, and in his commentary on the Epistle to the Romans. (For two of his other treatises on predestination, see Calvin 2006; see also Klooster 1977.) Swedenborg's main objections to Calvin and Calvinism concern Calvin's espousal of predestination as central to Christianity and Calvin's rejection of the worship of Jesus Christ; see §798. (4) The Synod of Dort (or Dordrecht) in the Netherlands (1618–1619) was a national synod (a council or assembly) of the Dutch Reformed Church, to which voting representatives from Reformed churches in other European countries were invited. The first of its five key resolutions or "canons" concerned predestination. (5) The Supralapsarians were Calvinists who believed that even before creation or the Fall, God had already predestined people yet unborn to either heaven or hell. (6) The opposing point of view was held by Infralapsarian Calvinists, who believed that predestination occurred only after creation and the Fall. [JSR, SS, FLS]

91 (in §486:2). Medusa, one of three sister creatures called Gorgons, is a figure in classical mythology. She was so fearsome to behold that she turned those who glimpsed her into stone. According to legend, the hero Perseus managed to strike off her head while looking at her reflection in a bronze shield; he later used her severed head as a weapon to petrify his enemies. Swedenborg would have known the myth from many sources, most notably Ovid *Metamorphoses* 4:604–5:249. [SS]

92 (in §486:2). Pallas Athena was a goddess of classical Greek mythology. She is described in Homer *Iliad* 5:736–742 and Ovid *Metamorphoses* 4:799–803 as wearing the aegis, a kind of protective armor, which is decorated with the head of Medusa, the Gorgon (see note 91). [Editors]

93 (in §486:3). On Swedenborg's use of the term *satans* to indicate a certain class of evil spirits in hell, see volume 1, page 679 note 18. [Editors]

94 (in §487:1). For a list of eighty-one Dutch and foreign members and sixteen deputies who participated in the decisions of the Synod of Dort, see *Iudgement* 1619, 58–67. [JSR]

95 (in §487:2). For more on Swedenborg's attitude to Calvinists, which underlies his characterization of them here as satanical, see note 90. [JSR]

96 (in §487:2). For more on Swedenborg's division of the mind into levels, see note 128. [Editors]

97 (in §487:3). For a statement in the Bible to the effect that God wants all to be saved, see 1 Timothy 2:3–4. [JSR]

98 (in §487:3). This translation sets some of the thoughts expressed by these predestinarians in parentheses, since they undermine the main points the speakers are making; the main points are predestinarian, while the material in parentheses, although spoken by the same people, is much closer to Swedenborg's theology. [JSR]

99 (in §487:3). The phrase "the small as well as the great" is an allusion to a biblical expression meaning people from all levels of society. It is found quite often in both the Old and the New Testaments; for example, in Deuteronomy 1:17; Psalms 115:13; Acts 26:22; Revelation 20:12. [JSR]

100 (in §487:3). In the eighteenth century, the term "subsolar" (Latin *sub sole,* literally, "under the sun") referred to all that was subject to the sun's influence, namely, the moon, the earth, and several atmospheres that were posited to exist between the sun and

the earth. One or more of these atmospheres was referred to as "the ether"; see volume 1, pages 696–697 note 116, and *Draft of "Supplements"* (= Swedenborg 1997a, 175–176) §320 [Rogers's numbering] = §312 [Potts's numbering]. Here, however, in the context of dizziness and lethargy the speakers are probably referring instead to the volatile liquid also known as ether. It was used as a solvent in Swedenborg's day and, although not employed as an anesthetic until the mid-nineteenth century, was already known to have intoxicative effects on the human body. [JSR]

101 (in §488). Although in many respects China evoked wonder and admiration in Europe in the eighteenth century, Swedenborg may be referring here to infanticide in that country. "In the seventeenth century, Jesuit missionaries . . . were horrified to find that in Peking alone several thousand [infants] (almost exclusively females) were thrown on the streets like refuse, to be collected each morning by carriers who dumped them into a huge pit outside the city" (Langer 1974, 354; see also 362 note 2 there). This practice continued into the 1800s. Similarly, in some parts of Europe in Swedenborg's time, newborns were not infrequently left in the streets or on the steps of churches to be raised by the church or the state. From ancient times until relatively recently, children were seen as the property of the parent, and no opprobrium attached to disposing of them immediately after birth. [JSR, SS]

102 (in §488). Swedenborg comments on this practice with similar horror in *Secrets of Heaven* 908:3. Examples of threats to expose a corpse to desecration by animals or birds can be found in Deuteronomy 28:26; Psalms 79:2; Jeremiah 7:33; Ezekiel 34:5, 8. Similar mentions can be found in the literature of other cultures; for example, Homer *Iliad* 1:4–5. [Editors]

103 (in §489:1). For more on the Council of Nicaea and Swedenborg's assessment of it, see §§632–634, and note 296 below. [JSR]

104 (in §489:1). For a passage that gives six examples of decisions arrived at by Roman Catholic councils, see §634:2; on Swedenborg's attitude toward Roman Catholicism in general, see note 69. [JSR]

105 (in §491:1). Neither the saliva nor any part of a crocodile in fact contains a toxin, though bacterial contamination from the teeth may cause a wound to become septic rapidly (Huchzermeyer 2010; see also Flandry and others 1989, 262–266). The legend may have entered the Western tradition with the Roman writer on natural history, Pliny (also known as Lacus Curtius Pliny, or Pliny the Elder [23 or 24–79 C.E.]), who refers to cures for the poison in the bite of the crocodile in his *Natural History* 32:17. (He speaks of crocodiles as sea creatures in 32:60.) Pliny was considered an authority on natural history well into the 1800s, and Swedenborg may have picked up this belief about the poisonous bite of the crocodile from him or from another author who drew on him. [SS]

106 (in §493). The term here translated "underlying reality" (Latin *esse,* literally, "to be" or "actual existence") has a long history in Western philosophy and theology. For more on this term and its pairing with the term "essence" (Latin *essentia*), see volume 1, pages 690–691 note 84. [KK]

107 (in §495). While some of the sacrifices mentioned in the Hebrew Bible were obligatory when conditions called for them, such as sin offerings (Leviticus 4:1–5:13; 6:24–30) and guilt offerings (Leviticus 5:14–19; 7:1–10), others were described as "freewill offerings." This is "a term applied to gifts presented out of the benevolence or religious

impulse of heart of the giver, and not in fulfillment of any obligation, promise, or vow" (*The Jewish Encyclopedia,* under "free-will offering"). Freewill offerings provided materials and support for both the tabernacle and the Temple (Exodus 35:4–29; 36:3–7; 1 Chronicles 29:1–9, 14–19; 2 Chronicles 31:14; Ezra 1:2–6; 7:15–17). They could also be offered by any of the people at will in the form of burnt offerings or fellowship (traditionally "peace") offerings (Leviticus 22:17–23; Numbers 29:39; Deuteronomy 12:6, 17; Ezra 3:5; Ezekiel 46:12). For more on freewill offerings, and on ancient Jewish sacrifices in general, see *The Jewish Encyclopedia,* under "free-will offering," "sacrifice"; for further discussion of sacrifice in the Old Testament, see Milgrom 1976, 763–771. [LSW, FLS]

108 (in §496:1). The assertion that few know that an animal adds elements to its body because it is continually rebuilding its component parts is an odd aside. A clue to the reason for the appearance of this statement here can be found in one of Swedenborg's scientific works, *Dynamics of the Soul's Domain* (= Swedenborg [1740–1741] 1955), part 1, §§247–315. In that passage, Swedenborg describes three types of growth—that of the embryo in the womb, that of an organism maturing after birth, and that involved in ongoing regeneration and repair of bodily tissues—as all relying on the same mechanism:

> The work of formation does not cease, but is still carried on, after the embryo is excluded from the womb; . . . for afterwards the animal enlarges and grows to maturity; . . . so that in the formed subject, formation and reformation [that is, building and rebuilding of bodily parts] still continue. . . . There is some formative substance and force, and . . . it is identical with that principle that repairs the dilapidations of the body, and when contingencies arise, renovates and perfects the system; and during formation makes one member succeed another. (*Dynamics of the Soul's Domain,* part 1, §§254, 255)

The mechanism by which this force works is that of successive addition of parts to an initial core; in Swedenborg's day it was called *epigenesis.* (The term has a slightly different application in current usage.) The theory of epigenesis stood in contrast to that of *preformation,* according to which life was reproduced through the growth of a minute but completely formed version of the final organism. In this passage in *True Christianity,* then, Swedenborg may be referring to the ongoing controversy between scholars who advocated for epigenesis and those who advocated for preformation: the few scholars who know that "the animal is continually adding elements to its body" by epigenesis are implicitly contrasted with those who believe the body is preformed and simply expands to its full-grown size. Some of the epigenesists Swedenborg may have had in mind here include Aristotle, William Harvey (1578–1657), Sir Kenelm Digby (1603–1665), René Descartes, Caspar Friedrich Wolff (1733–1794), and Voltaire. The preformationist camp included such luminaries as Nicolas de Malebranche (1638–1715), Gottfried Wilhelm Leibniz, Charles Bonnet (1720–1793), and Lazzaro Spallanzani (1729–1799). On preformationism as a theory, see Pinto-Correia 1997; Wilson 1995, 103–139. For Swedenborg's rejection of preformationism, see *Dynamics of the Soul's Domain,* part 1, §§249–250; *Divine Love and Wisdom* 432. Related philosophical themes in Swedenborg's works include the importance of sequential arrangement (see, for example, *Divine Love and Wisdom* 205); the theory of levels (on which in general see *Divine Love and Wisdom* 199–204, and compare also *True Christianity* 214:1); and his belief that by divine design the inner or center gives rise to the outer or periphery (compare *True Christianity* 35:7–13 and see note 458 in this volume). [SS]

109 (in §496:4). Swedenborg here refers to the complex and circuitous route by which fat is digested. Unlike sugars and proteins, which are absorbed by the blood vessels of the small intestine and delivered directly to the liver, fat is absorbed by lymphatic capillaries (lacteals) and turned into a milky substance called "chyle." The chyle then moves sluggishly through a dense network of lymph vessels in the folds of tissue within the abdominal cavity called the mesentery (see note 355). It proceeds not by action of the heart, but passively, by external muscular activity and a series of one-way valves. For other passages on the topic, see *Secrets of Heaven* 5173–5174 and *Divine Providence* 296:14. For Swedenborg's presentation and discussion of contemporary views on the mesentery and lacteals, see *The Soul's Domain* (= Swedenborg [1744–1745] 1960) §§141–157. [RPB, GMC]

110 (in §497:4). For more on how this individual judgment occurs, and the role of the individual's will in it, see *Secrets of Heaven* 4663:1; *Heaven and Hell* 545–550. [JSR]

111 (in §499:2). On the difference between noble and base natural objects, see volume 1, pages 703–704 note 159. [Editors]

112 (in §499:2). On ether, see volume 1, pages 696–697 note 116; and note 505 below. [Editors]

113 (in §499:2). Here Swedenborg describes the theory of *anathumiasis,* according to which minerals grow by the accretion of particles exhaled by the surrounding earth. The point of the illustrations in this passage is that the growth of anything by means of exhalations must be guided by something analogous to free will. A plant does not grow to become a stone, nor a stone a plant; it is the analogous "will" of these materials that guides the process of growth into a particular material through the absorption of exhalations. Anathumiasis, in its many variations, was widely accepted before the nineteenth century; the basis for it can be found in the Greek philosophers Aristotle and Theophrastus (around 372–around 287 B.C.E.); see particularly Aristotle *Meteorology* 378a–378b. The growth of plant seeds was thought to be analogous; for some further discussion of this process, see §§585:4 and 785 below. For extensive references in the literature of the period to this theory of the origin of metals, which extended to their recrudescence after mining, see Collier 1934, 417–427. Compare also volume 1, page 741 note 468. For Swedenborg's beliefs about how metals are created, including their growth from "seeds," see his preface to *Philosophical and Metallurgical Works III: Copper and Brass* (= Swedenborg [1734] 1938; also available in Swedenborg [1734] 1988a, 2:375–383). Also relevant are his paper on water as an agent in the growth of minerals (see *Miscellaneous Observations,* volume 2 [= Swedenborg [1722] 1976b, 117–127]) and his references to vapors from metallic veins in *Draft on Discovering Mines* (= Swedenborg 1992b, 51–64). For a similar contemporary theory of the growth of minerals and plants by the "attraction" of material, see Roe 1981, 24–25. [SS]

114 (in §499:2). Swedenborg does not elsewhere describe, in any thorough fashion, the fields (Latin *sphaera,* also translated "sphere," or "aura") that he theorizes belong to metals and other materials. Some understanding of them, however, can be gained from his descriptions of the field supposedly associated with the metal iron in his *Basic Principles of Nature,* part 2, chapter 1, §§28–30 (= Swedenborg [1734] 1988a, 1:239–243). They are clearly envisioned as fields of very fine particulate matter analogous to the

spiritual spheres or auras that play such an important role in Swedenborg's descriptions of spiritual phenomena. See, for example, *Divine Love and Wisdom* 293: "An outgoing wave is constantly flowing from individuals and from every animal, also from trees, fruits, shrubs, and flowers, and even from metals and stones. The physical world gets this from the spiritual world, and the spiritual world gets it from Divinity" (George F. Dole's translation). Compare *Secrets of Heaven* 10130:2 and note 164 below. [SS]

115 (in §500:1). For more on the concept of the divine design, see volume 1, page 678 note 13. [Editors]

116 (in §501:1). Swedenborg seems to suggest that skepticism about miracles was a recent phenomenon, but of course it was not; for example, in *City of God* 22:8:1 Augustine reports skeptics posing a similar question: "Why, they ask, are those miracles that you claim used to be performed no longer accomplished?" Here, however, Swedenborg seems to be making an understated reference to the general movement toward rejection of supernatural elements in religious belief during the Enlightenment. This was in part a result of the rise of Deism (see volume 1, page 684 note 46, and note 44 above) and other rationalistic modes of thought during that era. [SS]

117 (in §501:2). For a description of the composition of the inner church and its counterpart, the outer church, see note 231. [Editors]

118 (in §501:2). For the miracles in Egypt, see Exodus 4, 7–14. For the miracles on Mt. Sinai, see Exodus 19:16–19; 20:18–21; 24:15–18; see also Swedenborg's discussion in *True Christianity* 283–284. For the miracles performed by Elijah and Elisha, see 1 Kings 17–18; 2 Kings 1–8; 13:20–21. Many miracles of Jesus, involving healing, raising the dead, and controlling nature, are reported in the Gospels. [JSR, LSW]

119 (in §502:1). Swedenborg is here alluding to a New Testament parable (Matthew 25:31–46) in which sheep represent those who have served God by caring for others who are suffering and goats represent those who have ignored the suffering of others. On this symbolism, see volume 1, pages 705–706 note 170, and compare note 135. [JSR, KK]

120 (in §503:1). For a selective survey of the history of the much-vexed question of freedom of the will up to Swedenborg's time, see Dilman 1999, 11–140; for a recapitulation of the study of this question during the period of the seventeenth century, which was critical to the history of the discussion and formed the context for Swedenborg's thinking on this matter, see Sleigh and others 1998, 1195–1278. [SS, FLS]

121 (in §503:2). On the lack of true will in animals, see note 39. On the reason behind the negative representation of some animals in Swedenborg's theology, see §473 and note 66. Dogs in particular are often symbols of evil cravings or outright worthlessness in Swedenborg's works; a rare exception is *Spiritual Experiences* (= Swedenborg 1978) §4853, which explains that as symbols, dogs are good when they represent a desire for saying and teaching what is true, and bad when they represent a desire for saying and teaching the opposite. In nearly every passage in which dogs are mentioned in the Bible, the association is strongly negative; see, for example, Matthew 7:6; Revelation 22:15. [SS]

122 (in §503:4). This bracketed interpolation is Swedenborg's. Compare §463 above; the reference here as well is to *Concordia* 1756. (On the use of "Formula of Concord" to refer to the *Book of Concord,* see note 4.) The parallels in the modern edition of Kolb and Wengert 2000 to these page references are found at 544.7; 545.12–546.12; 548.20–549.25; 554.53–556.62. [Editors]

123 (in §503:5). For the meaning of the Christian theological term "justification," see note 291. [JSR]

124 (in §503:6). Although the exact force of the analogy contained in this sentence is no longer accessible today, context makes the main point clear: In the absence of free choice in spiritual matters, human beings would be deprived of their essential characteristics and the Word would be deprived of its essential meaning. Thus also the church would be unable to perform its essential function, like a hypothetical individual who, though a cleaner of clothes, is nevertheless apparently unable to clean even his or her own face. (Compare §484:1, where the church is likened to the relatively useless bark of a piece of wood.) [JSR, SS]

125 (in §503:6). On the phrase "a volume entirely without meaning," see note 86. [JSR]

126 (in §504:1). For more on the will and the intellect in Swedenborg, see volume 1, page 683 note 39. [Editors]

127 (in §504:1). By "the first type of sight (the sight of perception)," Swedenborg refers back to the ability to "perceive truths" with the higher faculty of the mind. Compare note 128 below and *Secrets of Heaven* 104, which defines perception as "an inner feeling for whether a thing is true and good—a feeling that can come only from the Lord." [SS]

128 (in §504:2). In Swedenborg's psychology, the human mind has higher and lower levels. The higher levels are devoted to higher forms of reasoning; the lower, to lower forms of reasoning. The memory occupies the middle ground. The region "above the memory," then, is where true reasoning and understanding occur. The region "below the memory" is the seat of false reasoning based on appearances and mistaken impressions from the bodily senses; it extends "downward" toward the level of the senses themselves. See *Survey* 55; *Draft of Five Memorable Occurrences* (= Swedenborg 1996c, 525) §11. For more on "higher" and "lower" in Swedenborg's theology, see volume 1, page 676 note 6. [Editors]

129 (in §504:4). On "producing good fruit," see Matthew 3:7–10; 7:15–20; Luke 3:7–9; 6:43–45; John 15:1–17 (some of which are quoted by Swedenborg in §483:2). On "believing in the Light," see John 1:1–14; 12:44–46. On "loving one another," see John 13:34–35; Romans 13:8–10; 1 Peter 3:8–9; 1 John 3:11, 23; 4:7–21; 2 John 1:5–6. On "loving God," see Deuteronomy 6:4–5; 11:1, 13, 22; 19:9; 30:15–20; Matthew 22:36–38; Mark 12:28–30; Luke 10:25–28. [LSW]

130 (in §504:4). For an extensive list providing some of the "thousand passages like this throughout the Word" (on obeying God's commandments and doing what is good), see *Life* 2. [LSW]

131 (in §504:4). The reference is to Genesis 3:24. The word here translated "angel guardian" is *cherub*, a Latin word based on the Hebrew כְּרוּב *(kərûb)*; it has traditionally been translated in English with the simple transliteration "cherub." That term, however, has misleadingly become attached to depictions of *putti* in art, winged infants or cupids. By contrast, angel guardians in the Bible were unearthly, winged, awe-inspiring figures; see volume 1, page 709 note 195. [JSR]

132 (in §504:6). Swedenborg's physiology held that there were three "bloods," or components of blood. They are named differently in different passages, but in *Draft on the Fiber* (= Swedenborg 1976a) §299 they are listed in order of purity as (1) the soul's essence, (2) the soul's spirits, and (3) the red blood. At various points in the body the

blood as a whole is filtered, in essence, by being forced into narrower blood vessels; in this way, the less pure elements are removed and the more pure pass through to fulfill a specific function. It is to a blockage at this sort of narrowing of the blood vessels that Swedenborg is referring here: as a result of disease, the impure blood clogs the opening of the smaller vessels. Such blockages could be illustrated from many passages in the anatomical works of Swedenborg; for example, in *Draft on the Fiber* (= Swedenborg 1976a) §441, coma is described as a disease that "arises from a thickened blood which is denied passage through the smallest arterioles, though passage through the larger ones still remains." For discussion of the components of blood in Swedenborg's theory, see [Acton] 1923, 7–11; Odhner 1933, 218–223, 234–249. See also *True Christianity* volume 1, pages 745–746 note 506. [SS]

133 (in §504:8). In the zoology of Swedenborg's day, a "prester" was a serpent whose bite was believed to cause death by swelling. [JSR]

134 (in §504:8). The statement that a spirit accompanied Swedenborg "home" suggests that the spirit journeyed either to Swedenborg's home in the physical world or to a corresponding site in the spiritual world. For a description of spirits following Swedenborg home and interacting with him there, see *Marriage Love* 329:1, 3, and *True Christianity* 159:7. On the existence of parallel sites in the spiritual and physical worlds, see *Spiritual Experiences* (= Swedenborg 1978) §§5092–5094. [JSR, KK]

135 (in §506:1). This memorable occurrence will be better understood if it is read in connection with Matthew 25:31–46. In that passage Jesus presents a picture of the Son of Humankind (on this term, see volume 1, page 675 note 1) coming in his glory and sitting on his throne with all the nations gathered before him. The Son of Humankind separates the people from one another as a shepherd separates sheep from goats. The sheep on his right represent those who have done good things for others, while the goats on his left represent those who have *not* done good things for others. Once their character has been made clear, the "goats" go away to eternal punishment, while the "sheep" go to eternal life. A summary of the characters and events of this memorable occurrence is as follows: Swedenborg sees from a distance a herd of goats and a flock of sheep. On closer approach, he sees that the "goats" are actually people who are devoted to the teaching that we are justified by faith alone (on "justification," see note 291), while the "sheep" are people who believe that faith must occur together with goodwill. Swedenborg addresses the "goats," who are mostly learned clergy, asking them why they are meeting. They respond that they are gathered to consider a written piece (see note 136) they have come across; it states that what Paul says in Romans 3:28 about "faith" and "the works of the Law" has been badly misinterpreted. Swedenborg withdraws until they finish their deliberations, and then approaches them again and asks them what they have concluded. When they state their conclusion, an angel suddenly appears, standing between the herd of goats and the flock of sheep, and warns the "sheep" not to listen to the "goats." The sheep are then divided into two flocks, one on the left and the other on the right, according to their support or lack of support of the goats. A conversation ensues involving the two flocks of "sheep," the "goats," and the angel. The sheep on the right are represented by one clergyperson who is among them, and by another outspoken person. Once all have had their say, most of the flock of sheep on the left, along with some of the clergy who had been among the goats, join the flock of sheep on the right, speaking out in

favor of faith together with doing what is good. The rest of the clergy in the herd of goats leave, loudly proclaiming their allegiance to faith alone. [LSW]

136 (in §506:2). The text at this point presents a statement that is similar to material in §288 above. The original Latin is somewhat ambiguous as to what kind of statement it was, whether written or oral. The abundant biblical references in parentheses, the interpolation by Swedenborg giving a cross-reference to another passage in *True Christianity* (see note 138), and the material added at the end all seem more characteristic of a written statement. Yet the Latin is clear that its recipients *heard* (rather than *read*) it. Perhaps readers are to think that it was a written statement that was communicated orally. [JSR]

137 (in §506:2). The phrase "the works of the Mosaic Law given for Jews" refers to the detailed prescriptions for sacrificial ritual, personal cleanliness, and diet attributed to Moses and given in the Pentateuch, or Torah (a body of work that also appears as the first five books of the Christian Old Testament). For more on the interpretation of the term *the Law* in this context, see *Divine Providence* (= Swedenborg [1764] 2003b), pages 365–366 note 103. [Editors]

138 (in §506:2). The material in brackets here is not in brackets in the first edition. Nevertheless it is clearly an interpolated reference to another passage in *True Christianity* rather than part of the original statement. Concerning the difficulties in interpreting this entire statement, see note 136 just above. [JSR]

139 (in §506:3). Following the practice of his times, Swedenborg refers to the books of the Bible ascribed to Paul simply as "Paul." Compare the reference to Galatians in §675:2 and to Colossians in §[852]. [Editors]

140 (in §506:5). The Latin word *pastores* is translated here as "pastors" and just below in §506:10 as "shepherds," the latter being the primary meaning of this Latin word. Its use in medieval and neoclassical Latin, as well as in English, to refer to ordained clergy who lead or "shepherd" Christian congregations is based on similar uses of the word "shepherd" in the Bible. See, for example, Psalms 23; 80:1; Isaiah 40:10–11; Jeremiah 3:15; 23:1–6; Ezekiel 34; John 10:1–18; 1 Peter 2:25. [LSW]

141 (in §506:7). Wild grapes are typically sour in comparison to domesticated grapes. The imagery of the wild grape here evokes the parable of the Lord's vineyard in Isaiah 5:1–7, in which the wild grapes that grow in place of the sweet grapes expected by the owner of the vineyard symbolize the fruit of willful unrighteousness. See also the ancient proverb mentioned in Jeremiah 31:29–30 and Ezekiel 18:2, in which the taste of sour grapes is symbolic of the consequence of unrighteous actions. [SS]

142 (in §507:4). Isaiah 14 addresses the downfall of the king of Babylon using imagery of the fallen Lucifer, whose name means "bringer of light," and who is referred to in verse 12 as "Day Star, son of Dawn." Lucifer, a god in Canaanite mythology, is cast into hell as punishment for attempting to usurp the throne of the Most High. The Isaiah passage taunts the king of Babylon for similarly boasting that he will make himself "like the Most High," only to be brought down "to the depths of the Pit" (verses 14, 15; New Revised Standard Version). Swedenborg points out below that this spirit is not Lucifer but simply imagines that he is. [KK]

143 (in §508:1). The description of the walls as consisting of "continuous" windows is remarkable, as this type of structure is unknown until the mid-1800s. Swedenborg here

finds it necessary to specify that the glass is "crystal clear" because in earlier times references to glass did not necessarily imply something fully transparent (see volume 1, pages 700–701 note 138). Compare §839:2, where similar walls and windows are mentioned. [JSR, SS]

144 (in §508:1). Note the parallel to Revelation 21:21, which says of the New Jerusalem, "And the twelve gates were of twelve pearls. Each of the gates is a single pearl." On the meaning of "pearls" as knowledge of what is good and true, which involves knowledge and experience of the Lord, see *Revelation Unveiled* 727, 899, 916. [JSR, LSW]

145 (in §508:1). Compare this passage with §209, where Swedenborg describes the Word and the true things from the Word as shining "like a giant star." [JSR]

146 (in §508:4). Swedenborg is probably here repeating the charge made by many Protestants of his time that Catholics do not read the Bible. For more on this accusation, see volume 1, page 743 note 486. [JSR]

147 (in §508:6). *Heaven and Hell* 29–40 presents a schema of three heavens, each one within or above the next. (For a similar equating of what is "within" and what is "above," see *True Christianity* 214.) The third heaven is the central or highest heaven. The "heavenly angels" who live there accept divine inflow directly into their lives by taking it into their intentions and putting it directly into action. The second heaven is the intermediate or middle heaven. The "spiritual angels" who live there accept divine inflow into their memory and from there into their discernment, thus intending and acting on it by an indirect and more intellectual route. The first heaven is the outermost or lowest heaven. The "spiritual-natural" and "heavenly-natural" angels in the first heaven live good and moral lives and believe in God with no particular interest in learning. The idea that there are three heavens does not appear first in Swedenborg; the apostle Paul speaks of a third heaven in 2 Corinthians 12:2. [LSW, LHC]

148 (in §508:6). For more on the curved letters used in the higher heavens, see §§241, 278, 280:4; *Heaven and Hell* 260–261; *Sacred Scripture* 71. [LSW]

149 (in §508:6). The plural pronoun "they" here reflects a plural pronoun in the Latin. This switch from singular ("an angel") to plural ("they") and the reverse are quite common in Swedenborg's accounts of his spiritual experiences (see, for example, §74:2). It may reflect the involvement of a so-called agent, envoy, or emissary spirit or angel, who represents and speaks for a larger group; see *Heaven and Hell* 255:3, 601, 603:9. [JSR]

Notes to Chapter 9, §§509–570

150 (in §510:2). For John the Baptist's preaching of repentance while baptizing, see Matthew 3:2; for his baptism being called a baptism of repentance, see Mark 1:4; Luke 3:3; Acts 13:24; 19:4. Other assertions about the Bible in this subsection are based on broad or implied themes for which specific verse numbers cannot readily be given. [JSR]

151 (in §510:2). For more on the Jordan as a border of the land of Canaan, which symbolized the Lord's kingdom, or the church, and on the Jordan therefore meaning one's entrance into it, see *Secrets of Heaven* 901:4, 1585, 4255, 8940:2; *Revelation Unveiled* 367. [LSW]

152 (in §511). In Greek and Roman mythology, the Furies (alluded to previously in §380:3) were the avenging spirits of violations against kinship and social order. Swedenborg's somewhat ironic use of them as an illustration here draws on folk beliefs

about hauntings by spirits of the dead rather than on his own theology of the afterlife. [KK, SS]

153 (in §512). "The consolation of the Gospel" is a phrase that, although not strictly biblical in origin, has been a commonplace of Christian devotional literature for centuries. The word "Gospel" as used in this phrase has a special Protestant sense of "the doctrine of salvation solely through trust in the merit of Christ's sacrifice" (*Oxford English Dictionary*, under "gospel"). "The consolation of the Gospel," then, means the reassurance and relief of anxiety afforded by this belief. At the end of the next paragraph in the translation Swedenborg indicates that acquiring this faith and receiving the consolation of the Gospel is considered (by the Protestant Christian world) to be equivalent to one's being renewed, regenerated, sanctified, and saved without any cooperation of one's own. [JSR]

154 (in §514). This figure of speech may be suggesting, within the ironic context of the passage, that the sulfurous stones represent our evils because they reek (as does sulfur) and are heavy or burdensome. At the bottom of the ocean, they still exist but are covered over so thoroughly that they are no burden and are of no consequence. [SS]

155 (in §515:1). Vesuvius and Etna are volcanoes located in Italy and Sicily, respectively. [KK]

156 (in §515:1). In Swedenborg's day "Tartary" (Latin *Tartaria*) was the name for a vast area north of the Great Wall of China. [JSR]

157 (in §516). The parallels in the modern edition of Kolb and Wengert 2000 are found at 318.36–37; 321.1–2; 361.24–362.29. For the names of the thirty-two signers Swedenborg alludes to at the beginning of the paragraph, see Kolb and Wengert 2000, 344; McCain 2006, 306. The statements he quotes or paraphrases here, however, are actually those of Luther himself, from the Smalcald Articles and the Small Catechism. [JSR]

158 (in §517). The "scribes" in ancient Judaism were professional interpreters of the Law, the Hebrew text that corresponds to the first five books of the Old Testament (see volume 1, page 731 note 387). Scribes were often linked with "Pharisees," a Jewish sect known for scrupulous observance of written and traditional law. In the New Testament both groups are frequently identified with hypocrisy. [JSR]

159 (in §519). The dragon appears in Revelation 12:3–4, 7–9, 13–17; 13:2, 4; 16:13; 20:2–3, 7–10, and in Revelation 12:9 and 20:2 is equated with the Devil. (On Swedenborg's understanding of the Devil, see §476:2.) Swedenborg defines those who are associated with the dragon in various ways throughout his works, but the definition in *Revelation Unveiled* 537:5 can be taken as representative: there he says that they are "people who are devoted to faith alone and who reject the works of the law as not effecting salvation." (Passages of *Revelation Unveiled* in these notes were translated by George F. Dole.) The chimerical monsters called locusts appear in Revelation 9:3–11; in *Revelation Unveiled* 424:1, Swedenborg interprets them as symbols of "people who have become sense-centered and see and judge everything on the basis of the physical senses and their illusions." [SS]

160 (in §519). In Swedenborg's theology, nocturnal birds and bats are symbols of false thoughts arising from evil desires; compare §42; *Revelation Unveiled* 757; *Marriage Love* 233:7. For more on Swedenborg's categorizations of animals into positive and negative representations, see note 66 above. [KK]

161 (in §519). The "vestments of the sons of Aaron" were sacred priestly garments; see Exodus 28:4. [KK]

162 (in §520:1). For an example of such teaching from Lutheran confessional texts, see the following statement in the Apology of the Augsburg Confession: "It is further taught that since Adam's fall all human beings, who are naturally conceived, are born in sin. From their mother's womb they are all filled with evil desire and the inclination toward evil" (McCain 2006, 76.2). [JSR]

163 (in §520:2). For an example of passages that describe "the first church" in symbolic terms, see Swedenborg's exegesis of Genesis 2–5 in *Secrets of Heaven* 73–165, 190–313, 324–442, 460–536. For more on the nature of this church, see *Secrets of Heaven* 1114–1129. [LSW]

164 (in §521:1). "Native character" refers to general character traits that people inherit from their parents. In this context it refers especially to character traits that are considered common to the parents' nationality. The "sphere of life that emanates" from this character is the way the particular native character expresses itself in the spiritual "sphere" or "aura" that surrounds each person. Swedenborg describes this aura in *Marriage Love* 171:1: "A spiritual aura goes out in waves from everyone, an aura that comes from the feelings of our love and surrounds us. It makes its way into the earthly aura that comes from our bodies and unites with it." (Passages of *Marriage Love* in these notes were translated by George F. Dole.) For more on this spiritual aura and its various effects see the remainder of *Marriage Love* 171; *Secrets of Heaven* 1048, 1316:2, 1383–1400, 1504–1520, 4464:2–3, 5179, 5725, 7454, 8794, 9109–9110, 10130; *Revelation Explained* (= Swedenborg 1994–1997a) §865:1. Swedenborg took it as a given that the people of each nation share specific character traits that set them apart from other nations. The "native character" of various nationalities can be seen dramatized in a memorable occurrence recorded in *Marriage Love* 103–114. This concept of national character also undergirds a description of the positions of various nationalities and groups in the spiritual world presented in §§800–845 below. [LSW]

165 (in §521:3). Judah had five sons in total. The first three were borne by his wife, who was the daughter of Shua, a Canaanite. Of these sons, the first two, Er and Onan, died childless. The third, Shelah, became the father of his own lineage. (See Genesis 38:2–10; Numbers 26:19–20; 1 Chronicles 2:3; 4:21–23.) The remaining two sons, Perez and Zerah, were twins that Judah fathered with his daughter-in-law Tamar (see Genesis 38:6–30 and note 511 below). They also fathered children (Numbers 26:20–21; 1 Chronicles 2:4–6). The phrase "three lineages," then, refers to the clans of Judah's three surviving sons: Shelah, Perez, and Zerah (Genesis 46:12; Numbers 26:20; see also *Secrets of Heaven* 4818:2). Though Swedenborg did have some awareness that at least two other tribes might have survived as part of the Jewish people (see §845:2; *The Old Testament Explained* [= Swedenborg 1927–1951] §3276), he generally accepts the view, common in his day, that since the time of the Assyrian exile of the northern tribes of Israel described in 2 Kings 17:1–6, the Jewish people have consisted primarily, if not entirely, of the descendants of the southern tribe of Judah. See, for example, *Secrets of Heaven* 3858:5, 4333, 4842; *Revelation Explained* (= Swedenborg 1994–1997a) §§430:3; 433:8, 23. [LSW, JSR]

166 (in §522). "That same chapter" apparently refers to the chapter on faith, which is the sixth chapter of *True Christianity* (§§336–391); see especially §§347–348, 368–372. The chapter on free choice follows it, but not immediately; it is the eighth chapter of the work (§§463–508). [JSR]

167 (in §524:3). Swedenborg begins the comparison by offering the illustration of "good" branches grafted onto a "bad" base (paralleling the practice of grafting the fruitful

cultivated olive branch onto the unproductive wild olive tree), but in developing it he turns the metaphor about so that by the end it is the bad (that is, we ourselves) who are being grafted onto the good (the Lord). The two processes are "similar" only inasmuch as they both involve grafting, literal or figurative; as far as the orientation of good and bad is concerned, the processes are the reverse of one another. Compare §584:2. For biblical precursors to this simile, in addition to the cited reference to John 15, see Paul's assertions in Romans 11:16–17: "If the root is holy, then the branches also are holy," followed by his description of the "wild olive shoot" (the Gentiles) being grafted onto Christ to "share the rich root of the olive tree" (New Revised Standard Version). [KK]

168 (in §525). It has been traditional in all major Christian denominations to give children instructions in the Ten Commandments, the Lord's Prayer, and other basics in the form of stock questions and answers to be memorized. These are usually presented in a small volume called a "Catechism," from a Greek word for echoing back and forth, or an "Enchiridion," from the Greek word for a handbook. For a Lutheran example that has been in use for the past five centuries, see Luther's Small Catechism in the *Book of Concord* (Kolb and Wengert 2000, 347–375; McCain 2006, 313–348). [JSR]

169 (in §526). "Holy Supper" (Latin *Sancta Caena*) is Swedenborg's preferred term for Holy Communion or the Eucharist, on which see §§698–752. [JSR]

170 (in §526). The text quoted here is retranslated from Swedenborg's Latin rendering from the Anglican Book of Common Prayer. The original English of the 1711 version, which Swedenborg is known to have owned (Alfelt 1969, 119), reads as follows:

> . . . that ye . . . be received as worthy partakers of that holy Table. The way and means thereto is: First, to examine your lives and conversations by the rule of God's commandment; and wherein soever ye shall perceive your selves to have offended, either by will, word, or deed, there to bewail your own sinfulness, and to confess your selvs to Almighty God, with full purpose of amendment of life. And if ye shall perceive your offences to be such as are not onely against God, but also against your neighbours, then ye shall reconcile your selvs unto them, being ready to make restitution and satisfaction according to the uttermost of your powers, for all injuries and wrongs done by you to any other: and being likewise ready to forgive others that have offended you, as ye would have forgiveness of your offences at God's hand: for otherwise the receiving of the holy Communion doth nothing else but increase your damnation. Therefore if any of you be a blasphemer of God, an hinderer or slanderer of his Word, an adulterer, or be in malice, or envy, or in any other grievous crime, repent you of your sins, or else come not to the holy Table, lest after the taking of that holy Sacrament, the devil enter into you, as he entred into Judas, and fill you full of all iniquities, and bring you to destruction both of body and soul.

This passage is referred to in §§621:10 and 812, and repeated, with some minor variations, in §722:3. In *Life* 5–6, Swedenborg gives the English of the same passage and translates it into Latin. For other mentions of this prayer, see *Divine Providence* 114, 258; *Revelation Unveiled* Protestant 8:2, 224:10; *Spiritual Experiences* (= Swedenborg 1978) §6098:4; *Draft of "Supplements"* (= Swedenborg 1997a, 137–138, 143) §§212, 224 [Rogers's numbering] = §§214, 227 [Potts's numbering]. The biblical allusions are to Luke 22:3: "Then Satan entered into Judas called Iscariot"; John 13:2: "The devil had already put it into the heart of Judas son of Simon Iscariot to betray him"; and Matthew 10:28: "Fear him who can destroy both soul and body in hell" (New Revised Standard Version). For a somewhat similar prayer against the Devil, see *Revelation Explained* (= Swedenborg 1994–1997a) §1148:4. [SS, JSR, LSW, GFD]

171 (in §527:3). Swedenborg is using the word "chyle" here in its usual sense of the emulsified or dissolved form of fatty substances that have been reduced for absorption via the lacteal lymph vessels in the small intestine. In one of his published pretheological works on anatomy, *The Soul's Domain,* Swedenborg lists some substances that can remain impure in the chyle even after the food they come from has been digested in the stomach: "The chyle itself has not always been completely purified. It sometimes contains crude emulsions from vegetables, or vapors, juices, or insipid elements from unfermented wine, rotten fruit, or unfermented or unclarified beer" (*The Soul's Domain* [= Swedenborg [1744–1745] 1960] §168 note u). As Swedenborg there goes on to say, such substances cause the chyle to "stick in the narrow passages, apertures, and nodules of the duct" that carries the chyle through the body. See also note 109 in this volume. [JSR]

172 (in §530:2). The eighteenth-century Lutheran practice of infant (and adult) baptism included a question regarding renunciation of the Devil. In the Anglican tradition of infant baptism, the godparents were likewise asked, "Dost thou in the name of this child renounce the devil and all his works?" (*Book of Common Prayer* 1711, 34). [JSR]

173 (in §530:2). The warning that Swedenborg mentions here has a biblical basis (see, for example, 1 Corinthians 11:27, 29) and was therefore common in one form or another among Christians of all kinds. For an example from just one faith tradition, see the statement read before communion to Anglican congregations, as quoted by Swedenborg twice in this work (at §526 just above and §722:3 below). See also §812. [JSR]

174 (in §530:2). By "six" commandments against doing evil things, Swedenborg is probably referring to the prohibitions against murder, adultery, stealing, and bearing false witness, and the two commandments against coveting what belongs to others; see §§309–328. (On Swedenborg's numbering of the commandments, see volume 1, page 740 note 465.) [KK, JSR]

175 (in §531). The Latin words here translated "owls and vultures," *ochim et tziim,* are transliterations of the Hebrew terms אֹחִים (*'ōḥim*) and צִיִּים (*ṣiyyîm*), which occur in Isaiah 13:21, a passage to which Swedenborg is clearly alluding. Schmidt 1696, a Latin Bible that Swedenborg favored, uses similar Hebrew transliterations (*Ochim et Zijim*) in this passage, no doubt because their exact meaning has long remained obscure. The word *ochim,* considered onomatopoeic, is taken to mean creatures that make a lamenting or ululating sound. The root meaning of the word *tziim* is "dryness"; the related word צִיָּה (*ṣiyyā*) means aridity. Therefore these are taken to mean creatures that inhabit dry places. Elsewhere Swedenborg clearly shows that he considered both *ochim* and *tziim* to be types of birds (*Marriage Love* 430; see also §661:12 in the present work). As for the Latin word here translated "satyrs," *satyri,* Swedenborg uses it in two overlapping ways. In Greco-Roman mythology the word is used for half-goat, half-human woodland creatures that are followers of Dionysus associated with revelry and lechery. The word also has a biblical use; Swedenborg follows Schmidt 1696 in using it as a Latin translation of the Hebrew שְׂעִירִים (*śə'irîm*) from Isaiah 13:21, which has traditionally been translated "wild goats." Its root relates to hairiness. [JSR]

176 (in §533:1). In Greek mythology, sirens were women (in some accounts birdlike in form) whose singing lured mariners to shipwreck: see, for example, Homer's *Odyssey*

12:39–45, 158–200. For more on sirens in Swedenborg's works, see §80:1 and volume 1, page 713 note 221. [KK, SS]

177 (in §534). In ancient Hippocratic medicine, the four "humors," or fluids, of the body were black bile, yellow bile, phlegm, and blood; their relative balance determined health and temperament. The reference here seems to be rhetorical: Swedenborg does not subscribe to the theory of humors, or at least not in its classical form. For more on Swedenborg's understanding of physiology, see *Secrets of Heaven* volume 1 (= Swedenborg [1749–1756] 2008), page 646 note 466. [SS, KK]

178 (in §534). Ophir was a city renowned in biblical times for its wealth, which included gold, silver, precious stones, sandalwood, and ivory. See 1 Kings 9:28; 10:11; 22:48; 1 Chronicles 29:4; 2 Chronicles 8:18; Job 22:24; 28:16; Psalms 45:9; Isaiah 13:12. [KK]

179 (in §534). "Jehovih" is an alternate spelling of "Jehovah" (see volume 1, page 677 note 9). Swedenborg distinguishes between the inner meaning of the two forms of the name in various places; see, for example, *Secrets of Heaven* 1793. [Editors]

180 (in §535:1). On the levels of the mind from the will at the highest level or core, down through understanding, reason, and knowledge in the memory, all the way to the life of the senses and the senses themselves at the lowest level or periphery, see note 128. As stated just above in §532, a person's actions come from that person's intentions, whose seat is the will. Therefore rebuking oneself for one's own evil and sin requires a change of will, which is at the very core of one's conscious life. However, rebuking others simply requires sensory observation of their actions and evaluation of those actions according to standards of good and evil previously learned and residing in memory. As this process engages only the lowest levels of the mind, it requires no fundamental change in oneself. [LSW]

181 (in §536:1). For what Swedenborg means by "the belief of today's church as it is applied to those three [that is, the persons of the Trinity] in sequence," see §633 below. [JSR]

182 (in §536:2). This view of Jesus' birth is in contrast to the account in Matthew 1:18–25; Luke 1:26–35. Though this rationalization of the Virgin Birth is here ascribed to certain individuals in the spiritual world, it was common also among Deists and other opponents of Christian belief during the Enlightenment. For instance, in *The Age of Reason,* which is a virtual compendium of Deist argumentation of the preceding century, the famous American polemicist Thomas Paine (1737–1809) says of the Virgin Birth that it is a "story . . . blasphemously obscene" (Paine [1794] 1995, 792) and "a theory which . . . is as fabulous and as false as God is true" (Paine [1794] 1995, 775). [SS]

183 (in §536:2). On the people associated with the dragon, see note 159. [Editors]

184 (in §536:2). By "the outer boundaries of the so-called Christian world," Swedenborg is referring to a region of the spiritual world that corresponds to the "Christian world" on earth—that is, to Europe and its colonies, or, in nongeographical terms, to the world's Christians themselves (and perhaps its Jews: see *Sacred Scripture* 54; *Spiritual Experiences* [= Swedenborg 1978] §5619). For more on the correspondence between regions in the spiritual world and various places and peoples on earth, see §§792–845; *Supplements* 32–90; *Draft of "Supplements"* (= Swedenborg 1997a, 57–108) §§1–132 [Rogers's numbering] = §§1–133 [Potts's numbering]. [LSW, SS]

185 (in §536:2). On the founding of a new heaven during the Last Judgment, see §§115 and 773. For descriptions of the "old heavens" in Swedenborg's works, see the references given in note 490. [Editors]

186 (in §536:3). The term "Jehovah Sabaoth" means "Jehovah of the Legions"; it is sometimes translated "Lord of Hosts." For more on "Jehovah," see volume 1, page 677 note 9; for more on "Sabaoth," see volume 1, page 715 note 232. [Editors]

187 (in §536:3). The interpolation "that is, the church" is Swedenborg's. The interpolation "commit adultery" in the next sentence is supplied by the translator from Jeremiah 7:9. [JSR]

188 (in §538:1). "The New Covenant" in this context is an alternate term for "the New Testament." The Old Testament and New Testament in the Bible were so named because of the covenants (or testaments) made between God and humanity in each. In the Old Testament this covenant is referred to frequently, and is renewed and modified many times. A prime example can be found in Exodus 24:1–8. Compare the "new covenant" pronounced by Jesus in Luke 22:20. [LSW]

189 (in §538:1). On the notion that sight involves a ray sent outward from the eye, see volume 1, pages 731–732 note 388. [Editors]

190 (in §560). In the first edition §560 immediately follows §539, more likely because of a numbering error than because of any omission of material. [JSR]

191 (in §562:2). Canon 21 of the Fourth Lateran Council in 1215 affirmed the necessity for all adults to confess their sins to their own priest at least once annually. Since the same canon required the taking of the Eucharist "at least at Easter," meaning between Easter Sunday and Pentecost Sunday, and since anyone who had sinned was not to take the Eucharist without first confessing that sin, confession was considered part of the so-called Easter Duty. Confession at more frequent intervals was encouraged by the church. [JSR, SS]

192 (in §563:1). The term "forerunner" here refers to a herald or "advance man" who went on foot before the vehicles of famous persons to prepare others to receive them. Compare Shakespeare's *The Merchant of Venice* 1:2:136: "There is a forerunner from . . . the Prince of Morocco, who brings word the prince his master will be here tonight." [SS]

193 (in §564:1). It is clear that the terms "earthly," "sense-oriented," and "bodily" (Latin *naturalis, sensualis,* and *corporeus,* respectively) are used here to describe three stages in a progressive decline or movement away from a spiritual or heavenly state, once the inner areas of the mind are blocked off. It is difficult, however, to determine precisely what each term means and what distinguishes the terms, since elsewhere Swedenborg uses them individually or in pairs or as a triplet in a great variety of ways and contexts, including contexts in which they seem synonymous and others in which they are neutral or even positive. For example, other passages speak of "bodily" and "earthly" phases that everyone goes through as part of an orderly progression in early life (see, for example, *Marriage Love* 59:1). A perhaps related passage may shed some light on the usage here. In *Marriage Love* 442 Swedenborg mentions three descending levels with the same names, but adds some description: People on the highest level of the three, the "earthly," have a rational perspective on their own insane thoughts but are nevertheless carried away by the pleasures that accompany those thoughts (for a possible example, see §662:5–7 in the present work). People on the next level down are "sense-oriented" because

they make observations and draw conclusions based on the evidence of their senses alone, and therefore reject notions like God and life after death. Those on the lowest or "bodily" level exercise no judgment at all and are carried away by cravings they feel in their bodies. See also *True Christianity* 402; *Secrets of Heaven* 6315–6318; *Divine Love and Wisdom* 248–255. For more on the meaning of "earthly," see *True Christianity* volume 1, page 681 note 29. On the meaning of "bodily," see *True Christianity* volume 1, page 683 note 38; *Secrets of Heaven* volume 1 (= Swedenborg [1749–1756] 2008), pages 599–600 note 23. [JSR]

194 (in §564:3). Swedenborg commonly refers to the cerebrum (Latin for "brain") and cerebellum (Latin for "little brain") as the "two brains." (For definitions of these brain parts, see volume 1, page 697 note 121.) When he assigns functions to these parts, it is usually voluntary control of the body that is assigned to the cerebrum and involuntary control that is assigned to the cerebellum (for examples, see *Secrets of Heaven* 4325, 9670:2). By contrast, when he assigns intellect and will, it is usually to the left hemisphere of the entire brain that he assigns the former and to the right hemisphere that he assigns the latter (for examples, see *Secrets of Heaven* 641, 644, 3884:1, 4052, 4410). The assignment of the intellect to the cerebrum and the will to the cerebellum in the current passage, however, is paralleled in *Divine Love and Wisdom* 384. For more discussion, see *Secrets of Heaven* volume 1 (= Swedenborg [1749–1756] 2008), pages 635–636 note 356. Compare also *Divine Love and Wisdom* 362; *Marriage Love* 444:6; *Soul-Body Interaction* 13; *Spiritual Experiences* (= Swedenborg 1998–2002) §§1023, 1027; *Revelation Explained* (= Swedenborg 1994–1997a) §§61, 316:16. [SS]

195 (in §565:1). The material in this passage has a fairly lengthy provenance in Swedenborg's corpus. It first appeared in *New Jerusalem* 50 as part of a topical index of sorts, with abundant references to *Secrets of Heaven*. Swedenborg then copied that material over into *Revelation Unveiled* 424:4, with some editing, rearrangement, and occasional additions, as a comparison of the two passages shows. It appears that he then copied *Revelation Unveiled* 424:4 in turn into *True Christianity* 402, with fairly extensive further cutting, including the deletion of all references to *Secrets of Heaven*, as well as further rearrangements and additions. Finally, in writing the present passage it seems that he went back to *Revelation Unveiled* 424:4 and copied it once more, again deleting the references to *Secrets of Heaven*, and again adding some new material not in any previous version, but on the whole doing less editing and rearranging. [JSR]

196 (in §565:2). The Latin phrase here translated "through a kind of back door" is *a tergo*, literally, "from the back" or "at the back." The same phrase is used in §402:8. [JSR]

197 (in §565:2). It is important to note that this describes the way things appear *in the light of heaven*, which Swedenborg also refers to as "the light of truth" (§186). He explains elsewhere that in the faint, deceptive light of hell, things look more agreeable and normal to the spirits there (§281:12). [JSR]

198 (in §565:2). By "the ancients" here Swedenborg presumably means people who lived at some period before the Flood. Swedenborg reports that the most ancient of these people were anything but fixed on sensory impressions: though fully able to perceive physical objects around them in the natural world, they were able at the same time to keep their thoughts fixed on the higher symbolism of the things they saw (see *Secrets of Heaven* 241). [JSR, SS]

199 (in §566:1). The word "satyriasis," which appears at the end of the previous sentence in the translation text, is a transliterated Greco-Latin medical term for a condition of pathological or uncontrollable sexual desire. The term "Saint Vitus's dance," which is now often understood to mean Huntingdon's chorea, referred to a different malady in Swedenborg's day: *choreomania* ("dancing frenzy"), an emotional affliction in which those affected appeared to dance uncontrollably; see volume 1, pages 754–755 note 582. [GMC, SS]

200 (in §567:1). Revelation 11:8 reads, "Their dead bodies will lie in the street of the great city that is spiritually called Sodom and Egypt." Swedenborg mentions below (§841) that there are actually two cities in the spiritual world that used to be called Jerusalem; it seems that he is using this allusion to refer to one of the two. [LSW, JSR]

201 (in §567:1). Swedenborg's assertion that these events occurred at the same time he was writing out the exegesis of Revelation 11 has reference to the similarity between his report and the events described in Revelation 11:1–14. In that story, two witnesses prophesy for the Lord, but are eventually conquered and killed by a beast that comes up from the bottomless pit. Their dead bodies lie in the street of the great city for three and a half days, while people from many nations gaze on them, mock them, refuse them burial, and celebrate their death. However, after the three and a half days they are resurrected and carried up to heaven as their enemies watch. A great earthquake then destroys a tenth of the city, killing seven thousand people. The rest of the people, terrified, give glory to God. For the original account of the experience Swedenborg recounts in this passage, see *Revelation Unveiled* 531. [LSW]

202 (in §567:2). For examples of the Lord preaching these things, see Matthew 4:17; 11:20–24; Mark 1:14–15; Luke 13:1–5; John 8:24. For examples of the Lord commanding his disciples to preach the same message, see Mark 6:7–13; Luke 10:1–21; 24:46–49. For additional references, see §528. [LSW]

203 (in §567:4). For more on these workhouses in the caves of hell, see §§281, 570:7; *Revelation Explained* (= Swedenborg 1994–1997a) §1194; *Sketch on Goodwill* (= Swedenborg 1995) §196. [LSW]

204 (in §567:5). The "ground" mentioned here presumably means the surface of the world of spirits (see note 34). Swedenborg presents both hell and the so-called lower earth as being underground worlds beneath the world of spirits. See volume 1, page 708 note 182; *Heaven and Hell* 428; *Draft of Five Memorable Occurrences* (= Swedenborg 1996c, 529) §18. [JSR]

205 (in §567:7). Since Swedenborg's first editions generally do not utilize quotation marks in the manner in which such marks are used today (see note 512 and volume 1, page 718 note 260), it is difficult at times to determine when a given speech ends. Such is the case in this passage. It is possible, although unlikely, that subsection 7 is to be read as part of the statement made by the "voice from heaven" mentioned in subsection 5. However, the tone of the words "I have asked many Protestants in the spiritual world about this" (compare the first words of §562) and the general similarity of subsection 7 to §§561–562 make these remarks seem more likely to be Swedenborg's than those of the voice from heaven. [JSR]

206 (in §567:8). Swedenborg is referring here to the two stone tablets on which the Ten Commandments were written (Exodus 34:28–29), specifically the fifth through tenth commandments on the second tablet. In *Revelation Explained* (= Swedenborg 1994–1997a) §1026:3, he clarifies that the first three commandments relate to loving

God and therefore appear on the first tablet, the fifth through tenth commandments relate to loving our neighbor and therefore appear on the second tablet, and the fourth commandment applies to and mediates between both types of love. This implies that the fourth commandment was written in such a way as to bridge the two tablets. [JSR]

207 (in §568:2). "Substantial" is used here, as often in Swedenborg, to refer to the spiritual equivalent of matter. For more on Swedenborg's concept of substance, see volume 1, page 691 note 85; and note 48 above. [Editors]

208 (in §568:5). On this shift from the plural "angels" (see subsection 4) to the singular "I," see note 149. In the next paragraph, the plural returns. [JSR]

209 (in §569:5). There are references to Jehovah smelling a pleasing aroma from burnt offerings and sacrifices in Genesis 8:20–21; Exodus 29:18, 25, 41; Leviticus 1:9, 13, 17; 2:2, 9; 3:5, 16; 4:31; 6:15, 21; 8:21, 28; 17:6; 23:13, 18; Numbers 15:3, 7, 10, 13, 14, 24; 18:17; 28:2, 6, 8, 13, 24, 27; 29:2, 6, 8, 13, 36; see also Ephesians 5:2. [JSR]

210 (in §570:2). The Roman deities Venus and Cupid (Aphrodite and Eros in Greek mythology) were gods of love and desire, respectively. The expression "the games of Venus and Cupid" was a hackneyed euphemism for amorous interaction between the sexes in general and for sexual intercourse in particular. The term "game of Venus" in this sense was very old even in Swedenborg's day; for example, it occurs in poem 142 of the anonymous poetic miscellany *Carmina Burana,* a collection that dates from 1000–1250 C.E. [SS, KK]

211 (in §570:3). "Angelic spirits" are defined in §387:1 as "people in the world of spirits who are being prepared for heaven." See also §156; *Divine Love and Wisdom* 140. On the preparation of angelic spirits for heaven, see *Heaven and Hell* 512–520. (In *Secrets of Heaven,* Swedenborg uses the term to mean permanent inhabitants of either the middle heaven [*Secrets of Heaven* 459] or the lowest heaven [*Secrets of Heaven* 9543:1, 9741:1]; there he also speaks of "the heaven of angelic spirits" [*Secrets of Heaven* 996:2].) [LSW, JSR]

212 (in §570:3). The Latin terms translated here, and generally throughout this volume, as "results," "means," and "purposes" are *effectus, causae,* and *fines.* These terms, which usually occur in the reverse order, have traditionally been translated as "effects," "causes," and "ends," respectively. [JSR]

213 (in §570:7). On "the lower earth," elsewhere in this edition sometimes rendered "the underground realm," see volume 1, page 708 note 182; for more, including the biblical basis for the term, see *Secrets of Heaven* volume 1 (= Swedenborg [1749–1756] 2008), pages 617–618 note 169. [JSR]

214 (in §570:7). The divine sphere of doing good is understood by Swedenborg to flow from the Lord into the entire universe. Its domain includes all of heaven, where it embraces the angels and protects them from the influence of hell; and it includes all of hell also, where it is distorted by the evil spirits and turned into its opposite, becoming a sphere of doing evil. For more on the divine sphere, see §§44, 308; *Secrets of Heaven* 8209, 9490, 9492, 9498, 9534, 10188; *Heaven and Hell* 595. [LSW]

Notes to Chapter 10, §§571–625

215 (in §572). The work mentioned here was published by Swedenborg in 1766. [Editors]

216 (in §572). John 6:63 reads, "It is the spirit that gives life; the flesh is no help. The words that I speak to you are spirit and are life." [JSR]

217 (in §572). Biblical references to "children of God" (or "sons of God") occur at Hosea 1:10; Matthew 5:9; Luke 20:36; John 11:52; Romans 8:16, 21; 9:8, 26; Galatians 3:26; 1 John 3:10; 5:2. References to those "born of God" occur at John 1:13; 1 John 3:9; 5:4, 18. References to our having a new heart and a new spirit can be found at Ezekiel 11:19; 18:31; 36:26. [JSR]

218 (in §573). "Jah" is a short form of the name Jehovah, on which see note 29. Swedenborg identifies this shortened form with the divine truth that stems from the Lord's divine humanity; see *Secrets of Heaven* 8267:2. [Editors]

219 (in §573). Passages in which the Lord is called Creator, Shaper, or Maker include Isaiah 17:7; 22:11; 40:28; 42:5; 43:1, 15; 44:2, 24; 49:5; 54:5. [LHC]

220 (in §574:2). On satyrs, see note 175. Priapus was the Greco-Roman god of procreation and was associated with the male genitalia; Swedenborg uses the plural here to mean lascivious male creatures. Satyrs and priapuses are symbolic of sinful people in other passages as well; see, for example, *Divine Providence* 117; *Revelation Unveiled* 655. The Latin here translated "crawling reptiles" is *quadrupedes lacerti;* literally, "four-footed lizards." The purpose of the metaphor seems to be twofold: we are born animals (like quadrupeds that creep on the ground), and what is worse, we are no better than the "worst" of those quadrupeds, reptiles. [JSR, SS]

221 (in §574:2). In the eighteenth-century notion of a hierarchy within all of nature, called the Great Chain of Being (see volume 1, pages 703–704 note 159), monkeys were seen as occupying the top of the animal scale just below the human level; see Lovejoy 2009, 233–236. [KK, JSR]

222 (in §577:1). The Latin phrase here translated "height of foolishness" is *vanitas vanitatum,* literally, "vanity of vanities," an expression used twice in Ecclesiastes 1:2 and once in 12:8. [JSR]

223 (in §577:2). For more on Swedenborg's views and those of his contemporaries on how arteries cooperate with the heart in circulating blood, see *Dynamics of the Soul's Domain* (= Swedenborg [1740–1741] 1955), part 1, §§172–173, 182–186. [JSR]

224 (in §577:2). By "the air pressure . . . acts upon the lungs," Swedenborg refers to the fact that the only force that expands the lungs is that of the air that fills them; the lungs are not attached to the inside of the chest cavity and cannot be "drawn" open by muscular action. By contrast, the ribcage is capable of forcing the lungs to exhale, an action that Swedenborg here describes as "the ribs working the lungs." In one of his anatomical works he states the situation thus: "The lungs contract through an effort of their own, but are opened through the force of the entering air," which acts under atmospheric pressure (*Dynamics of the Soul's Domain* [= Swedenborg [1740–1741] 1955], part 1, §353). See also *The Soul's Domain* (= Swedenborg [1744–1745] 1960) §394, (= Swedenborg 1744–1745, §332). [SS]

225 (in §577:2). Swedenborg believed that the brain possessed an independent motion comparable to that of the heart and lungs. (For a summary of the various components of this motion, see Fuller 2008, 626–634; for a passage in which Swedenborg describes it, see *Dynamics of the Soul's Domain* [= Swedenborg [1740–1741] 1955], part 2, §§1–68.) In this he joined other early researchers, including Thomas Bartholin (1616–1680), Humphrey Ridley (1653–1708), Raymond de Vieussens (1641–1716), and Giorgio Baglivi (1668–1706 or 1707). For some of the original anatomical sources that convinced Swedenborg of the

existence of this motion, see *First Draft of Three Transactions on the Brain* (= Swedenborg 1976d, vol. 1) §§127–136. [SS]

226 (in §577:2). For more detailed examples of this action and cooperation in the human body, see *Divine Providence* 180:2–4. These facts were all well attested in the anatomical science of Swedenborg's day. [JSR]

227 (in §577:3). By "the spiritual organic structure underlying our brain," Swedenborg is referring to the structure of the mind as it exists in spiritual substance, as opposed to physical or material substance. In *Divine Providence* 279:7–9, he describes the physical and spiritual structures of the mind as identical in function, adding that they "act as a unity" by means of correspondence (on which see *True Christianity* volume 1, page 682 note 35). [SS]

228 (in §578). In his anatomical works, Swedenborg several times describes the material brain as being essentially helical or spiral in form; see, for one example, *First Draft of Three Transactions on the Brain* (= Swedenborg 1976d, vol. 1) §409. In several passages in the theological works, he says or implies that the spiritual brain (see note 227 above) likewise has a spiral form. For an example of one such passage, offering further details, see *Divine Providence* 319:2–4. For a passage relating experiences of the kind of torment mentioned here, see *True Christianity* 739:4, 5. [SS]

229 (in §579:1). For a discussion of the word "glorify," which here signifies to "render glorious" or "transform," see volume 1, pages 677–678 note 11. [JSR]

230 (in §579:2). For more on the statement that "without the Lord's Coming no one could have been saved" see §§2–3, 118–120. [LSW]

231 (in §580:1). In general, according to Swedenborg, people who constitute the Lord's outer church are those whose religious observances are focused on taking part in the ritual practices of their church and obeying the Lord's commandments in their words and actions, without paying attention to the deeper aspects of the church. People who constitute the Lord's inner church are those whose religious observances are focused on love for the Lord and goodwill toward the neighbor, and on learning spiritual truth and guiding their lives by it, while still obeying the Lord's commandments in their words and actions and taking part in the ritual practices of their church. For more on the inner and outer church and the character of the people who constitute each, see §674; *Secrets of Heaven* 1062, 1083, 1098, 4292, 6587:2, 7840, 8762. [LSW]

232 (in §581). In actuality, the chapter in question has little to say on the topics mentioned; see note 314. [Editors]

233 (in §581). "The tip of one letter" is a reference to the tiny stroke at the top of each Hebrew letter. [Editors]

234 (in §582:1). This comparison is particularly apt because in the eighteenth century the paper used to wrap market goods such as spices, cheese, and fish was often waste paper from printing houses and therefore had printing on it. This practice of "recycling" paper covered with printing or even handwriting is mentioned frequently in literature and histories, and occasionally gives rise to similar ironic juxtapositions of the mundane item wrapped in the paper and the sublime writing on it. For example, the *Saint Matthew Passion* by J. S. Bach (1685–1750) is said to have survived only because the sheets on which it was written were rescued from a cheesemonger. [SS]

235 (in §582:1). For more on indulgences granted by the Roman Catholic pope, see volume 1, page 734 note 406. [JSR]

236 (in §583:2). "Sin" (Hebrew סִין [*sîn*]) was an Egyptian city located on the Mediterranean coastline just east of the Nile River delta, also known by its Greek-derived name of Pelusium. Its name has no connection or association with the English word "sin." "No" (Hebrew נֹא [*nō*]) was an Egyptian city more commonly known as ancient Thebes, which was located along the Nile River in Upper (southern) Egypt. Its name likewise has no connection or association with the English word "no." [LSW]

237 (in §583:2). For biblical references to "children of God" and "those who are born of God," see note 217. [JSR]

238 (in §584:1). By "human seed" Swedenborg does not mean "sperm-bearing fluid," but a vital essence that has no match in current biology. The description of seed in this sense as originating in the intellect is paralleled by Swedenborg's theories in his scientific works. In *Draft on the Origin of the Soul* (= Swedenborg 1984b, 70), he writes that the brain's simple cortex, whose "operation is intellectual or rational," is the place where the first essence of the soul is "conceived and procreated," adding that "in this way is the soul procreated in every animal." In *Draft on the Reproductive Organs* (= Swedenborg 1928), he explains how this essence is carried by fibers from the brain as it is taken up by the blood and borne to the testicles. This "first essence of the seed . . . supplies that which is the vital essence, that is to say, life itself and the principles and commencements of bodily life" (§43). It is "extracted in the testicle [and] is afterwards enwrapped in a regular series of envelopes," or coverings, in the epididymides, the seminal vesicles, the prostate, and the urethra (§41). This composite fluid is what we would call semen; the spermatozoa themselves Swedenborg dismisses as a deceptive appearance brought about by the active movement of the living seed (§§171–174). Thus it can be seen that his description in the current passage, though somewhat metaphorically expressed, is based on his understanding of the physical process by which semen originates. It is very much in line with the theories of human reproduction offered in his time. For more on these, see Roe 1981, Pinto-Correia 1997, Cobb 2006. On the ancient belief that human seed originates in the brain, see Onians 1951, 109–115, who actually links the word *cerebrum* with the Latin verb *creare*, "to create" (125, 150), though etymologists do not. The belief that the soul was transmitted from parent to child, as opposed to being spontaneously created by God at the act of conception, is called traducianism; on this belief, see Almond 1994, 9–13. [SS]

239 (in §584:2). Compare §524:3 above, as well as *Secrets of Heaven* 45, where bad and good animals are differentiated on the basis of tameness, which equates with domestication, or utility to humankind. Similarly here, Swedenborg calls "bad" the type of uncultivated tree that serves as hardy rootstock, but does not produce useful fruit without grafting. This badness is more than a bare reference to the relative utility of plants and animals, however; it reflects the evil in the universe that arose from the errors of humankind. On this, see note 66 and the references in volume 1, page 705 note 167. [SS]

240 (in §585:1). Although there was some recognition of genderlike distinctions between plants in ancient times, it was not until the late 1600s that reproduction in plants was described by researchers as analogous to sexual reproduction in humans. Some of the notable naturalists who espoused this view were Sébastien Vaillant (1669–1772) and Claude Geoffroy (1685–1752) in France, and Nehemiah Grew (1641–1712) in

England. This theory of sexuality in plants was well known, although not completely accepted, by the time Swedenborg's cousin-in-law Carolus Linnaeus (Karl von Linné; 1707–1778) began working out his taxonomic system based on the reproductive parts of plants. See Schiebinger 1993, 18–19. [SS]

241 (in §585:1). Swedenborg's assertion about the gender of plants offers a striking contrast to the system of classification established by Linnaeus (see note 240): the original basis of Linnaeus's system was an analogy between plant parts and the male and female reproductive parts of humans, so in his system plants may be male or female. (Swedenborg in fact refers to this sort of analogy at the beginning of this section.) In Swedenborg's day, Linnaeus's system did not have the monolithic authority we now ascribe to it: though it began to gain acceptance as early as the late 1730s, during the 1700s as a whole it had competition from some fifty other systems (Schiebinger 1993, 14). An identification of the earth as mother can also be seen in Aristotle—for example, *Generation of Animals* 716a [= Aristotle 1984, 1:1112]; and in the alchemical tradition— for instance, in the writings of the German alchemist Michael Maier (1569–1622); see Schiebinger 1993, 56–57. For a statement that seems to imply that the plant kingdom includes both genders, see *Marriage Love* 222:3. [SS]

242 (in §585:2). Swedenborg, like other physiologists of his time, saw the circulatory system of the body as a system of filtering devices that separated pure from impure elements (see note 132). The purest form of blood, the end product of several filterings, was the animal spirits, the "fluid of the soul" (see volume 1, pages 745–746 note 506). It is to the animal spirits that he is implicitly comparing "the purified sap" here. [Editors]

243 (in §585:2). The currently accepted analogy holds that the fruit is the developed ovary of a plant. Swedenborg's analogy compares the fruit to the testicle because he saw that organ as the place in which an essential seed that originated elsewhere in the body is wrapped in enveloping matter and matures, just as the seed of an apple, for example, matures within the fruit. On Swedenborg's theory of the development of human seed, see note 238. [SS]

244 (in §585:2). On the notion of the "plant soul"—a kind of nutritive force that keeps living things alive at a basic level—see volume 1, page 707 note 175; on the connection between the plant soul and the sap of the plant, see volume 1, pages 740–741 note 467. [Editors]

245 (in §585:3). On Swedenborg's interest in bees, and in particular Jan Swammerdam's account of them, see volume 1, page 687 note 58. [Editors]

246 (in §585:4). On the theory that exhalations are a driver of mineral and plant growth, see §785 and note 113. See also the statement in one of Swedenborg's early scientific works that "there are effluvia of innumerable kinds proceeding from every body" (*Basic Principles of Nature,* part 2, chapter 2 [= Swedenborg [1734] 1988a, 1:245]). Here the source of the emanations from grains of dirt is said to be heat seeping through from the spiritual world itself; the passage is remarkable for this oblique mention of an interface between the spiritual and the material. [SS]

247 (in §587). For more on the philosophical term "intermediate cause," see volume 1, page 703 note 157. [JSR]

248 (in §590:2). The Latin word for beetle here *(cantharis)* may refer specifically to *Lytta vesicatoria,* the blister beetle or Spanish fly (sometimes erroneously identified as *Cantaris vesicatoria*), used for medicinal purposes. It is more green than gold in color.

There are also, however, New World scarab beetles that have an uncanny appearance of being made of pure gold; for example, *Chrysina resplendens, Chrysina chrysargyrea, or Chrysina limbata* (Carlton 2011; Ivie 2011). Some of these were used as ornaments by the Indians of the Americas. Swedenborg may have seen such beetles in a museum or in one of the cabinets of curiosities that were popular at the time (Kors 2003, 2:23–24, 29, 446–447), and in which Swedenborg took a documented interest (Tafel 1877, 6; for examples of his visits to museums, see Tafel 1877, 15–16, 37, 73, 79–80). On the glow of swamp light, see volume 1, pages 702–703 note 149; the glow of rotten wood described here could stem from any of various kinds of phosphorescent fungi. White elemental phosphorus will undergo chemiluminescence (glowing that derives from a cold chemical reaction) on exposure to air; this property was discovered over a century before *True Christianity* was written. [SS]

249 (in §591:1). The "common saying in the church" that the inner self must be reformed before the outer is based on Matthew 23:25–28, especially the metaphor in verse 26, which reads, "You blind Pharisee! First clean the inside of the cup and of the plate, so that the outside also may become clean." For related statements in the Christian Scriptures, see Luke 11:37–41; Romans 2:28–29; 2 Corinthians 4:16. See also note 351. [LSW, RS]

250 (in §596:1). The Latin term here translated "a crisis of the spirit," *tentatio,* is used in a particular way in Swedenborg's theology, yet the process to which it refers is sufficiently multifaceted that no single English equivalent will suffice in all contexts. It has traditionally been translated "trial" or "temptation," an echo of its use in the Bible (see, for example, Psalms 95:8; Matthew 26:41; Luke 4:1–13; James 1:2–3, 12–14; Revelation 3:10). In the present work it is at times alternatively translated "inner conflict" or "assault," depending on context; elsewhere in this edition it is rendered "struggle," "crisis," "test," "trial," "temptation," or "enticement." *Tentatio* has six major meanings in Swedenborg's theology, all of which relate to its root meaning of "trying," and all of which are used to express various aspects of a human being's experience during a crisis of the spirit. It denotes: (1) "an assault" or "attack," because this is how Swedenborg says such a crisis begins—as an attack from hell (*Secrets of Heaven* 1690); (2) "an attempt," because such attacks are an attempt on the part of hell to control the individual (*New Jerusalem* 190); (3) "a putting to the test" or "a being put to the test," because although hell may not have a "putting to the test" as its goal, spiritual crises serve to test the individual, and in them one could be said to succeed or fail (in the sense that either one allows the Lord to be victorious or one succumbs; see *New Jerusalem* 192); (4) "an enticement to evil," because enticement is an aspect of the assault: hell attacks the good things that the individual's inner self loves by inflaming desires and stirring up unclean thoughts and impulses that still reside in the outer self (*New Jerusalem* 196); (5) "a battle" or "combat," namely, between heaven and hell, because a struggle occurs as heaven resists and counters the attack from hell (*Secrets of Heaven* 6657:2; *Revelation Unveiled* 100); (6) "a harrowing, painful, trying experience," usually culminating in utter despair and followed by consolation (*Secrets of Heaven* 1787:1; *New Jerusalem* 196), because this is how a spiritual crisis feels to the individual. Perhaps the three meanings used most commonly in Swedenborg's theology are the first, the fifth, and the sixth: attack on, battle within, and harrowing of the individual. For a general overview of this topic with abundant references to *Secrets of Heaven,* see *New Jerusalem* 187–201. [JSR]

251 (in §597:2). Swedenborg does not specify here what he means by this "crisis of a [truly] spiritual sort" (Latin *quandam spiritualem tentationem*). Compare the assertion he repeats elsewhere that, especially in recent times, "few" have been brought into crises of the spirit, or spiritual temptations (*Secrets of Heaven* 4274:2, 8164, 8965; *New Jerusalem* 193; *Revelation Explained* [= Swedenborg 1994–1997a] §897:2). For more on the council of Nicaea introducing a belief in three gods, see §§632–634 below. [JSR]

252 (in §597:2). For a passage that gives more detail about a conversation in the spiritual world concerning contrition, see §515 above. [JSR]

253 (in §602). Though the reference to a two-headed offspring is symbolic here, Swedenborg's choice of symbol reflects the tremendous interest in so-called monsters, or malformed humans and animals, during the Enlightenment. Their corpses were collected and studied carefully in the hope that they would yield clues about embryology and even about religious issues. For example, those who believed that humans grew from miniature, "preformed" individuals that had been passed down intact from the womb of Eve were challenged to explain the existence of malformed offspring: How could God allow such "monsters" to come into being? For a researcher's drawing from approximately this period, showing a set of conjoined twins sharing a common chest, and thus giving the appearance of a "two-headed offspring," see Roe 1981, 134. For more on monsters, see Pinto-Correia 1997, 144–182; Roe 1981, 124–125, 132–135. On the belief that birth defects resulted from irregular sexual unions, see *Secrets of Heaven* volume 1 (= Swedenborg [1749–1756] 2008), page 645, note 456. [SS]

254 (in §604). On the ancient image of the human being as microcosm, and on Swedenborg's reference to a "microheaven," see volume 1, page 708 note 184. [Editors]

255 (in §605). The original Latin text seems flawed here; the sentence as it stands appears to be missing a clause. Translators have either left this sentence and the next out (as does Clowes in Swedenborg [1771] 1781) or devised various alternate readings. The original reads *Accedit, quod fallacia hoc confuderit, quae est, quod quia homo intellectu ascendere potest, paene in lucem Caeli, & inde ex intelligentia cogitare & loqui de spiritualibus, qualiscunque Amor voluntatis ejus sit;* which could be translated, "In addition, a mistaken impression has caused confusion in this regard—the impression that, *because* we can rise up with our intellect almost into the light of heaven and therefore think and speak intelligently about spiritual matters, no matter what the love in our will is like . . ." (emphasis added). The long subordinate clause beginning with "because" is never completed by a clause stating what the resulting mistaken impression is; presumably, it would be the impression that *we have been reborn and are now spiritual, when in fact we have not been reborn and are still infernal.* The translation here, in effect, ignores the word *quia* (meaning "because"). [JSR]

256 (in §606:1). For examples of biblical passages that relate sleep to earthly life and wakefulness to spiritual life, see Mark 13:32–37; Romans 13:11–13; 1 Corinthians 15:33–34; Ephesians 5:1–16; 1 Thessalonians 5:6–8. See also *Revelation Unveiled* 158; *Revelation Explained* (= Swedenborg 1994–1997a) §§187, 1006:1. [LSW]

257 (in §606:1). The objects mentioned here are associated with the tabernacle, the sacred tent placed at the center of the tribes of Israel when they encamped during their wandering in the wilderness; see Exodus 25:8–9. The lampstand and its lamps and oil are described in Exodus 25:31–40; 27:20–21; 37:17–24; Leviticus 24:1–4. For a detailed explanation of the spiritual meaning of these items, see *Secrets of Heaven* 9547–9577,

9778–9789. The table for the showbread and the showbread itself are described in Exodus 25:23–30; 37:10–16; Leviticus 24:5–9. For a detailed explanation of the spiritual meaning of these items, see *Secrets of Heaven* 2177:7, 7978, 9526–9546, 9993:5. See also *True Christianity* 707. The altar of incense and the incense itself are described in Exodus 30:1–10, 34–38; 37:25–29; an explanation of the spiritual meaning of these objects can be found in *Secrets of Heaven* 10176–10213, 10289–10310. [LSW]

258 (in §607:1). The work mentioned here, *Marriage Love,* was published by Swedenborg in 1768. [JSR]

259 (in §607:3). For more on the expression "gathered to their people," see volume 1, page 688 note 68. [Editors]

260 (in §608:1). *Soul-Body Interaction,* a pamphlet of twenty-three pages in its original edition, was privately distributed by Swedenborg in 1769 (Hyde 1906, 519). [JSR, SS]

261 (in §608:2). This saying about the body of Christ is based on Romans 12:4–5; 1 Corinthians 12:12–27; Ephesians 4:1–16. Though the assertion that "Christ is the life within this body" is more implied than explicitly stated in these passages, it can be gathered from various other passages in the New Testament, such as John 1:1–5; 15:1–8; 17:2–3; 20:30–31; Romans 6:23; Galatians 2:20; Colossians 3:4. [JSR, LSW]

262 (in §611:2). The "worms" Swedenborg is alluding to in this analogy are probably the larvae of the codling moth, which is native to Europe; they are well known for making apples "wormy." The larvae's heads are distinctly darker than their bodies (Carlton 2011). [SS]

263 (in §614:1). The traditional Christian concept of sins being washed away by the blood of Christ is based especially on Hebrews 9:11–27; 1 John 1:5–10; Revelation 1:5; 7:14. For additional commentary on this subject, see §§567, 706; *Secrets of Heaven* 7317–7318, 9014:3; *New Jerusalem* 166; *Revelation Unveiled* 19, 378–379, 838; *Revelation Explained* (= Swedenborg 1994–1997a) §§30, 475–476. [LSW]

264 (in §614:2). On the discarding of waste matter outside the Israelite encampment, see Deuteronomy 23:12–14; see also Exodus 29:14; Leviticus 4:12. For additional commentary and biblical references on the subjects of waste and its disposal outside the camp, and on the symbolism of the camp as heaven and the desert as hell, see §569:5; *Secrets of Heaven* 10037–10038; *Marriage Love* 431; *Revelation Explained* (= Swedenborg 1994–1997a) §922:1. [LSW]

265 (in §614:3). For more on the "dragon's gang," made up of those who form the dragon described in Revelation 12:3–4, see note 272 below. [Editors]

266 (in §615). Swedenborg alludes here to Jesus' conversation with Nicodemus concerning rebirth in John 3:3–8. Although the relevant original Greek (specifically, of John 3:7) of the words uttered by Jesus is γεννηθῆναι ἄνωθεν *(gennethênai ánothen),* meaning "to be born again," the actual Latin word *regeneratio* does not generally appear anywhere in John 3:3–8 in Latin Bibles; nor does the English equivalent of the Latin, "regeneration," generally appear there in English Bibles. However, the English word does appear in English versions of Titus 3:5, where it translates a different Greek expression, namely, the single word παλιγγενεσία *(palingenesía),* "rebirth." [JSR, SS]

267 (in §617). Throughout the complex and interwoven string of similes contained in this paragraph, the actor remains the human being described in the opening clause— even when that human being is compared in quick succession to a ground-traveling

animal, a caterpillar, and a reptile. For more on the use of simile in this work, see volume 1, page 676 note 4. [LSW]

268 (in §618:1). For references to many passages from the Bible relating to these and other teachings about the Lord, see §§81–108; *The Lord* 1–45. [LSW]

269 (in §618:3). Though the precise wording of the statements that follow does not occur in the chapter on faith (§§336–391), similar statements do appear in §§349, 353, 354:3, 360–361, 367:2, 385. See also §392 in the chapter on goodwill and good actions (§§392–462). [LSW]

270 (in §619:1). "The valley of Hinnom" refers to the Valley of the Children of Hinnom (גֵּיא בֶן־הִנֹּם *[gê ben-hinnōm]*) south of Jerusalem, where the Israelites once sacrificed their children to Moloch, the god of the Ammonites (2 Chronicles 33:6; Jeremiah 32:35). Josiah, king of Judah, obeying the commands of the recently rediscovered Torah, defiled this site in his campaign against idolatry (2 Kings 23:10). In keeping with this historical defilement, it was later used as a refuse dump, and also became a place for common burial (Jeremiah 7:31–33). By New Testament times "Gehenna" (derived from the Hebrew for "valley of Hinnom") had become more or less synonymous with hell, and in some versions of the Bible today is so translated. See, for example, Mark 9:43, 45 in the New Revised Standard Version. Given this biblical background, being "buried among the bones in the valley of Hinnom" connotes being mingled with the evil and falsity of hell. On the spiritual significance of the valley of Hinnom, see *Secrets of Heaven* 1292:3; *Revelation Explained* (= Swedenborg 1994–1997a) §659:25. [LHC, RS, LSW]

271 (in §619:4). Torches, which were carried in wedding processions, were a symbol of weddings from ancient times onward; for examples, see Vergil *Eclogues* 8:29; Ovid *Metamorphoses* 10:6. "The marriage of truth and goodness" is a core concept in Swedenborg's theology, which holds that everything in the universe is created from the union or marriage of love (goodness) and wisdom (truth) in God, and is therefore an expression of that marriage. Thus everything in the universe also has that marriage within itself. In an individual human being this marriage is experienced as the union of will and intellect, or of goodness and truth; this is the "marriage" that is overcome by the third sphere mentioned here. For more on the marriage of goodness and truth (also called "the heavenly marriage") and its relationship with interpersonal marriage, see *Secrets of Heaven* 2508, 3952, 3960, 9961; *Heaven and Hell* 366–386; *Marriage Love* 60–67, 83–102. For more on goodness and truth, see *True Christianity* volume 1, page 676 note 7. [LSW, SS]

272 (in §619:5). The "dragon's gang" is made up of those who form the dragon described in Revelation 12:3–4. In Revelation 12:7–9 the dragon is cast down to the earth after losing a battle with Michael and his angels. Revelation 12 ends with the dragon still on earth making war against "those who keep the commandments of God and hold the testimony of Jesus" (Revelation 12:17; New Revised Standard Version). The dragon remains on earth until the events of Revelation 20:1–10, culminating in his being "thrown into the lake of fire and sulfur" where he is to be "tormented day and night forever and ever" (Revelation 20:10; New Revised Standard Version). Swedenborg identifies the dragon as "the people in the Reformed church who divide God into three [persons] and the Lord into two [natures] and who separate charity from faith, making the latter saving without the former at the same time" (*Revelation Unveiled* 537). For a

description of how the final judgment on this group was carried out in the spiritual world, resulting in the freeing of many good spirits from the sphere of the dragon, see *Supplements* 14–31. By Swedenborg's account there the dragon had been defeated in the spiritual world. He adds here that the dragon's influence still remained in the physical world. This is in accordance with the description of these events found in Revelation 12:7–9. [LSW]

273 (in §619:6). The Latin here translated "Baltic Sea" is *mari Orientali,* literally, "the East Sea." On the use of this term in Swedenborg's era, see Helander 2004, 241–242, 263. The term lives on in the modern Swedish word for this sea, *Östersjön* ("Eastern Sea"). The Latin *mari Occidentali,* here translated "the North Sea," literally means "the West Sea"; it refers to the body of water situated between Scandinavia and northern Europe on the east and Great Britain on the west. The North Sea, including the Kattegat and Skagerrak (two North Sea straits near Sweden), is still referred to as "the West Sea" *(Västerhavet)* by the Swedish. See Alexandersson 1982, 27. As Swedenborg's comparison here suggests, the view between the Baltic Sea and the North Sea is blocked by intervening land. [LSW, SS]

274 (in §620:1). The point of the comparison is not that the sun would appear like cloth, but that it would appear black; in the passage from the Book of Revelation Swedenborg mentions here, Revelation 6:12, the sun is specifically described as "*black* as sackcloth.*" Sackcloth (Hebrew שַׂק *[śaq];* Greek σάκκος *[sákkos]*) was a coarse cloth made of hair, usually black goat's hair, worn in ancient times as a sign of mourning or repentance. [LSW, SS]

275 (in §620:2). The Latin phrase here translated "transparent blockage" is *gutta serena,* meaning "unclouded disease." Swedenborg describes this condition in §645 below; see also §346 in volume 1. [JSR]

276 (in §621:2). The account here mentions four main categories of Christians in Great Britain: Roman Catholics and three types of Protestants. The identity of Roman Catholics is clear enough. The people the British refer to here as "our own holy ministers" would presumably be Anglican; "others who also call themselves Protestants" would likely mean Presbyterians; the "Protestant Dissenters" (Latin *sectarii*) probably means the smaller Protestant denominations in Great Britain at the time, such as Quakers and Moravians. [JSR]

277 (in §621:10). There is a slight disjunction between the question as phrased and the response the spirits receive. The spirits essentially ask if the ability to act "*as if* on one's own" is innate in humankind. The question is equivalent to: "Is it an inherent attribute of humanness that we are able to draw on divine qualities and strengths in our actions?" The angels do not respond to this question directly. They answer a different question, as it appears: whether we can act on our own at all. The implication is that we could not act on our own even so far as to draw on divine qualities and strengths. The angels then add that this inability does not matter, because (by implication) in supplying us with the ability to act at all, God supplies us with the ability to draw on his qualities and strengths. [SS, JSR]

278 (in §621:10). The angels are apparently referring (appropriately, considering that they are addressing British spirits) to the same Anglican text that Swedenborg quoted in §526; for discussion, see note 170. Strictly speaking, the material in question is not a prayer, as the angels suggest, but an exhortation from the minister to the congregation. [SS]

279 (in §621:10). The Latin expression *reus fieri* is used in this passage in the sense of "coming into fault"; it refers to the assignment of guilt in a courtroom after the fact; or, when used in the negative *(non reus fieri),* to the declaration of innocence. Elsewhere Swedenborg uses similar language of the assignment after death of guilt or innocence for one's actions during life on earth (*Marriage Love* 530:1). The implication seems to be that the individual both takes an action and takes a stance in regard to that action; and it is the stance that determines the individual's spiritual culpability for that act. In other passages, Swedenborg asserts that culpability results only when the will and the intellect collude; see *Secrets of Heaven* 9009:2–3; 9012. For related passages see §154:4; *Secrets of Heaven* 6324, 9075, 9132; *Heaven and Hell* 302; *Divine Providence* 290, 294, 320–321; *Revelation Explained* (= Swedenborg 1994–1997a) §1147:3–4. [JSR, SS]

280 (in §621:12). For the historical context of this reference to sculptures that speak, see volume 1, page 694 note 103. [Editors]

281 (in §621:12). Swedenborg briefly mentions such atheists in §§12:10, 382, 695:5, 759:3. For his description of their appearance "in spiritual light," see *Divine Love and Wisdom* 357. For some of the major atheist voices of his time, see volume 1, page 758 note 600. [Editors]

282 (in §621:13). The reference here to "something flamelike" coming down "from heaven" is reminiscent of an event recorded in Acts 2:2, 3, in which the apostles had a vision of tonguelike flames touching them on the Day of Pentecost. [JSR]

283 (in §623:1). For more on justification by faith alone, see note 291. [JSR]

284 (in §623:4). In this sequence of three, "the Creator and Preserver" refers to the Father as seen in traditional Christian theology, "the Redeemer and Savior" refers to the Son, and "the Enlightener and Instructor" refers to the Holy Spirit. [LSW]

285 (in §623:5). On the ancients assigning independent divine status to the various attributes of God, see volume 1, page 684 note 45. [Editors]

286 (in §624:1). In this spiritual experience Swedenborg can wake up "in the middle of the night" on earth and yet see a piece of paper "shining brightly" in the sun of heaven because the sun never sets there (*Secrets of Heaven* 10134:10; *Marriage Love* 137:5). [LSW, JSR]

287 (in §624:3). For more on the terms "underlying reality" and "capacity to become manifest," see volume 1, page 691 note 86. [JSR]

288 (in §625:1). The Latin is ambiguous; the Latin word *caelum,* here translated "heaven," also means "sky." [LSW]

289 (in §625:2). Alpha and omega are the first and the last letters of the Greek alphabet. For an explanation of their meaning and significance, see §19:2. [JSR]

290 (in §625:3). As is the case with forty-seven out of the seventy-seven accounts of memorable occurrences in this work, the account here is repeated from an earlier book published by Swedenborg. Cole 1991 points out that a mistake in the first edition at this particular reference to the Book of Revelation suggests how Swedenborg went about supplying the printer with the text of such repeated accounts. Expressed as usual in a combination of roman numerals for chapters and arabic numerals for verses, the reference reads, "XII: XXI: 1. 2. 9. 10," meaning "chapter 12 chapter 21, verses 1, 2, 9, and 10." The erroneous double chapter number can be traced to a mistaken catchword on page 63 of the first edition of *Marriage Love* 81. (In eighteenth-century printing, it was

customary to print a "catchword," consisting of at least the first few letters of the first word of a given page, in the right-hand lower corner of the previous page below the last line.) The first word on page 64 of *Marriage Love* is "XXI," correctly referring to chapter 21; but the typesetter of that volume mistakenly set "XII," or 12, as the catchword at the bottom of the page 63. It would appear, then, that when Swedenborg was publishing *True Christianity* and decided to include this account from *Marriage Love* 81, rather than writing it out by hand he gave the typesetter a copy of *Marriage Love;* and the typesetter, noticing that two different chapter numbers were given by the catchword and the text proper, but not knowing which was correct, copied both into *True Christianity.* [JSR]

Notes to Chapter 11, §§626–666

291 (in §626). Here and throughout this work, Swedenborg uses the word "justification" (Latin *justificatio*) not in its normal English meaning but as a Christian theological term. Justification is the action or process by which a given individual is freed from the penalty of sin and either deemed or actually made "just," meaning righteous and therefore worthy of salvation. In Swedenborg's time, a major focus of theological debate and disagreement between Roman Catholics and Protestants concerned the role of good works in this process; Roman Catholics laid great emphasis on good works, but Protestants used Romans 3:28 and other scriptures to argue that faith by itself (that is, "faith alone") without good works was the sole agent of justification and therefore the sole prerequisite for salvation. For a brief overview of the Protestant use of this term, see Muller 1985, 162–163; see also the introduction to volume 1, pages 90–92, and page 717 note 252 there. For a different interpretation of Romans 3:28, see §506:2–3. [JSR]

292 (in §627). For more on the promised, but never completed, appendix to this work, see volume 1, page 689 note 71. [JSR]

293 (in §629). It is difficult to convey in English the full force of the Latin play on words in this paragraph. The Latin words for "double" *(duplex)* and "doubleness" *(duplicitas)* have an even wider range of meanings than the related English words do. They have a straightforward sense like our words "double," "twofold," and "dual"; they have several negative connotations, similar to the related English expressions "duplicity," "double dealing," and "a double standard"; but the Latin words include a positive meaning that English does not share, which is that of "broadness" and "inclusivity" (see Littleton 1723, under *duplex*). Swedenborg here repeatedly plays these positive and negative meanings off against each other. [JSR]

294 (in §630). Beelzebub was the god of the city of Ekron in the Old Testament. In 2 Kings 1, King Ahaziah attempts to inquire of him, rather than of Jehovah, whether he will recover from a sickness, thus incurring the contempt of Jehovah and the prophet Elijah. The name Beelzebub means "Lord of Flies" in Hebrew. He is called the Prince of Devils in Matthew 12:24, and in later Christian tradition he was a lieutenant of Satan among the fallen angels (see Milton *Paradise Lost* 1:81). [JSR, SS]

295 (in §631). Swedenborg here refers to the practice among the ancient Romans of observing birds to determine whether some intended action was permitted by the gods on a particular day. In addition to the flight of wild and tame birds, their number, position, cries, and feeding were also believed to be significant. [SS]

296 (in §632:1). Constantine the Great lived from around 285 to 337 C.E. Alexander, usually referred to as the patriarch of Alexandria in Egypt, seems to have held office

beginning in 312 C.E., and may have died as early as 326. His date of birth is not known. Arius lived from around 250 to around 336 C.E.; as Swedenborg indicates, he was a presbyter, or elder, of the church at Alexandria, but he went down in church history as the originator of the Arian heresy mentioned here. Swedenborg saw the First Council of Nicaea (325 C.E.) as a turning point in Christian history of even greater significance than the Protestant Reformation; in §760 below he divides almost 1800 years of Christianity into two major phases, one before and one after the Council of Nicaea. [JSR, SS]

297 (in §632:1). For the full text of the Nicene and Athanasian Creeds in English, see Kolb and Wengert 2000, 22.1–25.40; McCain 2006, 16–18; on the Athanasian Creed, see also volume 1, pages 680–681 note 25. [JSR]

298 (in §632:2). The parallel for this extract in the modern edition of Kolb and Wengert 2000 is found at 22.1–23.4, 7. [JSR]

299 (in §632:2). The word "catholic" in this passage means "universal." The parallel for this extract in the modern edition of Kolb and Wengert 2000 is found at 24.3–4, 18–19. [JSR]

300 (in §633:3). By "all three continents," Swedenborg here means Asia, Africa, and Europe. Compare §§632:1, 636:1. [JSR]

301 (in §634:2). The Roman Catholic teaching that the pope is the vicar of Christ (meaning an agent or substitute for him) is based on two passages in Scripture: Christ's command to Peter to tend and feed his lambs and his sheep (John 21:16–17), and his assertion that Peter is the rock on which he will build his church, and therefore to Peter he grants power both on earth and in heaven (Matthew 16:18–19). The papacy was seen as inheriting these powers from Peter, and the pope was referred to as the vicar of Christ sporadically from the fifth century and regularly from the thirteenth. The invocation of saints, or calling on them to offer intercessory prayers to God, was sanctioned in Session 25 of the Council of Trent. For more on the veneration of relics, see volume 1, page 725 note 326; and on the removal from the laity of one of the elements of the Eucharist, see volume 1, page 734 note 406. The Protestant Reformers challenged the validity and scriptural soundness of all these practices. [JSR]

302 (in §634:2). Purgatory (see note 69) was mentioned in the Decree of Union drawn up at the Council of Florence (1438–1445). A decree concerning purgatory and another concerning indulgences were issued as part of Session 25 of the Council of Trent (December 3–4, 1563). For more on indulgences, see volume 1, page 734 note 406. [JSR]

303 (in §634:2). For more on the Synod of Dort and predestination, see note 90 and volume 1, page 734 note 407. [JSR]

304 (in §635). This is not the only passage in which Swedenborg refers to "seven chapters of the Book of Revelation" without specifying which chapters he means (see §179 and volume 1, page 735 note 412; *Survey* 76, 88). From the context here and elsewhere it is clear, however, that material in the nine chapters Revelation 8 through 16 is relevant. It remains uncertain if he meant to include all nine of those chapters and simply miscounted, or, if he was not referring to all nine, what specific material he would have excluded to reduce the count to seven chapters. [JSR, LSW]

305 (in §635). The name "Reed Sea" (*mare Suph* in the original Latin) is a biblical allusion to what is more generally known as the Red Sea. [JSR]

306 (in §636:2). The statement here that the Apostles' Creed was named for the so-called apostolic church implies that it was not named for the apostles themselves. This

may be a reference to the issue of the creed's authorship. In earlier centuries, Christians believed that the creed had been written by the apostles themselves; but this began to be questioned in the fifteenth century (Kolb and Wengert 2000, 20). In the appendix to the edition of the *Book of Concord* owned by Swedenborg, Rechenberg includes a lengthy discussion of issues surrounding this creed (*Concordia* 1756, appendix pages 40–106), and cites as evidence that it was not written by the apostles the fact that the creed is nowhere mentioned in the Acts or Epistles (*Concordia* 1756, appendix page 41). Nevertheless, it was recognized that this creed had originated in material from before the Council of Nicaea. [JSR]

307 (in §636:2). This, like many of Swedenborg's other quotations, is condensed. (For Swedenborg's treatment of quotations, see pages 13–14 in the list of short titles and conventions.) A parallel for this extract in the modern edition of Kolb and Wengert 2000 is found at 21.1–3, 22.7. [JSR]

308 (in §636:2). The other two creeds Swedenborg refers to here are the Nicene Creed and the Athanasian Creed. [JSR]

309 (in §637). In Homer's *Odyssey* 12:85–110, 222–259, 426–446, Charybdis is a whirlpool that destroys ships, and Scylla is a monster who lurks in a cliff opposite the whirlpool to seize and devour passing sailors. [SS]

310 (in §637). At the end of this string of references to "clear statements in the Old Testament," the first edition includes a phrase that is problematic in several ways and is therefore not represented in this translation: *his adde Joh. IX. 15* ("to these [passages] add John 9:15"). For one thing, it is odd, and unparalleled in Swedenborg's published works, to tell the reader to add a biblical reference to the text. Swedenborg may instead have written this as a reminder to himself or an instruction to the typesetter; and of course the typesetter may have misread or misunderstood what Swedenborg wrote. For another, John 9:15 is not part of the Old Testament and has no apparent bearing on the issue in question. It seems that other editors and translators as well have found the reference problematic. Clowes (Swedenborg [1771] 1781) omits it altogether. Worcester (Swedenborg [1771] 1833) leaves it as John 9:15. Foster (Swedenborg [1771] 1869) and Dick (Swedenborg [1771] 1950) change it to John 1:14. Ager (Swedenborg [1771] 1906–1907) expands it to read "John 1:14, 19:15." Bayley (Swedenborg [1771] 1933) has John 1:15. Chadwick prints John 9:15 but adds a footnote saying it is a "wrong reference" and that it is "possibly to be corrected to John 1:15" (Swedenborg [1771] 1988b, 2:677). Fitzpatrick's recent Latin edition (Swedenborg [1771] 2009, 2:194) corrects it to John 4:42 with a footnote. In addition to these, there are two other possible but unlikely solutions. Swedenborg may have meant to refer to John 8:58 (which in the Latin original would have been *Joh. VIII: 58*), but that would mean he committed five errors in a single reference. Another alternative is Job 19:25, a reading suggested in Swedenborg's own copy of the first edition, which was given to his heirs after his death, and which then passed through various hands. This copy (now housed in the Swedenborg Library in Bryn Athyn, Pennsylvania) contains emendations and marginal notes, many of which are clearly not in Swedenborg's own handwriting. The reference in question is emended in that copy: the printed characters representing the book, the chapter, and the verse have been directly altered in pen and ink to read *Job. XIX. 25* (Job 19:25). This reference is, on the one hand, arguably a plausible substitution: it is an allusion to the Old Testament, which seems to be required here; it is solidly on topic; and the same

reference also occurs in a similar list of passages in *Secrets of Heaven* 6281:3. However, there remain two reasons for questioning whether this correction was written by Swedenborg himself: (1) These corrections are drawn right on top of the printed text itself, whereas Swedenborg's usual practice was to indicate changes less intrusively in the margin. (2) Almost always throughout this volume and Swedenborg's other theological works he uses the abbreviation "*Hiob.*" rather than "*Job.*"; in almost two hundred references, the abbreviation "*Job.*" appears just three times, in *Secrets of Heaven* 728:5, 2864, and 8106:4. [JSR]

311 (in §638:1). The "garden of God" is the Garden of Eden. See §467:1–2 and the references there. [Editors]

312 (in §638:1). The Latin phrase here translated "until late afternoon" is *ad decimam horam,* literally, "until the tenth hour." From the sequence laid out in this paragraph, it seems clear that Swedenborg is here using the ancient Jewish reckoning of the day, which consisted of twelve "hours" of variable length between sunrise and sunset, whenever they occurred (for biblical examples see Matthew 20:3, 5, 6; 27:45; John 11:9). For example, if the sun rose at 6:00 A.M. (on a modern clock) and set at 6:00 P.M., the tenth hour would be from 3:00 to 4:00 P.M.; if the sun rose at 4:00 A.M. and set at 8:00 P.M., the tenth hour would be from 4:00 to 5:20 P.M. When Swedenborg elsewhere uses the same Latin phrase for the "tenth hour" but applies it to the modern clock, he makes this clear by adding the words *ante meridiem* (A.M.) or *post meridiem* (P.M.); see *Spiritual Experiences* 5099. [JSR]

313 (in §639:3). Swedenborg refers several times to the belief that nature created the universe (and thus "created itself") as a hallmark of atheism. (For more on atheists, see note 281). The belief that God came into existence after nature usually relies on the chain of reasoning that nature created humankind and humankind created the concept of God; for gods as figments of the human mind, see, for example, *On the Nature of Things* 5:1161–1240, by the Roman poet Lucretius (around 94–51 B.C.E.). On pantheism, which could be briefly if incompletely described as the belief that God and nature are the same thing, see volume 1, page 685 note 49. [SS]

314 (in §640:1). In actuality, the material on redemption in §§114–133 mentions regeneration only briefly, in §123:6. Keeping the commandments is mentioned nearby in §135:5. In the sixth chapter on redemption (§29) outlined in *Sketch for "True Christianity"* (= Swedenborg 1996a, 177–239) §29 (chapter 6), Swedenborg includes the proposition, "Through these acts [of redemption] Jehovah God took on the power to save all who believe in him and do what he prescribes." However, this proposition was not included in the published version of *True Christianity.* At the time of his death Swedenborg was in the process of rectifying this omission, taking up the subject in his *Draft for "Coda to True Christianity"* (= Swedenborg 1996b, 23–106). In §21 of that draft he offers eleven summary propositions about the Lord's redemption, the last six of which concern the regeneration of human beings. If Swedenborg did write the intended fuller explanation of those propositions as part of that draft, it has been lost with the portion of the manuscript that is known to be missing. The subject is treated briefly in §579:2 above in the chapter on reformation and regeneration. See also *Secrets of Heaven* 2954, 10152:2. [LSW]

315 (in §640:2). One important commentary on the Council of Trent was that of Giovanni Bellarini (1552–1630); see Bellarini 1603. Presumably, by the commentary or

commentaries on the Augsburg Confession (on which see note 6) Swedenborg means the Apology of the Augsburg Confession by Philipp Melanchthon (1497–1560), and perhaps also other documents that were eventually brought together with it to form the *Book of Concord;* see Kolb and Wengert 2000, 109–294. [JSR]

316 (in §640:3). The text here reproaches Protestants by asserting that these teachings of theirs verge on those of Roman Catholicism, to which they are assumed to be inimical. Swedenborg targets the Protestant notion that Christ's merit could be assigned, attributed, or applied to us, suggesting that it is only one step short of the Roman Catholic concept that the pope is the vicar of, that is, substitute for, Christ; see note 301. On Swedenborg's attitude toward Roman Catholicism in general, see note 69. [JSR]

317 (in §641:2). Spiritual auras or atmospheres are the phenomena in the spiritual world corresponding to the ether and air of the material world, which Swedenborg believed to be the carriers of material heat and light. (On the origin and transmission of material heat and light, see note 55). [SS]

318 (in §642). For Swedenborg's references to and summaries of passages on these subjects from the Council of Trent and the *Book of Concord,* see *Survey* 5b, e, and f; 11c; 12a. [JSR]

319 (in §642). For the biblical roots of this saying, see Proverbs 11:22, "Like a gold ring in a pig's snout is a beautiful woman without good sense," and Matthew 7:6, "Do not give what is holy to dogs, and do not throw your pearls before swine, or they will trample them under foot and turn and maul you" (New Revised Standard Version). [Editors]

320 (in §643:1). Swedenborg does not specify that the assignment of spiritual credit or blame occurs after death until the first sentence of §646 below. The translator has inserted the phrase "after death" in square brackets here and elsewhere in §§643–645 for the sake of clarity. [JSR]

321 (in §647:3). By the "Greek church," Swedenborg probably means Eastern Orthodox Christianity in general. Although Swedenborg frequently mentions Protestant and Roman Catholic Christianity, the only other mentions of the "Greek church" (Latin *Ecclesia Graeca* or *Graeca Ecclesia*) in his published theological works occur in §153:3 and *Survey* 18. He did, however, take some notes in 1748 on the structure, beliefs, and practices of Greek Orthodox Christianity. Still extant, these notes go by the short title *Greek Orthodox Religion* (see Acton 1922; Swedenborg 1922). [JSR]

322 (in §649). This is a reference to Revelation 12:3: "Then another portent appeared in heaven: a great red dragon, with seven heads and ten horns, and seven diadems on his heads" (New Revised Standard Version). For more on the symbol of the dragon, see note 272. [LSW]

323 (in §650). See, for example, Deuteronomy 6:14–15; 29:25–28; Isaiah 13:1–13; 34:1–8; 63:1–6; Jeremiah 7:20; 33:1–5; Revelation 6:15–17; 14:9–11. For commentary on these and other Bible passages that attribute anger and wrath to God, see *Secrets of Heaven* 5798; *Revelation Unveiled* 635, 658; *Revelation Explained* (= Swedenborg 1994–1997a) §§357:23, 960. [LSW]

324 (in §653). The context of the biblical passage quoted here in the text shows that Jesus' statement was directed specifically to Pharisees; see Matthew 12:24, 25. On Pharisees, see note 158 above. [JSR]

325 (in §654). Of the points listed so far in this paragraph, only one of them resembles any of the points made in the chapter on faith. The point here that reads "Faith without goodwill is not real faith, because it is not spiritual; goodwill without faith is not real goodwill, because it has no life" is like item 5 in the list in §336:3, which is explained fully at §§355–361: "Faith without goodwill is not faith. Goodwill without faith is not goodwill. Neither of them is living unless it comes from the Lord." It is possible that the previously unattested propositions given here were taken from a draft of *True Christianity* that is no longer extant. [LSW, JSR]

326 (in §655). The first three deities listed are gods and goddesses of Greco-Roman mythology by their Roman names. Jupiter was the supreme god. Juno was the chief goddess, wife and sister of Jupiter, and the goddess of marriage. Apollo was the god of prophecy, music, medicine, poetry, and the sun. Dagon was a principal god of the Philistines, who lived along the Mediterranean coast in southern Palestine in biblical times. See Judges 16:21–24; 1 Samuel 5:2–7; 1 Chronicles 10:8–10. Baal was a male fertility god often portrayed as a bull; he also had power over thunder and lightning. As the god of various Canaanite nations, sometimes worshiped by the Israelites themselves, he is mentioned many times in the Old Testament; for examples, see Judges 2:10–15; 6:25–32; 1 Kings 18:16–40; 2 Kings 10:18–28. Furthermore, various local Canaanite deities also bore the name of Baal; among these was the Baal of Peor mentioned here (see Numbers 25:1–5; 31:16; Deuteronomy 4:3; Joshua 22:17). On Balaam and his relationship with local deities, including Baal of Peor, and with the God of Israel, see Numbers 22–25; 31:7–16; Deuteronomy 23:3–6. The gods of Egypt are mentioned in Exodus 12:12; Numbers 33:4. [JSR, LSW]

327 (in §661:1). The Latin word here translated "homes" is *mansiones*. This is likely a reference to John 14:2, "In my Father's house there are many dwelling places," and to John 14:23, "Those who love me will keep my word, and my Father will love them, and we will come to them and make our home with them" (New Revised Standard Version). The Greek word μονή (*moné;* "dwelling place," "home") occurs only in these two verses in the New Testament. Swedenborg consistently translates it into Latin as *mansio* when quoting these verses. [LSW]

328 (in §661:7). The square hat or cap (Latin *pileus quadratus*) was a symbol of high status in the Europe of Swedenborg's time; it was worn mainly by clergy, but also by members of the nobility and government leaders. Here it is a sign that this devil was a member of the laity, just as the bishop's miter mentioned in subsection 9 just below marks that devil as a member of the clergy. In these contexts, such hats are of course grotesquely incongruous. [JSR]

329 (in §661:10). The reference here to "the keys" and "the power of binding and loosing" is an allusion to Matthew 16:19; see also Matthew 18:18; Isaiah 22:22. These verses figure in the claim made by some Christian churches to have a continuous succession of authority from Jesus through Peter to later church leaders. This authority is understood to provide efficacy in "binding and loosing" individuals to or from certain consequences in the next world that may accrue from their sinning in this one. Compare note 301. [LSW, SS]

330 (in §661:12). In the original Latin here Swedenborg uses transliterations of two plural Hebrew nouns: *ochim* and *ijim*. Elsewhere in the present work these are rendered

"owls" and "shrieking night birds," respectively. For more on *ochim* see note 175. The *ijim* (Hebrew אִיִּים‎ [*'iyyîm*]) are creatures mentioned in Isaiah 13:22; 34:14; Jeremiah 50:39. Their exact identity is unclear, but their name seems to be an onomatopoeic reference to howling or screeching. Although most English Bible translations render them as animals ("wolves," "hyenas," or "wild beasts of the islands"), this passage makes it obvious that Swedenborg takes them to be birds. [JSR]

331 (in §664:1). Examples of passages in which the Bible refers to "the elect" are Isaiah 45:4; 65:9, 22; Matthew 24:22–24, 31; Luke 18:7. [LSW]

332 (in §665:1). Context shows that in this passage "down" means not down to the physical earth but down to the world of spirits below the heavens; see note 34. [JSR]

333 (in §665:2). This paragraph centers on a commonality among three Latin words that is not fully representable in their English renderings. The Latin words here translated "conscience," "knowing," and "conscious" are *conscientia, scire,* and *conscire,* respectively, which all come from a root *sci-* that has to do with knowledge and awareness. [JSR]

334 (in §665:2). Compare §570:2, a passage in which delight is defined by some idlers in much the same terms. On the meaning of the cliché "games of Venus and Cupid," see note 210. [JSR, SS]

335 (in §665:3). On this comparison between the world and the stage, common from ancient times but especially beloved by early Enlightenment Neo-Latin writers, see Curtius 1953, 138–144, and Helander 2004, 422–424. Swedenborg himself made frequent use of this imagery throughout his works, but particularly in his prose poem of 1745, *Worship and Love of God.* [SS]

336 (in §665:4). On the two brains, see note 194. [Editors]

337 (in §665:4). The description of the causes of sadness, grief, and anxiety here does not perfectly match the account of these ailments as given in Swedenborg's anatomical work *Draft on the Fiber* (= Swedenborg 1976a) §§481–508. There are, however, strong similarities between the two accounts. For example, Swedenborg there writes that "In true melancholic diseases the red blood is harder, insoluble, [and] . . . mixed with fragments of bile," which causes the brain fibers to become "somewhat hard, tenacious, not easily mutable in respect to their state of expansion and constriction, but sluggish and stiff in action. This is the reason why melancholic subjects are fixed in one object of thought" (*Draft on the Fiber* [= Swedenborg 1976a] §484). The melancholic person is there similarly described as "obstinate and tenacious of purpose," and as clinging "to certain objects and to them alone" (*Draft on the Fiber* [= Swedenborg 1976a] §481). [SS]

338 (in §665:4). On the animal spirits, a superfine fluid permeating all parts of the body, see volume 1, pages 745–746 note 506. For related information, see also notes 132, 242 in this volume. [Editors]

339 (in §665:4). *Ataxia* is incoordination resulting from a nervous disorder. *Lipothymy* (now "syncope") is chronic susceptibility to fainting. [RPB]

340 (in §665:5). The *epigastric* is the anatomical region above the stomach, below the sternum. The *hypogastric* is the anatomical region below the stomach. [RPB]

341 (in §665:5). *Cacochymy* is an obsolete term denoting an impurity of the fluid in the interstices of the body resulting from a disease of the internal organs. [RPB]

342 (in §665:5). The phrase "humors . . . saturated with black, yellow, or green bile" refers to the characteristic jaundice of liver disease, from obstructed excretion of bile. *Cachexia* is a malnourished state seen in chronic wasting diseases. *Atrophy* is muscle

wasting from disuse in consequence of paralysis, debilitation, and the like. *Symphysis* is the fusion of parts from invasive inflammatory process; it is now called "adhesions." *Pseudopneumonia* is a chronic lung disease, now called "chronic bronchitis" or "chronic obstructive pulmonary disease" (COPD). The term "ichorous, acrid lymph" refers to lymph fluid carrying the waste products of infection. [RPB]

343 (in §665:5). The three terms mentioned are names for localized bacterial infections in three locations: within an organ ("empyema"), within a body cavity ("abscess"), and between two organs ("aposteme"). [RPB]

344 (in §665:6). The physicians Hippocrates (active around 400 B.C.E.), called "the Father of Medicine," and Galen (129–around 200 C.E.) are named here as the two foremost exemplars of ancient Greek medicine. The demurral "That is Greek to us" is ironic, inasmuch as Swedenborg himself was highly competent in both Greek and anatomy. [Editors]

345 (in §665:6). The medical treatment described here, of applying irritating chemicals to the skin to cause blisters, had been widely used for thousands of years. The underlying theory held that disease toxins or the defective bodily vapors ("spirits") that caused the disease would be drawn out of the body through the skin. A commonly used ingredient in the poultices applied to cause the blisters was cantharidin, an extract of the blister beetle (Moed and others, 2001, 1357–1360; compare also note 248). Perhaps the most famous historical example of blistering is that of the treatment of the "madness" of King George III of Great Britain (1738–1820); see Trench 1964, 110–111, 120–121, 133, 148–149. [SS]

Notes to Chapter 12, §§667–697

346 (in §667:1). Swedenborg here, as throughout his theological works, asserts that there are only two sacraments: baptism and the Holy Supper (also referred to as the Lord's Supper, the Sacrament of the Altar, Communion, and the Eucharist). The Roman Catholic, Orthodox, and Anglican traditions recognized seven sacraments. The Lutheran tradition he grew up with had fewer than seven, although the exact number was not fixed: in the Large Catechism in the *Book of Concord,* Luther referred to baptism and the Holy Supper as "our two sacraments" (Kolb and Wengert 2000, 456.1), but the Augsburg Confession (see note 6) in the same volume recognized absolution as a third sacrament (Kolb and Wengert 2000, 219.4; see also 193.41). [JSR]

347 (in §667:1). The term "elements" here refers to the bread and wine of the Holy Supper. As for the claim that proximity of the Word makes the elements sacred, this may be a reference to passages such as Luther's Large Catechism in the *Book of Concord,* in which he quotes Augustine as saying, "When the Word is joined to the external element, it becomes a sacrament" (Kolb and Wengert 2000, 468.10; compare McCain 2006, 432.10). [JSR]

348 (in §669). On the ancient practice of reading omens in the flight of birds, compare note 295 above. Another form of ancient divination was that in which the entrails of a sacrificed animal were examined for monitory signs from the gods. For classical arguments for and against these and other types of prophecy, see Cicero *On Divination.* [SS]

349 (in §669). The objects mentioned here parallel items associated with the tabernacle in the Old Testament. The table of showbread (Exodus 25:23–30), the golden incense altar (Exodus 30:1–10), the golden lampstand (Exodus 25:31–40), and the ark of

the covenant with its mercy seat and two guardians made of gold (Exodus 25:10–22) were the only furnishings in the two areas inside the tabernacle proper (excluding the court). On the veil and the arrangement of furniture within the tabernacle, see Exodus 26:31–35. For more on the first three items, see note 257. [JSR, LSW]

350 (in §673). Washing soda (Latin *nitrum;* Hebrew נֶתֶר *[neṭer]*) is a naturally occurring white powdery substance consisting primarily of sodium carbonates. In ancient times it was mixed with oil to form a soap used for household and personal cleaning. In the Hebrew Scriptures the word for it occurs only in Jeremiah 2:22 and Proverbs 25:20, where it has been variously rendered into English as "lye," "niter," "natron," "baking soda," and "soda." Hyssop was a fragrant herb (not the same herb known today as hyssop) that was used in ancient Judaism as part of various rituals of cleansing. See Leviticus 14:1–7, 48–53; Numbers 19:1–8, 17–19. [LSW]

351 (in §674). Since the fifth century, Christian thinkers have spoken of an internal church (Latin *ecclesia interna*) and an external church *(ecclesia externa),* also referred to respectively as the "invisible" church (meaning the church as a spiritual body of true believers) and the "visible" church (meaning the church as a worldly body of professed believers). This layered concept seems to be derived from the New Testament. For passages on the existence of an inner and an outer self within each individual, see Romans 7:22–23; 2 Corinthians 4:16. In Romans 8:1 the inner self (mentioned in Romans 7:22) is aligned with "the spirit" and the outer with "the flesh." Romans 2:28–29 differentiates between outward and inward practice of religion. On Swedenborg's use of the terms *inner church* and *outer church,* see also note 231 and the cross-references there; on inner and outer selves in the Bible, see also note 249. [JSR]

352 (in §674). Swedenborg uses the term *Jewish church* to mean the Judaism of biblical times as the third in a grand sequence of five "churches" (see §§760, 786–788). In this view, the earthly life and death of Jesus Christ marked the end of ancient Judaism's, and the beginning of Christianity's, role as "the church." [JSR]

353 (in §678:1). For a more detailed description of the placement in the spiritual world of people of various religions and nationalities, see §§792–845. See also *Last Judgment* 48; *Sacred Scripture* 105. On the difficulties offered the modern reader by such characterizations, see the translator's preface to this volume, pages 2–4. Compare also note 354 below. [LSW]

354 (in §678:2). Swedenborg's comments here, which seem to play to a Christian xenophobia, are obviously aimed at a Christian readership. Given the geographical separation of Christianity and Islam at the time, not to mention language barriers between them, Swedenborg could reasonably assume that all of his readers would be Christians and none would be Muslims. This is not the only passage that will be offensive to Muslims; a section below on Muslims in the spiritual world (§§828–834) contains much that is offensive and problematic. Nevertheless, Swedenborg certainly does not see Muslims as evil. He writes that there is a multileveled Muslim heaven to which Muslims go who are saved (§832; compare *Divine Providence* 255:5); the Muslim heaven and the Christian heaven are separate from each other, yet the higher levels of each share similar (but not identical) practices and beliefs. He also writes that Islam came about as the result of divine providence, and that it successfully replaced and vanquished idolatry in the countries where it is found, which are more numerous than those of Christianity (§833). In §831 he even reports Muslim criticisms of Catholic and Protestant Christians

for their idolatrous practices and trinitarian beliefs, criticisms with which he himself apparently agrees wholeheartedly. [JSR]

355 (in §679:1). The mesentery and mesocolon are the broad, sheetlike connective tissues that provide attachment and support for the intestines. Each is named for the part that it supports: *mes-* (from the Greek for "in the middle" or "between") + *enteron* ("intestine") = *mesentery,* which supports the small intestine; and *meso-* (the combining form of *mes-)* + *colon* = *mesocolon,* which supports the large intestine, or colon. [RPB]

356 (in §682:2). For this use of the sign of the cross in Lutheran baptism, see Kolb and Wengert 2000, 373.12. [JSR]

357 (in §685:1). Here Swedenborg enumerates the causes in a chain using designations common to Scholastic argument: the first, often identified with God; the middle, generally seen as an efficient cause (on which see volume 1, page 754 note 576); and the last, or final, generally identified with purpose. (The Latin here translated "intermediate cause" is *causa media,* literally, "middle cause"; although the common English meaning of "intermediate" is accurate here, a *causa media* is technically different from what was referred to in Latin as a *causa intermediata,* which is a cause in indirect connection to its effect.) [SS, FLS]

358 (in §685:2). As part of his geometrical style of argumentation (see volume 1, page 681 note 27), Swedenborg heavily cross-referenced his first Latin editions. Here, late in his last published theological work, he briefly adopts a system for cross-referencing not used elsewhere in his published theological corpus: he refers to material by ordinal number of heading and section: "the fourth section above under the second heading in this chapter." He uses this method of cross-referencing only three times in *True Christianity:* here, in the next section (§686), and in §730:1. It is possible that this alternate reference system is a remaining artifact of last minute changes and revisions, perhaps compounded by haste in production; see the translator's preface to volume 1, pages 28–29. [JSR]

359 (in §685:2). This is a truncated account, but it does follow the outlines of a Lutheran baptism in Swedenborg's day. For a more detailed account, see Kolb and Wengert 2000, 373.11–375.31; the elements Swedenborg mentions appear there in 373.12, 374.20–375.25. [JSR]

360 (in §687:2). Chyle (see note 109) renews the body by carrying nutrients; see *The Soul's Domain* (= Swedenborg [1744–1745] 1960) §202. Animal spirits (see notes 242 and 338) are described in Swedenborg's *Dynamics of the Soul's Domain* (= Swedenborg [1740–1741] 1955), part 2, §219 as "a most pure fluid" of the body that "irrigates, nourishes, actuates, modifies, forms, and renovates everything therein." [SS]

361 (in §689:2). In the first edition this Latin sentence is incomplete. The material supplied in brackets here is based on the end of §688. [JSR]

362 (in §691:3). On the delivery of the Ten Commandments and their mode of production, see Exodus 19; 20:1–21; 31:18; 32:19; 34:1–4, 28; Deuteronomy 5; 9:9–11; 10:1–2. On their placement in the ark and the ark's construction, see Exodus 25:10–22; 37:1–9; Deuteronomy 10:1–5. On Aaron's approaching the ark once a year, see Leviticus 16; Hebrews 9:7. [LSW]

363 (in §692:1). The word "Olympic" is used very vaguely here. It probably connotes a place where contests—presumably intellectual in nature—took place (with reference to the Olympic athletic games in classical times). The word here translated "halls" is

gymnasia, which has ancient connotations of athletic contests and in Swedenborg's day denoted schools. [SS]

364 (in §692:1). The Latin words here translated "New Athens," "New Parnassus," and "New Helicon" are, respectively, *Athenaeum,* or "like Athens"; *Parnassium,* or "like Parnassus"; and *Heliconeum,* or "like Helicon." Each of the originals of these locations represented Greek learning in some way: Athens was, among other things, the location of two of the greatest schools of ancient philosophical thought; Parnassus was a mountain sacred to the Greek god Apollo and the Muses, goddesses who fostered the arts; Mount Helicon was another mountain sacred to the Muses. The relative heights given here are curiously reversed: Mount Parnassus is actually the higher of the two landforms at 8,200 feet (about 2,500 meters), while Mount Helicon is only 5,868 feet (about 1,800 meters). The inversion may simply represent the discrepancy between natural and spiritual worlds. [JSR, SS]

365 (in §692:1). These four individuals were all Greek philosophers in ancient times. Pythagoras lived in the mid- to late 500s B.C.E.; he was a half-legendary figure, both a religious leader and a famed scientist and mathematician: the Pythagorean Theorem is named after him. Socrates (469–399 B.C.E.) was a central inspirational figure in Athenian philosophy, though he himself left no written work. His associates Aristippus of Cyrene (435–366 B.C.E.) and Xenophon (around 430–after 355 B.C.E.) left accounts of his teachings in the form of dialogs and memoirs, though it is the reports of Socrates' student Plato (see note 366) that have formed posterity's understanding of Socrates' thought. Swedenborg is known to have read Plato extensively, and would certainly have been acquainted with the works of Xenophon. The writings of Aristippus did not survive intact to modern times. [SS]

366 (in §692:1). The Greek philosophers Plato (427–347 B.C.E.) and Aristotle (384–322 B.C.E.) are here presented as focused on intellectual and rational philosophy *in contrast to* ethics. This is a surprising characterization. In Plato and Aristotle, reason is clearly understood to be a prerequisite to achieving virtue and being able to live a moral life, and to some extent the chief purpose of defining and mastering the use of reason lies in the attaining of virtue. Plato deals with ethical questions in many works, and very explicitly in the *Gorgias, Meno,* and *Protagoras,* while Aristotle confronts them in his *Nicomachean Ethics.* However, it is the limitation of the focus of non-Platonic and non-Aristotelian schools to moral praxis, rather than any failing of Plato and Aristotle to explore ethical issues, that seems to be the basis of the distinction made here. For example, one major school of ancient times, the Epicureans, explicitly emphasized morality as the chief end of study (Diogenes Laertius *Lives of the Eminent Philosophers* 10:30). Another school, that of the Stoics, was in its early form deeply involved in the exploration of logic, but later adherents, such as Seneca (Lucius Annaeus Seneca; born between 4 B.C.E. and 1 C.E., died 65 C.E.), Musonius Rufus (before 30 C.E.–before 101 or 102 C.E.), Epictetus (active mid-first century to second century C.E.), and Marcus Aurelius (121–180 C.E.), tended to focus on Stoicism as a way of life rather than as a pure study of logic. [SS, FLS]

367 (in §692:2). On the association of laurels with victory, and in particular with university degrees as a form of academic success, see volume 1, page 713 note 223. The palm was similarly associated with victory in ancient times, though it later became a symbol of Christian festivity and pilgrimage. [SS]

368 (in §692:3). In ancient times, a palladium was a statue of the warlike Greek goddess of wisdom, Pallas Athena; one was kept at Athens. It was believed to protect a city from capture. The use of the term in the context of this memorable occurrence loosely suggests that the very existence of this city depends on wisdom. [JSR, SS]

369 (in §692:3). On the discovery and investigation of two feral individuals, Peter of Hanover (discovered 1725) and Marie-Angélique Memmie Leblanc (who re-entered human society in 1731), see volume 1, page 704 note 160. For an example of the contemporary interest in such individuals, see the account by the English author Daniel Defoe (1660–1731) in Defoe 1726. Defoe makes the same claim about Peter of Hanover as the speakers do below: "He neither judged what to eat, or what to drink" (Defoe 1726, 24). [Editors]

370 (in §692:4). Swedenborg and other scientists of his time believed that plants and even animals could be reconstituted from their own ashes into some semblance of their previous form; see *Draft of "The Infinite" on the Soul-Body Mechanism* (= Swedenborg 1992c) §37; *Draft of a Rational Psychology* (= Swedenborg 2001) §517; *The Old Testament Explained* (= Swedenborg 1927–1951) §3061 (= Swedenborg 1847–1854, vol. 2 [bound as vol. 3], §1377); *Draft on Divine Wisdom* (= Swedenborg 1994–1997b, 491) §8 [heading] = §110 [Mongredien's numbering]; and *Marriage Love* 151b:5 (which is a previous telling of this same account). See also Howard 1927, 262–269, who quotes experimental results from the polymathic scholar Athanasius Kircher (1602–1680) and the philosopher and scientist Sir Kenelm Digby (1603–1665). These experiments involved the application to plant remnants of vaporizing heat or freezing cold, and supposedly produced a vague but recognizable representation of the original plant. Howard also notes that the efforts of the British chemist Robert Boyle (1627–1691) to reproduce this phenomenon left Boyle unconvinced. [SS]

371 (in §692:7). On Golden Age imagery, see volume 1, page 683 note 41. The Roman god Saturn was supposed to have ruled over the Golden Age, and sometimes gives his name to it, as here. [SS]

372 (in §692:7). For more on the spiritual decline of humanity from ancient times onward and the resulting cessation of communication with God and angels, see *Secrets of Heaven* 2995, 6628–6632, 7802, 8118, 10737, 10751; *Heaven and Hell* 252–253. [LSW]

373 (in §693:1). Demosthenes (384–322 B.C.E.) was a politician of ancient Athens; he is sometimes called the greatest orator of that city. He campaigned in vain for Athens to remain free of the political domination of nearby Macedonia. Diogenes (around 412 or 403–around 324 or 321 B.C.E.) was the founder of the Cynics, a philosophical school which emphasized living according to nature rather than convention, and which valued ethical practice over philosophical speculation (compare note 366). Epicurus (341–270 B.C.E.) was the founder of the Epicurean school of philosophy in Athens, which was focused on practices that would secure happiness in life. [SS]

374 (in §693:2). Pegasus was an immortal winged horse in Greco-Roman mythology. It was said to have created the Hippocrene spring sacred to the Muses (here called the nine maidens) with the first imprint of its hoof as it was landing on Mount Parnassus (compare note 364). [JSR]

375 (in §693:5). The Latin word here translated "somewhere-or-other" is *Pu;* the word is the transliterated form of the Greek interrogative and indefinite adverb ποῦ, meaning "where?" or "somewhere." It is used by Swedenborg to express an uncertain

location, approximately in the sense of "limbo" (see §769, where the two terms are equated; see note 444 for discussion of the term *limbo* itself). Though it may be translated in any of several ways, it appears in the Latin in the same sense in §§29, 769, 771; *Supplements* 4, 6; *Divine Love and Wisdom* 350; *Marriage Love* 28, 29, 182:5. See also Helander 2004, 137–138. [SS]

376 (in §693:5). The figure of six thousand years for the previous duration of the world reflects the chronology proposed by Archbishop James Ussher (1581–1656), which was arrived at by totaling the spans of time noted in the Bible. The resulting date of creation was 4004 B.C.E. It is difficult to know whether Swedenborg himself shared the common belief in this chronology; he nowhere challenges it directly, though he does seem to have accepted some form of an alternate theory that people had existed before Adam (see note 28). For other references to this timeframe, see *Heaven and Hell* 415 and *Marriage Love* 29, 39, 182:5. [GFD, SS]

377 (in §693:6). The belief in these massive cataclysms is based on biblical passages such as Isaiah 13:9–13; 34:1–4; Revelation 21:1. In particular, the belief that the stars will fall is based on a literal interpretation of such biblical passages as Matthew 24:29; Mark 13:25; Revelation 6:13; 12:4. Swedenborg mentions the absurdity of believing stars will physically fall onto the earth in several passages, including *Marriage Love* 182:6. [LSW, SS]

378 (in §693:6). On the consumption of ground-up Egyptian mummies as medicine, see volume 1, page 731 note 381. [Editors]

379 (in §693:6). The paradise of Greek mythology was called the Elysian fields (see volume 1, page 744 note 496). [Editors]

380 (in §693:8). Democritus (born 460–457 B.C.E.) was a Greek philosopher most famous for his atomic theory. He did, however, also write works on ethics; one of his moral maxims emphasizes the necessity for "cheerfulness." He was thus called "the laughing philosopher." Heraclitus, also a Greek (active around 500 B.C.E.), was renowned for his haughty and cryptic philosophical epigrams. He was called "the weeping philosopher" for various trivial reasons; see Kirk, Raven, and Schofield 1983, 183, for a full explanation. The names and ascribed characteristics appear in an unusual *ABba* order (chiasmus) in the first edition. [SS]

381 (in §694:1). For more on the analog of physical space in the spiritual world, which involves differences of emotional and mental states rather than fixed and measurable distances, see §29; *Secrets of Heaven* 1273–1277, 1376–1382, 3356, 5605; *Heaven and Hell* 191–199; *Divine Love and Wisdom* 7–10, 69–72; *Divine Providence* 48–51. [LSW]

382 (in §694:5). On the origination of physical things from spiritual substance, see note 48. [Editors]

383 (in §694:6). The names of these various games all refer to the Muses, Greek goddesses who fostered the various arts. See note 364 on Helicon and Parnassus; see note 374 on the Hippocrene spring. The association of the Muses with Athens is a nonclassical coinage, formed on the model of their association with Parnassus, Helicon, and the Hippocrene. [SS]

384 (in §695:3). Swedenborg here refers to the notorious "mind-body problem" that is still debated by philosophers: How can an apparently nonphysical entity, the soul or mind, interact with a physical entity, the body? It is striking that he recasts the debate as a question of which particular form of inflow causes the action of the body, and reinterprets the three major schools of thought on the issue strictly in those terms: (1) The theory of *occasionalism* (here referred to as "occasional inflow") held

that it is God who both makes us think and brings about the physical actions that we seem to perform as a result of thought; it was advanced by such scholars as the Cartesian Arnold Geulincx (1624–1669). (2) Aristotle and the Scholastic philosophers argued that there is some *physical inflow* by which a material component of external objects flows into the body and then into the soul. (3) Leibniz (see note 389) advanced another theory, called *preestablished harmony,* which holds that God does not act to make us think and move in each instance, but instead has established the harmony, or simultaneous occurrence, of all future mental and physical activity at the beginning of the world. To put it another way, changes in substances take place spontaneously because of the nature of those substances, not because the changes are caused by other substances; causation is thus only an appearance that emerges as spontaneous actions occur in parallel in separate substances. The further assertion of the speaker that "all three camps consider these forms of inflow as occurring within nature," that is, as purely within the physical world, does not seem a fair characterization, at least of occasionalism and preestablished harmony, which require at some point the action of a supernatural deity. For more on Swedenborg's view of the soul-body question, see his various writings on the topic from his scientific period onward: his unpublished *Draft of "The Infinite" on the Soul-Body Mechanism* (= Swedenborg 1992c, 123–146); the second chapter of his 1734 book *The Infinite* (= Swedenborg [1734] 1965, 143–232); *Draft on the Soul and the Body* (= Swedenborg 1984c, 21–64), from before or during 1742; *Draft on Action* (= Swedenborg 1984a, 117–142), likewise from before or during 1742; and the privately distributed *Soul-Body Interaction* (1769). There are also relevant passages in *Secrets of Heaven* 6053–6058, 6189–6215, 6307–6327, 6466–6496, 6598–6626. [SS]

385 (in §695:3). Beliefs of this sort about the soul stemmed from long before Swedenborg's time, but could also be heavily illustrated from the intense conversation about the nature of the soul still ongoing in his day. To give just a few examples, from both ancient and Enlightenment times: the pre-Socratic Greek philosopher Anaximenes (sixth century B.C.E.) and the Skeptic philosopher Aenesidemus (first century B.C.E.) believed the soul was air or ether (Tertullian *On the Soul* 9); the English physician Henry Power (1623–1668) similarly claimed that life was produced by an "aetherial substance" (Thomson 2008, 71). Heraclitus (active around 500 B.C.E.) and Hipparchus (active 146–127 B.C.E.) asserted the soul was made of fire (Tertullian *On the Soul* 5; perhaps also referred to by Aristotle, *On the Parts of Animals* 652b). The latter belief was called psychopyrism, and constituted the charge leveled by the Neoplatonist Henry More (1614–1687) against other theorists of the soul such as the Calvinist theologian Richard Baxter (1615–1691) and the English anatomist Thomas Willis (1621–1675); see Thomson 2008, 75, 82. The French philosopher René Descartes says of his own early thoughts of the soul that he "imagined it to be something tenuous, like a wind or fire or ether" (Descartes *Meditations on First Philosophy,* second meditation = Descartes [1642] 1984, 17). [SS, FLS]

386 (in §695:3). Various locations in the brain were proposed as the "seat of the soul" by scholars in Swedenborg's time and before. For example, Thomas Willis thought it was in the corpus callosum (Zimmer 2004, 222). For a compendium of some of these theories, see §697:4–5. Swedenborg's own opinion on this location varied over time. In his last work before the visionary period, the quasi-scientific prose poem *Worship and Love of God,* he at least metaphorically assigned the soul a dwelling in the cerebellum

(*Worship and Love of God* 50:6). He also stressed the importance of what he called the cortical glands in the cerebrum as the seat of rational understanding (*Worship and Love of God* 41 note z). [SS]

387 (in §695:3). Trees seem to have been chosen somewhat randomly here as an example of a nonhuman part of nature; the point is that everything in the universe, from humanity to trees or any other item one could name, receives divine inflow. [SS]

388 (in §695:5). Swedenborg expatiates on the remarkable habits and activities of caterpillars, butterflies, bees, silkworms, and spiders in §§12, 335:3–4. [JSR]

389 (in §696:1). Swedenborg here identifies three philosophers as founders of various schools of thought. The Greek Aristotle gave rise to the Peripatetic, or Aristotelian, school of ancient times, which in turn was in many respects the intellectual progenitor of the medieval Scholastic philosophical school (see note 391). The French René Descartes is the originator of Cartesian thought. The German Gottfried Wilhelm Leibniz was a key figure in the German rationalist movement. For more on Leibniz, see volume 1, page 751 note 552. For more on some of the particular ideas of these three schools, see note 384. [SS]

390 (in §696:1). Christian Wolff (1679–1754) was a German philosopher and a contemporary of Swedenborg's. On his supposedly subordinate relationship to Leibniz, see volume 1, page 751 note 552. [Editors]

391 (in §696:2). The Scholastics were medieval Christian thinkers who developed a unique and rich synthesis of various philosophies. They drew logical elements from Aristotelianism; mystical elements from Pythagoreanism, Platonism, and Neoplatonism; practical and ethical elements from Epicureanism and Stoicism; and religious elements from Scripture and the church fathers, in particular Augustine. The teachings ascribed to the exemplars in this passage are indeed highly Scholastic; a common saying among them was *Nihil est in intellectu quod prius non fuerit in sensu*—"There is nothing in the understanding that has not first been in the senses" (De Wulf 1956, 133). [SS]

392 (in §697:2). For information on the structure of formal debate in the European academic tradition, which this debate mirrors, see volume 1, pages 749–750 note 542. [Editors]

393 (in §697:2). The passage that follows, which consists of responses to the question posed by the speaker here, forms a selective survey of speculations about the soul from ancient times to Swedenborg's day. For example, the Greek physician Galen (129–around 200 C.E.) localized its faculties in the solid part of the cerebrum; the Christian church fathers, and most medieval scholars, placed them in the ventricles (Gross 1998, 31, 34). Others divided the soul's functions among various organs: for instance, Thomas Willis localized the common meeting area of the senses in what he called the *corpus striatum*, or "striated body" (Gross 1998, 43, 45). For other examples, see note 386; for details on ancient views of the soul, see Tertullian *On the Soul* generally, and chapter 15 in particular. The account here also includes some theories Swedenborg himself at one time espoused. For instance, he once described the blood as "the external form of the soul" (*Draft on the Fiber* [= Swedenborg 1976a] §374); at another he said that the soul "is everywhere in its body" (*First Draft of Three Transactions on the Brain* [= Swedenborg 1976d, vol. 1] §83); at other times he claimed that it was in cortical material (see note 386). The refutation of these theories by the authoritative figure of the elder in §697:10 is thus a significant repudiation of Swedenborg's own earlier attempts to locate the seat of the soul. Swedenborg is in accordance with his times in growing weary of such

speculation: Voltaire similarly ridicules contemporary theories about the soul (Voltaire [1764] 1962, under "soul"). [SS, FLS]

394 (in §697:5). The ancient Greeks cast ballots in an election by dropping a pebble in an urn—a white pebble to vote yes and a black pebble to vote no. The speaker here means that there are good reasons to favor each of the various conjectures. [JSR, SS]

395 (in §697:7). The early Christian writer Tertullian (around 155 or 160–220) reports that the ancient philosophers Strato (died around 287–269 B.C.E.), Aenesidemus, and Heraclitus believed the soul was "diffused over the entire body" (*On the Soul* chapter 14 [= Tertullian 1997, 193]). Even Augustine could have been the "ancient" intended here; in his *Quotations on Various Philosophical and Theological Topics* (= Swedenborg 1976c, 14), Swedenborg quotes Augustine *On the Immortality of the Soul* 50:15 (= Augustine 1938, 83 = chapter 16, §25): "The whole of the soul is present in the whole body, and in all its several parts." For other passages from Augustine that involve similar statements, see further in *Quotations on Various Philosophical and Theological Topics* (= Swedenborg 1976c, 15, 23). [SS, FLS]

Notes to Chapter 13, §§698–752

396 (in §699). For a particularly acerbic example of such criticism in Swedenborg's day, see Voltaire [1764] 1962, under "transubstantiation." [SS]

397 (in §700). In Scholastic philosophy, an essential cause is one that depends on its own intrinsic character (essence) and not on any extrinsic circumstance; it is the precise cause required for producing an effect. Swedenborg here explains that in traditional Christianity, Christ has been worshiped only as an "intermediate cause," or one in a chain of factors, leading to our salvation, rather than as the precise cause of our salvation in and of himself. That is, Christ has been worshiped as the Son, as a component of the Trinity, and not "as the only God, the One in whom the divine Trinity exists." [SS]

398 (in §705:1). If Swedenborg were following his usual practice here he would have highlighted the seven instances of the word "flesh" in the two ensuing biblical quotations. Instead he highlights the phrases "the feast of the great God," "my sacrificial meal," and "a great sacrificial meal." From the last sentence of this subsection we gather that these phrases were highlighted here in order to support a point made there. [JSR]

399 (in §705:1). The eating of fat and the drinking of blood in this passage from Ezekiel are, although obviously symbolic, still intended to be shocking. Fat was seen as a desirable foodstuff among the active peoples of ancient times because of the sustaining properties of its high caloric content (see *Secrets of Heaven* volume 1 [= Swedenborg [1749–1756] 2008], page 623 note 226). However, both the eating of fat and the drinking of blood were specifically outlawed in Leviticus 3:17; 7:23–27. (For an earlier prohibition against consuming blood, see Genesis 9:4.) [SS]

400 (in §722:3). On this quotation from the Book of Common Prayer of 1711, see note 170 on §526, where the same passage is given. Apparently Swedenborg retranslated or at least edited the passage for this second occurrence; there are slight differences in the Latin of the two passages. Except for the added text shown in square brackets, the variations are not significant and so are not indicated. [SS]

401 (in §726:1). The name Jesus ('Ιησοῦς *[Iesoûs]*) is a Greek form of the Hebrew Joshua (יְהוֹשֻׁעַ *[yəhôšûaʻ]*), meaning "Jah saves," "Jah" being a shortened form of "Jehovah." (On the name Jehovah, see note 29; on "Jah," see note 218.) [LSW]

402 (in §732:5). The belief on the part of some Christians that in heaven they will sit on thrones reigning as kings with angels ministering to them is based on biblical passages such as Matthew 19:28; Luke 22:30; Romans 5:17; 2 Timothy 2:12; Hebrews 1:13–14; Revelation 1:6; 3:21; 5:10; 20:4–6; 22:5. [JSR, LSW]

403 (in §734:1). The six groups whose views of heavenly joy and eternal happiness were detailed above in §732 are now dealt with one by one, but in the following order: the second (here in §734), the third (§735), the fifth (§736), the fourth (§737), the sixth (§738), and finally the first (§739). [JSR]

404 (in §735:1). This is the third of the six groups introduced in §732; see note 403. [JSR]

405 (in §735:2). Starting in the seventeenth and continuing throughout the eighteenth century, edible "dessert pyramids," or arrays of numerous fresh fruits, small cakes, or sweetmeats of various kinds, stacked loosely or fastened together with sugar icing into a roughly pyramidal or conical shape, were European table decorations associated with the finest dining. Starting in the mid-eighteenth century, desserts were also sometimes presented on a pyramid of salvers or stemmed plates of decreasing diameter, one on top of another. Swedenborg could mean either of these types of dessert pyramids here, although both might seem somewhat out of place at a feast with biblical patriarchs. His having written of the pyramids as being "*with* desserts" (Latin *cum condituris*) rather than "*of* desserts" makes the second type seem more likely. See Glasse [1760?], 263. [JSR]

406 (in §736:1). This is the fifth of the six groups introduced in §732; see note 403. [JSR]

407 (in §736:1). For a list of the relevant Bible passages, see note 402. [Editors]

408 (in §737:1). This is the fourth of the six groups introduced in §732; see note 403. [JSR]

409 (in §737:1). The Latin word here translated "excellent" is *nobilium,* literally, "noble." On the concept of noble and ignoble plants and animals, see volume 1, pages 703–704 note 159. For an example of a hierarchy of trees from ignoble to noble, see §94. Another example can be seen in §815:2, where the horse chestnut is indicated to be inferior to the laurel. [JSR]

410 (in §738:1). This is the sixth of the six groups introduced in §732; see note 403. [JSR]

411 (in §739:1). This is the first of the six groups introduced in §732; see note 403. [JSR]

412 (in §740:1). The word "prince" here (Latin *princeps*) is used in its older sense to mean a sovereign, chief, or leader rather than merely any male member of the royal family. [JSR]

413 (in §740:2). The meaning of the term *heavenly form* is never explained in Swedenborg's works, though it is used many times. For some discussion, see volume 1, page 732 note 390. [Editors]

414 (in §741:2). On the concept of the relative excellence of various trees, see volume 1, pages 703–704 note 159, and note 409 in this volume. [Editors]

415 (in §746:2). By this point in the argument, the speakers have apparently modified the definition of the fourth type of usefulness. It is no longer "loving to maintain ourselves for the sake of the higher forms of usefulness," but just "loving to maintain ourselves"; that is, for our own selfish benefit. [JSR]

416 (in §747:2). The Latin word here translated "young women" is *virgines,* the plural of *virgo,* a word from which our English word "virgin" derives. Although the meanings of the Latin word and the English word overlap to some extent, they differ in their semantic ranges. The Latin word *virgo* connotes someone who is marriageable, young, and female, while the English word "virgin" has evolved to mean a sexually inexperienced person of either gender and any age. (Compare, however, 1 Corinthians 7:25–26; Revelation 14:4.) The Latin word appears a number of times in §§747:2–749, including in plays on words that unfortunately cannot be effectively rendered with a single English equivalent. Here and throughout this translation, wherever possible the closest English equivalent, "young woman," has been used; but where context implies sexual inexperience, "virgin" or "virginal young woman" has been used. For more on this Latin word, see *Secrets of Heaven* volume 1 (= Swedenborg [1749–1756] 2008), page 607 note 80. [JSR]

417 (in §747:2). In this context (see §748:1) an "ephod" refers to a priestly garment described in Exodus 28:6–8; 39:2–5 as a cloth piece made of gold metal threads worked in among blue, purple, and scarlet threads and twined linen. It was fastened over the chest by means of shoulder straps and an attached waistband of similar workmanship. [LSW]

418 (in §747:3). In this description of a wedding ceremony in heaven, the fact that the bridegroom's role is apparently the more active does not imply any endorsement of a lack of mutuality in marriage relationships. As is reflected in this passage, Swedenborg does accept and endorse the traditional societal view that it is the role of the man to propose and initiate marriage and marital relations, and the role of the woman to accept and respond. In his discussions of this view in *Marriage Love* 221, 296–297, he offers a rationale for these differing gender roles based not only on his view of the differing natures of the male and female psyches, but also on prevailing societal attitudes about men, women, and marriage. However, far more essential to Swedenborg's view of marriage is an insistence on the necessity of mutuality and mutual consent in the relationship. One such statement occurs just below in §748:4, in the discussion that follows the wedding ceremony: "[The couple's] consent is the essential ingredient in a marriage; all the other aspects of marriage that follow from consent are just the various forms that that consent takes." For more on the essential role of mutual consent in marriage, and the destructiveness of inequality and striving for dominance, see *Secrets of Heaven* 2731–2732, 3090; *Marriage Love* 248, 257, 299–300. [LSW, SS]

419 (in §748:2). On the representations and inner character of men and women and the reversal of their representations in various contexts, see volume 1, page 702 note 144. [LSW]

420 (in §748:3). For references to Bible passages containing these phrases, together with commentary on those passages, see *Secrets of Heaven* 2362, 3081; *Revelation Unveiled* 620; *Revelation Explained* (= Swedenborg 1994–1997a) §863. [LSW]

421 (in §749). All major Christian traditions recognize chastity as a term applicable to faithful marriage, though some important Christian thinkers have judged such marital chastity inferior to a condition of complete sexual abstinence (see, for example, 1 Corinthians 7 in general; Augustine *On Virginity* 19; Aquinas *Summa Theologiae* 2:2:152:4). By contrast, Swedenborg defines chastity exclusively with respect to the faithful sexual relationship between husband and wife (*Marriage Love* 139), including as chaste those single people who have a desire and respect for such a relationship (*Marriage Love* 150). It is in this sense that the word "chaste" is used in the current passage.

For more on his application of the terms *chaste* and *unchaste,* see *Marriage Love* 138–155a. [SS, LSW, FLS]

422 (in §751). The priest's closing thought about people who are in the Lord and whom the Lord is in is an allusion to such passages in the Bible as John 6:56; 15:4, 5; Revelation 3:20. For more such passages, see §371:1. [JSR]

Notes to Chapter 14, §§753–791

423 (in §754:1). Underlying the discussion of the biblical image of Babylon here is the assumption—common among Protestants in Swedenborg's day—that it represents the Roman Catholic Church (compare *Revelation Unveiled* 631). For an extended interpretation of Revelation 17 and 18 in terms of this symbolism, see *Revelation Unveiled* 717–802. For balancing statements on the spiritual state of good and conscientious Roman Catholics and their entry into heaven after death, see §§820–821; *Revelation Unveiled* 786:3; *Survey* 105, 108; see also note 69. [SS, LSW]

424 (in §754:2). The "churches that separated from Babylon" are the Protestant denominations that diverged from the Roman Catholic Church. On this meaning of "Babylon," see note 423. [JSR, LSW]

425 (in §757). "The actual destruction of Jerusalem" refers to the siege and sacking of Jerusalem by the Roman army in 70 C.E. [LSW]

426 (in §757). On the prophetic mode, see *Secrets of Heaven* 66, which discusses its use as one of the four modes of writing in the Word. There it is said to be inspired by the writing of the people of the earliest church, in which "spiritual and heavenly things [are] represented by the earthly, mundane objects they mentioned." Being written in this symbolic or correspondential way, the prophetic mode is "almost completely unintelligible except on the inner level, which holds profound secrets forming a well-connected chain of ideas." [LSW]

427 (in §757). By "there" Swedenborg means in Matthew 24 (exclusive of the first two verses of that chapter). Specifically, *Secrets of Heaven* 3353–3356 explain Matthew 24:3–8; §§3486–3489 begin with a discussion of verse 8 again and explain Matthew 24:8–14; §§3650–3655 explain Matthew 24:15–18; §§3751–3757 explain Matthew 24:19–22; §§3897–3901 explain Matthew 24:23–28; §§4056–4060 explain Matthew 24:29–31; §§4229–4231 explain Matthew 24:32–35; §§4332–4335 explain Matthew 24:36–41; and §§4422–4424 explain Matthew 24:42–51. [JSR]

428 (in §758:2). For more on the promised, but never completed, appendix to this work, see volume 1, page 689 note 71. [JSR]

429 (in §759:1). The Christian practice of blaming Jews for Jesus' crucifixion began shortly after the Crucifixion itself and is reflected in New Testament accounts. On Swedenborg's harsh statements about Jews, see volume 1, pages 718–719 note 262; *Secrets of Heaven* volume 1 (= Swedenborg [1749–1756] 2008), pages 52–55. [JSR]

430 (in §759:1). On "the church that the prophets and the Book of Revelation call Babylon" as the Roman Catholic Church, see note 423. On "the churches that separated from it" see note 424. For Swedenborg's attitudes toward Roman Catholicism in general, see note 69. [LSW]

431 (in §759:2). On the idol of Dagon, see 1 Samuel 5:1–5. The Palladium in this passage is the statue of Athena, or Minerva; see note 368. [JSR]

432 (in §759:3). The technical terms for such disturbances in the sense of smell are *parosmia* and *dysosmia*. The Latin here translated "hysteria," *uterino morbo,* could be literally and accurately translated "uterine disease," but Swedenborg is likely thinking of the vast range of abnormal conditions formerly classified under the heading "hysteria," a word that comes from the Greek word for uterus (and is also cognate with the Latin and English word *uterus*). For thousands of years, hysteria was believed to be caused by a "wandering" of the uterus in the body and the subsequent impairment of normal function; see Veith 1965, 3–5, and compare Plato *Timaeus* 91. One of the many disorders that may have been included under hysteria in early medicine was what we now know as temporal lobe epilepsy, which is a common form of focal epilepsy. Its attacks are frequently preceded by episodes of parosmia and can produce exaggerated sensory stimuli, particularly of olfactory perceptions. Though we cannot be sure Swedenborg was referring to this particular form of epilepsy here (and epilepsy had long been considered a separate disease from hysteria; see *Draft on the Fiber* [= Swedenborg 1976a] §§457–463), it is a good example of the currently recognized causes of parosmia that he might well have referred to as "hysteria." Another possibility is that he has in mind the belief, dating from Egyptian medicine and persisting in altered form into the twentieth century, that the womb is attracted to pleasant smells and repelled by foul smells (see Veith 1965, 3–4). Physicians used this supposed susceptibility to odors in an attempt to lure or drive the womb back into its proper position. The great seventeenth-century English physician Thomas Willis wrote of hysteria that "sweet things held to the Nose bring on the fit, and stinking things drive the same away" (quoted in Lennox 1955, 93). The implication here would be that women with hysteria react with aversion to a pleasant fragrance because they can feel that it is exacerbating their condition. [SS]

433 (in §760). For lists of the Bible books Swedenborg included in these subdivisions of the Word (the historical Word and the prophetic Word), see volume 1, page 739 note 458. For an explanation of the distinction he made between them, see *Secrets of Heaven* 66. Compare also note 426 in this volume. [LSW]

434 (in §762:1). This passage is obviously expressed from the point of view of an inhabitant of the northern hemisphere. Not only was such a point of view natural to Swedenborg, but his reasonable expectation would have been that his immediate readers would share it. Note that for an observer in the northern hemisphere, the sun would be "in the north" when it is behind the earth, and therefore not visible. As a resident of Europe, and especially northern Europe, Swedenborg would have been very aware of the light that "leaks" around the earth through the polar regions at night during the summer months; this would reinforce his tendency to describe the sun as being "in the north" at night. [GFD, LSW, SS]

435 (in §762:2). Swedenborg seems to be loosely including poets under the rubric of philosophers here. The Roman poet Ovid (43 B.C.E.–17 C.E.), for example, recounts the four ages in his *Metamorphoses* 1:89–150. The Greek poet Hesiod (flourished around 700 B.C.E.) in his *Works and Days* 109–224 adds an Age of Heroes after the Bronze Age and counts the Iron Age as the fifth. Compare also *True Christianity* volume 1, page 730 note 375. [SS]

436 (in §763:1). In Aristotle's *Sense and Sensibilia* 439b (= Aristotle 1984, 698), colors are hypothesized to arise from mixtures of white and black in specific ratios. For further

information on Swedenborg's theory of color, see the endnote on this subject in §1042:2 in *Secrets of Heaven* volume 2 (= Swedenborg [1749–1756] 2013). [SS]

437 (in §763:2). For more on the juxtaposition in paintings of beauty and ugliness, see §465 and note 26. [JSR]

438 (in §764:1). On the significance of the four seasons in the Bible, see *Secrets of Heaven* 935, 2323, 2905; *Revelation Explained* (= Swedenborg 1994–1997a) §610:6. On the significance of the four times of day, in addition to the passages cited just below in the text, see *Secrets of Heaven* 3693, 8211; *Revelation Unveiled* 476. [LSW]

439 (in §766). There is no §765 in the first edition. [Editors]

440 (in §767:3). What Swedenborg is describing seems to be a putative effect of the solar vortex on oceans and the sandbars they contain. (The vortex theory of planetary motion, to which Swedenborg subscribed, posited a whirlpool-like current around the sun that swept planets along their paths perpetually.) Compare Swedenborg's 1719 work *Height of Water,* Second Edition (= Swedenborg [1719] 1992a, 23–24), in which he ascribes the disposition taken by sandbars to winds and to "the sea [that] has rolled with the sun." On the similarity between the vortex motion of the solar system as a whole and smaller "vorticles" within it, see *Basic Principles of Nature,* part 3, chapter 1, §1 (= Swedenborg [1734] 1988a, 2:232). [SS]

441 (in §768). The belief on the part of some Christians that at the time of the Last Judgment the Lord will appear in the clouds of heaven with angels and the sound of trumpets is based on biblical passages such as Daniel 7:13–14; Matthew 24:30–31; 26:64; Mark 14:61–62; 1 Corinthians 15:51–52. [LSW]

442 (in §768). A stadium (plural: stadia) was an ancient Greek unit of distance equal to about 607 feet, or 185 meters. A distance of twelve thousand stadia is approximately 1380 miles, or 2220 kilometers. [JSR]

443 (in §769). This section presents a somewhat random mélange of ideas held about the future state of the soul from antiquity to Swedenborg's time. Some of these theories are not easily traced and may be folk beliefs or merely fanciful, but others were quite serious. For the history of the idea of the soul in the early Enlightenment, with special reference to theological and sociological trends, see Thomson 2008. For a philosophical treatment, see Goetz and Taliaferro 2011, 65–130. Compare with §695:3 and note 385 there; and also §697. [SS, FLS]

444 (in §769). For an example of a work by a major thinker that maintains that souls are kept in the middle of the earth, see *On the Soul* 55 by the church father Tertullian; similarly, the Eastern Orthodox Church held that souls went to the abode of the dead, also called Hades, to await the Day of Judgment. On the "somewhere-or-other" mentioned here, see note 375. The "limbo of the fathers" refers to one of two different locations called limbo in the other world, according to Roman Catholic teaching: in one, just souls await the day when they can join in the beatific vision of God. In the other, the "limbo of children," the souls of children and others who have died unbaptized but without committing grievous sin are held in a state of perpetual happiness. See *The New Catholic Encyclopedia,* under "limbo." [SS, JSR]

445 (in §769). The belief that souls would sleep "in storage" until Judgment Day is called mortalism or soul-sleeping. Sometimes it is confusingly referred to by the Neo-Greek term psychopannychism ("soul-all-night-ism"), from the title of a book John Calvin wrote against the belief. It has sparked intense religious controversy from early

Christian times to today, and has been traced in thinkers as disparate as Martin Luther (1483–1546), Thomas Hobbes (1588–1679), John Milton (1608–1674), and John Locke (1632–1704). For a full discussion of the debate as it occurred in England, see Burns 1972; see also Jolley 1998, 382–385, and Thomson 2008, 42–44. [SS, FLS]

446 (in §770). The arguments reported by Swedenborg here are drawn from the stock atheistic and Deistic objections to the conventional understanding of the Last Judgment. Voltaire, for example, says: "Men and the other animals are really fed by, and get their growth from, the substance of their predecessors. The body of a man, reduced to ashes, scattered in the air and falling back to the surface of the earth, turns into a vegetable or wheat. . . . Now, when the time of resurrection comes, how shall we allot to each the body that belongs to him without losing a part of our own?" (Voltaire [1764] 1962, under "resurrection"). Many Christians affirmed this very belief, however challenging it was; for example, the English writer Thomas Browne (1605–1682) asserted: "I believe that our estranged and divided ashes shall unite again; that our separated dust, after so many pilgrimages and transformations into the parts of minerals, plants, animals, elements, shall at the voice of God return into their primitive shapes, and join again to make up their primary and predestinate forms" (Browne [1643] 1869, part 1, §48). [SS]

447 (in §770). On the belief that the stars will fall to earth, see note 377 above. [Editors]

448 (in §771:2). Swedenborg is most likely referring here to his works *Heaven and Hell* and *Last Judgment,* both published in 1758; and possibly his 1763 work *Supplements,* which contains additions to those works. For his publication explaining the Book of Revelation, see the 1766 work *Revelation Unveiled.* [Editors]

449 (in §772). In this edition the second of the works Swedenborg mentions here is referred to by the short title *Supplements* (see note 448 above). For reports in the present work concerning the spiritual events known collectively as the Last Judgment, see §§95, 115–124. [Editors]

450 (in §773:2). In this verse from Isaiah, Hebrew, Greek, Latin, and English Bibles usually have a phrase with the meaning "your name," not "my name," as Swedenborg's text does here. Furthermore, the reading "my name" (Latin *nomine meo*) is unusual even in Swedenborg's other translations of this verse. [JSR]

451 (in §776:3). The Latin word here translated "goodwill" is *charitas* (see volume 1, page 679 note 19). It is possible, however, that *claritas,* "clarity," was intended instead, given the context and the similarity of the words. This alternate reading was originally suggested by editor Samuel H. Worcester in Swedenborg [1771] 1906. [JSR]

452 (in §777:1). The phrase "truly I say to you" (here rendered "*Amen* I say to you") occurs over sixty times in the Gospels. For the first few instances see Matthew 5:18; 6:2, 5, 16. In the Gospel of John the phrase is "truly, truly, I say to you." See, for example, John 1:51; 5:19, 24, 25. The Greek word for "truly" in almost all of these cases is ἀμήν (*amén*), which is simply transliterated into English as "amen." The word was carried over into New Testament Greek from the Hebrew word אָמֵן (*'āmēn*), which is generally used as an adverbial exclamation affirming the truth of a statement, but is occasionally used as a noun, as in the phrase אֱלֹהֵי אָמֵן (*elōhê 'āmēn*), "the God of truth" (Isaiah 65:16). [JSR, LSW]

453 (in §779). Swedenborg refers to himself as "Servant of the Lord Jesus Christ" also on the title page of the first edition of *True Christianity* (volume 1, page 113 in this

edition). For a discussion of the positive inner meaning of the term *servant,* which may be used of the Lord, angels, and any who are in a good manner useful to others, see *Revelation Explained* (= Swedenborg 1994–1997a) §§6, 409. [SS]

454 (in §779). The number of years Swedenborg is referring to here is difficult to pinpoint, but it is around twenty-seven. In §12:8 he writes that he has been aware of and has sensed an inflow from what is divine through the spiritual world continually for twenty-six years; in §157:1 he writes that he has been "in the spirit" for twenty-six years; and in §851:1 below he writes that he has been in the spiritual world with angels and at the same time in the physical world with people for twenty-seven years. (The discrepancy may be a result of the passing of time between the writing of the last reference and the writing of the two previous.) The exact point of commencement of this visionary period is variously stated in his writings: in an early passage in a diary, he explicitly indicates that it dates *a medio Aprilis 1745,* "from mid-April 1745" (*Spiritual Experiences* [= Swedenborg 1998–2002] §[8a]), whereas in two later passages, one in a theological manuscript and one in a letter, he points to 1744 (*Draft on Divine Wisdom* [= Swedenborg 1994–1997b, 480] = §7 [heading] = §95 [Mongredien's numbering]; Acton 1948–1955, 627). See also note 455 just below. [JSR]

455 (in §779). In his published theological works, Swedenborg frequently reports what angels have said to him and to others (for a few of many examples in this work alone, see §§78, 134, 188, 506:6–7, 507:1–3, 621, 734:3, 735:5–6), and most of that reported discourse seems instructional in tone. Yet here Swedenborg strongly testifies that he has accepted nothing regarding the teachings of this church from any angel; and elsewhere he maintains that spirits do not dare, and angels do not wish, to teach people on earth about theology or the meaning of the Bible (*Divine Providence* 135, 154–174; *Revelation Unveiled* preface:4; see also *Draft of "Sacred Scripture"* [= Swedenborg 1997b, 33] §13:[2] [Swedenborg's numbering] = §29 [Hayward's numbering]). Furthermore, the statement here that he has learned from the Lord alone while reading the Bible is consistent with the learning process he describes elsewhere. See in particular his letter of February 1767 to his friend Gabriel Beyer (1720–1779): "When heaven was opened to me, I had first to learn the Hebrew language, as well as the correspondences according to which the whole Bible is composed, which led me to read the Word of God over many times; and as God's Word is the source whence all theology must be derived, I was enabled thereby to receive instruction from the Lord, who is the Word" (Tafel 1877, 261). [JSR]

456 (in §782:3). The word "your" here (Latin *tuo*) could be a typographical error for "his" (Latin *suo*), since the latter reflects the wording of the Hebrew Bible and other translations. [JSR]

457 (in §782:5). With the phrase, "where Jews once lived," Swedenborg refers loosely to the period when Jerusalem was controlled by people of the Jewish faith. At the time of the writing of *True Christianity,* this was far in the past: the last of the great Jewish temples there was destroyed in 70 C.E.; the last even nominally Jewish ruler, Herod Agrippa II, died before 93 C.E.; and Jews were forbidden to live in Jerusalem in 135 C.E. Thereafter they periodically returned and were expelled several times over the centuries, by Romans, Crusaders, and Muslims. Throughout Swedenborg's lifetime the city was under Muslim control. [SS]

458 (in §784:1). The statement that "this inner level has to be formed before the outer level" reflects Swedenborg's basic tenet that God has constructed the universe in such a way

that the outer levels of everything that has real existence are formed from and sustained by its inner levels. See, for example, the discussion in *Divine Love and Wisdom* 363–370, which presents the idea that love and wisdom constitute the very life and core of a human being, and that both the lower levels of the mind or spirit and the entire body are formed by and from that deepest core. This premise renders it impossible for any external church to be formed without there first being an internal church. It is possible for the external church to be separated from the internal church after it is formed; however, this results in the destruction of the church. For more on these concepts see *Secrets of Heaven* 1587, 3498, 5337, 5841, 10420; *New Jerusalem* 125. With respect to the new church in particular, the above principle is given even more force in *Revelation Unveiled* 918: "In that church there will be nothing on the surface that is separated from what is within." The idea that inner is primary and outer secondary became part of established Christian belief based on biblical passages such as Matthew 23:25–28; Luke 11:37–41; Romans 2:28–29; 2 Corinthians 4:16. On those who constitute the inner church and those who constitute the outer church, see note 231. [LSW]

459 (in §785). On the theory that exhalations are a driver of mineral and plant growth, see §§499:2, 585:4, and note 113. [Editors]

460 (in §785). Swedenborg generally divides animals and plants into good kinds that are beneficial to the human race and to other animals and plants, and bad kinds that are harmful to humans and to other animals and plants (see §78:5; *Secrets of Heaven* 45–46; *Divine Love and Wisdom* 331, 336, 338; *Revelation Explained* [= Swedenborg 1994–1997a] §1201:3). However, he was also aware of the need for predatory animals to control the populations of other animals (see §32:3). [JSR, LSW]

461 (in §786:1). Several passages in the Bible suggest that God is not "visible" or able to be seen as an object of intellectual thought, but that the Incarnation of Jesus made him visible: in addition to Exodus 33:18–23, which Swedenborg cites just below, see John 1:18; 14:7–9; Colossians 1:15; 1 Timothy 6:16. See also Job 37:23; John 1:14; 1 Timothy 1:17; Hebrews 1:3; 11:27; 1 John 4:12. An explanation of how God nonetheless became visible to various figures in the Old Testament follows just below in the main text here. For a memorable occurrence in the first volume of the current work exploring the issue of God's visibility and invisibility, see §159. [JSR]

462 (in §786:1). God appears to Moses throughout the Book of Exodus. See especially Exodus 3; 24:9–18; 33:7–23. For stories in which God appears to Abraham and Sarah, see Genesis 18; 22:1–19; to Hagar, see Genesis 16; 21:8–20; to Gideon, see Judges 6, 7; to Joshua, see Joshua 5:13–15; to the prophets, see, for example, Isaiah 6:1–8; Jeremiah 1:4–10; Ezekiel 1:25–28; Daniel 3:19–25. A careful reading of these texts shows that the figures appearing to these biblical personalities are sometimes referred to as "men," sometimes as "angels," and sometimes as "the Lord" (or "Jehovah"), and that the angels in these cases are often presented as speaking for the Lord. For Swedenborg's discussion of the process of the Lord speaking through angels by filling them with the divine presence, see *Secrets of Heaven* 1925; *Divine Providence* 96:6; *Revelation Unveiled* 465; *Revelation Explained* (= Swedenborg 1994–1997a) §§412:16, 1228. [LSW]

463 (in §786:1). The ideas found in this sentence are said to be "well known" because of the material in Hebrews 4–10, in which the author of that letter presents the details of the ancient Jewish tabernacle and the sacrifices that took place there as symbolic of Christ's sacrifice, which fulfills and supersedes everything contained in the tabernacle and its sacrificial worship. [LSW]

464 (in §786:2). For a listing of passages in which the prophets say that Jehovah himself is going to come and become the Redeemer, see §§82–83. [LSW]

465 (in §787:2). For a listing of Bible passages saying that the Father and the Lord are one, see §§98–99. For a listing of Bible passages to the effect that one has to believe in the Lord in order to have eternal life, see §107. [LSW]

466 (in §791). The gap of almost exactly a year between the date given just below in the text (June 19, 1770) and the date of publication (just before June 18, 1771) suggests that the completed "work" (Latin *opus*) mentioned here actually turned out to be the penultimate draft, not the final draft. For more on the date of publication and the extensive redrafting of the work beforehand, see the translator's preface in volume 1, pages 17–29. [JSR]

Notes to Author's Additional Material on the Spiritual World, §§792–851

467 (in §792). For the problematic and sometimes even offensive nature of much of the material in §§792–845, see the translator's preface to this volume, pages 2–4. [JSR]

468 (in §792). For a description of the states people go through after death, see *Heaven and Hell* 445–452, 491–520. [LSW]

469 (in §793). Although the biblical text sometimes refers to them not as angels but as "men" or "holy ones" or the like, angels appear to Abraham in Genesis 18:2; to Hagar in Genesis 16:7–13; to Gideon in Judges 6:11–22; and to Daniel in Daniel 8:15–17; 10:5–7; 12:5–7. One or two angels appear in or near the tomb of Jesus in Matthew 28:2–5; Mark 16:5; Luke 24:4 (compare Luke 24:23); and John 20:12. Angels are mentioned more than sixty times in the Book of Revelation; John explicitly mentions *seeing* angels in Revelation 5:2; 7:1, 2; 8:2; 10:1, 5; 14:6; 15:1; 18:1; 19:17; 20:1. Swedenborg's point is that the Bible presents these angels as human beings. [JSR]

470 (in §795). For more on Faustus Socinus (also known as Fausto Sozzini; 1539–1604) and Laelius Socinus (also known as Lelio Sozzini; 1525–1562) and their followers the Socinians, and on Arius and his followers the Arians, see §§94, 380:2–4, 632:1, 633:3, 636–638, and volume 1, page 716 note 245. [JSR]

471 (in §796:1). Martin Luther (1483–1546) was the founder of the branch of Protestant Christianity that bears his name. [JSR]

472 (in §796:6). Luther lived from 1483 to 1546. The rulers of Saxony during this period were Frederick III, also called the Wise (1463–1525); John the Constant (1468–1532); and John Frederick I (1503–1554). It would be difficult to decide which of these rulers is intended here; all three were protectors of Luther and personally acquainted with him. They were "princes" only in a loose sense of that term. See also note 530. [JSR, SS]

473 (in §797:1). Philipp Melanchthon (1497–1560) was a friend of Luther's and author of the first systematic presentations of Reformation theology. [JSR]

474 (in §798:1). On Calvin, see note 90. [JSR]

475 (in §798:2). For a list of some proponents of the doctrine of predestination since ancient times, see note 90. [Editors]

476 (in §798:2). On Gottschalk, see note 90. [Editors]

477 (in §798:2). This is a rare instance of Swedenborg's transcribing a word from the language of the spiritual world into earthly language. Other examples are found in *Marriage Love* 183, in which the spiritual word *Adramandoni* is said to mean "the delight of the love of marriage"; and in *Draft of "Supplements"* (= Swedenborg 1997a, 180) §332

[Rogers's numbering] = §324 [Potts's numbering], in which the spiritual word *scapuleja* is said to mean "to cast out" and *wita vella* is said to mean "to be at a distance." For more on the universal language of the spiritual world and its use by angels and spirits, see *Secrets of Heaven* 1634–1649, 1757–1764, 5225; *Heaven and Hell* 234–245; *Spiritual Experiences* (= Swedenborg 1978) §§1146–1148, [1221a]–1225, 4184–4186, 5112–5114, 6084. [LSW, JSR]

478 (in §798:10). On the *Formula of Concord,* by which Swedenborg means the *Book of Concord,* see note 4. [JSR]

479 (in §798:10). These pages in *Concordia* 1756 occur in the Saxon Visitation Articles, which for several centuries were part of the *Book of Concord* in electoral Saxony, although not elsewhere. The first quotation is point 6 of the refutation of Calvinist teaching concerning the person of Christ; the second is points 1–4 concerning predestination. Modern parallels in English can be found in McCain 2006, 657, 658. [JSR]

480 (in §800). The intended passage in *Heaven and Hell* is likely §308; compare with *True Christianity* 268. [LSW]

481 (in §801). This statement and another in the last paragraph of the section reflect a refrain that was common in Christian Europe, to the effect that contemporary Jews were miserly and self-serving. For Swedenborg's portrayal of Jews in the spiritual world, see §§841–845. On the problematic and offensive nature of much of the content of §§792–845, see the translator's preface to this volume, pages 2–4. For more on Swedenborg's attitude to Jews in this work, see volume 1, pages 718–719 note 262. [JSR]

482 (in §802:2). On the terms "essence" and "person" here, see volume 1, page 678 note 12. [JSR]

483 (in §803). Cocceians were followers of the Dutch biblical scholar and theologian Johannes Cocceius (1603–1669). [JSR]

484 (in §806). In the supplement to *Heaven and Hell* (*Supplements* 32–90) in which this material was first published, the sections on various national and religious groups appeared in a somewhat different order (see the translator's preface to volume 1, pages 19–21). Although the general introductory remarks here at §806 may seem somewhat out of place, preceded as they are by headings concerning Luther, Melanchthon, Calvin, and the Dutch (§§796–805), in their original location they came before all such material, since there the British were the first to be discussed. [JSR]

485 (in §807). With the expiry of the Regulation of Printing Act in 1694 there ceased to be prepublication censorship of the press in England. The relative freedom of the press was unique in Europe at the time and continued to be unparalleled throughout most of the eighteenth century; see Siebert 1952, 260–263; Black 1987, 8–12. [JSR]

486 (in §809). Although Swedenborg was a Swede, he was familiar with London; he lived there on nine occasions for a cumulative total of seven years, including the last seven months of his life. The Latin phrase here translated "where [the earthly] London has its meeting place for traders called 'the Exchange'" is *ubi in Londino est Conventus Mercatorum, qui vocatur Exchange.* By "traders" here (Latin *mercatores*) Swedenborg may mean merchants in general or stockbrokers in particular; by "Exchange" he may mean either the Royal Exchange, a vibrant shopping and social district with merchandise from around the world, or the group of one hundred and fifty brokers then meeting in Jonathan's coffee house and soon afterward to become the London Stock Exchange. In any event, the area of London to which he refers is clear, and is the same in both cases: the area around Cornhill, due north of what was then the London Bridge. [JSR]

487 (in §812). The statement from the Anglican service here referred to is the one given in §526 and again in §722:3; on which see note 170. [Editors]

488 (in §815:1). On Pegasus, Mount Parnassus, and the Muses, see note 374. [Editors]

489 (in §817). On Swedenborg's attitude toward Roman Catholicism in general, see note 69. [JSR]

490 (in §818). For more on the nature and location of these artificial heavens (also called "former heavens"; compare §771:2) and their abolition at the time of the Last Judgment, see *Last Judgment* 65–72; *Supplements* 8–22; *Revelation Explained* (= Swedenborg 1994–1997a) §§391–392, 394, 397, 497; *Draft of Five Memorable Occurrences* (= Swedenborg 1996c, 532) §24. [LSW]

491 (in §819:1). For more detailed statements of this charge that the popes transferred the Lord's power to themselves, see *Divine Providence* 257; *Revelation Unveiled* 717, 729. See also note 301 above. For an exception to the rule that no one who had actually been a pope in the world is allowed any authority in the spiritual world, see §820; *Revelation Unveiled* 752. [LSW, JSR]

492 (in §820:1). The time frame suggested here and certain facts given about this pope elsewhere confirm that Swedenborg is referring to Clement XII (1652–1740), who was pope from July 12, 1730, until February 6, 1740. These facts are: (1) references to a specific date (1738) in the pope's tenure, for which see *Draft of "Supplements"* (= Swedenborg 1997a, 82, 95) §§61, 102 [Rogers's numbering] = §§60, 102 [Potts's numbering]; (2) a reference to this pope's blindness in old age, for which see *Spiritual Experiences* (= Swedenborg 1978) §5272; *Draft of "Supplements"* (= Swedenborg 1997a, 95) §102 [Rogers's numbering] = §102 [Potts's numbering]; (3) a reference to the identity of his successor, for which see *Draft of "Supplements"* (= Swedenborg 1997a, 96) §103 [Rogers's numbering] = §103 [Potts's numbering]. [JSR]

493 (in §822). For more on the nature of unrestrained love of domination, see §§400:7, 661:4–12. [JSR]

494 (in §822). In classical mythology, Atlas was a Titan; his most well-known mythic role is that of holding up the sky, or as here, the world itself. (For that reason his name is used in English for a collection of maps.) For a brief but full discussion with references to ancient literature, see the *Oxford Classical Dictionary,* under "Atlas." Apollo was the god of the sun, conceived of as driving the chariot of the sun across the sky; see the *Oxford Classical Dictionary,* under "Helios." [SS]

495 (in §823). Though the phrase "papal bull" has acquired a more limited technical sense during the many centuries of its use, in early times it could refer to any papal document. The "bull" was originally the lead seal, so called from its similarity to a bubble (Latin *bulla*) on a flat surface, but in time the term was transferred to the document itself. [SS]

496 (in §824:2). The Roman Catholic Francis Xavier (1506–1552) was one of the original members of the Society of Jesus and a missionary in India, Malaysia, and Japan. He was canonized in 1622. [SS]

497 (in §826). Geneviève (419 or 422–512) is the patron saint of Paris, famed for her piety, her austere way of life, and her many works of charity. The church housing her relics was being rebuilt during the last years of Swedenborg's life (from 1764 on). [SS]

498 (in §828). In *Divine Providence* 255:1, Swedenborg maintains that "most" Muslims (that is, in the mortal world) view Jesus as greater than Muhammad, an erroneous

statement that seems to be based on misinformation concerning Islam that was current in Europe at the time. (See *Divine Providence* [= Swedenborg [1764] 2003b], 378 note 229.) [Editors]

499 (in §829). Further identification of this individual is not possible, but no small number of Europeans were captured and enslaved by Algerian Corsairs, also known as Barbary pirates. Such individuals then might well convert to Islam, willingly or unwillingly. The Barbary pirates were active from the 1500s through the early 1800s and conducted slaving raids on coasts as far away as Ireland and Iceland. Furthermore, some historically verifiable accounts read much like the brief biography of the individual mentioned here by Swedenborg. For example, the Netherlander Jan Janszoon van Harlem (1570–after 1641), also known as Murad Reis, was similarly captured, and he too converted to Islam. He eventually became President and Grand Admiral of the Corsair republic of Salé in North Africa. Thousands of other Europeans—called "renegadoes"— became Corsairs in the 1600s. For a colorful account of this phenomenon, with bibliography, see Wilson 2003. [SS]

500 (in §830). On the problematic and offensive nature of much of the content of §§792–845, see the translator's preface to this volume, pages 2–4. [JSR]

501 (in §833:2). Swedenborg here echoes the prevailing view of his times that Egyptian hieroglyphics were purely a symbolic and pictorial language, a concept that dates back to the Greek historian Diodorus Siculus of the first century B.C.E. and the Greek philosopher Plotinus (205–270). However, in contrast to pagan scholars, Swedenborg consistently refers the ultimate source of hieroglyphic symbolism to the ancient church; see *Secrets of Heaven* 6917:2, 7097. (On the members of the ancient church, or "the ancients," see note 198.) In his view, hieroglyphics were a medium for the transmission of the symbolic knowledge of the ancient church to modern times via the Hermetic tradition: in a unique passage he reports that the legendary originator of that tradition, Hermes Trismegistus, learned how to express mental perceptions by studying Egyptian hieroglyphics in the time of Moses (*Spiritual Experiences* [= Swedenborg 1978] §6083). Thus the Islamic tradition (described in this passage), the Hebraic tradition, and the Hermetic tradition contain parallel, if somewhat discrepant, streams of symbolic content. [JSR, FLS, SS]

502 (in §833:4). What is now known as Islam was in Swedenborg's day referred to as Muhammadanism. [JSR]

503 (in §834). The significance of this ivory spoon can only be conjectured. Such spoons may have been associated with Islam because of Arab trade in elephant ivory items from Africa and India; they may have been sold in Europe as implements to take snuff. The association seems weak, however. Elsewhere Swedenborg reports seeing an ivory spoon (in both instances the Latin phrase is *cochleare ebenum*) as an indication in the spiritual world that the people associated with it were Chinese (see the following passages, which are parallel to one another: *Spiritual Experiences* [= Swedenborg 1998–2002] §3066; *Secrets of Heaven* 2596; *Heaven and Hell* 325). In fact, Chinese ivory spoons used for inhaling snuff are extant from Swedenborg's day, and Swedenborg would certainly have been familiar with such utensils, as he was known to use copious amounts of snuff. (In fact, so much snuff fell on his manuscripts in the course of his writing them that one of his editors later claimed that the tobacco actually preserved the paper from bookworms [Tafel 1877, 544 with note].) On the use of snuff spoons during

this period, see Hill 1900, 589–590. On the translation of *ebenum* as "ivory" rather than "ebony," see Chadwick and Rose 2008, under *ebenus*. [JSR, SS]

504 (in §834). Swedenborg's only published memorable occurrence discussing odors in the spiritual world occurs in §569 of this work. He may also be thinking of the post-chapter essays in *Secrets of Heaven* 1504–1520, 4622–4634, which provide detailed accounts of odors and the sense of smell in the spiritual world. Swedenborg does speak of spiritual-world odors many times in the expository and topical sections of his published works. See, for example, *Secrets of Heaven* 925:2, 3577; *Divine Love and Wisdom* 420; *Divine Providence* 304; *Revelation Unveiled* 394; *Marriage Love* 430, 524:4. Accounts of odors in the spiritual world in his unpublished works occur in *Spiritual Experiences* (= Swedenborg 1998–2002) §323; Tafel 1877, 768–770. [LSW]

505 (in §838:2). The natural philosophers, or physicists, of Swedenborg's day conceived of ether as a superfine substance that interpenetrates the entire universe. In Swedenborg's account of the origin and character of air in his *Basic Principles of Nature,* part 3, chapter 7 (= Swedenborg [1734] 1988a, 2:303–310), he describes air as being different from ether only in having an increased "magnitude and dimension" (2:305). When he here says that ether is "thickened with air," he is probably thinking of a mingling of ether and air that results in a substance thicker than ether alone would have been. The point of the illustration is that air mediates for ether the way the Son mediates for the Father. On ether, compare also note 55. [SS]

506 (in §839). It appears from the context of this and other passages that by "reversed vision" here (Latin *visio praepostera*) Swedenborg means seeing dark as light and light as dark. Compare, for instance, the mention of "backwards faith" (Latin *fides praepostera*) at the end of §345, which is defined as faith that "presents falsity as truth and bolsters it with clever argumentation." See also §§162:2, 5; 334:3; 759:1. [JSR]

507 (in §839:2). On the remarkable specification of walls of clear glass, see note 143. [Editors]

508 (in §840). Even with the mention of a long-deceased person in the next paragraph (Augustine), it is difficult to tell from context whether Swedenborg is referring here to the geography of the Africa in the physical world or the geography of the Africa in the spiritual world or both. On the external similarities between the two worlds, see §§794–795. [JSR]

509 (in §840). Swedenborg was well acquainted with the writings of Augustine, the celebrated church father; extracts from some twenty-eight of Augustine's works are cited in Swedenborg's commonplace book, *Quotations on Various Philosophical and Theological Topics* (= Swedenborg 1976c). [SS]

510 (in §841). On the problematic and offensive nature of much of the content of §§792–845, see the translator's preface to this volume, pages 2–4. For more on Swedenborg's attitude to Jews in this work, see volume 1, pages 718–719 note 262. [JSR]

511 (in §845:2). The levirate law in Deuteronomy 25:5–10 states that if brothers reside together and one of them dies without a son, the remaining brother must marry the widow, and the first son born in that marriage will carry the deceased brother's name. This is the law referred to here as "the brother-in-law's obligation." As recounted in Genesis 38, Er, Onan, and Shelah were the three sons of Judah by his wife, who was a Canaanite. When Er died childless, neither Onan nor Shelah performed the levirate duty with Er's wife Tamar. Some time later Tamar heard that her father-in-law Judah

would be passing through her area. She posed as a prostitute and slept with him. When Judah heard that Tamar was pregnant, he ordered her burned for prostitution. But when she presented evidence that Judah himself was the father, he relented. Tamar bore twin boys named Perez and Zerah who became part of Judah's tribal lineage. For more on Perez and Zerah, see note 165. [LSW]

512 (in §846:1). In the first edition, §§846–851 are highlighted with double quotation marks at the beginning of each line of text, presumably to indicate that much of this material is copied from an earlier work (for details see the table of parallel passages on pages 629–638). For more on this method of highlighting text, see volume 1, page 718 note 260. [JSR]

513 (in §846:1). Since Swedenborg uses the term "church" (Latin *ecclesia*) in a variety of ways (see volume 1, pages 675–676 note 3), it is difficult to tell here whether he means "since Christianity first came into existence" or "since the earliest church first came into existence." [JSR]

514 (in §846:2). It is unclear whether Swedenborg has a more specific time period in mind here than simply "thousands of years" ago. The date (as well as the authorship) of Job was a matter of scholarly debate in the seventeenth and eighteenth centuries, as it still is today. For example, Sebastian Schmidt (1617–1696), in his influential commentary on Job, notes the wide range of opinions then in circulation and draws hesitant conclusions: the writing is definitely ancient; perhaps Moses himself either wrote or translated the work; and in any event, "for various reasons it is most probable that Job did not live after the time of Moses; neither did he live many centuries before" (Schmidt 1670, 4). For a history of views on the date and authorship of Job from the ancient rabbinic schools to the mid-twentieth century, see Pope 1965, xxx–xxxvii. [JSR]

515 (in §846:6). For more on what Swedenborg means by "levels that are prior" and "levels that are subsequent," see *Divine Love and Wisdom* 184–185, 189, and the broader context of those sections in *Divine Love and Wisdom* 179–229. [JSR]

516 (in §846:7). The words printed in italics in this paragraph are set in capitals and small capitals in the first Latin edition, since capitals and small capitals are the convention that Swedenborg commonly, though not exclusively, uses to indicate titles of his works. In the current edition, the specific works mentioned here are titled, respectively, *Last Judgment, The Lord, New Jerusalem* (covering both "the new church" and "its teachings"), *Sacred Scripture, Revelation Unveiled,* and *Other Planets* (covering both "the inhabitants of other planets" and "the worlds in the universe"). [JSR, LSW]

517 (in §847). As in the case of the titles in the previous section (see note 516), "true marriage love" is set in capitals and small capitals in the first edition. This is a reference to Swedenborg's 1768 work *Marriage Love.* [LSW]

518 (in §848). For the meaning Swedenborg elsewhere assigns to the biblical phrase "a time and times and half a time," see *Secrets of Heaven* 9198:4; *Revelation Unveiled* 562; *Revelation Explained* (= Swedenborg 1994–1997a) §§610:4–5, 761. [LSW]

519 (in §849). The hardening of the hearts of Pharaoh and/or the Egyptians in response to the escalating series of miracles performed by Moses is mentioned nearly a score of times in the Bible; see Exodus 4:21; 7:3, 13, 14, 22; 8:15, 19, 32; 9:7, 12, 34, 35; 10:1, 20, 27; 11:10; 14:4, 8, 17; 1 Samuel 6:6. [SS]

520 (in §849). The making of the golden calf and the dancing of the Israelites around it are described in Exodus 32:1–8, 19; Deuteronomy 9:12–21. The burning of

Mount Sinai is described in Exodus 19:18; 20:18; and Jehovah's speech from the fire is mentioned in Deuteronomy 4:33; 5:4, 22–26. [LSW, SS]

521 (in §849). Swedenborg, like other writers of his time, did not use quotation marks to indicate where direct speech begins and ends. Thus in the Latin original it is not entirely clear whether the reader is meant to understand that this information about the spiritual meaning of the biblical golden calf was part of what Swedenborg said to those in the lower regions or something he added later for the benefit of his readers. The material in question is, however, set off by italics, which would suggest that it is an aside to the reader. [JSR]

522 (in §851:1). For more on the date (or dates) of Swedenborg's spiritual awakening, see note 454. [JSR]

523 (in §851:2). The expression "in the spiritual world and in heaven," implying that there is a distinction between the two, is somewhat surprising here, given that generally elsewhere Swedenborg uses "spiritual world" as an inclusive term for heaven, hell, and the intermediate "world of spirits." He may have meant "in the world of spirits and in heaven." Compare note 34. [JSR]

Note to the Author's Table of Contents

524 (in Author's Table of Contents 10:4). In the first edition this statement appears out of place and numerical sequence; it is found after the rest of the contents of chapter 10. It is presented in its correct numerical position here. [JSR]

Notes to the Author's Index to the Accounts of Memorable Occurrences

525 (in Author's Index to Memorable Occurrences §74). The translation here is based on reading "of love and wisdom" *(amoris & sapientiae)* for the first edition's "of love from [those?] of wisdom" *(amoris ex sapientiae),* a rather clumsy expression without parallel in Swedenborg's corpus. This alternate reading was originally suggested by editor J.F.I. Tafel in Swedenborg [1771] 1857–1858. [JSR]

526 (in Author's Index to Memorable Occurrences §112). The work mentioned here, referred to as *Survey* in the present edition, was published by Swedenborg in 1769. For more information, see the translator's preface, pages 10–13, and page 720 note 279, both in volume 1. [JSR]

527 (in Author's Index to Memorable Occurrences §508). It seems noteworthy that what is here in the author's index of memorable occurrences described as a "round" temple (Latin *rotundum*) is in the memorable occurrence itself (§508:1) described as a temple "square in form" (Latin *formae quadratae*). In other respects the descriptions align. [JSR]

528 (in Author's Index to Memorable Occurrences §692). The Latin word here translated "something" is *subjectum.* It seems to be used in the philosophical sense of "the recipient of change; the substrate; the recipient of any perfection or form" (Wuellner 1956, under "subject," definition 4). (A substrate is that in which attributes inhere [Wuellner 1956, under "substrate," definition 1].) However, the word *subjectum* also refers to a percipient or conscious being as opposed to the perceived object (Wuellner 1956, definition 3), and Swedenborg may be creatively combining these meanings to suggest that we are perceptive and conscious, as we have to be to possess wisdom, and yet we are also a subordinate substance that is susceptible to perpetual divine inflow. [JSR, SS]

529 (in Author's Index to Memorable Occurrences §848). There is a numbering problem here in the first edition. This sentence, which covers §848, is preceded by the number 9; and the final sentence in the paragraph, which covers §850, is preceded by the number 11; yet the material between the two, which covers §849, is not preceded by the number 10. Furthermore, in the main text of §§846–850, the numbering only goes up to seven; numbers 8, 9, and 11 in the index here represent no such numbers in the main text. The present edition takes a middle course and leaves the numbers on the first eight items in place here, because they constitute the list Swedenborg communicated to angels of "secrets revealed" in his published theological works; it removes numbers 9 and 11 because those experiences were clearly not part of the list Swedenborg reported to angels. [JSR]

530 (in §[852]). This extra memorable occurrence, added at the end of the index of numbered memorable occurrences within the main text, has provided editors and translators with some challenges in its placement; see the translator's preface to this volume, pages 1–2 note 3. Some information on the identity of the individual mentioned is warranted. The Holy Roman Empire was an umbrella political organization that existed in Europe for roughly a thousand years; it is customarily seen as coming to an end in 1806, when Francis II (1768–1835) of the House of Habsburg resigned the title of emperor. It was formed primarily of German states but sometimes included parts of Italy, France, and other states in western and eastern Europe. The electors of the empire were ecclesiastical and/or civil leaders of the highest rank below the emperor himself; when the emperor died, even if his successor was hereditarily predetermined, they were responsible for electing him. There were three duke-electors (also called prince-electors) in Swedenborg's day: the Duke-Elector of Saxony, the Duke-Elector of Bavaria, and the Duke of Brunswick-Lüneberg, who was also Elector of Hanover. Of the many possible candidates, both of the electors of Hanover may be ruled out on the grounds that they were also kings of Great Britain (George I [1660–1727] and George II [1683–1760]) and surely the title of "king" would trump "duke-elector." The duke-electors of Bavaria may also be ruled out, since they were Catholic and the mention of "faith alone" that occurs later in the passage lends this memorable occurrence a distinctly Lutheran flavor. Swedenborg, then, may be referring to a Protestant duke-elector of Saxony. There are some ten candidates, from John the Constant (1468–1532), who originally introduced Lutheranism to his territories in 1527, to John George IV (1668–1694), the last Protestant duke-elector to pass away before Swedenborg. The second of these, John Frederick I (1503–1554), and the fourth, Augustus I (1526–1586), had significant involvement in ecclesiastical leadership during their earthly lives. John Frederick I may also be alluded to in §796:6; see note 472. Therefore John Frederick I may be the duke-elector referred to here. [JSR, SS]

531 (in §[852]). Although English translations of Philippians 3:9 do not use the exact phrase "the God of faith," the Latin expression here, *Deus Fidei,* does reflect the anomalous reading of Schmidt 1696, a Protestant Latin Bible. See also §354:2, which includes a longer quotation from the same verse and uses the same phrase. [JSR]

Works Cited
in the Notes

A list of the works of Swedenborg that are mentioned in the endnotes to this volume can be found on pages 15–22.

Acton, Alfred. 1922. "The Greek Religion." *The New Philosophy* 25:138–140.

[———]. 1923. "The Three Bloods." *The New Philosophy* 26:7–11.

———. 1948–1955. *The Letters and Memorials of Emanuel Swedenborg.* 2 vols. Bryn Athyn, Pa.: Swedenborg Scientific Association.

Alexandersson, Gunnar. 1982. *The Baltic Straits.* The Hague: Martinus Nijhoff.

Alfelt, Lennart O. 1969. "Swedenborg's Library: An Alphabetical List." *The New Philosophy* 72:115–126.

Almond, Philip C. 1994. *Heaven and Hell in Enlightenment England.* Cambridge: Cambridge University Press.

———. 1999. *Adam and Eve in Seventeenth-Century Thought.* Cambridge: Cambridge University Press.

Aquinas, Thomas. 1952. *Summa Theologiae.* Translated by the Fathers of the English Dominican Province and revised by Daniel J. Sullivan. Vols. 19–20 of *Great Books of the Western World.* Chicago: Encyclopedia Britannica.

Aristotle. 1984. *The Complete Works of Aristotle.* Princeton, N.J.: Princeton University Press.

Augustine. 1938. *Concerning the Teacher and On the Immortality of the Soul.* Translated by George G. Leckie. New York: Appleton-Century-Crofts.

———. 1952. *The City of God.* Translated by Marcus Dods. In vol. 18 of *Great Books of the Western World.* Chicago: Encyclopedia Britannica.

———. 1997. *On Rebuke and Grace.* Translated by Peter Holmes and Robert Ernest Wallis. In *Saint Augustin: Anti-Pelagian Writings,* vol. 5 of *A Select Library of the Nicene and Post-Nicene Fathers of the Christian Church,* edited by Philip Schaff. Grand Rapids, Mich.: Wm. B. Eerdmans.

Bellarini, Giovanni. 1603. *Doctrina Sacri Concilii Tridentini et Catechismi Romani de Sacramentis, et de Iustificatione.* Brescia: Francesco Tebaldino.

Black, Jeremy. 1987. *The English Press in the Eighteenth Century.* Philadelphia: University of Pennsylvania Press.

Book of Common Prayer and Administration of the Sacraments and Other Rites and Ceremonies of the Church. 1711. London: Charles Bill and Thomas Newcomb.

Browne, Thomas. [1643] 1869. *The Religio Medici.* London: Sampson Low, Son, and Marston.

Burns, Norman T. 1972. *Christian Mortalism from Tyndale to Milton.* Cambridge: Harvard University Press.

Calvin, John. 1960. *Institutes of the Christian Religion.* Edited by John T. McNeill and translated by Ford Lewis Battles. 2 vols. Philadelphia: Westminster.

———. 2006. *Calvin's Calvinism: Treatises on the Eternal Predestination of God & the Secret Providence of God.* Translated by Henry Cole. Grand Rapids, Mich.: Reformed Free Publishing Association.

Carlton, Christopher. 2011. Personal communication with Stuart Shotwell, January 6, 2011.

Chadwick, John, and Jonathan S. Rose, eds. 2008. *A Lexicon to the Latin Text of the Theological Writings of Emanuel Swedenborg (1688–1772).* London: Swedenborg Society.

Chrysostom, John. 1843. *The Homilies of S. John Chrysostom on the Epistles of St. Paul the Apostle to Timothy, Titus, and Philemon.* Oxford: John Henry Parker, and London: J.G.F. and J. Rivington.

Cobb, Matthew. 2006. *Generation: The Seventeenth-Century Scientists Who Unraveled the Secrets of Sex, Life, and Growth.* New York: Bloomsbury.

Cole, Stephen D. 1991. "A Short Note on Swedenborg's Procedure in Repeating Memorabilia." *The New Philosophy* 94:638.

Collier, Katharine B. 1934. *Cosmogonies of Our Fathers: Some Theories of the Seventeenth and the Eighteenth Centuries.* New York: Columbia University Press.

Concordia: Christliche, widerholete, einmütige Bekentnüs nachbenanter Churfürsten, Fürsten und Stende Augspurgischer Confession und derselben zu end des Buchs unterschribnen Theologen, Lehre und Glaubens. 1580. Tübingen: Gruppenbach.

Concordia Pia et Unanimi Consensu Repetita Confessio Fidei. 1756. Edited by Adam Rechenberg. Leipzig: Johan Grosse.

Curtius, Ernst Robert. 1953. *European Literature and the Latin Middle Ages.* Translated by Willard R. Trask. Princeton: Princeton University Press.

[Defoe, Daniel]. 1726. *Mere Nature Delineated: or, A Body without a Soul; Being Observations upon the Young Forester Lately Brought to Town from Germany; with Suitable Applications. Also, A Brief Dissertation upon the Usefulness and Necessity of Fools, Whether Political or Natural.* London: T. Warner.

Descartes, René. [1644] 1983. *Principles of Philosophy.* Translated by Valentine Rodger Miller and Reese P. Miller. Dordrecht: D. Reidel.

———. [1642] 1984. *Meditations on First Philosophy.* In vol. 2 of *The Philosophical Writings of Descartes,* translated by John Cottingham, Robert Stoothoff, and Dugald Murdoch. Cambridge: Cambridge University Press.

———. 2001. *Discourse on Method, Optics, Geometry, and Meteorology.* Translated by Paul J. Olscamp. Rev. ed. Indianapolis: Hackett.

De Wulf, Maurice. 1956. *An Introduction to Scholastic Philosophy.* Translated by P. Coffey. New York: Dover Publications.

Dilman, Ilham. 1999. *Free Will: An Historical and Philosophical Introduction.* London: Routledge.

Duncan, Joseph E. 1972. *Milton's Earthly Paradise: A Historical Study of Eden.* Minneapolis: University of Minnesota Press.

Flandry, Fred, Edward J. Lisecki, Gerald J. Domingue, Ronald L. Nichols, Donald L. Greer, and Ray J. Haddad. 1989. "Initial Therapy for Alligator Bites: Characterization of the Oral Flora of *Alligator Mississippiens.*" *Southern Medical Journal* 82:262–266.

Fuller, David B. 2008. "Swedenborg's Brain and Sutherland's Cranial Concept." *The New Philosophy* 111:619–650.

Genke, Victor, and Francis X. Gumerlock, trans. 2010. *Gottschalk and a Medieval Pre-destination Controversy.* Vol. 47 of *Medieval Philosophical Texts in Translation.* Milwaukee, Wis.: Marquette University Press.

Glasse, Hannah. [1760?]. *The Compleat Confectioner: Or the Whole Art of Confectionary Made Plain and Easy.* London: I. Pottinger and J. Williams.

Goetz, Stewart, and Charles Taliaferro. 2011. *A Brief History of the Soul.* Malden, Mass.: Wiley-Blackwell.

Gross, Charles G. 1998. *Brain, Vision, Memory: Tales in the History of Neuroscience.* Cambridge, Mass.: Massachusetts Institute of Technology Press.

Helander, Hans. 2004. *Neo-Latin Literature in Sweden in the Period 1620–1720.* Uppsala: Uppsala University.

Hill, Emily. 1900. "Snuff and Snuff-takers." *The Gentleman's Magazine.* 289:588–596.

Howard, Wilfred. 1927. "The Resuscitation of Plants from Their Ashes." *The New Philosophy* 30:262–269.

Huchzermeyer, Fritz W. 2010. Personal communication with Stuart Shotwell, December 23, 2010.

Hyde, James. 1906. *A Bibliography of the Works of Emanuel Swedenborg, Original and Translated.* London: Swedenborg Society.

The Iudgement of the Synode Holden at Dort, Concerning the Fiue Articles. 1619. London: John Bill.

Ivie, Michael A. 2011. Personal communication with Stuart Shotwell, January 6, 2011.

The Jewish Encyclopedia. Edited by Isidore Singer. 12 vols. 1901–1906. New York: Funk and Wagnalls.

Jolley, Nicholas. 1998. "The Religious Background of Seventeenth-Century Philosophy." In vol. 1 of *The Cambridge History of Seventeenth-Century Philosophy,* edited by Daniel Garber and Michael Ayers. 2 vols. Cambridge: Cambridge University Press.

Kirk, G. S., J. E. Raven, and M. Schofield, eds. and trans. 1983. *The Presocratic Philosophers.* 2nd ed. Cambridge: Cambridge University Press.

Kirven, Robert H. 1965. *Emanuel Swedenborg and the Revolt against Deism.* Dissertation, Brandeis University.

Klooster, Fred H. 1977. *Calvin's Doctrine of Predestination.* 2nd ed. Grand Rapids, Mich.: Baker Book House.

Kolb, Robert, and Timothy J. Wengert, eds. 2000. *The Book of Concord: The Confessions of the Evangelical Lutheran Church.* Minneapolis: Fortress Press.

Kors, Alan Charles, ed. 2003. *Encyclopedia of the Enlightenment.* 4 vols. Oxford: Oxford University Press.

Langer, William L. 1974. "Infanticide: A Historical Survey." *History of Childhood Quarterly* 1:353–365.

La Peyrère, Isaac. 1655a. *Prae-Adamitae, sive Exercitatio super Versibus Duodecimo, Decimotertio, & Decimoquarto, Capitis Quinti Epistolae D. Pauli ad Romanos. Quibus Inducuntur Primi Homines ante Adamum Conditi.* [Amsterdam.]

———. 1655b. *Systema Theologicum ex Prae-Adamitarum Hypothesi.* N.p.

le Goff, Jacques. 1981. *The Birth of Purgatory.* Translated by Arthur Goldhammer. Chicago: Chicago University Press.

Leibniz, Gottfried Wilhelm. [1698] 1989. "On Nature Itself; or, On the Inherent Force and Actions of Created Things, toward Confirming and Illustrating Their Dynamics."

In *Philosophical Essays,* edited and translated by Roger Ariew and D. Garber. Indianapolis: Hackett.

Lennox, William G. 1955. "The Reign of the Uterus." *Epilepsia* C4(1):91–98.

Libri Symbolici Ecclesiae Evangelicae sive Concordia. 1827. Edited by Karl August von Hase. Leipzig: Johan Sühring.

Littleton, Adam. 1723. *Latin Dictionary in Four Parts.* 5th ed. London.

Lovejoy, Arthur O. 2009. *The Great Chain of Being.* New Brunswick, N.J.: Transaction Publishers. First edition: 1936, Cambridge, Mass.: Harvard University Press.

McCain, Paul Timothy, ed. 2006. *Concordia: The Lutheran Confessions. A Reader's Edition of the Book of Concord.* 2nd ed. St. Louis, Mo.: Concordia Publishing House.

Mercer, Christia, and R. C. Sleigh, Jr. 1995. "Metaphysics: The Early Period to the *Discourse on Metaphysics.*" In *The Cambridge Companion to Leibniz,* edited by Nicholas Jolley. Cambridge: Cambridge University Press.

Milgrom, J. 1976. "Sacrifices and Offerings, OT." In *The Interpreter's Dictionary of the Bible, Supplementary Volume.* Nashville: Abingdon.

Moed, Lisa, Tor A. Shwayder, and Mary Wu Chang. 2001. "Cantharidin Revisited: A Blistering Defense of an Ancient Medicine." *Archives of Dermatology* 137:1357–1360.

Muller, Richard A. 1985. *Dictionary of Latin and Greek Theological Terms, Drawn Principally from Protestant Scholastic Theology.* Grand Rapids, Mich.: Baker Book House.

The New Catholic Encyclopedia. 2003. 2nd ed. 15 vols. Detroit and Washington, D.C.: Thomson/Gale.

Odhner, Hugo Lj. 1933. "The History of the 'Animal Spirits,' and of Swedenborg's Development of the Concept." *The New Philosophy* 36:218–223, 234–249.

Onians, Richard Broxton. 1951. *The Origins of European Thought about the Body, the Mind, the Soul, the World, Time, and Fate: New Interpretations of Greek, Roman, and Kindred Evidence, Also of Some Basic Jewish and Christian Beliefs.* 2nd ed. Cambridge: Cambridge University Press.

Paine, Thomas. [1794] 1995. *The Age of Reason.* In *Thomas Paine: Collected Writings,* edited by Eric Foner. N.p.: The Library of America.

Pinto-Correia, Clara. 1997. *The Ovary of Eve: Egg and Sperm and Preformation.* Chicago: University of Chicago Press.

Pope, Marvin H., ed. 1965. *The Anchor Bible: Job.* Garden City, N. Y.: Doubleday.

Popkin, Richard H. 1987. *Isaac La Peyrère (1596–1676): His Life, Work, and Influence.* Leiden: Brill.

———. 1998. "The Religious Background of Seventeenth-Century Philosophy." In vol. 1 of *The Cambridge History of Seventeenth-Century Philosophy,* edited by Daniel Garber and Michael Ayers. 2 vols. Cambridge: Cambridge University Press.

Roe, Shirley A. 1981. *Matter, Life, and Generation: Eighteenth-Century Embryology and the Haller-Wolff Debate.* Cambridge: Cambridge University Press.

Russell, Bertrand. [1900] 2008. *A Critical Exposition of the Philosophy of Leibniz: With an Appendix of Leading Passages.* New York: Cosimo Classics.

Schiebinger, Londa. 1993. *Nature's Body: Gender in the Making of Modern Science.* Boston: Beacon Press.

Schmidt, Sebastian. 1670. *In Librum Ijobi Commentarius.* Strasbourg: J. F. Spoor.

———, trans. 1696. *Biblia Sacra sive Testamentum Vetus et Novum ex Linguis Originalibus in Linguam Latinam Translatum.* Strasbourg: J. F. Spoor.

Siebert, Frederick Seaton. 1952. *Freedom of the Press in England, 1476–1776*. Urbana, Ill.: University of Illinois Press.

Sleigh, Robert, Jr., Vere Chappell, and Michael Della Rocca. 1998. "Determinism and Human Freedom." In vol. 2 of *The Cambridge History of Seventeenth-Century Philosophy*, edited by Daniel Garber and Michael Ayers. 2 vols. Cambridge: Cambridge University Press.

Swedenborg, Emanuel. 1744–1745. *Regnum Animale, Anatomice, Physice, et Philosophice Perlustratum*. The Hague: Adrian Blyvenburg, and London.

———. [1771] 1781. *True Christian Religion Containing the Universal Theology of the New Church: Which Was Foretold by the Lord, in Daniel, Chap. vii. 5, 13, 14, and in the Apocalypse, Chap. xxi. 1, 2*. [Translated by John Clowes.] 2 vols. London.

———. [1771] 1833. *The True Christian Religion Containing the Universal Theology of the New Church Foretold by the Lord in Daniel VII. 13, 14; and in Revelation XXI. 1, 2*. Translated by T. G. W[orcester]. Boston: John Allen.

———. 1847–1854. *Adversaria in Libros Veteris Testamenti*. Edited by J. F. Immanuel Tafel. 4 vols. Tübingen: Verlagsexpedition.

———. [1771] 1857–1858. *Vera Christiana Religio, Continens Universam Theologiam Novae Ecclesiae a Domino apud Danielem Cap. VII: 13–14, et in Apocalypsi Cap. XXI: 1, 2. Praedictae*. Edited by J.F.I. Tafel. 2 vols. Tübingen: Verlagsexpedition, and London: Swedenborg Society.

———. [1771] 1869. *The True Christian Religion Containing the Entire Theology of the New Church, Foretold by the Lord in Dan. vii, 13, 14; and Rev. xxi. 1, 2*. Translated by R. Norman Foster. 2 vols. Philadelphia: J. B. Lippincott.

———. [1771] 1906. *Vera Christiana Religio Continens Universam Theologiam Novae Ecclesiae a Domino apud Danielem VII: 13, 14, et in Apocalypsi XXI: 1, 2, Praedictae*. Edited by Samuel H. Worcester. 2 vols. New York: American Swedenborg Printing and Publishing Society.

———. [1771] 1906–1907. *The True Christian Religion Containing the Universal Theology of the New Church Foretold by the Lord in Daniel VII. 13, 14; and in Revelation XXI. 1, 2*. Translated by John C. Ager. 2 vols. New York: American Swedenborg Printing and Publishing Society. Several reprintings, the most recent of which was a two-volume set issued as part of the Redesigned Standard Edition by the Swedenborg Foundation, West Chester, Pa., 1996.

———. 1922. "The Greek Religion." Translated by Alfred Acton. *The New Philosophy* 25:165–178.

———. 1927–1951. *The Word of the Old Testament Explained*. Translated and edited by Alfred Acton. 10 vols. Bryn Athyn, Pa.: Academy of the New Church.

———. 1928. *The Animal Kingdom, Considered Anatomically, Physically, and Philosophically, Parts 4 and 5: The Organs of Generation*. Translated and edited by Alfred Acton. Bryn Athyn, Pa.: Academy of the New Church. First edition of this translation: 1912, Philadelphia: Boericke & Tafel.

———. [1771] 1933. *The True Christian Religion Containing the Universal Theology of the New Church*. [Translated by F. Bayley], with an introduction by Helen Keller. London and Toronto: J. M. Dent and Sons, and New York: E. P. Dutton.

———. [1734] 1938. *Swedenborg's Treatise on Copper*. Translated by Alfred Hodson Searle. 3 vols. London: Swedenborg Society and British Non-Ferrous Metals Research Association.

————. [1771] 1950. *The True Christian Religion Containing the Universal Theology of the New Church Foretold by the Lord in Daniel vii 13, 14, and in the Revelation xxi 1, 2.* Translated by William C. Dick. London: Swedenborg Society.

————. [1740–1741] 1955. *The Economy of the Animal Kingdom, Considered Anatomically, Physically, and Philosophically.* Translated by Augustus Clissold. 2 vols. Bryn Athyn, Pa.: Swedenborg Scientific Association. First edition of this translation: 1845–1846, London: W. Newbery, H. Bailliere, and Boston: Otis Clapp.

————. [1744–1745] 1960. *The Animal Kingdom, Considered Anatomically, Physically, and Philosophically.* Translated by James John Garth Wilkinson. 2 vols. [Bryn Athyn, Pa.]: Swedenborg Scientific Association. First edition of this translation: 1843–1844, London: W. Newbery.

————. [1734] 1965. *Forerunner of a Reasoned Philosophy Concerning the Infinite, the Final Cause of Creation; Also the Mechanism of the Operation of the Soul and Body.* Translated by James John Garth Wilkinson, with an introduction by Lewis F. Hite. 3rd ed. London: Swedenborg Society. Revision of the 1847 edition, London: William Newbery.

————. 1976a. *The Economy of the Animal Kingdom, Considered Anatomically, Physically, and Philosophically, Transaction III.* Translated by Alfred Acton. Bryn Athyn, Pa.: Swedenborg Scientific Association. First edition: 1918, Philadelphia: Swedenborg Scientific Association.

————. [1722] 1976b. *Miscellaneous Observations Connected with the Physical Sciences.* Translated by Charles E. Strutt. Bryn Athyn, Pa.: Swedenborg Scientific Association. First edition of this translation: 1847, London: William Newbery.

————. 1976c. *A Philosopher's Note Book.* Translated by Alfred Acton. Bryn Athyn, Pa.: Swedenborg Scientific Association. First edition: 1931, Philadelphia: Swedenborg Scientific Association.

————. 1976d. *Three Transactions on the Cerebrum.* Translated by Alfred Acton. 2 vols. Bryn Athyn, Pa.: Swedenborg Scientific Association. First edition: 1938, Philadelphia: Swedenborg Scientific Association.

————. 1978. *The Spiritual Diary of Emanuel Swedenborg.* Vol. 4, pages 91–494, and vol. 5. Translated by G. Bush and James F. Buss. New York: Swedenborg Foundation. First edition: 1889, London: J. Speirs.

————. 1984a. *Action.* In *Psychological Transactions and Other Posthumous Tracts 1734–1744,* translated by Alfred Acton. 2nd ed. Bryn Athyn, Pa.: Swedenborg Scientific Association.

————. 1984b. *The Origin and Propagation of the Soul.* In *Psychological Transactions and Other Posthumous Tracts 1734–1744,* translated by Alfred Acton. 2nd ed. Bryn Athyn, Pa.: Swedenborg Scientific Association.

————. 1984c. *The Soul and the Harmony between Soul and Body.* In *Psychological Transactions and Other Posthumous Tracts 1734–1744,* translated by Alfred Acton. 2nd ed. Bryn Athyn, Pa.: Swedenborg Scientific Association.

————. [1734] 1988a. *The Principia; or, The First Principles of Natural Things.* Translated by Augustus Clissold. 2 vols. Bryn Athyn, Pa.: Swedenborg Scientific Association. First edition of this translation: 1846, London: W. Newbery.

————. [1771] 1988b. *The True Christian Religion Containing the Complete Theology of the New Church as Foretold by the Lord in Daniel 7:13,14 and in Revelation 21:2,3.* Translated by John Chadwick. 2 vols. London: Swedenborg Society.

————. [1719] 1992a. *Height of Water.* Translated by Joseph E. Rosenquist. In *Scientific and Philosophical Treatises (1716–1740),* edited by Alfred H. Stroh. 2nd edition edited and rearranged by William Ross Woofenden. Bryn Athyn, Pa.: Swedenborg Scientific Association.

————. 1992b. *Discovering Mines.* In *Scientific and Philosophical Treatises (1716–1740),* edited by Alfred H. Stroh. 2nd edition edited and rearranged by William Ross Woofenden. Bryn Athyn, Pa.: Swedenborg Scientific Association.

————. 1992c. *On the Mechanism of the Soul and the Body.* In *Scientific and Philosophical Treatises (1716–1740),* edited by Alfred H. Stroh. 2nd edition edited and rearranged by William Ross Woofenden. Bryn Athyn, Pa.: Swedenborg Scientific Association.

————. 1994–1997a. *Apocalypse Explained.* Translated by John C. Ager, revised by John Whitehead, and edited by William Ross Woofenden. 6 vols. West Chester, Pa.: Swedenborg Foundation.

————. 1994–1997b. *On Divine Love and Divine Wisdom.* In vol. 6 of *Apocalypse Explained,* translated by John C. Ager, revised by John Whitehead, and edited by William Ross Woofenden. West Chester, Pa.: Swedenborg Foundation.

————. 1995. *Charity: The Practice of Neighborliness.* Translated by William F. Wunsch. 2nd edition edited by William Ross Woofenden. West Chester, Pa.: Swedenborg Foundation. First edition: 1931, Philadelphia: J. B. Lippincott.

————. 1996a. *Canons of the New Church.* In vol. 1 of *Posthumous Theological Works,* translated by John Whitehead and edited by William Ross Woofenden. West Chester, Pa.: Swedenborg Foundation.

————. 1996b. *Coronis, or Appendix, to "True Christian Religion."* In vol. 1 of *Posthumous Theological Works,* translated by John Whitehead and edited by William Ross Woofenden. West Chester, Pa.: Swedenborg Foundation.

————. 1996c. *Five Memorable Relations.* In vol. 2 of *Posthumous Theological Works,* translated by John Whitehead and edited by William Ross Woofenden. West Chester, Pa.: Swedenborg Foundation.

————. 1997a. *The Last Judgment.* In *Three Short Works,* translated by N. Bruce Rogers. Bryn Athyn, Pa.: General Church of the New Jerusalem.

————. 1997b. *The Sacred Scripture or Word of the Lord from Experience.* In *Three Short Works,* translated by N. Bruce Rogers. Bryn Athyn, Pa.: General Church of the New Jerusalem.

————. 1998–2002. *Emanuel Swedenborg's Diary, Recounting Spiritual Experiences during the Years 1745 to 1765.* Translated by J. Durban Odhner. 3 vols. Bryn Athyn, Pa.: General Church of the New Jerusalem. The first three volumes, in English, of the six volumes of Swedenborg's Latin work *Experientiae Spirituales,* edited by J. Durban Odhner (Bryn Athyn, Pa.: Academy of the New Church, 1983–1997). Further volumes forthcoming.

————. 2001. *Rational Psychology.* Translated by Norbert H. Rogers and Alfred Acton. Bryn Athyn, Pa.: Swedenborg Scientific Association. Revision of 1950 edition, Philadelphia: Swedenborg Scientific Association.

————. [1763] 2003a. *Angelic Wisdom about Divine Love and about Divine Wisdom.* Translated by George F. Dole. West Chester, Pa.: Swedenborg Foundation.

———. [1764] 2003b. *Angelic Wisdom about Divine Providence.* Translated by George F. Dole. West Chester, Pa.: Swedenborg Foundation.

———. [1749–1756] 2008. *A Disclosure of Secrets of Heaven Contained in Sacred Scripture, or the Word of the Lord, . . . Together with Amazing Things Seen in the World of Spirits and in the Heaven of Angels.* Translated by Lisa Hyatt Cooper. Vol. 1. West Chester, Pa.: Swedenborg Foundation.

———. [1771] 2009. *Vera Christiana Religio Continens Universam Theologiam Novae Ecclesiae a Domino apud Danielem Cap. VII:13–14, et in Apocalypsi Cap. XXI:1,2, Praedictae.* Edited by Freya H. Fitzpatrick. 2 vols. Bryn Athyn, Pa.: Academy of the New Church.

———. [1749–1756] 2013. *A Disclosure of Secrets of Heaven Contained in Sacred Scripture, or the Word of the Lord, . . . Together with Amazing Things Seen in the World of Spirits and in the Heaven of Angels.* Translated by Lisa Hyatt Cooper. Vol. 2. West Chester, Pa.: Swedenborg Foundation.

Tafel, R. L. 1877. *Documents Concerning the Life and Character of Emanuel Swedenborg.* Vol. 2, parts 1 and 2. London: Swedenborg Society.

Tertullian. 1997. *A Treatise on the Soul.* Translated by Peter Holmes. In *The Ante-Nicene Fathers,* edited by Alexander Roberts and James Donaldson. Grand Rapids, Mich.: Wm. B. Eerdmans.

Thomson, Ann. 2008. *Bodies of Thought: Science, Religion, and the Soul in the Early Enlightenment.* Oxford: Oxford University Press.

Trench, Charles Chenevix. 1964. *The Royal Malady.* New York: Harcourt, Brace, & World.

Veith, Ilza. 1965. *Hysteria: The History of a Disease.* Chicago: University of Chicago Press.

Voltaire. [1764] 1962. *Philosophical Dictionary.* Translated by Peter Gay. New York: Harcourt, Brace, & World.

Wilson, Catherine. 1995. *The Invisible World: Early Modern Philosophy and the Invention of the Microscope.* Princeton: Princeton University Press.

Wilson, Peter Lamborn. 2003. *Pirate Utopias: Moorish Corsairs and European Renegadoes.* 2nd rev. ed. Brooklyn, N.Y.: Autonomedia.

Wuellner, Bernard. 1956. *Dictionary of Scholastic Philosophy.* Milwaukee: The Bruce Publishing Co.

Zimmer, Carl. 2004. *Soul Made Flesh: The Discovery of the Brain—and How It Changed the World.* New York: Free Press.

Index to Prefaces, Introduction, and Notes

References in this index correspond to page and note numbers in volumes 1 and 2 of *True Christianity*. References to the different volumes are indicated by the bold numerals "1" and "2."

Index to Scriptural Passages in *True Christianity*

The following index refers to passages from the Bible cited in the translation of *True Christianity,* volumes 1 and 2. The numbers to the left under each Bible book title are its chapter numbers. They are followed by verse numbers with the following designations: bold figures designate verses that are quoted; italic figures designate verses that are given in substance; figures in parentheses indicate verses that are merely mentioned in passing. Biblical references that are enclosed in square brackets represent the exact references supplied by the editors in passages that would otherwise contain only indirect allusions to Bible verses. The numbers to the right are section numbers in *True Christianity.* (Passages from the Bible cited in the preface, introduction, and notes can be found under the heading "Scripture references" in the separate index of those elements.)

Table of Parallel Passages

The following table indicates passages in *True Christianity,* volumes 1 and 2, that parallel passages in Swedenborg's other theological works. The table draws on John Faulkner Potts's *Swedenborg Concordance* (1902, London: Swedenborg Society) 6:859–864, and on the tables of parallel passages in the following editions of Swedenborg's works: *Apocalypsis Revelata,* edited by N. Bruce Rogers, vol. 2 (2010, Bryn Athyn, Pennsylvania: Academy of the New Church); *Delights of Wisdom Relating to Married Love,* translated by N. Bruce Rogers (1995, Bryn Athyn, Pennsylvania: General Church of the New Jerusalem); *Delitiae Sapientiae de Amore Conjugiali,* edited by N. Bruce Rogers (1995, Bryn Athyn, Pennsylvania: Academy of the New Church); *Sapientia Angelica de Divino Amore et de Divina Sapientia,* edited by N. Bruce Rogers (1999, Bryn Athyn, Pennsylvania: Academy of the New Church); *Sapientia Angelica de Divina Providentia,* edited by N. Bruce Rogers (2003, Bryn Athyn: Pennsylvania, Academy of the New Church); and *Vera Christiana Religio,* edited by Freya H. Fitzpatrick, vol. 2 (2009, Bryn Athyn, Pennsylvania: Academy of the New Church).

Reference numbers in this table correspond to Swedenborg's section numbers; subsection numbers are separated from section numbers by a colon.

True Christianity	Parallel Passage
§2	*Faith* 34–36; *Revelation Unveiled* 67; *Survey* 116
3:2	*Marriage Love* 82:1; *Survey* 43, 117:3
4:1	*True Christianity* 108, 791
12:1–4	*Divine Love and Wisdom* 351–352; *Marriage Love* 416
12:5	*Divine Love and Wisdom* 353; *Marriage Love* 417
12:6	*Spiritual Experiences* 2475; *Heaven and Hell* 108:2; *Revelation Explained* 1198:3; *Divine Love and Wisdom* 354; *Marriage Love* 418
12:7–8	*Divine Love and Wisdom* 355; *Marriage Love* 419
12:9	*Divine Love and Wisdom* 356; *Marriage Love* 420; *True Christianity* 13:3

198	*Sacred Scripture* 14
199	*Sacred Scripture* 17
200:1–3	*Sacred Scripture* 18:1–3
201	*Draft of "Sacred Scripture"* 7:[1–2] (Swedenborg's numbering) = 17 (Hayward's numbering); *Sacred Scripture* 20
203	*Divine Providence* 326:11–12
204	*Draft of "Sacred Scripture"* 7:[4] (Swedenborg's numbering) = 19 (Hayward's numbering); *Sacred Scripture* 22
205	*Draft of "Sacred Scripture"* 7:[5] (Swedenborg's numbering) = 19 (Hayward's numbering); *Sacred Scripture* 23
206	*Draft of "Sacred Scripture"* 7:[6] (Swedenborg's numbering) = 20 (Hayward's numbering); *Sacred Scripture* 24
207	*Draft of "Sacred Scripture"* 7:[8] (Swedenborg's numbering) = 21 (Hayward's numbering); *Sacred Scripture* 25
208	*Sacred Scripture* 26:1–2
209:3	*Revelation Unveiled* 566:5, 7
210	*Sacred Scripture* 27–28
211	*Sacred Scripture* 29
213	*Draft of "Sacred Scripture"* 20:[1] (Swedenborg's numbering) = 54 (Hayward's numbering); *Sacred Scripture* 33
214	*Sacred Scripture* 37–39
214:1	*Marriage Love* 314:2
215	*Sacred Scripture* 40–41
216	*Sacred Scripture* 42
217	*Sacred Scripture* 43
218	*Sacred Scripture* 44
219	*Sacred Scripture* 45
220	*Sacred Scripture* 46
221	*Sacred Scripture* 47
222	*Sacred Scripture* 48
223	*Draft of "Sacred Scripture"* 10:[3–4] (Swedenborg's numbering) = 25 (Hayward's numbering); *Sacred Scripture* 49; *Revelation Unveiled* 47
225	*Sacred Scripture* 50
226	*Sacred Scripture* 51:1–7, 9
227	*Sacred Scripture* 54
228	*Sacred Scripture* 52

812	*Draft of "Supplements"* 282 (Rogers's numbering) = 353 (Potts's numbering); *Supplements* 45
817–818	*Supplements* 56–57
819	*Last Judgment* 56:4–6
820:1	*Supplements* 59
822	*Supplements* 61
823	*Supplements* 63
824:1	*Draft of "Supplements"* 60 (Rogers's numbering) = 59 (Potts's numbering); *Supplements* 64
824:2	*Supplements* 65–66
826	*Spiritual Experiences* 6091; *Draft of "Supplements"* 62–63 (Rogers's numbering) = 61–62 (Potts's numbering); *Supplements* 67
827	*Spiritual Experiences* 5834, 5992; *Draft of "Supplements"* 69 (Rogers's numbering) = 68 (Potts's numbering); *Supplements* 66; *True Christianity* 102:3
828	*Supplements* 68
829	*Spiritual Experiences* 5667[a]; *Draft of "Supplements"* 80 (Rogers's numbering) = 79, 83 (Potts's numbering), 82 (Rogers's numbering) = 81 (Potts's numbering); *Supplements* 69
830	*Spiritual Experiences* 5666[a]; *Draft of "Supplements"* 79 (Rogers's numbering) = 78 (Potts's numbering); *Supplements* 70
832	*Marriage Love* 342:1, 343
833	*Divine Providence* 255:1–4; *Marriage Love* 342
833:4	*Spiritual Experiences* 5061; *Draft of "Supplements"* 85 (Rogers's numbering) = 85 (Potts's numbering); *Supplements* 71, 72:3
834	*Marriage Love* 344
835	*Supplements* 73
836	*Supplements* 74; *Divine Love and Wisdom* 11
840	*Spiritual Experiences* 4777; *Draft of "Supplements"* 118 (Rogers's numbering) = 119 (Potts's numbering); *Supplements* 76
841	*Draft of "Supplements"* 248 (Rogers's numbering) = 251 (Potts's numbering), 255 (Rogers's numbering) = 258 (Potts's numbering); *Supplements* 79

Index to *True Christianity*

Reference numbers in this index correspond to Swedenborg's section numbers in volumes 1 and 2 of *True Christianity*. The portion of a reference number following a colon indicates the subsection. Readers should note that references to §§1–462 can be found in volume 1 and references to §§463–852 can be found in volume 2.

the plant kingdom illustrating that our essence determines what we do, 145

the plant kingdom illustrating the state of being emptied out and state of being glorified, 106

the plant kingdom (plants) as activated by the spiritual world, 470:3, 695:6

the plant soul, 63, 585:2

plants meaning evils and falsities, 498:2

plants' varying reception to heat and light as analogous to free choice, 491, 496:1, 499:2

Plato, 9:3, 692:1. *See also* Philosophers

Platonist, 692:7

Pleasure, 79:8. *See also* Delight

the Lord leading us away from cravings and evil pleasures, 478:3

pleasure being in the outermost part of our will, 565:3

pleasure coming from love, 38

the pleasure of heaven, 694:3, 732:1, 737:3–4, 739:2, 819:2

the pleasures of the lower self (flesh), 119:2, 151, 849

Pluto, 178

Politicians (political leaders), in the spiritual world, 160:6, 665:1–3, 693:1, 693:3, 693:7

Politics, 55, 162:7, 186, 482:1, 808, 819:2

Polygamy, 380:1, 833:4–834. *See also* Marriage

Popes, 111:11, 821. *See also* Roman Catholicism

popes as representatives (vicars) of Christ, 177:4, 560, 634:2

popes in the spiritual world, 64, 819–820

Portuguese Jews, 841. *See also* The Jewish church

Power. *See also* Omnipotence

acting from our own power, 71:2–3, 74:3, 438, 457:4

the belief that heavenly joy is possessing power and wealth, 732:5, 736

love for ruling power, 400:8–9, 405:1–4

"power" meaning the Lord's power through the Word, 776:1

the power of truth, 87

Prayer, 110:2, 126, 137:12, 185:7, 297, 459:4, 518:1, 526, 568:1, 621:10, 744:1, 751

the belief that heaven consists of perpetual prayer, 695:1, 732:6, 738:1

the Lord's prayer, 112:6, 113:5–8, 299, 306, 459:12

prayer only being heard if we are purified from evils, 329:4

the prayers of those who do not believe in the Lord, 108

praying to saints, 825

praying to the Lord, 159:2, 570:1, 570:4, 621:1, 696:1

praying to three gods, 73:1, 133, 134:5, 623:6, 831

repentance as involving prayer, 530:1, 535:1, 539:1

Precious stones. *See* Stones

Predestination

belief in predestination arising from belief in the assignment of merit, 628

belief in predestination arising from denial of free choice, 486–488

Calvin believing in predestination, 798:2–4, 798:8–11

memorable occurrences concerning predestination, 71–73, 664, 803

the origins of Christian belief in predestination, 177:4, 183:3, 489:1, 759:2

Predestinarians, 378:2, 486:2, 798:3–4

Pre-established harmony. *See* Inflow

Priapuses, 388:1, 574:2

Priesthood (priests), 415, 504:3, 812. *See also* The clergy; Ministers

Aaron's priesthood, 218

hypocritical preachers, 381:2–4

inauguration into the priesthood, 297, 356, 815:2

the Lord's priestly role, 114

memorable occurrence concerning the priesthood of the new church, 508:2

priests acting with goodwill, 422

priests as spiritual thieves, 318

priests in the spiritual world, 160:6, 185:3, 281:8, 281:11, 663:2–3, 693:1–5, 748:4, 809–810, 815:2

"The Prince of This World," 116:3

Principle cause. *See* Cause

The Pronouncements, 265:1–2, 279:1, 279:3

Prophets

the false prophet, 108, 148, 179, 187:1–3, 635

the Lord as the greatest prophet, 126, 129, 130:3, 828, 833:1, 833:4

the meaning of "prophecy," 149

the prophetic mode in the Word, 757

Prophets *(continued)*
  prophets representing the state of the
    church, 129–130, 296:3
  prophets speaking on behalf of Jehovah
    rather than on behalf of the Holy Spirit,
    158, 188:9
  the visions of the prophets, 157:1–2, 786:1,
    793, 851:2–3
Protestants, 154:2. *See also* The Reformed
  church
  Protestant belief in the assignment of
    Christ's merit, 516, 520:1, 561:2, 562:1,
    581, 628–631, 640:2, 642
  Protestant beliefs about contrition, 512–515
  Protestant beliefs about repentance (self-
    examination), 526, 535:1, 561–562, 564:1,
    567:7–8
  Protestants believing that the Lord's soul
    came from Mary, 82:3
  Protestants in the spiritual world, 111, 391:2,
    621:2, 800, 817, 831
  the Protestant Reformation, 796:5, 797:3
    use of the Word resuming during, 270,
      508:4
  the split within Christianity giving rise to
    the Protestant church, 760
Providers of arguments, in the spiritual world,
  332:1, 334
Prudence, 205, 335:3, 418, 425 (title), 428,
  566:2, 660:2, 663:2, 692:4, 695:1, 734:1,
  849
Punishment, 79:8, 407, 498:3, 525, 531, 566:2,
  592
Purgatory, 475:4
Purging, ritual, 134:1, 135:3–6, 160:6
Purification. *See also* Evil
  circumcision and baptism meaning spiri-
    tual purification from evils, 671, 675:2,
    676
  the Holy Spirit purifying us from evils, 142,
    144, 149
  the Lord purifying us from evils, 150, 153:1
  the purifying operation of faith, 462:3
  purifying ourselves from sin with a power
    apparently our own, 71:2, 331:4, 436, 438
Purpose, means, and result, 13:3, 67, 210, 387:3
Pyris, 798:2
Pyrrha, 58

Pythagoras, 692:1
Pythagoreans, 692:7

Q
Quakers, 378:2
Quartodecimans, 378:2
Qur'an, 829–830, 833:1. *See also* Islam

R
Races, Swedenborg conversing in the spiritual
  world with people from different, 795
Rachel, 735
Rationality (the rational mind), 71:2, 178,
  771:2. *See also* The mind; Reason
  Assyria meaning rationality and understand-
    ing, 200:3, 247:2, 467:2
  the development of our rationality, 443:1–2
  earthly rationality, 384
  the light of heaven lighting up our rational-
    ity, 215:5
  memorable occurrence concerning rational-
    ity, 507:1, 507:4, 507:6
  our being in touch with heaven by means of
    our rationality, 402:13
  the rational faculty (capability), 12:3, 334:6,
    564:3, 620:2, 802:1, 840
  scholarly study, rationality, and spirituality
    becoming one after the Lord's Coming,
    200:4
  worldly (earthly) rationality *vs.* heavenly
    (spiritual) rationality, 564:2–566, 758:2
Rats, 78:5, 334:4, 568:2, 595:4, 617, 693:5, 770,
  846:3. *See also* Animals; Mice
  rats meaning the falsification of truths, 203
Reality, the underlying divine. *See also* Coming into being; The Divine; Manifestation
  God as the underlying divine reality, 28
  God as the underlying reality of creation, 13,
    19:1, 775:2
  Jehovah as the underlying divine reality,
    18–21, 81, 351:1
  memorable occurrence concerning a conver-
    sation between angels about the underly-
    ing divine reality, 25
  the underlying divine reality as even more
    universal than God's essence, 18, 36
  the underlying divine reality manifesting
    itself as substance and form, 20

Biographical Note

EMANUEL SWEDENBORG (1688–1772) was born Emanuel Swedberg (or Svedberg) in Stockholm, Sweden, on January 29, 1688 (Julian calendar). He was the third of the nine children of Jesper Swedberg (1653–1735) and Sara Behm (1666–1696). At the age of eight he lost his mother. After the death of his only older brother ten days later, he became the oldest living son. In 1697 his father married Sara Bergia (1666–1720), who developed great affection for Emanuel and left him a significant inheritance. His father, a Lutheran clergyman, later became a celebrated and controversial bishop, whose diocese included the Swedish churches in Pennsylvania and in London, England.

After studying at the University of Uppsala (1699–1709), Emanuel journeyed to England, the Netherlands, France, and Germany (1710–1715) to study and work with leading scientists in western Europe. Upon his return he apprenticed as an engineer under the brilliant Swedish inventor Christopher Polhem (1661–1751). He gained favor with Sweden's King Charles XII (1682–1718), who gave him a salaried position as an overseer of Sweden's mining industry (1716–1747). Although Emanuel was engaged, he never married.

After the death of Charles XII, Emanuel was ennobled by Queen Ulrika Eleonora (1688–1741), and his last name was changed to Swedenborg (or Svedenborg). This change in status gave him a seat in the Swedish House of Nobles, where he remained an active participant in the Swedish government throughout his life.

A member of the Swedish Royal Academy of Sciences, he devoted himself to studies that culminated in a number of publications, most notably a comprehensive three-volume work on natural philosophy and metallurgy (1734) that brought him recognition across Europe as a scientist. After 1734 he redirected his research and publishing to a study of anatomy in search of the interface between the soul and body, making several significant discoveries in physiology.

From 1743 to 1745 he entered a transitional phase that resulted in a shift of his main focus from science to theology. Throughout the rest of his life he maintained that this shift was brought about by Jesus Christ, who appeared to him, called him to a new mission, and opened his perception to a permanent dual consciousness of this life and the life after death.

He devoted the last decades of his life to studying Scripture and publishing eighteen theological titles that draw on the Bible, reasoning, and his own spiritual experiences. These works present a Christian theology with unique perspectives on the nature of God, the spiritual world, the Bible, the human mind, and the path to salvation.

Swedenborg died in London on March 29, 1772, at the age of eighty-four.

697